BEING GIFTED IN SCHOOL

second edition

second edition

BEING GIFTED IN SCHOOL

an introduction

to development, guidance,

and teaching

LAURENCE J. COLEMAN

& TRACY L. CROSS

PRUFROCK PRESS, INC.

Library of Congress Cataloging-in-Publication Data

Being gifted in school : an introduction to development, guidance, and teaching / by
Laurence J. Coleman and Tracy L. Cross.—2nd ed.
        p. cm.
    Includes bibliographical references and index.
    ISBN 1-59363-154-5
    1. Gifted children—Education. I. Cross, Tracy L. II. Title.

    LC3993.C587 2005
    371.95—dc22

                                                                            2005009386

Layout design by James Kendrick
Cover design by Marjorie Parker

Printed in the United States of America.

ISBN 1-59363-154-5

At the time of this book's publication, all facts and figures cited are the most current available. All
telephone numbers, addresses, and Web site URLs are accurate and active. All publications, organizations, Web sites, and other resources exist as described in the book, and all have been verified.
The authors and Prufrock Press, Inc., make no warranty or guarantee concerning the information
and materials given out by organizations or content found at Web sites, and we are not responsible
for any changes that occur after this book's publication. If you find an error, please contact Prufrock
Press, Inc.

Prufrock Press, Inc.
P.O. Box 8813
Waco, Texas 76714-8813
(800) 998-2208
Fax (800) 240-0333
http://www.prufrock.com

To those special teachers who inspired us

and to Tom Cross for his inspiration

CONTENTS

DEFINITIONS AND MODELS OF GIFTEDNESS

KEY CONCEPTS

- The basic concept of giftedness has existed in different societies throughout the world for thousands of years.

- Giftedness is viewed both positively and negatively by educators and the public.

- Stereotypes of giftedness are remarkably resistant to change.

- Giftedness is not a synonym for genius.

- Since the 1950s, new definitions of giftedness have become increasingly broad.

- The many definitions of giftedness may be grouped into categories.

- Gifted children come in countless varieties.

The idea that human beings possess a wide range of abilities and skills is not new. For centuries, societies throughout the world have recognized that some individuals are more successful at some tasks than others. To address the needs of those with high ability, societies have developed various organizational structures. Individuals with important and valued skills have received more recognition and support than others. Consequently, every society has gained from the efforts of gifted and talented individuals.

Because the recognition of people of high ability and talent is not new and because such recognition may benefit a society, it is not surprising that there is a history of organized programs for the identification and education of the gifted. In ancient Greece, Plato proposed a plan whereby gifted children would be identified and educated. He suggested that these children were to be found within all levels of society and that they could be identified by their abilities to learn through trial and error, notice superstition, and discern deceit. Those who met the criteria were to be educated in science and philosophy (Freehill, 1961).

Further indications of interest in the gifted can be found in later historical periods. In 8th-century France, Emperor Charlemagne is reported to have been interested in finding talent among the common man (Hildreth, 1966). In the 15th and 16th centuries, during the spread of the Turkish Empire, an effort was made to recruit talented children from all social classes. Scouts were to locate children among the subjugated Christian populations and bring them to a special school in Constantinople where they were to be trained in Islamic science, religion, and art and to serve the interests of the empire (Freehill, 1961; Hildreth).

Interest in the gifted in the United States can be found in the writings of its founders. Most notably, Thomas Jefferson proposed that tests be instituted to identify the talented and that they be educated at public expense. In this regard, Jefferson wrote, "We hope to avail the State of these talents which nature has sown as liberally among the poor as the rich, but which perish without use, if not sought for and activated" (Hildreth, 1966, p. 43). This line of reasoning advocated by Jefferson has persisted over the last 200 years with varying levels of interest. Efforts to identify and establish programs for gifted and talented children have occurred across the country, especially in the latter part of the 19th century (Tannenbaum, 1958). Many of the ideas inherent in these efforts have continued in somewhat modified forms until today, reflecting the variety of ideas that exist about the education of gifted and talented children (Passow, 1979).

Along with this variety of positive efforts can be found negative efforts, although the presence of novel abilities is not usually met with highly visible repressive acts. Instead, gifted people receive negative reactions that are expressed in much subtler ways from parents, educators, and society at large.

When prospective parents say, "I just want a normal, healthy child," they may be stating their fear of having a child with learning problems, as well as their fear of having a "different" child. Normality is attractive. Abnormality, even if it is supernormality, is not desirable. Consider this familiar statement, which might be overheard at a family gathering: "We love Mary, we love her for her abilities, but why can't she be like us?" What kind of subtle message is Mary likely to be receiving about herself? This discomfort with giftedness has also been observed when parents brag about their child to others while asking the child to be less visible.

Educators, too, have their own forms of negative reactions to gifted abilities. A most effective brake is put on ability when children are required to master underlying steps and knowledge after they have already demonstrated mastery at a higher level. One might suspect that the goal of creating well-rounded children has a concealed, homogenizing, negative effect on children with special abilities.

The presence of negative images about gifted people is obvious from many other sources. Popular sayings or proverbs such as "The cream always rises to the top" and "A flash in the pan" are prime examples. Other sayings like "Smart Alec" and "Don't get smart with me" are common criticisms in our society. Moreover, popular movies portray gifted people as frail (*Powder*, 1995); psychologically damaged (*Shine*, 1996); dysfunctional (*Little Man Tate*, 1991); idealistic, but misguided (*The Nutty Professor*, 1996); and even violent (*Good Will Hunting*, 1997). Perhaps the simplistic notion of compensation—that bright people are physically weak or socially inadequate—is a form of hostility toward high ability.

The persistence of these images and myths about the gifted is striking because evidence to the contrary has been present for 80 years (Terman, 1925). These myths or stereotypical notions pervade most areas of life. Some of them are summarized in Table 1.1 by Sellin and Birch (1980). Note how these myths cover schooling, family life, and interpersonal relationships.

TABLE 1.1

Persisting Myths About Gifted and Talented People

1. Parents of average or retarded children cannot have gifted children.
2. Gifted and talented people are physically weak.
3. Gifted and talented people are morally lax.
4. Gifted and talented people tend to be mentally unstable.
5. Gifted and talented people are socially inept and narrow in interests.
6. Most eminent men and women were indifferent scholars as children.
7. Most gifted and talented children are "flash-in-the-pan" performers.
8. Gifted and talented people have a single talent.
9. Gifted and talented people tend to be odd.
10. Gifted and talented people tend to feel superior to other people.
11. Grade skipping, or acceleration, harms gifted and talented children.
12. Gifted and talented children require a different curriculum.
13. Teachers are poor identifiers of gifted and talented children.
14. Special classes are to be preferred to inclusion in regular grades.
15. The identification of gifted and talented children should be delayed until grade 3.
16. Enrichment of the regular curriculum is not effective.
17. Parents of gifted and talented children are conceited.
18. An IQ test is the only identifier of giftedness and talent.
19. Gifted and talented people require no undue educational provisions.
20. Society has little need of its gifted and talented citizens.
21. College graduates are brighter than noncollege graduates.
22. Special education of the gifted and talented causes elitism among students.
23. Gifted and talented students dominate other students in regular grades.
24. Memory is the best index of human intelligence.
25. Interest in educating gifted and talented people has been of importance only since the 1960s.

Note. From *Educating Gifted and Talented Learners* (p. 29), by D. F. Sellin and J. W. Birch, 1980, Rockville, MD: Aspen Systems. Copyright ©1980 by D. F. Sellin. Reprinted with permission.

The persistence of these notions is the darker side of society's response to special abilities. Given these notions, it is no wonder that the talents of gifted children, especially young women and culturally different people, are frequently covered by a cloak of incompetence. After all, why should one deliberately choose to show off one's difference in an unaccepting environment? The impact of these popular stereotypical notions is examined at different points in this text in discussions about the impact of giftedness on the family and on the person.

WHO ARE THE GIFTED?

The concept of giftedness is commonly confused with the concept of genius. The two concepts are *not* synonymous, although they are frequently treated as such. The *Oxford English Dictionary* (Brown, 1993) defines *gifted* as "Endowed with a gift or gifts; *spec.* exceptionally talented or intelligent" (p. 1088) and *genius* as "Inborn exalted intellectual power; instinctive and extraordinary imaginative, creative, or inventive capacity . . . ; a person having this" (p. 1076).

Although not synonymous, the concepts are related to each other. Some of this confusion may come from Terman's practice of referring to very high IQ scores as being in the genius range of intelligence. In order to distinguish between genius and giftedness, consider the following statements. *A gifted child is rarely a genius.* This statement is true because gifted children do not make contributions that are unique to their time in history. *Prodigies are not geniuses.* They do remarkable things for their age, but rarely things that exceed what gifted adults achieve or they themselves produce later in life.

A genius may have been identified as a gifted child. The criteria and procedures that are used to identify high ability in children are not the same as those used to define genius. A gifted child may become a genius. And, while we would like to identify the seeds of genius in children, currently we can only show that gifted children are likely to become gifted adults. We cannot demonstrate that being gifted points in any significantly predictable way to genius.

These statements add up to the conclusion that more clarity can be brought to the concept of being gifted in America by disassociating the two terms. The distinction can be sharpened by remembering Bronowski's (1973) attempt to distinguish between being extraordinarily clever and being a genius: "he was a genius, in the sense that a genius is a man with two great ideas" (p. 443).

DEFINITIONS OF GIFTEDNESS

A closer look at the historical perspective on programs previously outlined reveals differing viewpoints on the identification of particular abilities. The disagreement about what constitutes giftedness has led to an almost bewildering array of proposals on how to define giftedness. These definitions are probably a consequence of the values of the person making the proposal, the social climate of the time, and the gradual changes in our knowledge about human abilities. The many varieties of definitions are organized in this section to illustrate their evolution and their differences. The historical point of departure is the end of the 19th century, and the definitions to be discussed are relevant to the United States. One should remember that a discussion about definitions of giftedness is inevitably tied to how one might identify people with gifted characteristics. The definitions of giftedness are summarized in Table 1.2.

Ex Post Facto

Before the 20th century, the majority of definitions could be called *ex post facto definitions* of giftedness (Lucito, 1963). These definitions designated a person as gifted when he or she made an outstanding and new contribution to society. If one were to identify the gifted using this definition, it would be appropriate to wait for the contribution to become readily apparent. This type of definition effectively eliminates most children from consideration because it is unlikely that a child would produce something that could be called new and outstanding for a culture. Incidentally, many gifted people were recognized only after their death. An example in this century is the composer Belá Bartók, who died unrecognized and in near poverty in 1945.

The ex post facto definitions are fatalistic because they suggest that giftedness will emerge over time. Those who argue that "true" giftedness will emerge are comfortable with this type of definition. People who subscribe to Galton's idea of "hereditary genius" (e.g., Herrnstein & Murray, 1994) like this type of definition. The continued appeal of ex post facto definitions may relate to their inherent reminder that giftedness is important to a society because its expression in adults helps to advance, or at least strengthen, a society.

Measurable IQ

After the turn of the 20th century, concern began to grow about educating all children and nurturing their abilities. Because the school was the major vehicle for educating children, it is not surprising that these new definitions centered around the continual debate over the purpose of education as it applied to the development of children's abilities.

One group of definitions proposed that high ability in reasoning and judgment was essential to any idea of giftedness. In France, a test was developed to distinguish between people who had sufficient reasoning and judgment to succeed in school and those who did not. The Binet-Simon test (Binet & Simon, 1905), one of the first attempts to develop a paper-and-pencil test of intelligence, was quickly recognized as a way to sample these intellectual abilities. It was adapted to the United States and gained widespread use as the Stanford-Binet. These definitions may be called IQ definitions because they became equated with high scores on tests that yielded IQ scores. These tests of intelligence were thought to be relatively independent of socioeconomic status and political considerations and, therefore, more fair than previous testing methods. Unfortunately, this was not the case.

TABLE 1.2

Definitions of Giftedness

Ex Post Facto	Designate a person as gifted when he or she has made an outstanding and new contribution to society.
Measurable IQ	Propose that high ability in reasoning and judgment are essential to any idea of giftedness.
Achievement	Stress general academic achievement and specific academic achievement.
Creativity	Creativity—the ability to do something new or novel in one's environment—is what distinguishes the truly gifted from those who are only very intelligent or are high achievers.
Social Talent	Recognize the social forces involved in the development of abilities. Propose that giftedness is marked by consistent high performance in a socially valued activity.
Interaction of Attributes	Conceptualize giftedness as the interaction among various attributes.
Percentage-Type	A certain percentage of any group should be viewed as gifted or talented.
Development	Precocity in a valued area indicates giftedness.
Omnibus	The demonstration of achievement, potential ability, or both in one or more specified areas.

The *IQ type of definition* was accepted in the 1920s and is still widely accepted today (Borland, 1989; Gagné, 1998; Gust, Waldron, & Cross, 1997; Silverman, 1993). Gross (2004), in her study of exceptionally and profoundly gifted children, purported that, although many definitions of giftedness have

acknowledged various domains of abilities, the domain of intellectual giftedness remains highly important. She also added that the intelligence quotient
remains a useful index. Continued acceptance of IQ definitions of giftedness
is also probably related to the "special" qualities of objectivity and validity
ascribed to these tests by the public, as well as their place in Terman's work.
The power and universality of these standardized tests within schools can also
be linked directly to their practical application as devices for classifying children into groups, presumably to facilitate instruction (Sattler, 1988).

Achievement

While IQ definitions were popular, not everyone found them to be satisfactory explanations of giftedness. One concern was the observation that intelligence tests were only fairly good at predicting school success (Getzels &
Dillon, 1973). People with the highest intelligence scores did not consistently
get the highest grades, and a better predictor of general school success was
previously earned grades. Likewise, there was doubt that high intelligence
scores were indicative of future potential in all academic areas. High IQ scores
were frequently inadequate predictors of performance in specific academic
areas (Stanley, 1973).

Given these concerns, proponents for this type of identification believe a
better definition might be one that stresses *general academic achievement* and
specific academic achievement. An achievement definition would make sense
because it applies to schooling. General achievement would serve as a direct
measure of how gifted children are expected to behave in school (Gallagher &
Gallagher, 1994). Specific academic achievement would serve as a predictor of
how someone could be expected to achieve in a more narrowly defined area,
such as mathematics (Stanley & Benbow, 1986). A logical end point would be
professional schools where success is predicted by academic aptitude and
where students are trained for future significant contributions.

Creativity

The IQ-type definition and the achievement-type definitions do not
include all the aspects of human ability that may be associated with or
described by giftedness. One additional aspect that has been repeatedly mentioned is *creativity* (Lucito, 1963). Proponents of this kind of definition are
persuaded that the ability to do something new or novel in one's environment
is the most significant of human abilities. It is creativity, proponents believe,
that distinguishes the truly gifted from those who are only very intelligent or
are high achievers.

While support for a creativity-type definition had existed for many years,
it was never dominant in practice. However, in the 1950s, J. P. Guilford's
research rekindled concern for creativity when he pointed out that IQ tests did
not tap this ability. Leaders in the field of gifted education seized upon this

observation and incorporated creativity into definitions of giftedness (Fliegler & Bish, 1959; Renzulli, 1977; Tannenbaum, 1997). The result was an explosion in research on creativity and human abilities. A perusal of any journal concerned with gifted children, especially in the 1960s and 1970s, attests to the pervasiveness of the creativity definition. In fact, it has probably surpassed the achievement-type definition in popularity.

Social Talent

While the four definition orientations—ex post facto, measurable IQ, achievement, and creativity—seem to address a wide number of questions about giftedness, a number of issues remain unresolved about what constitutes an adequate definition of giftedness:

1. Why do some people perform at a high level, but not score well on tests indicating high ability?

2. Why are some ethnic groups underrepresented in programs when it is clear that they possess many gifted and talented people?

3. Why are standardized tests unsatisfactory in identifying abilities such as artistic and musical talent?

4. Why is it that the range of talents recognized and rewarded in adults is much broader than those recognized in children?

Contemporary theorists recognize that these issues need to be considered when formulating adequate definitions of giftedness. Thus, *social-talent definitions*, which propose that giftedness is marked by consistent, high performance in a socially valued activity, acknowledge that social forces play a role in the development of abilities. Theorists also consider the distinction between giftedness and talent in their definitions. Bloom (1985) and Feldhusen (1993), for example, have proposed definitions of giftedness as manifestations of talent that should be or have been developed.

Gagné (1985, 1995, 2003) has proposed the Differentiated Model of Giftedness and Talent (DMGT; see Figure 1.1), which differentiates between giftedness (natural abilities) and talent (systematically developed skills). The model explores the developmental relationship between gifts/aptitudes and talents (i.e., that aptitudes are the constituent elements of talents), the important role of learning and practice in transforming abilities into developed skills, and the role of intrapersonal catalysts (e.g., motivation and volition) and environmental catalysts (e.g., significant people) to this developmental process.

Thus, the social-talent definition of giftedness has the advantage of recognizing the relativity of the concept of giftedness and of pointing out that

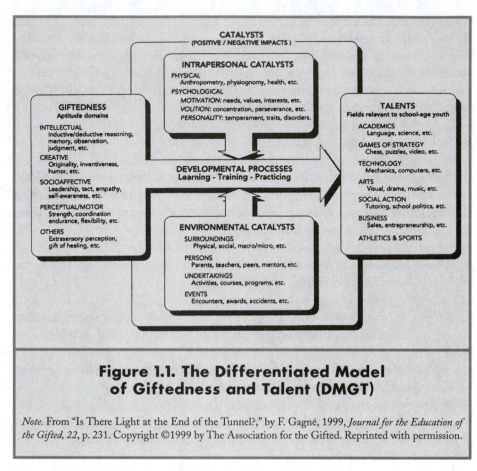

Figure 1.1. The Differentiated Model of Giftedness and Talent (DMGT)

Note. From "Is There Light at the End of the Tunnel?," by F. Gagné, 1999, *Journal for the Education of the Gifted, 22*, p. 231. Copyright ©1999 by The Association for the Gifted. Reprinted with permission.

the expression of giftedness is tied to what people are rewarded for in real life, as well as the environmental factors potentially influencing the successful development of talent (Coleman, Sanders, & Cross, 1997; Feldhusen & Treffinger, 1979; Sternberg & Zhang, 1995; Tannenbaum, 1997). Unfortunately, the very relativity of this idea makes some people who want a more absolute or objective definition uneasy because there might be inconsistency from one culture to another in the non-IQ intelligence definition of who is considered gifted.

Gardner (1983, 1993) acknowledges the social and cultural influences in defining intelligence in his book, *Frames of Mind*, in which he outlined his theory of multiple intelligences (MI). These include at least seven intelligences, or categories of human abilities, thought to be distinct from one another: logical-mathematical, linguistic, musical, spatial, bodily-kinesthetic, interpersonal, and intrapersonal. He has more recently added a naturalist intelligence and has proposed that existentialist intelligence be considered for future inclusion in these categories (Von Karolyi, Ramos-Ford, & Gardner, 2003). Gardner (1993) defined intelligence as "the ability to solve problems, or to create products, that are valued within one or more cultural settings" (p. x). He noted that individuals may have strengths or weaknesses in one or several areas and that an individual may excel in one category, but have no remarkable abilities in the other areas. Paired with the idea of multiple intelligences is the recognition that traditional means of intellectual measurements (such as IQ tests) would not be adequate for determining giftedness.

Subsequent to *Frames of Mind* came Sternberg's triarchic model of intelligence, which offers three kinds of giftedness: analytic, synthetic, and practical (Sternberg, 1985, 2003a). Analytic giftedness is the ability to take apart problems and understand the parts. Because conventional tests of intelligence place an emphasis on analytic reasoning, individuals with strengths in this area tend to do well on them. Synthetic giftedness is seen in individuals who are unusually creative and insightful, while practical intelligence centers on the ability to apply analytic and synthetic abilities to everyday, pragmatic situations. Like Gardner's theory, Sternberg noted that nontraditional means of identification were necessary for both the synthetic and practical areas of giftedness. An important difference between the two theories is that evidence of Gardner's theory can be seen in school-age students, while evidence of Sternberg's theory is more easily seen in adult populations. This is especially true for practical intelligence.

Another conception of giftedness as a manifestation of developing talent over time has been called the theory of deliberate practice or the novice/expert model (Ericsson & Charness, 1994; Ericsson, Krampe, & Tesch-Römer, 1993). In this model, the person is goal-oriented, and maintains conscious training over long periods of time. While expertise can be worked toward in virtually any area, societies will clearly impact the development of expertise by the way they do or do not support preferred areas of study. For example, the U.S. government is encouraging the development of language expertise in areas different from those it encouraged prior to the terrorists attacks on the World Trade Center and the Pentagon on September 11, 2001.

Interaction of Attributes

While Gardner's and Sternberg's theories emphasize areas of strength and weakness (i.e., an individual may be gifted in a particular area, but not another), other theorists conceptualize giftedness as *the interaction among various attributes*. Renzulli (1986), for example, views giftedness as the interaction among three clusters: above-average ability, task commitment, and creativity (see Figure 1.2). Tannenbaum (1983, 2003) similarly envisions giftedness as the center of five interacting elements: general ability, special aptitude, nonintellectual factors, environmental factors, and chance factors (see Figure 1.3).

Percentage-Type and Development

While most definitions of giftedness can be categorized within the five types of definitions described above, two other types have been presented in

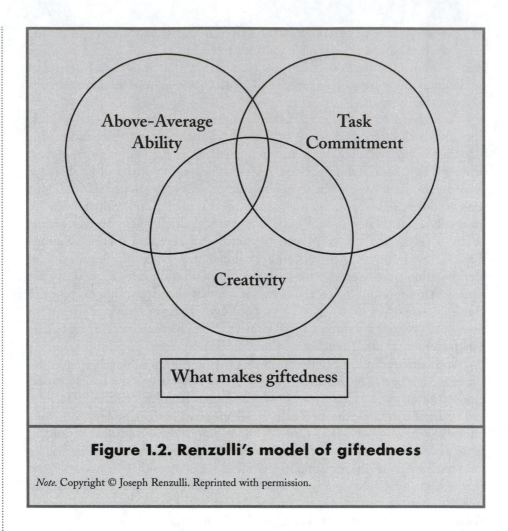

Figure 1.2. Renzulli's model of giftedness

Note. Copyright © Joseph Renzulli. Reprinted with permission.

the literature. Lucito (1963) reported a *percentage-type definition*, which argues that a certain percentage of any group should be viewed as gifted or talented. This type of definition creates a standard that fluctuates depending on the group and the trait measured. Getzels and Dillon (1973) have proposed another category, called the *development definition*, which points out that the gifted frequently are noticed because they accomplish certain tasks before their peers. It is their precocity in a valued area that makes them gifted.

Omnibus

By tracing these types of definitions, one can see that the notion of what constitutes giftedness has become more and more broad. Getzels and Dillon (1973) have called such broad definitions *omnibus definitions*.

This evolution was evidenced in the definition proposed by Fliegler (1961), which included elements of all the definitions. This definition pro-

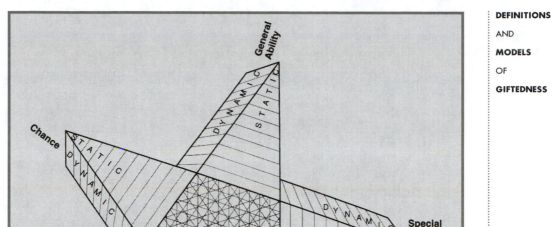

Figure 1.3. Tannenbaum's model

Note. From "Nature and Nurture of Giftedness" (p. 47), by A. J. Tannenbaum, in Handbook of Gifted Education (5th ed.), N. Colangelo & G. A Davis (Eds.), 2003, Boston: Allyn and Bacon. Copyright ©2003 by Allyn and Bacon. Reprinted with permission.

posed that a person was gifted when he or she demonstrated at least two of the following: high intelligence, high creativity, high achievement, or a talent. A more recent example was proposed by Marland (1972) in a report to Congress:

> Gifted and talented children are those identified by professionally qualified people who, by virtue of outstanding abilities, are capable of high performance. These are children who require differentiated educational programs and/or services beyond those normally pro-

vided by the regular school program in order to realize their contribution to self and society.

Children capable of high performance include those with demonstrated achievement and/or potential ability in any of the following areas, singly or in combination:

1. general intellectual ability
2. specific academic aptitude
3. creative or productive thinking
4. leadership ability
5. visual and performing arts
6. psychomotor ability.

It can be assumed that utilization of these criteria for identifying the gifted and talented will encompass a minimum of 3 to 5 percent of the school population. (p. 2)

This definition has been since restated in 1978 to exclude psychomotor giftedness.

THE VARIETIES OF GIFTEDNESS

As one reads the Marland (1972) definition, it is apparent that giftedness comes in many varieties. A person who has a suspected high ability in one area or a person who has many high abilities may both be considered gifted. Given all the possible combinations of abilities, one can locate many varieties of giftedness. Some of this variety is captured in the following seven case histories:

1. Dora—An Embarrassment of Riches.

2. Sarah—A Discrepancy in Ability.

3. Francine—A Talented Musician With a Moderate IQ.

4. Edwin—A School Failure With a High IQ.

5. Marshall—A Physically Handicapping Condition.

6. David—Underachievement With a Tradition of Education.

7. Dylan—A Shy Gifted Twin With Many Talents.

All of the people in these case histories meet the omnibus definition of giftedness. Some may seem surprising. Note the differences among the cases.

Case 1: Dora—An Embarrassment of Riches

In school, Dora was judged to be the brightest. At 8 years of age, she was doing fifth-grade work, and she had a Stanford-Binet IQ of 168. Her paternal grandparents, who had elementary school educations, raised her after her parents died when Dora was very young. Her two brothers had IQs of 129 and 155. Dora's aunt took particular interest in her development.

Dora taught herself to read at age 5. Reportedly, she could recite nursery rhymes at 13 months and complete songs when she began to talk. She was an avid reader. She had been characterized as having high ideals and as being friendly, conscientious, inquisitive, humorous, and mature for her age. Dora's interests were similar to those of other children, yet she preferred quiet games. In high school, those interests continued. She devoted time to reading, tennis, and piano. She was described as "very pretty."

Upon entering school, her abilities started to become apparent. She was the top student in her class. By third grade, she was observed reading advanced books and magazines such as *National Geographic*. Her success in school continued with achievement test scores that were 3 or more years ahead of her classmates. Although her work warranted it, her grandparents refused permission for her acceleration. In high school, Dora continued to get excellent grades.

Dora had always been popular with her classmates. She was friendly and outgoing. In high school, she was class president as a freshman and served on the school literary publications. She was attracted to Latin and Greek and wanted to be a teacher (Burks, Jensen, & Terman, 1930, pp. 252–255).

Case 2: Sarah—A Discrepancy in Ability

Sarah was a bright 8-year-old. At 7 years, she had a full-scale score of 121 on the WISC-R. Her verbal IQ was 131, but her performance IQ was 104—an unusual discrepancy.

She entered school at 5. In kindergarten, she was ready for reading at home, but her teacher was not responsive. The teacher expressed concern about Sarah's preference for talking to her even though Sarah was popular with her peers. Sarah never caused any classroom disturbances. Throughout school, she was observed to be immature in motor activities, and as a result she avoided such activities. At the end of second grade, she asked for harder work. At that time, she achieved at the 7.1, 6.2, and 3.5 grade levels on the WRAT in reading, spelling, and arithmetic, respectively. At the beginning of the next school year, her scores on the Metropolitan Achievement Test were consistent with previous tests.

Sarah was a middle child. Her parents were both professionals. Before the adoption of another sibling and the birth of a younger sibling, she was an only child for 5 years. Her parents supported her interests, which were primarily intellectual. In the midst of active playing with friends, she was observed to withdraw to do something by herself. Reading dominated everything. Sarah was quite opinionated and made connections among ideas readily. She had many friends.

Case 3: Francine—A Talented Musician With a Moderate IQ

Francine was tested at age 12 because of her unusually advanced musical ability. Her performance at concerts generated much public attention, and people spoke of her as having a "wonderful" future. Her family was very supportive of her talent, as they seemed interested in its financial value. Despite their modest economic condition, the family bought a grand piano and provided costly lessons. Her father and brother were tailors, and her sister had a small part in the Metropolitan Opera Company.

Francine had one primary interest: music. Her hobby was the piano, and she had little interest in school and was a poor student. At age 12, she scored 116 on the Stanford-Binet. She did best on subtests calling for imagery and problem solving and least well on verbal tests. Francine's physical development seemed normal. She seemed to have abundant energy. She was impulsive and very individualistic. She saw herself as someone who mattered. She definitely seemed to stand out (Root, 1931, pp. 91–93).

Case 4: Edwin—A School Failure With a High IQ

Edwin was a bright young man. At age 10, he had an IQ on the Stanford-Binet of 141. On a later testing at age 16, he had a similar score. Both of his parents were professionals, and they were ambitious about giving Edwin encouragement and help by providing rich cultural opportunities. In elementary school, he had an outstanding record. In sixth grade, he was reported to be brilliant and meticulous in his work. A similar report was available for 8th grade. At 12, he entered high school, and great success was anticipated. By 16, the school asked that he withdraw because he was failing three subjects and had already failed many others, including geometry, Latin, and literature. The school tried to help him. There was no ready explanation for his failures. Edwin said he did not like to study.

Edwin seemed to have the usual interests. He claimed he liked school, and he had many friends. Edwin was dismissed from the football team for poor grades (Burks et al., 1930, pp. 279–281).

Case 5: Marshall—A Physically Handicapping Condition

Marshall was identified with an IQ of 144 at 11 years of age. He had a frail physique because he had suffered polio as a baby. He walked with a pronounced limp.

Marshall came from a disharmonious family. His parents frequently quarreled, and they lived on the verge of economic disaster even with the children working to help support the family. His father was not interested in the family and physically abused the children, while his mother, who was reported to be unstable, was devoted to them, especially to Marshall. The other children, a sister and a brother, had normal and below-normal IQs, respectively.

In sixth grade, Marshall was several years ahead of his classmates on standardized tests. In high school, he began a chess club and was involved in the debating club. Marshall entered college and planned to became a lawyer. He joined the debating and chess clubs. He had a dean's list grade-point average. All this was accomplished while he supported himself through school.

Marshall was quiet, hard-working, and optimistic. He had a desire to do things well. At 15, he had to be hospitalized for a breakdown, which seemed related to his family situation (Burks et al., 1930, pp. 283–287).

Case 6: David—Underachievement With a Tradition of Education

David came to the attention of school authorities in first grade. The teacher was upset over his unorthodox and creative behavior. When tested, David was found to be functioning on the Stanford-Binet at about 140.

Although he followed two achieving sisters into school, school and David apparently did not mix. Throughout his academic career, he was a marginal student, and he was even held back in first grade. Few school subjects held any interest, although he loved creative writing. He particularly hated sports.

David was popular with his peers. He was elected class president, but declined the honor. He was characterized as generous, nonmaterialistic, opinionated, and quite concerned about the values operating in our urban, highly technical society.

David came from a family with a long tradition of education—five generations of educated African Americans. The family was oriented toward professional careers: The father was a university professor and the mother and two sisters were a librarian, a university professor, and an architect, respectively. The parents recognized David's talents and wanted him to be happy.

Since high school, David has been busy moving around. After he barely passed his freshman year of college, he joined the Coast Guard for 2 years. David returned to college, left again, and enlisted in the Navy. The Navy taught him to be a photojournalist, which he reportedly likes very much. David continues to write, but has submitted nothing for publication. At present, he is still trying to find himself.

Case 7: Dylan—A Shy Gifted Twin With Many Talents

Dylan was identified by his parents at age 4 with a highly developed receptive and expressive vocabulary. He was the younger of twins, and his brother was also identified as gifted. Both were assessed at age 6 to have WISC-III IQ scores greater than 137, and both spent their first 5 grades in a self-contained gifted program. The brother was outgoing and interested in other people. He became a leader in school, often drawing attention to himself. Dylan, on the other hand, was shy, with an advanced sense of appropriate behavior. He found most game playing to be childish and too unimportant to participate in. He grew contemptuous of athletics and what he perceived to be unwarranted attention and value placed on them by our society.

In school, Dylan struggled to find value and meaning in many class assignments. He could be noncompliant, creating tense situations between himself and his teachers and parents. His performance in areas of interest were regularly extraordinary. Writing book-length stories (his award-winning fourth-grade junior author story was 200 pages in length), art, and working on computers were his passions. Between his fourth- and fifth-grade years, Dylan composed three additional books of fiction exceeding 150 pages in length. Repetitive assignments in mathematics and highly structured assignments on any topic resulted in noncompliance.

To date, his teachers have recognized his multiple talents and have made some efforts to coax him along. His shyness, need for meaning in his work, independence, and passions make him a challenge to teach and a strong candidate for underachievement. The self-contained program for gifted students has been a place of acceptance and growth for his twin, while Dylan has struggled, sensing that some of the other students and specialty teachers (e.g., physical education) do not accept him.

Many other descriptions of individuals are possible because the Marland (1972) definition is such an expansive one. The omnibus definitions seem to be an attempt to reconcile the difficulties of formulating a definition that satisfies one's sense of justice and the practical requirements of setting up a program. Omnibus definitions have the advantage of recognizing that giftedness may be expressed in many ways and come from unlikely sources. The seven case histories are an attempt to illustrate this point. Three cases are recent examples, while the remainder represent children who have been identified as gifted over a 70-year period. If one wants a sense of a typically gifted child, then Dora probably comes the closest. The range of definitions and our case studies suggest that giftedness can be seen as existing across several dimensions, as illustrated below:

> many interests . . . . . single interest
> general ability . . . . . specific ability
> balanced . . . . imbalanced
> well-rounded . . . . . . unidimensional
> committed . . . . uninvolved
> demonstrated . . . . . . potential
> stability . . . . instability

The omnibus definition makes it possible to incorporate all these dimensions under one rubric. Other definitions would have varying degrees of difficulty adapting to the opposing points of each dimension. This list of bipolar descriptors is not meant to be exhaustive, nor is it meant to suggest that one group is preferable to another. The list is only means to represent terms commonly used in discussions about the meaning of giftedness.

FACTORS THAT INFLUENCE DEFINITIONS OF GIFTEDNESS

It is the very responsiveness of the omnibus definition that creates shortcomings. One problem is that the definition is difficult to put into operation because it recognizes so many varieties of giftedness. Each ability suggests a separate procedure for its identification (Chapter 3 on identification will expand on this idea).

Another problem is estimating how many people could potentially be identified as gifted. There is no real way to estimate the number of children who might be gifted. For example, the Fliegler (1961) definition suggests 20% of children are gifted, while the Marland (1972) definition suggests 3–5%. With an omnibus definition, one is faced with the absurdity that all children are to be considered gifted. While the notion of all children having talents is attractive and appealing, it is not a useful or a realistic definition. It is not useful in that the notion is so broad that it becomes difficult, maybe impossible, to discuss special provisions for the gifted and compare research and program effectiveness. It is not realistic because it avoids the issues of limited resources and the fact that societies do value some abilities more than others. The process of defining giftedness is never neutral.

What has given rise to these many proposals for defining giftedness? Several factors seem important to the process of continual redefinition.

First, there is our notion of intelligence (Borland, 1989; Gallagher, 1975; Plomin, 1997). Intelligence is no longer viewed as a unitary factor; rather, it is viewed as being composed of a variety of factors. Environment is now considered to be important to the development of intelligence. In fact, dissatisfaction with the operational definition of intelligence contained in the IQ test has continued to grow because of the failure to sample enough of what comprises intelligence. It is probable that this source of dissatisfaction will never diminish. Gardner's theory of multiple intelligences and Sternberg's triarchic model are current examples of the recognition that IQ scores represent only a small portion of what giftedness can be.

Another source of redefinition is largely sociopolitical. Since the early 1900s, cultural groups have wondered why so few of their numbers have been identified as gifted. The emerging consciousness and increased political power of these groups—including African Americans, Hispanics, people with disabilities, and people who are economically disadvantaged, among others—have kept the issue of an adequate definition alive. Their criticisms cannot be overlooked (Coleman et al., 1997; Howley, Howley & Pendarvis, 1995; Sapon-Shevin, 1994).

A third impetus for changing definitions has come from research into intelligence and creativity, which has shown that creativity is not synonymous with intelligence and that creativity may be nurtured. It has become apparent that intelligence test scores are not able to predict consistently who among the gifted will make the most creative contributions in many fields. Other evidence has indicated that successful artists and musicians do not necessarily have IQ scores in the gifted range, assuming the IQ criterion is two standard deviations above the norm.

A fourth source for change in the definition of giftedness has been our changing world. In the early 1900s, the United States was far different from what it is today. The explosion in information, the rapid rate of change, and the many technological advances of the 20th century have brought about significant changes in our lifestyle. These trends indicate that different abilities and talents are needed for success in today's society than were needed at the turn of the century. Toffler (1970) has written quite eloquently on this point.

A fifth source of influence has been follow-up studies of adults who were gifted students, and other studies considering potential and achievement. This research over the past 10 years has shed light on life experiences that successful adults attributed to their own development (Subotnik & Arnold, 1993), while other studies investigated the daily lives of gifted adolescents (Csikszentmihalyi, Rathunde, & Whalen, 1993). Combined, these two lines of research have illustrated the social and sociocultural dynamics involved in the successes and failures of students of high intellectual ability.

All the factors that have influenced the evolution of a definition make it apparent that giftedness is a relative concept. Its meaning is related to changes in our knowledge and to changes in our social and political lives. One should not search for an absolute definition of giftedness because it does not exist. Efforts to find the *truly* or the *really* gifted are shortsighted and misplaced when applied to children. Unless one uses an ex post facto definition, one must recognize that definitions applied to children are only statements about their probable functioning as adults. The definitions state that, at this time and place, a child exhibits characteristics or potentials denoting evidence of giftedness and evidence of special promise. Not all people of high ability achieve eminence, and no definition can predict with infallible accuracy those people who will be the greatest within a generation. However, a meaningful definition should be able to predict outstanding performance in a manner greater than chance alone.

A SCHOOL-BASED CONCEPTION OF GIFTEDNESS

Given all the issues involved in formulating a definition, one should be hesitant about proposing yet another one. Even so, a definition will be proposed here in order to clarify our perspective as the authors of this text. The concerns expressed throughout are premised on this one definition. Although other viewpoints are explored and expressed, the evidence is, of course, colored by our conceptions of giftedness.

Our school-based conception of giftedness (SCG) is intended to encourage clearer communication among educators, administrators, and school boards concerning the role and responsibilities of our schools in developing talent (Cross & Coleman, 2005). The SCG differs from other conceptions by proposing a change in the criteria that describes giftedness by accounting for changes in abilities with advancing age in school. The criteria become narrower with increased age, which means that, in the early grades, giftedness would appear more in the areas of general ability or specific skills; but, as the child moves through school, evidence of ability and achievement would manifest within specific areas of study (Coleman, 1985a; Coleman & Cross, 2000; Cross & Coleman). This is a developmental model that has roots in the writings of Feldman (1997), Fliegler (1961), Newland (1976), Renzulli (1977), and Simonton (1997).

In the SCG, preadolescent gifted children have potential or demonstrated high ability in two areas: general cognitive ability and creative ability. Adolescent gifted children have demonstrated ability in abstract thinking, have produced creative works in some worthwhile area, and have demonstrated consistent involvement in activities of either type. It is estimated that approximately 6% of the school-age population would fit the SCG because of the association between abstract thinking and creative production.

The elements in this definition have been selected for specific purposes. The distinction between preadolescent and adolescent children recognizes that a good definition should foster identification, nurture talent, and make a statement about future behavior. The SCG does these things by noting that general abilities are important signs of giftedness and that general abilities are nonspecific predictors of adult accomplishments. The inclusion in preadolescents of high-level general cognitive ability, creativity, or both recognizes the interrelationship between these abilities. While they are not the same phenomenon, they do seem to converge at some point beyond average ability, making them the bedrock upon which gifted behavior is based. However, the change in the criteria states that gifted children must, at some point in time, be expected to express their potential. The indication of potential is no longer sufficient for being considered gifted in adolescence. This change in the criteria is really a change to an adult, real-world standard of giftedness, which means demonstrating one's ability in a performance or in a creative product and demonstrating one's involvement in a field of knowledge.

This makes sense for several reasons. The SCG recognizes the relative stability of interests that are evident by age 12 in many people (Albert, 1980; Hildreth, 1966). Another reason is that it recognizes the cumulative effects of development that are relatively invisible before adolescence (Simonton, 1997). In this manner, the criteria pay attention to children who do not perform well on standardized tests, but show promise in specific fields (Wolf, 1981). The criteria recognize that involvement in a field of study becomes more evident as one begins to master that field (Bloom & Sosniak, 1981; Sosniak, 1997). This position is also consistent with information on the expression of creativity in various fields of endeavor (Feldman, 1997; Lehman, 1953). (Chapter 6 on creativity develops this point further.)

A final reason for the change in the criteria is the recognition that the peak performance in most gifted people's careers comes in early adulthood, and signs of this performance are evident in their youth. In her study of giftedness, Cox (1926) noted, "the superior youths . . . pursued high ideas, developed significant interests, and created new expressions of scientific and philosophical thought before they had reached the age of manhood" (p. 218).

See Cross and Coleman (2005) for a thorough description of the SCG. In that chapter, they conclude by claiming that

> Ultimately giftedness is a consequence of the development of the individual over time. Although people generally follow certain forms of universal development such as those described in developmental psychology, the pattern of those developing extraordinary talent is necessarily nonuniversal by its very nature (Feldman, 1997). It may represent common patterns within specific disciplines and therefore will be both idiosyncratic and normal. Hence, people may be born with the potential to be gifted, but many do not actually become gifted; because to be gifted means gifted at something.

In our society, not every talent domain can be the responsibility of schools to develop. The SCG helps clarify the role and responsibilities of America's schools in developing the talent of its students.

WHO IS NOT GIFTED?

An analysis of the varieties of giftedness might lead one to conclude that giftedness is everywhere, which is probably accurate. Giftedness may be found in all groups of humans. However, it is a mistake to conclude from this discussion that everyone is to be thought of as gifted. Not all people with high ability are to be considered gifted. Everyone has abilities, and everyone has worth. Everyone has the potential for making a contribution to the development of him- or herself and to the development of society. These contributions are a consequence of individual abilities and the conditions operating at the time. While all contributions may be valuable, not all contributions have equal value. Some contributions bring more benefit to a person and to a society than others. The people who make such contributions are the gifted, although no assumption should be made that those people were trying to make such a contribution. People who do not make such contributions are not gifted.

The point where this distinction about giftedness and nongiftedness blurs is in the discussion of children. It is obvious that children, especially young children, have a small probability of making such contributions. That is why our identification procedures should be broad and keyed to signs of giftedness. It is our task to cultivate these abilities so they may flower. Yet, it serves no honest purpose to claim that all these abilities have germinated or will germinate when it is readily apparent that it has not happened. The SCG proposes the point at which the gardener picks the flowers that are likely to be "best of show." Those who show their unique potentials have a greater probability of contributing to all of us. The gardener realizes that the best will sometimes be missed; but, in the long run, the mistakes will even out.

ARE THE GIFTED HANDICAPPED?

Giftedness is different from nongiftedness. It is the differences that permit us to identify the gifted, and while they are present throughout a person's life, they are not necessarily obvious. Gifted people do not experience life in the same ways as the nongifted because of their abilities. Chapter 5 is devoted to a discussion of this point.

It is not uncommon for people to ask whether these ability differences handicap the gifted. This question may arise because of the increased interest in the disabled and the fact that texts on handicapped or exceptional people include chapters on the gifted.

It is our position that the gifted are handicapped. They are handicapped because they meet two conditions.

The first condition is deviation from the norm. By definition, the gifted possess abilities that place them outside the normal range. In this manner, they are similar to the disabled. It makes no difference that their abilities may be thought of as strengths, rather than weaknesses. Sometimes, these strengths have been viewed as signs of weakness or disease, often carrying stigmatizing effects (Coleman, 1985a; Cross, Coleman, & Terharr-Yonkers, 1991). Indeed, as the text will later describe, these very strengths have often been interpreted by some as weaknesses.

The second condition is the inadequacy of the school program. The issue is whether the needs of the gifted can be met within the typical school program. One may say that needs have been met when social adjustment and learning are optimal. In an optimal situation, gifted children would be placed at their instructional level. Given the varied interests and learning rates of the gifted, it is difficult to see how the typical program with peers and with a carefully controlled curriculum can meet their needs at their instructional levels. In this manner, the gifted are similar to other children with disabling conditions in that the school environment inhibits their growth by not responding to their needs; thus, they need special services.

Given these two conditions, the gifted are handicapped. Their handicap is defined not by pathology, but rather by their differences and by the inadequacy of regular education to meet their needs. It should be possible to remove the second condition by modifying the school. At this point in history, there is little evidence to suggest that such modifications for the gifted will be extensive. However, it has been made clear in several government reports over the years (Martinson, 1972; U.S. Department of Education, 1993) that special education provisions benefit the gifted.

CONCLUSION

Chapter 1 has concerned itself with the many varieties of giftedness. Interest in the education and development of giftedness has existed since ancient times and has had both positive and negative effects on gifted people. Over the last century, interest has increased, and a bewildering series of definitions has been proposed as part of a larger evolutionary process tied to our new knowledge of child development, the emergence of a new social consciousness toward minority groups, newer technologies, and an increased understanding of giftedness. The result of the evolution is an expansion of the definition of giftedness to include multiple abilities and talents found across American society. The new expanded definitions have increased the complexity of the identification process because more decisions are required about the relative importance of several abilities. The question of measurement is ever present. In some ways, the expansion of the definition may be an illusion because the power of the IQ remains and the interrelationships among advanced abilities need to be explored. Many of the issues raised by the varying definitions will reappear throughout the text as information on identification, guidance, and programming is examined.

FOR **DISCUSSION**

1. How would you respond to an individual who claims that money directed at gifted education programs would be better spent elsewhere because "the cream always rises to the top"?

2. A number of myths about gifted and talented persons are presented in Table 1.1. Reflect on the myths associated with schooling and discuss the implications of these myths on classroom practice.

3. Reflecting on the information concerning definitions of giftedness, how would you respond to an individual who asks you what percentage of students are gifted?

4. Reflect on and discuss how changes in political and social climates have affected definitions of giftedness.

5. Considering the various definitions of giftedness, identify individuals (from the past or present) who would be considered gifted under a particular definition. Would these same individuals be considered gifted under more than one definition?

6. What are the educational implications for designating a person as gifted under one definition but not another.

7. In the conclusion, it is noted: "In some ways, the expansion of the definition may be an illusion. The power of the IQ remains." Do you agree or disagree with this statement?

chapter two

THE LIVES OF GIFTED PEOPLE

KEY CONCEPTS

- An unusually broad base of information has accumulated on gifted children.

- A profile of the gifted reveals an array of positive characteristics and abilities in diverse areas.

- A portrait of the gifted may be overgeneralized so that individual children rarely fit the picture.

- There are several issues that must be examined when considering the portrait of the gifted child based on the early research.

- Considering the portrait is essential to understanding much of what has occurred in gifted education in the United States since the 1920s.

- The recognized gifted child grows into an adult with undiminished abilities.

- Gifted children manifest their abilities in a variety of adult roles and careers, but the conventionality of their choices is linked to factors other than being gifted.

ifted children comprise a population that has an extremely wide range of skills and abilities. This range encompasses abilities of the nongifted and extends to the very highest and incomprehensible levels of knowledge and skill. The abilities of gifted people are expressed in all areas of human activity. It is very difficult to delineate the specific abilities or experiences that influence expression within a specific career. Interest in trying to find out about the lives of gifted people has been extensive. Even though we believe that the gifted population is a heterogeneous group of individuals, we include in this chapter a portrait of the life of a "typical" gifted child based on the early research on gifted children. This composite portrait is compared to a portrait of gifted adults to demonstrate the connection between gifted children and adults. The career choices and life satisfaction of these gifted adults are discussed in terms of these portraits.

The placement of this topic at this point in the text may seem unusual to some readers. Why not discuss identification before describing characteristics? The purpose of this organization is to help the reader understand the population known as gifted. It is assumed that, by understanding their lives, inferences can readily be made about identification and programming. The characteristics one is searching for determine who is selected, and the process of identification in schools is never value-free.

THE DATABASE

The information on characteristics of gifted people is quite diverse and extensive for both children and adults, although the information on children is more extensive. The centerpiece of this information is the *Genetic Studies of*

Genius, Lewis Terman's longitudinal study of 1,500 gifted people, which began in 1921–1922 (Terman, 1925) and is continuing today (Sears, 1979; Tomlinson-Keasey & Little, 1990). The subjects were contacted at least nine times over a 70-year period, which allowed a wealth of data to be gathered on their development. These studies are monumental in scope and thoroughness, with spin-off studies being published today (e.g., Rogers, 1999). Other longitudinal studies of gifted children have also been conducted (d'Heurle, Mellinger, & Hapgood, 1959; Hollingworth, 1942; Witty, 1940), and they have painted a remarkably consistent picture of the traits of the gifted (Getzels & Dillon, 1973). In fact, one could say the data are corroborative if not redundant. The information cited today is very similar to that published more than 75 years ago (O'Shea, 1924).

This early research on the gifted has provided us with high-quality information. The data are based on following the same people over a period of years so that inferences need not be made about what happened to the subjects. The redundant or consistent findings are another way of pointing out the replicability of the information. Data, as a rule, are considered more reliable and valid when they have been reproduced by researchers with different subjects and conditions over time. This is certainly true of the research on the gifted.

Gifted children come in a variety of sizes, shapes, and backgrounds. In the midst of this variety, one can find shared patterns and characteristics. In fact, "the developmental patterns true of one group of the gifted usually apply to another" (Gowan & Demos, 1964, p. 36). The following section describes these modal, or typical, patterns, although obviously no single individual fits these generalizations. The composite is based predominantly on the research of Terman and his colleagues (Burks, Jensen, & Terman, 1930; Terman, 1925; Terman & Oden, 1947) with significant newer contributions by Barbe (1963), Kaufmann (1981), and Torrance (1972, 1981). While Terman's research dominates the topic of giftedness, his studies did not include all types of giftedness. In fact, the subjects may be characterized as being middle-class Californians with high IQs. We will return to the issues associated with the Terman research.

EARLY RESEARCH: PORTRAIT OF A GIFTED CHILD

The early research portrays the gifted child as coming from a familial environment that indirectly encourages the development of giftedness. Both parents tend to have more formal education than families without gifted children. A disproportionate number of fathers are employed in professional, semiprofessional, or business occupations. The family income is usually middle to upper-middle class. The gifted come from "good" homes where children receive necessities, have parental supervision, and live where stimulating materials such as books abound. Terman and Oden (1947) reported that "as a rule the homes [of gifted children] themselves tended to be distinctly superior to the neighborhood in which they were situated" (p. 16). Based on Terman's data, the gifted child's family is stable in terms of a low incidence of divorce and separation, although it is questionable in the 2000s that this would still be the case.

The probability of a family with one gifted child having another gifted child is greater than chance alone. However, first-born children and only children have a greater tendency of being identified as gifted.

The gifted child, contrary to popular notions, is physically healthy. "In all respects the results of the measurements showed that the gifted group was slightly superior physically to the various groups used for comparison" (Terman & Oden, 1947, p. 20). However, significant exceptions to this finding have appeared (Goertzel, Goertzel, & Goertzel, 1978).

Apparently, gifted children have good prenatal care. Their mothers are healthy, the children are born after a full term, and they tend to have a larger birth weight than other infants. They are breast-fed. They tend to walk and talk earlier than usual. They are physically active. They may reach puberty a little earlier. There is an increased likelihood that they will wear glasses.

> The results provide a striking contrast to the popular stereotype of the child prodigy so commonly depicted as a pathetic creature, overserious and undersized, sickly, hollow-chested, stoop-shouldered, clumsy, nervously tense, and bespectacled. There are gifted children who bear some resemblance to this stereotype, but the truth is that almost every element in the picture, except the last, is less characteristic of the gifted child than of the mentally average. (Terman & Oden, 1947, p. 24)

The gifted child relishes learning. The gifted child enters school about the same age as other children. Many quickly advance to a higher grade. About half can read before entering school. Most are accelerated in schoolwork by one grade, although this pattern in recent years is likely changing given the myriad options available to schools. Their teachers recognize their need for more challenging work, but they tend to underestimate their achievement potential by several grade levels.

The overwhelming majority of these children like school, especially the girls, although one summary of biographies indicated that gifted students dislike school (Goertzel et al., 1978). These children are generally successful in school, although their grades frequently do not reflect their real achievement. Being gifted should not be equated with top grades, yet gifted students rarely fail courses. In high school, "the girls receive(d) a grade of 'A' in nearly three quarters of their schoolwork, the boys in 45 percent" (Burks et al., 1930, p. 108). In general achievement, the gifted tend to be substantially ahead of the nongifted. This observation does not appear to be due to practice at home. Below ninth grade, the gifted average less than 2 hours of homework per week, or 15 minutes per day.

The gifted child tends to achieve about 44% above his or her chronological age. In practice, the average gifted 10-year-old is 3 full years beyond his or her peers on standardized tests.

> It is a conservative estimate that more than half of the children with IQs of 135 or above had already mastered the school curriculum to a point two full grades beyond the one in which they were enrolled, and some of them as much as three or four grades beyond. (Terman & Oden, 1947, p. 28)

This finding has been replicated (Martinson, 1961) and widely reported (U.S. Department of Education, 1993).

These achievement patterns are not the same for all academic subjects. The gifted tend to do better in subjects requiring language and abstract thinking. Reading, language arts, mathematical reasoning, science, literature, and the arts are high-achievement areas for the gifted. In subject areas that do not require much abstract thinking, such as spelling and computation, they do not achieve as highly. Their performance is essentially average in handwriting, home economics, and shop training. Surprisingly, their superiority in history and social studies is not consistent with superiority in literature and science. Whether this relationship is due to some element of giftedness or to school practices is unclear. The pattern of differential strengths in various subjects should not suggest that the gifted display greater disparity or irregularities of achievement across subjects than the nongifted. However, this finding may be an artifact of the ceiling effect in tests, rather than a representation of the abilities of the gifted.

The success of gifted students in the more abstract subject areas may be associated with their interests. They appear to like practical subjects less than their peers do. However, both groups like games and sports. The gifted seem to be somewhat more interested than their peers in literature, dramatics, ancient history, and debating than in industrial arts and handwriting. When these practical subjects are put in a more exotic context, such as calligraphy instead of handwriting, the differences vanish.

Gifted children have many interests and they appear to be generally enthusiastic. They like active, physical games and prefer to play with one person. They, like the nongifted, would prefer not to play alone, but the gifted seem to cope with it better. In general, the gifted enjoy activities similar to those favored by other children, although they seem to have greater intellectual and social interests. The interests of gifted boys are decidedly masculine. The gifted seem to prefer games that older children like to play. In fact, they seem to like older playmates. There is a slight indication that gifted children may prefer activities that are less sociable and less active than other children. Goertzel et al. (1978) reported that the gifted have less interest in social and competitive activities, which may be accounted for by the fact that the gifted tend to be younger than their peers and they like two-person games. It is also likely that some of these children could be characterized as socially disinterested.

The gifted love to read and read a great variety of material. Parents and teachers indicate that gifted children are in the habit of reading. Parents report that children read approximately 6 hours a week at age 7, and the length of time increases with age.

A gifted person is a composite of many traits that are demonstrated in his or her daily life. It is clear that the gifted do not become less intelligent as they grow older. Intellectual characteristics are observed in the young gifted child. Parents frequently notice these characteristics, such as quick understanding, endless curiosity, large amounts of knowledge, extensive vocabulary, strong memory, and interests in numbers, maps, and encyclopedias. Teachers have noted that gifted children seem to be original in thought. They actively want to know, and they have common sense. Many of these traits are descriptive of creative behavior (Torrance, 1965).

Gifted children exhibit interesting qualities in terms of motivation. They seem to have will power and perseverance. They maintain a problem set, and they have endurance (Root, 1931). They wish to do well in their interest area. They seem to bring self-confidence and cautious planning to a situation. In conjunction with these motivational qualities, gifted children seem to be cheerful; they have a sense of humor and are optimistic. They appreciate beauty and music. From an ethical perspective, gifted children are truthful, conscientious, sympathetic, and somewhat generous. As leaders, they are recognized by others; they are popular, sensitive, and modest. The gifted are among the most popular students throughout their school years. At the elementary level, their popularity is the highest. At the secondary level, commitment to intellectual activities without other interests can lead to lower popularity. The "studious" subgroup is likely to be unpopular (Tannenbaum, 1962).

Taken together, these qualities suggest that gifted children

> are not as a group characterized by intellectual one-sidedness, emotional instability, lack of sociability or of social adaptability, or other types of maladjusted personality; indeed in practically every personality and character trait such children average much better than the general school population. (Burks et al., 1930, p. 473)

These personality characteristics are maintained into adulthood.

The portrait of gifted children from the early research is an impressive one. The case of Dora in the first chapter is an example. Although there is no one who precisely fits her case history, there are a large number of children whose case histories do closely approximate it. A graphic summary of this portrait is provided in Figure 2.1, which compares the average gifted to the nongifted child. The concentric circles illustrate departures from average performance. It is important to note that Figure 2.1 is a group, not an individual portrait. Many instances exist of gifted children who do not fit this picture.

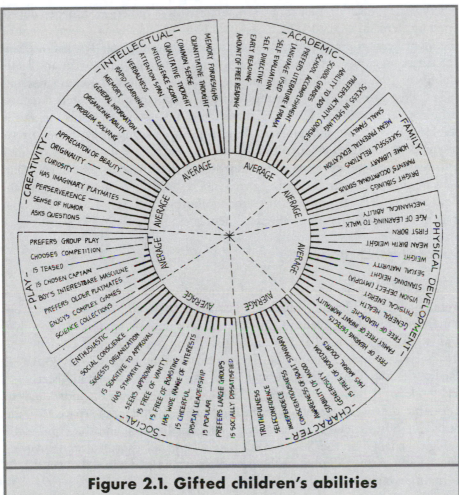

Figure 2.1. Gifted children's abilities

Note. From *Gifted Children*, by M. Freehill, 1961, New York: MacMillan. Copyright ©1961 by Office of the Superintendent of Public Schools of Ventura, CA. Reprinted with permission.

Other case studies reported in Chapter 1 illustrate this point. There are gifted children who have problems or come from backgrounds that complicate the identification of their giftedness. These groups are the nonmodal gifted. They are discussed in later sections of this chapter and throughout the text.

ISSUES IN THE PORTRAIT OF A GIFTED CHILD

Validity of the Portrait

Given that the portrait of the gifted child is based on data dating back to the 1920s, is it a valid portrait of gifted youth living today? This question can be addressed by considering more recent descriptions of the gifted.

A Scale for Rating Behavioral Characteristics of Superior Students, developed by Renzulli et al. (1971), has gained wide popularity as a component of the identification process of gifted children. The rating scale is a list of characteristics organized into four parts: learning, motivation, creativity, and leadership. Figure 2.2 is adapted from the scale. Note how the characteristics subsumed under each part are reminiscent of the portrait just created and confirm its relative stability. However, one should not assume that this portrait is stable for non-White and non-middle-class groups because they are underrepresented in the research literature. Thus, in the midst of this high-quality information, there are some significant issues that must be examined when considering the portrait of the gifted child based on the early research. Because the data is comprised of urban-suburban Whites, Terman's sample may not be representative of all gifted people.

Sociocultural Environment

Another issue is the sociocultural environment in which the early studies were conducted. The individuals studied by Terman and his associates were children in the 1920s, teens in the '20s and '30s, college students in the '30s, and adult workers in the '30s and '40s. Their lives were affected by the "macrosystem" and "chronosystem," terms Bronfenbrenner (1979, 1986, 1994) used to described the cultural influences of their place and time in his ecological model of human development. Much has changed since the individuals in Terman's study were of school age. World War II, Vietnam, the space race, the turbulent '60s, societal changes of the '70s, globalization, and the rapid technological changes in the '80s and '90s have all created a sociocultural environment with vastly different influences than those affecting the youths in Terman's sample.

Divorce rates are a good example. Practically unheard of in the '20s and '30s, a divorced family situation is commonplace today. The advancement of communication technologies over the past decades is another area of substantial change (Cross, 2004). Such influences are likely to have a significant impact on the gifted children of today.

Selection of Gifted Students

The selection process of gifted students has also changed since the 1920s. Terman selected his subjects solely through the use of IQ scores, a procedure that tends to exclude some people with high levels of talent. Furthermore, limited data are available on gifted people from rural backgrounds or gifted people with physical or learning problems. Much recent interest has been focused on these overlooked groups (e.g., gifted students who are diagnosed with Attention-Deficit Hyperactivity Disorder or learning disabilities and minority gifted students). Thus, in addition to changes in the macro- and chronosystems, changes in the way we define and identify giftedness needs to be considered when evaluating the early portrait of a gifted child. Such a portrait is essential to understanding much of what has occurred in gifted education in the United States since the 1920s. Thus, an appreciation of the current status of gifted education lies in the understanding of the early research.

In addition to the issues raised above, other considerations and questions may be raised about other areas of the gifted child composite. These areas are sex differences, the stability of intelligence, socioeconomic status and ethnic issues, special talents, emotional stability, and the creatively gifted.

Sex Differences

Are there any substantial differences between gifted girls and boys in the portrait? Significant differences do exist, but the meaning of these differences is not clear. The older research suggests that more boys than girls have high intelligence. For example, Root (1931) used the Stanford-Binet to find 53 "supernormal" children of various ages in which the ratio was 32 males to 21 females. Terman and Oden (1947) reported 557 males to 493 females, or a ratio of 1.13:1. Terman and Oden attempted to account for this finding by conducting additional analyses, but they failed to reveal any statistical bias related to selection of subjects. They also showed that boys had greater IQ variability in abilities than girls (i.e., more high and more low IQs). Incidentally, the three highest IQs were produced by girls. Terman and Oden noted that this sex difference was also shown with thousands of subjects in a Scottish study, which showed a male-to-female ratio of 1.34:1. Later research by Nancy Bayley (1970) showed no real sex differences in IQ scores. Analyzing sex differences in a study ranging far beyond IQ scores, Maccoby and Jacklin (1974) concluded that the overlap in abilities between the sexes would predict gifted behavior in women in all areas. Yet, other data revealed a general lowered achievement level in girls, especially after elementary school, when compared to similar ability in boys.

On the whole, gifted children of both sexes do significantly better than their nongifted peers on standardized achievement tests. Girls seem to do better in English, while boys achieve significantly better in science (Burks et al., 1930; Kelly, 1978) and math (Burks et al.; Fox, Brody, & Tobin, 1974). However, when grades are used as the criterion, girls receive higher average marks in everything, including science and math (Burks et al.; Kimball, 1989). Among the most mathematically gifted, "marked gender differences exist on the two major classes of special abilities critical for engineering and physical science achievement and excellence" (Benbow & Lubinski, 1994, p. 265).

An interesting and significant difference in scholastic interests appears when the gifted and nongifted are compared. The interests of gifted boys are more similar to those of nongifted boys than the interests of gifted girls are to those of nongifted girls. In this way, the gifted girls' interests are more like

Part I: Learning Characteristics

1. Has unusually advanced vocabulary for age or grade level.
2. Possesses a large storehouse of information about a variety of topics.
3. Has quick mastery and recall of factual information.
4. Has rapid insight into cause-effect relationships; wants to know what makes things (or people) "tick."
5. Has a ready grasp of underlying principles and can quickly make valid generalizations about events, people, or things.
6. Is a keen and alert observer; usually "sees more" or "gets more" out of a story, film, and so forth, than others.
7. Reads a great deal on his or her own; usually prefers adult-level books.
8. Tries to understand complicated material by separating it into its respective parts; reasons things out for him- or herself; sees logical and common sense answers.

Part II: Motivational Characteristics

1. Becomes absorbed and truly involved in certain topics or problems; is persistent in seeking task completion.
2. Is easily bored with routine tasks.
3. Needs little external motivation to follow through in work that initially excites him or her.
4. Strives toward perfection; is self-critical.
5. Prefers to work independently; requires little direction from teachers.
6. Is interested in many "adult" problems such as religion, politics, sex, race—more than usual for age level.
7. Often is self-assertive; stubborn in his or her beliefs.
8. Likes to organize and bring structure to things, people, and situations.
9. Is quite concerned with right and wrong.

Part III: Creativity Characteristics

1. Displays a great deal of curiosity about many things; is constantly asking questions about anything and everything.
2. Generates a large number of ideas on problems; often offers unusual, clever responses.
3. Is uninhibited in expressions of opinion; is sometimes radical and spirited in disagreement.
4. Is a high risk-taker; is adventurous and speculative.

5. Displays a good deal of intellectual playfulness; fantasizes; imagines; is often concerned with adapting, improving, and modifying institutions, objects, and systems.

6. Displays a keen sense of humor and sees humor in situations that may not appear to be humorous to others.

7. Is unusually aware of his or her impulses and is more open to the irrational in him- or herself (freer expression of feminine interest for boys, greater than usual amount of independence for girls); shows emotional sensitivity.

8. Is sensitive to beauty.

9. Is nonconforming.

10. Criticizes constructively; is unwilling to accept authoritarian pronouncements without critical examination.

Part IV: Leadership Characteristics

1. Carries responsibility well.

2. Is self-confident with children his or her own age, as well as adults.

3. Seems to be well liked by his or her classmates.

4. Is cooperative with teacher and classmates.

5. Can express him- or herself well; has good verbal facility, and is usually well-understood.

6. Adapts readily to new situations.

7. Seems to enjoy being around other people; generally directs the activity in which he or she is involved.

8. Participates in most social activities connected with the school.

9. Excels in athletic activities; is well coordinated and enjoys all sorts of athletic games.

Figure 2.2 Behavioral characteristics of the gifted

Note. From "Teacher Identification of Superior Students," by J. S. Renzulli, R. H. Hartman, and C. M. Callahan, 1971, *Exceptional Children, 38*, pp. 211–214, 243–248. Copyright ©1971 by the Council for Exceptional Children. Adapted with permission.

those of gifted boys than nongifted girls. "In other words, the scholastic interests of girls appear to be more influenced by superior intelligence than those of boys" (Terman & Oden, 1947, p. 31).

The performance differences that persist between the sexes and cannot be accounted for by levels of ability suggest the operation of social forces that have different effects on the development of talent in boys and girls. These forces are detailed in Chapter 4 on guidance. The differences between the sexes become sharper when we look at income, occupational achievement, and status in the portrait of gifted adults (Kaufmann, 1981; Tomlinson-Keasey & Little, 1990).

Stability of IQ

The question of what happens to the intelligence quotients of gifted children has long been of interest to researchers. Burks et al. (1930) devoted an entire chapter to this question. Subsequent studies have also looked at this issue in terms of adults (Terman & Oden, 1947) and found that the IQs of gifted children change. For some individuals, the change is remarkable. When the entire group is considered, it becomes clear that the majority of gifted children maintain their relative superiority over the nongifted. A relatively small number fall below the IQ range usually classified as the gifted.

Some current studies, on the other hand, have indicated that IQs remain stable over time. Spangler and Sabatino (1995), for example, gathered longitudinal data to investigate the temporal stability of gifted children's intelligence. They reported statistically stable verbal, performance, and full scale IQ scores.

Socioeconomic Status and Ethnic Issues

The gifted are found in all segments of society. Socioeconomic status and race are discussed together because they tend to confound each other. It is clear that "no race or nationality has any monopoly on brains" (Terman & Oden, 1947, p. 14). Nevertheless, a disproportionately high number of people from the White middle class are found in studies of gifted children. Furthermore, a disproportionately high number of Jewish and Chinese children are found among the gifted (Martinson, 1961; Terman, 1925). Why this happens is not clear, although many different hypotheses have been offered. It is likely that the values reflected in the composition of tests and the learning reflected in the performance of children interact in a manner that conceals the abilities of children from non-middle-class families. This is a serious problem that has led to many proposals, and it demands resolution (Bernal, 1979; Cooke & Baldwin, 1979; Ford, 1996). At present, the portrait of gifted children is seriously flawed by the lack of information about these groups. When the discussion turns to the process of identification, creativity, and guidance, this issue will be looked at in-depth.

Special Abilities and IQ

According to our composite portrait, gifted children have many strengths. This picture of a broad range of highly developed abilities obscures the fact that children with unusually advanced ability in a narrow area are also found among the gifted. In fact, some people believe that it is a special ability, rather than many high abilities, that makes one truly gifted (e.g., Stanley, 1979; Stanley & Benbow, 1986).

Terman (1925) was aware of this distinction and sought to find children who exhibited special abilities. He searched for examples of special ability in art, music, manual training, domestic science, and agriculture because he believed that this search would help locate children with very high intelligence. Only 26 cases were nominated. They had a mean IQ of 114, and the special abilities were distributed as follows: 15 had artistic ability, 10 had musical ability, and 1 had mechanical ability. Six years later, 19 of these children— 12 artistic and 7 musical—were in a follow-up study. The findings indicated that fewer than half of the subjects remained more than slightly interested in their area of special ability. Interest in musical ability seemed to be more permanent. Interestingly, none of these special ability subjects, except for one musician, had achieved in or outside of his or her field of interest in a manner comparable to the regular gifted group.

These data suggest that (1) the special ability cases may not really have had special abilities, (2) special abilities in nonacademic areas were not identified, or (3) "without the support of high intelligence, special talent is not likely to mature into achievements of very unusual merit" (Burks et al., 1930, p. 243).

This third possibility is supported by Cox's (1926) retrospective study of 300 geniuses. All these people had unquestionable special abilities and varying degrees of estimated general intelligence. Cox's data showed that high intelligence is a highly probable concomitant of outstanding achievement and that this level of intelligence is noticeable before the age of 17. Incidentally, a fascinating sidelight to the Cox data was an indication that the IQ of eminent people increased with age. Since the earlier IQs for some people were estimated to be between 120 and 135, this level of IQ might have excluded such people from a study like Terman's. However, it is likely that these estimates are a little low.

The relationship between IQ and special ability is far from clear. Retrospective studies suggest that people of special ability are likely to be brighter than their peers with no special abilities. Goertzel et al. (1978) suggested that special abilities are noticeable at an early age, but they did not directly address the question of a relationship to intelligence. Hildreth (1966) commented that the mean IQ of the student body at the High School of Performing Arts in New York City was about 121. These students are certainly highly talented and have special abilities. Other work by Stanley (1980) and Robinson, Roedell, and Jackson (1979) suggests that, even though high general ability and special academic abilities are associated in children, they are not the same thing. Golomb (2004) noted that the data on artistically gifted normal children and the findings on autistic savants (mentally retarded autistic children whose drawings greatly exceed the standards attained by normal children) highlight the tenuous relationship between intelligence and artistic achievement.

In conclusion, it appears that much remains to be learned about the relationship of IQ to special abilities and IQ to academic abilities. It is probable that talents that make use of abstraction and projection may require more general intelligence than other talents. It is also possible that some level of "minimum" general intelligence is needed before special abilities can be fully developed. Lastly, it is possible that too high a level of general intelligence works against the development (in some areas) of special abilities (Feldman, 1980). All these possibilities complicate the process of identifying gifted children.

Emotional Stability

The accuracy in our portrait of the emotional stability or general emotional development of gifted children is commonly questioned. Conventional wisdom suggests that gifted people are generally unstable and crazy and that gifted children will eventually become that way.

Terman (1925) expended much effort in an attempt to understand the relationship between intellect and emotional development using a battery of seven paper-and-pencil tests. Eighty-five percent of the gifted subjects between the ages of 10 and 14 were scored as being more stable than average (the data on younger subjects were not reliable). Overall, the data indicated that the gifted had developed to a level of maturity typical of older children. These findings corresponded to ratings given to the gifted children by teachers and by parents. The raters were in general agreement on 12 different traits, and these ratings were found to be consistent over a 6-year interval. The gifted as a group were found to be emotionally stable (Burks et al., 1930; Terman). Later studies of Merit Scholarship winners confirmed the finding (Nichols & Davis, 1964; Warren & Heist, 1960). These findings for the group show the gifted to be developing healthier personalities than their nongifted peers.

In a review of the literature, Neihart (1999) noted two contrasting positions about the psychological well-being of gifted children. One is that giftedness enhances an individual's resiliency; the other is that giftedness increases vulnerability. She concluded that neither viewpoint is adequate for understanding the influence of giftedness on an individual's psychological well-being. Rather, positive or negative psychological outcomes seem to depend on the type of giftedness, the educational fit, and the personal characteristics (e.g., self-perceptions, temperament, and circumstances) of the gifted child.

As Neihart's conclusions suggest, all gifted children do not have similar developmental courses. The gifted as a group present a wide range of abilities and traits, and within this group are atypical people. One such subgroup are the people with IQs three or four standard deviations above the mean. Terman studied subjects with IQs of 170 or above, and on the basis of data gathered in 1922, 1928, and 1940, these subjects received personality ratings "almost identical" to the whole gifted group (Terman & Oden, 1947). In terms of social adjustment, the findings were similar. Other authorities have suggested that this group may experience more problems, but not necessarily emotional instability, because of their inability to find peers of similar abilities and interests or because of the varying expectations, often antithetical, placed on them in differing environments (Coleman, 1985a; Cross, 1997b). Hollingworth (1942) suggested that, at an IQ of 160, the difficulty begins. Martinson (1972) suggested that these problems, if any, are a result of family background and educational circumstances and not of IQ. Regarding educational circumstances, Gross (1998, 1999) noted that highly gifted children as young as kindergarten age may conform to the social or behavioral norms of their age group once they become aware of the differences between their abilities and those of their peers.

The Creatively Gifted

Within the gifted there is a subgroup of people who possess one characteristic in such abundance that their collective portrait might depart from the one we have drawn. This group is the creatively gifted. Torrance (1979b) believed the creatively gifted have unique needs. As a consequence, they experience their giftedness in an unconventional way and make less-orthodox career and life choices. In essence, the interaction between creative potential and social norms means that the creatively gifted find themselves to be "a minority of one" more frequently than other gifted children. One can infer from this situation that the portrait of the creatively gifted contains more evidence of social disinterest, greater attention to the pursuit of solitary interests, less evidence of full social acceptance, and more conflict than the general portrait of the gifted. Whether these possibilities lead to a clearly different portrait than that constructed for the total group of gifted children is arguable. The discussion in Chapter 5 on guidance and Chapter 6 on creativity provides evidence on this issue.

THE GIFTED AS ADULTS

The gifted child has the potential to become a gifted adult. Do gifted children fulfill this promise? Do they tend to disappear into obscurity? What is known about their functioning as adults? How do they view their lives? This section explores the provocative data on gifted adults. Evidence is presented to address these questions.

An entire section devoted to the gifted as adults may seem unwarranted in a text focusing on schooling. The reason for its inclusion is that information on adults is a significant source of background material that one needs for understanding later chapters. For example, data on sources of life satisfaction and career choice are useful for comprehending the discussions on guidance and on families. The data on career portraits and predictors of accomplishments are relevant for following the discussions on identification and on educational programs.

Definitions

It is more difficult to create a modal portrait of the gifted adult than the gifted child because of the variability of characteristics within the adult population. The historical circumstances and the careers available in a particular epoch have an undeniable influence on the manifestation of abilities. With the "standardizing" influence of schooling, patterns of child rearing, and the dependency of youth removed, the lives of gifted adults go in myriad directions. However, it is possible to group the careers of adults; in this way, we may be able to make certain generalizations about the gifted as adults.

The evidence on gifted adults may be conceptualized as "Terman" and "non-Terman." The non-Terman sources are many. One such source is bibliographic studies that examine historical information on people judged to be gifted. The following are examples of some excellent studies: *Age and Achievement* (Lehman, 1953); *Cradles of Eminence* (Goertzel & Goertzel, 1962, 2004); *300 Eminent Personalities* (Goertzel et al., 1978); *Beyond Terman: Contemporary Longitudinal Studies of Giftedness and Talent* (Subotnik & Arnold, 1993), and *Women's Lives Through Time: Educated American Women of the Twentieth Century* (Day Hulbert & Tickton Schuster, 1993). Another source is studies concerned with people in a specific field or career. Examples include *The Making of a Scientist* (Roe, 1953) and *The Scientific Elite* (Zuckerman, 1977). A third source is research on creativity (Bullough, Bullough, & Mauro, 1981; Torrance, 1972, 1981), scholarship winners (Kaufmann, 1981), and semifinalists and finalists in the Westinghouse Science Talent Search (Subotnik, Stone, & Steiner, 2001).

The Terman sources are the continuation of the monumental study of 1,500 gifted children. The samples obtained in 1922 have been followed up to the present, and data on the subjects are available from 1945, 1950, 1955, 1960, 1972, and 1986. Taken together, these sources complement each other and present information that has widespread implications for the identification, guidance, and education of gifted children. The points at which the information is contradictory are noted.

A discussion of the gifted as adults requires that an effort be made to clarify the meaning of the terms *adult* and *gifted*. *Adult* refers to people who have attained the age of 17 or older. Seventeen is an appropriate age because most gifted children have left secondary school or have left their parents' homes by then. This age was also used by Cox (1926) in some of her analyses. The term *gifted* may present some problems to readers because it is not used by all the authors cited in this section; however, a perusal of these references will show that the definition proposed in this text clearly defines these people as being gifted.

A Brief Sketch

The gifted as adults face as many crosscurrents of life as do the nongifted. In this sense, their experience is similar to that of everyone, yet they experience life in a different way because their abilities make them more sensitive, may make them more visible to others, and can help them realize a wider range of expression. The most eminent among the gifted seem to be cognizant of the effect they have on others.

The gifted as adults demonstrate many of the qualities they did as children. The activities they were attracted to and interested in continue in the careers they choose (Oden, 1968; Torrance, 1981). The gifted do not suffer from a diminution in their abilities as they age; rather, they love to continue learning about what interests them. Their abilities seem to crystallize and expand. Although much of their most original and highest quality work is accomplished in their adult years prior to age 30, they continue to make significant contributions long afterward. Frequently, the most productive period in terms of quality comes early in their careers; in terms of quantity, it comes later in their careers.

The gifted adult tends to associate with people who have similar interests and abilities. When the restrictions imposed on social behavior in childhood are removed, this tendency becomes very clear. The foremost scientists, writers, and musicians in a period are frequently acquainted. Without meaning to oversimplify, it seems that something more than accident is occurring when various cities, universities, or even sections of cities become the places where many of the top people in a field can be found (Bullough et al., 1981). This tendency is being modified due to increased mobility, telecommunications, and the Internet. An interesting point is that, when gifted people associate with each other, the magnitude of their differences tends to be less evident.

High ability does not lead to success in all areas of life. Some of the gifted purposefully choose to adopt lifestyles that do not tax their abilities. They choose careers that leave them time to pursue a wide variety of outside interests.

Gifted adults seem to need periods of isolation to be able to pursue their thoughts or work on a subject. This, as well as a strong commitment to a particular endeavor, may make them difficult to live with. Gifted adults tend to marry and have children. The conventionality of their lifestyle, or its lack thereof, seem to be related to factors of family background, sex, career choice, and perhaps creativity. Overall, gifted adults seem to derive considerable satisfaction from their lives; but, one should not conclude that they are happy or unhappy. Gifted adults are complex people who lead complex lives.

Sources of Life Satisfaction

The brief sketch of gifted adults sets the general pattern of their lives, but it fails to get at specifics. Do these people of outstanding ability value life in a way that differs from the nongifted? As their achievements gain them recognition and perhaps fame, are they seeking different satisfactions? Answers to what they value and how they conduct their lives are given in this section. Information comes from Terman's research and that of others, and each source of data is presented separately.

The Terman Group

Again, the Terman data are a rich source of information on these questions. Data gathered in 1940, 1960, and 1972 form the basis for the following discussion.

In 1972, the Terman group completed questionnaires on how they viewed major areas of their lives: occupational success, family life, friendships, richness of cultural life, total service to society, and joy of living (Sears, 1979). The 916 respondents were divided almost equally by sex. The subjects who were in their 60s were asked to make a judgment about how important these areas were to them as young adults and to what degree they felt satisfied in these areas. There were significant sex differences, as the men valued occupation much more than the women, who placed significantly more importance in all the other areas. The exception was total service to society, where there was no difference. Both sexes valued family life the highest. Sears observed that, between the sexes, "women evidently planned in early adulthood for a more varied or multifaceted type of life" (p. 81). The areas in which they believed themselves to be most successful also showed significant difference between the sexes. Men felt more successful than women in occupations, while women felt more successful with friendships and richness of cultural life. On family, service, and joy of living, the sexes were not significantly different.

These findings can be misleading if one forgets the relationship between importance and success and if one ignores the difference in occupational history of the sexes. In an effort to deal with these problems, a special scale was constructed to account for the confusion in comparing one's success in areas of unequal importance. The new variable confirmed the findings on differences in ratings of success and importance between men and women. Again, family life was found to be the highest area of life satisfaction for both sexes.

The vocational history of the men and the women might account for the significant difference in how they rated the importance, success, and life satisfaction of an occupation. Since more than half the women had a limited history as income producers, even though they were active outside the home, they were removed from the comparison. Therefore, 43% of the women who were defined as income workers were compared to the men. Even in this comparison, the men continued to attach significantly more importance to occupation than did the women, but there was no significant difference between the sexes on success achieved in an occupation nor on general satisfaction in the occupation (Sears, 1979).

The contrast in occupational importance and work roles of men and women prompted a further inquiry into factors leading to occupational satisfaction for men and women. It appears that gifted men who felt successful in work continued to work longer and put off retirement. These people tended to be better educated and had higher occupational status. They seemed to be more involved in their work. Interestingly, money was not a significant factor (Sears, 1977).

The data on women are most provocative because of the mixed roles women perform—homemaker, career worker, noncareer worker, homemaker-career worker—and the relationship of their roles to satisfaction with life. It had been hypothesized that women who had a "full life," including marriage, children, career, and a good income, would be more satisfied with life than those who did not have such a "full life." For the Terman women, this was not the case. Apparently, being married, having a career, and not having children are aspects that are connected to higher life-satisfaction scores. One should not conclude that family and children are not important, but rather "a satisfying style of work [as viewed at about 60 years of age] apparently does not need to be that full!" (Sears, 1979, p. 87).

Family life has been shown from these data to be the most highly rated area of life satisfaction (Oden, 1968) and the most satisfying area for the Terman group at around age 60 (Sears, 1979). For these reasons, family life is examined more closely. About one quarter of the sample group had been divorced. Stability of the marriage is related to economic factors. Mates tended to have similar personalities, and they had IQs comparable to the average college graduate. Most couples had children, who tended to have above-average intelligence, and the familiar regression effect was observed. Marital happiness seems comparable to the nongifted group (Sears, 1979).

Non-Terman Data

Ratings of life satisfaction are not directly available from non-Terman data because the gifted adults were not asked to respond to that question. Instead, data were gathered from biographies and other sources, thus making a few tentative generalizations possible.

Gifted adults tend to work in urban environments. They are deeply and actively concerned about their personal lives. They continue to be active searchers for knowledge. The urge to succeed or, at least, "do their own thing" seems to pervade their lives. Their choice of career or occupation seems to provide more opportunity for autonomy, which is very important to gifted adults (Goertzel et al., 1978; Roe, 1953).

The gifted tend to have conventional lifestyles, yet they are "much more likely to be divorced or to remain single than other adults, and they are likely to be inadequate as parents" (Goertzel et al., 1978, p. 338). Gifted women who are famous seem to experience difficulty in family life. These women are divorced more than men. Interestingly, a large proportion of gifted women had no children: "Only seven of the eighty-one women were able to combine marriage, children, and a career" (Goertzel et al., p. 347). It was not possible from these data to determine if the husbands were gifted, too.

Summary

These findings seem to be somewhat contradictory. The Terman data suggest much more satisfaction from family life than the non-Terman and

45

Kaufmann data. Both indicate life satisfaction may be more difficult for women, especially since involvement and commitment to career is an important aspect of satisfaction (Kaufmann, 1981). Upon reanalyzing the Terman data, Tomlinson-Keasey and Little (1990) reported that their work "adds a third longitudinal study documenting the importance of personal determination in maintaining intellectual skills and interests [over a long career]" (p. 451). Considering the fact that the career is so important to the gifted and is a major part of their adult lives, an examination of career accomplishment is warranted in order to comprehend more fully the texture of their lives.

Career Choices and Accomplishments

People spend the majority of their lives involved in a chosen career, and this choice has an obvious effect on them. The gifted seem to prefer some careers more than other careers. However, it is not possible to describe the composite gifted adult career because people change careers over the years, economic and political conditions change, and the continuous standardizing influences of school and family are no longer felt. Once again, the two major sources of information are considered separately.

The Terman Data

The careers of the gifted may be categorized on several bases. Terman is a major source of information on careers and career changes over the years (Oden, 1968; Terman & Oden, 1947, 1959). The data on occupational types are quite consistent over time. Table 2.1 and Table 2.2 contain a breakdown of the variety of occupations held by employed men and women in 1960. The majority of the gifted are in professional or semiprofessional occupations. The next largest group is in business occupations. Relatively few are engaged in other occupations. Note the greater variety of occupations among the men than among the women (in 1960). This finding is probably a consequence of social conditioning, as well as opportunity.

Two measures of achievement are occupational status and income. Even though the Terman group was selected on a very stringent IQ criterion in 1921–1922, "20 years later they ranged in vocational success all the way from international eminence to semi-skilled labor" (Terman & Oden, 1947, p. 311). Forty years later, in 1968, this range was still evident (Oden, 1968).

That statement applies predominantly to men. A similar statement might be made about the gifted women as adults, but in 1945 few gifted women entered professional careers. Most became housewives, and Terman did not study this group. The 1960 and 1970 data indicated that women entered a variety of occupations, ranging from professional-managerial to clerical. However, their career choices seem narrower, excluding the fact that many remained housewives throughout their lives (Oden, 1968; Sears, 1979).

When compared to the general population of their generation, the gifted men were quite different from their peers. Seventy-one percent of the gifted were professional and semiprofessional compared to 14% of the nongifted. Only 6% of the gifted were in semiskilled or unskilled occupations, compared to almost 50% of the general population. (Interestingly, only 1% were unemployed during the Great Depression.) The proportions remain fairly constant over the next 20 years; yet, some individuals made large changes. A slight decrease in trends in semiskilled and unskilled occupations and an increase in professional work is evident (Oden, 1968; Terman & Oden, 1959).

Seventy percent of the gifted were college graduates, 10 times above the average for the general population. They also earned significantly more honors in college. Sixteen percent earned Phi Beta Kappa or Sigma Chi honors. Twenty-nine percent earned one or more graduate degrees, compared to 3% of the general population. Given the occupational status of the group, it is apparent that many earned Ph.D.s or other doctoral, medical, or law degrees (Terman & Oden, 1959; see Table 2.2)

The income difference between the gifted and nongifted is also evident. In 1944, the gifted earned approximately 1.7 times more than the average person. The proportion of gifted men earning more than $5,000 was six times the national average. However, gifted women earned salaries close to the average population (Terman & Oden, 1947). Overall, the gifted men earned an income that exceeded their nongifted peers (Terman & Oden, 1959).

When the numbers of publications written and patents obtained are compared, further differences emerge. In 1945, when the gifted were about 35 years of age, they "had published about ninety books or monographs and approximately 1,500 articles in scientific, scholarly or literary magazines" (Terman & Oden, 1947, p. 300). The publications covered all fields of endeavor. More than 100 patents were granted, but 50 were from just two men. Terman and Oden believed that the numbers would have been greater if World War II had not required that gifted men's energies be directed elsewhere. The figures clearly outstrip the national average, but none of the publications or patents was of "epoch-making importance" (Terman & Oden, 1947). The 1968 data confirm this notion.

The Terman study has clearly made a significant contribution to our society in this century. One can say a high IQ in the 1920s was a useful variable for predicting success, although it is clear that high IQ is insufficient to the task of predicting success among the gifted. It is also apparent that high intelligence does not automatically lead to the level of achievement exemplified in the work of Curie, Mozart, Einstein, Picasso, Brontë, Marx, and Freud, among others. On the other hand, to expect one region of America, in this case California, to contain children in a 50-year period capable of such feats of intellect and creativity is highly improbable. Moreover, it is clear that the patterns of the occupations noted have been affected by the historical zeitgeist experienced by the Terman group subjects' cohort.

TABLE 2.1

Occupations of Employed Men—1960

Occupation	No. in Terman Group Employed	%
I. Professional		
Lawyers (includes judges)	77	10.4
Engineers	56	7.6
Members of college or university faculties	54	7.3
Physical and biological scientists (includes geological scientists)	41	5.6
Physicians (private practice)	39	5.3
Educational administration or teaching below four-year-college level	32	4.3
Authors or journalists	17	2.3
Architects	10	1.4
Economists or political scientists	7	1.0
Clergymen	4	0.5
Psychologists (private or institutional practice)	3	0.4
Other professions	4	0.5
II. Official, Managerial, Semiprofessional		
1. Higher business:		
Business and industry: managers and supervisors (middle management)	48	6.5
Banking and finance, insurance, land development, investments (executives and owners)	45	6.1
Business and industry: officials and executives at policy-making level (top or near-top management)	31	4.2
Accountants, tax consultants, statisticians, etc.	28	3.8
Sales: sales managers, sales engineers, technical representatives	24	3.3
Office workers at supervisory and managerial levels	24	3.3
Advertising promotion, public relations (executives and owners)	15	2.0
Building and construction (owners or officials)	5	0.7
2. Arts and entertainment:		
Motion pictures, radio, or television: writers, artists, producers, directors	16	2.2
Performing arts: musicians or actors	5	0.7

3.	Officials or managers in administration, public or private: public utilities, research institutions, philanthropic organizations, social security administration, local or state government	15	2.0
4.	Army, Navy, or Air Force officers	12	1.6
5.	Officials in federal government: State Department, Defense Department, Foreign Service officers	6	0.8
6.	Miscellaneous business owners	6	0.8
7.	Miscellaneous semiprofessionals	14	1.9

III. Retail business, Clerical and Sales, Skilled Trades

Clerical, sales, and related	33	4.5
Skilled trades and crafts (foremen and supervisors)	25	3.4
Retail business (small) (owners or managers)	10	1.4
Protective services	6	0.8
Professional services	6	0.8

IV. Agriculture and Related Occupations

Ranchers and orchardists	9	1.2
Dairy farmers	2	0.3
Landscape gardeners and horticulturists	1	0.1

V. Minor business or clerical and semiskilled occupations	8	1.1

Total Employed	738

Note. From "The Fulfillment of Promise: 40-Year Follow-Up of the Terman Gifted Group," by M. H. Oden, 1968, *Generic Psychology Monographs, 77*, p. 3–93. Copyright ©1968. Reprinted with permission of the Helen Dwight Reid Educational Foundation. Published by Heldref Publications, 1319 18th St., NW, Washington, DC 20036-1802.

Non-Terman Data

The careers of the gifted can also be tabulated by examining the people studied in the work of Goertzel et al. (1978), who studied 317 eminent personalities, each of whom had been the subject of a biography. These people represented an international sample, but the majority were from the United States and Western Europe. They constituted a heterogeneous group composed of both sexes, and they were certainly eminent and very attractive to some segment of our society. The group was categorized into four career areas: literary, political, artistic, and other. They included

TABLE 2.2

Occupations of Employed Women With Full-Time Employment

Occupation	No. in Terman Group Employed	%
I. Professional and Semiprofessional Occupations		
Teachers (elementary and secondary schools)	58	22.9
Members of college or university faculty	21	8.3
Librarians	15	5.9
Social workers or welfare personnel	14	5.5
Authors or journalists	11	4.3
Physicians	6	2.4
Pharmacists, nurses, or laboratory technicians	6	2.4
Members of junior college faculty	5	2.0
Educational administration or supervisory positions	5	2.0
Economists, political scientists, and related	5	2.0
Physical scientists (industry)	2	0.8
Lawyers	2	0.8
Psychologists (private practice)	2	0.8
Theater arts related	2	0.8
Music teachers	2	0.8
Other professions	3	1.2
II. Business Occupations		
Secretary, bookkeeper, accountant, or related office work	54	21.3
Executive or managerial positions in business or industry	23	9.1
Real estate, insurance, investments	7	2.8
Public relations, promotion, advertising	5	2.0
Miscellaneous	5	2.0
Total Employed	253	

Note. From "The Fulfillment of Promise: 40-Year Follow-Up of the Terman Gifted Group," by M. H. Oden, 1968, *Generic Psychology Monographs, 77,* pp. 3–93. Copyright ©1968. Reprinted with permission of the Helen Dwight Reid Educational Foundation. Published by Heldref Publications, 1319 18th St., NW, Washington, DC 20036-1802.

- 92 literary, including fiction, drama, poetry, and nonfiction editors;
- 77 political, including all political viewpoints, spies, assassins, reformers, and generals;
- 75 artistic, including musicians, directors, and graphic artists; and
- 73 others, including scientists, athletes, religious philosophers, labor leaders, mystics, therapists, and doctors.

Cox (1926) provided another source of career data. Although this study is part of the Terman series, the data are not based on Terman's subjects; therefore, the study is defined as non-Terman. These data are similar to the Goertzels' because they, too, are based on biographical and historical accounts. Cox attempted to group her 300 male geniuses into 10 categories, excluding statesmen and soldiers who inherited their positions (p. 35):

- 52 imaginative writers, including poets, novelists, and dramatists;
- 43 statesmen and politicians;
- 43 writers, including essayists, critics, scholars, and historians;
- 39 scientists;
- 27 soldiers;
- 23 religious leaders;
- 22 philosophers;
- 13 artists;
- 11 musicians; and
- 10 revolutionary statesman.

The categories represent a large number of careers.

Later evidence on careers and accomplishments can be found in a longitudinal report on the lives of Presidential Scholars who were nominated in 1968. Kaufmann (1981) reported that the sample continued to be successful academically through college, and many earned advanced degrees. Seventy-six percent of the subjects were in high-status occupations, although they extended across the occupational spectrum. Most common occupations were college professors (20%), medical doctors (13%), and lawyers (9%). Women tended to be unemployed or employed in clerical positions more frequently than men. Annual income of the entire sample was substantial, but women tended to earn less money. Achievements since high school that the subjects mentioned most frequently were the following: acceptance and implementation of their ideas by colleagues or superiors (46%); publication of journal articles (42%); instruction of coworkers in in-service sessions (35%); presentation of original scholarly papers (3%); and receipt of research monies (27%). One quarter of the sample volunteered information on family, political, religious, and other creative activities. In general, the adult accomplishments of this group are impressive. Considering the age of the sample, many additional accomplishments are likely to occur in the future.

Arnold (1993b) reported on the early adult careers of valedictorians who graduated in the state of Illinois in 1981. No simple formula could be constructed to account for the various choices in careers as school success could not predict professional accomplishment. Among the entire group, the academically outstanding young women were found to lower their intellectual self-esteem as they progressed through college, and movement into a career was convoluted (Arnold, 1993a).

A comparison of these different sources of data using the Goertzel labels (Goertzel & Goertzel, 1962; Goertzel et al., 1978) as the standard for defining categories reveals that the biographical and historical data are more similar to each other than the Terman data in terms of literary and political careers. This may reflect a bias in the sampling procedure of the studies. Literary careers comprise the largest category, approximately one third of each sample. Political careers make up the next largest category, approximately one quarter of the two groups. When searching for these categories in Tables 2.1 and 2.2, it becomes obvious that the Terman group did not enter these careers in the same proportions. Exact comparisons are not possible because of the variations in the definitions by the authors. However, using a liberal yardstick, it would appear that fewer than 15% of the Terman group might be considered literary people (professors, authors, political scientists, artists), and fewer than 20% might be considered political (lawyers, administrators, military professionals). The Kaufmann (1981) data have even smaller percentages.

It is in the artistic category that the greatest differences appear between the Cox (1926) study and the Goertzel studies (Goertzel & Goertzel, 1962; Goertzel et al., 1978), comprising approximately 10 to 23%, respectively, of their samples. The reason for this difference is not apparent. When these figures are compared to the Terman data, very few people (fewer than 5%) could be considered to have artistic careers. The Others category is the third largest category for Goertzel and Cox, with the latter's sample having a slightly larger percentage. It is for the Terman data and the Kaufmann data that the Others category is the most extensive. If semiskilled and agricultural occupations are discounted, inspection of Tables 2.1 and 2.2 shows that professional and semiprofessional careers are peculiar to the 20th century. It is in this century that technology, big business, and big government have appeared, and these changes may account for the growth of the Others category and for the expansion of what gifted people might consider to be appropriate careers for the expression of their abilities.

Summary

These findings should not be overinterpreted. Results may be due to a variety of other factors related to changing values and sample selection. Differences may be due to changes in societal values that occur over time, and the similarity in categories may be due to an unspoken bias among biographers and publishers as to which literary and political figures are worth writing about. Differences may also be due to a lack of representation by biographies of talented, perhaps gifted, people who did not make it. One must be careful in comparing the biographical data to the Terman group. The former represents the cream of many centuries of civilization. The latter represents children living in California in the 1900s.

In sum, two statements are clearly appropriate: (1) IQ is an insufficient predictor of career attainment and eminence, and (2) the gifted have the potential for success in many careers. In this century, the number of possible career opportunities is greater than ever. The promise of gifted children is evident. With special programs, their promise can be enhanced.

Career Portraits

It would appear that different careers require different constellations of talent and are associated with differences in background and lifestyle. In this section, we use the bibliographic data to construct a portrait of the career categories outlined by Goertzel et al. (1978). The distinguishing characteristics of the life histories of career groups will be described based upon the studies cited at the beginning of the chapter, as well as a reinterpretation of the Cox data by Walberg, Rasher, and Parkerson (1979). Regardless of career, gifted people have much in common, and these common factors are discussed in a final section on predictors of success.

Career Portrait—Literary

Literary careers are common among the gifted. Writers may be more homogeneous than people in other career groups. They have the ability to capture in words the conflicts in our lives, and their own backgrounds and personalities enhance this ability. Nonfiction writers are somewhat different from fiction writers.

Literary figures are likely to have been only children who were cognizant at an early age of conflict within their families. Their childhoods are commonly unhappy, even though the parents are likely to be described as "humanitarian" and "idealistic." Parental alcoholism is present to an unusual degree. Literary figures are less likely to be socially attractive as children than political figures; they tend to have been continually rejected by others. More than those in other career groups, literary figures are avid readers as children. They seem to need to relate to peers less than other children. It is not uncommon for them to have created fantasy worlds, and daydreaming is common. They seem to be acute and sensitive observers of life. Nonfiction writers tend to have been more precocious in childhood. Future writers seem to dislike school, but they love learning. The structure of school seems to be quite distasteful to them, for it interferes with reading and writing. They generally do not like arithmetic or competitive games. Their physical condition is likely to be frail. Cox (1926) pointed out that they are less active than children from other career groups.

Literary people do not develop their skills on the bedrock of familial talents. In comparison to other portraits, they seem to have difficult lives as adults. More literary people remain single, and when they do marry their marriages tend to be unstable. They are more likely to attempt suicide, and they are also more likely to have divergent sex lives (Goertzel et al., 1978; Ludwig, 1995).

In the midst of their departure from social norms, literary people tend to have characteristics similar to other gifted people, especially love of learning, a drive to write, and the energy to continue their efforts.

Career Portrait—Political

People with political careers include heads of state, reformers, and revolutionaries of various political persuasions. Politically gifted people make themselves apparent early in their lives. They are usually male and tend to be the middle child in their families. The reformers and revolutionaries tend to have fathers who are politically liberal.

The politically gifted like school and excel in it. They select the debating team, the school newspaper, the yearbook committee, and other clubs for their extracurricular activities. They possess characteristics such as honesty, obedience, popularity, and calmness, and they are rarely delinquent. In short, they are well-rounded individuals (Walberg et al., 1979). These qualities seem to make them attractive to others. During their school years, they acquire leadership skills that are conducive to building organizations and influencing others. In secondary school, they begin to emerge. Later in their careers, it is not uncommon for their followers to begin to doubt their motives as their power grows (Goertzel et al., 1978; Ludwig, 1995).

These political figures' marriages are significantly more stable than those of other groups. It is rare for them to be sexually divergent. It has been suggested that political figures have conservative family relationships (Goertzel et al., 1978; Ludwig, 1995).

In other ways, the politically gifted are similar to those in the other career areas. They learn from their families to love learning, are energetic, and possess great drive.

Career Portrait—Artistic

The artistic careers described by Goertzel et al. (1978) include painters, sculptors, musicians, dancers, and other performers. While there is overlap in their characteristics, there are also some significant variations that make it difficult to develop a fair portrait of the group.

Artistic people seem to construct a world in which they can live and find fulfillment. Walberg et al. (1979) described them as brooding and less wholesome than other career groups. Artistic people seem more likely than other gifted groups to be precocious. Their IQs, according to Cox (1926), seem to be lower than those of writers. Their families run the gamut from supporting them to rejecting them, although the former is more common. The economic and emotional support they need in order to develop their talents frequently comes from siblings.

Artistic people do not like school, nor are they likely to be voracious readers. They are not likely to be well-rounded students. Because their school records are erratic, it is not surprising that their level of schooling is lower than that of other gifted groups. Relatively few have attended college. On the other hand, they seem to profit from special schooling. The artistic, unlike other groups, often have early, special training in their fields.

Family structures developed by artistic people offer a wide range, from the conventional to the most divergent. No one pattern clearly dominates. Their devotion to their work seems to ensure considerable strain in personal relationships. It is probably most accurate to characterize their lives as complex and filled with emotional highs and depths of despair (Ludwig, 1995).

Career Portrait—The Variegated Others

It is obvious that many careers exist outside the literary, political, and artistic arenas, and the variety of careers available for the expression of great ability frequently results in samples that are too small to permit reliable comparisons. Generalizations about the "others" category are very similar to the brief composite sketch of the gifted adult presented at the beginning of this chapter. Consequently, at this time, relatively little can be determined from biographies of the lives of educators, businesspeople, athletes, and others, although Walberg et al. (1979) offered some interesting data on 11 different careers.

One group that has received much attention (e.g., Roe, 1953; Zuckerman, 1977) is composed of scientists. Considerable interest in this group appeared after the Soviet Union launched Sputnik, the first-ever satellite, in 1957, thus ushering in the era of the space race. Scientists are likely to be independent and dutiful. They believe that logic, reason, perseverance, and self-control can lead to the solution of problems. They are intellectual, have high IQs, and are heavily committed to their work. Social activity does not hold much interest for them, so they have only a few close friends. They are not rebellious. Interest in the opposite sex comes late, and the scientist is likely to marry the first person to whom he or she becomes attached. Scientists seem to avoid emotional introspection. Their lives are quite conventional (Ludwig, 1995, also discussed this pattern). In a recent analysis of the Terman data, Tomlinson-Keasey and Little (1990) found that "sociability" was negatively associated with maintaining intellectual skills as adults.

Summary

When these portraits are considered in light of the general data on career accomplishments and the provocative similarities and differences between subgroups of gifted people, it becomes clear that the gifted are a very heterogeneous group. Many factors must be involved in the development of successful gifted people, which brings up a number of questions. Are there any discernible patterns that lead to success? Is it ability alone? Is it perhaps luck that explains why some gifted children become eminent adults? These questions are of prime importance to educators of gifted children. If we postulate that giftedness can be recognized and nurtured, then the variables or circumstances that predict adult accomplishment need to be identified to ensure appropriate programming.

Predictors of Adult Accomplishment

A basic assumption about the gifted is that giftedness can be recognized and nurtured. Given the description of successful gifted adults, what predictors can be located? Once again, the evidence comes primarily from the analysis of biographies, the Terman research, and specific talent areas.

Cox (1926) concluded that three factors are important to the emergence of giftedness. One factor is "superior advantages in early environment." Gifted people tend to come from family backgrounds that provide for the development of skills and knowledge. These people had early educational opportunities, but not necessarily formal schooling. A second factor is that gifted people exhibit the behavioral characteristics of those with "unusually high" IQs. They were precocious in their mental development, productivity, and rate of progress. The third factor is "persistence of motive and effort, confidence in their abilities, and great strength or force of character" (p. 218). These qualities are consistently evident. Reinterpretation of the data using psychological traits found in an earlier study of gifted adolescents essentially reaffirmed Cox's findings (Walberg et al., 1979). And, even more recently, Tomlinson-Keasey and Little (1990) lent support to the importance of these three factors.

Cox's research was part of the Terman project and, as such, probably reflects its bias. On the other hand, Goertzel and Goertzel (1962; 2004) and Goertzel et al. (1978) used a different framework. They were interested in looking for commonalities among a group of unique individuals who had achieved some measure of fame. Similar conclusions were yielded by both projects:

1.   a love of learning is acquired in the home;

2.   has a clear, strong dislike of school, especially rote learning;

3.   tends to be firstborn;

4.   exhibits familial characteristics of being verbal, experimental, curious, and active, and shares and sets goals;

5.   has brothers and sisters who are supportive;

6.   likes to be left alone to work;

7.   has difficult peer relationships in secondary school;

8. has a father who is either failure-prone or famous;

9. has a "need to compensate for physical and environmental handicaps" (Goertzel et al., 1978, p. 340);

10. has neurotic, rather than psychotic, emotional problems (if any, depression is most common); and

11. uses fantasy and imagination.

The overlapping findings of Cox (1926) and Goertzel and Goertzel (1962; 2004) suggest that, as children, gifted adults possess personal and familial characteristics that are possible predictors of success. The three factors that seem to be present are evidence of intellectual ability and active learning, creativity, and involvement in their interests. There is less overlap on other factors.

The Terman data show other possible predictors that both supplement and contradict some of this evidence. The Terman group did well when compared to their nongifted peers. Within the gifted group, the lives they chose followed a variety of paths. Some achieved eminence, while others did not do so well. The issue of success is perplexing because it is difficult to define its parameters. One does not have the perspective of history, as in the historical and biographical research. A series of value decisions must be made, and these depend upon the cultural milieu and personal feelings of those making the decisions. Of course, more contemporary studies have the advantage of being able to obtain a complete set of data on subjects.

With full recognition of this difficulty, Terman and Oden (1947) made an effort to define achievement in order to look for predictors of success. They defined achievement as "the extent to which a subject had made use of his superior intellectual ability" (p. 312). A panel of three judges ranked the male subjects on the basis of this criterion. The group was then divided into the top group (A) and the bottom group (C), with the middle group excluded from further analyses. The comparisons were done in 1940 and in 1960, and the number and composition of the judges were not the same on both occasions, nor were the subjects.

One should not assume that the C group was composed of failures or of people with semiskilled or lower occupations. People who were judged to be functioning well below their career peers were given C ratings. The data in Table 2.3 illustrate the differences in occupational status over a 20-year interval. Note that the A group tends to be in the high-status occupations, but it is clear that some C subjects also belong in these categories. The C group has a wider range of achievement. Two points cannot be seen in Table 2.3. The first is that both groups earned an income above the national average. The second is the change of personnel within groups from 1940 to 1960. Approximately 45% of the original A and C groups were reclassified in the same category over

TABLE 2.3

Occupational Status of A and C Groups—1940–1960

Status	1940 % A n = 150	C n = 150	1960 % A n = 100	C n = 100
Occupational classification				
Group I: Professional	68.7	9.3	59	5.0
Group II: Official, managerial, and semiprofessional	30.7	7.3	40	13.0
Group III: Retail, business, clerical, and skilled trades		48.7		62.0
Group IV: Agricultural and relate		1.3		1
Group V: Semiskilled		22.0		8.0
Others classification				
Unskilled, irregular employment, unemployed, retired	0.7	11.3		2.0

Note. From *The Gifted Child Grows Up: Twenty-Five Years' Follow-Up of a Superior Group. Genetic Studies of Genius Vol. IV* (p. 92), by L. M. Terman, and M. H. Oden, 1947, Stanford, CA: Stanford University Press. Copyright ©1947 by Stanford University Press. Reprinted with permission.

the 20-year interval. Some of this may have been due to the smaller samples in 1960. It may also have been due to the number of raters. Interestingly, no person rated C in 1940 received an A rating in 1960, but two were very close. Four of the 1940 A group were classified as C in 1960. All four had serious alcohol or, in two cases, marital problems (Oden, 1968).

A search for predictors that distinguish the A group (who lived up to their superior intellect) from the C group (who did not) can lead in many directions. The wealth of data accumulated over 50 years on these subjects is hard to comprehend, so to facilitate a comparison, the findings will be reviewed selectively. No meaningful differences exist in IQ, health, and interests, according to ratings in childhood by others and to autobiographies written in 1950. There are few clear trends. Reliable differences between the A and C groups were found on personality, and there were familial differences between the groups. At some points, the distinction between familial and personality differences is for convenience. For a more extensive look at family considerations, see Chapter 4 on families.

Parent-teacher ratings obtained in 1922, when the mean age of the subjects was 11, and again in 1928, when the mean age was 17, reveal some interesting differences. The group in 1928 was superior to the C group in intellectual, volitional, and moral/social traits. The traits were ordered from highest score to lowest score, and both groups received ratings above-average for their ages. It is in social traits that both are nearest the average; in intellectual traits, they are most extreme compared to the nongifted. Note that three of the four variables are nonintellectual and suggest creative potential. These traits seem to continue into adult careers. In other research, Torrance (1981) has demonstrated that creativity test scores may be predictive of adult performance. Other indications from parental ratings show that 57% of the A group "strongly liked school," compared to 42% of the C group. The A group also seemed to have more than one special ability. The C group was rated as being more headstrong (30%) than the A group (13%).

An interesting point is that, in 1950, a greater proportion of the A group said they felt different from their classmates than the C group did (63% vs. 48%). This self-rating about feeling different in a general sense was greater than individual ratings about feeling different in terms of intellectual, physical, and social considerations. In all cases, the A group felt more different than the C group. Such feelings do not apparently lead to maladjustment or lack of success.

The subjects in 1950 filled out biographical information on their familial relationships. While few significant differences emerged between the two groups, one area of difference that was found was that parents of the A group encouraged initiative and independence. The parents of the A group were also more likely to encourage children to "forge ahead" in school, get good marks, and attend college. However, they were definitely not excessive in their encouragement, according to their children.

When selecting careers, the A group was more likely to follow parents' choices, but the majority of parents did not suggest a preference. In other research, it appears that gifted children commonly accept implicit family values that point to their talent (Bloom & Sosniak, 1981). The A group picked careers based on interest, while the C group attended to financial necessity. In later research, the predictive quality of adolescent interests to later adult accomplishment is evident (Milgram & Hong, 1993). Significantly more of the A group considered their career choice before age 18. The A group clearly derived greater satisfaction and interest in work than the C group did (78% vs. 22%). Nobel laureates in science sound very much like the A group (Zuckerman, 1977). Incidentally, neither group was particularly interested in making money.

Summary

It is possible to identify indicators of future success by studying the childhoods of gifted people. Certain characteristics appear in all accounts. The gifted give signs of being advanced in knowledge and skills that they have acquired—sometimes in unforeseen ways—from early experiences. Early training and experience pays off. They are committed to learning about topics that interest them, and they devote considerable energy to this search.

It is difficult to determine whether or not the gifted like school. Because general public education is relatively new, it is inappropriate to make comparisons with earlier centuries. The gifted do seem to profit both historically and currently from specialized attention, which is appropriate to their accelerated pace of learning. Length of schooling and early career activity are important predictors of success. It is apparent that artistic and literary people like school the least. It is surprising that the Terman study found that more successful adults remembered "strongly liking school," even though they received little attention and the elementary school was out of step with their abilities.

Successful gifted adults have little interest in social activities, according to all the sources, although politicians are notable exceptions. The evidence from childhood shows that involvement and concern for social activities is mixed. It seems to be more a case of indifference than disinterest for many of them. They are popular with their peers in elementary school, but problems may develop at the secondary level. Perhaps their creative abilities and involvement in work are not congruent with social activity. Torrance (1979b) has noted that gifted people must struggle to develop their creative potentials.

Emotional instability is not a characteristic of the general population of successful gifted adults, and Terman's data show that the same is true for most gifted children. This finding is provocative because the gifted person seems to be very aware of being different. (Chapter 4 on guidance explores this issue further.) If the gifted adult has an emotional problem, it is likely to be depression. Another emotional trait that is a strong predictor (perhaps the strongest) is will power or persistence. The ability to focus one's energies on the resolution of a problem, whether scientific, artistic, or political, predicts success. All the data point in this direction. A committed person is able to withstand the disappointment, the dead ends, and the elusive sense of completion that is necessary for outstanding performance.

Creative work seems to demand this quality of perseverance. The phenomenon of creativity has been referred to directly and indirectly, using labels such as *original, curious, inventive,* and *daydreamer.* All the people in the historical studies were undeniably creative, and their unique works or actions led to their recognition. The point is so obvious that it is frequently overlooked. Creativity is a characteristic of giftedness in children and adults, and during the 1960s and 1970s, the data on giftedness were dominated by the study of creativity (Guilford, 1959; Torrance, 1962a, 1962b, 1965, 1968). Chapter 6 is devoted to this topic.

THE NONMODAL GIFTED

One should realize that giftedness comes in a variety of forms, and generalizations have been used in this chapter to illustrate various points. No typical gifted person exists. Although such a tautological statement may seem unnecessary, unfortunately it *is* necessary because the stereotype Terman was trying to eliminate through his research may have created a new, more sophisticated stereotype of giftedness, which might be called the "Terman stereotype" (Whitmore, 1980). In this stereotype, the gifted child has become the all-American, middle-class child who does everything well, is physically attractive, and is liked by all. This new picture of giftedness does a disservice to all because it tends to ignore the many varieties of giftedness.

The gifted child most likely to be overlooked is the child who is handicapped by learning or behavioral problems; the child from a poor, rural background; or the child belonging to a minority. These are the nonmodal or atypical gifted. Throughout the text, we will discuss these groups in terms of identification, guidance, and programming. The nonmodal gifted are ignored or overlooked because their attributes are viewed as being inconsistent with those of the gifted. Instead of looking at their differences as possible sources of strength or as cloaks hiding their strengths, they are viewed as signs of weakness. These ideas of weakness may be part of an unintentional social phenomenon, or they may be tied to the prejudice and racism implicit in some segments of American society. It is possible to change this situation, and specific suggestions are presented throughout the text.

CONCLUSION

The examination of the lives of gifted people in this chapter is intended to serve as a means for understanding the gifted and the significant factors in their development. Armed with this knowledge, better programs can be planned.

From this review, one can see that there is a constellation of factors that shows some continuity from child to adult, although the knowledge base outlining the relationship between childhood characteristics and adult performance is far from perfect. The factors of motivation, intelligence, and creativity seem most critical. A gifted child does not automatically grow into a successful gifted adult. Neither do the best environments ensure success. While giftedness exists at all levels of society, it is not recognized in all segments of society. Giftedness will not emerge unless it is encouraged. The cream does not always "rise to the top."

When a person is identified as gifted, it should not be assumed that joy and happiness are inevitable concomitants. Being gifted presents unique problems to oneself and to those in one's environment. What is remarkable is the range of variability in people with supposedly similar abilities. It is this variability that this book is trying to encourage.

FOR **DISCUSSION**

1. The chapter mentions the low incidence of separation and divorce among the families in Terman's studies and that it is questionable whether this would be the case in the 2000s. Reflect on and discuss how sociohistorical changes may impact the portrait of a gifted child in the 2000s.

2. What are the educational implications of the finding that more than half of the gifted children with an IQ of 135 and above are in grades in which they have already mastered the curriculum?

3. How would you respond to an individual who asked you to describe a gifted child?

4. Some researchers have suggested that gifted children may experience more problems, not necessarily because of emotional instability, but because of their inability to find peers of similar abilities and interests. What steps can teachers, counselors, and/or parents take to reduce potential problems for gifted children?

5. The non-Terman data is rich in information about the lives of gifted individuals. Much of this information, however, is gathered from biographical sources. What are the problems associated with gathering data about gifted individuals from these sources?

6. How would you respond to an individual who asks you the question: "Do gifted children become gifted adults?"

7. The chapter mentions that the nonmodal gifted are gifted children who have problems or come from backgrounds that complicate the identification of their giftedness. As a teacher or counselor, what practices may be taken to ensure that nonmodal gifted children are not overlooked?

chapter three

IDENTIFYING THE GIFTED

KEY CONCEPTS

- A comprehensive system of identification requires that school personnel make many complex decisions.

- All sound identification schemes operate on the basis of five universal assumptions.

- Given the same group of children, no two school systems will determine identical children to be gifted.

- The means by which a school decides to measure giftedness is the real meaning of that school's definition.

- Schools have a wider range of options in selecting measurement techniques than is commonly believed.

- Intelligence tests are not suitable for measuring creativity and achievement.

- Teachers, parents, and gifted people have different capacities for recognizing giftedness.

- Traditional assessment approaches reflecting historical conceptions of giftedness tend to value factors that underrepresent nonmodal gifted students.

- Nonacademic abilities, motivation, and identification at the preschool and secondary levels need to be considered in designing identification procedures.

The identification of gifted children is a challenging and perplexing problem for people interested in promoting the development of high ability. This identification will continue to be a problem until attitudes, psychometric techniques, and educational practices come together around a common definition of giftedness. The likelihood of such a confluence is slim, given the sociopolitical context in which definitions are proposed. The process will continue to be perplexing as long as the identification of gifted children is expected to be a value-free, or at least a neutral, enterprise. While one may strive for the ideal means of definition, commitment to the education of gifted children dictates that identification decisions must be made, often on the basis of imperfect information.

The placement of a chapter on identification after a discussion of characteristics may strike some readers as unusual, as it is more conventional to reverse this arrangement. The typical sequence is developed from the standpoint that identification procedures lead schools to select students with specific characteristics. The problem with this sequence is that it overlooks or ignores the fact that the characteristics describing giftedness are largely determined before the identification process actually begins. The chapter on characteristics is placed before the chapter on identification so that schools or other organizational groups who wish to identify the gifted will consider these data prior to fashioning an identification program.

The influence of values upon imperfect information surrounding the identification of gifted children is the underlying reason for the placement of this chapter. Identification procedures are inescapably value-laden. While the definitions that have been discussed and the characteristics of gifted children are useful sources of information for schools wanting to develop an identification system, these sources are not definitive.

Neither the definitions nor the characteristics were derived from a value-free situation. However, the quality of objectivity should not be confused with a value-free system. The proponents of the various definitions had specific philosophies about who the gifted are or should be. The arguments for various positions make this clear. The researchers who have studied the characteristics of gifted people also have conceptions of who the gifted are or should be. The selection of measurement devices is tempered by some notion of what qualities are worthy of study. The result is that one tends to find what one thought would be found. The important work of Terman, Torrance, and other pioneers in this field illustrates this point. Nothing is wrong about this circumstance. Everyone starts with a point of view. In this regard, school systems that are attempting to identify gifted children are similar to researchers. Any endeavor requires that one start with a set of assumptions based upon one's values and knowledge, and these unspoken assumptions are generally not a problem when conducting research because most consumers of research are trained to be alert to this situation.

However, they become a problem in the real work of identifying children in schools because they perpetuate controversy. For example, if one believes that math or creativity or intelligence are true signs of giftedness, then one will be dissatisfied with a system that overlooks or downplays these qualities. On the other hand, if one believes that giftedness is evenly distributed across society, then one will be upset by identification procedures that do not select equal numbers of girls and boys, well-to-do and poor children, and so on. Unless these assumptions are made explicit and unless they are resolved in a reasonable manner, programs for gifted children will be in continual jeopardy. Of course, not all differences can be easily compromised. Traditionally, a school system reaches agreement on a definition before proceeding with the development of identification procedures. The purpose of this chapter is to discuss these sources of conflict and offer a rational means of identifying gifted children in schools.

UNIVERSAL ASSUMPTIONS

A general discussion on the development and implementation of a system for identifying gifted children infers a series of assumptions that underlie all identification systems. Some may seem minor or even unnecessary to some readers. However, they are stated in the interest of clarity because, without these assumptions, identification systems need not be created.

1. *Giftedness exists and is recognizable.* Giftedness is a psychological and socially contextualized construct. Like all constructs, it does not exist as a directly measurable quality or behavior; rather, giftedness is identifiable because certain qualities describe the construct. It is the particular configura-

tion of qualities that represents the reality of any single construct. Examples of constructs are creativity, reading readiness, and freedom. Each of these is described by a different set of qualities. With this assumption, one is asserting that a series of qualities may be differentiated from the general characteristics of human beings in order to locate giftedness. Giftedness exists in many settings. If the characteristics are not observable, then giftedness may not exist.

2. *Identification plus programming nurtures giftedness.* A system of identification should be created to achieve certain results within the context of a program. Identification without a program is useless and potentially harmful to a child and to the future development of a program. The program influences the definition. Identification promotes the development of special abilities that would be less likely to develop without it (Stanley, 1976). A common belief is that the self-concept of children will be improved and serious maladjustment may be prevented (Martinson, 1975). Another belief is that society will be able to profit from the achievements of gifted people. Involved in this assumption is the notion that the earlier the identification, the better it is for the child (Roedell, Jackson, & Robinson, 1980).

3. *There must be commitment to identification.* A system of identification must assume that all participants in the process are committed to the education of gifted children. The commitment takes precedence over allegiance to personal, idiosyncratic views about giftedness. Without a willingness to hear different viewpoints and to strive for an agreement, the development of an adequate system of identification is impossible. Identification systems should be open to modification as the effects of various decisions become known. Commitment means continual efforts to improve the system of identification. Change is valued, and research is encouraged.

4. *The system can be made reliable.* A rational identification scheme can be constructed. The reasons for particular procedures can be explicitly stated. A system is organized to minimize error in selecting children who should be in the program for the gifted, but error cannot be completely eliminated. This system does not require that an absolute definition of giftedness be formalized; instead, it needs a definition that is agreeable to concerned parties and is consistent with the program's purposes. Different programs are best for children with certain abilities. A child may not be gifted within the definition of all programs. Legislative mandates should be considered, but definitions should not be limited by legislative rules and regulations.

5. *The child becomes an adult.* Implicit in an identification system is the idea that the abilities we see exhibited by children are related to their accomplishments as adults. Accordingly, all gifted children are potentially

gifted adults. When children are identified, they implicitly have a higher probability of behaving like gifted adults than other children do. This is an assumption because the data relating childhood and adult performance are inconsistent (McClelland, 1958; Perrone, 1991). It is easier to make statements about groups than about individuals. However, when identification takes place, individuals are selected. The issue is always deciding which qualities or characteristics should receive the most attention. This assumption asserts that it is advisable to give preference to indicators that are most closely related to adult success in a given field. These preferred characteristics might vary depending upon the forms of a program. For example, a creative writing program might be suitable for a candidate with a different constellation of abilities than a candidate for a math-oriented or music-oriented program.

These five assumptions seem to be characteristic of strong identification systems across a variety of settings. School systems that get involved in identification tend to forget that decisions have been made prior to the actual implementation of the system. These unseen decisions govern future procedural and policy decisions, thus school systems need to become aware of how they influence the operation of their identification systems.

PROCEDURAL CONCERNS

A good system of identification for the gifted is similar to other identification schemes in schools. A good system will select children to meet the purpose of the program. Given the same group of children, not all schools will designate the same children as gifted due to differences in measurement techniques, screening procedures, definitions, and program objectives. Each of these differences is discussed later in this chapter. In this section, procedural concerns are described. These procedures should be part of any system of identification, regardless of the particular orientation of the program for which the identification is being conducted. Attention to procedural concerns can improve an identification system, but cannot ensure the best one for every school.

1. The first procedural concern is that an identification system should be *comprehensive*. Data on the abilities that are specified in the definition should be gathered. There is no point in stating that an ability is an attribute of giftedness (e.g., creativity) and then ignoring it in the selection process. If a definition proposes multiple criteria for selection, then there should be a search for all the criterion abilities.

2. An identification system should be *inclusive*. All children in a school system should have an initial chance to be included in the selection process.

69

Preemptive decisions can result in overlooking children who might be eligible for the program. It is likely that preemptive decisions have contributed to the low numbers of nonmodal gifted children—including those with disabilities or those who are from culturally different backgrounds—being identified for programs.

3.   A program of identification should begin as *early* in a child's life as possible, and it should be reinstituted at regular intervals. Early identification helps promote development and circumvent behaviors that tend to obscure giftedness. The search for gifted children who might have been overlooked at an earlier time should be continued at regular intervals. Yearly searches are advisable until fourth grade, then biannual searches through secondary school. Special attention should be given in junior high school for nonmodal gifted students because the effects of impoverished environments, atypical developmental experiences, or both may be less visible. It is in the later years of schooling that most identification programs cease.

4.   Implied in this continuous process is the idea that the system is *open-ended*. Children who have been included, as well as excluded, may change over time. The reality of dealing with children and families who were at one time included and at a later time excluded is a most uncomfortable one.

5.   A program of identification should use a *screening* procedure that is appropriate to the program's objectives and to the composition of the school's student body. The screening procedure is that part of the identification process by which the total number of students who are eligible for the program is reduced to a manageable number for more intensive study of each student. Screening may be carried out in one or more steps. For example, a school may use teacher nominations for screening whereby all students not mentioned are screened out. Another school might first use a cutoff group intelligence test score of at least 115 to lessen the number of eligible students and then use teacher nominations to further reduce the number of students for final study.

One should infer from this description that screening is a crucial point in the process because it can eliminate a child from further consideration; consequently, it is advisable to set the initial screening thresholds liberally to ensure that a school is less likely to miss students who belong in a program. As the process continues, the criteria should be made more restrictive. In school districts with significant proportions of educationally disadvantaged children or nonmodal children, screening decisions are particularly important because gifted children from these backgrounds are more likely to be overlooked and prematurely excluded. Ways to deal with this situation are described throughout this chapter.

6.   The final identification decision should be made by a *group or team*, which should use all the information gathered on each child. A group decision is preferable because it allows people with various perspectives to consider the same information, thus minimizing choices made on irrelevant data. This practice also serves to increase the numbers of people who have responsibility for a good program, although unfortunately, in some schools, it is used to displace blame. The team should be composed of people who have direct knowledge of the children, meaning the composition of the team might change from child to child. For example, an identification team may be broadened by adding a coach, a shop teacher, and a minister, all who may have valuable information about a child.

The statement recommending that all the information available be used by the team may seem unnecessary. After all, why would one *not* use all the information? In the enthusiasm to adopt an inclusive identification plan, schools gather as much data as possible from teachers, parents, peers, past records, psychologists, and so forth. When all these data descend on those making the final decision, they need to order the data from most important to least important in order to digest it all. In the process, one realizes that some data were unnecessary or of minimal value. This is an important finding, but it tends to create a morale problem that may hurt later efforts to identify children. School staff resent participation when they realize that the extra energy expended in reporting on certain children was not used in the identification process.

In one situation, for example, the entire faculty of a school was asked to fill out a 45-item rating scale on each child in their homerooms, the average size of which was 25 students, making the effort equivalent to taking 25 twenty-minute tests. The results on these rating scales were used in the final selection decision after achievement and IQ-test data were used to reduce the number of children to be considered. Since only 10% of the school population of 1,000 was selected, the amount of data that was not used and the amount of wasted energy was inordinately high. The school system had great difficulty recruiting teachers to participate in the identification process 2 years after this occurred. In order to prevent problems such as this and to make the process more efficient, school systems must make decisions about the degree of emphasis intended for different types of data. By following that practice, they can make use of all the information at their disposal and minimize problems.

These components do not guarantee an appropriate identification procedure for a program. The consideration of these six procedural concerns can only improve an identification process. They deal indirectly with the time needed for a good identification system and with the issue of measurement. The time needed for a good identification program is valuable. It may be as long as a year, or it may only take several weeks. Regardless of the time, these concerns can improve the process. The time taken should be long enough to meet the purposes of school programs. The measurement of giftedness is a major issue that requires extensive decision making. This issue will occupy much of the remainder of this chapter.

MEASUREMENT

Who Controls the Process?

A definition of giftedness makes a statement about what abilities or qualities constitute giftedness. Such statements are usually in language that makes their meaning understandable and acceptable to a wide range of people. While the ability to generalize is good for discussion purposes, it can be too open to varying interpretations to be adequate for the goal of identification. To be useful, abilities have to be translated into operational terms. Of course, the operational meaning of any ability is defined by how we choose to measure it (Gallagher, 1975). There are many different ways to measure each ability—standardized tests, rating scales, observations, work samples, and so forth—and, subsequently, there is great confusion about how to measure the abilities associated with giftedness (Alvino, McDonnel, & Richert, 1981; Richert, 1991). This confusion is apparently related to a misunderstanding or lack of knowledge about what constitutes appropriate measurement techniques for these abilities.

One consequence of the confusion about general statements of abilities and operational statements is the misuse of measurement techniques. Another consequence is that school personnel forget that the technique for measuring an ability determines what that ability means. It is not the rhetoric or general definition that in practice defines giftedness. In reality, what your technique measures is what you get. If one is not sensitive to this point, then the tool or measuring device largely controls the selection of children, which is disadvantageous because it relinquishes control of the identification program to the developers of the measurement devices. This problem is compounded when school personnel use devices for purposes for which they were never intended. Such ignorance needs to be eradicated.

In order to get this problem under control, people concerned with the identification of gifted children need to be more aware of the appropriateness of various techniques for identifying the abilities or qualities that define giftedness in their school system. Procedures are available to measure all the abilities contained in federal or state definitions, as well as any other abilities a school district might wish to measure. Some procedures are better than others for identifying gifted children, and some constructs (e.g., leadership abilities) are more difficult than others to measure and, therefore, it is more difficult to find valid and reliable instruments that measure them.

A good measuring device is one that reliably selects the children for whom a program is intended. The precision of this standard varies according to the ability being measured and the purposes of the selection. A problem with this relative standard is that it impedes comparisons among programs and among groups of gifted people because of the variability of operational definitions and their concomitant measurement techniques. The problem could be resolved in an ideal manner through agreement about appropriate techniques to use for measuring any ability.

Types of Measurement

Because the variety of procedures available for measuring various abilities is so extensive, they will be grouped under three headings for purposes of analysis and discussion: standardized tests, rating scales, and work samples. The advantages, disadvantages, current practices, and research evidence of these types of measurement are discussed below.

The measurement devices in this discussion are used solely for the purpose of classifying individuals. No attempt is made to discuss diagnostic tests or criterion-referenced tests in any systematic manner. Criterion-referenced tests are often misnamed and are designed primarily for purposes of instruction. The identification process is only indirectly concerned with instruction. School personnel who are looking for such information from an identification process have expectations that cannot be met. While it is true that information relative to instruction is a desirable goal, the devices used for identification were not designed for this purpose.

The measurement devices used in these categories are considered to be attempts to meet the definition of testing proposed by Newland (1980): "Testing is the controlled observation of the behavior of an individual to whom stimuli of known characteristics are applied in a known manner" (p. 76). The three categories can be considered in light of this definition. In all cases, it is presumed that these tests were developed to show the differences among individuals, not within an individual.

Standardized Tests

The largest category is standardized tests. Tests can be found that purport to measure all the abilities in the federal definition (Coleman, 1976). Standardized tests are the most frequently mentioned technique for measuring abilities (Alvino et al., 1981; Richert, 1991). However, they are not the technique used most frequently for every ability. General intellectual ability, specific academic aptitude, and creative or productive thinking abilities are measured using standardized tests more often than other abilities. For this reason, standardized tests in these areas will be discussed. The reader who wants information on standardized tests in other areas is advised to consult Buros' *Mental Measurement Yearbooks*, *Tests in Print*, and *Test Critiques*.

Standardized tests have qualities that approximate Newland's (1980) definition of testing, and they are commonly referred to as "objective tests." Objectivity has a specialized meaning in testing and should not be considered the opposite of subjectivity. The objectivity of standardized tests derives from

73

the fact that explicit directions are provided on how to administer a standard stimulus. The behaviors indicated by the scores are interpreted in terms of the "norms" that were established by testing a group of people who are described in detail in the manual. Data are provided on consistency (reliability) of scores, how well the test measures what it claims to measure (validity), and the amount of error there is likely to be in a score. According to Hammill (1987), the criteria for defining a standardized assessment are (1) a set of precise administration procedures, (2) objective scoring criteria, (3) a specified preferred frame of reference, and (4) evidence that the measure is reliable and valid. Therefore, it is important to note that a criterion-referenced measure can be considered standardized.

These qualities combine to make a test objective in the sense that the user can better estimate whether or not the differences revealed among children are due to real differences or to other factors. Given these qualities, one can understand why standardized tests are used. However, one should be wary of the claims made by test publishers. There is a considerable range of quality among standardized tests. Just because a test alleges standardization does not make it a good test. Furthermore, do not assume that, because a test is called by a particular name, such as the Xanadu Intelligence Test, that it measures what other intelligence tests do or that it even measures intelligence.

Even with the information supplied—both by publishers and by test evaluators such as Buros' *Mental Measurement Yearbook*—on specific tests and even with the good intentions of school personnel, standardized tests are frequently misused. The following are some common mistakes.

1. Tests are administered to groups of children for whom the test was not designed—rural, disadvantaged, learning disabled, and so forth. The section in this chapter on nonmodal gifted children discusses this problem.

2. Tests designed to measure one ability are used to measure another. For example, creativity tests are used to measure intelligence, or achievement tests are used to measure general intellectual ability. When this occurs, one is not measuring what one thinks is being measured. A good test can be invalidated by this practice.

3. Tests with questionable reliability and validity and with an inadequate ceiling are used as the major criterion for screening and selecting children for a gifted program.

Because standardized tests are used most frequently for the measurement of general intellectual functioning, specific academic aptitude, and creativity, each ability area will be reviewed individually. The precise differences among standardized tests in these areas are primarily due to the specificity of the content and the degree to which the developers assumed the existence of a specific course of instruction (Anastasi & Urbina, 1997). In this manner, general intelligence tests and creativity tests tend to measure broader, heterogeneous samples of behavior than do specific academic aptitude tests. All these tests should conform to the technical details involved in test construction.

Intelligence tests. Tests of general intellectual functioning attempt to sample a large number of behaviors related to school learning. Some behaviors that are frequently sampled on these tests are discrimination, generalization, motor behavior, general information, vocabulary, induction, comprehension, sequencing, detailed recognition, analogies, abstract reasoning, memory, and pattern completion (Salvia & Ysseldyke, 1995). These behaviors are not sampled in all tests, nor do they have the same emphasis in all tests. Thus, IQ scores derived from various tests taken by an individual have somewhat different meanings depending upon the specific test. It is always advisable, therefore, to specify the test along with the IQ score. Furthermore, intelligence tests come in two major varieties designed for different purposes: group tests and individual tests.

Group intelligence tests are useful for obtaining scores on a large number of children for preliminary selection or screening. Group tests differ in administration time, number of subtests, and scores yielded. The group test selected should provide data consistent with the purposes of a program. Some of the more popular tests are the following:

- Raven's Progressive Matrices (Raven, Raven, & Styles, 1998);

- Cattell Culture Fair Intelligence Test (CFIT; Cattell, 1950);

- Cognitive Abilities Test (CogAT; Lohman & Hagen, 2001);

- Lorge-Thorndike Intelligence Tests (Lorge & Thorndike, 1954);

- Differential Aptitudes Test (DAT; Bennett, Seashore, & Wesman, 1990);

- Goodenough-Harris Drawing Test (GH; Goodenough & Harris, 1963); and

- Otis-Lennon School Ability Test (OLSAT; Otis & Lennon, 2003).

Some tests are better than others for specific purposes, and the relative merits of these tests will be briefly reviewed.

The first two tests on the list were developed for use with nonmodal gifted children. For example, the Raven's Progressive Matrices' minimal language requirements make it well suited for measuring the intelligence of individuals

75

with handicapping conditions (Pratt & Moreland, 1998) and non-English-speaking children (Kamphaus, 2001).

Selection of a particular group test may be based on the desire for a single global score or multiple scores. Several scores permit the user to see the variance in separate abilities instead of a single score favoring people with overall strength. The Cognitive Abilities Test (CogAT) is a product of work on the Lorge-Thorndike Intelligence Test. The CogAT may be used in grades K–12, and it "yield[s] three scores—verbal, quantitative, and nonverbal—and [has] separate level tests for each grade, three through twelve" (Hagen, 1980, p. 45). A positive feature of this test is that it permits the teacher to administer levels of difficulty appropriate to student ability, which should minimize the problem of an inadequate number of easy items. A global score is not to be used. The test has good reliability, but limited data on validity.

Another instrument that yields various scores rather than a global score is the Differential Aptitudes Test (DAT). While it provides eight scores for high school (grades 8–12), only four subtests—verbal reasoning, abstract reasoning, space relations, and numerical ability—are useful for identifying the gifted. Hagen (1980) warned that the test "does not differentiate the top ability levels very well" (p. 45). The reliability and validity of this test are well documented.

The Goodenough-Harris Drawing Test (GH) is for use with children 3–15 years of age. The student draws a man, a woman, and a self-portrait. Scores are based on the male and female drawings and are determined according to directions in the manual. The GH has adequate reliability, but the description of the normative sample is too sketchy. The test appears most appropriate for children younger than age 8. It also may tend to underestimate drawings of women, given the changes in mores since the norms were published in 1963.

The Otis-Lennon School Abilities Test (OLSAT) is currently in its eighth edition. It does not yield an IQ score, but rather what is entitled "a school ability index," which has a mean of 100 and a standard deviation of 16. The test has seven levels, extending from grades K–12. The levels for first, second, and third grade require no scaling. The levels for fourth grade and upward seem to measure reasoning and competence in verbal and quantitative areas. The OLSAT has reasonable reliability and validity data obtained from a national sample. Because the test yields a global score, Hagen (1980) noted that it may result in screening out those with an outstanding skill in one area, but low or average scores in others.

In sum, group tests provide a relatively inexpensive and efficient way to obtain information on children for making preliminary decisions in the identification process. They have the advantage of requiring children to perform in a situation that approximates the way in which learning takes place in school. At the same time, however, these tests may present problems for children who are very bright, but who do not function well in a test-taking setting. Group tests also tend to "stress verbal ability and thus penalize certain groups, although this problem may be greater at the elementary than at the secondary level" (Martinson, 1975, p. 42). Martinson recommended that group tests be used in combination with other measures before decisions are made about individual children.

Individual tests of general intellectual functioning make up the heavy artillery found within the arsenal of tests available for use in the identification process. Unfortunately, these tests constitute the only means of measurement in some identification procedures, as many systems use individual intelligence tests as the final determinant of giftedness.

Individual tests have definite advantages over group tests. The conditions are optimal for getting an accurate picture of a child's intellectual abilities. The examiner is specially trained to administer and score the test, thus problems of low motivation and confusion over directions can be ameliorated. As the child takes the test, the examiner is able to observe qualitative aspects, largely missed in group testing, of the child's performance. If an answer seems incomplete, an examiner may probe further. The test format is more advantageous because a broader sampling of behavior can be examined. On group tests, responses are limited to simple words or to the completion of computer-scored sheets. On individual intelligence tests, children may be asked to describe pictures, rearrange puzzles, explain situations, manipulate objects, and define words.

Although there are many individual tests of general intelligence, the real workhorses of past years have been the Stanford-Binet Intelligence Scale, Fourth Edition (SBIV; Thorndike, Hagen, & Sattler, 1986) and the Wechsler Intelligence Scale for Children–III (WISC-III; Wechsler, 1991), both of which were revised in 2003. Given that many schools continue to use earlier editions of a test despite the publication of a revised version, the previous and current editions of the Stanford-Binet and Wechsler will be overviewed. They will be described separately, and then the relative merits of each will be appraised.

The Stanford-Binet Intelligence Scale has been used in the United States and has gone through several revisions since it was introduced by Terman in 1916. Terman developed the test on the basis of the Binet-Simon Scale, originally developed in France, by adding, discarding, and rearranging items and by standardizing the new version on an American sample. Specific instructions for administering and scoring the test were provided and the concept of an Intelligence Quotient (IQ) was included.

The SBIV samples a wide range of behavior. The items are arranged according to age level from 2 years to superior adult levels. Each level includes a group of items that the majority of people at that level could pass correctly. For any given age level, the items are varied. Children are not administered the entire test; rather, they are only presented items that are between the point at which they get every item correct (the basal) and the point at which they fail to get any item correct (the ceiling). A child earns credit for passing items in each level. The total number of points may be interpreted in a table as a mental age score or a deviation IQ score. The average IQ is 100 with a standard deviation of 16. The SBIV has a long history and is widely accepted in psychological testing.

The latest version is the Stanford-Binet Intelligence Scale, Fifth Edition (SB5; Roid, 2003). The test is designed to measure cognitive abilities and intelligence in children and adults (age range 2 to 85+ years). The SB5 samples behaviors in verbal and nonverbal domains. All individuals are administered two routing subtests at the beginning of the assessment to determine the developmental starting point for the remaining subtests. As with the SBIV, a child is not administered the entire test. Rather, the basal is determined by the routing subtests, then the child continues until he or she reaches the ceiling.

The other widely used individually administered intelligence test are the Wechsler scales for children, which have recently undergone revisions. The Wechsler Intelligence Scale for Children–III was updated to the fourth edition (WISC-IV) in 2003 (Wechsler, 2003), and the Wechsler Preschool and Primary Scale of Intelligence–Revised was updated to the third edition (WPPSI-III) in 2002. Another Wechsler measure is the Wechsler Adult Intelligence Scale–Revised (WAIS-R). These tests are to be used with people of different ages: The WAIS-R is for those over 16 years of age, the WPPSI-III is for those from 2 to 7 years of age (the previous edition was from ages 3 to 7), and the WISC is for the intervening years, from 6 to 16.

The organization of the WISC-III is similar to the group tests observed earlier. Age scales were discarded in favor of a scheme that groups items into a series of subtests of similar content. These items are graded for differentiating within a single subtest, and the person moves from one subtest to another. The WISC-III has 10 subtests and two supplementary subtests, all of which are grouped into verbal and performance categories. The scores are determined by changing the subtest raw scores into scale scores, which are combined to yield three IQ scores: a verbal IQ, a performance IQ, and a full-scale IQ. The deviation IQs have a mean of 100 and a standard deviation of 15. The WISC-III was revised and reintroduced in 1991. Evidence of reliability and validity is satisfactory.

Changes to the WISC-IV include incorporating current research on cognitive processes and development, updating norms, adding new subtests, and dropping others. Also, instead of scale scores being combined into a full-scale IQ, a verbal IQ, and a performance IQ, the scaled scores are summed into four index scores: Verbal Comprehension Index (VCI), Perceptual Reasoning Index (PRI), Working Memory Index (WMI), and Processing Speed Index (PSI). The full-scale IQ score is retained. Evidence of reliability and validity is also satisfactory for this edition.

IQ tests compared. The WISC and the Stanford-Binet are the two tests chosen by most school systems for measuring intellectual ability in children. In many schools, these tests are the final criterion for determining giftedness.

Consequently, general intellectual functioning is viewed as the hallmark of giftedness. This practice is what gives intelligence-type definitions, described in the first chapter, a high emphasis. While both tests measure similar abilities, they do not measure the same abilities in the same age groups of children, nor are these tests equally sensitive to differences within age groups. Choosing which test to use is really a decision concerning what bias one wishes to impose on a program for gifted children. This statement underscores the fact that test selection does inevitably influence who is identified. All measurement and selection has error, thus the object is to try to have errors occur in directions that are considered acceptable.

Comparing the WISC-III to the SBIV, the Wechsler tests are attractive because they are organized to yield scores on particular subtests, which permits the examiner to get a better look at variation in verbal and nonverbal abilities. The SBIV does not produce such information. The WISC-III produces more information on nonverbal abilities than the SBIV (with children below age 9, assessing general intelligence is especially difficult). On the other hand, the SBIV has been recommended because of its greater ability to show differences among young children (Hagen, 1980; VanTassel-Baska & Baska, 1993).

Other issues involved in test selection and the reasons for selecting a particular test over another are illustrated in a study by Freeman (1979). When comparing the previous versions of each test, she selected the Stanford-Binet for the following reasons:

1. The Binet measures children more precisely in the higher ranges of ability than the Wechsler. Measurement of the top intellectual range is clearly important, and Wechsler himself doubted the efficiency of his scales at the higher levels.

2. The Binet is much less likely than the Wechsler to discriminate between the sexes on grounds of general ability. (p. 107)

Practitioners are currently assessing the recent editions of the Wechsler and the Stanford-Binet, both of which are commonly used for assessing high ability. To this end, the SB5 features high ceilings, continuous testing of abilities from early childhood through late adulthood, and extended IQ scores (Ruf, 2003). The WISC-IV has been praised for the increased ceilings (i.e., increasingly difficult questions were added at the upper ends) on a number of subtests (Gilman, 2004). There is some concern about the use of the indexes in assessing giftedness. For example, Gilman asserted that, while the WISC-IV's VCI and PRI are good indicators of giftedness, the WMI and the PSI are not. The concern is that the WMI and the PSI will confound (or weight down) the full-scale IQ. Given that the full-scale IQ is typically used as the standard for entrance to gifted programs, children deserving of gifted services may be overlooked.

Overall, there are advantages and disadvantages to any intelligence test selected. The reasons developed by Freeman (1979) may not be the reasons you would use to select one of these measures of general intelligence. However, the point remains that the identification team has reasons for selecting the test it chooses. Even if legislative mandate or state law advocates the use of a specific test, the users should be prepared to deal with the inherent biases.

Before concluding this brief review of individual general intelligence tests, it is important to mention additional tests. The Woodcock-Johnson III (WJ III; Woodcock, McGrew, & Mather, 2001) is noted for its suitability in assessing intellectually gifted students (Gridley, Norman, Rizza, & Decker, 2003). Gridley et al. noted that the battery reflects current intelligence theory (i.e., the Cattell-Horn-Carroll [CHC] model of cognitive abilities), is designed to assess multiple abilities, and has favorable technical characteristics (such as adequate ceilings, acceptable reliability, and documented content and construct validity). Tests not recommended for the identification of gifted children (Borland, 1989) include the Slosson Intelligence Test for Children and Adults (Slosson, Nicholson, & Hibpsham, 1991) and the Peabody Picture Vocabulary Test (Dunn & Dunn, 1997; Hagen, 1980).

Specific academic aptitude. Standardized tests are used most extensively to measure general intelligence. One may infer from this that multiple-criterion definitions of giftedness are either not followed in practice or are really dominated by one ability: general intelligence. For this reason, we have devoted considerable space to its measurement. Not all people concerned with identification perceive that the IQ test is the best way to determine giftedness, as specific academic aptitude may be a more reliable indicator of gifted behavior (Stanley, 1980). Specific academic aptitude (achievement) and creativity are also measured by standardized tests, but much less widely. Intelligence tests do not measure either of these areas, thus it is inappropriate to use intelligence tests to measure achievement or creativity.

Achievement tests have been used for decades in gifted education to determine specific academic aptitude, although this practice has been questioned by psychometric experts. For example, Anastasi and Urbina (1997) stated that "[a]ptitude tests measure the effect of learning under relatively controlled and unknown conditions, whereas achievement tests measure the effects of learning that occurred under partially known and controlled conditions" (p. 475). In addition, achievement tests generally represent an evaluation of a person's status after training or instruction, thus the emphasis is on what a person can do at a particular time. Achievement tests differ from intelligence tests in that they are designed to make judgments about how well someone has learned a particular content area or, in some cases, subject matter when compared to others of comparable age or grade. Achievement tests were not designed to measure general intelligence and should not be used for that purpose because such use increases the potential for misuse of scores.

Achievement tests are typically, but not always, group tests. They should be viewed with all the reservations afforded intelligence tests. For example, the extent to which knowledge in a particular content area is revealed depends largely upon how the items designed to sample that area are developed, the number of areas to be assessed, and the age ranges for which they are intended. A test that is designed to assess achievement in reading, language arts, and mathematics in grades 4–9 will necessarily present relatively fewer items in any one content area than a test intended to measure only reading in primary grades. Fewer items will necessarily limit both the precision with which achievement is estimated and subsequent placement decisions. For screening purposes, this might not be a problem. Nevertheless, when choosing an achievement test, be sure to examine the content to see if it is related to the program.

The inability of a test to sample all the behaviors in an area is likely to result in a ceiling effect when trying to locate high achievers. When students score at or above the 90th percentile on most achievement tests, it is probable that the ceiling effect is in play. If identification is to be made using cutoff scores above the 90th percentile, it is advisable to administer a test with averages based on the scores of older children, a practice commonly referred to as "out-of-level testing." Keating (1975) presented data showing the utility of this practice for students between the 90th and 99th percentiles, and it is used in the national talent searches (Jarosewich & Stocking, 2003; Lupkowski-Shoplik & Assouline, 1994).

Numerous tests covering many curricular areas are available. Within these, tests that measure reading, language arts, and mathematics are probably better designed and more useful than those covering more specific areas, such as social studies or natural sciences, when evaluating elementary school children. On the whole, they are well-developed group tests that should be valid and reliable measuring devices, and several are used in a variety of settings across the nation:

- Woodcock-Johnson III Tests of Achievement (Woodcock, McGrew, & Mather, 2001);

- Wechsler Individual Achievement Test–Second Edition (WIAT-II; Wechsler, 2001);

- California Achievement Test, Sixth Edition (CAT/6; CTB/McGraw-Hill, 2003);

- Iowa Tests of Basic Skills (ITBS; Hoover, Dunbar, & Frisbie, 2001);

- Metropolitan Achievement Tests, Eighth Edition (MAT/8; Harcourt-Brace Educational Measurement, 2001);

- SRA Achievement Series (Science Research Associates, 1992); and

- Stanford Achievement Test (SAT; Harcourt-Brace Educational Measurement, 1996).

These achievement tests cover multiple curricular areas in grades K–12. All claim to be useful as either norm-referenced or criterion-referenced tests. For a full description of these tests, consult such guides as Buros' *Mental Measurements Yearbook, Test Critiques,* or *Tests in Print* or the test manuals.

The use of all standardized achievement tests for identifying gifted children is not universally recommended. Hagen (1980) cautioned against their use without consideration of other indicators of giftedness. She was especially hesitant about the use of criterion-referenced tests in academic areas because they are based on the notion of minimal competence. They do not assess the higher level competencies associated with giftedness. Other writers have stated that achievement tests are not the most efficient or effective means for identifying gifted children. This issue will be discussed after we conclude our review of measurement devices.

Creativity. The final ability that standardized tests are prominently used to assess is creativity. Tests of creativity differ from achievement tests in that they try to measure a broad area of functioning that is independent of traditional content areas.

The increasing interest in creativity since the mid-1950s has led to the development of tests that, in turn, have influenced the very definition of giftedness (Coleman, 1985a). Some authorities have asserted that "both measures of IQ and measures of creativity appear to be essential in identifying giftedness" (Gowan, Khatena, & Torrance, 1979, p. 200). The conclusion that creativity is a major criterion for identifying the gifted seems warranted by the results of a survey in which creative ability was most frequently cited after intelligence as an indicator of giftedness (Alvino et al., 1981). The same survey also indicated that only one third of the citations used creativity tests to measure creativity. Some of the following tests were mentioned:

- Guilford Tests of Divergent Thinking;

- DFU Subtest of the Meeker SOI Learning Abilities Test;

- SOI Screening Test; and

- Torrance Tests of Creative Thinking.

These tests have much in common because Guilford's notions of divergent thinking seem to serve as tentative models for the development of the other tests. Even under these conditions, one should not assume that the development of these tests has resulted in greater precision in the measurement of creativity than in intelligence and achievement. If anything, the measure of creativity is a more controversial area because of its problems regarding definition, criteria, validity, and reliability. Because creativity is such an important area, a chapter of this text is devoted to a comprehensive discussion of the topic.

There is considerable debate about whether or not creativity tests measure what they claim to measure. Torrance, who has developed the most widely used and thoroughly researched test for children, believes he has demonstrated the utility of his test, not only in terms of measuring creativity, but also as a culturally nonbiased means of assessing minority youth (Torrance, 1972, 1977). Hagen (1980), on the other hand, has taken the opposite view and suggested that general tests of creativity add little of significance to our search for gifted students.

For a variety of reasons, it is probably wise to avoid basing the selection of students solely on a measure of creativity. As we turn to other forms of measurement, we will see that creativity emerges again as a major area of interest.

Summary of standardized testing. Standardized tests remain a cornerstone of the identification process. They may be used to assess a wide number of abilities related to the many definitions of giftedness. Standardized tests are employed primarily to assess the abilities of general intellectual functioning, specific academic aptitude, and creativity, although there are tests available for the measurement of other abilities. Certain qualities of standardized tests render them desirable. These are norm groups, rules for administration and scoring, estimates of reliability and validity, and general public acceptance. Some standardized tests also have disadvantages, including inadequate description of norms and technical data, differing types of content from test to test, a lack of items of sufficient difficulty, and a tendency to yield consistently low scores for the nonmodal gifted. The advantages will continue to provide the rationale for adopting standardized tests in identification procedures. On the other hand, the disadvantages will continue to supply the momentum for developing alternate means to measure abilities.

Rating Scales and Checklists

Measurement techniques to be used in a system of identification may include devices other than standardized tests. One category is rating scales and checklists. The number of measurement techniques included in this category probably exceeds the frequency of using standardized tests in the United States (Alvino et al., 1981). The size of this category is related to the variety of techniques subsumed within it.

These devices are grouped together under "rating scales" and "checklists" because they share common properties. Rating scales and checklists meet Newland's (1980) definition of testing proposed earlier. A rating scale or checklist requires making a judgment or series of judgments about people on the basis of a stated criterion along a continuum (Borland, 1989).

The criterion may be broad (e.g., "exhibits creative behavior") or specific (e.g., "reads five books each week"). In practice, there are usually many statements used to evaluate a person. The person who makes the judgments may be a parent, a peer, a teacher, or the person him- or herself. The literature on rating scales and checklists frequently cites the rater in order to describe the technique—teacher ratings, parent ratings, peer nominations, or self-report technique.

Advantages and disadvantages. The popularity of rating scales and checklists is related to factors dealing with attitudes toward standardized testing and the fallibility of identification procedures, although reactions against testing alone are not sufficient to explain the popularity of this category of techniques. Rather, rating scales have a number of unique attributes that make them attractive to schools.

The history of the use of such procedures dates back to the 1920s when there was an upsurge of interest in research on gifted children (Terman, 1925). The increased use of standardized tests coincided with the need to reduce the number of children to be tested, and rating scales provided such a service. They were inexpensive, easily understood, and could be used by people who were uneasy or uncomfortable with standardized tests.

Rating scales are readily modifiable, and they may be constructed to measure abilities related to local circumstance and geographic variation. They may also be modified to be responsive to expanding notions of giftedness. Rating scales have demonstrated predictive abilities relative to school performance, job performance, and creativity (Hong, Milgram, & Gorsky, 1995; Institute for Behavioral Research in Creativity, 1974; Schaefer & Anastasi, 1968). These scales have been based on biographical data, situation-related behavioral data, and personality data.

Even with this positive picture of the performance and attractiveness of rating scales, one should be aware of their many faults before making a decision about their utility and accuracy (Anastasi & Urbina, 1997). Rating scales frequently suffer from an unclear definition of the quality to be evaluated. For example, an item from a popular rating scale (Renzulli et al., 1971) reads as follows:

The terms in the statement are subject to different interpretations. What is perfection? Is it related to being satisfied? What if the child is not satisfied with achievements in math, but is satisfied with achievements in stamp collecting? The intent here is not to disapprove of this item, but rather to illustrate how different raters might interpret it. An allied problem that may compound ambiguity is the nature of continuums or scales upon which the ratings are made. As in our example, different interpretations may also be placed on the meaning of "occasionally" or "considerable." (p. 245)

All ratings are related to the opportunity to observe and scrutinize the behavior. If the rater has had limited opportunity, the rating may not have much meaning. For this reason, some scales provide space to indicate insufficient experience to judge.

Rating scales are also susceptible to several other well-known errors. The most prominent is the "halo effect," which occurs when the rater is overinfluenced by one trait and evaluates other traits accordingly. In this situation, the rater tends to rate all items in a similar manner. Some people do not like children who ask too many questions and, upon rating that characteristic, may tend to give lower ratings to associated characteristics. The opposite is possible when a favorable quality is rated. Other problems with rating scales include the tendency to give a neutral rating and the tendency to avoid giving too many negative ratings.

The general advantages and disadvantages of rating scales should be weighed against the purpose for which the scales are intended. The utility of rating scales and checklists can be more accurately assessed by examining how they have been used in identification schemes and evidence of their usefulness.

General and specific abilities. Rating scales and checklists have been most prevalent in the identification of giftedness where giftedness is conceived of as a general referent to high ability. In other terms, giftedness is viewed as a unitary phenomenon, as opposed to the discovery of children with specialized talents or abilities. In his pioneer investigations, Terman (1925) used a general approach in which teachers were asked to name the brightest children. Other investigators have followed this pattern. Since Terman, researchers (Borland, 1978; Gear, 1978) have tended to be more specific in their description of giftedness and have been more concerned with improving the performance of raters than narrowing the abilities to be identified.

Research on the use of rating scales to locate specific abilities has been conducted. Renzulli et al. (1971) proposed a scale to look at characteristics organized into four ability categories: learning, motivation, leadership, and creativity. It is toward these last two areas that energies of most researchers have been directed (Anastasi & Schaefer, 1969; IBRIC, 1974). The trend appears to favor becoming more specific about abilities (artistic-creativity, scientific-creativity), rather than using the broader category (creativity). Some of the newer efforts make rating scales more like standardized tests. This line of research seems quite promising.

Rating scales and checklists have been developed for use by people who have enough knowledge of and experience with a child to be able to make accurate ratings. The people interact with the child at home, at school, and in the community. Thus, the rating scales are directed at the teacher, the parent, the peers, and the child. Evidence of the effectiveness of the rating scales when used by these people is examined with an eye toward making recommendations about the appropriate use of rating scales and checklists.

Teachers as raters. The literature on teacher rating, sometimes called teacher nomination, is the most extensive. Writing and research on this topic have looked primarily at whether or not teachers can identify the gifted, as well as some designated criteria, such as IQ tests. Sometimes, a placement committee or an achievement test is the criterion for designating who is gifted.

While there have been numerous studies in this area, the study by Pegnato and Birch (1959) is considered to be the classic. It reported that classroom teachers were not good at identifying gifted children, a finding that upset educators. It is a significant problem because the teacher sits in the center of the child's school life, and much research on teacher ratings has been directed at clarifying this finding or at improving teacher ratings of children. The study was conducted in a junior high school (grades 7–9) in Pittsburgh that served a generally advantaged, high-socioeconomic community. The criterion for being classified as gifted was an IQ of 136 on the Stanford-Binet. Seven sources were compared to this criterion: (1) teacher referral, (2) honor role, (3) creative ability in music and art, (4) student council memberships, (5) mathematics performance, (6) group IQ test of 115 on Otis Quick Scoring, and (7) group achievement test (math and reading averaged to be 3 grades beyond on the Metropolitan Achievement Test). The results indicated that teachers' referrals were neither efficient nor effective in identifying children with IQs of 136 on the Binet. In fact, teachers referred only 45.1% of all the children identified as gifted. Even more surprisingly, 31.4% of those they referred had IQs in the normal range, 115 or below. Several of the other referral sources were also really teacher referrals—creativity in art and music, and math achievement—and it appeared that teachers were not good sources of reference. Incidentally, a combination of the IQ test and achievement was 96.7% effective in identifying the gifted.

The results mean that, under conditions set by Pegnato and Birch, teachers have trouble picking out gifted children. How were the ratings made? The teachers were given the following instructions: "Name the children you consider mentally gifted in your homeroom or in any of your classes. Make a statement as to why you judge the child to be mentally gifted." No definition was given; each teacher was free to interpret the term *gifted* in his or her own way (p. 30). No limit was put on the number of children they might identify. Despite the concerns raised by Pegnato and Birch, other authors (e.g., Borland, 1989) have claimed that teacher nominations can be much more accurate if they are provided forms with specific behaviors to be considered. The ensuing discussion illustrates the nature of the problem teachers face when recommending children as being gifted.

Following the discussion of shortcomings of rating scales, one can see that the very ambiguity of the term *gifted* might be unduly influencing the selection process. The practice of using such a broad term may seriously underestimate the utility of teacher ratings, as well as a teacher's true ability to rate children (see Figure 3.1). Gear (1976) reviewed the literature on

	Seldom	Occasionally	Considerably	Almost Always
Strives toward perfection				
Is self-critical				
Is not easily satisfied with his speed or products				

Figure 3.1. Example from "Teacher Identification of Superior Students"

Note. From "Teacher Identification of Superior Students," by J. S. Renzulli, R. H. Hartman, & C. M. Callahan, 1971, *Exceptional Children, 38,* p. 245. Copyright ©1971 by The Council for Exceptional Children. Reprinted with permission.

teacher nominations and concluded that teacher ratings at primary, elementary, and secondary levels were usually low and not to be recommended. However, some of the studies hinted that teachers might be better at identifying the gifted under different circumstances and that teacher ability to identify them might be improved. The circumstances that seemed to be working against effective teacher identification were the global description of giftedness, the age of the children to be identified, and the teachers' lack of knowledge about gifted children's behavior. A few studies have examined these circumstances. Borland (1978) developed a three-interval teacher rating scale for children in elementary school containing 15 behaviors with varying weights assigned to each one. Giftedness was defined by IQ, achievement, and teacher ratings. Borland reported that teacher ratings were predictive of IQ scores, efficient, and sensitive to gender and achievement differences, thus suggesting that teachers are better at identifying the gifted than was previously thought. The study tended to confirm the probable value of rating scales that describe more specific behaviors associated with giftedness.

In a study using a different approach to improving ratings over five sessions, teachers were trained in order to improve their ability to identify gifted children who were culturally disadvantaged (Gear, 1978). Giftedness was determined by a team judgment, although the WISC-R was also administered. The mean IQ of the group was 133, and the range extended from 124 to above 145. Trained teachers were found to identify significantly more children (85.5%) than untrained teachers (40.3%). The efficiency of the teacher groups was similar. The efficiency and effectiveness of teachers has also been studied with positive results by others (Chambers, Barren, & Sprecher, 1980; Renzulli & Smith, 1977b).

A variable that may be important to teacher ratings is the age of the children being identified, as the findings of some studies imply that teachers may be less able to pick out gifted children in the early school years than they are at the secondary level. While Pegnato and Birch (1959) reported that secondary teachers were less than 50% effective in picking out the gifted, Cornish (1968) found that teachers correctly identified only 31% of those designated as gifted at the sixth-grade level. In a later study, Jacobs (1971) found teachers to be a mere 9.5% effective in identifying kindergarten-age children designated as gifted on the WPPSI.

The research on teacher use of rating scales is difficult to summarize, although in general one can say that the evidence is not very positive for teachers. How comfortable one feels about using teacher rating seems to be related to what one is willing to accept as evidence. The results are conflicting because different standards are employed to form the criterion group against which comparisons are made. One group of studies that assumes giftedness is best revealed by an individually administered IQ test finds teacher ratings to be generally unsatisfactory. On the other hand, a second group of studies assumes giftedness is not best indicated by an individual IQ test, contending instead that giftedness manifests itself in more ways than general intellectual functioning, and therefore should be found in more children who are not from middle-class backgrounds than is presently the case. This position is associated with criterion groups formed on the basis of varied procedures such as achievement tests, assessment team reports, group IQ tests, creativity tests, and even teacher recommendations to identify giftedness. Studies based on this conception of giftedness create the impression that teachers should be given more credit for identifying children as gifted. Since the criterion groups differ in composition, it is really not possible to compare the results.

All of this is confounded even further by the problem of constructing rating scales. Given this situation, it is probably safest to say that teachers can supply information about specific characteristics and abilities, while standardized tests cannot. The position of this information in the identification process is best related to program objectives. Why teachers are not better than they are at picking out the gifted is not clear. It is likely that typical classrooms do not tap the talents of children in a way that is readily observable. Even in specific subject areas, such as math and art (Pegnato & Birch, 1959; Stanley, 1976), it may be because the curriculum is too easy.

Parents as raters. Because parents often have unique opportunities to observe a child's behavior in many settings, one would assume they are excellent sources of information as raters. School personnel, however, have ambivalent feelings about consulting parents. On the one hand, a good identification system calls for a variety of information. Parents may have information about hobbies, interests, advanced abilities, or social activities that are not apparent in the school. School personnel, on the other hand, are sometimes reluctant to raise inquiries because of the anticipated wishful thinking by parents or because of the problem of answering questions about why one's child is not considered gifted. Although no empirical evidence is cited, it seems likely that these concerns may account for the limited amount of research in this area.

Ciha, Harris, Hoffman, and Potter (1974) compared the effectiveness of kindergarten teachers and parents in rating children as gifted on the basis of stated criteria. Parents effectively nominated 67% of those who were identified as gifted using the Slosson Intelligence Scale, while the teachers were 22% effective in selecting the gifted. The study indicates that, for kindergarten youngsters, parents are more effective identifiers than teachers. However, parents tended to nominate many more nongifted than the teachers did. The excess of nominees suggests parents are inefficient sources of data.

Somewhat contradictory findings were reported in a thorough study by Jacobs (1971). All the children entering kindergarten in a school district were administered the WPPSI. Out of 654 children, 19 reached the criterion of an IQ of 125. Parents and teachers were asked to nominate children based on a general statement. The parents were 76% effective, while the teachers were only 9.5% effective. Interestingly, none of the parent ratings agreed with the teacher ratings. Jacobs concluded that parents were much more conservative than teachers in nominating children.

Based upon these studies, it would appear that parents may supply useful information, but they certainly should not be the sole determiner of giftedness at the kindergarten level. The research on parents as identifiers has been questioned because of the use of the Slosson Intelligence Test, the cutoff used with the Wechsler scale, and the global description of giftedness given to the parents. Nevertheless, parents may be able to report the presence of behaviors that school personnel are not in the position to observe. It is likely that parents, who have frequent, prolonged interactions with their children, will be one of the best sources of information. Because virtually all of the research has been conducted with primary-grade children, information is needed on the effectiveness of parents as identifiers when children are in elementary and secondary schools.

Despite the research findings on the effectiveness of teachers and parents as raters, it is common practice for teachers and parents to complete rating scales designed to identify gifted students. Instruments designed to assess general characteristics of gifted students include the Scales for Identifying Gifted Students (SIGS; Ryser & McConnell, 2003) and the Gifted and Talented

31. Has anyone in your immediate family participated professionally in an artistic (music, dance, art, drama, writing, etc.) area?
   A. Yes
   B. No

60. When working on an interesting report or paper, how often do you do it over and over until is it [sic] as good as you can make it?
   A. Once is enough
   B. Sometimes
   C. Frequently

96. Which of the following best describes your study habits?
   A. I do not do much studying because I do not want to.
   B. I do not do much studying because of other activities.
   C. I do not do much studying because it isn't necessary.
   D. I study hard but only before examinations.
   E. I study regularly throughout the school year.

Figure 3.2. Example of self-rating questions

Note. From *Identification of Academic, Creative, and Leadership Talent From Biographical Data: Final Report* (pp. 36, 39, 42), by The Institute For Behavioral Research in Creativity, 1974, Raleigh, NC: Department of Public Instruction. Copyright ©1974 by the Department of Public Instruction.

Evaluation Scales (GATES; Gilliam, Carpenter, & Christensen, 1996), both of which are used for identifying gifted students between the ages of 5 and 18 years. Other instruments are designed to assess children's performance in particular academic areas. The Test of Mathematical Abilities for Gifted Students (TOMAGS; Ryser & Johnsen, 1998), for example, measures mathematical problem solving and mathematical reasoning at the Primary Level (grades K–3) and the Intermediate Level (grades 4–6).

Peers as raters. A third source of information is the rating of children by their peers, who may be able to supply important data (Gagné, 1993). Particularly in the search for ways to identify leadership abilities, peer ratings may hold special promise. Peer ratings have also been used to measure general intellectual ability, creativity, performing arts, and leadership ability with disadvantaged and rural populations (Alvino et al., 1981). Baldwin (1977) reported the use of peer ratings as an alternative to using only standardized tests in order to identify Black children for a gifted program. In a similar vein, peer nomination has been proposed by Cooke (1976), who suggested that "although results are not conclusive, it appears that an overlooked two percent of a given school's population may be identified" (p. 3). Renzulli and Smith (1977b) also viewed peer nomination as a promising practice. However, children above the age of 10 may be better raters than younger children (Hagen, 1980).

Peer ratings are usually seen as a means to circumvent or supplement the traditional methods of identifying giftedness. Numerous references appear in the literature on peer nomination that have not been cited here, but may be described in this manner. The utility of this practice, however, remains to be seen. It is likely that this procedure will have to be more carefully researched before it is considered a reliable technique.

Self as rater. A direct way to discover giftedness is to ask someone if he or she considers him- or herself to be gifted. However, this is not the way self-ratings commonly work. Instead, people are asked to respond to a series of descriptive statements about such things as habits, preferences, interests, and abilities (Figure 3.2 supplies examples of such statements). Given this format, older children make better candidates for self-ratings because they can more readily be introspective and have a more extensive history about themselves to draw from than younger children are likely to have.

The literature on self-ratings describes rating scales that may be offered on a continuum from informal, unstructured techniques to formal, standardized techniques. The informal rating scales are subject to the problems inherent in any rating scale that has not been empirically validated. The informal scales provide data that are difficult to interpret and use in an identification process. At the other end of the continuum, the formal, standardized rating scales seem to offer more promise for uncovering giftedness. Several studies stand out in this area, all of which follow similar procedures for building the rating scales. A group of children is identified as being gifted, either in general or in some specific ability (creative ability is the most studied area). This criterion group is compared to a nonselected group by scrutinizing their responses to a series of statements. The statements, which discriminate between the gifted group and the nongifted, are used to construct one or more scoring keys. The same rating scale would be scored for different types of gifted abilities, such as creativity, academic aptitude, and leadership (IBRIC, 1974).

Anastasi and Schaefer reported two studies using self-ratings for identifying creativity in boys and girls in high school (Anastasi & Schaefer, 1969; Schaefer & Anastasi, 1968). Students responded to items about family history, educational experiences, physical traits, leisure-time activities, and so forth. The researchers were able to distinguish between creative and noncreative people in art and science for boys and in art and writing for girls. The criterion groups were drawn from advantaged schools, which tended to encourage creative behaviors.

The Institute for Behavioral Research in Creativity (1974) instituted a study to identify academic, creative, and leadership abilities without using traditional measures, which tend to be culturally biased. The criterion group was selected from the North Carolina Governor's School by teacher nomination

4.   Travis is often the first person to answer questions asked of the class. _____ Travis is a lot like me.

12. Davis has organized a successful campaign which has ensured the integration of the history of minority groups into the curricula of his high school. Bill would never organize such a movement but would support the campaign. Byron sees no reason why people should bother about changing what is taught in school. _____ I am more like Davis than like either Bill or Byron.

21. Luddy often makes creative things in her free time. Vivian often reads about things that interest her during her spare time. Sheila usually talks with her friends during her free time. _____ I am more like Luddy or Vivian than like Sheila.

Figure 3.3. Example from RAP Inventory

Note. From *RAP Inventory* (pp. 1–2), by T. E. Grant and J. Renzulli, 1981, Marlborough, CT: RAP Researchers. Copyright ©1981 by RAP Researchers. Reprinted with permission of Joseph Renzulli.

for special abilities in art and music. The validity coefficients produced between the self-ratings and the three abilities were at the .70 level, which is an unusually high value. Several items from this scale are included in Figure 3.3.

Other self-rating instruments that have received attention in the literature tend to follow a similar format. An exception is the Relevant Aspects of Potential (RAP) Inventory, an instrument developed to assess minority youths with potential for college success (Grant & Renzulli, 1981). The rating scale was constructed by comparing responses of various groups to a pool of items. The scale employs an interesting format for some items, in which students are asked to respond on a scale from *strongly disagree* to *strongly agree* on items such as those in Figure 3.2. This format may engage the rater's interest in a more realistic manner, and it may also provide a comparative standard from which the rater may make a better judgment. Although additional research is needed to validate this instrument, it serves as a provocative idea that should receive greater attention than it does.

Self-ratings in response to biographically oriented statements are sources of potentially valuable data. Their power may be related to the old maxim that says that the best predictor of future behavior is past behavior. The rater may be the best source of information about experiences that other raters, parents, or peers can rarely observe. It is in determining abilities other than academic or intellectual abilities that self-ratings seem most promising. Recognition of this fact may be partly responsible for the use of self-ratings in measuring the six abilities mentioned in the federal definition (Alvino et al., 1981), with creativity being the most researched ability in this area.

Self-ratings have been recommended as a valuable source of data (Hagen, 1980), especially when trying to identify leadership (Friedman, Jenkins-Friedman, & Van Dyke, 1984) and creativity (Hong, Milgram, & Gorsky, 1995; Runco, 1987). However, research is needed to determine at what ages and for what abilities this technique is most appropriate and how assumptions such as the rater being a good reader affect its usefulness. The effectiveness of this technique for identifying a child for placement in a program has not been established.

Work Samples and Pupil Products

The measurement of abilities may be accomplished by using standardized tests and rating scales or checklists. Both techniques have received much attention in the literature on identification and are used widely in schools across the nation.

However, researchers and practitioners continue to seek alternatives to these traditional forms of assessment. Kanevsky (2000), for example, has noted the benefits of dynamic assessment, an interactive methodology that focuses on the *processes* involved in intellectual development, as a means of identifying gifted students. VanTassel-Baska, Johnson, and Avery (2002) developed performance assessment tasks to facilitate the identification of underrepresented populations in gifted programs. As Johnsen (2003) pointed out, however, a number of factors continue to impede the use of nontraditional forms of assessment, particularly in the area of talent development. That is, traditional forms of testing continue to be supported because of contextual beliefs, technical qualities, and diversity within talent development areas.

One nontraditional assessment technique is a work sample, a general term applied to the products of a child's efforts in specific areas. These products or accomplishments are available for others to observe. They may be brought to a place for examination, or they may be produced in a controlled situation under the scrutiny of judges. Work samples are appropriate measuring devices in the same sense that standardized tests and rating scales are because they are intended to show differences among individuals. However, these differences extend from more to less with no standard zero point. Work samples are used in many different areas of life as a means for measuring performance. Wherever they are used, they assume that performance is the best measure of ability. The work sample has potential for accurate measurements that are not provided by standardized tests and rating scales.

To clarify what a work sample might be, several examples follow that illustrate the application of this technique in different fields of endeavor—fashion modeling, dancing, and sculpting. The model would compile a portfolio containing examples of recent work to present to agencies. The sculptor would follow a similar path, but because it is not feasible to carry a truckload of statues around, he or she would present a portfolio of slides and photos. The dancer would attend auditions and collect clippings about past performances. These examples typify the work-sample technique.

The products of one's efforts are presented to an authority in the given field for evaluation. Central to this technique is the role of the authority or expert. The role implies that the expert has had much training and gained significant knowledge in some field, which gives him or her specially enhanced skills for judging high-quality activity. A nonexpert would not make judgments based on the same criteria because he or she would not be properly trained to observe. The meaning of the difference between expert and nonexpert can readily be seen in the Olympics. The gymnastic events are filled with outstanding performances, but the expert commentator can describe why one performance is superior to another by pointing out improperly executed techniques. The non-experts are caught by the beauty of the performance and are unaware of those subtle, yet significant, differences. When the area of endeavor becomes more and more interpretive, relatively speaking, as in music and art, it is harder to illustrate the expertise in operation. Nevertheless, it is there.

The work-sample technique harnesses the abilities of experts to identify those with special talents. This practice has been recognized by people interested in the arts (Barren, 1968; Kay & Subotnik, 1994) and in science (Zuckerman, 1977). The work-sample technique can assess a variety of abilities and test them under conditions that are associated with the real-life demonstration of the ability. Abilities in leadership, creativity, visual and performing arts, and school learning have been assessed using this technique (Alvino et al., 1981).

The following are examples of products, many of which are commonly judged in schools today, that might be included under the work sample: prizes in competitions, exhibits in the school or community, diaries, poems and essays, hobbies and collections, elected offices, inventions, committee work, extracurricular activities and club memberships, autobiographies (written or recorded), popularity polls, and school work in relevant classes. Some of these products have already been evaluated; others would need to be submitted to a panel of judges.

While the work-sample technique seems to have the advantages of (1) requiring children to produce in a manner that corresponds to program objectives and (2) being flexible for use with various abilities, it has several disadvantages. For one, it focuses on demonstrated ability, rather than potential ability, which many standardized tests claim to measure. It is not easy to assemble a panel of experts to judge a product, and people often disagree about expertise. The process is time-consuming and may be costly when the experts are paid for their services. Another possible problem is that the experts may reflect the prevailing prejudice about certain products and not be able to recognize originality.

The work-sample technique is a procedure that has been neglected in systems of identification. It has the potential for assessing aspects of performance—persistence, organizational ability, imagination, and self-criticism—

recognized to be attributes of giftedness that receive little attention (Kay & Subotnik, 1994). The utility of this procedure probably increases with the age of the child. Like the other techniques, more research is needed; in fact, the work sample seems to be the least-researched measurement technique. Although much has been written in recent years, there has been little in the way of empirical study on its reliability and validity for identification. If school personnel wish to use this technique, it is advisable to select carefully the judges and be specific about which abilities they are to judge. It is important to remember that the judges will rank the work samples from most evidence to least evidence of specific ability. Once again, final identification for a program should be based on multiple criteria.

Typical Identification Systems: A Summary and Critique

The complexity of the identification process is difficult to grasp without actually experiencing it. The benefit of certain procedures and measurement techniques and the shortcomings of others may not be apparent from our discussion at this point. In order to bring out the problems inherent in identification procedures, three systems are presented. These are typical of practices we have observed in school systems in four states. These practices represent reality, not necessarily preferred practices. For the sake of brevity, presume that each district is attempting to follow the criteria outlined earlier in this chapter and that the school district selects the appropriate measurement devices.

Table 3.1 outlines the procedures, including the school's definition and criteria for screening and placement. All these systems are appropriate if they meet the objectives of the school district's program. Schools A, B, and C have the following similar procedures, although not in the same order: (1) intellectual ability as the primary ability, (2) use of group tests, (3) use of individual IQ tests, (4) use of teacher ratings, (5) screening procedure, (6) multiple criteria for selection, (7) process started at the third-grade level, and (8) IQ score as final determinant. These practices are commonly used by school districts. Again, if the school program objectives are met, then the system is appropriate.

There may be more efficient ways to identify children in some of these districts. Sometimes, a district may be following procedures that are unnecessary in terms of their definition. School B uses a creativity test, but the definition doesn't mention creativity. School C may be using too many procedures given its definition. All the practices of the districts are restricted to traditional procedures. Notice also that Schools A, B, and C do not use work samples and only collect ratings from teachers and ignore other raters—including peers, parents, and the children themselves.

Even though there are differences in procedures between Schools A, B, and C, they are likely to select similar kinds of children. These children are all-around well-balanced, achieving children, usually from advantaged homes. At the same time, the differences result in some schools selecting a more hetero-

TABLE 3.1

Typical Identification Procedures

	School A	School B	School C
Definition	Children who have potential for high creative performance and have high intellectual abilities that demand special education.	Children who possess high general intelligence and are capable of outstanding performance.	Children who have unmet educational needs and score at least two standard deviations above the mean on an individual IQ test.
Screening	Group achievement test in third grade. Score at 90th percentile or 2 years above peers. Teacher nomination based on: "Who is gifted?" by teachers in art and music, on those reaching achievement cutoff.	Teacher nomination by third grade based on school-devised checklist of "gifted behaviors." A group creativity test only to those nominated above. Cut-off at 85th percentile for the school district.	Group IQ test in third grade. Score 130 IQ. Teacher nomination: Confirm child has high ability in all classes. Group achievement scores in school records at 96th percentile.
Placement	Individual IQ test: Binet IV IQ of 132.	Individual IQ test: WISC–III IQ of 130.	Individual IQ test: WISC–III IQ of 130.

Note. From *Schooling the Gifted* (p. 87), by L. J. Coleman, 1985, Menlo Park, CA: Addison-Wesley. Copyright ©1985 L. J. Coleman. Reprinted with permission.

geneous group than others. Schools B and C select a more varied group than School A, with School B having the most diverse combination of children. Remember the admonition that the chosen measurement techniques create the reality of any district's definition of giftedness. The actual definition of giftedness used in a school is made operational by the placement of certain measuring devices at specific points in the identification process. The procedures in Table 3.1 tend to screen out particular children due to the properties of each measurement device. The review of these measures clearly supports this statement. All three schools utilize teacher nominations, yet research indicates that teacher ratings are not very good at the elementary school level. Using traditional definitions of giftedness, they are likely to miss more than 70% of gifted children. Achievement tests are quite unreliable at picking out the traditionally defined gifted, although they are somewhat better than teacher ratings. Group IQ tests at the 130 IQ level in School C will probably overlook 50–70% of those who are identifiably gifted according to a traditional definition. The creativity test has questionable utility when used to discriminate between gifted and nongifted. Given the order of the measurement technique in the process and its own particular properties, certain children are eliminated from consideration, are not likely to appear on instruments designed to corroborate giftedness, or both.

For example, in School A, achievement tests and teacher ratings in art and music are not likely to identify many children because ability in art and music is not measured by high scores on achievement tests. Thus, achievement tests that do not reflect ability in art and music combined with the general problem inherent in teacher rating should dramatically narrow the number of children eligible for the individual IQ test. A somewhat similar case can be made for Schools B and C. The result is that many children may not be identified as gifted when, in fact, they are. The converse may also happen. These circumstances are probably responsible for the familiar refrain heard when programs are developed: "These children do not behave the way I expected they would." While this comment is not unanimous, it is heard with surprising frequency.

Circumstances converge to identify children who are more likely to fit the Terman type of giftedness than the expanded notions of giftedness that recognize abilities in leadership, creativity, and the visual or performing arts. The complexity of the identification process has intensified with this expanded notion of giftedness. It seems that more decisions need to be made about abilities for which limited information is available. The complexity is compounded by the fact that problems inherent in identification using conventional notions of giftedness have not been adequately resolved (Coleman et al., 1997).

One conclusion is clear: Identification systems tend to select the Terman-type gifted child having multiple strengths expressed in ways that permit relatively easy recognition and they often fail at finding children who depart from this picture. One of the hottest issues in identification is how to find these people who don't fit that mold (Ford, 1996; Sato, 1974). While the problem is recognized by all, it is not a major issue to everyone concerned with the development of gifted children (Stanley, 1976).

IDENTIFYING THE NONMODAL GIFTED CHILD:
A CONTINUING DILEMMA

The goal of a complete identification system is to identify all the children who should be. It is not possible, except in a theoretical sense, to estimate how many children this would be in any school district; yet, we keep striving to improve our procedures. The general need for improving identification systems is evident from these persistent factors:

1. The number of children represented in gifted programs from non-White, non-middle-class, nonurban backgrounds is disproportionately low, given their numbers in the general population.

2. With the diversity of our population of school-age children increasing, the loss of talent to society makes the search for giftedness more important than ever, and the need for appropriate means for identification approaches crucial.
3. Many adults who are recognized as gifted were not identified as gifted children.

4. Many gifted adults who went unidentified had learning and behavior problems as children.

The presence of these facts, as well as the general description of the children who are identified, makes it clear that children who depart from the portrait developed by Terman and others are most frequently missed. The more readily identified are modal gifted children, who are the ones with the most commonly occurring pattern of characteristics (Coleman, 1985a). Those who are missed in traditional identification systems are the nonmodal gifted children, who do not possess the common pattern of characteristics. The only common characteristic is that nonmodal children display behaviors that decrease the likelihood they will be recognized as being gifted until after they should have been identified. These behaviors include the use of language. As noted by Slocumb and Payne (2000), many gifted students from impoverished backgrounds may have limited exposure to language that enriches their vocabularies and models a formal style of speech. The adoption of more casual speech by these students, including the use of slang words and incorrect grammar, may result in others perceiving them as being of lesser ability than those who speak more formally.

Traditional assessment approaches reflecting historical conceptions of giftedness tend to value factors that underrepresent nonmodal gifted students. This implies that some nonmodal children get identified, but it is believed that more exist than are found. The paradox within our identification procedures from Terman's time until now is that the intention is to remove bias in selection. While this has been successfully realized for some individuals, the practices of identification have led to new lines of stratification in schools (Sapon-Shevin, 1994). Standardized tests have received the bulk of criticism in our failure to identify the nonmodal gifted, but other factors are at work. For example, the sociocultural context in which the IQ tests were developed and implemented in arenas such as Terman's study may have had an influence on the perpetuation of the Terman stereotype, the impact of which may be significant on nonmodal gifted children. It must be considered that the bias in identifying nonmodal gifted children may not be only from tests, but may be present in all facets of the identification and placement processes.

Why are these groups so difficult to identify? A sufficient explanation is one that looks at the enormity of the problem. Primarily, the identification problem is a consequence of the characteristics of nonmodal children; secondarily, it is a consequence of the way the identification system is designed, as in Schools A, B, and C. Neither cause, by itself, is sufficient to explain the ineffectiveness of our provisions for identifying this group.

The nonmodal gifted individual has characteristics that simultaneously confirm and dispute the notion of giftedness in a manner that defies common sense. This amorphous group tends to have broad characteristics that, when coupled with the term *gifted*, create an oxymoron. When the terms *gifted* and *disabled* are combined to yield the term *gifted disabled*, they produce discomfort because they do not seem to belong together. One's discomfort is not relieved when this group is further divided to create more or less specific categories, such as *gifted learning disabled*, *delinquent gifted*, *physically impaired gifted*, and so forth. Each one of the terms used to modify *gifted* needs additional explanation in order to clarify its meaning. Perhaps the fuzziness of these terms contributes to the problem of identification and also perpetuates the apparently endless debate. For purposes of discussion, the nonmodal gifted group will be classified into two broad categories, which are not mutually exclusive: (1) gifted disabled and (2) culturally different gifted. Within each category, there are additional subdivisions, and there is much overlap.

Gifted Disabled

The gifted disabled are children who may be defined as being both gifted and disabled. Various estimates have been offered about how many children fit this category. In 1981, Whitmore reported estimates ranging from 120,000 to 540,000 children, which were based upon the percentage of children with disabilities (1–2%) who might be gifted. The real percentage, however, is unknown. It is likely to be nearer the lower limit because the total number of children with disabilities includes a large number of people classified as mentally disabled, who would rarely be found to be gifted, and people with speech impairments, who are also members of other categories of disabled.

TABLE 3.2

Characteristics Impeding and Revealing Giftedness

Impeding characteristics	Characteristics revealing giftedness
Little or no productivity in school—cannot read, write, spell easily or accurately ("learning disabled"). Poor motor skills, coordination—writing is painfully slow, messy: often child is easily distracted from tasks and described as inattentive (neurologically impaired, "minimal cerebral dysfunction," developmental delay in motor area).	Superiority in oral language— vocabulary, fluency, structure. Memory for facts and events. Exceptional comprehension. Analytical and creative problem-solving abilities. Markedly advanced interests, impressive knowledge. Keen perception and humor. Superior memory, general knowledge.
Absence of oral communication skills (e.g. cerebral palsy, deafness).	Drive to communicate through alternative modes—visual, nonverbal body language. Superior memory and problem-solving ability. Exceptional interest and drive in response to challenge.
Disordered behavior—aggressive, disruptive, frequently off-task.	Superior verbal skill, oral language. Exceptional capacity for manipulating people and solving "problems." Superior memory, general knowledge.
Extremely withdrawn, non-communicative.	Most difficult to identify— the only key is response to stimulation of higher mental abilities unless superior written work is produced.

Note. From "Gifted Children with Handicapping Conditions: A New Frontier," by J. R. Whitmore, 1981, *Exceptional Children, 2*, p. 106. Copyright ©1981 by the Council for Exceptional Children.

Even though the exact number is unknown, it is clear that gifted-disabled people exist and are largely ignored. History provides evidence of the existence of gifted-disabled children from the biographies of famous people such as Aldous Huxley, Albert Einstein, and Helen Keller. Interest in the identification of individuals with disabilities along with gifted abilities has been growing (Baum, Emerick, Herman, & Dixon, 1989; Brody & Mills, 1997; Fox, Brody, & Tobin, 1983; Frierson, 1968; Maker, 1977). An array of conditions of disability are identifiable and were codified in PL 94–142—The Education for All Handicapped Children Act (Blake, 1981), recently reauthorized as the Individuals With Disabilities Education Act (IDEA) in 1997.

When one reads these definitions, it is obvious that they describe incompatibilities between a child's characteristics and the structure of the school. The terms *gifted* and *disabled* overlap in this regard. The identification of children with disabilities follows procedures similar to those recommended for identifying the gifted, although it focuses on a child's inability to perform various tasks. The general remediation model adopted by special education sets the norm, or average, as the educational goal for students with disabilities. This tunnel vision may help explain why some children who are both gifted and disabled are missed. However, a better explanation that is probably more fair is that the characteristics of the children and the nature of the identification process itself interact to overlook these children. Table 3.2 shows one conception of how characteristics of children with disabilities and those usually attributed to the gifted do not correspond. Reasons why the identification system may not be up to the task of identifying these children are obvious.

One factor is that the nearly invisible learning disability can confound the most experienced teacher when it is paired with gifted abilities. The competing abilities and disabilities may interact in such a way that they mask each other, resulting in a gifted child who struggles (and often succeeds) to attain average performance. Vail (1979) offered the following examples of students with abilities and disabilities in the same learning system:

1. In the visual learning system, a talented art student may have trouble recognizing printed letters or words.

2. In the motor system, an exquisitely coordinated athlete may have barely legible handwriting.

3. In the auditory learning system, a student with perfectly good hearing may not remember oral instructions.

4. In the language system, a student who speaks fluently may have trouble organizing written work or comprehending written text (p. 37).

Another factor is that the tests used to identify disabilities were not developed for spotting high-ability differences within any one disability group. Instead, they were developed simply for classifying the disabilities. In addition, if a handicapping condition masks or depresses performance so that special abilities are hidden, then it takes an astute observer to note discrepancies that indicate high ability (Coleman, 1985a). The problem is most acute in assessment where "developmental delays occur in early childhood as a consequence of specific handicaps" (Whitmore, 1981, p. 109).

Consider the problems of evaluating a child with a learning disability, a child with spastic cerebral palsy, a child with a hearing impairment, or an emotionally disturbed child. The tests used to assess these children for their disabilities are not commonly used to identify the gifted. Furthermore, identification systems for children with disabilities typically ignore assessment of abilities associated with giftedness, such as creativity and artistic ability. Pollard and Howze (1981) reported an effort to identify deaf students of high ability that illustrates the complexity of a good assessment program for the hearing-impaired.

The inadequate identification of the gifted disabled may also be due to a lack of opportunity to demonstrate their giftedness because of the curricula in special-education programs. Because programs for children and youth with disabilities focus on the development of basic academic and social skills, the child who has ability in the arts, language, science, or mathematical reasoning cannot show this potential. Even in programs for the mildly mentally disabled, the attention to the remediation of weaknesses with little regard for strengths works against the interests of the child.

If the gifted disabled are ever going to be identified in numbers that correspond to estimates of their population, then special efforts will have to be made to include the search for strengths as part of the identification process. Efforts should be made not to be premature in screening children with disabilities out of consideration for gifted programs. This requires setting cutoff scores, interpreting performance discrepancies in a positive direction, and clarifying ill-defined categories. The search for the gifted disabled will always be a difficult undertaking because of all the factors discussed in this section. Without continuous efforts, little progress can be expected.

Culturally Different Gifted

The most significant proportion of the nonmodal gifted group is composed of the culturally different, who Sato (1974) defined as having "membership in a culture other than the dominant culture in society" (p. 573). The definition in this discussion is more narrow in that it includes only children who come from backgrounds that diverge from the Caucasian, middle-class norm. These people are frequently members of minority groups defined by race or language differences. However, a person may be a member of a minority group and not be considered culturally different according to this definition.

The identification of culturally different gifted students is a perplexing problem because their average performance on aptitude and achievement tests

TABLE 3.3

Trends in the Representation of Minority Students in Gifted Education Programs, 1978–1992

Student population	1978	1980	1982	1984	1992
Hispanic American	6.8	9.0	8.6	13.2	13.7
	5.2	5.4	4.0	7.2	7.9
	(u = 25%)	(u = 40%)	(u = 53%)	(u = 45%)	(u = 42%)
American Indian	.8	.7	.5	.8	1.0
	.3	.3	.3	.3	.5
	(u = 62%)	(u = 57%)	(u = 40%)	(u = 62%)	(u = 50%)
Asian American	1.4	2.2	2.6	3.7	4.0
	3.4	4.4	4.7	6.8	7.0
	(o = 59%)	(o = 50%)	(o = 45%)	(o = 46%)	(o = 43%)
African American	15.7	20.1	25.8	24.5	21.1
	10.3	11.1	11.0	12.9	12.0
	(u = 33%)	(u = 45%)	(u = 57%)	(u = 47%)	(u = 41%)

Note. Percentages are rounded; top number indicates percentage of student population and middle number represents percentage of gifted education. "o" indicates overrepresentation; "u" indicates underrepresentation. Percentage of underrepresentation was calculated using the following formula: 1 - (percentage of gifted education program divided by percentage of school district). Source for 1978–1984 data: Chinn & Hughes (1987). Source for 1992 data: OCR Elementary and Secondary School Civil Rights Compliance Report (1992).

From "The Underrepresentation of Minority Students in Gifted Education: Problems and Promises in Recruitment and Retention" by Donna Y. Ford, 1998, *The Journal of Special Education, 32*, p. 7. Copyright ©1998 by PRO-ED.

tends to be one standard deviation below the mean when general norms are used (Borland, 1989; Samuda, 1975). If standardized tests are used in the conventional manner, it is probable that many culturally different children will not be identified as gifted.

Several means for dealing with this disquieting fact have been suggested. One provision is concerned with the inadequacy of standardized tests—including intelligence, aptitude, and achievement tests—to measure ability in many culturally different groups. Some studies have examined the content of these tests, including specific test items, to ascertain if they are unfair to any particular group (Torrance, 1977). Other studies have examined whether or not predictions about future school performance made on the basis of test performance were biased (Samuda, 1975). The research efforts in both areas have produced inconsistent and confusing findings that may be interpreted in contradictory ways. Thus, the search to prove that tests are inadequate because they are biased has been moderately successful or unsuccessful, depending upon your point of view.

Clearly, culturally different children are underrepresented in programs (see Table 3.3). The complete abandonment of tests is not the answer because some culturally different children are identified as gifted who would not have been identified without them (Coleman, 1985a). In addition, a newer statistical approach for considering test bias called Differential Item Functioning is showing great promise in providing additional information for those selecting instruments to assess gifted children.

A major effort for dealing with the marked discrepancy in scores between culturally different children and White, middle-class children has been to improve standardized testing. For more than 50 years researchers have been trying to develop culture-free or culture-fair tests, especially general intelligence tests, that produce similar scores for varying cultural groups. Culture-fair tests contain more items, have different instructions, and sometimes have different time limits than regular tests. Samuda (1975) summarized the results:

> It is the consensual opinion of psychometricians and psychologists that culture-free or culture-fair tests have proved disappointing and have fallen short of their goals; for minority students have been shown to perform, if not more poorly, at least just as badly as they do on conventional intelligence measures. (p. 142)

Thirty years later, the situation has not changed. Because these efforts to devise better measures of intelligence have not been successful, other solutions have been tried, which are documented in the section on solutions for identifying the nonmodal gifted child.

The attempt to devise solutions and understand the complexity of our identification procedures is hampered by two factors that are sometimes overlooked. One is the fact that there are variations within any group. As Baca (1980) cautioned,

> The reader should be careful not to generalize from one diverse population to another. It is even difficult, if not impossible, to generalize within a single minority group because of the regional, cultural, linguistic, and other types of differences that prevail. (p. 583)

If this is the case, then modifications in an identification system must be flexible enough to deal with many variables. Whether such flexibility is possible is, again, a question of who defines the standards.

The second factor is that, as stated earlier, bias in identifying nonmodal gifted children may have its origins in the sociopolitical context in which our measurement instruments and methods were developed. With this recognition, it may be possible to work around the errors such bias injects. For example, tests are abused when they are employed as the sole criterion of giftedness (Shore, Cornell, Robinson, & Ward, 1991). By utilizing multiple criteria in the identification process, this abuse can be reduced. Test scores may continue to have value in identifying the culturally different gifted, but only with specialized interpretation of their results. The point at which cutoffs are established for including or excluding children from gifted programs needs to be researched. It is generally recommended that cutoff scales be more liberal when a specific test is known to have problems of reliability and validity when used with samples outside of the norm group. However, the effect of liberalizing cutoff scores is not known.

Solutions for Identifying Nonmodal Gifted Children

Possible remedies for deficiencies in identification systems have been proposed. Some of the most promising remedies attempt to deal with the design of identification systems overall, while some are designed to deal with the specific performance, namely low scores on standardized tests for subgroups of nonmodal gifted children.

Test Modifications: Development and Scoring

A number of projects have concentrated on culturally different groups. E. P. Torrance worked for at least 30 years to develop tests of creative ability, not intelligence tests, that would minimize cultural differences. The attention to creativity was based on his idea that creative ability is responsible for what is recognized to be outstanding in adults. Torrance believed he had been successful in this enterprise (Torrance, 1980). A colleague of Torrance's, Bruch (1971), has walked a different path in dealing with the culturally different by improving the use of standardized tests. She proposed that the Stanford-Binet should be scored in a way that would pinpoint the strengths of minority youths.

The development of a useful screening device has been another way to attack the identification problem. Johnsen and Corn (1987, 1992, 2002) created the Screening Assessment for Gifted Elementary Students (SAGES) to accomplish this purpose by assessing students in three areas. The instrument seems to function in a fair manner when screening Hispanic and Anglo American children in grades 3–5 (Runnells & Martin, 1993).

Efforts to modify standardized tests to assess culturally different groups in a more effective manner have been consistent with the "culture-specific movement" in testing (Samuda, 1975). The culture-specific movement accepts the premise that cultural differences do exist and will continue to exist. In fact, one can argue that general intelligence tests are culture-specific to White, middle-class children. Some noteworthy efforts have been conducted in this area. Mercer, who was originally concerned with the misplacement of minority youths in programs for the mentally retarded, developed the System of Multicultural Pluralistic Assessment (SOMPA) for assessing the performance of Hispanic and African American children in California (Mercer, 1973),

105

which has clear implications for the gifted child (Mercer & Lewis, 1978). Mercer's approach is to use conventional tests in a culture-specific manner. The SOMPA proposes that valid estimates of ability may only be made when comparisons are drawn to one's sociocultural group. In the SOMPA, data are obtained using assessments from traditional tests and by using interviews to gather assessments about the child's adaptive behavior in terms of cultural background. These data are combined to produce an estimate of a child's learning potential that may be used to identify him or her as gifted.

While Mercer's approach has been applied to the identification of culturally different gifted children as an afterthought, Bernal devised a procedure for identify giftedness among primary-school-aged, Spanish-speaking Mexican Americans residing in Texas (Bernal & Reyna, 1975; Reyna & Bernal, 1974). The direction in this project was to develop alternate identification procedures. Children were defined as gifted if they scored above the cutoff score established by a rater on one of five measures: WISC—verbal, WISC—performance, Torrance Tests of Creative Thinking—Verbal, Torrance—Figural, or DeAvila's Cartoon Conservation Scale. Thirty-four children were subsequently identified as gifted. Parents were interviewed using a behavioral and an adjectival checklist describing giftedness that was developed after extensive interviews in the Mexican American community. Due to problems in obtaining data from parents, 22 gifted children were compared to 32 normal children on these checklists. Results indicated that gifted children did exhibit behaviors that enabled parents to distinguish between the two groups. The authors concluded that the development of rating scales that are culture-specific is "worthy of further study."

This conclusion is consistent with efforts to identify culturally different high school children using the Institute for Behavioral Research in Creativity (IBRIC), described earlier in this chapter. On the other hand, the many compromises and departures from conventional identification practices and methodology described by Reyna and Bernal suggest this promising means of identifying culturally different gifted children is fraught with problems. A study by Chambers, Barren, and Sprecher (1980) illustrates other problems in developing rating scales geared to specific cultural groups.

The system of identifying nonmodal gifted children has also been improved by combining measurement techniques in a way that uses the best features of each. This procedure involves combining rating-scale techniques, work-sample techniques, and standardized tests to evaluate the abilities of nonmodal gifted children at varying grade levels. The joining of two or more measurement techniques has the potential for improving the identification of nonmodal gifted children because it attempts to sidestep the problems of standardized testing.

In a study by Maker, Morris, and James (1981), kindergarten and first-grade culturally different children were presented a standard lesson in a small-group setting. Observers rated performance on the Torrance Checklist of Creative Positives. These data were used as part of the screening procedure. In more recent work, Maker and her colleagues have continued the effort to invent ways to identify culturally different children (Maker, 1992; Maker, Rogers, Nielson, & Bauerle, 1996).

The DISCOVER (*D*iscovering *I*ndividual *S*trengths and *C*apabilities through *O*bservation while allowing for *V*aried *E*thnic *R*esponses) project, funded as part of the Jacob K. Javits Gifted and Talented Education Act, has abandoned the notion of general intelligence in favor of Gardner's ideas of multiple intelligences. Three of the seven types of intelligence are assessed: spatial, logical-mathematical, and linguistic. Five assessment activities or tests are designed to determine children's problem solving in the classroom. Three of the activities (Pablo, tangrams, and storytelling) are performed in small groups, while two activities (math and writing) are performed with the whole class. Reliability and validity data on this new system is beginning to emerge (Sarouphim, 2001, 2002, 2004), and this promising procedure is being used in some school systems.

A much more indirect format was developed to identify Mexican American children in grades 3–5 by Chambers et al. (1980). They, too, were trying to locate gifted children with creative ability. A rating scale was constructed with items based on traits of gifted adults. Teachers were trained to use the scale by comparing the child's traits to those of his or her peers. If a child received the highest rating, then the teacher supplied an example of the child's work that demonstrated high ability.

Two recent approaches modify forms of measurement and acknowledge the classroom and other real-life settings as locations for gathering information on the talents of culturally different children. One approach designed to fit the identification process to the environment of the children is Project Synergy (Borland & Wright, 1994), which uses a combination of traditional and nontraditional measures to identify kindergarten students living in New York City in poor economic circumstances. The project had three phases. The first phase screened children using observation, teacher nomination, enrichment lessons, portfolio assessment, and a standardized drawing test to determine a candidate pool. The second phase, diagnostic assessment, used a combination of dynamic assessment tasks, standardized tests, and interviews to produce an academic profile. These data were used in the third phase, where needs were determined and placement was decided. Data reported by the developers indicate that children can be identified by these methods.

Another approach that developed new instruments and procedures was Early Assessment for Exceptional Potential of Young Minority and/or Economically Disadvantaged Students (EAEP), another Javits-funded project (Coleman, 1994). This project used portfolio assessment as the centerpiece of the identification process. The developers assumed that there are 18 universal signs (identifiers) of exceptional potential. They developed authentic examples of these identifiers that were rooted in the life of the child in the school, home, and community. Training procedures were developed to help teachers recognize these children in their classrooms. EAEP demonstrated that children can be found using the procedures.

In addition to attempting to prove the inadequacy of tests and develop new or improved procedures, there is another approach that deals openly with the average discrepancy in scores between culturally different groups and White, middle-class groups: the establishment of different cutoff scores on tests for various cultural groups. Although this proposal has been discussed most frequently in terms of the criteria used for admission, it also has direct application to the identification of gifted children. It is not widely discussed in the literature on gifted children, but this approach is explained here as a possible solution for identifying nonmodal gifted children.

The argument for different cutoff scores is based on what is considered to be the fair use of test scores. *Fair use* is a match between the proportion of people whose scores predict successful performance in a given situation and a probable number of people whose performances would be successful in that same situation if people were selected at random. For example, imagine the following: A group of children are selected at random and placed in a program. Those who perform successfully remain in the program; the others leave. At this point, one can calculate the proportion of children from varying cultural backgrounds who were successful. In a fair use of the test, the cutoff scores should admit the proportion of applicants from various backgrounds that corresponds to the children who were actually successful in the program. The procedure for using different cutoff scores would probably result in more culturally different children being identified as gifted, and it would probably reduce the number of White, middle-class children in the program. At the same time, it would also be likely to increase the number of children who would be unsuccessful in the program (assuming the program stays the same). This approach is controversial because it raises real sociopolitical issues embedded, though often ignored, in identification systems.

The identification of gifted-disabled children may be made possible by modifying the use of measurement devices. One obvious modification has to do with using tests, whenever possible, that have scores based on averages for specific disability groups. Most of the tests that are available are nonverbal tests for those with sensory disabilities. An example of a nonverbal test is the third edition of the Test of Nonverbal Intelligence (TONI-3; Brown, Sherbenou, & Johnsen, 1997). Designed to assess special populations of students (such as those with limited exposure to U.S. culture, learning disabilities, and limited English proficiency), the TONI-3 uses abstract-figural content to measure intelligence, aptitude, problem solving, and abstract reasoning. The Naglieri Nonverbal Ability Test (NNAT; Naglieri, 2003) is another nonverbal measure that has shown promise for identifying diverse students for gifted education programs (Naglieri & Ford, 2003). Tests such as the TONI-3 and the NNAT are recommended for comparing children with disabilities to peers of similar ages and disabilities. When such tests are not available—which happens frequently—it is useful to have an examiner who has had extensive experience with children who have disabilities.

The process of studying each individual child deemphasizes the global score on a standardized test and focuses instead on the child's performance on subtests and specific items. Average or above-average performance in a specific area may be an indicator of giftedness (Wolf & Gygi, 1981). Unusual discrepancies may also be indicators of giftedness. When interpreting scores, one should note how physical disability and sensory impairment may interfere with the ability to comprehend or respond to an item (Maker, 1981). It is possible that a technique developed in Israel by Feuerstein (1980) may be an important tool for identifying the gifted disabled and culturally different gifted. This technique incorporates the idea of teaching a child to perform the task that one wants to measure.

Rating scales, another important measurement technique, can be altered for the purposes of identifying gifted-disabled students. Individuals with specific disabilities have a unique perspective on people like themselves, thus they should not be ignored as a data source. The most productive way to use rating scales may be in conjunction with an interview format.

The modification of measurement techniques may be extended to changing the cutoff scores on specific tests. For example, one possibility could be to lower the IQ cutoff scores on the full-scale WISC-R from 130 to 110 for children with a given disability. Mauser has identified a large number of learning-disabled gifted children by ignoring the full-scale IQ scores and using the performance IQ or the verbal IQ scores. When a child with a learning disability attains an IQ score of 120 on either scale, he or she is considered gifted. Inherent in such a practice is the implication that different standards are appropriate for people with disabling conditions because the conditions inhibit performance on standardized tests. It is not clear how this practice relates to how these gifted-disabled people will function as adults. In discussions about identifying typical gifted children, the utility of a definition may be questioned by invoking this qualification about adult performance. One could argue that a qualification should be introduced here, too. If it is admitted as a valid concern, then future research should demonstrate that using different cutoff scores yields minimum benefits to the individual and to society.

A final way to modify instruments for identifying children with disabilities is to apply a standard that assumes that the highest score a child attains is the best indicator of a child's potential in a given area. In this manner, one moves away from looking at averages and instead looks at the full array of scores achieved by the individual.

Redesign the System

Identification of nonmodal gifted children may be improved by redesigning the typical identification system, which assumes that the mechanics of the process can be studied and improved. The intent is to improve the reliability of the system, as well as to deal with many of the issues discussed in this chapter.

The problem of the predictive power of low scores for some minority students on standardized tests has been described by Baldwin (1977), who proposed a "kaleidoscopic approach" for identifying children that takes into account the child's social background. The system, entitled the Baldwin Identification Matrix (BIM), organizes scores obtained from measuring the abilities contained in the federal definition. The scores on each instrument are ranked from average to above-average. The scores are summated by rank. The total score permits "any child from a different culture an opportunity to compete for recognition in a specialized program" (Cooke & Baldwin, 1979, p. 392). The BIM system has been criticized (Borland, 1989) because of the manner in which scores from different instruments are combined and compared. Feldhusen, Buska, and Womble (1981) criticized the BIM in a general article on how to synthesize the various pieces of data in an identification program in order to have a more reliable and valid system. They advocated that standard scores be calculated on all children measured in order to have a more precise picture of the performance of any individual when compared to the group. Final selection is made by adding up all scores and establishing a suitable cutoff point to fit the program's resources. When one can agree on the appropriate measures, the use of standard scores is a helpful suggestion to the extent that it addresses the problem of combining and comparing scores. However, as the authors point out, "the thorny issues of weighting the scales, establishing cut-off points, and determining test validity relative to our success criteria are still with us" (p. 181).

As previously noted, the establishment of more liberal cutoff scores tends to increase the effectiveness of our procedures; but, it is not a completely satisfactory solution because it also tends to keep IQ and achievement measures, with their attendant limitations, in place. An alternative is to use less traditional measures, as well as expand the criteria used in screening. In our example of Schools A, B, and C, screening was done quickly, usually with a single measure. This practice could be altered to be less traditional and more inclusive. Several projects concerned with identifying nonmodal children have made such changes.

Project RAPYHT (Retrieval and Acceleration of Promising Young Handicapped and Talented) has identified preschool gifted-disabled children (Karnes & Bertschi, 1978), and the Eugene Field Project has identified culturally different gifted kindergartners and first graders (Maker et al., 1981). This latter project employed measures of creativity, intelligence, and leadership. At least three measures of each ability were obtained, and these multiple criteria were organized into the Baldwin Identification Matrix to make screening decisions. The children selected in this manner were studied further to identify them as gifted. The identification step used two additional pieces of information—the Peabody Picture Vocabulary Test and scores on either the Leiter, WISC-R, or WPPSI—that were placed in the BIM format for final decision by a team of specialists. This brief description illustrates how the system may be redesigned to become attuned to the particular abilities contained in a program's definition of giftedness. The degree of satisfaction one might feel depends upon how well the children identified by the redesigned system fit a school district's standards.

Because identification takes place in the real world, factors such as time and cost are important considerations in the identification process. In particular, two concepts are crucial to real-world identification systems: efficiency and effectiveness. Both these issues were mentioned in regard to the utility of group tests and teacher ratings earlier in this chapter. An important study on this issue was conducted by Renzulli and Smith (1977b), in which they compared a traditional identification procedure to a case-study approach. A traditional approach was defined as using a group test for screening and an individual IQ test for selection. This is somewhat similar to the methods used by Schools A and C in Table 3.1. In the case-study approach, data are gathered from many sources—standardized aptitude or achievement tests; teacher, parent, and self-ratings; and information from the cumulative folder—and data are reviewed by a selection committee. Renzulli and Smith drew several conclusions from their findings: (1) A variety of data is best for identifying children; (2) additional sources of information were not expensive in terms of time and money; (3) standardized test data were valued in both systems; (4) case studies were much less expensive; (5) case studies did not get an excessive number of nominees; and (6) case studies were "more sensitive" to culturally different children.

However, not all these conclusions are warranted. The conclusions that standardized tests are valued and the case-study approach does not get an excessive number of nominees are supportable. One cannot conclude, though, that the case-study approach identified children who were comparable to those identified in the traditional approach because the criteria for selection were different. Furthermore, the case-study approach cannot be compared to the traditional approach used in earlier research because the ages of the subjects and the meaning of the terms *efficiency* and *effectiveness* differ. On the other hand, Renzulli and Smith's (1977b) study does show that a team of individuals can select gifted children, as can tests alone, in a manner that is acceptable to school districts without incurring high costs. A school that desires to adopt such a procedure using the Renzulli and Smith assumptions should consider the case-study approach as a legitimate option that may be more sensitive to the problem of identifying nonmodal gifted children.

Another way to improve the identification system is to train teachers to be better identifiers of the gifted (Borland, 1989; Maker, 1981). The principle here is to improve the accuracy of teacher ratings through training. For example, Gear (1978) doubled the effectiveness of a group of teachers in identifying gifted students using Wechsler IQ scores by conducting five-session training programs.

A report by the National Research Center on the Gifted and Talented, *Contexts for Promise: Noteworthy Practices and Innovations in the Identification of Gifted Students* (Callahan, Tomlinson, & Pizatt, 1996), describes several

TABLE 3.4

Suggestions for Change: From Traditional to Contemporary Beliefs and Practices

Gifted education considerations	Traditional beliefs and practices	Contemporary beliefs and practices
Focus of testing	Focus solely on identification, which does not suggest how to meet students' needs.	Focus on assessment that is diagnostic and prescriptive.
Emphasis on testing	One test is sufficient to identify gifted students. One number (IQ or achievement test score) identifies gifted students. The best measure of giftedness is a test.	Giftedness is multi-dimensional; therefore, multiple methods (qualitative and quantitative) are used, and more information is gathered from multiple sources (teachers, parents, community members, etc.). No "one-size-fits-all" test exists.
Perceptions about giftedness and test scores	Giftedness is equated with a high IQ or achievement score. A cutoff score determines giftedness.	The limitations of test scores are recognized, especially among culturally diverse students. Gifted students can have low test scores.
Views about ability and effort	Ability is rewarded; students must demonstrate their ability.	Effort is valued and rewarded. Educators recognize that high-quality educational experiences can help students reach their potential.

Note. From "Beyond Deficit Thinking: Providing Access for Gifted African American Students," by D. Y. Ford, J. J. Harris III, C. A. Tyson, and M. F. Trotman, 2002, *Roeper Review, 24*, p. 56. Copyright ©2002 by The Roeper Institute. Reprinted with permission.

TABLE 3.5

Percent of District Students Certified as Gifted by APA Subgroup

APA Subgroup	No. Assessed	No. Certified	% Certified
Asian Indian	55	25	45.45
Chinese	214	108	50.47
Japanese	92	38	41.30
Korean	78	37	47.44
Cambodian	151	19	12.58
Hmong	85	12	14.12
Laotian	171	27	15.79
Vietnamese	504	150	29.76
Other Indochinese	56	14	25.00
Filipino	1,093	306	28.00
Guamanian	41	9	21.95
Hawaiian	25	7	28.00
Samoan	41	3	7.32
Other Pacific Islander	18	1	5.56
Total, including non-APAs	14,778	3,108	21.03

Note. From "Are Asian and Pacific Americans Overrepresented in Programs for the Gifted?," by M. K. Kitano and M. DiJiosia, 2002, *Roeper Review, 22,* p. 77. Copyright ©2002 by The Roeper Institute. Reprinted with permission.

projects funded by the Javits Act Program that were aimed at creating means to identify nonmodal gifted students. Although the projects varied in numerous ways, they did reflect an important attitudinal change from previous practices by attempting to situate identification within communities by drawing groups of stakeholders together to create the process to be used. Although the results are too recent to assess fully, the projects hold promise for future practice.

Focus on the Underlying Assumptions

Many researchers note that underrepresentation of diverse students in gifted programs "extends beyond identification instruments and assessment procedures" (Ford, Harris, Tyson, & Trotman, 2002, p. 52). Although the field of gifted education has evolved in terms of beliefs and practices (see Table 3.4), the necessity of examining the underlying assumptions of educational systems remains. The Association for the Gifted (TAG; 2001) addressed this issue in a national action plan on diversity and developing gifts and talents. Calling for a "radical shift" in thinking, the action plan focused on the preparation of teachers, the development of learning environments and curricula, and the recognition of student potential as areas in need of change.

In other areas, researchers have emphasized the need to examine how the politics of race and culture impact the education of African American students (Morris, 2002), the role of social support systems on talent development (Olszewski-Kubilius, 2003), and the influence of ethnic identity on achievement (Rowley & Moore, 2002). Ford et al. (2002) argued that recruitment and retention of African American students in gifted programs is limited by educators' adherence to a "deficit perspective," that is, educators tend to interpret differences as deficits or disadvantages, instead of focusing on the strengths of individuals. Further, Bernal (2002) noted the need for recruiting and retaining gifted education teachers from minority ethnic groups and establishing multicultural programs in schools. Kitano and DiJiosa (2002) have investigated the percentages of Asian and Pacific American (APA) students in programs for the gifted and found that, despite the common perception that APA students are "overrepresented" in gifted programs, there are a large number of *subgroups* encompassed in this category (see Table 3.5). Clearly there are many issues that need to be addressed when considering the underrepresentation of nonmodal students in gifted programs.

Summary of Identification of the Nonmodal Gifted

The nonmodal gifted child is the source of much concern in discussions about identification. The nonmodal gifted are children who may be described as having disabilities, being culturally different, or both. They may come from rural, suburban, and urban areas. The concern for the nonmodal gifted is related to the belief that a disproportionately low number of them are found in programs for the gifted.

The general identification problem is that these children produce low scores, average scores, or uneven scores on typical measures of aptitude and performance. When a child does well on such measures, we have little problem assuming high ability. With the nonmodal child, we have the problem of determining whether low scores are proper indicators of low ability or incorrect estimates of what is actually high ability.

The plain fact is that we have not been able to come up with a generally satisfactory means of handling the situation (Coleman, 1985a; Frasier, 1997). This is going to persist as long as measurement techniques remain at their present primitive stage and definitions remain unsettled. It is clear that methods do exist that can be implemented to improve the chances of identifying nonmodal gifted children. For example, modifications to existing measurement techniques hold much promise, as do the redesign of identification systems to improve screening procedures, the use of multiple criteria, and the use of assessment teams to keep the system open-ended. The combination of rating scales and work samples is another promising area for research.

Considering the literature, the identification of nonmodal gifted children should probably focus on two times in nonmodal children's lives: when they enter school and at the beginning of adolescence (Coleman, 1985a). These points in a child's life may offer the best opportunity for spotting signs of giftedness. Entry into school seems an opportune time to be on the alert for children who get excited and devour information because they may soon lose those inclinations. Adolescence seems to be another good time to look at the specific interests of children. By this time, they have had an opportunity to develop the information and skill bases that come only from persistent and long-term interest in a subject. They have also had a chance to overcome developmental delays. Of course, the areas of interest are unlikely to be typical school subjects, but rather such subjects as fishing, automobiles, rock music, horror films, or gardening. It does not seem sensible to expect nonmodal gifted children to become typical gifted children.

The problems in identifying nonmodal gifted children are immense. Restated, the problem is that tests confirm what we already know: Real differences exist between groups in American society. How are we to act on this knowledge? If children are identified in the conventional manner, there will continue to be only a small number of nonmodal children identified. This problem is especially acute with culturally different children.

The danger of present practices is that they may perpetuate the system of limited opportunities for nonmodal youths. It is preferable to admit as many children as possible to programs for the gifted, although the limited resources available in many school systems make this difficult. If nonmodal children are to be admitted in greater numbers, then it is possible that a typical gifted child with a higher score on a single test would become ineligible. This scenario underscores the importance of moving toward measurement techniques that correspond more closely to the performance of gifted adults or to programs that serve everyone.

SPECIAL ISSUES IN IDENTIFICATION

A comprehensive discussion of the identification of gifted children would be incomplete without consideration of five questions that influence the design of any system of identification.

- How does one identify children with nonacademic abilities, such as those in music or art?

- How does motivation fit into identification?

- At what ages can we begin to identify gifted children?

- Is there some sort of interaction between abilities that should receive attention within an identification system?

- How should identification procedures be fashioned at the secondary level?

Identifying Nonacademic Ability

The discussion of giftedness and identification has centered on only three abilities described in the federal Marland definition: general intelligence, specific academic aptitude, and creative or productive thinking. Two remaining abilities—leadership and ability in visual or performing arts—have received little attention in this chapter because most of the identification literature has largely overlooked them. Many factors may be responsible for this situation.

One factor is that these areas of functioning have been called *talents*, rather than *abilities*, and have been viewed as peripheral to the academic role of the school. This situation may be due to the fact that nonacademic abilities are valued less by American society and are not, therefore, nurtured in children. Perhaps there is a general conception that these abilities naturally accompany the more valued and recognized abilities. The lack of effort in identifying these abilities may be a result of school personnel, especially psychologists and guidance counselors, having little familiarity or confidence with measurement techniques in these areas.

Whatever the reasons, children with these talents are identifiable, and these abilities may be nurtured within a school program. When identifying these nonacademic abilities, one can look for (1) signs of accomplishment, such as awards, poems, and offices; (2) characteristics associated with the ability, such as collections, club memberships, and lessons; and (3) results of tests that measure potential (Getzels & Dillon, 1973). More specific means of identifying these abilities are examined in the following sections.

Leadership Ability
Interest in leadership ability as a component of giftedness predates the federal interest in 1972. The 57th yearbook of the National Society for the Study of Education mentioned leadership as an important talent (DeHaan & Wilson, 1958). Elizabeth Drews (1963) noted that leadership is one type of giftedness found in adolescents. Others have argued that the world needs gifted leaders (Karnes & McGinnis, 1995).

Although no one would quarrel with the idea that leaders can be identified, there is much argument about who is a good leader and what qualities comprise good leadership (Roach, Wyman, Brookes, Chavez, Heath, & Valdes, 1999). Stogdill (1974), recognizing this problem, reviewed almost 30 years of research and produced a list of six general factors related to leadership, but no unity to the concept of leadership. Even an examination of childhood experiences of leaders does not lead to a clear pattern of abilities and experiences. Because we are concerned with identifying children with potential for leadership, the state of the art does not provide much guidance in formulating a program for identification.

Standardized tests are available that measure traits that may presumably be related to leadership giftedness, namely personality tests (Plowman, 1981). Measurement alternatives to these tests are work samples and rating scales. While there is no record of the direct use of work samples in the literature, rating scales have been recognized as a source of data by several authors (Hagen, 1980; Hildreth, 1966). Rating scales are viewed as appropriate techniques to be administered by parents, peers, and students themselves, as well as by community and school personnel familiar with specific students (Plowman). A subscale of the Scale for Rating the Behavioral Characteristics of Superior Students (SRBCSS) is organized to give a rating on leadership ability (Renzulli et al., 1971), and a more formal measure of leadership for high school students, based on biographical data, has been developed by the Institute for Behavioral Research in Creativity (1974). Sociometric-type rating scales may be another source of information. For example, Khatena (1982) has proposed a means of organizing data on characteristics associated with leadership.

The literature on leadership ability is a complex mixture of conjecture and conflicting research that stems back to differences in desirable leadership qualities among children, youth, and adults (Roach et al., 1999). Thus, the school that wishes to identify children with leadership abilities is hard put to find real help in the literature. The rating scales are probably the most usable form of information. Given the questionable assumptions involved in developing these scales, a school district may wish to create its own rating scale in accordance with its needs and intentions.

Ability in the Visual and Performing Arts

Identification of ability in the visual or performing arts is problematic. The same general disarray surrounding leadership ability is multiplied by the large number of talents included under the rubric of visual and performing arts. When one examines performance in these related fields—composition, conducting, sculpting, graphics, painting, to name a few—it becomes apparent that a complex interaction of personal and aptitude factors account for success. Possession of general ability in the visual and performing arts is insufficient to predict success within all related professions, and the problem is compounded when one tries to identify these abilities in young children (Winner & Martino, 1993). The pattern of high ability seen in young children may not be continued with age (Terman, 1925) because the mastery of specialized knowledge and skills may be influenced more by opportunity in young children than it is in older children.

All these factors should be kept in mind as we examine these areas. Our discussion will be confined to identification of those children with musical and artistic abilities because measures in these areas are widely reported.

Musical ability. Early identification of musical ability is difficult in part because of the universal appeal of music and the fact that all children show sensitivity to music (Winner & Martino, 1993). The identification of musical ability by schools generally follows the same procedures used to identify other abilities, and efforts have concentrated on the development of standardized tests and the use of work samples. Interest in the construction of tests of musical ability dates back to the beginning of this century. And, while many tests are available that purport to measure musical abilities, they all suffer from a variety of limitations (see Lehman, 1968).

A broad spectrum of abilities may be assessed by the Musical Aptitude Profile (Gordon, 1995), which includes a series of subtests that require the subject to listen to musical selections played on a piano or a violin and cello in order to measure aspects of music appreciation and musical production. The tests are appropriate for children at or above fourth grade. Reliability and validity data are stronger for these tests than for the Seashore test (Anastasi & Urbina, 1997), with the Musical Aptitude Profile being the stronger of the two.

The assessment of musical talents may also be aided by using work samples. Demonstrations of ability can be in the form of auditions, records of awards, and recommendations from experts in the field. These measures give a strong indication of a child's skill level, as well as commitment to music (Kay & Subotnik, 1994). Schools that specialize in music have long made use of such techniques. Work samples of musical ability seem to be particularly effective with older children who have had the opportunity to develop their abilities. A child who has undeveloped abilities due to geographical or socioeconomic circumstances may be missed by such a procedure. Perhaps some combination of work sample and controlled observation may aid in solving this problem.

Artistic ability. It is clear that artistic ability is manifested for varying reasons, and most identification systems are not likely to be sensitive to these variations. According to Clark and Zimmerman (1987), there are three primary means of identifying artistic ability: (1) standardized tests, (2) informal tests or checklists, and (3) combinations of other approaches such as recommendations, work-sample portfolio reviews, peer nominations, and interest inventories.

Standardized tests have attempted to assess the primary artistic abilities that underlie the many artistic professions. According to Clark and Zimmerman (1987), however, there is not sufficient evidence to conclude that standardized instruments predict success in art programs.

One approach to assessment is to have subjects produce a product to be judged on the basis of explicit criteria. This approach links work sample with standardized test procedures. Another approach is to combine different measures. For example, in Project ARTS, Clark and Zimmerman (2001) used locally designed identification measures (such as student portfolios and out-of-school projects) along with standardized measures to identify artistically talented students in rural communities.

Summary. The identification of nonacademic abilities is a precarious under-taking given the present state of our knowledge about measuring leadership and abilities in the visual and performing arts. It is likely that schools will avoid look-ing for these abilities in children as long as this condition exists. The develop-ment of special programs for these abilities may bring enough resources together to make use of work samples and rating scales in the identification process.

Motivation and Identification

A means of incorporating the concept of motivation in the identification process is of continual concern to school personnel and researchers. Since the increase in interest in gifted children at the beginning of the 20th cen-tury, terms such as *persistence*, *motivation*, and *commitment* have been put for-ward as important qualities of giftedness. Terman was well aware of this factor in the early years of his study (Cox, 1926), and Renzulli (1977) included in his well-known definition "task commitment" as one of three qualities of giftedness. The definition in this text also attends to this dimen-sion of giftedness.

The emphasis on motivation is an attempt to comprehend why high abil-ity in a homogeneous group is an insufficient predictor of later success. It is striking, considering the attention paid to this variable, that a direct procedure for measuring motivation has not been developed. The situation is probably related to several factors. For one, motivation is a construct that can only be described by stating a series of specific examples of people behaving in a moti-vated manner. These examples combine to produce a commonality to the meaning of motivation, but that commonality is insufficient to describe moti-vation. For example, a motivated artist, a motivated scientist, and a motivated teacher act differently because the situation itself helps shape what is done. Without describing the situation, one would lose part of the meaning of moti-vated behavior. Given this caveat, one can carefully and hesitantly describe motivation in a manner common to the artist, the teacher, and the scientist. Two qualities cut across situations: time and complex performances. People who devote more time to an activity are more likely to be motivated. An indi-cation of how free time is used relates to one's priorities. The successful per-formance of complex tasks probably requires more motivation because one must direct energy toward mastery and must overcome obstacles to achieve that mastery.

If these qualities are used to identify a motivated student, where should these data come from? Sources of information about motivation can be best obtained by examining past accomplishments, observing performance in a particular time period, and recording statements about the future. Examples of past accomplishments include hobbies, collections, awards, and products. Observing performance requires setting up a situation in which behavior can be observed over several months. There are obvious problems in setting up such a situation. First, it would be difficult to rate time and complex perform-

119

ance as qualities of motivation in young children. But, the difficulties go beyond problems of logistics. Children may have insufficient background skills to maintain interest in undirected activities, insufficient exposure to situations that might engage their attention so that they might demonstrate motivation, and insufficient access to necessary materials and experiences to continue to develop their interests. Lastly, given age considerations, they may have had limited time to show evidence of sustained activity.

These realities seem to point in the direction of standardized tests, but few tests measuring motivation are available (one recently developed example is the Children's Academic Intrinsic Motivation Inventory [CAIMI]; Gottfried & Gottfried, 2004). However, such standardized tests are generally inadequate for all the same reasons previously mentioned about their shortcomings. Further, tests of the need for achievement and aspiration are too global and have not been shown to have much utility with young children.

These circumstances lead to the conclusion that it would be virtually impossible to identify highly motivated children before the beginning of adolescence, or, let us say, sixth or seventh grade. This may suggest a different identification procedure when one is considering secondary school programs.

Early Identification

The previous discussion of identification noted that early identification is advisable for encouraging the widest and most expansive development of ability. *Early identification* in this section refers to searching for children before school age (first grade), which is clearly possible (Sisk, 1997), although some have proposed the need to identify children as young as several months of age (Gelbrich, 1997). The early years are an opportune time to observe the emergence of special abilities (Gardner, 1997). Many famous personalities gave evidence of their ability before age 6.

The rationale for early identification is based on the notions of prevention and maximization. *Prevention* refers to helping children cope with life before their unusual abilities lead to problems of maladjustment and limitations imposed by certain habits. *Maximization* refers to the optimum development of a child's potential. Without recognition, high ability can diminish over time.

An identification system needs to give preschool children the chance to show their abilities, allow for the wide fluctuations found across many tasks, and provide a place for parent input (Robinson et al., 1979; Smutny, 1997). It should assess children on the abilities relevant to program objectives, which usually focus on intellectual ability, creative ability, academic ability, or a combination of these abilities.

Early identification systems are faced with the general problem of the greater unreliability of scores for younger children than for older children. In practice, this means that scores in the gifted range at 4 years on the Binet may drop by age 7 into the normal range; similarly, scores below the gifted range at age 4 may rise to the gifted range at age 7. Scores obtained at ages 2 and 3 are even less stable. This circumstance is a consequence of the tests, the process of development, and, probably even more so, the problem of eliciting top performance from young, active children. When factors such as cultural differences and handicaps are present, the problem of obtaining an accurate measure of functioning is compounded.

In order to combat these problems, a variety of measures should be used. The examiner should be particularly alert to signs of inattention and best performance in specific areas. Group testing cannot meet these criteria and is probably inappropriate for use in the final selection of very young children (Roedell et al., 1980). However, some programs have found a use for group tests in the screening phase of identification (Hughes & Killian, 1977; LaRose, 1978). Portfolios are also recommended as a means to gather and organize information needed to identify gifted young students (Coleman, 1995; Kingore, 1997). There should be no assumption that a child who is not selected at one time cannot be reevaluated at a later time.

Abilities that are academically oriented may also be assessed through standardized testing or rating scales. One should not assume that measures of general intellectual ability identify all the children who perform in an outstanding manner on measures of academic ability.

Assessment of reading and math abilities is difficult because few tests are available for measuring them in preschool children. Schorr, Jackson, and Robinson (1980) reported that the Peabody Individual Achievement test was a satisfactory means for measuring reading and math abilities in gifted preschoolers. Several other tests or parts of tests, such as the arithmetic subtests of the Wechsler Preschool and Primary Scale of Intelligence or the numerical memory subtests of the McCarthy Scales of Children's Abilities (Robinson et al., 1979), may be used. If one wants additional data on academic ability, informal assessments, such as giving a child a book to read or a situation to describe, can provide valuable data.

Parents are an important source of data on their children. The use of rating scales by parents, reviewed earlier in this chapter, showed parents to be more accurate than teachers in identifying giftedness in young children. Parents are also able to observe children in a wider arena than do examiners in the testing situation. The value of parent nominations can be increased by asking for examples of behavior (Robinson et al., 1979), although there is some indication that socioeconomic status may influence parents' tendencies to nominate their children (Ciha et al., 1974) and some parents may employ unrealistically high criteria. Therefore, parents may need some direction in spotting high ability. Continued efforts to improve rating scale formats should lead to better identification procedures (Roedell et al., 1980). Teachers are another source of information, especially with the increase in the number of preschool programs (see Karnes & Bertschi, 1978, for an approach to obtaining valuable information about preschoolers).

Interrelationship Between Abilities and Identification

The relationship between gifted people's abilities is an important subject in any discussion about identification. If a significant relationship exists, then it might be possible to select people based upon one or two variables with the best predictability. If there is no such relationship, then a broader system of identification is necessary for effectively selecting the gifted. A third possibility is that, if there is little relationship, selection on one ability will tend to exclude other abilities.

The notion that abilities are interrelated is an old one in psychology. Generally, it is recognized that positive relationships exist among most abilities (Guilford, 1967), which also appears to be true of the gifted if one accepts the findings from Terman and others who found that "children selected for any one superiority ordinarily are above average on other characteristics" (Hauck & Freehill, 1972, p. 3). This statement affirms that the relationship among abilities of the gifted is positive when IQ is the selection variable. It does not say that superiority in one ability leads to superiority in another ability. The statement admits the possibility that abilities may be coupled in some more precise arrangement so that certain cognitive or affective abilities consistently cluster together to a high degree.

Some research is available on the relationships among particular sets of cognitive abilities. Measures of specific abilities or aptitudes are constructed to be minimally related to measures of general ability; but, measures of specific ability might be related to each other. Freeman (1979) reviewed her own and other research on the relationship of musical to mathematical ability and of musical to artistic ability. She concluded that little relationship could be found in children and in adults between musical and mathematical ability, although she found a moderate relationship between artistic and musical ability. The Institute for Behavioral Research in Creativity (1974) found a similar relationship using self-reports. These findings suggest that selection for one ability is not likely to find a paired ability.

A number of studies have examined the relationship between creativity tests and general intelligence (IQ) in children. A small positive relationship exists; but, for the gifted, there is a negligible correlation in both children and adults. Whatever general intelligence tests measure, it is not the same as what creativity tests measure in gifted children (Crockenberg, 1972; Getzels & Dillon, 1973).

Although research on cognitive abilities of gifted children reveals a small relationship among abilities, it is possible that a more significant relationship is present between affective characteristics, such as personality traits or values. The research in this area has looked primarily at factors that seem to be related to gifted performance because, for many years, it has been observed that people of apparently equal ability do not succeed in an equal manner (Cox, 1926). Although a large number of personality variables have been associated with high performance, none has emerged as predominant. The situation may be summed up by a new, but familiar-sounding statement: "The combination of great ability and personal eagerness to accelerate virtually guarantees success" (Stanley, 1976, p. 236).

The question about how high abilities in gifted children are related to each other is clouded by the way tests are constructed and by the fact that the gifted already comprise a specially selected group. Thus, a ceiling effect and the restricted range of abilities contribute to the largely inconclusive findings. Under these circumstances, it is possible that some abilities occur together with greater frequency than others in gifted children and adults, but research techniques obfuscate the point.

It is obvious that high intellect and persistent creative activity do appear together at the same time. Realizing this congruence of abilities is important, even though it does not appear in some ordered manner that would produce a correlation. The fact that certain abilities appear again and again is the relevant fact about determining giftedness. This is what Cox (1926) must have been observing when she wrote, "High, but not the highest, intelligence, combined with the greatest degree of persistence will achieve greater eminence than the highest degree of intelligence with somewhat less persistence" (p. 187). One can infer from this statement that intelligence is necessary, but not all-important, and that some point exists where general intelligence is no longer a primary determinant of gifted behavior. Later data from Hollingworth (1942) and Terman and Oden (1959) indicate that high IQ (above 170) does not ensure the greatest success.

At the same time, it is hard to find someone who would argue that general intelligence has no predictive validity. It may be, as McClelland (1958) wrote, that intelligence is a threshold type of variable; that is, once a person has a certain minimal level of intelligence, his or her performance beyond that point is uncorrelated with his or her ability (p. 12). Subsequent research has suggested that IQ might well be a threshold variable (Hauck & Freehill, 1972). Crockenberg (1972) reviewed research using the Torrance Tests of Creative Thinking, which indicated that an IQ of 120 might be the threshold. Others have indicated similar values with adults (Getzels & Dillon, 1973). Two studies of artistic ability (Anastasi & Urbina, 1997) indicated that high average intelligence is an important concomitant of artistic success; in one study, the mean IQ was 119 on the Stanford-Binet, and in the other, the IQ range was from 111 to 166. Hildreth (1966) reported that the mean IQ of students at New York City's High School of Performing Arts was about 121. It is probable that abilities that make greater use of verbal abstractions may require more general intellectual ability for successful functioning than the level suggested by this evidence.

Although the evidence is incomplete on this point, there are enough data to warn that unduly high IQ cutoffs could severely restrict the variety of abilities present in students within a program. If this possibility is ignored, it will not be surprising if the children in the program act differently from what is expected. This evidence provides a good rationale for using an identification team to consider multiple criteria before final identification. At the same time,

123

though, it suggests that intellectual ability is an important component of gifted performance.

Secondary School Identification

The literature on giftedness seems to concentrate on identification during elementary school. A substantial amount of recent writing deals with identifying preschool-age children, but there is little on identification at the secondary level. Why this situation exists is not certain. One possibility is the supposition that most gifted children will be found during the elementary years and their high performance will continue into high school. Another possibility may be a belief that the organization of the secondary school already provides services to gifted students. Although the reasons for this lack of emphasis are cloudy, it is clear that gifted children have needs that are not met at the secondary level and programs are needed.

Identification procedures at the secondary level should follow the outlines of any good identification program, but it should differ from identification at the elementary level. It should be more attuned to the manifestation of ability in terms of specifics, rather than to the indicators of general ability shown at the elementary level, which is consistent with the definition of giftedness proposed in Chapter 1. At the secondary level, one should also be able to distinguish definite signs of long-term involvement in some area of talent or field of knowledge. If identification at the secondary level is to attend to the presence of special abilities and involvement in some area, then procedures should be adopted that are sensitive to both. Incidentally, it might be wise to avoid making entrance into secondary programs automatically contingent upon earlier identification.

The identification of special abilities requires the development of a measurement technology that is equal to the task of assessing specialized, instead of global, strengths. The Study of Mathematically Precocious Youth at Johns Hopkins University has proposed the administration of standardized tests, such as the Differential Aptitude Battery or the Scholastic Aptitude Test (mathematics or verbal), as instruments for discovering high academic ability in children entering secondary schools (Stanley, 1979). The tests are useful for distinguishing ability differences among children who perform at the ceiling of other conventional measures (Keating, 1975). If one wishes to assess abilities such as leadership, creativity, or performing arts or personality traits such as motivation, then standardized tests leave much to be desired. Where appropriate, work samples, including evaluation of student products and auditions, would be a valuable source of information.

Silverman (1980) pointed out that secondary programs should allow students to be more actively involved in the identification of giftedness. Because older students tend to have more insight into their own talents than do younger children, they are important sources of information. Silverman suggested that self-nomination, peer nomination, interviews, and auditions be included in a comprehensive identification system. The actual procedures a school district wishes to utilize should reflect the objectives and philosophy of a program (Shore et al., 1991). Some procedures used for special programs are described in a publication of the National/State Leadership Training Institute on the Gifted and Talented (Tews, 1981), in Stanley (1979), and in Gerencser (1979). Given the resurgence of interest in the gifted, more writing on this topic should be appearing.

WHAT IDENTIFICATION CANNOT DO FOR TEACHERS

It is important to keep in mind that there are many things that even the best identification system cannot do. Specifically, all the energy necessary for a sound identification system does not transform itself directly into an effective educational program: "Identification per se does not improve learning" (Martinson, 1975, p. 135). This is because identification is primarily a classification process, not a diagnostic process, because the information obtained about a student is not specific enough to begin instruction in a subject area or field. Diagnosis, on the other hand, typically leads to specific interventions or instructions because it provides specific information on strengths and weaknesses in particular areas. Children are classified as gifted on the basis of a limited number of extremely broad characteristics, such as high intelligence or creativity. An IQ score of 150 yields scant information on which to base instruction, although one could surmise that the child is likely to be a rapid learner.

This situation changes somewhat when a program is organized in reference to a specialized area of knowledge. In this circumstance, identification is closer to instruction. Programs such as the Study of Mathematically Precocious Youth have a closer tie between identification and instruction than is usually the case. Another variable that closes the gap between instruction and identification is the age of the students. By early adolescence, a child is likely to have developed enough knowledge and skills in a particular domain so that an instructional program can be designed based upon identification-type information.

The relative discontinuity between identification and instruction is the major criticism teachers have against identification procedures, which is valid based on their role of implementing service. From the administrator's perspective, though, it is not a fair criticism because identification systems are for the purpose of distinguishing between students whose needs are or are not being met by regular instruction. Their interest is clearly one of classification. By isolating the group whose needs are not being met, specific funds and other resources may be allocated to it. Identification systems are good at finding children, and they serve this purpose quite well. This scenario implies that tension will continue between teachers and administrators on how satisfied they may be with an identification system. As long as both parties are interested in improving the quality of instruction to gifted students and in increasing the quantity of resources, programs will improve. This process may be hastened if teachers and administrators can keep in mind each other's priorities.

WHY DO CHILDREN GET MISSED?

This chapter has presented an elaborate discussion on how to organize an effective program of identification to locate gifted children in a school system. The length of the chapter implies that giftedness is not obvious in many children. Many factors hinder identification:

1. The situation at home or at school may not present opportunities for children to demonstrate their giftedness. When challenging situations are not available, one does not need to stretch to perform. After all, average behavior is desirable.

2. The behaviors exhibited by a child may be termed undesirable or not indicative of giftedness when they are actually manifestations of daydreaming or sex-role stereotyping.

3. Children may exhibit appropriate behaviors and seem average because of subtle adjustments in their patterns of behavior to meet the demands of a situation. For example, a child remains quiet and avoids a confrontation with the teacher because his or her parents would not approve, or a child does not ask a question because he or she senses that the teacher does not have the answer.

4. Children may choose not to be obvious because their peers, family, or culture would not understand or approve.

5. Teacher judgment has too prominent a place in the determination of who is gifted.

6. The instrument selected for measuring various abilities is inappropriate for measuring that ability and inappropriate for the group being measured.

This chapter has described a variety of means for identifying children fairly, and these procedures suggest a degree of sophistication in the use of measurement techniques, the logistics of gathering and organizing information, and the operation of a definition. However, less complex means are available for identifying gifted and talented children. Two means may be inferred from the discussion and are offered for consideration.

System I: A school system constructs a large sign like the one on the next page.

Gifted Program: Apply Here

The program will consist of special activities in _____

Sign here: _____

Names

1. _____

2. _____

3. _____

4. _____

System II: A school opens a classroom one day a week for 50% of the students for half a year. In the class, they are challenged by a rigorous curriculum as if they were in a gifted program. Those children who seem to thrive in this environment are selected for the formal program.

Both these suggestions are filled with problems. However, many children would be correctly identified by these simplified procedures. Some children would certainly be missed, but this is true of any system.

CONCLUSION

Identification is an important issue in the education of gifted children, and information about the process can aid students who are unaware of their potentials and help them secure assistance from schools and families in developing their talents. Parents who are knowledgeable about their children's abilities may be better able to provide support for advanced study. Schools, when made aware of the needs of gifted children, also tend to provide more meaningful experiences for the gifted.

FOR **DISCUSSION**

1. How would you respond to an individual who asserts that gift-
    edness is evenly distributed across society and that identifi-
    cation procedures in schools need to reflect this?

2. Investigate the procedures for identifying gifted students in
    your school district. Are the procedural concerns discussed in
    this chapter met in the identification process? What is the
    measuring device(s) used to identify gifted students?

3. How would you respond to an individual who states that only
    the full-scale IQ score from an intelligence test should be used
    for assessing high ability?

4. How would you respond to the comment that teacher ratings
    are the best choice for evaluating students for giftedness?

5. Reflect on and discuss the advantages and disadvantages of
    using nontraditional forms of assessment in identifying gifted
    students.

6. Upon testing a struggling student, a school psychologist
    reports that the child has a learning disability. The child's cog-
    nitive ability scores indicate that her full-scale IQ is 142, plac-
    ing her in the gifted range. What are the educational
    implications of this finding for the student?

7. Considering the discussion of the problems in identifying cul-
    turally different gifted students. What is the best solution to
    this situation?

chapter four

FAMILIES:
GUIDANCE
CONSIDERATIONS

KEY CONCEPTS

- It is axiomatic that the family has a significant role in the development of giftedness.

- The data on families with gifted children are confounded because they are based primarily upon retrospective accounts of middle-class families.

- A common characteristic among the gifted is that they come from environments that nurture their gifts.

- The variability in familial characteristics highlights the problem of generalizing about family backgrounds.

- Some families feel an urgent need to respond to their child's giftedness; others do not. Some families fail to notice that their child is gifted.

- Parents must contend with the rapid development of their child.

- Parents experience difficulty talking to others about their child.

- Parents must accept the lack of empirical information on the rearing of gifted children.

- The relationship between school and family can be volatile.

- Advocates are needed to promote education for gifted children.

Lhe importance of the family's involvement in the early experience of and support for the development of giftedness cannot be overestimated. In this chapter, the family will be studied in more detail than it has been in other chapters. While Chapter 5 will concentrate on guidance from a school perspective, this chapter will discuss guidance in terms of the family.

A discussion of the families of gifted children is complicated by numerous issues, including the perennial problems of definition, identification, and research design. Questions may be raised about the ability to apply pre-1970 research findings to present families because newer, expanded definitions of giftedness may not be related to similar familial characteristics. Questions may also be raised about the evolving nature of the family. In the last 30 years, many changes have occurred, and the effects of these changes on the development of giftedness have not been researched. It is obvious that changes have different effects, but it is not possible to pinpoint which changes have specific effects. Questions may be raised about how the information on families was researched, particularly because the data are based primarily on retrospective judgments about family life. Although measurements on important variables are obtained from rating scales and interviews, research on the actual interactions in homes with gifted children is meager, making the accounts of family dynamics sketchy. One is hard-pressed to find substantial amounts of data on non-White and non-middle-class families. Given the concern for identifying and encouraging gifted children from all backgrounds, this is a serious void. Of course, in all fairness, the lack of data on non-middle-class families is not a problem unique to the field of giftedness.

The paucity of contemporary research makes apparent many unanswered questions that illustrate the incomplete nature of our information on families. Why, then, do we devote a chapter to the family? The answer is that the family continues to be the primary socializing agency in the life of the growing child (Olszewski, Kulieke, & Buescher, 1987). Its influence is felt throughout the individual's life, and the decisions a family makes can be improved by examining the data that are available. Teachers, school administrators, and prospective parents who read this chapter may gain an understanding of the family and the difficulties involved in raising a gifted child.

GENERAL FAMILIAL DESCRIPTORS

Gifted children come from backgrounds that encourage the development of giftedness. Several factors emerge when group comparisons are made between the gifted and nongifted, and the influence of genetic and environmental interactions cannot be separated in this discussion.

Firstborn children and only children are more likely to be identified as gifted. Kaufmann (1981) found that 62% of the Presidential Scholars were firstborn children and 10% were only children, and Gross (2004) noted a strong tendency for firstborn children among her study population. Albert's (1980) data also supported this finding and went on to suggest some similarities in the backgrounds of his subjects' parents. These studies reported family size to be small to average. A somewhat different finding has been reported by Benbow and Stanley (1980), who found families with gifted children to be larger than the national average and more of their gifted sample to be second-born children.

Historically, parents of gifted children have tended to have more formal education than parents of nongifted children (Burks et al., 1930). Research on Presidential Scholars reported that 60% of the fathers and 73% of the mothers had attended college (Kaufmann, 1981). Advanced degrees were earned by 44% of the fathers and 15% of the mothers. Similar findings have been reported for another sample (Benbow & Stanley, 1980). Albert (1980), in part of a longitudinal study of mathematically gifted and intellectually gifted (150+ IQ) students, found both parents to be above the national norms in education. Interestingly, he noted that the grandparents also attended school for a longer period of time than others of their generation, and the results suggested that mathematically gifted children come from families with two generations of commitment to education, while high-IQ subjects do not. Evans, Bickel, and Pendarvis (2000) and Dai and Schader (2001, 2002) noted high educational levels amongst the parents of the musically talented students in their studies, and Gross (2004) noted that the parents in her study of exceptionally gifted (160+ IQ) children in Australia had "unusually high" educational status.

An unequal proportion of gifted children come from families where the father is employed in a professional, semiprofessional, or business occupation. The resultant income is middle to upper middle class, which, given the educational backgrounds, is not surprising (Albert, 1980; Benbow & Stanley, 1980; Burks et al., 1930; Olszewski et al., 1987; Gross, 2004). These family

characteristics reflect two problems with the research base: (1) the disproportionate representation of middle- and upper-class students as subjects and (2)
the paucity of research on gifted children from lower socioeconomic and culturally diverse backgrounds (Howley et al., 1995).

Gifted children do not always come from respectable, middle-class families, however. The Goertzels (Goertzel & Goertzel, 1962, 2004; Goertzel et
al., 1978) found, from studying the biographies of famous people, that gifted
children may come from atypical backgrounds, such as alcoholism or poverty,
that are not associated with conventional wisdom about nurturing giftedness.
However, the same atypical families were able to promote a love of learning
(not to be confused with love of school) that despises rote learning. The gifted
children in these families tended to be firstborn. In general, the families had
verbal, experimental, curious, active, and shared-goal characteristics, and some
had severe emotional conflicts. The fathers were typically either famous or
failure-prone. The latter group was composed of men who had a succession of
setbacks that kept the family in economic ruin. In each case, the situation was
thought by the Goertzels to allow the child to develop independence at an
early age.

One can infer from the Goertzels' data that families of gifted children
provide opportunities for the children to behave in a gifted manner. The very
characteristics of the family sound like characteristics of the gifted. Other
research on familial background reinforces the interpretation that the family
provides experiences that demand gifted behavior from its younger members.
Walberg, Williams, and Zeiser (2003), for example, studied the biographies of
256 eminent women and noted that 30–50% of them had strong encouragement (or direct teaching) from the father, mother, or another adult, and 70%
noted clear parental expectations for their conduct. Also, approximately 50%
of the women came from financially and culturally advantaged families. It is
important to note, however, that being from an educated, middle-class family
does not ensure the development of giftedness. A number of factors—including luck and opportunity—play an influential role throughout a gifted individual's life (Walberg et al.).

These findings also raise the provocative question of whether or not parents of gifted children must be gifted themselves. Silverman (1997a) has
claimed that "when a child is identified as gifted, the parents are probably
gifted too" (p. 393). Plomin (1997) noted that "family studies show that intelligence does indeed run in families" (p. 68). Terman's research indicated that a
family with one gifted child had a greater likelihood of having another gifted
child. The fact that giftedness does not automatically occur in families suggests that potential and opportunity must meet. Because the family supplies
both, it is impossible to address the question in absolute terms. Some data
indicate that parents of the gifted tend to be above average in cognitive ability. Albert (1980) compared creativity scores of parents and gifted children in
his longitudinal study, the results of which suggested that the family has
potential for creativity. Albert's study is intriguing because the construct of

creativity is frequently described by the characteristics (verbal, experimental, curious, active) that the Goertzels enumerated as familial characteristics. Studies on family patterns with gifted students have found that parents demonstrate a high level of involvement with their gifted children (Kulieke & Olszewski-Kubilius, 1989; Robinson & Noble, 1991). When considered together, these findings make it appear as if gifted children live in family environments where opportunity for the development of creativity is enhanced by the lifestyles of the families and, perhaps, by certain familial predispositions.

One should not conclude that all the evidence on family characteristics determining giftedness is in. More research in needed in many areas, including understanding the familial factors that contribute to giftedness in women. Many of the studies examining family characteristics have had a much higher percentage of men than women in the sample. For example, in Goertzel and Goertzel's 1962 sample, only 14% of the subjects were women. The updated edition of that study (Goertzel, Goertzel, Goertzel, & Hansen, 2004) noted that the low percentage in the 1962 sample reflected a societal gender bias, but even then the percentage of women in 2004 sample only rose to 27%. Thus, generalizing these findings may be problematic.

A further problem with the evidence on how family characteristics determine giftedness is that it suggests that a unified set of characteristics is responsible for the emergence of advanced ability and, ultimately, high accomplishment. A similarity certainly exists across backgrounds when descriptions are broad; but, just as certainly, there are significant differences. The lack of similarity in background is evident when gifted individuals with particular talents (e.g., literary, artistic, scientific) are studied. The differences in background, which were discussed in Chapter 2 in reference to predicting adult accomplishment, are fascinating.

A few examples of the variability in familial characteristics should highlight the problem of generalizing about family backgrounds (Cox, 1926; Goertzel et al., 1978; Roe, 1953). People who become well known for literary contributions often come from unstable families that have frequent conflicts of which the child is very aware. The parents are interested in others and are idealistic. Writing skill is not a family trait. These children are less social than other children and hate school, which are behaviors the parents accept. Social leaders, on the other hand, come from backgrounds that are relatively stable and similar to the general picture of family characteristics. Those with artistic talents in painting, music, or dance come from varied backgrounds—some families are supportive, others reject. Precocious talent comes from a supportive environment and is more common. Siblings frequently provide the emotional and economic support for the development of artistic talents. Scientists come from families that are stable, honor intellect, and view life in a fairly conventional way, although alcoholism is present to an unusually high degree (Ludwig, 1995).

These statements about family background are too brief and are based on too little data to draw a set of conclusions about familial characteristics rele-

135

vant to the development of giftedness. However, these statements serve as a reminder that it is too simple to say gifted children only come from one type of family.

Familial Patterns of Behavior

General descriptors associated with giftedness provide an incomplete picture of family interactions in terms of nurturing giftedness. It is the specific patterns of interaction, rather than general descriptions of home background, that are necessary to provide a meaningful basis on which to counsel families. When patterns of interaction are evident, they are never so specific as to describe who says or does what to whom in a problem situation. These data are almost impossible to obtain at this time. As yet, research has not permitted us to connect specific events in childhood to gifted behavior displayed 10 years later. The time span, with many intervening variables, prevents us from obtaining such specific information. Even in studies covering shorter time frames, it is possible only to describe general patterns of behavior. Most studies on family behavior of the gifted are retrospective, in that they ask gifted people to describe their past experiences. Other studies ask family members to complete rating scales, questionnaires, and so forth, from which comparisons are made. Studies that involve observation of gifted children in the home environment are rare. Research is needed to look at short-term comparisons of families with and without gifted children and tie family interaction to adult accomplishment. While the picture of family interaction is incomplete, useful information is available on family patterns associated with the development of remarkable abilities. These data will be described in the following pages, although it is important not to overgeneralize from them.

The development of advanced ability is clearly associated with an early opportunity to be involved in a specific area (Pressey, 1949). Performance beyond age expectation is the criterion of advanced ability in children. Child prodigies, who are the most extreme examples of advanced ability, only emerge from environments where opportunity for development is available and actively assisted (Feldman, 1980), which are typically provided by families.

Children who have unusually advanced abilities and accomplishments, but are not designated as prodigies, also come from homes where their strengths are actively encouraged (Bloom & Sosniak, 1981). Studies of musically gifted students, for example, report that parents attribute their children's musical accomplishments to family (and friends') encouragement (Evans, Bickel, & Pendarvis, 2000). Even children who have advanced abilities in more general areas (indicated by IQ, achievement, or creativity scores) than prodigies have come from encouraging environments. One cannot escape the conclusion that experience in any area is a necessary requisite for advanced development. Experience, however, may be relatively unfocused in that it is not grounded in one area of skill and knowledge, but cuts across several areas.

Bloom and Sosniak (1981) described a generalized pattern of family inter-action associated with the development of advanced ability in three fields of endeavor (artistic, psychomotor, and cognitive). Data were gathered by inter-viewing subjects who were less than 35 years of age and had earned the high-est form of recognition in their respective fields. The subjects could be called, in more common terminology, "world-class performers." Concert pianists, Olympic swimmers, and research mathematicians comprised the fields, with 25 subjects in each group.

Commonalities emerged about their family experiences. First and foremost, opportunity for learning was available. In most families, at least one parent had an interest in the field; occasionally, a sibling or a relative provided this back-ground factor, and sometimes, the entire family was involved. Early on (3 to 7 years), the child was encouraged to join the family exploring the area. Sometimes, the parents were above average in the field. Overall, the family pro-vided a model of behavior that permitted the child to observe a set of values important to that field and a set of examples of the qualities and lifestyle of those engaged in it. The family assumed the child would naturally master the language associated with the area and with the talent. Children were not consulted about this goal. Learning in the area was initiated by the child or another family mem-ber. Rate of learning seemed related to an imprecise family standard of what constituted an appropriate level or next step in that field. Teaching about the field was informal in that the child learned through modeling, differential rein-forcement, and direct teaching when it was considered appropriate. At some point, the parents recognized the child's growing competence in the area and arranged for formal lessons. The child was expected to learn the talent, and instruction proceeded in a highly individualized manner. In the beginning, the family followed the teacher's guidance in helping the child by monitoring prac-tice and providing correction. There was consistency between the home and the lesson. At around ages 10 to 12, the child surpassed the parents' expertise. The child, in order to continue, needed specialized instruction. The influence of the home diminished as the child adopted the standards and values of the teacher, high-ability peers, and the field itself. The talent area dominated the child's life, and he or she was expected to practice and strive for excellence. The parents con-tinued to supply encouragement and resources. Family advice and many of the child's decisions centered around whether or not a particular decision or behav-ior was likely to help or hinder development in the area.

In sum, the Bloom and Sosniak (1981) interviews showed children acquir-ing advanced skill and knowledge in a field within the context of the family's long-term commitment to their development. The subjects in the study devel-oped in an environment of shared goals where active exploration and pursuit of one's interests were encouraged and increased independence and competence in an area were expected. It is not surprising that the children developed a love of learning, at least in their specific fields of interest. Since the Bloom and Sosniak study, others have pursued similar questions (e.g., Bloom, 1985; Kulieke & Olszewski-Kubilius, 1989; Robinson & Noble, 1991).

Gifted people lead highly successful lives in many different fields, which brings up the question of whether they come from similar experiences. While it is likely that similarities exist between and among families with children of different talents, dissimilarities must also exist. Although hard data are not available on these differences, a reading of the literature on counseling and guidance suggests that many families do not marshal their resources in a direct manner for development in any single talent area. Rather, family resources are spread over a wider band of abilities. While relatively few families have a clear set of values along with a sense of commitment to particular ability areas, many with gifted children have a commitment to providing the best opportunities possible for learning and becoming successful human beings. The concern of such families is evident in gifted children's recollections of family life (American Association for Gifted Children, 1978), adult recollections of growing up, family attendance at school or club activities, and families looking for advice and assistance with their children (Freeman, 1979).

Family Member Concerns

The presence of a gifted child can affect the relationships among family members and how they think about them (Cornell, 1984). Changes are a product of the family rearranging itself to deal with a member who presents a behavioral pattern that departs from typical expectations (Moon, Jurich, & Feldhusen, 1998; Ross, 1979). These changes in relationships probably begin to occur in the natural course of family interaction before the child is recognized as being different.

Once a child is suspected of being different, parental concerns begin to surface. These concerns are enhanced, even exaggerated, as the differences between the gifted child and other children become more clear and the parents feel the need to respond in some special way. The intensity of their need to respond is probably influenced by specific familial values. Some families do not feel an urgent need to respond because they do not regard their child as being different, which contrasts with outsiders who see the child as atypical. Such families do not have the concerns discussed here. However, for most families, the intrusion of official recognition by the school can create concerns that were previously dormant or nonexistent.

Teachers and counselors should be aware of family members' concerns in order to deal with related issues and problems as they develop. In this section, some of these concerns are discussed. Later sections discuss special problems that interfere with good decision making by the family and suggestions that teachers and counselors can make to families.

Parental Concerns

Parents see themselves as responsible for making sure the family functions smoothly, as well as for the development of the child. They are concerned with obtaining understandable information on the child's abilities. In addition, parents' concerns revolve first around the question of whether or not the child is gifted (Gold, 1965; Gust et al., 1997), which is followed by concerns about what they can do to help the child, the nature of communication within the family, and the child's present and future behaviors.

Parents want to do what is best for their children (Silverman, 1998), thus the issue of whether or not their children are gifted is important to them. Parents may recognize that a child has high ability, and they may want to encourage it, but the possibility of the child being gifted raises doubts about the proper course of action to take (Dettman & Colangelo, 1980; Solow, 1995). They believe that a clearer view of their child's abilities will help in decision making. Unfortunately, the imprecise nature of identification, especially at early ages, may leave the parents dissatisfied and confused about what their role in identification should be. Parents of only children appear to experience more difficulty developing an accurate appraisal of their child's ability than do parents with several children (Hitchfield, 1973).

Confirmation that a child is gifted can heighten a family's sense of responsibility (Greenstadt, 1981; Silverman, 1998), resulting in a change in orientation from concern for the normal to concern for the atypical or, in this case, the supernormal. The meaning a family attaches to this change is difficult to fathom. Both positive and negative changes are possible, but one thing is certain: The family cannot remain as it was unless it denies the new knowledge. It is important in the family's evolution that the parents maintain clear communication about what giftedness means to them so that they may keep a realistic perspective on both the family unit and individual members.

The loss of perspective on defining giftedness is associated with parental attitudes and behavior that interfere with child-rearing practices. Some parents develop a fear of "stunting the child's growth" (Greenstadt, 1981; Ross, 1979). The realization that their child has unusual potential propels the parents into a relentless search for educational opportunities. A desire to provide lessons and additional learning opportunities can become almost pathological when it stretches family resources and interpersonal relationships beyond the normal scope of family activities and values. An example would be a working-class family who buys a piano and the *Encyclopedia Britannica* for their daughter upon learning she is gifted. Another example is a middle-class family who supplies a continuous series of lessons and club activities. Neither of these decisions is wrong in itself, as many families can handle such changes in stride. It is when the typical family relationships become suddenly distorted, instead of having time to evolve, that the perspective is lost. Some of this pressure to provide opportunities may be tied to misconceptions about early development and later eminence and to misguided responsibility. Lost opportunities do not lead automatically to lost abilities, and parents are not responsible for all that their children become. If clear and unmistakable relationships could be drawn from family to child, there would be no need for this chapter.

Feelings that parents have about themselves and their own childhoods may present problems in maintaining a perspective on their child's abilities.

Parents may begin to mix their childhood dreams and memories into their needs for their children (Greenstadt, 1981). Decisions that are based on unrealistic expectations about a child's development can lead to pressure on the child to perform and almost certain disappointment for the parent. Other choices may be made as a result of disguised competition between parent and child because of present circumstances or childhood memories. When parents interpret a young child's behavior as an attack or as competition, it is time for them to reconsider their actions and attitudes.

While parents need to maintain a perspective on the meaning of giftedness, they also have real concerns about their child's behavior. These concerns are punctuated by the recognition that the child is gifted. In addition, they are mediated by the social values they have internalized about child rearing and giftedness (Colangelo, 1997; Ross, 1979). Parents' conceptions of the gifted role and sex roles are an inextricable part of how they relate to their child. The behaviors that most bother parents seem to be those that are inconsistent with their ideas of giftedness. Of course, these concerns are related not only to learned values, but also to the behaviors they observe in their children.

Parents of gifted children have expressed concern about the fact that their children do not take risks, misuse leisure time by watching TV, and are critical of those who do not learn as they do (Fisher, 1981). These concerns are similar to those expressed by parents in general, but they seem to have a special urgency when expressed by parents of gifted children. Other behavioral areas that are frequent causes of concern are achievement, discipline, and sibling rivalry (Clark, 1988; Dettman & Colangelo, 1980; Webb, Meckstroth, & Tolan, 1982). More specific concerns about behavior were described in a study conducted in Great Britain comparing gifted children identified by their parents to both children with IQs roughly similar to the gifted and to nongifted children from similar school environments (Freeman, 1979). Parents of the gifted said their children felt different 17 times more frequently than the two control groups. They also described their gifted children in the following manner: very different (22%), particularly sensitive (44%), very emotional (19%), difficulty with sleep (50%), sleeps little (7%), very independent (49%), feels "different" (51%), no friends (7%), friends older (36%), extraordinary memory (40%), excellent school progress (43%), prefers educational-type TV (11%), and wide reading range (61%). While these data may depart from findings with a U.S. sample, it is clear that they are similar to many issues recorded in Terman's classic research.

Sibling Concerns

Parents of gifted children often have concerns about the nongifted siblings feeling left out (e.g., when the gifted child monopolizes the dinner conversation). They are also uncomfortable when they must help older siblings deal with a younger child's greater competence (Ross, 1979). Sometimes, a sibling may feel pressure to do as well as the gifted child (AAGC, 1978).

The extensiveness of these concerns for families is not obvious. The data are also incomplete on defining the concerns of siblings. This information is important in terms of guidance because it appears that brothers and sisters can be supportive to the development of gifted siblings (Goertzel et al., 1978). Variables that might affect sibling relationships, such as family size, socioeconomic status, and ethnicity need to be examined.

The Gifted Child's Concerns

The concerns of gifted children seem to be the same as those of other children. Primarily, they want caring parents. They want their parents to provide encouragement and support for their interests, trust and respect them, keep awards in perspective, see them as individuals, give love and affection, let them be unscheduled, be patient, respect their privacy, and act as models (AAGC, 1978; Delisle, 1987; Galbraith, 1985).

Summary

While some information is available on parental concerns, relatively little is known about the concerns of gifted children themselves, nor about the concerns of their siblings. It is clear that the family undergoes changes with the recognition of a gifted child. Relationships change as the family becomes concerned with its atypical members. The parents' search for information to help resolve their new concerns is likely to be frustrated because the present data, which are useful, are not sufficient to the task of providing a coherent framework for family decision making.

Special Problems for Parents

Parents must deal with three special problems related to their gifted child: the child's rapid development; how to tell the public about their problems with the child, as well as about their pride in the child; and the lack of empirical information on the rearing of gifted children.

Gifted children progress through various stages of development at a rate that results in the accomplishment of tasks and the development of interests beyond children the same age. The speed of development in all cases makes it difficult for parents to maintain an accurate view of the child's abilities, especially when the parental notion of development is based upon the norm. Some stages of development are more acceptable to parents than others (Greenstadt, 1981). For example, early interest and enthusiasm for a musical instrument is more acceptable in a young child than long hours of practice and concentration to the exclusion of other interests in a teenager. A preschool child continuously demanding to be read to is exhausting and bothersome to the parent, while extensive reading at age 8 is acceptable. Verbalization about incongruities in social mores are cute in 7-year-olds and disrespectful in adolescents.

Gifted children can develop values that are in conflict with the family (Parker & Colangelo, 1979). Rapid development in a special area may result in the child internalizing the values of people who have similar interests, rather than those of the family. Thus, the development of special talents can hasten the distance between the child and the family (Bloom & Sosniak, 1981).

The parents who experience problems in raising their child must deal with the social realities of qualifying their enthusiasm (Ross, 1979), being reluctant to boast (Hitchfield, 1973), and being wary of asking for assistance. After all, they might reason, don't parents of children with disabilities have more serious problems than we do with our gifted child? Aren't these less-fortunate children more deserving of attention?

This dilemma faced by parents of gifted children is part of the phenomenon of acquiring social values as a by-product of living in a society. The discussion of guidance centers on this phenomenon. Parents, too, learn the social values about the meaning of difference. Their feelings about having children with advanced abilities are mediated by the same social values. The apparent conflicts between individual and group needs, excellence and equality of opportunity, and humility and pride are part of their experience, as well as their children's. Parents of gifted children need to be told that there is no merit to the argument that other children are more deserving of special provisions than their children. Gifted children also need assistance in developing their abilities.

The problem of dealing with a child's giftedness is probably multiplied when the child is a nonmodal gifted child who is, for example, disabled or culturally different. In those instances, the parents must overcome their own, as well as others', preconceptions about the lack of high abilities in nonmodal children. If a parent notices signs of high ability, their tentative overtures may be ignored or overlooked by the more knowledgeable "experts" who discount the possibility of high ability in such children. Parents of children with disabilities have a real obstacle in this regard (Boodoo, Bradley, Frontera, Pitts, & Wright, 1989; Whitmore, 1981).

Parents of culturally different children face a different problem than those of children with disabilities because they may have prejudices to overcome. Stereotypical notions about the abilities of ethnic groups can interfere with identification procedures (VanTassel-Baska, Patton, & Prillaman, 1991). Communication between the family and the dominant culture, as represented by the school, is frequently inadequate due to contrasting value systems, language differences, and previous school experiences (Marion, 1980), which can hamper the efforts of parents who are trying to gather information in order to make wise choices (Ford, 1996).

Child-Rearing Problems

Parents of gifted children face some unique child-rearing problems created by the interplay between their children's characteristics and society's values. To deal with these problems, parents need good information so that they may make wise decisions for the child and for the family. Unfortunately, parents and their advisors are confronted with an obstacle: Simply stated, it is that little substantive information is available on these issues for solving problems (Sandborn, 1979b), and most of the information that is available is not specific to gifted children. Further, families that seek specialized counseling services to deal with psychosocial issues associated with giftedness may encounter family therapists who have little expertise in this area (Moon & Hall, 1998). Gifted students require a developmental counseling program that includes a focus on the cognitive and affective needs of the child (Colangelo, 2000, 2003), and few family therapists receive the necessary training to differentiate therapy for gifted and talented individuals and their families from the general population (Moon & Thomas, 2003).

It is no wonder parents are frustrated and searching for help. The need for parent support groups is obvious in this situation. While efforts are ongoing to provide means for parents to work successfully on behalf of their gifted children (Damiani, 1996), educators need to maintain open lines of communication with parents and be frank about the scarcity of empirically validated specialized information (Shore, Kanevsky, & Rejskind, 1991).

THE PARENT/SCHOOL RELATIONSHIP

The school can play a valuable role in assisting families with gifted children. Our discussion on patterns of, and concerns about, family interaction provides a background for the information and procedures teachers and other school personnel can use in consultations with parents. The intent is to facilitate communication between the school and the family. Because parents are powerful forces in a child's development, meaningful communication can assist everyone (Damiani, 1996). The discussion does not assume families consist only of parents and children.

General Principles

Meaningful communication between the parent and school personnel must occur in an atmosphere of openness and honesty. Each party needs to accept that the other is honestly concerned about the welfare of the child and come to an agreement about which aspects of a child's life at home and at school are open to influence.

Within this broad context, Sandborn (1979b) has proposed three generalizations about working with parents. These generalizations are a result of 20 years of dealing with families in more than 16,000 conferences.

- There are often very strong differences of opinion among parents and children about which courses of action to take in response to giftedness or talent.

- Parents are more likely to take action on suggestions made by the school when these suggestions are highly specific and instructions are clear.

143

- Parents are likely to take action on school suggestions that are clearly predicated on specific knowledge of their child (p. 398).

These generalizations are significant because they point in the direction of action. The consultant needs to obtain information on points of conflict between family and child. One cannot supply the family with needed information unless the problem is clarified. Teachers must realize that sometimes a sympathetic listener is all that is needed, and action is not required. When suggestions are being solicited, the teacher needs to be specific whenever possible. Being specific when suggesting alternatives and in citing examples of the child's behavior demonstrates real concern to the parents and to the child. Teachers should prepare for meetings with parents to help clarify the child's performance. This preparation adds to the probability that the conference will be successful.

Family Relations With the School

In our society, the laws of compulsory school attendance mean that contact between the school and the family must occur. The quality of that contact is up to the participants.

It is inevitable that some contact will be stressful. Occasional disagreements are likely, even if it is assumed that the participants want to make the best possible decisions. Given the various concerns of the three parties (the parents, the school staff, and the child), areas of misunderstanding and conflict are likely to exist. The continuous process of change over the years of schooling contributes further to the potential for disagreement. Thus, it is important to keep the lines of communication open. As usual, this openness is easier said than done.

The Parents' Perspective

The parents' primary responsibility is to the child. Their need for information about the child's behavior and about options available for educating the child is paramount. However, they may find that the school fails to deal with their questions (Dembinski & Mauser, 1978), and as a result they do not feel satisfied after an exchange with school personnel (Mathews, 1981).

Parents believe it is the school's responsibility to provide clear answers, but often find that the school furnishes them with ones that are vague and jargon-laden (Bostick, 1980). According to parents, school often refuse to recognize that a problem exists and resist the idea that parents might have valid information on their child's needs. Parents report feeling that the school implies that the problem is of their making or that the problem is due to some intractable, intrinsic characteristic of the child and not the school system itself (Hall & Skinner, 1980). Moreover, schools often have no plan for how to offer services.

The parents' persistence is the most important factor in determining whether a successful relationship is forged with school personnel.

The School's Perspective

It is difficult to characterize the school's perspective because the stated philosophy of the school sounds very much like that of the parents' in terms of individualization and maximizing the potential of children. School personnel believe that the task of carrying out such goals in the real world complicates the situation. They have no desire to conduct themselves in ways that are antithetical to the school's expressed goals. However, the resolution of parental concerns is frequently seen as beyond the control of the individual school principal or teacher. Successful resolution is seen as a political question tied to budgets, taxes, and board policies about class size, materials, and the like. School personnel tend to feel overburdened, underpaid, and unappreciated. They see themselves as experts, and they want to be regarded as such. When new problems are brought to their attention, they see them as exceptions.

They wonder why parents never praise them for what they do, and when parents raise questions, they are sometimes seen as pushy and self-serving. Such parents exist, but this image, at least as seen by the children involved, is inaccurate and unfair. Parents of exceptional children are not encouraged to participate in decision making about placement (Mathews, 1981; Yoshida, 1978). If school personnel are ever open to criticism, it is when it is accompanied by constructive suggestions. Parents who complain without being able to supply at least a partial description of what they consider to be a reasonable solution are viewed as adversaries.

Schools want solutions. However, the less changes interfere with general operating procedures, the more easily they are accepted. Above all, the school contends that it is concerned with all children, not just one child.

The Advocate's Perspective: The Educator

A third perspective is that of the educator or teacher of the gifted who functions as an advocate for quality education. The teacher should facilitate the communication process by clarifying the perspectives of each party and providing needed suggestions. Shore et al. (1991) noted that well-trained teachers of the gifted were needed because they could identify gifted students better than other teachers and because their training and working with gifted students led them to become advocates.

The characterization of the parents' and the school's perspectives dramatizes the volatile nature of the home/school relationship. Meaningful interaction can be effected when all participants recognize the following limitations: (1) a perfect solution is a myth; (2) any given issue is likely to return again in another form; and (3) all parties believe that their perspective is legitimate.

The advocate can advise the participants to prepare for the meeting. School personnel should review records before a conference and have alternatives ready for discussion. They can help themselves by attending to the following list of recommendations for conferences compiled from parental surveys in California and Illinois (Dembinski & Mauser, 1978):

1. Keep the parents informed about their child's progress or the lack of it.

2. Allow the parents to ask questions.

3. Show the parents reports on their child and explain them.

4. Allow the parents to contact the school when needed.

5. Tell the parents how their child gets along with others in his or her class.

6. Tell the parents if their child gets into trouble.

7. Tell the parents of any special adjustment problems their child is having.

8. Be willing to discuss the child's needs and progress with other professionals involved.

9. Tell the parents if the school thinks the child is in the best possible educational setting.

10. Tell the parents if the school thinks the child is progressing at a reasonable rate.

11. Use terminology the parents can understand.

12. Give the parents the school's impression of the parental role in the child's learning process.

13. Inform the parents of the school's most successful techniques in working with the child.

14. Require the parents to attend parent conferences.

15. Give the parents suggestions to enrich their child's home life.

16. Tell the parents what to expect their child to learn and when.

17. Give the parents material to read.

18. Show the parents how to teach things to their child.

19. Help the parents accept their child as normal.

20. Require the parents to discuss their concerns with the school.

21. Put the parents in touch with other parents who have similar concerns over their gifted children (p. 11).

Parents, in preparation for a conference, should arrive with some alternatives and should push for clear answers. The possibility for a successful conference is increased when schools furnish parents with information about the program before the meeting. In an exchange, most parents are at a disadvantage because they have limited experience in conferences with school personnel and limited knowledge of educational jargon. Hall and Skinner (1980) suggested that parents practice being at a meeting by role-playing. Some suggestions for parents arguing their case are provided in Table 4.1. Hall and Skinner also provided an "Everyman's Guide to Educational Jargon," which parents might find helpful as background for a meeting. Kitano (1991) recommended that schools recognize the strengths of families while appreciating the variation in access to resources when working on behalf of children. With reasonable preparation and good faith on both sides, it is usually possible to effect a solution to the situation.

The Advocate's Perspective: Groups

Parents seeking answers to questions about how to educate their gifted children may wish to join or start an advocacy group. Such groups are formed in order to further opportunities for gifted youths. Advocacy groups may be found within organizations, such as parent/teacher associations and school advocacy groups, or they may be separate entities devoted solely to gifted children. Membership may or may not include professional educators. In recent years, the number of advocacy groups has grown. Parents have become increasingly aware of the need for mutual support and the need for organized efforts to get things done. Parents have learned that they have more influence when they operate together in an organization than they have as individuals and that advocacy does makes a difference (Bostick, 1980). Involvement in group activity also makes a difference by broadening the parents' concern to include people outside the family (Nathan, 1979).

The formation of an advocacy group requires hard work and a group of committed individuals. Specific details about how to form a group is available in the literature. The American Association for Gifted Children sponsored a publication entitled *Reaching Out: Advocacy for the Gifted and Talented* (Tannenbaum & Neuman, 1980). The success of a California advocacy group has been documented (Bostick, 1980). In addition, Kaufmann (1976) has some useful suggestions, and Gowan et al. (1979) have enumerated some "unorthodox rules for forming a group" (pp. 249–250). Organizations may also be contacted for assistance: The Association for the Gifted (TAG), the National Association for Gifted Children (NAGC), and the American Association for Gifted Children (AAGC), as well as universities and colleges.

TABLE 4.1

How to Argue Effectively for Gifted Education

School Argument	Parents' Response
We are the experts. We educators know best, and you do not understand all the complex issues involved.	We know our child's needs. It is your responsibility to design a school environment that meets the needs of all children.
Do you have any proof that gifted children have special problems or needs?	We are prepared to defend and define the problem with documentation. We have done our homework and know what is happening nationally, as well as in our state and locally.
The examples you cite are exceptions. Giftedness certainly isn't widespread.	Each child in the school is important. Can you prove there aren't more gifted children?
We really can't do that much for gifted students.	Blaming the child rather than the system, which may be structured to create problems, is a common way to avoid facing real problems.
Yes, we know the problem exists, but we need time to figure out the best thing to do.	We want to know exactly what is being done. We want your plans in writing, specifically how the plan will be implemented, and who is responsible for it.
It's an unimportant problem.	We believe the problem is important because it affects the children directly.
We aren't doing worse than any other schools.	Just because other schools aren't doing anything different for the gifted does not excuse this district from providing for the needs of the gifted.
We have no money.	This may be true, but free and appropriate education of all children is the district's responsibility. Money should be sought from other sources, and present priorities reexamined.

Note. From *Somewhere to Turn: Strategies for Parents of the Gifted and Talented* (p. 21), by E. G. Hall and N. Skinner, 1980, New York: Teachers College Press. Copyright ©1980 by Teachers College Press. Reprinted with permission.

The building of an effective advocacy group is an important objective. The influence of such organizations can be positive in terms of improving family mental health and effecting educational changes. Families discover that they are not alone—others have dealt with similar problems. Parents are also surprised at how the previously recalcitrant school can become a partner in improving opportunities for gifted children. In some instances, advocacy groups have found it necessary to create alternative programs in order to aid children. An interesting side effect of advocacy is that it helps to nourish and sustain those individuals in school who, in the past, were lone voices in support of education for the gifted.

THE TEACHER AND FREQUENTLY ASKED QUESTIONS BY PARENTS

Teachers of the gifted find themselves in a special position in the lives of gifted children. Not only do they have the role of teacher and perhaps counselor to the child, they are also required to furnish advice to parents and friends of parents who are seeking information on giftedness. In an advisory role, the teacher of gifted children is an expert in gifted education and is expected to possess special knowledge on issues that concern the parents. Young teachers are sometimes surprised at how parents who are older than themselves ask for and rely on their opinion. Certain issues come up with enough frequency to warrant brief discussions to provide some additional insight for teachers and other school personnel into family dynamics.

How Can We Tell Whether Our Child Is Gifted?

Identification is an issue of great concern to parents. The question of identifying giftedness is frequently directed at parents of already identified children and teachers of gifted children (Gust et al., 1997). The question comes most often from parents of preschool- and elementary-age children.

Although an absolute answer to this question is impossible, parents want some information so they may decide whether or not to pursue the issue further or to make some special educational considerations. Abraham (1977) proposed a simple list of characteristics of young gifted children as a guide to help parents (see Table 4.2). He suggested that a child who is strong in at least half of the characteristics is surely a bright child. A more specific guideline for looking at developmental milestones in preschool children has been presented by Hall and Skinner (1980), who constructed developmental guidelines on general motor ability, fine motor ability, and cognitive language. An unusual feature of their guidelines is that the normal developmental schedule is presented, as well as the time at which a child is indicated to be "30% more advanced." They, too, suggest that, if a child reaches the criterion of "30% more advanced" on a majority of items, the child may be gifted.

TABLE 4.2

Characteristics of the Young Gifted Child

1. Started to walk and talk before most other children you know about.
2. Is at least a little taller, heavier, and stronger than others his or her age.
3. Shows an interest in time—clocks, calendars, yesterday and tomorrow, and days of the week.
4. Learned to read even though not yet 5 years old. Likes to read.
5. Arranges toys and other possessions, putting the same kinds of things together.
6. Knows which numbers are larger than others.
7. Can count and point to each item as he or she correctly says the number.
8. Creates make-believe playmates as he or she "plays house" or different games.
9. Is interested in what is on television and in newspapers, in addition to cartoons and comics.
10. Learns easily, so that you have to tell him or her something only once.
11. Shows impatience with jobs around the house that seem to have no meaning—such as putting toys away when he or she is just going to have to take them out again.
12. Asks "Why?" often and really wants to know the answer. Is curious about a lot of things, from a tiny insect and how it's "made," to a car and how it works.
13. Doesn't like to wait for other children to catch up.
14. Sticks with a task longer than others do. Won't give up easily.
15. Does things differently in ways that make good sense, whether it's piling up blocks, setting the table, or drying dishes.
16. Likes to be with older children and can keep up with them.
17. Collects things, likes to organize them, and doesn't want anyone to mess them up—but doesn't always collect neatly.
18. Can carry on a conversation and enjoys it. Wants your ideas and likes you to listen to his or hers. Uses big words and knows what they mean.
19. Shows an interest in drawing and music, knows colors, and has rhythm.
20. Makes up jokes—has a good sense of humor.

Users of these guidelines should remember that there are variations at different ages.

What Can We Do to Help Our Child Develop?

Recognition that a child is bright or has been identified as gifted increases parents' concern about being a "proper parent." Parents seem to forget that they must have been doing something right because, after all, giftedness does not emerge in a vacuum. Families should continue to do what they've been doing and integrate into that pattern the knowledge that their child is gifted.

Writers on this topic have offered tips on how to live with gifted children. While these tips will not solve every problem faced by families, they are useful in helping parents regain their sense of perspective on the child and the family. Teachers should be aware of these points and introduce them into the discussion whenever possible.

Gifted Children Are Children

Gifted children have the same needs as other children (Cross, 1997a, 1997b; Gowan et al., 1979). Maslow (1968) conceptualized needs as existing on a hierarchy of five levels. A person has a tendency to move upward, but unmet needs inhibit development. The levels of needs, simply stated, are (1) basic physiological needs, which include getting food, shelter, and clothing; (2) safety needs, referring to emotional safety and security; (3) belonging needs, including respect and appreciation as a valued group member; (4) love and self-esteem, referring to sharing love and affection; and (5) self-actualization, including self-awareness, openness to experience, and thrill of growth. Providing for these needs for all family members is an important goal. Being gifted does not exclude one from having these needs. The ability of a gifted child to make use of special abilities is influenced negatively when the needs are unmet. Remembering that a gifted child is a child also reminds parents that gifted children should have the same family responsibilities and are subject to the same rules as other family members. The routines of life apply to all family members.

Gifted Children Are Gifted

That gifted children are gifted may seem obvious at first, but is crucial that the strengths or advanced abilities of these children are acknowledged as real. They do not go away. Some of these abilities permit gifted children to have more insight into their unmet needs mentioned above. Sometimes, these abilities help the child work out solutions. At the same time, advanced abilities demand expression. Exercising strengths leads to a clearer view of one's self and the world. One cannot make wise choices if one's sense of self and knowledge of the world are inaccurate.

The Child Is Gifted, Not You

The parents' role is to help the child deal with being different. It is not the parents' role to be gifted. In terms of immediate concerns, only the child is gifted. Even with support, the child is still alone. Parents may bask in their child's successes and suffer with their child's failures, but in neither case is the parents' reputation at risk. Children have enough difficulty managing their differentness and learning to be responsible for themselves (Coleman & Cross, 1988). Additional pressures are unnecessary and unfair. The ability to separate oneself as a parent from the child is not an all-or-nothing condition. Children want their parents to be involved, but they also want them to be distant (AAGC, 1978; Delisle, 1987; Silverman, 1993). The line between involvement and freedom is very fine. Teachers, too, would do well to keep these notions in mind.

The Model Is the Message

Because of their sensitivity, gifted children are great observers of what is happening around them. Many of the behaviors they acquire come from observing what others do. Fisher (1981) reported instances of parents discovering that negative behaviors in their children, such as inappropriate use of leisure time and dependency, were modeled by them in the home. "Do as I say, not as I do" is never a good strategy with children, especially gifted children.

Summary

These four general suggestions are useful for parents and teachers to share. They illustrate that raising a gifted child is not an issue that can be separated from the realm of child development. These statements provide a base for keeping the process of child-rearing in perspective. More specific ideas about how giftedness may be nurtured follow.

What Should We Do at Home to Promote Giftedness?

The development of very advanced abilities in children follows the pattern described by Bloom and Sosniak (1981) and Pressey (1949). Talents, according to their research, are developed within a familial framework, which provides continuous, individualized attention to the mastery of a relatively narrow range of abilities comprising a talent area, such as swimming, piano, or mathematics. The child's talent is recognized early in life, and in those early years, the nurturing process is informal and individualized, yet purposeful in terms of the family's values. As the child grows older and more proficient, the process of encouragement becomes more formal and eventually moves beyond the family circle into the realm of experts. The process is one of long-term commitment, which is modeled by the family and internalized by the child.

The general literature available to parents on what can be done to promote giftedness presents a somewhat different view (Delph, 1980; Kanigher, 1977; Kaufmann, 1976; Miller & Price, 1981). The issue of long-term commitment to a specific talent area is mentioned primarily in the context of career choice and secondary education, thus it is rare to find it discussed in articles about pre-school- and elementary-age children. Why this is the case is not apparent. Nevertheless, it is an issue that confuses parents. It is likely that educators contribute to the notion that long-term commitment only applies to older children due to the social values against such development in most schools and colleges of education. Family can certainly provide opportunities and circumstances that enhance the development of gifted children. Suggestions for families in the professional literature on intelligence and creativity correspond closely to recommendations that appear in popular magazines such as *Redbook* or *Woman's Day*. The general, recipe-like nature of the suggestions is typical. The generality reflects difficulty in providing specific information to a broad audience, as well as the limited state of our knowledge about family dynamics. Professionals need to understand this situation and realize that parents are distressed by it.

Kaufmann (1976) has provided a description of creativity and recommendations for setting conditions for its growth:

- Provide materials that develop imagination, such as open-ended stories or drawings.

- Provide materials that enrich imagery, such as fairy tales, folk tales, myths, fables, and nature books.

- Permit time for thinking and daydreaming. Just because a child does not look like he or she is busy does not mean that his or her mind is not.

- Encourage children to record their ideas in binders, notebooks, and the like. Even playing secretary for your child by having him or her dictate his or her stories to you can be a special way of showing that his or her ideas are valuable and that you care about what he or she is thinking.

- Accept and use his or her tendency to take a different look. There are really many things one can learn about the world by standing on one's head.

- Prize, rather than punish, true individuality. It is always possible to find little details about a child's work or behavior that might make him or her feel as though you noticed him or her as a special person.

- Be cautious in editing children's products. Sometimes a word corrected in the wrong place or too many times can stifle a child's creative energy and feeling of worth as a creator.

- Encourage children to play with words. Even in such common settings as a car ride or shopping trip, word games like rhyming, opposites, and puns can be used to their full advantage (p. 14).

153

Kaufmann (1976) went on to say that, in addition to setting these conditions, a parent can deliberately teach creative thinking and problem solving (many of these ideas will be reviewed in the chapters on creativity and instruction). Parents who wish to explore other ideas are referred to Delph (1980), Hall and Skinner (1980), Vail (1979), and Walker (1991). One approach, the SCAMPER method (Eberle, 1996), has received considerable attention due to its flexibility as a teaching technique (Kaufmann; Sellin & Birch, 1980). Materials that parents can use to foster the development of talents are available in magazines from advocacy groups and others such as *Gifted Child Today*, *Highlights for Children*, and *Parenting for High Potential*.

Cassidy (1981) proposed other ways in which parents can further their child's education in the school setting by adopting one or more of five potential roles. Two roles have already been described in this chapter: The advisor/advocate role supplies valuable background data on the child's strengths and learning style and acts as an advocate for the child with the school; the parental guide role provides learning opportunities at home and outside school. There is also the mentor role, in which parents share their expertise in some field with their child or other children who have special interests in this area. The classroom-aide role is one in which the parent assists in a program, especially with independent study projects. Finally, in the materials-developer role, the parent prepares materials under the teacher's direction so that the school program may provide instruction aligned with the known interests and abilities of the class.

What Do Those Test Scores Mean?

Standardized tests have become a staple in U.S. schools. Many issues are defined and decided by such tests, including identification, achievement, and program success. The benefits and shortcomings of standardized tests have already been described in the chapter on identification. The question of test scores is raised here in regard to the results of IQ tests and achievement tests. Each is discussed separately.

The question of the meaning of an IQ score is valid and natural. Parents and sometimes children themselves want to know its meaning. An IQ score alone cannot supply anything specific about an individual child except that he or she may meet a state's definition of giftedness, and it serves as a rough approximation of general learning rate. After that point, the score is rather misleading because it ignores the margin of error in any score and the narrow definition of intelligence found in IQ tests. Gold (1965) recommended that parents be given "the percentile band in which a score falls" (p. 374). This procedure is the most accurate way of interpreting a score because it shows the possible range of a child's performance at the time the test was given in comparison to peers.

If parents want estimates of a child's future performance in school, it is better to look at past school performance than IQ scores. Gifted children frequently do well in school, but a significant number do not. IQ is not the sole factor related to school achievement. The probability of getting high achievement scores using IQ as the predictor variable "in a number of different subjects . . . [is] very small indeed" (Hitchfield, 1973, p. 34). If parents want an estimate of their child's future profession, the IQ test cannot provide that information. The fairest answer is that future choices are not restricted and that factors beyond IQ such as interests and opportunity will shape these possibilities.

Due to misinformation, parents occasionally ask whether or not it is true that their 10-year-old child is thinking like a 14-year-old. Such a notion is too broad and conveys an erroneous interpretation of the meaning of mental age scores derived from intelligence tests. A score is a result of performance on items scattered across a variety of subtests. A score summarizes a child's performance and ignores variations among items of varying content and complexity. Thus, children with the same IQ score can exhibit considerable variation in abilities (Guilford, 1967).

A problem in all discussions of test scores, including intelligence and achievement tests, is that parents mistakenly believe that psychological and educational tests are as precise as tests used in chemistry or engineering. The lack of precision in these tests seems to be responsible for a considerable amount of confusion.

Grade-level scores cause problems for parents and children alike (Coleman, 1983). When academic achievement is presented in grade-level scores, the meaning of achievement scores is confused because parents incorrectly assume that a sixth-grade reading score in a second grader means the child is reading like a sixth grader. It is possible, but unlikely. The child is not asked to read all the third- through fifth-grade material. On one test, the child may be required to read some items from each grade level; on another test, the child may not. On either test, the child's performance is compared to typical second graders who are supposed to be reading at the second-grade level. In the example, the child is so superior in reading that the performance is extrapolated to be at the sixth-grade level. Thus, the primary meaning of the grade score is that the child is a superior reader for a second grader.

These points about the meaning of test scores are difficult to communicate to parents. A continuous dialogue between school and home is necessary to keep these matters clear.

Why Isn't Our Child Well-Rounded?

Another question that has considerable currency is the parents' concern that their child is spending too much time pursuing personal interests that tend to be abstract and apart from those of peers. The parents would like their child to have more social contact, wider interests, and so forth. In short, they want the child to be balanced in terms of intellectual, social, emotional, and physical pursuits, which they see as somehow related to being a normal human being.

While this concern is real for many parents, it is also an unrealizable ideal for most gifted children. Being in balance is impossible because gifted children by definition are out of balance. In a preceding chapter, it was proposed that gifted children are developmentally advanced; they have a need to further their development in interest areas. To ignore or downplay this point is to deny the child's uniqueness and to inhibit the self-development of strategies for managing differentness.

The child and the parents have to learn to cope with this differentness. Part of coping is realizing that being different is okay. Parents and educators alike need to learn that some children are socially disinterested, and such disinterest may be perfectly natural. Social disinterest is misinterpreted to be the same as social isolation. Furthermore, the excitement of pursuing advanced interests is overlooked as a valuable consequence of being gifted. It is very reinforcing to have such feelings. Parents must deal with the "unfortunate" fact that some interests require more solitary work than others.

The concern for balance would be more profitable for the family if the parents saw the problem as existing outside their child. However, there are limited opportunities for the child to have contact with others of similar ability and interest. Looking for such opportunities, helping to create social opportunities, and joining advocacy groups to provide additional opportunities are constructive ways to improve the situation for the child (Coleman & Cross, 1988; Cross, 1997b). After all, the making of friends and the development of values happen most naturally in the context of mutual interest and experience.

This response is unsatisfactory to parents because they do not see being balanced as an issue of denying one's abilities, but rather as a concern or fear about their child's future adjustment and happiness. They see well-rounded individuals as being happy. They wish to protect their children from themselves. The parents, in this case, have created for themselves an impossible task.

Should We Accelerate Our Child?

The issue of acceleration is a constant in gifted education because gifted children are advanced in their development. Acceleration refers to a number of educational options that have as their common denominator increased speed through a body of information in order to advance children beyond their peers. The most frequently cited examples of acceleration advance the child across all school subjects by grade skipping, early admission, or double promotion. Acceleration may also include advancement only in particular subject areas, such as going to higher grades for reading or mathematics or taking Advanced Placement tests. It is advisable for teachers to determine what the parents think acceleration is.

The empirical evidence on this topic is quite clear. The general-education literature is not. Research indicates that acceleration is beneficial to children in that it has positive academic and social effects and shows little evidence of maladjustment (George, Cohn, & Stanley, 1979; Kulik & Kulik, 1984, 1997).

(For a more complete discussion of this topic, the reader should refer to the chapter on programming.) Knowledge of the benefits has limited value for the parents. They appreciate knowing what the benefits are in general, but such group findings are indirectly related to the needs of their child, for whom they wish to make the best decision.

As it is with most issues, the correct decision is unclear. The situation is complicated by parents' experience and by the viewpoint of school personnel. The parents' experience, in terms of either their observation of others who were accelerated or their own acceleration, can be positive or negative. Professionals should recognize, not dismiss, the validity of the parents' experience. The role of the teacher or counselor is to help parents consider the evidence and look behind the generalizations to their child's situation. The school's view tends to be against acceleration, a view that is typically based upon little knowledge of research evidence, an imprecise belief about balanced development, and a desire not to disturb the status quo. Both parties—parents and school personnel—are unlikely to abandon their views.

The root of the parents' concern is related to the aforementioned issue of being balanced. Concern about acceleration eventually becomes a pointed question of future social adjustment; it is the anticipation of problems the child may experience in high school or college. Parents remember their own adolescent years and the trauma associated with them. The thought of their child having to cope with those problems at a younger age seems overwhelming. Parents, quite understandably, want to protect their children from more problems. While this altruistic motive is commendable, it is also impossible. It is doubtful that parents can minimize, much less protect their children completely from the strains of growing up.

An alternate concern parents should consider is the problems exaggerated by not allowing their child to accelerate. The problem of growing up gifted, as outlined in the chapter on counseling, is inevitable. It is true that acceleration adds strains to growing up that would not ordinarily be there, but it is equally true that acceleration reduces conflict.

How is a family to decide? Of course, the child's desires and abilities, the school's flexibility, and the family as a whole need to be considered in terms of the support the child needs and its availability. Acceleration without guidance sometimes works, but it is usually most successful when support is present. The support of teachers, counselors, and administrators is important, and the support of the family is absolutely crucial. The ability of the family to support the child if difficulties arise would seem to be the determining factor in making a decision.

FOR **DISCUSSION**

1. How would you respond to an individual who asks you to describe the typical family background of a gifted child?

2. The chapter mentions that less is understood about the familial factors that contribute to giftedness in women. Reflect on and discuss how family characteristics (historically and currently) may impede the development of giftedness in females.

3. Reflect on and discuss how differing family values may influence the way a family responds to their child's giftedness.

4. An individual comments that raising a gifted child is no different from raising a nongifted child. How would you prioritize the points mentioned in this chapter to convince this person that that may not be the case?

5. Conduct Internet and/or library searches to identify advocacy groups around the country. Discuss the similarities and differences of these groups.

6. The chapter mentions that magazines such as *Gifted Child Today*, *Highlights for Children*, and *Parenting for High Potential* contain ideas parents may use to foster the development of talents. Look at one or all of these magazines and find three ideas that would be beneficial to share with parents.

chapter five

COPING WITH GIFTEDNESS:
GUIDANCE AND COUNSELING CONSIDERATIONS

KEY CONCEPTS

- The prevalence of severe emotional disturbances among the gifted has not been proven to be any different than that of the general population.

- Gifted children experience a higher potential for conflict in their lives than the nongifted.

- Giftedness is stigmatizing. The child copes by managing identity.

- A guidance program can help children develop strategies that preserve identity and do not inhibit development.

- Managing identity is especially complicated for the nonmodal gifted.

- Underachievement is an example of an unsuccessful management strategy.

- Guidance procedures that develop from a unifying theoretical perspective are more likely to have coherence and direction.

- Theoretical models have implications for guidance programs.

Gifted children grow up in a complex world where their talents are encouraged, praised, ignored, and treated with disdain. In this chapter, the life of the gifted child is examined in terms of the child's and others' responses to giftedness within the community at large and the school in particular.

This chapter serves to acquaint the reader with the benefits and liabilities of being gifted as one grows up. Gifted individuals are presumed to experience more conflict in their lives and, consequently, more difficulties in self-development than do nongifted people. Conflict is produced by a lack of congruence between a gifted child's advanced development and the social norms, rather than as a consequence of possessing certain special traits. Gifted children are thus faced with the general problem of managing development and maintaining identity in the face of these conflicts.

DEFINING THE TERRITORY

Guidance and coping with giftedness suggest many topics, ranging from psychosis to career choice. Several assumptions underlying the format and content of this chapter are presented for the sake of clarity.

This chapter provides a perspective on guidance for teachers and counselors; it is not an exhaustive review of counseling procedures. One will not become a counselor from reading this chapter. However, one can gain some information that has significant implications for guidance, counseling, teaching, and programming.

Despite public perception of a link between genius and insanity, no link has been established for gifted children. In 1891, two books appeared that studied the lives of famous male historical figures and reported a disproportionate number of cases of emotional instability (Tannenbaum, 1958). Forty years later, Cox (1926) reported contradictory findings. More recently, Goertzel et al. (1978) analyzed the biographies of eminent men and women and concluded that "some experienced mental illness, but as a group they have little in common with the psychopathological" (p. x). Empirical research on the gifted from childhood through adulthood has also confirmed that emotional disturbance is not a common correlate of giftedness (Lajoie & Shore, 1981; Neihart, 1999; Sears, 1979; Terman & Oden, 1947; Yewchuk, 1995).

Children who have severe emotional problems are candidates for psychotherapy, not for guidance. Therapy for these individuals generally follows the procedures advocated for anyone else with emotional problems. The concern of this chapter is the general problem of dealing with differentness as perceived by the gifted and placing the concerns of the gifted within the realm of normal development.

Our contention that the incidence of emotional disturbance among the gifted is comparable to that of the general public and the fact that the gifted generally make good adjustments is surprising to some because it seems to contradict common sense. If the gifted are deviants by definition, then why aren't the incidence figures higher? This may be due to many factors:

1. Giftedness does not lead to social and emotional problems.

2. The "truly" gifted are not being studied.

3. The measurement of social and emotional adjustment is too primitive to be respected.

4. The gifted can reason out and provide the answers for which researchers are looking.

All of these explanations contain some validity, but the first is the best supported. The other explanations imply that the figures should reflect a higher incidence of problems, but they are of the "catch-22" variety because they cannot be directly proven and are circular. Given our present level of knowledge, it could be argued that gifted children experience either less stress or more stress because of their giftedness. One could also argue that being gifted provides one with the opportunity to profit from conflict and become better adjusted.

While it is clear that gifted children have a similar, and possibly lower, incidence of severe emotional problems when compared to groups of nongifted children, one might ask whether the absence of mental illness means the gifted are happier or more content than other children. Such a question is unanswerable. Comparisons are based upon limited samples of gifted children and upon relative norms, rather than on absolute standards of emotional health and stability. However, on balance, it is reasonable to assert that the gifted, on the whole, are well-adjusted and happy (Neihart, 1999; Terman & Oden, 1959; Tidwell, 1980; Yewchuk, 1995). Of course, within this generalization, considerable variation in adjustment occurs for gifted individuals. It is apparent that gifted children have problems growing up. Some exhibit disturbing behaviors, but the meaning of these individual cases should not be generalized to reflect on the whole group and should not be considered typical.

Consideration of the development of gifted students necessitates examining the literature on social/emotional development. Coleman and Cross (2000) noted three viewpoints on development: *universal* (gifted children develop like all children); *universal with special characteristics* (gifted children develop like all children, but with special characteristics); or *non-universal* (development is linked to advanced abilities or talents in relatively few people). The position taken in this chapter is that coping with giftedness is part of the general problem of living in a society, as well as a special problem for a person developing advanced abilities. The fashioning of an appropriate guidance model should be based on an understanding of how gifted children cope and with what they must cope. Problems encountered by gifted children are assumed to be caused by the incongruities between their developing abilities and interests and society's expectations. There is no assumption that the gifted have a unique system of needs or develop in a manner that differentiates them from other children. Their needs are as varied as any group. Their stages of growth are similar to any group of children, although their rate of development is more rapid (Zaffrann & Colangelo, 1979). However, their rate of development exists on a continuum from slow to fast, and it cannot be generalized across all domains of development.

SOURCES OF CONFLICT
IN THE LIVES OF GIFTED CHILDREN

All children experience difficulties in growing up. There is nothing unique about this phenomenon. Gifted children, however, also have to deal with a number of issues unique to their situation. One issue is that gifted students must compete with a number of widely held myths and associated practices that may affect their social and emotional development (Cross, 2004). Also, gifted children must deal with more potential conflicts in school and in the community while growing up than nongifted children. Strang (1960) saw the conflict as an undeniable product of being gifted in a nongifted world. Twenty years later, Whitmore (1980) noted that the gifted were generally vulnerable to environmental influences. More recently, Cross discussed influences of macrosystems, exosystems, mesosystems, and microsystems on the lives of gifted students. The social milieu of the school, for example, may be a source of conflict for a gifted student, especially since schools have been criticized as being anti-intellectual enterprises (Howley et al., 1995). A reasonable assumption is that, if schools are anti-intellectual in orientation, academically gifted students will experience conflict.

TABLE 5.1

Traits Meet Social Expectations and Are Interpreted as Possible Problems

Positive traits		Social Expectations	Interpretations
• Sensitive • Independent • Sees relationships • Logical • Analytical • Creative thinker • Persistent • Has special interests • Has a broad information base • Strives for mastery	MEETS	• General mixed messages • School structures • Gifted role • Sex role	• Possible attendant problems

Note. From *Schooling the Gifted* (p. 161), by L. J. Coleman, 1985, Menlo Park, CA: Addison-Wesley. Copyright ©1985 by L. J. Coleman. Adapted with permission.

Much of the conflict in gifted students' lives is a consequence of their advanced developmental rate accompanied by the emergence of more complex abilities and interests, which is incongruent with the behavioral expectations set out for them. The source of conflict is not something inherent in the traits of gifted children, but rather in the interplay between the individual and his or her surroundings.

Frequency of conflict or heightened potential for conflict is an outgrowth of how specific social roles and conditions resist the gifted child's developed abilities. A person may have a variety of roles, including gender, race, and age, and a person is supposed to behave in ways that are consistent with each role. Giftedness is one such role that contains a series of expected behaviors for the gifted and by the gifted. It is others' interpretations of the child's behavior, as well as the child's view of others in his or her world, that promotes conflict.

On the following pages, a series of social messages are depicted as the sources of conflict. As noted in Table 5.1, these social messages may be categorized as general mixed messages, gifted-role messages, sex-role messages, and school-role messages. Some messages are not recognized or encountered by all gifted children, and it is unlikely that any single gifted child would encounter all them. These messages need not lead to open confrontation, but they may well function as continual prods to move the child in some "correct" direction. These categories of messages are neither mutually exclusive nor exhaustive. The categories are also inconsistent in the sense that they may be considered as strictly positive or unquestionably negative statements relative to giftedness. Inconsistency is an important quality of social expectation because it places the gifted child in a quandary about how to respond. A range of responses is possible, although in responding, some behaviors are encouraged more than others.

General Mixed Messages

The general mixed messages are statements that are related to one's social attractiveness. A person's acceptability to others and to oneself is associated with social attraction and the pressures of conformity. These messages are mixed because they illustrate discrepancies between social rhetoric and social reality as perceived by gifted children. The power of these messages to produce conflict occurs as children come to accept and believe them. Because the messages are abstractions of reality and, as already noted, contradictory, it is easy for gifted children to misinterpret and overgeneralize the situation and themselves.

One pervasive message is that one should remain within one's chronological age group. A child's friends, interests, and abilities are expected to be on a certain level. However, gifted children develop faster than other children and have interests that differ from their nongifted peers, differences that continue through the school years (Bachtold, 1978). Many young, gifted children tend to have friends who are at their mental age level, rather than at their chronological age level. This tendency obviously corresponds to their ability to deal with greater abstraction. Older friends and advanced thinking levels encourage consideration of issues and topics in ways that differ from the considerations of classmates who are the same age. Gifted children raise sophisticated questions about topics that are ahead of their years, such as questions of morality, politics, and future problems. Reactions to such inquiries naturally vary. Questions raised about death by a 4-year-old may be cute. Similar questions by a 10-year-old or adolescent can provoke negative reactions.

"Be independent" is another message that is conveyed to gifted children. This message is usually tempered by the unspoken, yet dominant view that independence in thought is more desirable than independence in action. When a child interprets independence as going one's own way, the child is met by "sanctions against divergence," a problem of which children are very aware (Torrance, 1962a). Because independence and creativity are coequal parts of our definition of gifted behavior, the potential for conflict is increased. Gifted children's striving for independence is similar to that of the nongifted; however, for gifted children, there are more clashes with existent modes of thought and behavior due to their greater interests and advanced talents. Because gifted children have a propensity to move faster through various informational areas, these clashes happen with greater frequency. Many gifted children possess a sense of potential success that may propel them to more encounters with the status quo (Rice, 1970). From this point, one should not assume that gifted children are, on most issues, less conforming than others. Most evidence is based on rating whether or not a child is independent, and evidence gathered outside the laboratory in real-life settings under experimental conditions is rare.

Problems of definition further confound the issue. Independence is more than a reflexive reaction to social or situational moves, but it is less than a stage of life. Independence is conscious action to pursue a line of thought or to entertain a strange idea despite the sanctions against such thoughts or ideas. Thus, an independent child may follow a path well ahead of peers or forge a new path ahead of almost everyone. The likelihood of the latter possibility increases as children move into adolescence, as does tolerance for such movement.

"Be a balanced, well-adjusted individual" is another message broadcast to children. Some gifted children may well fit the notion of the "all-American" boy or girl, especially those who fit the portrait of giftedness constructed by Terman and his associates. Other gifted children definitely do not fit the well-rounded mold (Torrance, 1962a). The child who has one interest or several consuming interests is regarded in a questionable manner, (e.g., "She spends all her time reading" or "He is only interested in computers"). Being too involved in one thing, as some children are, is to be discouraged (Getzels & Jackson, 1962).

The ideal is to be a well-rounded and multifaceted person who is sociable and has social facility and numerous friendships. The concern for sociability is pervasive in school settings, as well as in the home. There appears to be some ungrounded belief that happiness with self or in life is reflected primarily by the number of friends one has. For the gifted child who has time-consuming interests and is generally socially disinterested, not socially isolated, there is pressure to make friends. Given the restricted number of gifted peers and opportunities to meet gifted peers, this is a problem, especially if the child is sensitive to these concerns in others.

The gifted child's plight is paradoxical. If great interest in one area or more competency than peers in an area is exhibited, the child is moving toward being defined as imbalanced. Because imbalance is to be avoided, the child is encouraged to work on weak areas, such as handwriting or making friends, and to neglect strong areas. One might conceptualize this situation as asking a child to deny his or her special qualities or uniqueness. The process of systematically moving a child away from strengths toward relative weaknesses is likely to generate tension and confusion. A more reasonable position is to encourage and nurture interests in children, rather than sending the message that they are unacceptable as they are. For example, encouraging gifted children to attend residential summer programs can do wonders to broaden interests within a community where they feel emotionally safe and accepted for who they are (Cross, 2004).

The American meaning of excellence is a mixed message for gifted children. American society cannot seem to come to a consensus about the values of individual excellence and social equality (Gardner, 1961; Tannenbaum, 1998). The situation takes form in the way we tell gifted students to do well in intellectual pursuits, but not too well, and always be humble. The admonition to be humble applies to all pursuits, including athletics, but it seems to be especially important to cognitive pursuits. The message is relatively clear: To be socially attractive, one should be slightly above average and downplay one's accomplishments.

Children who are gifted develop more rapidly than other children in specific areas. Therefore, they are automatically likely to stand out from their peers. As the years go by, the discrepancy between a gifted child's accomplishments and those of nongifted peers become more obvious. When these accomplishments are visible in subject areas in the school, the child is freed from the problem of doing too well. A variety of responses, ranging from increasing one's obvious strengths to concealing them, are possible. Choices along this continuum may be necessary at varying ages for children with special strengths. In adolescence, it becomes a greater problem for the studiously inclined gifted child because intellectual pursuits become less acceptable to peers (AAGC, 1978; Austin & Draper, 1981; Coleman & Cross, 1988; Tannenbaum, 1962). A child with multiple interests and talents or less-advanced development would be likely to experience relatively fewer problems in the typical school milieu.

Some gifted children who are very creative may experience the problem of doing too well in a different manner than other children because of the way they express their competence (Torrance, 1962). If advanced ability is manifested in the form of a highly unusual product, it may be evaluated as a sign of low ability. Likewise, the display of humor by gifted children may be interpreted as a sign of insufficient seriousness, rather than as a sign of giftedness. In the updated edition of Goertzel and Goertzel's *Cradle of Eminence* (2004), Goertzel and Hansen mention Woody Allen's experiences in a gifted classroom: "The strictures of the classroom did not allow him to express himself in his own way or to use his imagination in his lessons. Instead, he expressed his creativity by becoming a troublemaker and was dropped from the gifted classes" (p. 314). This example illustrates how a lack of recognition results in labels such as "deviant," "troublemaker," or "clown," which are replete with their own role considerations. Baum and Olenchak (2002) also noted the possibility of gifted children being misdiagnosed and given labels (such as Attention-Deficit/Hyperactivity Disorder) that do not serve them educationally.

The admonition to be humble requires special mention because it places special demands on gifted children. Most children, gifted or not, deal with the issue of being very good in some situations. The problem is especially taxing to gifted children because they are more likely to do well in one or more areas than other children are. To ask gifted children to deny their competence when confronted with real evidence of it is to ask them to create a fictional view of themselves. In some ways, it contradicts the often-expressed moral values of truthfulness and openness. Given gifted children's heightened awareness of moral issues, they are faced with a series of dilemmas ranging from frank expression to concealment, and from pride to shame. Perhaps the general confusion many gifted children have about themselves is tied to this problem.

In sum, the messages transmitted to gifted children about what constitutes social attractiveness and desirability are mixed in that they propose contradictory values and relative standards of behavior. The gifted child, due to advanced abilities, comes into frequent conflict with messages about age-appropriate behavior, independent thought, social adjustment, and excellence. The problem of growing up gifted is coming to terms with these expectations and other messages contained in the roles described in the following sections.

Gifted-Role Messages

Sources of conflict come not only from the general mixed messages transmitted in American society, but also from the roles gifted individuals are expected to fulfill. There is a gifted role that sets specific patterns of behavior and expectations, and gifted children are expected to behave in a manner befitting the role. Thus, there is conflict to whatever degree the child departs from the role expectancies in particular social contexts.

Role relationships involve the communication of messages. Unlike the discussion of general mixed messages, which were ambivalent, the messages associated with the gifted role are much clearer and they encompass a more definable set of expectations. When these messages become rigid, a stereotype exists. Such stereotypes are created by overgeneralizations or superstitious thinking on the part of others, including peers, friends, parents, teachers, and experts on the gifted (Casserly, 1979). These overgeneralizations become problems for gifted children when they have to deal with the faulty, stereotypic expectations of others and begin to internalize or accept them. While it is difficult to specify the particular dimensions of a gifted stereotype, it is possible to describe some aspects of the gifted role and its associated characteristics.

One is the belief that gifted people do not study or work hard. It just comes to them; therefore, those who do study can't really be gifted. How this far-fetched notion ever came into existence is unclear. A brief reading of the biography of any gifted person reveals the implausibility of such an expectation. Nevertheless, some gifted children accept part of this notion because they see intelligence as an attribute of those who get high grades without working for them (Coleman, 1975). The separation of the expression of intelligence from persistent effort is pernicious. Many gifted children recognize that they spend time and effort in order to learn within a general area, such as schoolwork, as well as within specific areas of interest, such as chess or poetry. This confusing background of expectation makes it difficult for gifted children to integrate self-notions of ability and worth.

Another aspect of the gifted role is that gifted children are supposed to have multiple strengths. This notion may be called "the Terman stereotype" because it is an overgeneralization of Terman's findings. Holding to this notion lends one to expect that the gifted will do well in everything, an expectation that operates in different areas of a gifted child's life. So, for example, during the process of identification, typical questions emerge: "How can Jake be gifted when he fights with other children?," "Caroline is poor in math. How can she be gifted?," or, "Sam has little interest in what we do in class. How can he be gifted?" The common denominator in these questions is the implausibility that a poor student or an ill-behaved student can be gifted. The expectation for multiple strengths is also observed in comments about how children who have been identified as gifted perform in class, for example, "Josh never completes his spelling. He can't be gifted" and "Sarah has terrible handwriting and poor manners. What is she doing in that program for gifted children?" The common denominator in both situations is the expectation of multiple strengths in the gifted.

The expectation of multiple strengths also creates a series of limiting expectations that may be problematic for gifted children. These negative expectations mean that gifted children are supposed to be gifted all of the time. As a consequence of being gifted, a child may forfeit his or her right to be noncreative and the privilege of failing or having difficulty mastering something (AAGC, 1978). Imagine the pressure of having to perform successfully in all situations. Furthermore, being very good all the time implies that being depressed, disinterested, and unenthusiastic are inappropriate behaviors. In some ways, it is as if the presumption of strength carries certain expectations for the fulfillment of one's promise in terms of self and society. Writers on this topic are particularly concerned about gifted children's underachievement and their place as future leaders (Havighurst et al., 1958; Passow, 1979; Rimm, 1997; Silverman, 1993). Considerable discussion among professionals in the field concerns wasted talent and improper career choice, and the gifted role may circumscribe the range of careers deemed suited for the gifted (Rodenstein, Pfleger, & Colangelo, 1979). The expectancy to fulfill one's promise can, in inexperienced adults, become overstressed, and such prescriptions for behavior can increase conflict in the lives of gifted children.

Some aspects of the gifted role are definitely negative in that the gifted are expected to behave in an antisocial or asocial manner. For instance, Freeman (1979) reported on parents who had difficulty conceptualizing their children as gifted because the children were happy. In addition, gifted children are often accused of being immodest, egotistical, isolated, snobbish, obstinate, verbose, argumentative, off-the-track, domineering, bizarre, pedantic, irrelevant, and overly logical. Interestingly, the actual behaviors that are interpreted as deserving of these negative labels may conversely be interpreted as expressions of positive traits, such as inquisitive, persistent, independent, and creative (Rice, 1970; Webb et al., 1982; Whitmore, 1980). It is possible that the behavior of gifted children is interpreted in a negative manner when their identification is public knowledge. For example, the nongifted are often permitted to be immodest about their accomplishments, while gifted children have less license to act immodestly because, after all, they are gifted. We will return to these possibilities when the stigma of giftedness is discussed.

In sum, the role of giftedness creates expectations for behavior. The child who is gifted is faced with developing a personality and dealing with the pressures resulting from the role expectations of giftedness.

Gender-Role Messages

Among the many roles in one's life, the influence of one's gender role is pervasive. Boys and girls are expected to behave in mutually exclusive ways. The less a child is sex-typed in behavior (or the more androgynous the child's behavior is), the greater the problem for either sex. Children who have interests within traditional roles experience less conflict.

Much recent literature has been concerned with the role of women and how traditional roles work against the emergence of gifted women. The American female role has subtle expectations for women (Blaubergs, 1978; Reis, 1998). Women are not expected to achieve as much as men, even when the work produced is identical. Furthermore, they are expected to succeed with less frequency on a given task. Such expectations are related to the perception that femininity is equivalent to passivity, noncompetitiveness, and selflessness. A girl with interests and abilities beyond these expectations must deal with some formidable obstacles in the development of her giftedness (Wolleat, 1979). These obstacles include consequences of gender socialization, societal stereotypes, and the relationship between career development and achievement and other life roles (Hollinger, 1991). Further, many gifted females struggle with feelings of self-doubt in their abilities and may tend to attribute their successes to external factors such as luck or chance, rather than their abilities (Callahan, Cunningham, & Plucker, 1994).

Rodenstein et al. (1979) noted the following direct conflicts between female-role and gifted-role expectations:

1. A gifted student is expected to develop his/her own talent and to be selfish in energy use, yet a woman is expected to be selfless, nurturing, and giving.

2. A gifted student is expected to be active, exploring, and assertive in his/her demands, yet a woman is expected to be passive and dependent.

3. A gifted student is expected to pursue a challenging career, yet a woman is expected to run a household.

4. A gifted student is expected to develop his/her talents, yet a woman is expected to put her career second to "her man's" career.

5. A gifted student is expected to succeed in the traditionally male-dominated careers, such as science, medicine, math, and business, yet a woman is expected to be feminine. (p. 385)

These statements strongly suggest that gender-role considerations and gifted-role considerations may interact to produce increased conflicts for gifted girls. While many of these conflicts still exist, the language used to discuss these issues and the context of the issues themselves have evolved. Awareness of these issues and the development of promising methods of guidance for helping gifted females deal with their conflicts have also evolved (Kerr, 2000).

In recent years, research attention has begun to focus on gender-role expectations for males, as well, evidenced in published case studies of male students from diverse backgrounds (Hébert, 2002; Hébert & Beardsley, 2001). Also, a number of books (e.g., Kerr & Cohn, 2001; Kindlon & Thompson, 1999; Pollack, 1998) and articles have recently been written that explore males' experiences. In their overview of gender and giftedness, Kerr and Nicpon (2003) noted special issues associated with giftedness in males, ranging from gender-role socialization (e.g., boys are discouraged from participating in play activities considered "feminine"), to the ramifications of gifted men feeling pressure to conform by choosing traditionally masculine careers, rather than pursuits such as arts and music (see also Goertzel et al., 1978; Kerr & Cohn; Wolleat, 1979). More about gender roles is described in a later section of this chapter on managing identity.

Summary

The gifted live in a world filled with expectations for behavior, and the interaction between their developing abilities and these expectations is a constant source of conflict. Gifted children need to maneuver through a contradictory web of exhortations about how they should behave. The gifted role and gender roles present special conflicts for children because they tend to obscure the child as an individual. To learn and develop oneself in these circumstances is difficult, and guidance counselors can help children find themselves by recognizing the dynamic nature of the situation.

TRAITS AND GUIDANCE PROBLEMS: AN INTERACTIVE VIEW

The interactive position stressing advanced development and social expectations as a basis for guidance is different from looking at adjustment problems relative to specific characteristics of the gifted. The interactive position is sometimes hard to follow because one tends to think of specific traits leading to specific problems. The interactive position plays down these traits and highlights the interpretation of behavior in social context. However, the practice of listing specific traits associated with problems brings certain clarity to discussing intervention.

In this discussion, positive traits and attendant problems are seen as points of conflict between the gifted individual and the world. Several authors have done an excellent job of listing those traits (Clark, 1992; Rice, 1970; Whitmore, 1980). Table 5.1 presents some of these traits and categories of social expectations that differ from other such conceptions. It does not include specific descriptions of problems because such a list would hide the fact that traits have different meanings to others at various points in a person's life and in different contexts.

The social values attributed to the traits, not the traits themselves, are the problem. For example, being independent is not a continuous irritation to others in the environment. Independence has a different meaning when gender role is considered, such as independent young women being considered antisocial. When there is a small list of traits that refers to a narrow time frame, such as elementary school, then the relationship between a trait and a problem is easy to conceptualize. When the list expands in number of traits and in time frame along with a corresponding increase in interpretations, overlaps are created among the traits and the associated problems. This overlap raises questions about the meaning of the traits and their utility as harbingers of potential difficulties. The point can be illustrated by placing trait names on a set of index cards and concomitant problems on another set of cards. Mix the cards and try to match each trait to the appropriate problem. The result is confusing and unsystematic.

The sorting task illustrates the limitation of the trait-problem approach, namely, the difficulty with the definition of trait and of problem, the association between traits and problems, and developmental changes over time. Therefore, the trait-problem approach is not presented. Nevertheless, it is useful because it points out that advanced development is exemplified by a loose configuration of behaviors. The approach taken here is to view the development of giftedness as a continuous interaction between developed abilities and social expectations, both of which are constantly changing. This point becomes clearer as one tries to understand the experience of being gifted.

Managing Identity

Children who are gifted must deal with more instances of conflict in their lives than the nongifted because their advanced development in general and in specific talent areas does not coincide with certain role expectations for behavior. Furthermore, they may be required to play an extra role—that of the gifted—that nongifted children do not have to play.

These circumstances make it difficult for gifted children to come to an understanding of who and what they are. The problem for the child is fashioning an emerging identity in the midst of conflicting social demands (Cross, 2004). The child needs to develop an appreciation that the problem exists more in the environment than in him- or herself. Because this sophisticated notion is beyond the abilities of gifted children, at least until adolescence, the child has the problem of ascribing meaning to feelings of differentness. Many gifted children seem to sense differentness, but they cannot attach a clear

173

meaning to it (Coleman & Cross, 1988; Cross, Coleman, & Stewart, 1993). The meanings that develop are not predetermined.

The school can play a useful role in helping the gifted child. The guidance function requires an understanding of the process of dealing with differentness. The literature on giftedness presents models of development, but the models are not relative to the issue of understanding differentness.

In the following section, a descriptive and heuristic model is proposed on how a gifted child, assuming the goal is accepting his or her identity as a gifted person, manages the special problem of differentness. This model was influenced greatly by the work of Goffman, especially the work on stigma (1963).

Stigma of Giftedness

Being different is problematic in that differentness prevents, or at least interferes with, full social acceptance and personal development. Because the social group forms the context in which differentness may exist, it is the social value judgment of difference that is at issue. The sources of potential problems for gifted individuals are the same signs of advanced development that are interpreted both positively or negatively depending on the social context. Comprehending the meaning of differentness for the gifted requires recognition of the fact that people possess implicit notions about how characteristics (real or imagined) of others interfere with normative social interactions. The gifted introduce an element of differentness because their characteristics disrupt, or they are believed to have the potential to disrupt, normal social interactions.

The "tainted" characteristics, in general, may or may not be readily visible. For example, physical deformity is fairly visible, but personality variables such as addiction, intellectuality, homosexuality, radical political belief, and giftedness are less visible. All of these characteristics suggest that the person is dangerous or is capable of atypical behavior, which calls for unusual behavior on the part of others. After all, how can one so young possess such knowledge? It is not right. It is strange! As a gifted child put it, "Being one of the smarties isn't easy. Actually, it is on the same wave length to some people as a man with only one leg, it's a social handicap and everyone stares" (AAGC, 1978, p. 23). The less visible characteristics of giftedness are potentially discrediting to the child because such information may become known and change their normal social interaction into something less normal.

To gifted children, there is no doubt about feeling different. As one put it, "Now, let's be blunt: We are not 'normal' and we know it; it can be fun sometimes but not funny always" (AAGC, 1978, p. 9). However, feeling different should not be equated with feeling one is gifted. "I've never felt gifted" (p. 7) or "I never considered myself to be gifted or talented, but I try hard to enhance my own natural abilities by bettering them" (p. 5) are examples of statements where the definition of self is not that of giftedness, although it appears that these children recognize their differentness and deal with it. They also recognize that people overgeneralize about them based upon their having "extraordinary abilities."

The feeling of differentness may be magnified by the school. Gifted children, like all children, learn how to be students within their particular school's environment. They pay attention to the messages sent to them by students, teachers, and other adults. Thus, children's understanding of how to be gifted students is learned in the environment in which they are schooled (Cross, 1997b). The feeling of differentness may also be magnified by special programs. Chan (2004), for example, noted that the growing number of programs for gifted students in China increased educators' concern with the psychological effects on students of being labeled gifted and coping with giftedness. Indeed, he noted a connection between social coping strategies and psychological distress in his study of 527 Chinese gifted students. The presence of an official label is likely to raise issues about differentness that one had previously been able to avoid. Identification can also lead to increased social isolation. Consider these statements on the term *gifted* written by gifted children:

> Probably the only single thing all twenty of us agreed on . . . in our lives was that we hate the word "gifted." It's flattering, it's pleasing, but it alienates us from friends. (AAGC, 1978, p. 4)

During a panel discussion on being gifted, a child said:

> I would like to comment on the word "gifted" in this sense. I mean, if a school were to be founded for the gifted, I would suggest . . . not calling it for the gifted because of social adjustment, that kind of puts somebody way above the clouds. (Stark & Stanley, 1978, p. 228)

As these quotations make clear, many adolescent youths feel strongly about being labeled gifted.

Giftedness is a special type of differentness because it alternately leads to praise for and condemnation of strengths. The case has already been made that social roles and messages cause problems and lead to conflict, for example, when the child who has "too much of a good thing" is required to be modest or is expected to perform well all the time, even in areas extending beyond his or her strengths. These general values are learned by gifted children, too, and can lead to feelings of self-hate (AAGC, 1978). If the gifted child is to reconcile these notions with recognition of differentness, then the child must adopt strategies that deal with these external exhortations about conduct while maintaining a sense of self. It is here that management of one's identity as different is paradoxical because one's strengths and failings are sometimes the same thing. It is alternating between praise and disdain for one's qualities that makes others' knowledge of one's giftedness threatening. In short, being known as gifted is potentially discrediting.

Gifted children must contend with the fact that they do not know whether others have labeled or will label them as gifted. Further, they do not know if knowledge of the label will affect how others will deal with them. Gifted children do know from experience that both praise and disdain are possible. Given this situation, gifted children who desire social acceptance must be aware more continuously than other children of their effect on others, peers, and teachers and be prepared to respond to the behavior of others accordingly. The child knows from experience that "when you exhibit extraordinary abilities, other people tend to exaggerate them" (AAGC, 1978, p. 31). Thus, others often unrealistically expect gifted children to be constant achievers. A gifted child may experience great difficulty in learning something, but the degree of difficulty is not recognized by others. A gifted child may be greeted with amazement when a task is difficult for him or her to accomplish.

The problem of managing one's gifted identity is a real one for a child who has received a lot of recognition. The child has limited opportunity to counteract faulty impressions imposed by others because of reduced social contacts and preconceptions. As one child stated, "They've heard of me but they don't know me in person; they've read the reviews and think they've read the book" (AAGC, 1978, p. 20). This occurrence is similar to the problem celebrities have in that they are known for their achievements, not for themselves. The public assumes they know a gifted child's interests, which is particularly problematic in adolescence when others assume that the high-ability student is not interested in sports, sex, or parties. Gifted children with less public recognition face this same problem. When the gifted child is able to break this cycle, he or she is likely to hear, "Hey, you are really an okay person!" This remark clearly implies that an alternate expectation was held. It is another indication of the tentative nature of gifted children's social acceptability.

The problem of differentness is continuous throughout a child's life, reaching its apex during adolescence, when the internal pressures to develop conflict with the social expectations of peers and teachers. Given the notion of discreditability, the child has numerous opportunities to manage the information people have. The extent to which a child engages in strategies to minimize discreditability may be an indication of successful adjustment. For many, the process of managing one's identity begins in early elementary school.

Upon school entrance, knowledge of one's differentness becomes apparent as the opportunity for comparison with others increases. It is through comparison with others that much self-knowledge is possible (Coleman, 1975). In elementary school, the problem of differentness is minimal because the developmental tasks are less focused, the latitude for acceptable behavior from peers is less restrictive, and the notion of self is still being developed. Nevertheless, recent research has indicated that gifted students at the elementary level often confront stressful situations and must develop coping strategies to deal with them. Swiatek (2002) reported the use of social coping strategies by gifted elementary school students, and Preuss and Dubow (2004) reported that gifted fifth and sixth graders use more problem-solving strategies than typical students to deal with daily stressors.

In junior and senior high school, the problem of managing one's identity becomes acute for the gifted student. At this stage in life, the developmental tasks become sharply focused, the range of acceptable behavior from peers becomes narrower, and the implications of one's ability and differentness can be grasped. It is in adolescence that the gifted student is faced with the conflict of developing abilities in opposition to demands for socially acceptable behavior (Coleman & Sanders, 1993). In a study that asked special-program graduates to reflect on their past, Bachtold (1978) reported that the secondary school years were "the worst of school," with intellectual starvation and alienation from peers being the primary problems. This is consistent with reports on adolescence by gifted adults (Goertzel et al., 1978; Roe, 1953), but it is not consistent with Terman's and others' research (Tidwell, 1980). This discrepancy may be due to the way attitudes are measured.

In a survey of approximately 1,600 10th graders in an urban California school system, Tidwell (1980) used a series of standardized measures of self-concept, self-esteem, locus of control, and several questionnaire-type scales on school attitude, self-concept as a learner, and a general survey she developed on interest and activities. The results on the standardized tests showed that the gifted had comparable or higher-than-average (the norm) feelings about themselves. However, on some of the questionnaire data, Tidwell reported a surprising finding: two thirds of the sample perceived themselves as "unpopular." Another unanticipated finding was the gifted students' hesitancy to admit having special talents. The willingness to admit to unpopularity and the reluctance to admit special abilities fits the gifted role (Coleman, 1985a). These admissions are opposite of what one might expect a nongifted child to report. That is, a nongifted child would tend to deny unpopularity and claim special abilities. After all, the strengths that the gifted students knew they possessed were the same things that led to their unpopularity.

In retrospect, adults who are gifted may be able to reflect on the role their strengths played, while children who are gifted cannot. To adults, their adolescence stands out as a time when they were confronted with difficult choices in managing their identity in the face of peers who devalued their abilities and their popularity being diminished compared to what it was in elementary school (Austin & Draper, 1981; Coleman, 1975). The pressure for choices or compromises between one's own interests and peer values is fraught with conflict and danger. Ziv (1977) described the dilemma for the gifted child in these terms: "He can adopt the same perceptions and interests as his peers and probably abandon his intellectual interests and scholarly achievements, or he may ignore his peers' preference and continue as he is" (p. 34). Because neither choice is satisfactory, the problem of managing one's identity is never finished; it continues throughout the course of adolescence as individual needs and priorities change with the social situation. The problem of managing one's identity was captured by one gifted girl:

As I sit in a classroom of a small town high school, I am listening to the teacher begin a lecture for the day. He asks a question regarding the assigned homework, Chapter 25 in our book. I raise my hand and respond correctly to his query. He continues to ask questions and I continue to answer them. After a couple of rounds I begin to look around sheepishly to see if anyone else has his hand raised. No one does so I answer again. I hear annoyed mutterings from my classmates. I just know they're thinking, "She thinks she knows everything." So in a futile effort to conform and satisfy them, I sink down in my seat just a little and let the rest of the questions slide by. The teacher becomes angry that no one has read the assignment and feels he must repeat the chapter. And another day is wasted. So goes it, and unfortunately, too often. As a result, I do not feel challenged nor do I attempt to be when I find myself in such a class. One alternative, which in my school is extremely limited, is to sign up for those courses which are designed for people planning to major in that specific area. But alas, not enough teachers, nor enough money in the budget for books or supplies. So suffer, kid! (AAGC, 1978, p. 24)

The Teacher's Reaction

Managing differentness is not only a factor in the gifted child's relationship with peers, but also in the child's relationship with teachers. Teachers, like gifted children, have grown up in a society that conveys mixed messages about excellence and equality and the expectations of behavior in certain roles. Our knowledge of the influence of these messages on interactions with gifted children is limited.

Teachers, in general, seem to favor education for the gifted. Rubenzer and Twaite (1979) surveyed 1,200 teachers and found that they strongly favored special provisions. In an earlier study, Smidchens and Sellin (1976) found that teachers enrolled in college courses saw the gifted as "positive to teach, but not a high priority for service" (p. 111). Teacher conception of giftedness is indirectly indicated by the literature on teacher nomination and identification of gifted children reviewed in Chapter Three. Teachers have a nebulous view about the gifted. They tend to identify children who do well in schoolwork, many of whom are not gifted, using the IQ criterion. Teachers are frequently surprised by actual selection results.

The precise dimensions of the teachers' view of the gifted is unsettled. House (1979) provided some preliminary evidence in her study with people training to be teachers of gifted children. The 24 subjects rated students in a 150-word adjective checklist. Teachers checked many more favorable than unfavorable adjectives and rated girls more favorably than boys. In addition, children under 12 were evaluated more favorably. Two adjectives emerged as unfavorable descriptors of typical gifted children: *argumentative* and *opinionated*. The favorable descriptors were not enumerated. In another study,

Smidchens and Sellin (1976) asked 116 teachers enrolled in college courses to respond to a trait list in which only two traits were positive. The responses indicated that the gifted cannot generally be described as having negative characteristics, except for some minor dispositions toward the aggressive behaviors of showing off, bullying, or fighting. It is not clear how the subjects defined giftedness.

On the basis of limited evidence, it is difficult to discern whether or not this generally favorable attitude of teachers is revealed in their direct interactions with children. Verbal expressions of beliefs are not the same as active expressions of beliefs. Given the fact that teachers are supposed to like children and favor individualized education based on individual needs, it is probable that their verbally expressed beliefs about gifted children are skewed in a positive direction. However, active expressions may be otherwise, especially in light of repeated reports from gifted children of the resentment and hostility teachers have toward them (AAGC, 1978) or from parents repeating what their children say (Freeman, 1979). As part of a larger project, Whitmore (1980) reported that, in interviews, teachers revealed discomfort and irritation at the behavior of gifted children. This situation should not be interpreted to mean that gifted children face a relentless series of rebukes from teachers. More often, children feel their differentness is highlighted by unnecessary teacher praise or by using their performance as a standard for others to emulate. Gifted children interpret this as rejection; at best, it is unthinking behavior on the part of the teacher. Other actions in which teachers engage, such as insisting that all work missed while out of the classroom in a special program be made up or that all schoolwork and homework be completed, can be interpreted as signs of rejection, as well (Coleman, 1985a).

On-Grade Behavior

In order to understand the problem for gifted children and their teachers, it is necessary to return to the underlying problem for gifted children: the incongruity between their developmental status and role expectations. Teachers tend to think of on-grade behavior in terms of attentiveness, skill level, knowledge level, and compliance to rules. The closer a child is to on-grade expectations, the less conflict he or she might experience.

Unfortunately, the gifted child cannot meet these expectations. The passage of time brings maturity and knowledge. The gifted child, at varying rates in different areas, rapidly develops beyond the typical on-grade expectations. The student's advanced interests mean there is less likelihood of being attentive to already acquired knowledge. Acquired skills make it difficult to comply with usual classroom procedures. For many gifted children, development at the time of school entrance is already beyond grade level. Small discrepancies become magnified as the child passes through school. The further one outdistances his or her peers, and even teachers, in specific curricular areas, the more different he or she appears and the more his or her attention is directed toward managing that differentness. Children with single abilities, especially nonschool abilities, have different management problems than children with multiple abilities, some of which are school-related. Children who are identified as gifted by the school have experiences that differ from gifted children who are not identified. Most of the information available is on the identified group.

Working With the Teacher

The major problem in managing differentness with teachers is presenting oneself in such a way that the teacher does not get angry, defensive, sarcastic, or neglectful. There seem to be two aspects to this problem. One is the reality of advanced knowledge in an area, and the second is the reality that one is not advanced in every area or in all facets of a single subject. Both of these aspects will be considered.

The child with advanced knowledge is functioning below the instructional level because the material being covered is known. Making it obvious that the work is known may engender negative reactions. Some teachers make sarcastic remarks, while others assign busywork. The child can handle this situation by asking for more advanced work or sitting back and waiting for something more interesting. As one child has said, "I do my best to maintain tranquility between myself and the teacher" (AAGC, 1978, p. 30).

A particular problem is evident for the gifted child who is enthusiastic and involved in a particular subject area. The child mistakenly thinks the teacher is equally interested and fascinated by the subject and offers creative interpretations in the area. Because these offerings are the ideas of exploring children, they tend to be unfinished and inexact—and sometimes outlandish. The teacher who is generally irritated by this behavior can respond to these explorations with ridicule and sarcasm instead of encouragement. Torrance (1962a) documented these reactions and speculated on the long-range effects of them on the growth of creativity. However, the reaction by teachers to advanced thinking and interests need not be actively negative to make the child feel rejected. As one child noted, "I wish teachers would explain more fully; they don't like insatiable appetites!"(Cohen & Frydenberg, 1996, p. 192).

In environments such as this, boredom is likely to ensue and students learn that being passionate about learning is not valued in school; in fact, it may be counterproductive. Knowledge of the most rudimentary facts and processes are believed to be more valued and welcome in the classroom than advanced knowledge or skills. Compliance, complacency, a friendly outgoing personality, and enthusiasm for working in groups are valued, as are in-the-moment, teacher-led activities and "going along." Add to these in-class perceptions the mixed messages gifted students often perceive, such as "all kids are gifted," "no kids are gifted," "gifted kids have unfair advantages," and "gifted kids can get it on their own," and you have the confusion of a gifted child's perceptions. Children learn these lessons even when they are unintended (Cross, 2004).

Gifted children need to be appreciated, but expressions of interest by the children seem to work against this need. Some teachers have the mistaken notion that gifted children do not need their help (Casserly, 1979).

The second reality—that a child may not be equally advanced in many areas or proficient in all parts of a given area—is difficult for the child to manage. Children frequently report that teachers are surprised at how such a smart person could make such simple mistakes. This reaction may contribute to the difficulty many gifted children have in dealing with subject matter they cannot learn quickly (Zaffrann & Colangelo, 1979). The reaction of teachers to a child's errors can be embarrassing, especially when the child is singled out for attention. In one case, a child described the teacher's reaction to missed work as "wrath"; in another case, the child saw the teacher as a "bully" (AAGC, 1978). What is confusing to the child is the inattention and lack of challenge on the one hand and the overattention to error on the other hand. Many children simply keep a low profile in order to "maintain tranquility." When combined with the pressure from peers to conform, it is clear that gifted children experience more conflict than other children (Delisle, 1992).

PROBLEMS FOR SPECIAL GROUPS

How does membership in a subgroup affect the problem of working with one's differentness? *Subgroup* in this sense refers primarily to the category presented in Chapter Three, the nonmodal gifted, and other categories, including the creative gifted and the special-ability gifted. The effect on development of multiple labels (e.g., female culturally diverse gifted) is not known with any precision. The appearance in recent years of increased attention to some subgroups implies that membership in one of these subgroups does affect experience. Much of the literature concerning subgroups deals with identification and instruction, but there is relatively little information on the experience of being gifted (Coleman & Cross, 1988). Of course, research that does cover the nonmodal gifted experience suggests prior identification.

Culturally Diverse Gifted

The culturally diverse category is broad with much variety, which makes it difficult to make generalizations about students' experiences being gifted and how they manage their giftedness. The variables of racial diversity, socioeconomic deprivation, and geographic isolation can be used to define culturally diverse children (Baldwin, 1977; Ford, 1996). Each variable, in turn, can be further divided into subunits based on variables such as ethnic background or environment (urban or rural). These variables correlate to produce a great assortment of circumstances that affect giftedness. Nevertheless, the term "culturally diverse" refers most frequently to specific ethnic groups: African Americans, Puerto Ricans, Hispanics, Native Americans, and Asian Americans.

While the variables hinder generalizations and require attention to the individual, it is possible to state the major issue common to all: Does being gifted affect the usual pattern of social interaction so that the child has problems gaining full social acceptance in a special environment? If the child's abilities and interests are in tune with subgroup values, then the issue of cultural difference in terms of managing identity is largely irrelevant to this discussion. Such a child should be considered as having experiences similar to mainstream gifted children. In other words, one should not assume that all culturally diverse gifted children face added adversity in their lives (Kitano, 1997a). On the other hand, if a child's abilities and interests are not synchronous with subgroup values, then he or she must face the problems of gaining acceptance of his or her giftedness by both society and by members of the subgroup. Acceptance by general society seems to be a more pervasive problem than subgroup acceptance, as inferred from Frasier's (1981) conclusion that culturally diverse gifted children are "more like gifted children in the general population than they are like their nongifted peers in their own . . . group" (p. 54).

The extent of the problem of managing giftedness and its dynamics is far from obvious. Assuming that being different from a group elicits social comparison processes (Festinger, 1954), then many culturally diverse gifted youths must come to terms with their differentness. Evidence on the phenomenon is difficult to locate when describing giftedness in culturally diverse children. The literature on cultural difference, reviewed in Chapter Three on identification, emphasizes strategies for nurturing these children and focused discussion on the issue that behavior taught by a culturally diverse group might be antithetical to conventional notions of giftedness (Ford, 1996; Kitano, 1997b; Torrance, 1977). Ford and Harris (1999) noted that, for some gifted minority students, an incongruity between the values, attitudes, and behaviors of their home and those of the school may result in considerable stress. This stress may be exacerbated when cultural differences are ignored or trivialized by the school. Some information may be obtained from biographies (Frasier & McCammon, 1981), films (Hébert & Speirs Neumeister, 2001), and novels (Potok, 1972) detailing the clash between ability and notions of accepted behavior in a cultural group.

It would appear from the general tone of the literature that culturally diverse gifted children have greater problems developing a clear idea of their abilities and fighting off feelings of alienation and inadequacy. More research on this issue is clearly needed.

Gifted Women

It is axiomatic that women and men are different. While Simpson (1979) has hypothesized that women pass through developmental stages in a manner that differs from the way men pass through the same stages, others have proposed a different developmental path altogether (Gilligan, 1982). The concern here is whether or not being female and being gifted results in a special set of experiences.

Terman's studies showed that women chose to use their abilities in occupational areas that differed from those chosen by men, even though they had high ability, and they, too, suffered from no diminution of abilities with age (Oden, 1968). Other researchers have shown how achievement patterns in science (Adams, 1996; Kelly, 1978) and in math (Benbow & Lubinski, 1997; Fox, Brody, & Tobin, 1974) are not readily explainable by ability differences. These findings suggest that young women display their high ability in ways that differ from young men. It may be that gifted women attach different importance to various aspects of living, such as family, occupation, or friendship (Sears, 1979). For example, Fleming and Hollinger (1994) noted that many of the women in their Project CHOICE study chose to reduce or interrupt their careers for family responsibilities. These acquired values, when expressed in terms of life choices, mean that gifted women experience life differently than gifted men. Reflecting on talent realization in gifted women, Reis (2003) commented, "There is not a clear path for any of us [gifted and talented women], as our lives and creativity are both more connected with our love for our family and our friends and are more diffused than the lives and creativity of our male counterparts" (p. 155).

In the earlier discussion on sex roles, the conflict between being female and being gifted was presented as a battle between the gifted role and the female role in American society. It would appear that successful gifted women have worked out some accommodation between these roles because their personality characteristics tend to be androgynous (Bachtold, 1976; Bachtold & Werner, 1970, 1972, 1973). One implication of this is that the discrepancy between the female role and the gifted role is greater and more problematic than the discrepancy between the male role and the gifted role, although data on this implication are very imprecise. On the other hand, researchers such as Raffaele Mendez (2000) have noted androgynous self-perceptions in gifted girls and the positive psychological qualities associated with this personality characteristic.

Nevertheless, gifted women still face obstacles in developing their abilities and must navigate around them to manage their identity as highly able people (Reis, 1998). The obstacles for women are not biologically based, but rather socially imposed and therefore institutionalized in the social setting:

1. American women expect lower educational achievement in general and in specific areas such as science (Kelly, 1978) and math.

2. Success of women in America is attributed to effort and luck, rather than the presence of high ability.

3. There are insufficient numbers of female role models in nontraditional occupations in life and in fiction.

4. There is a lack of institutional support directed toward the development of talents considered to be sex-typed.

5. Career development requires a long-term, uninterrupted commitment that is inconsistent with women's expectations for marriage and family (Hoyt & Hebeler, 1974).

Although other obstacles might be listed, these five represent much of what is in the literature (Kitano, 1998; Shore et al., 1991). Taken together, these obstacles exert considerable pressure on women to meet social expectations and deny their abilities. These pressures are partially responsible for the encouragement and acceptance of attitudes that work against the fulfillment of the promise indicated by women's high abilities. They also influence how gifted women are likely to manage their feelings of differentness.

Horner (1972) conducted a study with college-age women and men in which the subjects completed a story based on a fictional statement about a woman in medical school who was at the top of her class. After analyzing the imagery, Horner concluded that women had a greater motive than men to avoid success. Thus, the excellent performance of this fictional woman was accompanied by the women's descriptions of social rejection, unfemininity, and negative labels, including "unhappy" and "aggressive." The female subjects predicted that the fictional woman would intentionally lower her grades, worry whether school was worth it, get noticed only to help others with homework, drop out to get married, and help her less-competent boyfriend.

Of course, these are fictional predictions of the consequences of excellence. The extent to which these women would make use of these strategies in real situations is questionable. Nevertheless, these accounts of feminine behavior are reminiscent of strategies actually employed by young women (Kranz, 1975). Considerable research and debate has occurred about whether Horner's finding of fear of success is unique to women. Blaubergs (1978) cited studies that suggest that, as gifted girls advance from elementary to secondary school, they use different strategies for managing their giftedness. In one study, Kimball and Leahy reported that high school girls who were in college prep courses had more fear of success than girls in secretarial courses. In another series of studies, Baruch reported strategies of girls in 5th grade and in 10th grade that indicated that older girls may learn to cope with their fears (Blaubergs). Clearly, the social acceptability of girls among peers in general, and among boys in particular, is a continuing problem, one that is lodged in both male and female attitudes in American society. The gifted young woman's situation is somewhat paradoxical: She may have to devote more energy than males to gain recognition for her high ability and she may have to combat the negative evaluation of other females.

In case it is not obvious, the attainment of excellence is similar to the achievement of any goal. It is in the movement toward excellence that gifted women have some difficult chores because they must, in some cases, reject the female role or at least redefine it in some way. The following strategies gleaned from the research are indicative of what some women have done: (1) reduced the "masculinity of achievement"; (2) asserted their femininity by "marrying and then getting on with achieving"; (3) picked a partner with outstanding ability or drive in order to hide their own aspirations; or (4) selected a "feminine" occupation (Blaubergs, 1978). It is also likely that some gifted girls adopt behaviors that provide them with acceptable methods for being successful and feminine at the same time.

Gifted Students With Disabilities

Gifted students with disabilities are a heterogeneous group made up of individuals with a variety of handicaps, including learning disabilities, behavioral disturbances, and physical impairments. While giftedness can coexist with nearly any disability (Silverman, 2003), the primary subgroups of gifted students with disabilities are: learning disabilities, ADHD, hearing impairments, visual impairments, and intellectual disabilities (i.e., savants; Yewchuk & Lupart, 2002). Common learning disabilities in the gifted are sensory integration dysfunction, ADHD, auditory processing disorder, visual processing deficits, dyslexia, and spatial disorientation (Silverman).

Estimating the numbers of gifted students with disabilities in the population is difficult because of the heterogeneity of the group. In 1981, Whitmore noted that roughly 120,000–540,000 children might be in this group. Yewchuk and Lupart (2002) overviewed research reporting percentages of gifted students with disabilities that ranged from 2% to 9.2%. Estimating the proportion of individuals in disability categories, however, is far from precise. Conventional wisdom about large numbers of delinquent and disturbed people who are gifted is probably overstated (Lajoie & Shore, 1981).

The gifted student with a disability must handle two conflicting roles—being gifted and having a disability—that seem to be mutually exclusive. While empirical research on the management of differentness for these subgroups is limited, the phenomenon of gifted individuals with disabilities is mentioned in the gifted literature. For example, Goertzel and Goertzel's (1962, 2004) surveys of eminent men and women noted that many suffered from physical handicaps. Researching gifted students with disabilities is complicated by the dissimilarity among disabilities, which may mean the problem differs from subgroup to subgroup.

One should not assume that being gifted-disabled means having more limitations on development. It is possible that having a disability might make it more acceptable to be gifted because people want to believe in compensation—if you have lost one ability, nature will supply you with another, stronger ability, as the blind are believed to be compensated with heightened aural perception.

Other possibilities indicate that individuals with disabilities have social limitations on development. One such limit is "star-of-the-handicap" role. The person is viewed as a fine example of what people with disabilities can become. This characterization gives one a status that is less than full social

185

acceptance. The problem of managing differentness in the face of condescending attitudes is obvious.

Another limit is that special education or rehabilitation agencies may concentrate so hard on the deficiency that opportunity for maximizing strengths is restricted or not provided at all. For a person with a disability, getting support for development in strong areas or getting recognition from others poses real problems. Much research is needed before this phenomenon is fully understood.

Special-Ability Gifted

The special-ability category is another heterogeneous group that includes children with very high IQs, the highly creative, children with ability in visual or performing arts, and children with ability in social leadership. These subgroups are composed of people with more specific gifts, suggesting that they may experience differentness in a manner that distinguishes them from other gifted children.

Extremely High IQ

The extremely high IQ group has long been a source of interest (Burks et al., 1930; Gross, 1993, 2004; Hollingworth, 1942; Morelock, 1997; Terman, 1925). The Terman data showed that "the members of the gifted group whose IQs are in the neighborhood of 170, 180, or 190 tend to have considerably more difficulty in making social adjustments than do the more typical members of the gifted group" (Burks et al., p. 183). The increased number of problems was attributed to the relatively low frequency of peers with comparable mental abilities. For example, a 10-year-old child with an IQ of 170 would, very roughly speaking, find mental-age peers who were 17 years old. Thus, children of high ability are inclined to seek out play companions older than themselves. For example, the exceptionally and profoundly gifted children in Gross' (2004) study preferred the company of children 2 to 4 years older than themselves. The obvious discrepancy in physical development, however, may lead to adjustment problems. The 35 extremely high IQ children in Terman's study had few friends and tended to play alone. In her work with children whose IQs were 180, Hollingworth (1942) confirmed that the gifted played little with other children and spent considerable time in solitary pursuits.

Terman reported that 64% of his sample was rated as making fair to good social adjustments, while 36% was making poor to very poor social adjustments. Incidentally, more were rated as making excellent social adjustments. The extremely high IQ children were very similar to the typical gifted in terms of their expressed preference for spending time alone, with one person, or with several people. In short, they, too, liked social interaction.

The data suggest that extremely-high-IQ children may have problems managing their differentness. The high-IQ children's problems do not automatically lead to poor adjustment; they are able to come to terms with their differentness. Whether they experience their giftedness differently than other gifted children is unclear. Logic would suggest that it is harder for them to deny their difference than it is for other gifted children.

Highly Creative Gifted

The basic problem for highly creative gifted children is managing the uneasiness of being different in the face of the following obstacles:

1.   sanctions against divergency;

2.   alienation of friends;

3.   pressure to be well-rounded;

4.   gender-role norms;

5.   individual style of learning;

6.   attempts at tasks that are too difficult;

7.   seeking a purpose;

8.   having different values and motives; and

9.   seeking individual uniqueness.

The interaction between children's abilities and social norms can lead to problems for those who choose to continue to express their abilities and for those who repress those abilities. Both groups are of concern to guidance personnel (Colangelo, 1991; Silverman, 1993). Piirto (2004) noted that many creative children are considered odd because they do not feel to need to conform to social expectations. The pressures to conform, however, may produce conflict in these children. The children who cope with these conflicts work out strategies of "productive nonconformity" in managing their differentness (Pepinsky, 1960). The development of such strategies again illustrates that gifted children, including those who are highly creative, must manage their differentness from others.

Other Special Abilities

The last subgroup of gifted people with special abilities includes those with high ability in visual or performing arts (Winner & Martino, 1993), social leadership ability, and ability in specific academic areas. These special abilities involve better-than-average intellectual ability as measured by IQ tests with scores that are frequently less than two standard deviations above the mean and high ability in a specific area. How those with relatively special-

187

ized abilities develop is difficult to document because of the variety of abilities, the instability of some of these abilities over time (Burks et al., 1930), and the infrequency with which single abilities occur.

If the opportunity for developing special potential in receptive environments is basic to the emergence of special abilities (Feldman, 1980), then it is likely that the energy involved in managing differentness is directed more toward interactions with others of special ability, many of whom are adults of special ability, than at general problems of managing differentness. This may mean that, as adults, these people will have to learn interpersonal skills that they did not find necessary to develop earlier. For those who become "superstars" in their field, dealing with differentness is an even more complex situation. Although outside the scope of this text, some provocative notions can be found in works by Roe (1953), Zuckerman (1977), and Goertzel et al. (1978).

Summary

Given the different circumstances and patterns of abilities, children in each of the aforementioned subgroup experience being gifted in a manner that is relatively unmatched by other gifted children. Their experiences may give rise to different strategies for managing differentness. Whether this assertion is the case or not is hard to determine based on the available evidence. It is possible that the experience of being a member of one of these subgroups is so unique that the experience is described better within a discussion of giftedness in general. More research on these subgroups is certainly needed.

STRATEGIES USED IN THE PROCESS OF MANAGING IDENTITY

Recognition that managing identity is a continuous thread in the child's development has relevance for building a guidance program. This can be made obvious by examining the process in more detail and noting the strategies that children employ in different circumstances. Remember, the child is striving to maintain a sense of self amidst a feeling of differentness while developing within a world of conflicting expectations. The range of behaviors that can be deemed as coping efforts range from acting out to gain attention, to remaining quiet rather than revealing that one knows a correct answer to a question in a class, to underachieving in school, to the most serious effort at coping—suicide (Cross, 1997b). Figure 5.1 is an illustration of an Information Management Model (Coleman & Cross, 1988) developed to depict the lives of gifted students and how they deal with the mixed messages they perceive from society.

The Information Management Model (IMM) provides a useful visual to illustrate the temporal nature of the interactions gifted students have in and outside of school. Each period in the model is noted with the letters A, B, C and represents a time when gifted students make decisions about how to cope with their giftedness. The model is based on a social-cognitive framework

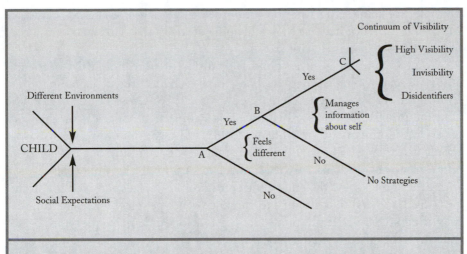

Figure 5.1. Information management model

Note. From "Is Being Gifted a Social Handicap?," by L. J. Coleman and T. Cross, 1988, *Journal for the Education of the Gifted, 11*, p. 44. Copyright ©1988 by The Association for the Gifted. Adapted with permission.

(Bandura, 1986) that assumes people are active agents in constructing their world. For example, their social goals are deemed important and related to their subsequent behaviors. The IMM is helpful in understanding the interaction between gifted students' perceptions of the expectations for them within their school environments and how they choose to cope with potential conflict.

To follow the IMM, one must read from left to right, first noting the gifted child approaching a specific setting or event (e.g., school, out-of-school activity) that, in the student's mind, carries social expectations. To raise children, parents and teachers spend a great deal of time and energy teaching them how to act/behave in different settings (e.g., school, church, in a restaurant). As the child develops, he or she comes to believe that certain expectations and social mores exist in school. Much of what is being discerned is how they should behave in this particular setting in order to be successful or to avoid pain. The extent of a gifted student's feelings of differentness from other students affect his or her behavior in school. In the IMM, if gifted students do not feel different (point A), then they will have little need to develop a system of social coping strategies. There is evidence that some gifted students do not feel different from their nongifted peers (Coleman & Cross, 1988; Cross et al., 1993; Manor-Bullock, 1995). However, this research indicates that this group is relatively small in proportion to the gifted population as a whole.

The next decision point (point B on the IMM) illustrates that there are gifted students who do feel different, but seemingly do not develop social coping strategies, per se. "This claim is arguable since many forms of coping strategies are quite subtle and may originate as a strategy and later become a common part of the child's behavioral repertoire" (Cross, 1997b, p. 191). For example, spending extra time on schoolwork (Tomchin, Callahan, Sowa, & May, 1996) can originate as a social coping strategy that later becomes a part of the child's regular behavior pattern.

Point C is where a gifted child feels different from nongifted peers and utilizes social-coping strategies that can be characterized as falling on a Continuum of Visibility (Coleman, & Cross, 1988; Cross et al., 1991). The Continuum of Visibility (see Figure 5.2) is a construct that draws on the work of Erving Goffman's Stigma Theory (1963). The continuum reflects that, as people act, they reveal social goals that range from standing out further from other groups of students (high visibility) to becoming invisible (blending in with other groups). At the end of the continuum is a place reserved for strategies (disidentifiers) that attempt to convince other people, by association, that the gifted student is really more like a group of students stereotypically not thought to be gifted (e.g., burners, dopers, skateboarders, jocks) than he or she is like gifted students (Coleman & Cross; Cross et al., 1991). Combined, the behaviors of gifted students in school mirror their self-perceptions about feeling different or the same, and how they choose to act in order to maintain as much social latitude as they desire. A more detailed depiction of the three positions on this continuum follows.

The Continuum of Visibility

The strategies children use in managing identity are roughly grouped along a continuum ranging from standing out among students (high visibility), to blending in among all students (invisibility), to becoming totally invisible (disidentifying; Coleman & Cross, 1988). A range of behavior is possible within each category, and it is the child who decides his or her visibility.

High Visibility

Strategies that fit the description of "high visibility" are those that permit others to see one's differentness. *High* is a relative term, meaning that giftedness is readily observable more than it is hidden.

Some children choose to flaunt their differences as if to say, "I'm different, so there." They use their differentness as an explanation for undesirable behavior, for example, a child defending his behavior by accusing others of envy. The differentness in this case provides a special license for outrageous behavior. Of course, this behavior may serve as a signal to attract others with compatible feelings. Being highly visible is also associated with what others describe as an overbearing, obnoxious manner. In older children, it may be related to getting attention; but, the strategy is more likely to be used by children who are unaware of, or generally unconcerned with, their effect on others. It is the eagerness to share information and pursue interests that is misinterpreted by others. Older children who are highly visible by being obnoxious or the class clown use such tactics to signal their feelings about being held to the slow pace and tight structure of the regular program.

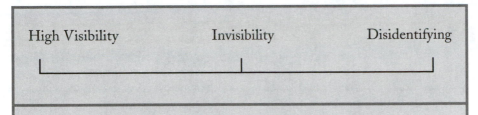

Figure 5.2. Continuum of visibility

Note. From "Is Being Gifted a Social Handicap?," by L. J. Coleman and T. Cross, 1988, *Journal for the Education of the Gifted, 11,* p. 44. Copyright ©1988 by The Association for the Gifted. Reprinted with permission.

Some children are visible because they are involved in many activities. These children seem to be everywhere. Their enthusiasm can be wonderful. For some of these children, though not all, the very breadth of their activities may be limiting in that they have little time to become outstanding at any one thing. In a sense, their proliferation of talents makes it difficult for them to choose to develop any single talent. Contending with this "embarrassment of riches" is hard (Gowan & Bruch, 1971, p. 35). The scope of the activities may reflect children's real interests and abilities. At the same time, it is a means for postponing decisions about their high abilities and their futures.

Gifted children may engage in highly visible behaviors, assuring their recognition. Paradoxically, when used to excess, these same behaviors may present potential problems. These problems occur when the child habitually uses a strength to the exclusion of other abilities. Excessive reliance on a logical, rational approach to solving problems is one example (Rice, 1970). Strength in the ability is not the problem; rather, it is the limits the child places on him- or herself through overreliance on the ability, which, in turn, precludes the use of other abilities appropriate for solving problems.

Some gifted children are less visible than others. There is little effort on their part to draw attention to themselves, yet they seem to accomplish things that have that effect. Their work is characterized by its completeness, as well as by its creativity. Some of these children seem almost frenzied in their efforts to start new projects. Other children, in a somewhat different manner, frantically scurry around in a disorganized fashion as they begin new projects. These behaviors may signify attempts to fight off depression, which commonly follows a major effort. Children need to be made aware that depression is not unusual and that it will pass. These behaviors are also indicative of the tendency to be simultaneously attracted to and fearful of moving into unknown areas where one is alone, unsure of the next step, and in danger of being a "minority of one" (Torrance, 1962a). Most gifted children experience this dilemma, but indicate their anxiety in less-obvious ways.

Being a gifted child ensures being in a state of discomfort more frequently than those who are not gifted. This discomfort is associated with their faster developmental rate in general and in specific areas. As they move through dif-

TABLE 5.2

Invisibility Strategies

- Don't carry a calculator.
- Miss a few answers on a test.
- Wear contact lenses.
- Don't volunteer answers.
- Don't admit a test was easy.
- When asked about accomplishments, be noncommittal.
- Avoid asking questions about moral or ethical concerns.
- Ask questions to which you know the answer.
- Go out on a date with a "dumb" kid.
- Don't tell your age if you were accelerated.

Note. From *Schooling the Gifted* (pp. 181–182), by L. J. Coleman, 1985, Menlo Park, CA: Addison-Wesley. Copyright ©1985 by L. J. Coleman. Reprinted with permission

ferent developmental levels, gifted children spend relatively more time in transition between stages than do nongifted children, who pass through fewer stages in the same period of time. If the transition between developmental levels is viewed as a period of instability and inconsistency (Feldman, 1980), then gifted children certainly must come to terms with discomfort. This point underscores the fact that managing differentness means dealing with feelings that have more to do with personal growth than with social attractiveness.

Invisibility

The strategies gifted children use to be "invisible" attempt to hide or minimize differentness. Invisibility strategies, or aspects of them, are used more often than other strategies, especially as the child enters the secondary school years. A common theme is to cover up or camouflage high abilities and advanced interests in order to appear to conform and "pass for normal" (Freeman, 1979, p. 252). These strategies are acquired over time as children experience the negative social value attached to differentness. Many of these values have been stated earlier in this chapter in the discussion of mixed messages, gifted roles, gender roles, and problems of special groups; they will not be repeated here. Instead, the general characteristics of the process will be presented to illustrate how children manage their differentness, or, in other words, camouflage their competence.

The reader should not assume that these strategies are fixed once they are acquired. The process of developing strategies continues until children understand themselves and the world well enough to move beyond many of these tactics. It is doubtful that all strategies will be abandoned because the social

TABLE 5.3

Disidentifiers

- Be seen with people who are not gifted.
- Ask silly or crazy questions.
- Tell jokes.
- Go out for extracurricular activities for which you have little talent.
- Be very pleasant.
- Claim a test was difficult.
- Feign interest in small talk.
- Make fun of other gifted kids.

Note. From *Schooling the Gifted* (p. 182), by L. J. Coleman, 1985, Menlo Park, CA: Addison-Wesley. Copyright ©1985 by L. J. Coleman. Reprinted with permission

reality is that giftedness is not quite normal or acceptable (Cross, Coleman, & Stewart, 1995).

The process of camouflaging one's competence takes various forms, which are reactions to the values discussed earlier and are dependent on the child's past experience. For example, a child can choose to become invisible by avoiding the display of behaviors that might point out differentness. Table 5.2 lists some examples obtained from conversations with students.

Disidentifying

The third position on the continuum reflects a gifted student's desire to present "disidentifiers" (Goffman, 1963). Here, the gifted child makes some effort to present cues to others that are associated with another stereotypical role that the gifted child perceives to be more acceptable than being thought of as gifted. Table 5.3 includes some examples of disidentifiers.

The effort to camouflage one's differentness becomes another matter when a child has been "officially" designated as gifted and placed in a special program. Knowledge of the effects of special placement is severely limited. The conditions change for the child because a select set of other gifted children are now available for comparison, and a set of implicit expectations about how gifted children should act both inside and outside the program are brought to bear. The management of one's differentness is complicated in that new obstacles and benefits are apparent. Many of the covering strategies listed in Tables 5.2 and 5.3 are still possible in a special program. One's notion of one's abilities, or differentness, is complicated by placement in a special program. It has been demonstrated that the narrower comparison group is related to lower self-concept scores, suggesting that the value of one's differences undergoes modification (Coleman, 1981).

193

The expectations within the special program may influence children's notions of the value of their differentness. A benefit of identification is that their giftedness is out in the open. Engaging in activities that are more abstract and age-advanced is now permissible. Others with similar abilities and interests can identify them, and special opportunities for contact are possible. In this sense, visibility is provided for them. On the other hand, a new problem is created because of the expectations embedded in the gifted role. Gifted children soon learn that the regular program and the special program are different contexts for displaying their abilities. In the special program, individual styles of learning and expressions of unusual ideas are permitted and encouraged, whereas in the regular program, these same behaviors are cues to differentness and the children avoid them. A particular problem is that no other program provides the opportunity not to be gifted. One wonders if the gifted role takes over some children's lives.

A program of guidance must recognize the signs of children managing their differentness by making themselves more or less visible under certain circumstances if that program is to intervene meaningfully when unsuccessful strategies are adopted. A single strategy or combination of strategies may be unsuccessful when a child's growth in areas of personal strength is inhibited. An understanding of this notion can be clarified by looking at successful strategies.

Successful Strategies: Implications for Guidance

A successful strategy (1) enables a child to continue to develop areas of strength, usually by using those strengths; (2) is directed toward meeting a perceived, reality-based need; and (3) does not continue to a point where future growth is stunted. The extent to which a strategy approximates these idealized criteria defines its success. Any strategy that denies strength and limits development is considered to be less successful. Throughout the chapter, the strategies have not been labeled as good or bad because they are in a state of flux as the child learns different ways of dealing with the world. Knowledge of the strategies used by adults is too limited to be helpful.

In essence, coping with one's giftedness means accepting that the rewards of giftedness are worth the loss of being normal and the loss of complete social acceptance. A group of gifted children commented on the situation:

> For what it's worth, when we wonder whether or not being gifted is worth the extreme depression, excruciating sensitivity, inability to relate, and/or tendency to over-analyze, all of us vote "yes." The elation that comes with rapid comprehension, the wide range of understanding open to us, the self-satisfaction that comes from developing a talent, and the ability to empathize easily do make the "lows" bearable. So we hope that you will come to feel that way, too. (AAGC, 1978, p. 37)

Children and adults have been developing strategies for many years to be themselves and to live in the world. A guidance program should note successful strategies as prototypes for other gifted children to emulate. Some interesting statements about coping can be found in *On Being Gifted* (AAGC, 1978) and are paraphrased below:

- When you feel down, get involved in a hobby, one of many.

- Reading is a great vehicle for leaving the limits of school, entering another's exciting thought, and learning.

- When life seems futile, go to sleep. Upon awakening, you will see a way out.

- As you switch from feeling talented to feeling like a failure, try to do your best. Don't be too serious about yourself.

- We all have limits.

- By understanding yourself, you can relate to others. Beware of too much self-study.

- Learn to listen to others. Relax, you don't have to be up on all the latest jargon.

- Find a person who takes an interest in you and who wants to help— a parent, teacher, friend, or guidance counselor.

- Learn to do things peers value, but don't give up yourself.

- Make your own decisions and take your own initiative, no matter what your situation is.

- The basis of all successful learning is self-discipline.

- Most defeats in learning or changing something are only temporary.

There are other means of coping, as well. Some children resort to using jokes and being class clowns to win acceptability (Torrance, 1962a). One child reported that she imagined writing down her feelings on a piece of paper whenever she became angry at someone at the school. Marie Curie, the famous scientist, described hiding her emotions with laughter: "This is something I learned to do when I found out that creatures who feel as keenly as I do, and are unable to change this characteristic of their nature, have to dissimulate it at best as much as possible" (Bachtold, 1980, p. 244).

Evidence of another sort comes from a study on how gifted college women function in groups. Pepinsky (1960) studied how women who were judged to be successful, independent, and innovative behaved in campus activity-oriented groups. The following are some of the strategies used by these women:

- modifying one's language so that ideas were seen as contributing to the group;

- offering constructive criticism;

- showing belief in something the group could respect;

- listening to others and not invoking feelings of personal threat;

- earning credit with the group over time by good service;

- sticking to the task and avoiding "personality" issues and self-promotion; and

- being aware of when to time remarks and actions.

These strategies were apparently learned by these women without direct instruction, but a study of their backgrounds revealed that they had an opportunity to learn to be independent. These statements are strategies that gifted individuals have employed to manage their differentness. It is striking how conventional the statements are. They may reflect how difficult it is to discuss or describe in general terms how one copes with life. Of course, these statements are indicative of problems of developing oneself in the real world. It may be that these strategies are what a successful program of guidance should realistically be expected to accomplish. One strategy that seems to be very difficult to modify is described in the next section.

Underachievement: An Unsuccessful Strategy?

The underachieving gifted child has been a source of concern to educators of the gifted for many years. Chapters in general texts on the gifted have been devoted to the topic (Delisle, 1992; Gallagher, 1975; Gold, 1965; Peters, Grager-Loidl, & Supplee, 2000), and there are texts focusing on the problem alone (Raph, Goldberg, & Passow, 1966; Rimm, 1990; Whitmore, 1980). The prominence and persistence of the topic justifies its place as a special guidance problem. Surprisingly, it is a difficult topic to discuss, even though there is a sizable amount of research and opinion.

The complexity of the problem of the underachieving gifted is seen in the confusion over the definition of the term. All definitions assume that it is possible to estimate accurately what a gifted child should achieve (Gallagher, 1975). Not only is there a dispute over that assumption, but there is also disagreement over what appropriate discrepancy between estimated and actual performance constitutes underachievement (Gowan, 1955). Reis and McCoach (2000) noted that three themes emerge from the many definitions of gifted underachievement. Underachievement is depicted as (1) a discrepancy between potential (or ability) and performance (or achievement), (2) a discrepancy between predicted achievement and actual achievement, or (3) as a failure to self-actualize. If the situation is not already confusing enough, there also are problems in specifying the ability areas in which one should be achieving, such as academic subjects, general academic achievement, art, music, leadership, and problems in specifying the characteristics that consistently distinguish underachieving children from modal and nonmodal gifted children. One final uncertainty is that discussion of underachievement mixes the issue of low scores inhibiting identification with low scores signaling untapped potential. Hitchfield (1973) has discussed the problem of estimating achievement levels for any given level of potential.

This confusion makes it obvious that, when someone uses the term *underachievement*, it is always a good idea to check out what he or she is assuming. This discussion will focus on the issue of untapped talent in children already identified as gifted using the conventional meaning of underachievement—unsatisfactory academic achievement in terms of one's estimated school learning potential as indicated by an IQ score—while recognizing its imprecision. The issue of underachievement in other areas is recognized as an interesting area of speculation and potential research. However, given the difficulty of getting a handle on the parameters of the conventional meaning, discussion of other areas is premature. The research on underachievement has been concerned with understanding the causes and evaluating treatment programs. Interpreting these findings is complicated by the lack of comparable groups from study to study. Despite these problems, many children belong in the category.

Several conclusions are warranted on the basis of the research. First, there is a general consensus that underachievement exists. Studies, using our loose definition, have reported that underachieving children tend to have a pattern of personal and familial characteristics that may be said to be relatively independent of socioeconomic factors and the nonmodal groupings of gifted children. These characteristics have been summarized in various combinations by different authors (Baker, Bridger, & Evans, 1998; Gallagher, 1975; Peters, Grager-Loidl, and Supplee, 2000; Shore et al., 1991; Whitmore, 1980). Underachievers, who are usually boys, tend to have some of the following characteristics: low self-esteem, feelings of alienation and hostility, deficient academic skills, disturbed family relationships, and negative responses to school organization and curricula. These characteristics interact in complex, unknown ways to produce underachievement. McCoach and Siegle (2003), in a study of 56 gifted underachievers and 122 gifted achievers, noted that the underachieving gifted students differed from the high-achieving gifted students in attitudes toward school and their teachers, motivation and self-regulation, and goal valuation. Their academic self-perceptions, however, were not different.

Other researchers have spent less time searching for characteristics associated with underachievement and have concentrated instead on eliminating it. Intervention efforts have been made in two general directions: counseling and modifying the educational environment. Evidence for the success of either approach has been less than positive (Raph et al., 1966; Shore et al., 1991). The prevailing view is that, by secondary school, the probability of effecting changes in underachievement is diminished. Although no approach or combination of approaches has yielded consistent results, effective intervention seems to involve three factors: (1) early identification and guidance; (2) a supportive teacher or counselor; and (3) remedial-skills training in a sympathetic atmosphere (Gowan et al., 1979, p. 265).

In 1980, Whitmore provided new evidence on the modification of underachievement in elementary children in her book *Giftedness, Conflict, and Underachievement.* She defined gifted children in a manner consistent with a loose definition of the term and detailed the causes of underachievement as aspects of handicaps, including learning disabilities, behavioral disorders, emotional disturbance, neurological handicaps, and minimal brain damage, as well as an aspect of the paralyzed perfectionist. Her approach was to place these children in self-contained classes for intensive instruction in personal development, social skills, and academic skills. Counseling was viewed as an integral part of the classroom program because the classroom is the context in which the problem exists. Evidence of the effectiveness of the 2-year program was primarily in the form of anecdotal records, which revealed improved functioning in class, in school, and at home; measures of self-perception that tended to corroborate these observations; and measures of academic performance that showed improvement. In sum, the mixed results of this project offer some provocative insight into the dynamics of underachievement and the difficulties, which persist over time, in effecting changes.

As a whole, the literature on underachievement is unsatisfactory (Delisle, 1992; Shore et al., 1991). Problems of definition and measurement abound. Information on etiology and intervention is confused. The meaning of underachievement seems to elude our grasp. It is more than getting poor grades, an issue with which it is usually confused. Rather, underachievement is a problem of unfulfilled potential. While this is a concern one could have about all children, it apparently has more import for the gifted because of the loss of talent to American society. Some of the confusion about this concept may be traced to an inherent conflict between the individual child's desire and the gifted role.

Given the state of the field, a reconceptualization of the phenomenon of underachievement is needed. Whitmore's (1980) work implies that underachievement of the gifted fits first within the general problem of underachievement and then within the problem of being gifted. This second problem is in keeping with the emphasis in this chapter on gifted children managing their differentness. Underachievement for many gifted children is likely to be one means of camouflaging competence.

Although there is no desire to end this discussion of underachievement on a pessimistic note, the research indicates that altering the behavior of under-achievers is easier said than done. The simple and disturbing fact is that, by the secondary school level, a pattern of underachievement is not likely to be broken unless the student is lucky enough to get into a situation where an empathetic person with whom he or she can identify to some degree exhibits behaviors the student can try to emulate.

DEVELOPMENTAL MODELS AND GUIDANCE

The presentation on managing giftedness has the advantage of stressing the interaction of the individual and the environment in terms of a series of interlocking and overlapping conflicts in the gifted child's life. Guidance procedures need to attend to this phenomenon. On the other hand, the presentation has the deficiency of downplaying the long-term developmental processes operating within children as they grow through the school years.

The Place of Models

The construction of a meaningful guidance program cannot ignore models of development, nor can it occur in a theoretical vacuum. In this section, models that are relevant to guidance and counseling are examined. Practices that develop from the unifying perspective of developmental models are more likely to have a cumulative effect over the long term because theory brings coherence and direction to our efforts. Theory is especially useful because "we know very little that is specific about the genesis of guidance problems of the gifted child" (Gowan, 1977, p. 283).

Three models, along with their advantages and disadvantages, are presented in this section. The models are the Universal Developmental Model, the Behavioral-Cognitive Model, and the Domain-Specific Developmental Model. Other models could have been chosen, but these three have implications for guidance. They are useful for comprehending the problems of being gifted and for effecting meaningful guidance techniques. Only one of the three models has been particularly visible in the literature on guidance of the gifted. The other two models contribute new perspectives on the development and nature of giftedness. The models have heuristic value.

The Universal Developmental Model

In actuality, there is no model with the precise name of Universal Developmental Model (UDM). Rather, the UDM is intended to symbolically integrate various stage models of development that are commonly referred to in discourse on the development of gifted students: affective development (Erickson), cognitive development (Piaget), moral development (Kohlberg), conative development (Perry), and transcendent development (Dabrowski). Our purpose is neither to review each model, nor to recommend one over another. Each has made a significant contribution to our knowledge of human development. Our intent is to clarify what the five models have to tell us about the development of gifted and talented individuals. These models have much in common, which leads to the name Universal Developmental Model. We borrow the idea of melding developmental models from Gowan (1972) and Simpson (1979), and the idea of universality from Feldman (1980).

Development is viewed as "a staircase-like parameter of hierarchical nature with discrete levels" (Gowan, 1972, p. 25). Using an analogy from physical science based on water changing from its icy state to its gaseous state, Gowan postulated that developmental stages lock in and accumulate energy periodically in order to transform the person into a new stage of development. One characteristic is predominant at any stage, and the preceding stages of that theory are relatively less important.

A person's upward movement is never smooth; each emergent stage incorporates and transforms the previous stage. Gowan (1972) argued that transition from stage to stage proceeds according to five components:

1. *Succession*: a fixed order of hierarchical stages.

2. *Discontinuity*: a discrete stage with relatively stable characteristics.

3. *Emergence*: the faint outlines of a stage seen in an earlier stage become obvious.

4. *Differentiation*: the shift to a new stage with fixed characteristics.

5. *Integration*: a synthesis of all elements in the stage.

These characteristics of development contribute to the notion of universality. Because these components are believed possible for everyone, universality is an appropriate descriptor for these models. Children are assumed to be impelled to master tasks relevant to each stage. The fact that this is supposed to happen across normal circumstances and culture is another feature that makes the five theories universal. An interesting aspect of the models is how development is never really finished.

When a person does not move from one stage to the next, problems develop for that individual, such as negativity, guilt, or alienation. In a later writing, Gowan introduced the term "developmental dysplasia" to describe problems in development. The two types of dysplasia are "an absolute dysplasia, in which there is a disparity between the age of the individual . . . and the different stage he is actually in" and "a relative dysplasia in which there is a disparity between the cognitive and the affective stages. These are never more than two stages apart" (Simpson, 1979, p. 376). The idea of uneven development has been modified and extended recently by theorists interested in asynchrony. This idea, which is embraced by interpreters of Dabrowski's ideas, has combined the idea of unevenness with a special kind of emotionality (Silverman, 1993).

The UDM has implications for understanding the development of giftedness and the strategies children employ to manage their differentness. The following are some of its advantages:

1. Aspects of development are integrated so that cognitive, affective, moral, and conative build in conjunction with each other.

2. Attention is focused on the predominance of certain needs at different stages (the universal).

3. The invariant sequence is outlined so that sequence is more important than chronological age (the universal).

4. The concept of uneven development is normal.

5. Development is anticipated to go beyond the school years.

The following are some of its disadvantages:

1. Important differences among individual theorists is not evident. The evidence on each theory is far from complete.

2. The concept of state and stage transition as it applies to these theories is not well understood. It is too difficult, if not impossible, for a teacher to determine at what stage a child is functioning.

3. Intervention strategies are difficult to formulate based on the model because the definitions are too general.

4. Too much of the model is concerned with guidance issues that are beyond the range of the time a child is in school.

The Universal Developmental Model, on balance, offers a perspective on the overall development of children. For gifted children, it indicates the tasks in which they are likely to be advanced, points out the direction in which they are growing, illustrates where development might be impeded, and provides few specifics for practitioners.

The Behavioral-Cognitive Model

The second perspective on the gifted, the Behavioral-Cognitive Model, is rarely cited in the literature, which is surprising given the amount of literature on learning and counseling that refers to behaviorism. Although the reasons are far from obvious and have not been researched, it may be a result of a dislike for behaviorism as a theory of human development in general or a result of the apparent inability of the model to account for the development of creativity, problem solving, or intelligence in a manner that makes sense to people in gifted education. Whatever the reasons, the model is considered here.

The Behavioral-Cognitive Model is a convergence of cognitive theorists, who generally talk about hidden mental structures or processes that account for human behavior, and behavioral theorists, who generally talk about observable, external events that account for human behavior. The model seeks to bring these two schools of psychology together by recognizing that unobservable events such as cognitions determine what people do; by recognizing that equipotential for accomplishing certain tasks may not exist throughout one's life; and by recognizing that external events are powerful influences of human behavior (Stone, 1980). The Behavioral-Cognitive Model accepts the import of the mediational process (nonobservable, cognitive effects) on how people cope with life, yet continues to emphasize the place of environmental conditions (contingencies) on perception and behavior.

The Behavioral-Cognitive Model was conceptualized by Stone (1980) as revolving around several characteristic themes:

> The world of experience is mediated by the person who experiences it; the person primarily responds to mediated information about his or her world rather than to the physical world; such information is more or less actively constructed by the person; however, such information is generated within a person-environment context in which the thoughts, feelings, and activities of the person are related to the stimulus environment; information is the basic factor in most human learning; the response system of the person, including cognition, emotion, and motor behavior, are interdependent. (p. 4)

These themes show the interdependence of the person and the environment. The theory sees emotion and intellect as being linked. The person is seen as an active force in personal achievements and habits. The problems that children experience are seen as consequences of the way they see the situation and the way their responses are received in the situation. Changes can be made in behavior and in feelings about oneself by modifying cognitions in regard to these themes.

One example illustrating the behavioral-cognitive approach was formulated by Williams and Long (1991). The model presumes that people can take an active stand in shaping their own lives by deliberately analyzing their attitudes and achievement and applying behavioral-cognitive principles. Williams and Long consider that certain areas of personal concern, such as interpersonal relationships, academic achievement, health, creativity, assertiveness, and stress come under the purview of the model. They see the model as being consistent with American ethics of responsibility to oneself and of the ability to make choices. People can take more control of their lives and become who they wish to be through awareness of the events and situations that influence their behavior. Taking more control, in Williams and Long's view, means learning how to modify one's own behavior. People have the ability to change most, not all, behaviors because most behaviors are situation-specific and mediated by thought.

The model describes a six-step process through which one can effect changes in oneself. The step-by-step model is a general outline and should not be interpreted to mean that all steps must be used. Williams and Long (1991) pointed out that changes frequently occur in the opening steps. The model follows the general notion that a person (1) selects personal behavior to change; (2) studies the circumstances in which desirable behaviors are infrequent; (3) records these instances; (4) alters the situations to avoid the undesirable behavior or becomes more aware of it by arranging consequences to encourage the desired behavior; (5) increases awareness of these consequences; and (6) continues until the desired changes have occurred. Throughout the process, it is important to record one's behavior.

In effect, this model presents a rational, organized strategy for dealing with specific problems at any point in one's life. Incidentally, it is interesting to note the similarity between this model and the descriptions of problem solving and creativity in the literature on these topics.

The Behavioral-Cognitive Model has several important advantages in understanding a person's behavior and in helping people understand their own behavior.

1. It emphasizes the interaction between person and environment in determining behavior.

2. It proposes a practical, definitive approach to modifying one's behavior.

3. It recognizes the active role one can take in self-development.

4. It recognizes that different environments (school, home, club, etc.) encourage particular kinds of actions and attitudes.

5. It is an optimistic system.

The Behavioral-Cognitive Model also has disadvantages:

1. It does not recognize that the potential for acquiring certain knowledge and skill varies at different times.

203

2. It does not recognize the existence of stages of development.

3. It treats all aspects of development, such as emotional, social, and language, by using the same procedures.

4. Most of the model is built on research with adults.

5. It does not deal with people coming to terms with their limits.

The Behavioral-Cognitive Model implies that a child's feelings of differentness and notions of abilities are a result of learning to interpret behavior through interacting with the environment. The interpretations and the associated behaviors are subject to change if the person follows certain procedures. In terms of counseling, the model assumes the person wants to change. Thus, the value of any change is really in the mind of the person.

The Domain-Specific Developmental Model

The third theoretical perspective, the Domain-Specific Developmental Model, or nonuniversal model, is a relatively new addition to the literature on child development and giftedness. The model may better be called the Feldman theory, after its originator (Feldman, 1980); however, it has been renamed to help differentiate it from the other theories presented in the section.

The Domain-Specific Developmental Model is a cognitive developmental theory that incorporates the concept of stages and the gradual increase of competence in a person. It departs from the Universal Developmental Model in that "to some extent it takes the stage out of the child's 'mind' and represents it as existing instead within a body of knowledge" (Feldman, 1980, p. 3). Thus, in order to discuss developmental stages, one must simultaneously discuss the child and the domain of knowledge and skill. Feldman believes that this position makes sense because it is unnecessary to argue for the existence of a whole structured stage (a fact that research has not been able to establish) that cuts across broad areas of human endeavor. In order to avoid confusion with the word usage, Feldman prefers the word *level*.

Feldman claims that developmental theories, as presently construed, are unable to deal with domains of knowledge and skills that are nonuniversal, that is, areas that are culturally based or subject-matter-based and comprise much of what children and adults are expected to learn in school and society. Examples of nonuniversal domains are reading maps, riding bikes, building bridges, and writing books. Developmental theories cannot deal with nonuniversal domains of knowledge because they assume that, for something to be developmental, it must be universally achievable by all people in all cultures; be acquired spontaneously without any special environmental circumstance; be in an invariant sequence where everyone starts at the same place, moves through all stages, and does not move backward; and be integrated in a hierarchical fashion according to transitional rules.

Together, these assumptions define developmental theory as being appropriate only for describing skills and knowledge that are inevitably learned by everyone. The four assumptions deny the reality that important changes in thinking occur in some individuals and not in others, and not everyone in a society masters the same fields of knowledge. Furthermore, nonuniversal achievements seem to occur in specialized environments. Do the gifted who accomplish nonuniversal achievement belong outside the realm of ordinary development because their achievements do not meet the assumption? Or should special qualities be ascribed to people who do nonuniversal things? Feldman believes that unusual accomplishments properly belong in the area of development and can be considered as such by retaining two of the assumptions—sequentiality and hierarchical integration—and discarding universality and spontaneity.

Feldman's perspective has important implications for guidance of the gifted. It has always been difficult to account for giftedness within normal development. Attempts to prove that gifted children move through universal stages any faster than normal children have yielded mixed findings. On the other hand, it has been demonstrated that the gifted move faster through different domains and produce more novel thoughts (Porath, 1996). In specialized circumstances and in specific domains, they may progress even faster than previously thought possible. An idealized set of levels can be specified within nonuniversal categories.

> These nonuniversal domains are not necessarily mastered at the highest (or even initial) levels by all children in all cultures, nor are they achievements which can be acquired spontaneously, independent of the environmental conditions prevailing in a particular culture in a particular moment in time. (Feldman, 1980, p. 8)

The nonuniversal categories may be tentatively placed on a continuum to illustrate how knowledge and skills move from the universal to the unique. The universal is knowledge and skills that everyone attains, and it meets the four assumptions of general developmental theory. The other regions on the continuum show that fewer and fewer people attain certain levels. "Cultural achievement" refers to the things that all children in a culture are expected to master, but not necessarily to the highest degree. Some examples in American culture are reading, writing, and understanding capitalism. "Discipline-based achievement" refers to skills and knowledge related to more specialized areas, such as chess or medicine, that are attainable by relatively fewer people. Discipline-based achievement can cross cultural lines. "Idiosyncratic achievement" is open to even fewer people. It is usually a specialty within a discipline that a person pursues independently, attaining high levels of mastery. Child prodigies fall into this category. "Unique achievements" are accomplishments that are novel for a given domain of knowledge or even initiate a new domain. These achievements are relatively rare, and relatively few people accomplish them.

Bound to this model is the idea that environmental conditions influence development, serving as catalysts for different levels. Ideally, environmental conditions that stimulate the development of levels of knowledge and skill should be identified. Feldman believes that conditions can eventually be specified for all these levels. At present, there is stronger information promoting universal and cultural achievements than idiosyncratic and unique achievements. This model makes no assertion about what happens when someone does not reach the next level. It does imply that transition through levels means the child must live in an unsettled state in order to move forward. The child in this situation has the potential to make more contradictory responses than a child who is not in the process of transition to a higher level. The child must also recognize that present strategies or understandings are inadequate for the situation and need to be changed. The conditions that could encourage such movement still need to be delineated.

The Domain-Specific Developmental Model has certain advantages that help gifted children come to terms with their differentness:

1. The development of outstanding talent belongs within the developmental domain.

2. The importance of environmental conditions to advanced development in varying domains is highlighted.

3. Progression through a domain means a child will be at a mixture of levels, producing contradictory responses.

4. The model implies that guidance must be affected when the help has expertise in the areas of a child's strengths.

5. The attainment of a level makes it difficult for a child to reconstruct being at a more primitive level.

6. The placement of creativity is within a domain and is an integral part of the mastery of that domain.

7. An explanation of how disparity in development can occur from domain to domain in one person is possible.

The model also has certain disadvantages:

1. The model considers affective considerations primarily in terms of how they may relate to cognitive development.

2. The meaning of disparities in an individual's development across different domains needs to be explored.

3. The model provides little direct information on how intervention strategies might be formulated.

On balance, the Domain-Specific Developmental Model draws attention to the emergence of high performance in specific domains and maintains that such behavior is in the province of developmental theory. Advanced development is seen to exist in a specific field of knowledge, as well as in the child. Environmental events interacting with ready abilities make advanced development impossible for all but a few people. The opportunity for experience is most important. It is possible that general high ability may work against unusual advanced ability in a specific area. It is also conceivable that advanced ability in different areas may be possible. Definitions of general high ability and advanced ability need to be refined.

Incorporating the Models in a Guidance Program

The three models on the development of gifted individuals were selected because they present perspectives that have implications for guidance programs in schools. These models have varying ranges of comprehensiveness. The Universal Developmental Model incorporates theories that account for the development of all individuals across broad developmental areas. The Domain-Specific Developmental Model describes general development in specific areas of knowledge and skill. Both models use the notion of stages or levels.

All the models, including the Behavioral-Cognitive Model, convey some idea of sequence, and they all note the presence of internal events; however, the Behavioral-Cognitive Model minimizes their roles, especially in broad areas of development. Although all three models offer hints about how gifted children experience life, they are not interchangeable, nor are they complimentary, even though the discussion may imply that they are. The models have different contributions to make to a comprehensive guidance program.

The Universal Developmental Model has an important place in a guidance program. It makes us aware of different needs and tasks to be accomplished at different periods in a child's life. However, the wide scope of the Universal Developmental Model makes its place within the context of the school difficult to comprehend. What is the place of this model in terms of a guidance program? Its very universality makes an excellent general guide for understanding how the needs of gifted children change and how development is not locked to age considerations. Furthermore, its universality serves as a reminder that curriculum development and administrative procedures should be fashioned in line with changes that all children experience. The Universal Developmental Model could be used more specifically if procedures for drawing definite correlations between a child's pattern of behavior in school, the universal developmental stages, and the school's objectives were available.

The Domain-Specific Developmental Model provides needed insight into development during the school years. The model views the development of specialized domains of knowledge and skill as an interplay between the child, the domain itself, and special environmental circumstances. The Domain-Specific Developmental Model removes much (but not all) of development from the unrelenting press of universal, internal processes and highlights the place of specialized environments in development. For example, the school is a specialized environment where culturally valued domains of knowledge such as reading, math, economics, and ethics are nurtured. The domains are developmental because a sequence of knowledge and skills gets increasingly complex and because mastery requires a child to pass through a series of stages. An implication for guidance is that sequence and hierarchical structure is present throughout the school.

The Domain-Specific Developmental Model is also useful for comprehending why the gifted are frequently referred to as being developmentally advanced in various domains. After all, many gifted children are recognized because they pass through the stages of a domain at a faster rate than other children.

The Domain-Specific Developmental Model also provides for a reconsideration of the meaning of uneven development. The model underscores the influence of teaching and opportunity on development. An explanation of how gifted children can be advanced in one area and not another is apparent. Furthermore, the model suggests why nonmodal gifted children show signs of advanced development in late in the elementary school years after they have had the opportunity to develop. With this theory, being developmentally advanced is not an aberration; it is a natural occurrence that can be explained to the child and to teachers.

The Domain-Specific Developmental Model also offers alternate explanations for several problems that gifted children face in managing their differentness. Some children are puzzled by limits on their development in a specific area of interest at a particular point in time. The limit exists in the domain of knowledge and not solely because of the child. Some children and some teachers are distressed when supposedly gifted children waiver between competence and sophistication in one area and incompetence and immaturity in another. Rapid movement through a domain places a child in stages of transition with more frequency. A characteristic of transition from level to level in a domain is a contradictory response to various situations. The persistence or commitment to mastering a domain may increase the frequency of transitions through stages or levels for gifted children compared to nongifted children over the same time frame.

The Behavioral-Cognitive Model offers little assistance to a child or counselor who is trying to understand developmental changes and problems. The model does provide a system for considering a child's behavior at a par-

208

ticular point in time and a strategy for affecting it. In a sense, the model can be thought of as problem-specific. Gifted children, in growing up, believe they are besieged by crises. Around fourth grade and at adolescence are especially worrisome times. Informing gifted children that "this, too, shall pass" is unsatisfying to the child and to the counselor, even if it is sometimes true.

The Behavioral-Cognitive Model points out that the way one thinks about oneself and one's environment is a powerful shaper of behavior. These factors are amenable to change, and if the child does not like the way life is at one time, then there are things that can be done about it. The child's choices may be restricted because of social and cultural constraints, thus it is up to him or her whether to go against, to circumvent, or to accept those limits at that time. The potential of the Behavioral-Cognitive Model to clarify the short- and long-term consequences of one's choices is important (Whitmore, 1980). The Behavioral-Cognitive Model also has the potential to use gifted children's strengths in analyzing and generating many ideas that will help them learn to deal with their problems.

A Program of Guidance

This chapter has advocated that a major task for gifted children is managing their differentness while growing up (developing) in a culturally based context (school). The problem for educators of the gifted is designing a guidance program that accounts for the problems of managing differentness. A good program of guidance and counseling in school will assist gifted children in coping with conflicts and help increase the probability that they will reach their life goals. A guidance system is concerned with nurturing giftedness. It is only a part of a total program for gifted children. It is a system that is neither exclusive nor inclusive of a total school program. The guidance system plays a vital role, but not the only role, in a gifted child's schooling. Guidance considerations are important in formulating effective identification and meaningful instructional systems. It is unfortunate that school personnel tend to divide themselves into separate and distinct roles to administer to these complementary systems.

A guidance system is the responsibility of the entire school staff; it is not the sole province of any one professional position. The allocation of responsibility across professional positions means that guidance is an ongoing process that is not confined to 20 minutes per week with the guidance counselor. While structured, planned sessions may certainly be beneficial to a child, meaningful guidance opportunities occur more frequently in spontaneous interactions through modeling and conversation.

A guidance program should not be confined to crisis-oriented situations. Developmental concerns and long-term planning should not be ignored. Planning and attention to developmental changes are crucial to a high-quality program. Guidance is assumed to be most effective when the overall school program is structured to minimize conflict and support personal growth and exploration. However, even the best-organized program will not prevent problems because the basis for many problems originates before the child comes to school or problems emerge as a result of circumstances outside the school. A well-organized program must deal with crises. Significant changes in personal development occur during times of crises or, at least, considerable discomfort. Counselors need to be able to help students profit from these crises.

The twin tasks of helping a child cope and helping a child expand his or her possibilities are major undertakings that can be in opposition when they reflect short- and long-term considerations. The possibility of opposition can be seen by realizing that guidance issues for a child can be categorized into three areas: personal concerns, academic (school) concerns, and career/vocational concerns. Personal concerns are those that deal with managing one's differentness and finding one's identity. They also include the normal developmental issues with which most children deal (e.g., puberty and separating from family). Many of these concerns continue throughout life. The successful strategies presented in this chapter highlight some of these concerns. The academic and career concerns are not considered to be continuous in this presentation. Academic concerns have to do with dealing with the school as a setting for guidance. Career/vocational concerns begin during the school years and continue beyond its time frame.

The discussion to follow will be confined to the school setting. The elementary and secondary years are considered separately. Preschool guidance is considered in the chapter on families. A somewhat different and more expanded guidance delivery system has been outlined by Safter and Bruch (1981).

The Elementary School Years

Entrance into school is an important time for children when they begin to appreciate their differentness (Coleman, 1985a; Cross, Coleman, & Stewart, 1993; Goffman, 1963). Opportunity for comparing themselves to others has previously been limited. The sense of self that emerges may have long-term effects on development.

Guidance at the elementary level is less clearly defined than at the secondary level because the child's abilities and interests are not well developed. Guidance is delivered in an indirect manner (Strang, 1960). Teachers should take the opportunity to use typical class activities to help gifted children construct an accurate picture of what their strengths, limitations, and possibilities are. Instructional activities should provide opportunities for exploring interests, discovering new interests, observing the differences between people, and interacting with other children.

In general, gifted children in elementary school have a positive attitude toward school and other children (Gallagher, 1975), thus the later development of negative attitudes can be attributed to their school experiences. One problem for gifted children is that their behavior is often interpreted as being negative, rather than positive (see Table 5.1). The major guidance problem for school personnel is understanding that gifted children's strengths are often interpreted negatively because the expectations for behavior are too narrow to accommodate gifted children's individual differences. Unless these expectations are eliminated, or at least modified, school life is likely to be a negative experience for gifted children. At the center of elementary school guidance is the discrepancy between the child's developmental level and the institution's norms. The ensuing conflicts have been cataloged in depth. Action must be taken to deliver appropriate guidance to the gifted with attention to problem areas.

It is also important for school personnel to consider the social milieu of the school and classroom through the eyes of the child. Often, the teacher and other school personnel have quite divergent views of what it means to be a student or a gifted student and what the social expectations for them are. Moreover, students hold a wide variety of opinions about what they think being a student means and how they should behave in various school settings. Therefore, talking openly about the expectations for students can help them feel more comfortable in the school (Cross, 2004).

Academic problems. The primary procedure for solving academic problems is to adjust the instructional level to the child. Let him or her proceed at a rate that eliminates unnecessary practice. Being asked to learn skills that are prerequisites to more complex skills that have already been mastered is deadening to a child (e.g., asking a child who can already read to learn the correspondence between letter and vowel sounds). Flexible scheduling is needed, as well as support for teachers who are willing to modify their programs.

A challenging program of instruction is an obvious, simple, yet powerful means of avoiding the development of poor study habits, inattention to detail, dislike for school subjects, conformity, and boredom. Exposure to alternate ways of looking at phenomena and learning independent study skills are also recommended. The essence is that the child maintain a zest for learning.

Personal problems. Gifted children need to learn that they are not alone and that others experience many of their feelings. Group discussions, values-clarification exercises, creative dramatics, and learning centers can do much to counteract feelings of aloneness. The emphasis is on appreciation of others' and one's own differences.

Having the opportunity to work or play with other gifted children seems to alleviate some of the pressures a gifted child feels. For example, gifted students often report feeling different from other students, except when they have time to be together. When together, they often comment on the profound sense of relief of knowing there are other people like themselves who have many similar interests and qualities (Cross, 2004). In late elementary school, with the approach of adolescence, the need to have a friend to talk to without having to moderate one's enthusiasm and abstractness seems to be especially important to children.

Attention should be paid to the overuse of a special strength by a gifted child in a manner that can be self-limiting over time, such as overreliance on logic, easy verbal explanation, quick memory, or the creative, funny answer.

The "paralyzed perfectionist" (Whitmore, 1980) is a special concern. Children sometimes need to be shown their impact on others and alternate ways of behaving. Puppetry and sociodrama are useful techniques for examining one's behavior and experimenting with new behaviors. Books describing the problems of growing up provide an excellent vehicle for guidance (Frasier & McCannon, 1981).

Career and vocational problems. Guidance in careers and vocations at the elementary level is frequently overlooked by school personnel. The opportunity to see the long-term implications of one's interests is part of this area, and other guidance areas provide important complements to it.

Efforts should be made to have children come into contact with people who have chosen a variety of careers. Whenever possible, these models should transcend sexual, racial, and occupational stereotypes. Visits to potential career sites beyond the fire station and post office are needed. The chance to see the enthusiasm and excitement of people in a variety of careers is important. Parents are often excellent sources of information.

Another aspect of guidance in this area is students' learning when to go along and learning when to raise questions in order to effect change. Such lessons are crucial to later independence and adjustment.

In sum, the elementary school years are an important time for guiding the gifted child because they set the stage for subsequent development. Specific guidance or counseling techniques relevant to teachers may be found in the discussion on instruction later in the text. Whitmore (1979) has provided a good discussion of discipline.

Secondary Programs

Guidance at the secondary level differs from guidance at the elementary level in that service is relatively more direct and the counselors are frequently more available to assume a more visible role. It is at this level that developmental acceleration in general and specific areas becomes most obvious, fewer special programs are available, questions of career choice are raised, and the internal and peer pressures for being socially acceptable are heightened.

Within these circumstances, a guidance program should help adolescent children maintain a perspective on who they are and where they are going. The need for good guidance at the secondary level is unquestionable when one considers that gifted children acknowledge this period to be the "worst of school" (Bachtold, 1978). The delivery of good counseling is not an easy task when one remembers that the range of individual differences among gifted children increases each year. Drews (1964) was cognizant of this fact and proposed that gifted adolescents be categorized into types. Her research revealed that three types—the creative intellectual, the studious, and the social leader—

TABLE 5.4

Profiles of Adolescence

Type Profile	Kind of Achievements or Motivational Emphasis
Creative intellectual	Drive to deal with intellectual and philosophical matters, to be both contemplative and independent. Oriented toward scholarship, theoretical, aesthetic, complex, humanistic, and original approaches.
Studious	Drive to perform, in outstanding manner, in the areas defined by parents and teachers as "school learning." Strong desire to get high marks and to measure up to the expectations of those in authority.
Social leader	Drive to acquire power and money, a need for social acceptance by peers, and a desire to be popular and to dominate and to engage in entrepreneurial activity. Strong interest in creature comforts.

Note. From "The Creative Intellectual-Style in Gifted Adolescents" (p. 21), by E. M. Drews, 1964, *Being and Becoming: A Cosmic Approach to Counseling and Curriculum* (3rd Report of Title VII, Project # 647-I, National Defense Act of 1958, Grant # 7-32-0410-140, Cooperative Research Project No. E-2, Contract SAE 9101 5-0400-2-12-1), pp. 21–22. Copyright ©1964 by the Department of Health, Education, & Welfare.

could be found when gifted high school students (IQ 120+) were given the opportunity to identify themselves (see Table 5.4). The studious comprised 60% of the sample, and the others approximately 20% each.

The differences among the groups in number and in motivation imply the need for different strategies in terms of academic and career and vocational counseling. The creative intellectual type needs assistance surviving in a world that does not encourage diversity and commitment. The studious need help in pursuing their interests against the prevailing peer values and help in moving toward more self-direction in learning. The social leaders need counseling in order to come to terms with the responsibility of leadership and the validity of intellectual pursuits.

Academic problems. The guidance considerations at the secondary level focus on assisting the student in obtaining a background that will promote later growth and study.

Advancement within specific subject areas for which the student has competencies is important for the prevention of alienation toward school.

213

Acceleration occurs more frequently in science areas than in social studies areas. Consideration of early college admission and grade skipping should not be dismissed. Recognition of special talents in various domains of knowledge is to be encouraged, as well as a realistic assessment of abilities.

Selecting from choices within the school is difficult for children with multiple strengths and abilities. Fortunately, inappropriate choices are not beyond repair. Out-of-school or extracurricular activities provide opportunities for the pursuit of special interests more than the regular school curriculum, with its timebound structured blocks of learning. Advocates for gifted children need to push for such opportunities.

Unfortunately, it is often in these special situations, rather than in school, that gifted children encounter adults who share a thirst for learning and an understanding of the problems one faces in trying to master a domain of knowledge. These mentors can play an invaluable role. In such situations, many of the most significant aspects of guidance can occur because behaviors and values are modeled within a context where counseling corresponds to real circumstances relevant to a knowledge domain.

Career and vocational problems. Secondary school is the place where most career counseling takes place. Although most of it is done by guidance counselors in a formal manner, the classroom teacher plays an important part in conveying attitudes and providing content-specific information. (*Formal* refers to the administration and interpretation of data, preparations for college admission, and so forth.)

In our society, the choice of a career is one of life's biggest decisions. Purposeful efforts should be made to aid gifted children in making choices (Sandborn, 1979a). Gowan (1977) has discussed some of the guidance problems in this area. The gifted child has multiple strengths, which make choices more difficult because a variety of possibilities and directions are open. The child needs to recognize this fact and withstand (if necessary) the pressure for an early choice.

Some children are very clear about their direction. Others know what they want to avoid, but not what they want to do. Gifted adolescents need to realize that knowing what to avoid is an important piece of information. A good approach in decision making is matching interests and aptitudes, which may not be correlated. Avoiding areas where aptitudes and interests are low is usually not a problem; however, when there is a divergence between these variables, the choices get tougher. A child, whenever possible, might consider joining two strengths in a career choice. One thing to keep in mind is that aptitudes can find expression in a vocational pursuit.

Upward social mobility is a real problem for nonmodal gifted children (Gowan, 1977) because they are universally expected to pursue stereotypical careers. Children who are moving away from norms feel they are wrong, or they are ambivalent about leaving their group. Children may react to these pressures with strategies that limit later development, including aggressiveness, denial of feelings, and manipulation of others. Counselors who work with nonmodal gifted children should provide them with information about future problems and, when possible, contact with others in similar circumstances. Sandborn (1979b) contended that special efforts need to be made on behalf of nonmodal gifted children. Frasier (1974) has described a counseling program for disadvantaged adolescents that has implications for career guidance.

Drews (1964) developed the means for delivering career guidance to adolescent youths in a programmatic form. She proposed that, through a study of role models (gifted people who were "being and becoming"), gifted children could find meaning in their lives, experience developmental patterns firsthand, and develop their own individual patterns of self-discovery. Drews created curricular materials and a set of films to accomplish this purpose. She believed that this approach should teach children to make decisions and think critically so that gifted adolescents might comprehend our rapidly changing world where careers evolve in the context of technological and personal innovation. Almost 20 years later, there were similar calls for career education (Sandborn, 1979a), yet few school systems to this day have career education programs.

Notes on Problem Behaviors

Gifted children sometimes exhibit behaviors that are problems to themselves and others. These problem behaviors have been viewed as the manifestation of their advanced development in conflict with social expectations for children. In essence, the major problem for the children is managing their identity as gifted people. The three theoretical models—the Universal Developmental Model, the Domain-Specific Developmental Model, and the Behavioral-Cognitive Model—presented earlier in this chapter are indirectly translated in this section into some techniques for dealing with gifted children.

Gifted children can exhibit problem behaviors that, if continued, can interfere with development. Some common problem behaviors are inattention, dominating discussions, tuning out discussions, being argumentative, refusing to comply with rules, inappropriately criticizing, being in continual motion and activity, teasing and ridiculing others, desiring to control others, and being messy with personal property and work (Whitmore, 1980). These behaviors are amenable to intervention strategies that pay attention to the strengths of gifted children and realize that problem behaviors are learned, rather than being innate.

One strategy for helping children is to have a continuous dialogue with them. A dialogue means the adult listens to the child. A relationship based upon mutual respect and trust is established. The development of a relationship takes place gradually, not immediately. On this foundation, the teacher can play back the child's perceptions of the situation so that he or she may identify the source of a behavior and its consequences. Whitmore (1980) reported that "the needs of children, which most often motivate inappropriate behaviors, are related to a strong desire for social approval, leadership roles, and successful mastery of knowledge and skills" (p. 25). A second strategy is

215

to use group instructional activities that permit children to share ideas and feelings about themselves and the world.

Class meetings (Glasser, 1969) and sociodrama (Moreno, 1952) are techniques that are especially useful for assisting children in realizing how others see the same phenomena in different ways. Another counseling strategy is the use of literature to address needs such as awareness, self-understanding (Ford & Harris, 1999), and identity development (Frank & McBee, 2003). These strategies are largely based on the idea that, as children develop insight into their behavior, they will change appropriately. Since gifted children are frequently insightful and verbal, these are useful techniques.

An allied approach is to have a child develop a rational understanding of the problem behavior (Whitmore, 1980). The purpose of this is to help children see their behaviors and their feelings as normal reactions to living that they can control. The children use analytical and evaluative abilities to see how their behaviors affect themselves and others. This knowledge can be used to change themselves or to change the situation through systematic or unsystematic means. The latter refers to a general, unfocused strategy in which results are left to evolve as they will.

Another strategy uses the rational approach within a system for changing behavior based on the principles presented in the Cognitive Model. In essence, a plan is formulated or a contract is made to change a specific behavior (Drew & Drew, 1979; Whitmore, 1980). The plan may be formulated by the teacher, by the teacher and the child together, or by the child alone. The idea is to move toward a plan that is developed entirely by the child. Through this process, the child can acquire skills in resolving problems, which may lead toward a self-managed lifestyle (Williams & Long, 1991). Torrance and Myers (1970) proposed a five-step problem-solving model that is similar to the Williams and Long proposal.

CONCLUSION

The experience of being gifted in American schools is a problem of managing one's differentness in the face of many sources of conflict. The clash between the gifted child's advanced developmental level and social expectations is the central problem of being gifted, which makes it crucial for gifted children to learn how to manage their differentness in order to maintain their identity. The strategies children use can range from high visibility, to invisibility, to disidentification. Underachievement is a special case of using a poor strategy to manage one's differentness.

The Universal Developmental Model, the Behavioral-Cognitive Model, and the Domain-Specific Developmental Model are theoretical frameworks that have particular advantages and disadvantages for use with gifted children. The Universal Developmental Model provides a general outline for a school program; the Domain-Specific Developmental Model furnishes a clearer explanation of advanced development than other approaches; and the Behavioral-Cognitive Model presents ways of using the gifted children's strengths to help them solve their problems. Use of these theoretical models in understanding how gifted children manage their differentness is a necessary foundation for the construction of a quality guidance program. In this sense, it is important to remember that guidance is part of all professional roles, not the exclusive property or domain of counselors.

FOR **DISCUSSION**

1. The chapter mentions the social milieu of the school as a potential source of conflict for a gifted student. Reflect on and discuss how different social milieus may impact a gifted child.

2. How would you respond to a gifted student who complains that she feels great pressure from her parents and teachers to engage in more social activities? She comments that she wants to spend her time on her artwork.

3. What can parents and/or teachers do to help gifted adolescents who struggle with the pressure of choosing between their own interests and those of their peers?

4. Biographies and films are mentioned as potential sources of information for culturally diverse gifted students. Compile a list of three (or more) biographies and/or films featuring culturally diverse gifted individuals. Share them with your classmates to compile a reference list.

5. What steps can you (as a teacher, counselor, and/or parent) take to ensure that gifted females successfully circumvent socially imposed obstacles to achievement?

6. What steps can teachers, counselors, and/or parents take to ensure that gifted children do not engage in strategies that result in them "blending in" or becoming "invisible"?

7. The chapter mentions three themes that emerge from the many definitions of underachievement: (1) a discrepancy between potential and performance, (2) a discrepancy between predicted achievement and actual achievement, and (3) a failure to self-actualize. Discuss the educational implications of viewing underachievement in one way and not another.

chapter six

CREATIVITY:
PSYCHOLOGY,
DEVELOPMENT,
AND TEACHING

KEY CONCEPTS

- Divergent thinking is not a synonym for the creative process. It is only a part of the process.

- Techniques for measuring creativity are plentiful. Each produces an incomplete picture of the creative process.

- Designating children as creative is a common belief, but it is debatable.

- Assigning the label on a sole measure of creativity is unwarranted. Talking about creativity as being unconnected to adult human activity leads to educationally blind alleys.

- The evidence that creativity is domain-specific is growing.

- The nature of the relationship between intelligence and creativity is unresolved; yet, finding a person who possesses a high level of creativity in the absence of above-average general intelligence is improbable.

- When techniques for teaching for creativity are grouped according to stages in the creative process, the preparation and incubation stages receive the most attention.

- The precise nature of the creative process is undetermined. The process is assumed to develop over time and becomes more centered in a field.

- Divergent-thinking scores and creative-like behavior can be improved. The link to real-life adult creativity is poorly understood.

Creativity is a broad construct that has multiple meanings. Like other constructs such as democracy and love, people have personal definitions for it, which provide fertile ground for strong opinions and misunderstandings, which extends into the field of gifted education.

Our decision to devote an entire chapter to creativity is intended to convey the significance of the topic to the field. Since Guilford's seminal paper in 1959, the topic of creativity has been a main part of the debate over the meaning of giftedness, although attention to it in the literature has been sporadic. It appears not only in discussions of the psychology of giftedness, but also in discussion of program goals and identification. While creativity is generally regarded as an aspect of giftedness and by some as a separate kind of giftedness, agreement about its definition, process, measurement, and how it should be nurtured is strained.

The purpose of this chapter is to gather the strands of information about creativity so that informed decisions can be made in schools. Because it is a chapter and not a text on a single topic, we do not present an exhaustive account, but rather a synopsis that includes both classic studies and new information. In short, in order to appreciate the present conception of giftedness, one must have an understanding of creativity and how it develops.

DEFINITIONS OF CREATIVITY

A single accepted definition of creativity does not exist, nor is there universal agreement about what relevant attributes are needed to define an act as creative. The difficulty of selecting relevant attributes underscores the problem of defining creativity.

The terms *originality* and *novelty* pervade the literature on creativity. They express a quantitative and a qualitative standard, but they fail to say to what criterion a person is being compared. Is originality determined by comparison to self, others, a situation, a point in time, a field of study, a cultural group, or a combination of these? The standard or criterion specified is important because the choice alters the meaning of creativity. If novelty means comparing a person to him- or herself, then creativity becomes possible for everyone because the definition is based on individual growth. On the other hand, if originality is tied to a point in time, to a specific content domain, or to others in a field, then creativity becomes more narrowly defined.

Problems of this sort affect the formulation of a suitable definition and lead to different recommendations for education. The lack of agreement probably undermines the consideration of creativity as a serious part of the curriculum by practically oriented school personnel.

Classifying Definitions

The lack of a universal definition for creativity is exemplified by the wide array of definitions found in the literature. Some writers have tried to bring order to this area by classifying the many theoretical perspectives. Classification schemes illustrate the commonalities and differences that exist among researchers.

Gowan (1972) proposed that definitions of creativity be organized on a continuum from rational or conscious, to irrational or unconscious. The ends of his continuum identify terms that reappear in many discussions of creativity. In a more complex scheme, Busse and Mansfield (1980) classified notions of creativity in terms of how they correspond to seven theoretical traditions in psychology. The psychoanalytic category indicates the importance of allowing the release of unconscious thought in order for new perspectives to appear. The gestalt category pinpoints how restructuring elements in a situation is part of creativity. The association category notes that ideas exist in hierarchical relation to each other and the creative person has access to them. The perceptual category asserts that openness to different perspectives is central to the creative process. The humanistic category highlights that creativity springs from the uniqueness of individuals and environments. The cognitive-developmental category identifies creativity as an irreversible process to which a person is drawn and to whom the creative solution, when found, seems obvious. The composite category attempts to unite some of these perspectives into one theory.

More recently, other schemas have been introduced into the literature. Csikszentmihayli (1996) wrote about two kinds of creativity: Creativity with a big "C" and creativity with a little "c." The former is the kind that changes a culture and alters the way we see the world. Examples might be Einstein's theory of relativity or Monet's impressionism. Big "C" makes one famous. The later is more personal and has to do with changes in a person's life. Little "c" has to do with changes in how one lives or experiences the world in a new original manner. Mumford (1998) offered two divisions: One is based on creativity being "an unconscious, uncontrollable phenomenon," the second is based on "active manipulation of available information using mechanisms such as analogical reasoning" (p. 14).

These classifying schemes are helpful because they illustrate basic points about creativity. Gowan's (1972) presentation illustrates that the rational-irrational dimension is powerful. Mumford (1998) contrasts unconscious forces or deliberate use of skills. However, the part played by the irrational and rational in a creative act is not clear. The Busse and Mansfield (1980) system shows how particular elements of the creative process are better represented in one theory and not another and, perhaps more significantly, how some theories align themselves better with one domain than another. For example, the psychoanalytical and humanistic categories fit artistic creativity better than other categories, just as the gestalt category seems to fit scientific creativity. Csikszentmihayli's (1996) distinction points out the sociocultural context such that famous creators change the world while others simply change themselves. Taken together, these classifications show the improbability of constructing a general theory of creativity, which is an especially difficult problem for writers who try to trace examples of creative behavior in children to adult activity in a specific field (Feldman, 1980; Gardner, 2000; Gowan; Sawyer et al., 2003). The field of gifted education needs to know more of such a connection—if one exists—in order to implement sound methods for nurturing creativity.

A Working Definition

A discussion of the creative process requires the formulation of a definition. The preceding section attests to the fact that there is not a single orthodox view of creativity. A single definitive statement about creativity is inconceivable based on our present state of knowledge. Yet, without some statement, our discussion would lack coherence and practicality.

A definition of creativity should be relevant to our topic of being gifted in schools, consistent with the state of our knowledge, and helpful in discussing the questions of measurement, process, and education. The definition should allow for rationality, intuition, personality, and motivation in the creative process. It need not assume universality across children, nor claim the process is identical for adults and children, two assumptions that are made by some.

Therefore, we offer the following definition: Creativity is a general process that is expressed in many aspects of life and is exhibited in increasingly more specific ways as age increases. In children, the creative process is expressed across a broad range of abilities, interests, and activities and may be evaluated by comparison to age peers. As one becomes more experienced and committed to various areas of knowledge and skill, the general process becomes transformed by parameters established by the field of interest or domain. The importance of the generalized process is diminished, yet it is not lost. Rational and irrational elements, which enhance the creative process, are associated with interest in particular areas of human endeavor. In other words, creativity becomes more field-related, and its presence may be judged in comparison to criteria relevant to a field of inquiry. Thus, the creativity of a scientist differs from that of an artist. Within those categories, creativity is further differentiated, so that physicists differ from biologists, and sculptors differ from painters. The generalized process is rarely completely integrated into a field of interest. It is probable that the less specialized the creative process, the less likely it is that one will be identified as making a big "C" creative contribution to society.

Our description makes creativity a developmental process that becomes refined and restructured over the long term. The implications for education are described later in this chapter. Although the process can be seen over the long term, it still lacks clarity. The image of the creative process may be sharpened by reading a fascinating account by Ghiselin (1952), a classic work by Wallas (1926), or more recent expositions (Amabile, 1983; Mumford, 1998; Sawyer et al., 2003).

THE BASIC QUESTIONS

Our review of definitions of creativity was intended to communicate the complexity of the topic as a basis for discussion of four pivotal questions:

- What does creativity look like?

- What is the relationship between intelligence and creativity?

- What is happening when creativity is occurring?

- What conditions are conducive to enhancing creativity?

These four questions may be restated in the same order as a question of measurement, a question of intelligence, a question of process, and a question of education.

The Question of Measurement

An extensive discussion of the identification of gifted children was presented in Chapter Three. In this section, we offer a focused discussion on the measurement of creativity. Measurement is the first of the questions we consider because much of our knowledge of creativity, especially in children, is based heavily upon how it is appraised. An understanding of measurement techniques should help clarify what are considered to be signs of creativity. Although, as we shall see, the issue of measurement is far from settled, some procedures have become routinely used and some aspects of creativity are more readily measured than others.

Measurement techniques used to identify creative children must meet the same standards of reliability, validity, and selection of norm group as any good test (Plucker & Runco, 1998; Treffinger & Poggio, 1972). At the heart of the issue of measurement is the problem of what external evidence verifies the presence of creativity. Evidence may be found in the immediate time frame of childhood or in a future time frame of adulthood. Unless there is agreement about the evidence, the test results remain muddled. Showing differences among children does not mean we understand what those differences mean.

The basic problem is specifying what characterizes behavior or performance as being novel or unique. (If the meaning of *novel* were absolute, then this problem could be quickly resolved.) An example might clarify the dimensions of the problem. Consider two children in slightly different situations. In the first situation, Sarah is 7, and you are her teacher. She calls you to her desk and shows you that she has discovered the Pythagorean Theorem ($c^2 = a^2 + b^2$). In the second situation, Ellen is 18, and you are her teacher. Ellen shows you that she has discovered the Pythagorean Theorem. Which girl is creative?

More people would say that Sarah is creative, while few believe that Ellen is creative. Because their behavior is identical, the distinction is based solely on the contention that Ellen had an opportunity to learn the theorem, while Sarah did not. Significantly, the criterion has changed due to the ages of the girls.

Other people might state that both are creative by arguing that both may have been taught the theorem, but that does not mean they ever learned it. These same people might say that both girls are creative because the novelty should be judged in terms of what is novel for that person.

A final group might insist that neither Ellen nor Sarah is creative. They might argue that creativity is not an aspect of mathematics, but only of art and music; the theorem was discovered 2,500 years ago; or a pattern of novel behaviors must be seen before one can claim that either girl is creative.

This example illustrates the relative meaning of the term *creativity*. The scope of the problem of setting an appropriate criterion for judging the presence of creativity is extremely complex. The criteria problem, as described here, is presented as an issue in an immediate time frame. In other words, was the person creative at that point in time? The criteria problem is also important in terms of future behavior. The identification of gifted children is based on concern for their immediate needs, as well as predictions about future development. The issue is whether children who are identified as being creative become creative adults. This does not mean that creativity in children looks like creativity in mature adults (Fishkin & Johnson, 1998; Sawyer et al., 2003). The relatively few studies available on the relationship between creativity measured in childhood and adult performance or accomplishment are tied to specific measures of creativity and are discussed later.

The measurement of creativity is an enduring topic in the literature, one that is characterized by caution and optimism. Actual measurements of creativity have outdistanced the present state of knowledge about the creative process and the building of a sound theoretical foundation for the tests. Even the impetus for practical application, such as identification and program evaluation, has not resulted in the development of high-quality measurement techniques.

The means for measuring creativity are organized into the three categories outlined in Chapter Three: standardized tests, work samples, and rating scales. Within each category, examples of instruments that are primarily used for children in school are presented.

Standardized Tests

Standardized tests are primarily measures of creative potential. Children are asked to respond to designated tasks that are presumed to elicit behaviors associated with creative traits. Responses are scored in terms of specific criteria. Typically, the child's responses are judged by the number of answers (fluency) and the infrequency of the responses in comparison to the norm group's responses (originality). Sometimes, scores are awarded for amount of detail (elaboration) and number of categories among the responses (flexibility). Standardized tests are designed for use with children, have a research base, and have some theoretical underpinnings. They assess creativity in a manner that is relatively independent of subject matter or academic disciplines. A compendium of tests with commentary on their strengths and weaknesses is available (Fishkin & Johnson, 1998).

Torrance Tests of Creative Thinking (TTCT). The Torrance Tests of Creative Thinking (Torrance, 1974) are the most important and widely used (Alvino et al., 1981) standardized tests. The research base of other tests cannot compare to that of the TTCT.

The TTCT are composed of three figural activities and seven verbal activities that are designed to be highly engaging to children and adults. Children are encouraged to produce unusual ideas or pictures that no one else would produce. The figural activities take about 30 minutes and require children to draw responses to abstract, nonspecific line drawings or shapes. The verbal activities take about 45 minutes and ask children to write clever and unusual questions, describe possible consequences of improbable situations, and so forth. Equivalent forms are available. They are administered to groups above the third-grade level. The items are generally scored for fluency (number of responses), flexibility (categories), originality (novelty), and elaboration (details). Scores are totaled across subtests. Special streamlined scoring procedures for the figural tests are available.

Because the TTCT are so popular for assessing creativity, they have been reviewed extensively (Anastasi, 1976; Crockenberg, 1972; Hagen, 1980). The reliability has been judged to be satisfactory, although verbal activities show higher reliability than figural activities, and the tests seem fair to different ethnic and socioeconomic groups. Scoring presents difficulty in tests like these because there is no single correct response. Because the scorer has to make decisions based upon specified criteria, training materials (Ball & Torrance, 1980) have been produced to improve scorer reliability. The use and meaning of the different scores for fluency, flexibility, originality, and elaboration have been questioned. Anastasi thought it was "inadvisable to derive more than one score from any one test or to treat similarly labeled scores from different tests as measures of a single trait" (p. 396). A number of studies have demonstrated that the fluency score contaminates the originality scores (Plucker & Runco, 1998). Research on assessing divergent thinking not using the TTCT has attempted to deal with this issue (Hong & Milgram, 1991; Runco & Mraz, 1992).

Questions have also been raised about the construct and predictive validity of the TTCT, although more than 1,000 studies (Torrance & Hall, 1980) contribute varying degrees of evidence for their validity. Positive indications of construct validity can be found in reports showing relationships between the TTCT and various personality traits and various educational procedures for a range of age groups. Reviewers in the 1970s found evidence for (Baird, 1972) and against (Anastasi, 1976) Torrance's construct. Since then, researchers into creativity have come to a consensus that the Torrance tests are a measure of divergent thinking or ideational fluency, an important aspect of creativity (Runco, 1993; Sternberg & Lubart, 1993).

Criticisms of predictive validity have been the strongest. At issue is whether the TTCT predict real-life achievements. Torrance and his associates have attempted to answer critics using data from a 22-year longitudinal study (Rieger, 1983; Torrance, 1972, 1981; Torrance & Wu, 1981), in which a remarkable 55% of the original sample was located and studied. These studies report significant correlations between a creativity index consisting of scores derived from various TTCT batteries and questionnaire data indicating adult creative achievement. Again, reviewers have differing views on the available data (Anastasi, 1976; Crockenberg, 1972; Hagen, 1980; Treffinger, 1980), but the consensus is that the predictive data are weak. A confounding validity issue is whether the TTCT measure something other than high general intelligence (Baird, 1972; Wallach, 1972).

In sum, the TTCT have a relatively long history of use. All reviewers believe Torrance has made a significant contribution to the study of creativity. These tests sample significant aspects of the creative process. Caution is advised in making identification decisions on the basis of these tests alone. The TTCT are most appropriately viewed as a valuable tool in the hands of discerning users.

Wallach-Kogan Test. Another approach to creativity conceptualizes it as being an associative process, which assumes that, for any stimulus, a series of associated ideas will be produced. The ideas are organized in a hierarchical fashion, with associated responses becoming more unique and less typical as the process continues.

The Wallach-Kogan Test (Wallach & Kogan, 1965) is based on this notion creativity, as are others (Mednick & Mednick, 1967; Torrance et al., 1973). It has a significant place in the literature on creativity (Crockenberg, 1972; Howieson, 1981; Wallach & Wing, 1969). The test consists of verbal and visual subtests that are untimed so that the creative process may occur. Children are asked to generate alternate uses of a verbally presented object, such as a newspaper, or to list meanings after looking at a line drawing. Responses are scored for number and infrequency. The test has reasonable reliability and is less related to IQ than the TTCT and Guilford measures. The validity of the test has been studied by using scores to predict the number of creative-like extracurricular activities for children at 5- to 7-year intervals. Scores seem unrelated to nonacademic attainment in schools and at graduation (Kogan & Pankove, 1974).

Summary. Standardized tests attempt to measure traits associated with creativity. The tests ask children to respond to stimuli that elicit a variety of responses. The emphasis is on the number of responses and on how infrequently they are made. The issue of qualitative differences is not dealt with in a direct manner; rather, the creative process is indirectly assessed. These tests are independent of subject matter or of specific areas of study (Plucker & Runco, 1998). They tend to assume the existence of a general process that occurs in the short term (minutes), as opposed to the long term (months or years). Different tests of creativity (divergent thinking) may not measure the same things, and the correlations among tests are very low. Evidence of the relationship between test performance and real-world creative performance is limited (Runco, 1993; Sternberg, 2003b).

The issue of what these tests measure is confounded by general intelligence. When test protocols are compared to the description of the creative process, it is highly probable that these tests measure only one aspect of the creative process: fluent responses. Other aspects of the creative process, such as sustained commitment, attention to real problems and products, and aesthetic judgment, are neglected (Kirschenbaum, 1998). Using Guilford's terminology, these tests are most accurately called tests of divergent thinking, rather than tests of creativity. This distinction needs to be maintained more clearly in any discussion of measurement by standardized tests.

Rating Scales/Checklists

Rating scales and checklists differ from standardized tests, although some rating scales have been through standardization procedures. In essence, rating scales ask a person to judge another person or oneself for the presence of certain attributes (see Chapter Three). Dissatisfaction with tests and a strong interest in identifying creative people are probably responsible for the rapid growth of rating scales and checklists.

Evidence appeared in the 1960s that biographical data were the strongest predictor of creativity in adults (MacKinnon, 1964; Taylor & Ellison, 1967), and those kinds of data distinguished adolescent boys and girls who produced creative products from those who were not creative in science, art, and literature (Anastasi & Schaefer, 1969; Schaefer & Anastasi, 1968). From 1969 to 1974, the American College Testing Program produced data showing biographical data to be useful predictors of college and postgraduate accomplishments (Hagen, 1980). It became clearer that biographical data were useful in spotting creativity in secondary-age students.

The interest in this area has resulted in the development of several devices that have wide distribution (Fishkin & Johnson, 1998; Hunsaker & Callahan, 1995). Several of the rating scales, such as the Scale for Rating the Behavioral Characteristics of Superior Students (Renzulli, Smith, White, Callahan, Hartman, & Westberg, 2002) and the Alpha Biographical Inventory (IBRIC, 1974) have wide currency. Some examples of this kind of approach are described below.

Checklist of Creative Positives. This is an extension of Torrance's (1962b) interest in moving away from standardized tests in the identification of talent, especially among culturally different youth. The checklist is composed of 18 characteristics that are strengths of culturally different groups. The list is based upon Torrance's record of research on tests, observing children, and review of the literature. The 18 characteristics (Torrance, 1969) are:

1. ability to express feelings and emotions;

2. ability to improvise with commonplace materials and objects;

3. articulateness in role-playing, sociodrama, and storytelling;

4. enjoyment of, and ability in, visual arts, such as drawing, painting, and sculpture;

5. enjoyment of, and ability in, creative movement, dance, dramatics, and so forth;

6. enjoyment of, and ability in, music, rhythm, and so forth;

7. use of expressive speech;

8. fluency and flexibility in figural media;

9. enjoyment of, and skills in, group activities, problem solving, and so forth;

10. responsiveness to the concrete;

11. responsiveness to the kinesthetic;

12. expressiveness of gestures, body language, and so forth, and ability to interpret body language;

13. humor;

14. richness of imagery in informal language;

15. originality of ideas in problem solving;

16. problem-centeredness or persistence in problem solving;

17. emotional responsiveness; and

18. quickness of warm-up.

No student is expected to possess all these traits. Torrance provided advice on how to identify these strengths and how to use the checklist. He also made useful suggestions for programming.

Group Inventory for Finding Talent. The Group Inventory for Finding Talent (GIFT; Rimm & Davis, 1976) was developed on the notion that personality traits and records of past creative activities are predictors of later creative accomplishments. These data may be gathered from children in grades K–2, 3–4, or 5–6. GIFT was revised in 1980 to include 25 items common to all levels and several additional items. Examples of items and the trait they are intended to measure are: "I like to paint pictures" (interest in art); "It is alright to sometimes change the rules of the game" (flexibility); and "A picture of the sun should always be colored yellow" (independence).

The authors reported reliability and validity of data determined in studies in the United States, Israel, and France. Reliability coefficients for the primary, elementary, and upper elementary levels of .55, .69, and .68, respectively, were reported from a pilot study (Davis & Rimm, 1979), as well as coefficients of .80, .86, and .88, respectively, in a later article (Rimm & Davis, 1980). The authors warned about the primary level of GIFT. Criterion-related validity was obtained by comparing scores to teacher ratings of creativity and to ratings by two others of student-written stories and art products. Over several studies, the majority of coefficients were around .30. The difficulty in establishing a criterion for judging creativity can be seen in these articles. The GIFT seems to be a promising tool when used in conjunction with other data. It has the advantage of providing the user with a description of what the GIFT might be measuring.

Additional rating scales are available to measure aspects of the creative process. These scales are generally used with adolescent and older students. Some are How Do You Feel About Yourself? (Williams, 1971), Statement of Past Creative Activities (Bull & Davis, 1980), Your Style of Learning and

Thinking (Torrance, Reynolds, Riegel, & Ball, 1977), and The Creative Perception Inventory (Khatena & Torrance, 1976).

Summary. Rating scales and checklists provide another means of identifying creative people. The scales presented here have a research base and some normative data. They make heavy use of biographical data and readily accept the person as the best judge of his or her background and past accomplishments. Concern over lying and distortion is not found in the literature on giftedness. The preference seems to be to give children the benefit of the doubt, rather than to make preemptory exclusions. Self-ratings seem to work better with older children. It would appear that the process of creativity needs time to become visible to oneself. The larger scales, as usual, are more reliable.

Rating scales and checklists have the dual advantage of using actual description of creative activity as the basis for judgment and being easy to administer. An obvious disadvantage is that one cannot rate oneself on actions that one's environment did not encourage or permit. The reliability and validity of rating scales are adequate and quite comparable to creativity tests. Identification decisions should not be made on the basis of a single scale. Practitioners should consider using rating scales in conjunction with some other creativity measure.

Work Sample or Creative Performance

The third category of measurement switches measurement from the person's traits or biography to performance in the area of interest, which allows for less distant inferences about creative tendencies. The work sample uses the products of creativity as the basis for comparison among people. It reemphasizes the problem of criteria, which was discussed earlier in this chapter, by placing the issue right out front. Simply stated, what makes a particular product creative? The continued interest in ways to judge creative performance has come not only from those interested in identifying creative people, but also from those who are seeking ways to evaluate the accomplishments of students in programs for the gifted.

The work-sample technique assumes that it is possible to evaluate what creative people do, that is, the products of their creativity. A creative product is tangible; others can sense and appreciate it. No direct assumption about the nature of the creative process is necessary, although it is assumed that creative people produce creative products (Renzulli, 1968). The influence of the social context and the predilections of the evaluators cannot be removed from judgment. The work-sample technique makes no assumption about its use for identifying gifted children; however, work samples are a potentially powerful tool for assessing creativity, as well as for studying the creative process (Runco, 1987).

The issue of what makes a particular product creative is extremely complex. Researchers into creative achievement in the past (Jackson & Messick,

1965; Lehman, 1953), as well as those trying to identify contemporary creative achievement (Bull & Davis, 1980; Gardner, 2000; Reis & Renzulli, 1991; Runco, 1987), have had to contend with this issue.

In an influential paper on assessing creative products, Jackson and Messick (1965) proposed four criteria for characterizing creative products: unusualness (novelty and surprise), appropriateness (fits the situation to perfection), transformation (breaking new ground and stimulating new work), and condensation (elegantly simple, yet powerful). Their criteria have been the basis for many discussions about assessing creativity, but general agreement about evaluating creative responses has been slow. Bessemer and Treffinger (1981), after reviewing more than 100 studies, formulated the Creative Product Analysis Matrix, which places a sample of creative work in a three-dimensional space where it is evaluated along the dimensions of novelty, resolution, and elaboration and synthesis.

The task of building a procedure for judging a sample of creative products that crosses academic disciplines is significant for the development of valid systems of identification and program evaluation. Central to evaluating work samples is the role of experts. Can anyone serve as a judge of creative performance? Bessemer and Treffinger (1981) found the evidence to be inconclusive; yet, Feldman (2000) argued that experts are able to make better judgments of creative performance than nonexperts and tests. He presented evidence showing that experts in the creative process are necessary for making suitable judgments about qualitative differences between children on standardized creativity tests. Feldman went on to posit that experts in a specific area of knowledge and with specific skills are needed if the creative process is to be evaluated using a wider perspective than those used on divergent-thinking tests. In his view, the role of experts is unavoidable:

> To put it more broadly the criteria for evaluation of creative works are inextricably entwined with the field of effort within which the work is produced. Hypothetically, Jackson and Messick's criteria can be applied to any domain. But practically, each domain utilizes the criteria unequally, and anyone proposing to apply the criteria must have reached a degree of mastery of the domain in question. (p. 103)

Gardner (2000) amplified this point: "Judgments of originality or creativity can be properly made only by knowledgeable members of the field, though that field can be ancient or newly constituted" (p. 79).

Self-reports or observations can measure students' creative production. Milgram and colleagues (Milgram & Milgram, 1976) have been using self-reports to study creativity, and Runco (1987) has extended this kind of research. In a recent study, Hong et al. (1995) demonstrated that young children can respond to a 60-item questionnaire on their out-of-school activities in six domains (art, music, sports, dance, drama, and literature). These studies provide support for the rating scales discussed above.

231

Direct observation of products is another way to judge creativity. This practice is done routinely in judging competitions in music, dance, painting, and so forth. In terms of more academic creations, rarely are studies reported. Baer (1994) assessed story writing, poetry writing, and storytelling in elementary school children and demonstrated that consensual ratings can be stable. Reis and Renzulli (1991) have observed that few instruments are available for judging creative products.

One such instrument is the Student Product Assessment Form (SPAF), which is an outgrowth of many people's interests in student creative products as being important outcomes of special programs. Reis and Renzulli (1991) developed the SPAF by drawing on their own and colleagues' experiences in the schools with student products that focused on Type III of the Enrichment Triad Model, as well as their familiarity with the literature. The SPAF consists of 15 items, each of which focuses on a characteristic of a product. It generates scores for the process of creating the product (eight scores), as well as scores for the final product (seven scores). Examples of the former items are "early statement of the problem," and "diversity of resources." Examples of the latter items are "originality of the idea" and "quality beyond age/grade level." After field testing and subsequent fine tuning, reliability was calculated for four raters by having them rate 20 products already created by students. Reis and Renzulli reported estimates of .96 and higher for interrater reliability for the total instrument; stability estimates also seem adequate. Content validity was established by obtaining evaluations from national authorities and 20 experienced Connecticut teachers of the gifted. The authors recognize that additional research on this instrument is needed.

Summary. The discussion of work samples and creative products illustrates the complexity involved in judging creative performance and makes it evident that people who are extremely sensitive to creative products are needed. Experts or highly trained personnel are necessary for making the work-sample technique successful. A distinct advantage for work samples is that judgments are made on the basis of real-life activity. This contrasts with inferences about future creative performance made on creativity tests where the situation is more contrived and the product is less real-world-oriented. A definite disadvantage is the problem of selecting experts. Any lessening in the use of divergent-thinking tests will probably be accompanied by a corresponding increase in the utility of the work-sample approach.

Summary of Measurement

Standardized tests, rating scales and checklists, and work samples are useful for studying creativity and the creative process in children. Recognition of the strengths and weaknesses of these forms of measurement must temper statements about identification and the nature of creativity. Selecting children for programs on the basis of any one technique is unwarranted. Multiple measures are better for making identification decisions. For elementary-age children, standardized divergent-thinking tests might be a reasonable choice when coupled with noncreative indications such as intelligence. For late elementary-age children, creativity tests and rating scales would be a useful combination. As children get older, reliance on work samples and products should be increased. If a program is designed for children who are creative in a specific area, measures of that area are more significant than divergent-thinking tests.

Discussion of the nature of the creative process should be guarded based on the limitations of measurement devices. Anyone who claims that the creative process is adequately revealed by any of these procedures is going beyond reason. Each category of measurement provides a brief look at some aspects of the process. Rating scales provide data on personal and affective characteristics and history. Work samples and products provide some indication of motivation and a hint of the end of the creative process. Standardized tests provide data on the number and unusualness of ideas one can produce in a short period. The meaning of the differences between children yielded by these measures is confused by questions of future (adult) behavior and conflicting theoretical foundations. A factor that further complicates the discussion of giftedness and creativity is the relationship between intelligence and creativity.

The Question of Intelligence and Creativity

From the 1960s to the 1980s, there was special interest paid to the question of the relationship between creativity and intelligence. The debate has cooled as some aspects have become accepted and ideas of general intelligence and general creativity have given way to more domain-specific notions of intelligence (Gardner, 1983) and creativity (Gardner, 2000; Plucker & Runco, 1998; Sawyer et al., 2003.).

Concern about the relationship between intelligence and creativity is not new. While this concern predates the development of IQ tests (Getzels & Dillon, 1973), most of the research done on it revolves around the question of who is gifted. Once again, Terman and his associates were influential in pointing out the inability of intelligence alone to account for outstanding performance. Cox's (1926) efforts to estimate the IQs of people noted for their unusual contributions imply that IQs of some highly creative individuals may be lower than expected considering their contributions to our culture. Other data in Terman's study show intelligence is not a reliable predictor of creative accomplishment among the gifted. In addition, Hollingworth (1942) noted that only 12 of her 36 children with IQs above 180 showed signs of creativity.

One inference from these findings is that creativity is not synonymous with intelligence; or, one may infer that variables such as motivation, schooling, or family, are more strongly related to outstanding creative performance. In 1950, J. P. Guilford, in his presidential address to the American Psychological Association, refocused interest in creativity by proposing the existence of a low to moderate positive correlation between IQ and creativity measures and suggesting that creativity was relatively independent from intelligence. Two decades of research followed that proposal. Since the 1980s, this issue has moved off center stage, but it is still alive and intriguing (Sternberg & O'Hara, 1999).

Separating the Issues

Several questions are posed to sort out the different issues in understanding the relationship between intelligence and creativity.

Is creativity the same thing as intelligence? The question is too general, and it is unanswerable because the terms are not defined. As soon as one defines creativity or intelligence as being either different from, or similar to, each other, then one has an answer. However, if the question is restated in terms of measuring the two variables, then it is possible to get closer to an answer.

Do measures of intelligence measure the same thing as measures of creativity? This question presupposes agreement about how to measure each variable. The discussion of measuring creativity illustrated the unsettled situation. Because creativity tests, rating scales, and work samples may not be measuring the same thing, one must be careful to make reference to the form of measurement when comparing intelligence and creativity. Unlike creativity, there is agreement that IQ tests are sufficient for measuring intelligence (regardless of the construct for IQ underlying the test). Of course, there are differences in group and individual measures.

The question needs to be restated again. *Do standardized tests of creativity—more properly named divergent-thinking tests—measure the same thing as IQ tests?* An answer to this question requires administration of both measures and inspection of the association between the two tests. Remember that Guilford (1959) expected a low correlation that could be interpreted to indicate little similarity between the two measures. Hundreds of studies have been conducted using divergent-thinking measures and IQ tests (Getzels & Jackson, 1962; Guilford & Christensen, 1973; Wallach & Kogan, 1965). Given the consistency of the findings of correlations at or below .26, IQ and divergent-thinking tests apparently measure different psychological variables. However, such a conclusion may be overgenerous for three reasons. First, measures of divergent thinking relate less to each other than IQ measures correlate to creativity. This means that divergent-thinking tests are more like general intelligence tests than like themselves. Another reason for caution is that the relatively high IQ levels and the restrictive range of children's abilities confound the issue (Crockenberg, 1972). Another qualification to this finding was shown by Martinson and Seagoe (1967), who compared high-IQ and average-IQ children on test scores and on creative products. They reported a significant relationship between IQ and judges' ratings of actual creative products, which suggests that high IQ is important for high ratings of creativity. They also found that creativity test scores were not significantly different between IQ groups, which suggests that divergent-thinking tests may be measuring something that is different from creative production.

Do Highly Creative Children and Highly Intelligent Children Differ?

The notion that highly creative children may not be the same kind of people as highly intelligent children is related to the idea that IQ and creativity (divergent thinking) tests may not measure the same thing. This is a most important question because it challenges the IQ as the sole determiner of giftedness while simultaneously suggesting a broader definition of giftedness.

More than 40 years ago, the issue was brought into focus in a classic study by Getzels and Jackson (1962). This provocative study is explained in order to clarify, first, what the issues were, and second, what questions were not really answered by that study and other studies that followed it. Students in grades 7–12 in a private school were administered five tests of creativity developed by the authors that comprised a creativity score. Cumulative records were used to calculate Stanford-Binet IQs. Children were assigned to two groups on the basis of IQ and creativity using contrasted patterns. The highly creative group (HC) was defined as scoring in the top 20% on creativity, but below the top 20% on IQ. The highly intelligent group (HIQ) scored in the top 20% on IQ, but below the top 20% on creativity. From about 500 students, they placed 15 boys and 11 girls in the HC group and 17 boys and 11 girls in the HIQ group. The groups were then compared to see if there were significant differences between the highly intelligent and the highly creative.

The highly intelligent group was found to have more conventional interests and attitudes than the highly creative group. Teachers liked the HIQ group better. Interestingly, school achievement of the two groups on standardized tests was comparable, and both groups were superior, even though a 23-point difference was apparent in IQ scores. The finding of comparable achievement was a source of much controversy. By contrast, the HC group was more imaginative and original, had fewer conventional interests, took greater risks, and preferred unusual occupations. Both groups seemed to understand what was expected of them, but the HC group chose a different path. These findings implied that secondary-age students with high IQs can have somewhat different personalities or attitudes than highly creative students.

Again, one must be careful about interpreting the findings. Critics of Getzels and Jackson's (1962) study have pointed out significant methodological problems: the way IQ scores were obtained was inappropriate, correlation between measures were incomplete, the school was atypical, and a special group (the highly creative and highly intelligent) was not studied. Lack of information on this unstudied group confuses the issue of whether or not HC children differ from HIQ children and whether or not the intellectually gifted differ from the creatively gifted.

It is easy to overlook the fact that Getzels and Jackson (1962) were not using an absolute standard for defining the groups. Instead, the groups were formed relative to the setting. The 20% cutoff was based on the range of scores within that school or sample. The terms "highly creative" and "highly intelligent" obscure the fact that, although the IQs of the highly creative were low in comparison to the IQ scores of the highly intelligent (average 127 vs. 150, respectively); the creative groups' average was still well above the national norms (average IQ of 100), that is, above the 90th percentile. Thus, one might say the highly creative are different from the highly intelligent, but it is incorrect to think of the them as having low intelligence. This point returns us to the problem of the relationship between measuring techniques. The lack of data on the highly creative group with high IQs makes it impossible to discern whether these children are different from either the highly creative or the highly intelligent.

Other studies on the issue of whether HC children differ from HIQ children (Torrance & Wu, 1981; Wallach & Kogan, 1965) have not clarified the issue. They, too, have methodological problems. Although they formed their groups using different procedures, their findings continued to support the idea that HC, HIQ, and the third group, HC-HIQ, were successful students. The Wallach and Kogan study shed some additional light on the issue of whether personality differences exist among the groups, as well as how gender influences this relationship. The characteristics of the highly creative and highly intelligent have some correspondence to stereotypical notions of these groups. The HC-HIQ portrait is striking on two counts. The boys and girls sound like integrated people, reminiscent of the humanistic perspective on creativity and the composite portrait of giftedness presented earlier based primarily on Terman's data. This point is fascinating when one considers the frequent and appropriate criticism about how Terman selected his children. One wonders about the kind of children he studied and about the meaning of the terms *intelligent* and *creative*.

In sum, these studies show that there is no clear, highly visible group of traits that distinguish highly creative children from highly intelligent children. Nevertheless, some characteristic differences are apparent in elementary and secondary school students, such as independence, desire to take risks, and unconventional interests. These findings point to the fact that noncognitive factors might be very important in the creative person. Some of the impetus for developing rating scales comes from these findings. While this research provides inconclusive evidence on distinguishing traits, the data do indicate that highly creative children are likely to experience adjustment problems related to teacher attitudes and school structure, even though their achievement ranges from satisfactory to superior (Getzels & Jackson, 1962; Torrance, 1979b, 1981). This likelihood has prompted development of programs of guidance.

Is IQ level related to creativity? In general, the high intelligence level of the samples has confounded the relationship of intelligence to creativity. One wonders if the relationship is consistently the same throughout the range of IQ scores and creativity scores. Perhaps the relationship is different at varying levels. The ability of one score to predict the other is important for understanding the development of the creative processes, as well as identifying creative people. Is it possible that there exists a point, or points, where the predictable relationship between IQ and creativity changes? Again, because different forms of measurement complicate the questions, the discussion is divided into two parts: (1) IQ and divergent-thinking test scores and (2) IQ and creative accomplishment or productivity.

IQ and Divergent Thinking

Earlier it was noted that an average correlation between .20 and .40 for creativity and intelligence has been reported. In order to study the question, one divides groups into IQ levels and looks for changes in the size of the correlation. For example, Yamamoto (1965) demonstrated correlations with the Torrance tests of .88 for children with IQs below 90, .69 for children with IQs of 90–110, and a correlation of -.30 for IQ scores above 110. The change in the size of the correlation indicates changes in the relationship, such that lower correlations mean greater variability at those levels. Fuchs-Beauchamp, Karnes, and Johnson (1993) studied preschoolers using different measures and reported that intelligence was significantly related to creativity when IQ was less than 120. The correlations were similar in size to those reported by Yamamoto.

Reviewing research on this topic has caused some writers to conclude that creativity is related to intelligence. Increases in IQ are related to increases in creativity scores, although the relationship seems to disappear at higher IQ scores. It would seem that low IQ operates against creativity (Freeman, 1979; Guilford, 1975). Crockenberg (1972) has suggested that "there might be a threshold above which there is little relationship between IQ and creativity" (p. 32). In this sense, once a person has a minimal amount of intelligence, his or her creative abilities may be very little or very great. Whatever the case, IQ cannot predict it. Several writers have proposed an IQ of 120 as being the threshold (Gowan, 1972; Simonton, 1979). Guilford and Christensen (1973) disputed the notion of a threshold, but others have confirmed it (Fuchs-Beauchamp et al., 1993; Sternberg & Lubart, 1993).

IQ and Creative Accomplishment or Productivity

Research on this line of inquiry with children is scarce as studies that report the outcomes of programs do not answer this question. While Martinson and Seagoe (1967) found a significant relationship between children's products and IQ, most of the research has been on adults with creativity being rated by colleagues in that field.

MacKinnon (1964) summarized his research with creative people in various disciplines, including writing, architecture, and mathematics, by noting that a high degree of intelligence is needed for creative work. Once a person reaches that degree, then higher degrees of intellect are not predictive of creativity. This finding parallels that for children and implies a threshold effect, as well. Whatever the relationship, intelligence and creativity apparently work together. As Albert (1980) has noted, "The interrelationship is twofold: creative performance requires intelligence for processing information and problems; and gifted intelligence is associated generally with a number of the same personality characteristics associated

237

with creative ability" (pp. 177–178). In response to the question of whether intelligence is needed for creativity, the answer is yes. In response to whether creativity and IQ are related, as Sternberg (2003b) noted, creativity "tends to be rather, but not totally distinct from psychometrically measured intelligence" (p. xvii).

A Question of Process

Up to this point, we have provided a definition for creativity and talked about the issues of measurement and the relationship between intelligence and creativity. In the midst of all this, we have skirted a basic question: What is the creative process? The fact that we could have a sustained discussion about creativity without dealing with such a basic question illustrates that it is possible to have incomplete knowledge about a phenomenon and still have a discussion on that basis. We also place the foundational question of process at this point because background information was needed in order to consider some of the debate among experts and to provide an orientation to the next major division of the chapter: education and teaching.

We present two models of the creative process. Each model conveys something about the issue. We begin with an old notion of the process that continues to have currency in the literature and follow it with exposition of a promising recent model.

The Wallas Model

According to Wallas (1926), the creative process occurs in four steps, each of which implies the operation of varying cognitive processes. Although cognitive processes are stressed in this depiction, one should recognize the weakness of that position because motivational considerations activate and sustain the process. We will use this model later as a means for organizing some of the literature on teaching for creativity.

Preparation. The preparation stage is easy to overlook in a discussion of creativity. It involves the identification of a question, paradox, or concern (e.g., how to show depth on a two-dimensional surface or calculating how many stars are in the sky). The person is engaged in considering the question from multiple angles. The person amasses knowledge, experience, and skills related to the problem. In other discussions of the process, the preparation phase has been described as problem finding, an ability associated with creativity (Csikszentmihalyi & Getzels, 1971; Runco & Nemiro, 1994).

Incubation. The person is unaware of a conscious attempt to solve the paradox; yet, incubation propels him or her toward a solution. Although the literature is filled with accounts of the incubation period, little experimental data are available on this stage. Guilford (1979) saw the stage as transformation of required information into something new. Arieti (1981) believed it to be a critical point in the creative process as a person becomes aware of elements in the situation.

Illumination. The illumination stage is commonly referred to as "the moment of insight" in which the solution suddenly presents itself. In a cartoon, a light bulb goes on above Bugs Bunny's head. This stage is mentioned frequently by creative people across various disciplines. The person senses that the illuminated idea—the insight—is the most appropriate one for the situation. The creator is surprised and delighted by the experience.

Verification. The point in the process where the person evaluates the merit of the idea is the verification stage. The final product, such as an idea, an experiment, or a painting, is reworked until the person is ready to reveal it to the world. The presentation of the solution gives one the opportunity to show off one's efforts. An inadequate expression of the creative act to others may mitigate against its acceptability.

The Investment Model

Sternberg and Lubart (1993, 1995) described the creative person as behaving in a fashion analogous to an investment banker: Creative individuals pursue or produce ideas that seemingly have little value (buy low), work toward perfecting those ideas, and eventually convince others of the merit of those ideas (sell high). They proposed that creativity occurs as a consequence of the interaction of six resources: intellectual processes, knowledge, intellectual style, personality, motivation, and environmental context.

The six resources are not simply added to make someone creative. Rather, they interact in some multiplicative way to increase creativity within the context of some domain. "Creative giftedness is rare . . . because so many resources combine interactively to produce it" (Sternberg & Lubart, 1993, p. 13).

Intellectual Processes. Creative people have intellectual processes that enable them to see and think about the world in a manner that is different than others who are less creative. "Creatively gifted people excel in the intellectual processes of problem definition, strategic use of divergent thinking, and selective encoding, selective combination, and selective comparison skills, which interact with and to a degree depend upon each other" (Sternberg & Lubart, 1993, p. 9).

Knowledge. Creative people must have information in order to produce novel events. Time and energy are required to master bodies of information so that they can comprehend what is missing in a field and learn from others. Paradoxically, an unspecified amount of knowledge prepares a person to be ready to capitalize on chance events that a less-informed person might miss, and too much knowledge might work against being open to new ideas.

Intellectual Style. The characteristic way a person behaves governs his or her behavior. Some styles may be more conducive to creative behavior than others. Using the three branches of our federal government and two modes of information processing (global and local), the theory suggests that a legislative, global style is more likely to characterize a creative person. People with these styles tend to like to work on wide-ranging, unstructured problems in which they make up the rules. Schools prefer executive and judicial intellectual styles.

Personality. Affective aspects are as important as cognitive aspects in the emergence of creativity. Some of these prerequisite attributes are tolerance for ambiguity, moderate risk taking, perseverance, willingness to grow, and a degree of self-esteem. Cognitive ability may be present in a person, but without the personality traits, creative production is unlikely.

Motivation. People are motivated by intrinsic and extrinsic forces. Intrinsic motivation seems to enhance creativity, and extrinsic motivation appears to be detrimental (Amabile, 1983), although, according to Sternberg and Lubart (1993), "extrinsic motivators are not inherently antithetical to creativity" (p. 12). For creative people, "task-focusing motivators," an intrinsic force, are more important than "goal-focusing motivators," an extrinsic, instrumental force. What is motivating can change over time, and different motivators might be important at different parts of the creative act.

Environmental Context. The culture and the time frame in which people live surround them. Some contextual elements, such as stimulating family, enriched classrooms and teachers, and environmental rewards, might be considered acceptable in one context and not in another.

The Propulsion Model of Creative Contributions

In more recent writing, Sternberg, Kaufman, & Pretz (2002) proposed the Propulsion Model of Creativity, which switches attention from the person to the creative product. Context is recognized as being a crucial part of the process. Creative contributions are placed into a taxonomy of eight kinds of contributions that share the common denominator of being products that "propel" or lead a field forward in some way. The contributions represent how the field is affected by their presence.

The forms of contribution and their effects are: *replication* (points to creative work that preserves the dominant paradigm and fleshes out the field); *redefinition* (changes the way a field is viewed); *forward incrementation* (encourages a field to move in the direction it is now going); *advance forward incrementation* (continues the forward movement, but moves out from the prevailing notions); *redirection* (moves the field into a new and different direction); *reconstruction/redirection* (moves the field back to an earlier point and takes it off into a new direction); *reinitiation* (takes the field back to a new starting point and moves the field into that direction); and *integration* (two opposing views are reworked to create a new product including both). Sternberg et al. provide examples from science and technology, arts and letters, and popular culture.

Notice that the emphasis here is on the creative product in reference to a domain. An interesting feature of the theory is that the same product can be judged differently based on the time at which it appears. For example, a new impressionistic style of visual art may be enthralling to us, but its place would not be the same as Monet's contribution a century ago.

Summary

Wallas' conception is a compelling and satisfactory way to conceptualize the creative process, but it is clearly not a description of it. It is primarily a rational view of creativity that does not describe the three elements that consistently reappear in discussions of creativity, namely, time, motivation, and irrationality. The first element is time. Over what length of time may a stage occur? Stages are variable. A stage may take years. Adjacent stages may be of varying lengths. The length of a cycle of creativity is indeterminate. These variations in time suggest a second element: motivation. Amabile (1983) asserted that motivation is the missing crucial element in most discussions of creativity. A person must be committed to the problem in order to concentrate his or her energies over short and long terms, be able to persist in the face of frequent opposition to new ideas, and to contend with his or her own limitations at any point in time. A third missing element in the Wallas model is irrationality and conflict in the process within the person. Different stages imply contradictory modes of behavior (Gallagher, 1975). Incubation and illumination imply a disorganized, partially formed, detached, illogical, scattered personality style, while verification and preparation imply an organized, complete, logical, and disciplined style. All of these traits are associated with creative people. Creativity seemingly is the melding of these conflicting elements so that they may coexist within the same person in a manner that does not degenerate into psychological impairment.

Sternberg and his colleagues' theory point out different sets of elements in the creative process. Affect, personality, and environment are seen more clearly in the process, although how the interaction takes place is fuzzy. The Investment Model (Sternberg & Lubart, 1993, 1995) describes the creative person as behaving in a fashion analogous to an investment banker: Creative individuals pursue or produce ideas that seemingly have little value (buy low), work toward perfecting those ideas, and eventually convince others of the merit of those ideas (sell high). A person uses six resources (intellectual processes, knowledge, intellectual style, personality, motivation, and environmental context), which are not simply added together, but rather, interact in some multiplicative way to increase creativity within the context of some domain.

The propulsion model switches attention to the contextual elements of a field and how a creative contribution can influence a field in various ways. All creative products change a field, but the quality cannot be judged outside the field.

These three theories deepen our appreciation of the creative process, yet none provides us with an understanding of the development of creativity in children. They illustrate that the deeper one's understanding grows, the more apparent is the complexity; thus, they should be kept in mind as we discuss the development of the creative process in the course of people's lives.

THE CREATIVE PROCESS AND DEVELOPMENT

Many abilities and skills are known to develop in children as they learn and mature. Can the same be said for the creative process?

The term *development* has more than one meaning. *Creative development* can mean an increase in creative functioning over time with unspecific attention to promoting growth, or it can mean increased competence with specific organized efforts to develop it. We make this fuzzy distinction in order to postpone a discussion of teaching for creativity until later in the chapter. First, we review what is known about changes in creativity over time, rather than deliberately teaching for creativity. Of course, this information has implications for teaching.

The development of creativity has been studied by looking for evidence of the progressive growth of psychological traits, examining the process itself, or trying to correlate sociocultural conditions with creative production. These perspectives are not mutually exclusive and were chosen to highlight meaningful differences in the research. Issues of definition and measurement confound our discussion.

The Trait Approach and Development

Trait-perspective studies of creativity search for certain personal traits or qualities as predictors, or at least associated characteristics, of creative behavior. A frequent, but not mandatory, assumption is that traits are normally distributed through society (Nicholls, 1972). Thus, people have creative traits in differing amounts, from a small number of people with a great deal, to a large number with moderate amounts, to a small number with few traits. People with more traits are likely to be eminent, and those with fewer are not. The traits may be generalized across situations and content areas. Proof that creativity is a trait is based upon demonstrating that those with more of the trait are more creative in a variety of situations. A common way to study the issue is to compare the traits of people divided into creative and noncreative groups. Note that, in using this approach, one may be able to predict who is creative, build a list of traits, and still gain little knowledge of the creative process.

The study of the development of creative ability in children takes a general strategy. Children are identified as being creative on the basis of some measuring device. Measurements are made at different ages. When the same children are retested at intervals to determine how the traits have changed, it is a longitudinal study. When children of different ages are tested at the same time, it is a cross-sectional study. Both studies expect increases in scores to correspond to increases in age. The studies ideally show that higher scores at one age are associated with higher scores at other ages. These studies also report data supporting the relationship between high scores and indices of creative performance. This latter point refers to the questions of validity, which was discussed under measurement and is indirectly related to the issue of development.

Information on the development of creativity is dominated by the work of E. Paul Torrance, who undertook cross-sectional studies using the Torrance Tests of Creative Thinking (TTCT) to document changes in creative ability. In general, the studies indicated a gradual increase in scores as children aged; yet, the upward trend was marked by periods of rapid growth, sudden decline, and slow recovery. Rapid growth was evident prior to grade 4 and around grade 11. Sudden decreases were found at grades 1, 4, 7, and 12. The worst slump was around fourth grade (Torrance, 1965). Intrigued by the slump, Torrance conducted a longitudinal study. Because this study is a classic, it is described in some length.

Torrance (1968) extracted a random sample of 100 children from a larger pool of students attending a university school and a Pueblo school from 1959 to 1964. Scores obtained from 45 boys and 55 girls when they were in grades 3–5 were transformed into standard scores using fifth-grade norms. Scores on fluency, flexibility, originality, and elaboration were analyzed for indication of drops or gains; a change of one-half standard deviation was judged as a change. Significant differences were found for all the variables. No scores dropped between grades 3 and 4, and more gains were made between grades 4 and 5. Further inspection of the data indicated that, overall, fluency did not return to the height achieved in third grade. Flexibility and originality showed no significant changes over the three grades. Elaboration scores, which were based on about half the sample, showed significant growth, and the fourth-grade scores exceeded those of the third grade.

At the fourth grade, a decline in creativity (fluency) appeared, which continued over several grades. Although Torrance's findings are cited extensively, few studies supplement them. Khatena (1972) reported decreases of original verbal images at fourth grade on two different measures, and in a 4-year longitudinal study, Khatena and Fisher (1974) reported slumps in scores that occurred at 9 or 10 years of age.

The fact that different measures of creativity were used makes it difficult to interpret the findings. Clearly, scores do increase as children age, and between ages 8 and 10 (fourth grade), creative traits are less evident. Over a 10-year interval, students who are noncreative (low scorers) produce more stable scores than creative students, which suggests the upward growth in fluency.

Because tests of creativity are constructed with the assumption that creativity increases, establishing the fact that scores increase is meaningful. Of further importance is showing that the scores are related to other indicators of creative behavior. The TTCT have served as the measure of creativity in several studies. Torrance reported studies that followed up on what children did in later years and compared that to creativity scores. In 1959, he obtained scores from seniors attending a university high school; in 1966, he used questionnaires about their activities; and, in 1971, judges rated their responses for signs of creativity (Torrance, 1972). The categories for which creativity was judged were family, writing, educational innovation, style of teaching, visual arts, creative photography, dissertations, research publications, music, self-discovery, human relations, and medical/surgical. Results indicated that high scorers became creative adults. The 12-year follow-up produced higher and more significant correlations than the 7-year follow-up, suggesting creativity continues to develop. Several other findings of interest were that highly creative people chose or aspired to unconventional occupations; took circuitous, yet constructive, routes to career choices; and reported more peak achievements.

In a third paper, Torrance (1981) reported a 22-year follow-up of all the elementary school children enrolled in two Minnesota schools. Scores obtained over 3 years were combined into a Creativity Index. Questionnaires were scored for 211 of the original sample of 400. Correlations were calculated between the index and ratings of five kinds of creative achievements. Highly significant correlations were reported to the number of creative achievements during and after high school, the number of "creative style of life" achievements, and the quality of aspirations. Correlations increased in size from high school into the adult years. Rieger (1983), using the same sample and procedures, split the girls into two groups based on the media scores on the Creativity Index with similar results.

A contradictory piece of evidence on the development of creativity in school is also available. Kogan and Pankove (1974), using a somewhat different measure of creativity, attempted to predict creative behavior in high school students from scores obtained in 1967 in fifth-grade classes from both large and small school systems. Children responded to the Wallach-Wing Inventory and to questions about participation in leadership, art, music, science, and dramatic arts. Achievement in these areas was unrelated to creativity scores.

The findings on the development of creativity using the trait approach and activities are based on self-reports that are typically difficult to interpret. Confusion exists between number and quality of activities, not to mention how the activities are categorized. The fact that one engages in many activities, which is similar to the idea of fluency on tests, is not the same as an evaluation of the quality of an activity that warrants the label of creativity. The description of how creative products were evaluated is not as rigorous as our description of how to identify using work samples. In general, the description of creative products and the products themselves seem to be rather weak descriptors of the creative process because they are dissimilar to records of creative work used when we refer to eminent creative people. More convincing evidence on development would be qualitative, as well as quantitative, demonstrating increases in creative activities as a person ages.

The Process Approach and Development

Do the results just reported mean that the development of creativity is not related to age? Such a conclusion would overstate what is known. Although evidence on the development of creativity (or, more precisely, creative traits associated with creative-like activities) could be stronger, other data do exist on the development of creativity in children and adults. These data say something different about the creative process than the trait approach. These studies present creative production during one's career and over one's lifetime, as well as information on the creative process itself. Although much of this information has no direct bearing on life in the classroom, it gives a perspective that is important for understanding giftedness, as well as creativity.

Are children more creative than adults? Is childhood creativity a precursor to creativity in adults? An answer to this question goes back to our distinction of originality being determined in terms of an individual or a discipline. This section does not answer that question, but it does provide information on whether there are periods in which people are more likely to be creative in a manner we would all recognize.

The classic work *Age and Achievement* (Lehman, 1953) is a retrospective study of the relationship of age to the amount of creative work and of age to the most significant creative work. The exceptionally creative participants were selected by expert opinion, study of histories, and analysis of people in various disciplines, including poets, physicists, educators, and novelists. The yardstick for the creators was published contribution, such as articles, books, paintings, and musical scores. The results are about groups of people, not any specific individual. Lehman believed his results to be powerful because of their consistency across time, culture, and field of study—in general, a rapid rise in creativity in a relatively short period of time and a gradual decline over a longer time period. Peak, high-quality achievements appeared relatively early in a person's 30s, with the interval from 30 to 35 slightly more productive than 35 to 40. Major contributors in a field tended to start earlier than minor contributors. Interestingly, creative peaks were field-specific. The peak for the natural sciences and mathematics was 5 to 10 years earlier than those in the social sciences. Poets peak earlier than novelists. Political leaders peaked around 60. However, the findings on peak should not be over interpreted, as opportunity to learn and become involved in a field is a significant intervening variable.

Other research reinforces Lehman's (1953) findings. A study of Nobel Laureates in science confirmed the points about early interest, peak productivity, and quantity of creative productions (Zuckerman, 1977). In another study covering two time periods separated by several centuries, peak productivity was before age 40 (Bullough et al., 1981).

245

A developmental pattern in creative production in adults is evident. Whether or not this pattern can be extended downward into childhood is a critical issue. If data could be produced showing changes in development in social, cognitive, or affective processes coincident with changes in creative activity, then the tie between the creative process in children and adults would be strengthened. We know that creative adults recognized by a field tend to have had extensive experiences in that field as children (Albert & Runco, 1986; Bloom & Sosniak, 1981; Subotnik & Arnold, 1993).

How this process might occur has been described by Gardner (2000) using hypothetical chronological markers. Gardner views 5-year-old children as unconcerned about domains or fields. Development follows typical patterns for children growing up in most cultural communities, and the milestones are relatively impervious to normal environmental variations. Sometimes, children are captivated by a domain, and this experience crystallizes to influence later development. Children can be observed doing impressive things that appear related to a field, but mostly they are indifferent to it. Thus, their productions are not really creative. Ten-year-olds want to know the rules of a domain as quickly as possible. The outlines of the domain become known through the child's commitment to it. The level of activity may be interesting and novel, yet the child's exploration of the edges of a domain is not grounded in extensive knowledge of the field. The foundation for later creative activity may be forming, but the activity itself does not deserve the label. The 15-year-old is at a vulnerable time for the development of creativity. Investment of time and energy in a field, as well as willingness to tests its limits, are needed for creativity to continue to develop. Many potentially creative children drop out at this stage because they cannot sustain the commitment and risk taking. The 30-year-old is immersed in a field, having taken a bold step and produced an idea that has the potential to change that field. If others recognize the product, the person is creative. Gardner's picture of the developmental process suggests that the developmental needs of children at different ages might require different kinds of experiences. In his view, the connection between childhood activity and adult creativity is significant.

Another piece of evidence on the connection between children and adults linking creativity across the life span is the work of Feldman (1980), who saw a coincidence between descriptions of cognitive development and creativity. Briefly, Feldman proposed that the creative process is generally analogous to Piaget's conception of equilibration and stage transition. The basic idea is that a child has a set of intrinsic rules for dealing with life. When a person encounters a problem believed to be solvable, but the person has no rules for doing it, he or she attempts to generate original (to that person) rules. Once these rules are shown to be successful, they become part of the person's way of dealing with the world.

The generation of original rules in the transition from the old way to a new stage is analogous to the creative process. The similarities are evident in the four attributes shared by creativity and stage transition: (1) the person is astonished by the new rule; (2) the new rule seems obvious; (3) the person feels almost drawn in some inevitable way to the solution; and (4) the achievement of the new way of behaving is irreversible and opens the way to new accomplishments. These four attributes are striking in their resemblance to descriptions of the creative process. The coincidence between the creative process and cognitive developmental processes is important, but one should not assume they are equated (Feldman & Fowler, 1997). When children construct new rules, the process is similar to creativity. However, the outcomes are dissimilar in that the creative process produces novel, more effective ways of doing things in comparison to self, society, and a particular field of interest, while the cognitive developmental process produces something novel in terms of oneself.

Summary

Clearly, creative performance continues throughout the adulthood of eminent, creative people. Whether the same may be said for less-creative people is an open question. Young adults tend to be most creative. A connection exists between childhood and adulthood; yet, the precise nature of that transition is not known. Experience in a field of study or domain of knowledge is necessary for later outstanding achievement. The disconnect between childhood and adult creativity may have more to do with our notion of creativity than the actual process. The creativity of a child would seem to be grounded in experience and spontaneity; the adult's in knowledge and persistent searching (Hildreth, 1966). The concept of creativity in childhood is frequently rooted in the idea of a normally distributed trait; the concept in adulthood is less so. Measurement of creativity in children is tied heavily to producing a large number of responses; in adults, fluency is less important than producing a limited number of well-conceived products. In other words, the criteria applied to children's creative productions are more generous than those typically applied to adults' work. Lastly, it appears that there is a general assumption that the creative process is the same at different ages and in different fields. This notion seems to be undergoing some change at this time.

Cultural/Historical Conditions and Development

The creative person grows up in a particular culture and time period. He or she has no control over the time of birth or the set of circumstances that will influence his or her development. The fact that opportunity affects development of creativity is repeated in human development (Gardner, 1983). Serious observers of history have noted that outbursts of creativity occur in certain places, in certain time periods, and in certain ethnic groups. The explosion of art in the Italian city of Florence in the 15th century is one example. Do these so-called "Golden Ages" have any common attributes? Is it possible to substantiate these observations and learn something from them about the creative process and the creative person?

Research on creativity from a historical perspective is complicated by the usual problems of definition, as well as the problem of obtaining enough data to make valid generalizations. Studies (Cox, 1926; Goertzel & Goertzel, 1962; Goertzel et al., 1978) may be criticized on this latter point.

Bullough et al. (1981) attempted to overcome these problems when conducting a study that looked at 290 people from 18th-century Scotland and 158 people from 15th-century Florence. Several important variables associated with creativity emerged in both places. Most of the creative people came from the middle class, which was attributed to the middle class defining achievement and supporting it. Relatively few were aristocrats, and few were poor; there was a "three-generational shift" in which the creative person's family was three generations removed from poverty. Significant achievements were found to rarely go beyond one generation, which was interpreted to mean that creativity was influenced by more than genetic endowment. Good health was important, and again, the most significant accomplishments occurred before age 40. Aging provided an opportunity to restate and amplify one's work. Length of schooling was found to be more significant than social class in encouraging creativity in both centuries. The authors were surprised by this finding and suspected the presence of some hidden bias. Urbanization was found to be a crucial factor in creative achievement. In fact, a commitment to education in association with urbanization was the single most important factor associated with the appearance of creative outburst. The Scottish data illustrate that operating schools in rural areas without local support had no effect on increasing creative work. Interestingly, schools with more than one teacher produced larger numbers of eminent people. Overall, creativity flourished most in an intellectual milieu with others. The authors concluded, "in general, our studies tended to indicate that intellectual and creative achievement is both an individual and societal effort" (p. 114).

Simonton (1979) attempted to understand the influence of cultural conditions on creativity by conceptualizing creativity as having two distinct phases—a developmental period and a productive period—each of which is affected differently by cultural forces. After conducting a series of studies, he reported that the developmental period was more susceptible to external events than the productive period. Illness and age negatively affected the productive period. Wars had a varied effect. Simonton, summarizing the factors influencing the developmental period, stated that formal education had a positive effect on creativity up to a point, after which it had an opposite effect. Social leadership was negatively correlated with longer time in school. The presence of role models was found to be quite important. The total number of eminent creators in one generation was strongly associated with the numbers in the preceding generation. The effects of role models varied according to the discipline. Simonton proposed other factors that influence creativity: the prevailing zeitgeist, political fragmentation, civil disturbance, and political stability. Most of these factors limit the development of creativity. In later work, Simonton has continued to study the historical and cultural context of creativity. His *Origins of Genius* (1999) is an intriguing argument for creativity as part of the evolutionary development using the story of Darwin as a creative genius.

Csikszentmihalyi (1996) argued that it is a mistake to think of creativity as the work of the lone creator. He proposed that creativity is context laden and as such takes place within a large system in which people interact within a domain that shapes the creative act, as well as what is deemed creative. In his view, it makes no sense to separate the person from his or her time or place. Feldman (2000) presented a strong case that the most extreme instances of creativity, such as that of Mozart, are a consequence of complex forces, which illustrates the fragility of creativity. The emergence of creativity is not predictable because social conditions nurture or inhibit creative production (see also Sawyer et al., 2003).

Summary

Creativity has been defined as a general process that becomes increasingly specialized within a particular field of study as one ages. This definition of creativity is consistent with the data on the relationship of childhood creativity measures and adult creative performance. The definition is also consistent with data on adult creative peaks and societal conditions promoting creativity. The creative process in children shares attributes of the creative process in adults. The connection between child and adult creativity is recognized, but the nature of the relationship is not clear.

THE QUESTION OF EDUCATION:
TEACHING FOR CREATIVITY

Creativity is a most complex topic. Knowledge of the process is contradictory, yet we do know that creativity does not happen in a vacuum. Some circumstances seem more conducive to promoting the development of creativity than others. In this section, we look more directly at how creativity may be encouraged by education. Earlier information is important for understanding this section; however, this section stands alone, which signifies the current disconnect between theory and practice. Teachers and parents looking for direction in making decisions will find some guidance in this section, which should put into perspective the large assortment of materials available from publishers that purport to teach for creativity.

The phrase "teaching for creativity" in the heading was chosen on purpose. It emphasizes that creativity can be enhanced, and teaching means arranging the instructional situation to stimulate creativity. The child is not conditioned; rather, conditions are established so that the child may be creative.

Theory as an Organizing Principle

Our review of the creative process and the uncertainty surrounding its development and maintenance implies that it is unwise to think there is only one way to enhance creativity. For example, believing one can increase creative performance by teaching to improve divergent thinking is simplistic. Mumford (1998) commented on this situation: "little guidance, either empirical or theoretical, is available to help us identify those [developmental activities] likely to make a real contribution to the development of students' creative thinking skills" (p. 14). Despite this situation, creativity can be enhanced (Plucker & Beghetto, 2003).

Given this lack of guidance, an organized approach is needed to put teaching procedures and materials into a comprehensive framework so that teachers will have a coherent program. Because of a general acceptance of the idea that process underlies performance, educational practice might be organized on the basis of some theory of the creative process. Precedence for using theory as an organizing principle for a discussion of creativity is evident in the literature (Coleman, 1985a; Mumford, 1998; Stein, 1974; Sternberg, 1999). Using a theory to organize the literature has the advantage of placing educational techniques within stages of development and providing a partial rationale for teaching practice by clarifying what the technique might actually be teaching.

The selection of a suitable description of the creative process to examine teaching procedures is a difficult undertaking because of the arguments that can be raised about making such a choice. One can argue that the process differs from person to person, that is, it is so idiosyncratic that selecting a theory is nonsense. Another argument is that the process is content-specific or domain-specific, so that the process is not comparable across areas. A third argument is that creativity occurs over a long period of time; therefore, it is meaningless to describe a process as if it is locked into a short time frame, such as a day or a week.

These three positions have validity. They include different implications for nurturing creativity because the transformation of a process into educational practice communicates to children what the process might be. The first argument, the idiosyncratic viewpoint, implies an unfocused, highly specific, eclectic approach. The second implies a focused, content-oriented approach. The last implies a choice between long-term and short-term involvement.

Because it is impossible to satisfy all these concerns, the Wallas model is used for this discussion. Use of the Wallas model has the disadvantage of tending to downplay the prime importance of affective or motivational aspects in the process. Unfortunately, assignment of affective forces to any stage is not readily apparent, although some scholars have made suggestions (Amabile, 1983; Gardner, 2000; Mumford, 1998; Sternberg & Lubart, 1993). The creative frame of mind suggests openness, flexibility, and receptivity to unusual and original thoughts accompanied by long-term involvement and perhaps single-mindedness in some areas of interest. These characteristics among others fuel the creative process (Gardner). How to teach affective or motivational characteristics is unclear. A reasonable way to organize instruction would be to teach children how creative people in a particular field behave by reading and discussing their lives (Drews, 1964; Feldhusen, Bahlke, & Treffinger,

1969). Another way is to expose them to models and mentors who display the characteristics. Teachers and parents should be aware that living with a highly creative person is not necessarily easy or pleasant.

The Nature of the Evidence

Each stage of the Wallas model is defined along with a review of techniques relevant to that stage. Some procedures have more implications for affective growth than others. Our review is not exhaustive; rather, samples the field in order to provide a sense of what teachers or programs could do to teach for creativity.

In general, the procedures of teaching for creativity try to press students to behave like they were creative under special conditions, try to imitate the creative process or presumed parts of the process, or both. To teach people to be original by asking them to reproduce or mimic creative behavior appears to be paradoxical. Copying the process is consistent with the time-honored teaching practice of having students model themselves after the masters in a field. However, in the situation with the master, the student is immersed in a situation surrounded by visible and tacit manifestations of creativity. In a typical classroom, it is doubtful that those conditions could be duplicated. Nevertheless, teachers should model creativity in their classrooms (Sawyer et al., 2003). This situation suggests that, when teaching for creativity, teachers should be careful not to overemphasize any part of the process.

Another point to keep in mind is the motivators that are present in the teaching environment (Amabile, 1983). Building intrinsic motivation is preferable to relying on extrinsic motivators to promote creativity. The former seems to be a prerequisite for creative activity, and the latter appears to short-circuit later displays of creativity. By constructing an environment that contains opportunities for choice, time for making decisions, and opportunities for self-expression and psychological support, teachers can promote the growth of intrinsic motivation.

Preparation Stage Techniques

The preparation stage is the time when the person acquires skill, knowledge, and attitudes that are useful later for creative activity, and it is the time when questions or problems are found or formulated. In a sense, a large part of the preparation stage occurs before the creativity process, relative to a particular field or product, is activated (Feldman, 1980; Stein, 1974; Sternberg & Lubart, 1993). The school might be more likely to influence positively in this stage than in the others.

The importance of the climate in the classroom and the school has been well documented (Amabile, 1983; Renzulli, 1992; Torrance, 1965). On this issue there is good news and bad news. The bad news is that schools spend the smallest part of their time on creative activities. Teachers primarily reward

251

conformity and are uncomfortable with creative students. The good news is that, when creative-like behavior is rewarded, children display it with greater frequency.

A significant aspect of the preparation stage is the development of knowledge and skills relevant to a field of study (Keating, 1980; Mumford, 1998). A person must be well versed in the fundamental concepts, as well as the most advanced propositions, within a field in order to do creative work (Sternberg, 2003.) The school can play an important role in permitting children to engage these concepts and develop more efficient ways of representing the information. Children should be actively involved in being responsible for mastering increasingly complex knowledge and, most importantly, for developing habits of questioning and searching for unresolved problems in an area. Problem finding incorporates these ways of thinking and acting.

"The ability to define or identify a problem prior to working on its solution" is what defines problem finding (Kay, 1994, p. 195), and it is crucial to the creative process. Problem finding can be enhanced in various ways. "Classrooms that are entirely 'open' and unstructured are *not* conducive to creativity. . . . Students can learn a great deal about problem finding and problem solving from lectures and explicit instructions" (Runco & Nemiro, 1998, p. 237). By presenting problems that are well-defined and problems that are ill-defined, students can practice dealing with both situations. Kay (1998) recommended that children have an opportunity to engage problems that are personally meaningful. Curricula can be designed to do that, for example, a "Discovery Center Unit" that promotes the development of this skill (Kay, 1994).

Associated with problem finding is the development of critical thinking skills. Scholars (e.g. Mumford,1998; Sternberg, 2003) have suggested that such skills are foundational, that is, creative thinking cannot occur unless one has learned or organized the relevant ideas and content. Choosing among various possibilities requires a critical eye.

Becoming aware of one's interests and values is an important part of preparation for creativity. It is through planned awareness activities that one can learn about oneself (Whitmore, 1980). Values clarification, role-playing, psychodrama (Ortman, 1966), and other training materials have application here (Callahan, 1978; Feldhusen & Treffinger, 1980; Torrance & Myers, 1970). However, if these activities are implemented as independent, disconnected activities, children may be engaged and adults fascinated, but the activities are unlikely to contribute to the development of creativity without being tied to meaningful problems.

Self-knowledge also means that one can learn to anticipate and, if desired, counteract the habits or thoughts that interfere with creativity; or, one can arrange one's life for work under optimal conditions. Many examples of preferred work or study conditions can be found (Stein, 1974). Some preferences suggested by gifted children are using well-sharpened pencils, working early in the morning, drinking soda constantly, keeping the stereo on, and not being interrupted by anyone. The teacher can help children become aware of their idiosyncratic ways of working and learning. Renzulli (1992) has recommended that such information be part of the process of teaching for creativity for many years. Being aware of oneself is a valuable asset.

Incubation Stage Techniques

The Journal of Creative Behavior (Brunelle, 1979) and *Gifted Child Quarterly* (Gowan, 1979) have devoted entire issues to the incubation stage. Incubation is invisible—a time when previous, sustained work on a real problem of interest is set aside. Something happens during this apparent inactivity that is revealed in the next stage, illumination. Olton (1979) distinguished between incubation and creative worrying. In the former, one who is highly motivated and knowledgeable in an area ceases to work on a problem after substantial previous activity. In the latter, one returns episodically to the problem until a solution emerges. Incubation occurs infrequently in this description. The length of time over which incubation may occur is unknown, but it is possible for it to last for a period of years (Arieti, 1981). Given the nature of incubation, the techniques used to foster it fall into two categories: those that help people turn inward and observe themselves and those that stimulate what is assumed to be happening by forcing associations.

Turning Inward. Many school practices run counter to conditions that stimulate creativity. The very idea of incubation—the notion that stopping work will lead to greater productivity and creativity—is contrary to typical school programs. Several values that promote creativity, but are in opposition to our action-oriented, direct style in schools, are daydreaming, solitude, inactivity, gullibility, and free thinking (Arieti, 1981). The common thread is the opportunity for a person to step outside the action and turn inward, where one's inner resources and past experiences may intrude on the conscious mind. Arieti saw the unconscious as the wellspring of valuable ideas. Coming from another perspective, Gruber noted that the generation of ideas requires time to be spontaneous and reflective (Kay, 1998). An environment that will promote creativity needs to make provisions for abandoning the typical practices in schools. Teachers can plan for such time in their classes.

Techniques such as hypnosis, meditation, relaxation exercises, and biofeedback are related to promoting incubation (Krippner, Dreistadt, & Hubbard, 1979; Stein, 1974; see Torrance, 1979a, for descriptions of other techniques used to heighten incubation.). In essence, these procedures have the person simulate assumed aspects of the process. Besides learning to set aside obvious concerns, there are other procedures that cause people to turn inward in a more direct way. These techniques ask people to pretend or imagine they are not themselves. One may become another person with different emotions, goals, and so forth through role-playing or psychodrama, or one may pretend to be an inanimate object or substance though personal analogy (Gordon, 1961). The premise behind these techniques is that the act of putting aside one's conventional self changes one's position in relation to a problem. A person can then perceive previously overlooked or prematurely discarded relationships among ideas. These techniques have been used successfully in industry (Stein, 1974) and have ready application in the classroom (Feldhusen & Treffinger, 1980).

Forcing Associations. A host of techniques are available that take a paradoxically direct approach to fostering incubation. These techniques are efficient means for increasing creativity, which is an inefficient process that proceeds at its own rate. These techniques force ideas and words to become visible and to become associated in unconventional ways, thereby breaking the bonds of habitual associations. The intent is to help people see old associations in new ways and produce many responses. The rational is harnessed to serve the irrational. All of these procedures have implications for succeeding stages of the creative process. Placing them under incubation forces relationships that a person might see spontaneously if left alone. Most of these techniques have been used to increase the creative output of groups of children and adults (Callahan, 1978; Feldhusen & Treffinger, 1980; Stein, 1975; Treffinger, Sortore, & Cross, 1993). Whether they increase the creativity of individuals is an open question, one that not everyone accepts (Paulus & Paulus, 1997).

Brainstorming is a technique with wide currency that was conceived in the 1930s by Osborn (1953), who believed people could be taught to become creative. Primarily, it is a group procedure for generating many ideas while suspending judgment. It is often used in conjunction with other procedures (Parnes, 1967). Brainstorming is built on two main ideas. First, the greater the quantity of ideas, the greater the likelihood that original, high-quality ideas will appear. (Note the idea that less commonly associated ideas are more creative.) The second idea is that deferring judgment increases creativity because evaluation tends to censor strange, but potentially creative, ideas. When used in classrooms, brainstorming usually proceeds in the following manner. The class is given an explanation of the rules. Criticism is ruled out; wild, crazy ideas are encouraged (the more ideas, the better); and combining ideas is welcomed. A problem is specified. All ideas are recorded. Evaluation follows the brainstorming session.

Much research has been conducted on brainstorming (Stein, 1975). Although people can be taught to produce more ideas (Parnes, 1967), it is less clear whether all the possible ideas are produced and whether the most original ideas are generated during brainstorming.

> Controlled studies comparing group brainstorming with individual brainstorming found that individuals in groups often generate 50% fewer ideas than solitary brainstormers and fewer high-quality ideas. . . . Even so, those who participate in group brainstorming rate their performance more favorably than those who perform alone. (Paulus & Paulus, 1997, p. 225)

Groups can be made more effective by employing teachers or facilitators who are adequately trained, by letting children choose to be in a group or be alone, and by holding individuals accountable for producing numbers, not quality, of ideas (Paulus & Paulus). The level of diversity in background, opinions, and ideas is most important in making creativity work in groups (Paulus & Nijastad, 2003).

Attribute listing is another technique for forcing associations. The procedure involves selecting an object or a situation that one wishes to change. The important characteristics of the object or situation are listed, and suggestions for change in each attribute are made without concern for evaluation or appropriateness (Callahan, 1978; Feldhusen & Treffinger, 1980).

Morphological analysis is a procedure that forces the user to bring ideas into new combinations that might otherwise be overlooked. The steps are: (1) identify the basic components or parameters of the problem; (2) list attributes of each parameter; (3) arrange the parameters and their attributes as dimensions of a grid or cube; (4) combine variables as they intersect in the grid; and (5) evaluate the results (Feldhusen & Treffinger, 1980). Morphological analysis can produce some clever ideas. One problem with the technique is that, because children are unable to visualize more than three dimensions, the larger grids become unwieldy.

Checklists are a group of procedures that direct a standard list of questions to a problem situation. The questions act as a stimulus for uncovering new relationships by forcing a change in the user's perspective on the problem, thus forcing the generation of new ideas. Osborn (1953) used questions to spur idea generation in brainstorming. Bondi and Koubik (1980) composed a checklist using key words (modify, adapt, rearrange, magnify, minify, combine, substitute, reverse) to apply as one reconsiders an object or event. The SCAMPER model uses this idea with children (Eberle, 1996).

The use of analogies and metaphors to enhance creativity has shown much promise. Gordon (1961, 1971) pioneered in this area with his Synectics program, which uses metaphor to break away from habitual thinking and increase one's receptivity to new ideas. Gordon's ideas are significant because the emotional side of creativity is recognized. He believed that people, in order to overcome emotional blocks to thinking, have always used metaphor. Analogy helps make the familiar strange and the strange familiar so that ideas are less threatening. Types of analogies include direct analogy, symbolic analogy, and personal analogy, and each has different effects. Personal analogy was described earlier in the section on turning inward. Direct analogy uses parallel examples from another field to solve problems, such as comparing a beehive to house construction. Symbolic analogy uses a compressed image of the problem in which words are in opposition (e.g., "burning ice" to convey the idea of heating and refrigeration). Callahan (1978) and Feldhusen and Treffinger (1980) have described the use of analogies and metaphors in a typical Synectics session. Castille (1998) reported using analogies in metaphorical comprehension with primary-age children.

Summary. In sum, methods to enhance the incubation stage of the creative process are organized into two types: turning inward and forcing associations. The former places more emphasis on the affective part of the process and attending to unconscious processes; the latter emphasizes the production of multiple uncommon responses. Both types help children move out of conventional thinking about themselves and problems. Many of the techniques use logical and analytical cognitive processes in the service of promoting illogical, potentially creative associations. All the techniques give students license to depart from normal practice.

Illumination Stage Techniques

The illumination stage is the moment of insight, marking the end of the incubation stage and the beginning of the verification stage. Illumination is the transition from inspiration to reality. Gruber described the feelings of that moment: "surprise is failure backward" (Kay, 1998, p. 108). In one sense, it moves back to the preparation stage and forward toward a potential solution. In another sense, illumination offers a glimpse of the creative product, although the product is rarely complete. A metamorphosis is occurring.

How does the creator know which one of the many possibilities is the one to pick? The procedures designed to foster incubation by generating new ideas provide no answers to this question. People do report moments of knowing or sensing they are on the right track. Apparently, in illumination, even though the final product is still incomplete, its outline is clear enough for the person to believe that progress is being made and success is ahead. Without this feeling of progress, the individual may be paralyzed by the number of choices.

Scant information is available on which to base an instructional procedure that would enhance illumination. In fact, direct approaches seem unlikely to work because the standard for judgment is fuzzy or unknown beforehand, and the creative process is uncontrollable. Moving too rapidly toward the verification stage is precisely what incubation techniques contradict in advance of the appearance of insight.

One teaching approach might be to focus on the preparation stage where a reservoir of knowledge and skills in a domain is being constructed. Perhaps it is in the problem-finding part of preparation that the recognition of the illumination stage is set. Famous creators, such as Albert Einstein (Getzels, 1979) and Pablo Picasso (Feldman, 1980), seem to have relied on the statement of the problem as the basis for a creative product. Educational procedures could provide opportunities for identifying problems in contexts similar to those faced by famous creators. Another approach might be to help individuals distinguish between problem-finding situations presented by others and self-selected problems. In problem-finding situations presented by teachers or employers, hints about an appropriate solution may be apparent. A willingness to wait and not rush toward the insight may also be taught. In our fast-paced world, that is difficult to do. An allied method is teaching individuals to trust their hunches and be willing to go toward their intuition in making choices.

Various counseling strategies work toward that end. Whether or not these approaches can foster illumination awaits further research.

Verification Stage Techniques

The creative product is evaluated and reworked until the creator believes it is ready to be presented to others. Verification rarely involves a single decision; instead, it incorporates a series of decisions and modifications as the work approaches final form. Verification differs from illumination as the completeness of the product becomes more and more apparent. The standards of judgment move from implicit, internal standards to more explicit, external criteria as the person is aware that others will see the work.

The dynamics of this stage are difficult to capture. The individual must be committed to a solution or final product for this stage to be operational, even if her or she has no intention of showing the work to others. Verification requires a special kind of discipline to continue in the face of uncertainty and question openly the worth of one's efforts (Runco, 1993). Many people probably hesitate and reject further work at this point (Amabile, 1983). Verification contradicts early stages in which evaluation is avoided in order to let a free exchange of ideas occur. Ready examples of change in creative work during verification can be found in reading versions of manuscripts for novels or records of scientific experiments.

Teaching for verification is problematic because evaluation is rational and intuitive when applied to creative activity. The rational part is a logical and critical analysis of the work based upon known technical and procedural principles in a field of study, and intuitive means it feels like it fits in that field. Teaching for critical thinking is also relevant to the verification stage because it requires learners to look with and beyond the problem situation (Feldhusen & Treffinger, 1980; Mumford, 1998; Sawyer et al., 2003). Another approach might be to teach a systematic procedure for testing all the possibilities, just as Thomas Edison did to find the proper substance for a light bulb filament. Runco (1993) made a distinction between valuative and evaluative thinking in judging the worth of a creative product. In the former, the child recognizes the appropriate fit of an idea for the situation; in the latter, the aim is to arrive at the best, most creative solution.

The intuitive or mystical part of evaluation is the aesthetic feeling accompanying the creative product that indicates the work is complete (Stein, 1974). These feelings are apparently similar to those of the illumination stage, but they operate at the end of the process when inspiration has been replaced by a feeling of "rightness," which the creator may share with observers of the creative work (Ghiselin, 1952; Kay, 1998). Teaching someone to tune in to their aesthetic sense might be accomplished by providing students opportunities to discuss their experiences while working on a creative product. Sensitizing individuals to signs of progress and completeness may be advanced in this way (Stein).

An Implied Stage: Showing One's Work

Verification is the final stage of the Wallas model. Implied in it is the need to communicate one's ideas to others. Someone may create something, but it will not be recognized as a creative event unless others learn about it. In this stage, we are not talking of the general acceptance that is needed to foster creativity, but rather, the fact that ideas and products have to be made accessible to others. As Sternberg and Lubart (1993) would say, you have to sell your ideas to others.

Children need to develop skills in presenting their ideas to others and gaining support for their creative efforts. Writing skills are particularly important in this regard. The presentation of a creative work to the public may entail communicating with a variety of intermediaries, such as gallery owners, experts, patrons, teachers, mentors, and managers. Facility in working with others is also important. Given the fact that many creative people tend to be loners, skills in communicating and gaining support are necessary parts of the curriculum, but relatively little attention has been paid to them.

One danger of categorizing teaching techniques in terms of a stage model is that readers may incorrectly conclude that each technique is only relevant to one stage. Knowledge of the creative cycle is not clear enough to make such a judgment. Our organization was intended to help practitioners recognize the rationale for many techniques and the limits of that particular procedure. Actually, many of the writers on creativity urge that a variety of skills be taught in order to foster creativity (Mumford, 1998; Runco, 1993; Sternberg, 1999). Programs or instructional systems are available that use many of these techniques and do not use the stage orientation used here.

Materials and Programs

A large number of materials and programs are available that claim to teach for creativity in children and adults (Davis & Rimm, 1989; Feldhusen & Clinkenbeard, 1986). While we advise readers to consult them for ideas, our caveat is that claims for the success of these materials exceed the evidence supporting their effectiveness. Of course, this is no different than the case with most commercially available materials.

The Future Problem Solving Program, Odyssey of the Mind, and CPS for Kids are popular programs that encourage children to develop positive attitudes about and skills for creativity that cut across the stages of the Wallas model. The first two are widely used around the country and involve thousands of children in creative problem-solving competitions. They are frequently used as activities within a program for the gifted.

Another major impetus for teaching for creativity comes from the programs that advocate that children produce real-world creative products. In various publications over many years, Joseph Renzulli, John Feldhusen, Donald Treffinger, George Betts, and James Gallagher have been proponents of creative products as an appropriate outcome for programs for the gifted and talented. In particular, Renzulli and his colleagues have published a number of studies demonstrating that children can produce creative products at all levels

258

of schooling (Burns, 1990; Delcourt, 1994; Renzulli, 1999; Shack, 1993; Starko, 1988). These studies illustrate that children can be taught in situations that promote the production of creative products. More about this model is discussed in a later chapter.

Summary

Research has been conducted on the effectiveness of teaching for creativity, but more research, especially on children, is needed. Evidence supporting training for specific stages of the creative process is less than overwhelmingly favorable. The preparation and the incubation stages have received the most attention from educators. The verification stage and the implied stage (communication of results) need to receive more attention if all aspects of the creative cycle are to be developed. Evidence supporting creativity programs is encouraging and mixed. The connection between performance on lessons designed to teach a technique or skill related to problem solving and creativity in a domain is not well established.

Clearly, we can increase creative-like behavior in children; for example, they can learn techniques that increase scores on divergent-thinking tests (Pyryt, 1998). Long-term programs are likely to produce better results than creativity lessons. Until more data on the effectiveness of various methods and programs are available, believing that one program is superior to another for use with children of all ages and ability is unwarranted. In fact, relying solely on one approach, given what little we know, might be harmful for the development of creativity. At the same time, a broad, eclectic approach should not be embraced as the best methodology. Given the definition of creativity as a generalized process that becomes increasingly specialized with a field or domain, schools might teach for creativity by giving general process instruction in the early years, which gradually gives way to field-specific instruction as children become more committed to a field of interest.

CONCLUSION

Creativity is one of the major topics in the field of gifted development. Conflicting views on definition, process, and education abound.

The problem of measurement of creativity is determining the characteristics of creative activity. What constitutes a valid criterion? Does the same criterion apply to children and adults? What connection, if any, should there be between the expression of creativity in children and adults? Uncertainty over these issues, as well as technical considerations, suggests caution in interpreting measurement. Creativity may be measured by standardized tests, rating scales and checklists, and work samples or products, each of which has advantages and disadvantages and no one of which alone gives a complete view of the creative process. Standardized tests measure traits associated with creativity. One trait, divergent thinking, stands out as a sign of creativity. Its place in the creative cycle is unclear. When is the best time to teach for this skill is not clear, but some recent recommendations are for later in the process. Qualitative differences in performance are indirectly assessed by these tests. Standardized tests have little relationship to each other, and there is limited evidence of their ties to real-world creativity. Rating scales and checklists are increasingly popular. Some have normative data. Rating scales make use of biographical information by asking the person or an observer to rate interests and past experiences associated with creativity. Self-ratings by older children are the strongest. Work sample or creative products differ from the other forms of measurement in that they inspect the outcomes of creativity in real-world terms. However, the problem of criteria and who should judge is persistent. Identification of creative ability can be helped by the use of these devices. Combinations of these techniques are probably the best ways to assess creativity. Obviously, at this time, these devices inadequately reveal the creative process.

The question of the relationship between creativity and intelligence is complicated. In essence, creativity and intelligence tests measure different phenomena, but the two variables work together in such a way that outstanding performance contains both. Perhaps there is a threshold phenomenon. Saying that highly creative people are not intelligent is incorrect. The nature of the relationship is not settled, and the question has changed as discussion of intelligence and creativity has become more and more domain-specific.

Creativity appears to develop across the lifespan. The connection between childhood and adulthood is not clear, although there is a connection. The creative traits of childhood are conservatively related to adult traits. Further, the relationships between traits such as divergent thinking and adult accomplishment are not strong. Whether or not the creative process works the same in children and adults is not clear. Some kind of interplay takes place between rational, logical forms of thinking and unconscious, emotional forms of thinking. Affective and motivational variables fuel the creative process. In adults, creativity is viewed as field-specific; eminent adults often become involved in their field relatively early in life and produce their most significant creations in early adulthood. A general tendency exists in cultures to encourage some aspects of the creative process and some field-related processes more readily than others.

The amount of literature on teaching for creativity is voluminous, and the number of materials available for use in teaching far outdistances the evidence of their effectiveness. The data available on some techniques are encouraging, but not heavily so. By having children behave as if they are creative, we have been able to show growth in creative products. Procedures for teaching creativity are most comprehensible when tied to real-world activity. There are no shortcuts to the development of creative ability.

FOR **DISCUSSION**

1. Would a universal definition of creativity be useful? Provide three reasons to support your position.

2. Imagine you actually had a class of children who were creative and exhibited all the personal characteristics associated with creativity. How would you organize instruction for that kind of group?

3. If creativity and intelligence cannot be separated, what implications does this have for education?

4. The chapter offers several classification schemes for thinking about creativity. It also used the Wallas model to organize teaching information. Which other classification scheme might you use to organize information about teaching?

5. Given the idea about the historical context for creativity, what forms of creativity are likely to flourish in the next 25 years?

6. Defend or refute: Creativity is present in every field of human endeavor.

chapter seven

ADMINISTRATIVE ARRANGEMENTS, PROGRAM PROTOTYPES, AND THE TEACHER

KEY CONCEPTS

- Program arrangements for the gifted are designed to meet the persistent challenges these children create for the school.

- Most current administrative arrangements have been operative in some form since the early part of the last century.

- Educational programs are built on three contrasting educational models: the Whole Child Model, the Talent/Multiple Ability Model and the Basic Skills Model.

- Enrichment, acceleration, and special grouping in settings are the variables used in program planning. They are not mutually exclusive.

- The benefits of acceleration are the best-kept secret in the educational community, and impeding implementation indirectly demonstrates the resistance to advanced development in society.

- Nine administrative options are available for incorporation in any program and may be used in varying combinations.

- The need to determine the effectiveness of various program designs is well recognized and underimplemented.

- The selection of quality teachers and mentors is a prime requisite for any program. Not everyone can teach children who are gifted.

The development of giftedness has been discussed in detail throughout this text. The case has been made that the gifted, as a group and as individuals, have characteristics that demand special educational arrangements if they are to realize their potentials. Our discussion of identification (Chapter 3) and guidance (Chapter 5) illustrated the problems a child might have in being gifted in American schools. The content of this chapter is directed toward organizing a program for the gifted.

Seven key features of programs for the gifted were identified more than 30 years ago and are still relevant today (Renzulli, 1968): (1) the teacher, (2) the curriculum, (3) student selection procedures, (4) a statement of philosophy and objectives, (5) staff orientation, (6) a plan of evaluation, and (7) administrative responsibility. Two additional features are (8) guidance services and (9) ability grouping, acceleration, or a combination of the two. Some features are discussed in other chapters. Student selection procedures and guidance services were discussed in Chapters 3 and 4. Curriculum is discussed in Chapter 8, and issues of teaching are in Chapters 9 and 10. The remaining features are essentially administrative arrangements that shape the environment in which teaching and learning take place.

An entire chapter is devoted to administrative options because organizational details bear considerable weight in a school district's decision to build a program for the gifted. Most descriptions of educational provisions for the gifted are portraits of how programs are organized in terms of these key concepts. In fact, more research has been conducted on the effects of programs than on the use of particular teaching or curricular practices. Our experience in countless meetings in school districts and in state departments of education reminds us of the fact that administrative arrangements are invariably mentioned with greater frequency than curricula and student learning.

In practice, there are a limited number of programmatic dimensions that American school systems consider when building the kind of program they want. Programmatic dimensions are useful for comparing different administrative arrangements. Gallagher (1975) named three dimensions: the content, the method of presentation, and the learning environment. These dimensions seem to be aimed at different aspects of programming and, for our purposes, are renamed *curriculum*, *teaching strategies*, and *administrative arrangements*. This chapter is devoted to administrative arrangements. The others are discussed in successive chapters. In actuality, the programmatic dimensions are intertwined and their relationship is confused. The logical order in which they are organized in this text is for pedagogical reasons and should not be assumed to be the order in which decisions are made in any school district. The reasons for this organization will become evident in each chapter.

CHALLENGES THE GIFTED PRESENT TO THE SCHOOL

The education of the gifted has a long history that extends back to at least the time of the Greeks (Tannenbaum, 1993). The general outline of administrative arrangements for the gifted that are practiced today were evident before World War I (Freehill, 1961). They emerged because gifted children presented problems for American schools that demanded resolution and because administrative arrangements are easier to put into practice than are curricular and instructional modifications. The problems are still with us and still stimulate the seemingly timeless practices of acceleration, grouping, special classes, special schools, and so forth (Howley et al., 1995).

All program modifications are directed at four persistent problems gifted and talented students present to the school: the students' wide range of abilities, teacher limitations in content areas, teachers' lack of special methods (Gallagher, 1975), and students' advanced rate of development (Coleman, 1985a). VanTassel-Baska (1994a) has suggested three somewhat related student characteristics (precocity, intensity, and complexity) that influence how a curriculum is enacted.

The persistent problems conveniently divide themselves into the categories of *student-oriented problems* (wide range of abilities, advanced rate of development) and *teacher-oriented problems* (limitation in content areas, lack of special methods). Student-oriented problems are inevitable because they are inherent in the expression of giftedness. These problems will continue to serve as an irritant to school systems because they can be neither changed nor eliminated. On the other hand, teacher-oriented problems are more amenable to change. Teachers as people are not the problem. Teachers are representatives of the educational establishment or community, which, in turn, reflects societal priorities and values. The educational establishment, rather than individual teachers, is responsible for limitations in content areas and for the lack of special methods. The educational establishment is responsible for the unavailability and inadequacy of teacher training programs (Feldhusen, 1994), the intransigence of school organizations, the lack of long-term research on educational practices for the gifted (Borland, 1989, 1996), and the limits on resources available for educating the gifted. Of course, the educational community is not monolithic. Pockets of excellence do exist and deserve to be emulated (some of them are described later in this chapter). Nevertheless, the complex source of the persistent problems makes it highly unlikely that they will disappear in the near future. Thus, schools will continue to grapple with them as best they can.

The schools' responses are likely to continue to be primarily administrative in nature and follow the outlines of practices developed in the last century. This reaction to persistent problems raises an intriguing question: Why do the responses persist in the same general forms? Perhaps, there is only a limited range of programmatic options for American schools, given the philosophical perspective of Western society as it relates to giftedness (Fetterman, 1988). This possibility was alluded to Chapter 1. Newland (1976), noting the rise and fall of interest in the gifted, suggested that the lack of a philosophical perspective on ability that leads to a commitment to educating gifted children is largely responsible for this situation. When programs are begun primarily because they are fashionable or because there are financial incentives without philosophical commitment and community support, it is not surprising that they are abandoned when fashion changes or money diminishes (Callahan, 1996).

Another possibility for the persistence of the problem is that the educational models educators have for dealing with giftedness and talent are inadequate and inappropriate for the task of meeting their educational needs. In the next section, we discuss three models that are embedded in the educational establishment and compete for control of teaching and learning.

THREE MODELS

Schools districts and state departments of education typically have available statements of goals and curriculum standards that are meant to apply to all children (U.S. Department of Education, 2004). Examples of typical statements are "to develop the capacity to function as citizens in a pluralistic society" and "to enable children to fulfill their potentials as persons to the fullest extent possible." These examples of goals and standards seem straightforward, and they sound as if the school would be responsive to developing giftedness. Yet, schools in general are not receptive to special programming. The discrepancy between statements of goals and actual practice with gifted students in most schools is clear (Gallagher, 2003).

Gifted and talented students are not thriving when it would seem they should be. The goals, in reality, hide the fact that contrasting educational models can support the same goal statements while having different philosophical orientations toward development, learning, teaching and so forth, which imply different implications for the gifted in school administrative arrangements. Not all administrative arrangements are amenable to the development of talents and gifts.

We offer three competing educational models and highlight the variance among them. The three models are the Whole Child Educational Model (WCM), the Talent/Multiple Abilities Model (TMM) and the Basic Skill Educational Model (BSM). The first two models were offered in the first edition of this text (Coleman & Cross, 2001); the BSM is new to this edition. In our view, only one model, the TMM, is oriented to the development of giftedness and talent and is consistent with our knowledge.

Table 7.1 illustrates the attributes of the three models. The models are compared in terms of goal orientation, time to begin instruction, rate of development, child's role in education, attitude toward ability, nature of creativity, teacher's role and expectations, attitude toward lack of growth, evaluation, implications and the availability of resources to foster development.

The goal of the Talent/Multiple Ability Educational Model is the maximization of a talent or a complex of abilities. An effort is made to uncover talents in individuals as early as possible, and the child's commitment to developing the talent is expected to be high. Abilities that are indirectly related to the talent receive little emphasis. Maximum talent development is expected to occur for that child. Evaluation is varied and frequently public. Creative ability is expected to emerge as the child becomes increasingly competent. The teacher is presumed to be an expert who will have a long-term involvement with the child, although he or she will pass the child on to another expert when it is appropriate. Lack of progress is thought to be the teacher's fault. The program structure implied in this model is individually oriented, and instruction is geared toward mastery and future development.

The Whole Child Educational Model is concerned with maximizing a child's potential as a whole person. This process begins at school entrance. The presence of high ability is accepted and reacted to when it is obvious. Major efforts are devoted to fostering the development of lesser abilities indicated by age and grade averages so that some sort of balance is maintained. Creativity is believed to be present in all children, and its emergence is possible in most instructional situations. Feedback about one's progress is commonly delayed, but public. The teachers are generalists who typically spend a year or less with a child. Lack of progress is the fault of the child, the family, or prior teachers. The program organization in the Whole Child Developmental Model is group-oriented and is administratively geared to managing groups of children as they develop in accord with age and grade expectations in multiple areas.

The Basic Skills Model is concerned with maximizing the development of basic skills with attention paid to other skills and ability if time permits. The process begins at school entrance when academic skills are introduced and encouraged. The child is seen as a member of a cohort that must reach a minimal level of competence as measured by standardized tests. Development is

TABLE 7.1

Contrasting Educational Models

Attributes	Talent/ Multiple Abilities	Whole Child	Basic Skills
Long-term goals	Maximize talents of person	Maximize whole person	Maximize mastery of basics, narrow the range
Beginning instruction	Informal, explorative, early as possible, individually oriented	Formal, school entrance, group oriented	Formal, school entrance, academics first, group
Developmental rate learning	Field-specific	Age/grade-specific	Age/grade-specific, basic skills
Child's role	Active, involved	Passive, involved	Passive, involved
Attitudes toward ability	Proactive, mastery	Reactive, balanced	Reactive, mastery of skills by group over individual, narrow the range
Creative potential	Province of masters in field, increases with competence	Normal, distributed, emerges in most situations	Irrelevant to mastery of skills, encourage afterwards
Teacher role	Expert, few teachers with multiyear contracts	Generalist, different teacher yearly	Manger and trainer, different teacher yearly
Teacher expectations	Child is committed, complete mastery	Some will, some won't do it, mastery related to chronological age	All children must reach minimal level, raising the lowest third of class comes first
Lack of growth	Teacher fault	Child, family, prior teacher fault	Educators' fault
Evaluation	Frequent, encouraging, immediate, relative to task	Infrequent, delayed, relative to age/grade	Frequent, age/grade-related, mastery, high stakes
Implication for programs	Primary instructional, individually oriented	Primarily administrative, group-oriented	Primarily administrative, group oriented
Resources	All that is possible, sacrifice is worth it	All that is available	Enough to meet the standards

Note. From *Schooling the Gifted* (p. 275), by L. J. Coleman, 1985, Menlo Park, CA: Addison-Wesley. Copyright © 1985 by L. J. Coleman. Reprinted with permission.

age/grade-specific as it applies to basic academics. The child is assumed to be passively involved in mastering academic knowledge. Creativity is of minimal interest. Teachers are managers of instruction who are expected to raise the level of the group, especially the lowest third. Average levels of achievement are more critical than expanding the upper range of performance. Evaluation is frequent and relies on standardized measures at specified intervals, usually toward the end of the school year. The program is primarily administrative and group-oriented. Resources are limited and forthcoming when successful and reallocated when not.

These three models have been represented as being very different for purposes of clarity in order to highlight that competing educational models move schools toward administrative choices. In reality, the differences are not so sharp and may be reconciled in different ways within programs, which will become clear when some programs are examined. Based upon the attributes in Table 7.1, it is apparent that the Whole Child Model and the Basic Skills Model are operating in most American schools. The Talent/Multiple Ability Model spawns rhetoric about attending to individual differences, but few schools use it in their administrative structure. The exceptions are special schools that are more ready to accept aspects of the TMA model. Among the three models, the Basic Skills Model is controlling the educational agenda today. This is not good news for gifted children.

In the next section we examine general variables that are used to shape administrative practices. Each model has attractive aspects for dealing with the problems presented by gifted children that help to sustain the unsettled state of programming. The hesitancy of schools to respond to the needs of gifted children and some of the problems of building community support can be linked to the acceptance of irreconcilable aspects drawn from the three models.

VARIABLES RELEVANT TO PROGRAM PLANNING

Three general variables are used to plan programs: enrichment, acceleration, and special grouping in settings. These three variables are able to deal with aspects of giftedness and fit within educational models. They are the *traditional* aspects of program planning. Each implies a set of educational decisions about curricula, student selection, evaluation, and funding. Selecting one variable as the basis for programming, however, does not automatically ensure these implied decisions were made. In fact, schools have come up with such an assortment and combination of plans that it is sometimes difficult to distinguish the predominant variable. Arguably, the most common program structure is eclecticism, which involves piecing together elements that seem to fit a school district. Sometimes, one aspect of a program can be in conflict with another, such as an enrichment-oriented math class in which the students want to move to more complex content and the program wants them to stay within the regular curriculum.

Understanding these three variables will clarify the basis for decisions a school has made in organizing its program for the gifted. A fourth variable, guidance (Kaplan, 1974), has been suggested as an important element in programming decisions. However, guidance is considered to be a curricular and instructional decision; therefore, it is outside the parameters of this chapter.

Enrichment

Enrichment is a broad term used to refer to program organization that extends, supplements, and sometimes replaces aspects of a school's structure. The emphasis in enrichment is generally to keep children with their peers and to foster the development of higher cognitive and affective processes. In essence, enrichment means that the time one spends in a course of study remains the standard length, but additional experiences are provided. In its broadest interpretation, enrichment encompasses a number of modifications in standard educational practices. In its narrowest interpretation, enrichment means providing interesting and stimulating tributaries to the mainstream of school. Enrichment can occur in a single lesson or class (Howley, Howley, & Pendarvis, 1986) or in an entire school (Betts, 1988; Renzulli & Reis, 1985, 1997).

Acceleration

Acceleration is a broad term that can refer to program organization in which the learner completes a course of study in less time than ordinarily expected. The emphasis in acceleration is on compressing time and early entrance into a career. Students spend more time learning new material and less time practicing what they already know. Acceleration in its broadest sense refers to an individual student moving ahead of peers in all areas of schooling. In its narrowest sense, acceleration is applied to a specific course of study or talent area where one moves ahead of his or her peers in selected areas. In essence, acceleration means that the time one spends in a course of study is shortened, and conventional experiences are compressed within that time frame (Schiever & Maker, 1997) so the child can move to a higher level.

Special Grouping in Settings

This is a form of program organization in which students are placed in physical proximity in order to provide entry to learning opportunities. The administrative emphasis of group settings is to maximize the number of students in programs in order to reduce program costs and produce specialized experiences. Placing students in a wide variety of settings is possible. There are very few settings that do not involve grouping children together on the basis of some common characteristic. Much of the discussion of settings is about the efficacy of various grouping arrangements.

Combining the Variables

The three variables—enrichment, acceleration, and grouping in settings—do not operate in isolation. In practice, they are combined to create program organizations. A key to deciding how to use each variable is the purpose or goal of a program. Teaching decisions and content decisions are secondary in this regard unless one is already committed to a particular means of instruction in a specific content area. For example, if one wants to use a seminar format while teaching Elizabethan literature, then many programming decisions are already completed. However, being committed to a particular subject area, such as mathematics, does not preordain the program structure. If it did, then the decisions would be simpler.

A closer look at what is involved in deciding on the administrative structure should help clarify this murky process. The acceleration-enrichment controversy will be discussed, followed by an examination of the issues related to the selection of grouping in settings. At the end of those sections, we return to actual examples of programs that use these variables.

The Acceleration–Enrichment Controversy

The controversy over acceleration and enrichment is an old one. Proponents of either position, as in most arguments, tend to make the other viewpoint look bad, although both positions have merit.

Within the community of scholars, teachers, parents, and researchers who are interested in gifted education, there is widespread acceptance of acceleration as a viable option for gifted learners alone and even more acceptance that enrichment and acceleration should be complementary programming variables. The disagreement in the field is more about for whom and under what conditions is acceleration a proper alternative (George et al., 1979; Schiever & Maker, 2003) and whether enrichment is appropriate solely for the gifted (Pendarvis & Howley, 1996). However, within the larger educational establishment or community, there is a general lack of acceptance of acceleration and a more ready acceptance of enrichment (Pendarvis & Howley). In the current situation, for many there is no controversy because it is simply a matter of when to use either; for others, the debate is emotionally charged because it goes to the heart of the argument on the nature of giftedness and gifted education. Once one arrives at an understanding of the elements in this debate, one has a deeper comprehension of the vitality and dialectic forces of the field.

In discussing the principal arguments, we start with acceleration and continue with enrichment, but readers will find the two topics being referred to in both sections. We chose to begin with acceleration because its proponents are typically on the defensive when explaining their position to the general education community. Review of the controversy uses the definitions proposed earlier in this chapter and proceeds to a series of questions asked first by general educators and then by gifted educators.

Social and Emotional Maladjustment

Concern for the social and emotional development of accelerated children is predominant among opponents in general education (Southern & Jones, 1991). The sentiments against acceleration are mostly concerned with what happens after acceleration. The fear is that the children will experience social isolation and develop unrealistic self-perceptions.

After reviewing 50 years of data on this question of adjustment and finding little evidence justifying the concern, Daurio (1979) stated that educators express a "disproportionate amount of caution" based upon relatively few, but highly visible, case histories and that educators use "selective bias" in interpreting the research. Daurio concluded that social and emotional adjustments associated with acceleration were clearly insignificant (Benbow & Lubinski, 1997). Gross and van Vliet (2003) concurred in their summarizing of the international research on students who left high school 3 or more years early. In sum, not only is achievement greater with acceleration, but negative affective consequences are not evident.

Yet, the social and emotional adjustment of gifted children as a consequence of acceleration remains a concern of some gifted educators. Their concern is not with maladjustment defined as emotional disturbance, but rather maladjustment defined as an insufficiently differentiated notion of oneself. These critics suggest that acceleration prompts children to recognize their capacity as skillful, rapid learners while ignoring motivational, creative, and idiosyncratic capabilities (Clark, 1997; Gold, 1979a; Piirto, 1999; Renzulli, 1979). Consequently, even with such strong evidence for acceleration, commitment to acceleration is qualified. For example, Cornell, Callahan, Bassin, and Ramsay (1991) noted the lack of research directly on acceleration's negative effects on affective development, and Silverman (1997b) noted a problem associated with asynchrony.

Appropriate for Whom?

The question "For whom is acceleration appropriate?" raises the problem of how to select children who might benefit from acceleration. In a significant manner, the question is linked to identification (see Chapter 3) because it, too, calls for a reliable and valid means of selection. Opponents of acceleration raise many questions about reliable selection procedures. Proponents of acceleration see the procedural question of choosing children for acceleration as a major stumbling block to its acceptance. Standardized individual intelligence tests (Daurio, 1979) and group-administered tests, such as the Scholastic Assessment Tests, Secondary School Admission Test, and PLUS Academic Abilities Assessment, among others, have been cited as reliable and valid tools for selection (Assouline & Lupkowski-Shoplik, 1997). These tests can effectively and efficiently identify highly intelligent and talented children.

Even so, the "appropriate for whom" question really has two parts because evidence must be provided to show the benefits of acceleration to those identified for it. The evidence strongly suggests that many children who have been identified for acceleration by those tests have benefited from being accelerated (Colangelo, Assouline, & Gross, 2004; Shore et al., 1991).

What is needed to satisfy critics is a more precise description of students' characteristics and program characteristics. For decades, the Johns Hopkins group and the talent searches that have spun off from it have been reporting impressive, positive data on mathematically talented and verbally talented youths who want to be accelerated (Colangelo, Assouline, & Cross, 2004; Lupkowski-Shoplik, Benbow, Assouline, & Brody, 2003; Stanley & Benbow, 1982; Swiatek & Benbow, 1991).

Acceleration Is the Same Old Thing, Just Faster

The concern that acceleration is simply a faster process comes from educators of the gifted, not general educators. Some perceive acceleration as addressing quantitative, but not qualitative, differences in learning. Their argument is much more sophisticated than the question of speeding up time in school.

The two related issues—qualitative differences in learning and curricular reform—need to be separated in order to increase understanding of the position. The definition of quality and assessing quality is slippery. The interjection of quality and quantity as considerations in the acceleration-enrichment debate is related to a basic assumption critics have about the nature of giftedness and its relationship to appropriate programming for children. These critics believe that there are qualitative differences between gifted and nongifted learners that must be attended to if a program is to be appropriate. The unique characteristics of the gifted, they believe, require a relatively unique program to strengthen their abilities. We infer an implied fear of superficiality in learning.

The issue of reform is aligned with the issue of quality in the minds of enrichment supporters because the continued use of the same dull curricula at a faster rate is really an administrative gimmick. It sidesteps the problem of inadequate and irrelevant curricula for gifted children (as well as others) who might not need acceleration, yet would benefit from enrichment (Gold, 1979a; Renzulli, 1977; Renzulli & Reis, 1985; Silverman, 1997b).

The proponents of acceleration dispute the existence of unique differences between gifted and nongifted children that require qualitatively different programs. On the issue of qualitative differences, researchers have found no evidence for this position (Achter, Lubinsky, & Benbow, 1996; Robinson, 1977). In other words, "Individuals classified as gifted in the narrow sense [using IQ scores] are not uniquely different from the rest of the population" (Jensen, 2004, p. 158). Taking a slightly different position, several authorities (Morelock, 1996; Silverman, 1997) maintain that qualitative differences are evident in some gifted children with extremely high IQs, yet they do not argue against the appropriateness of acceleration.

Curricular reform is not seen as a necessary requisite for providing qualitatively different programs (Benbow & Lubinsky, 1997; Cohn, 1979). Acceleration leads to excellence, which, in turn, leads spontaneously to higher levels of thinking and to creativity. George (1979) maintained that gifted children who have chosen acceleration do not learn superficially and do not feel their creative potential is left unstimulated. In fact, the proponents of acceleration proclaim that achievement gains that are a consequence of acceleration enable the person to enter a field of work and inquiry where real creative achievement can be realized.

The dispute among educators of the gifted may also be seen as a disagreement between experts who are knowledgeable in different subject areas, namely the natural sciences on the one hand and the humanities on the other. The evidence of the benefits of acceleration is more clearly demonstrated in math, natural sciences, and foreign language than in the humanities and social sciences. Thus, stronger advocates for acceleration are found in the natural sciences than in the humanities.

How the curriculum fits into programming is a strong undercurrent issue in the enrichment-acceleration debate. Enrichment can be treated as a programming variable, as we are doing in this chapter, or as a curricular issue, which we will do in Chapter 8. Understanding the meaning of enrichment is important because it is the most frequent term applied to programs for the gifted and its meaning is changeable (Cox, Daniel, & Boston, 1985).

Whether enrichment is viewed as an alternative to acceleration or as an educational partner is somewhat dependent on how the term is used. For those who see giftedness as primarily a quantitative difference in learning and development, enrichment that supports fast development is warranted. If it does not support fast development, it should not be implemented because it is not the best use of the limited time available in schools. Stanley (1976) found no use for enrichment that is nonaccelerating. Programs, Stanley argued, must lead to acceleration, or else the student is left with heightened interest and competence, but faces a blank wall. For those who see giftedness as situation-specific at different points in development, enrichment provides for flexibility to meet those situations and times. For those who see the standard curriculum as needing reform because it is inadequate to the needs of children, especially those who are gifted, something must be done to move children into more meaningful content.

By reflecting on these varying perspectives underlying enrichment, it is apparent that different forms of evidence substantiate the different positions. Furthermore, because enrichment takes forms ranging from modifications in general classes, to modifications requiring children to leave the general class, to whole-school modifications, it is extremely difficult to compare results when the perspectives just outlined are part of the dialogue. Thus, one cannot arrive at an answer to the question of which type of enrichment works best.

However, a more general question can be asked: "Do people learn more in enrichment-type programs than in general education situations?" The answer is a definite *yes* (Kulik, 1992; Rogers, 1991), but notice that our question does not compare enrichment to acceleration. Making such comparisons is risky and inappropriate unless both parties can agree on what the outcomes should be. Of course, one can insert any criterion for judgment one wants. When achievement on standardized tests and taking higher grade-level courses are the criteria for judgment, enrichment does not measure up to acceleration. When outcomes are based on the development of "creative" products or participation in nonstandard experiences, enrichment as a programming variable appears much stronger.

Given all this back-and-forth reasoning and evidence, how can a school resolve this issue? Although there is not unanimity, a strong consensus has emerged and is summed up in a proposal originally made almost 25 years ago:

> If *enrichment* is defined as the provision for learning experiences that develop higher processes of thinking and creativity in a subject area, and if *acceleration* is defined as the adjustment of learning time to meet the individual capabilities of the students, the two terms are complementary rather than conflicting. If one assumes that the goal of educational programs for the gifted is to meet their learning needs, *both* enrichment and acceleration are necessary. Thus, the gifted learner can proceed at a faster pace, to a higher level of content, and to more abstract and evaluative thinking than his or her age peers. (Fox, 1979, pp. 106–107)

Most people in the field would subscribe to this viewpoint today. However, like all consensus statements, it leaves a lot unspoken. Seeing the place of both of these approaches as programming considerations does not mean that they will be implemented in an even-handed and appropriate manner. Additionally, the third programming variable, grouping, to be discussed next, influences administrators' decisions to implement enrichment and acceleration. Clearly, the purpose of any program as expressed in its content or subject matter has an important place in the decision-making process regarding the use of acceleration and enrichment (VanTassel-Baska, 1993).

Grouping in Settings

It is quite difficult to separate out decisions about acceleration and enrichment from decisions about the setting for the program, which reinforces the point made earlier that the three variables involved in program planning (enrichment, acceleration, and grouping in settings) are linked. Concern about finding the most appropriate grouping in a setting is really a question of the efficacy of grouping patterns, which vary in terms of students' characteristics and the group's physical location. There are two subissues: Is one form of grouping with gifted students a more effective procedure than another form? and Is the setting itself an important consideration?

It is theoretically possible to group students on the basis of any characteristic or ability. In practice, though, very few characteristics are used. The typical school is organized by grouping students according to when they start school, and students are generally kept together throughout their schooling years. In effect, this amounts to grouping by age because school policy usually restricts school entrance to set times and school exit to the accumulation of credits.

275

Departure from this practice involves bringing students together according to some other criterion. Handicapped children, children with learning problems, and children with special interests (e.g., band, orchestra, sports, etc.) have all been grouped by criteria other than age. School systems have also grouped their populations on the basis of intelligence or achievement. This is sometimes called "tracking." All of these examples are instances of homogeneous grouping where like-ability, like-interest, or some combination is used to form the group.

The principle behind all these practices is that increased homogeneity in a group will narrow the range of variation and will produce benefits not possible with less homogeneity. The general evidence for the practice of homogeneous groups is compelling, yet the evidence is not interpreted unanimously. This seemingly contradictory state is a consequence of researchers having different perspectives, using different research methodologies, and studying classes having dissimilar curricula (Kulik & Kulik, 1991). In general, teachers like homogeneous grouping, but it does not have a uniformly beneficial effect on all children (Oakes & Lipton, 1992). An exception to this generalization has been evident for gifted children for 40 years (Borg, 1964). More recent research and analysis has confirmed and clarified this point (Colangelo, Assouline, & Gross, 2004).

Homogenous ability grouping does not seem to increase achievement in middle- and low-ability groups, but it does in high-ability groups. However, the difference is small, only measuring 1 month per academic year when the curriculum stays the same in all ability groups. When the curriculum is adjusted to meet the learning levels of the group, high-ability groups achieve around a year more than those without an altered curriculum. With adjusted curriculum in mixed-ability groups (i.e., groups that are more heterogeneous in terms of ability), the gains are more modest in elementary and middle school pupils (Kulik & Kulik, 1991).

These findings indicate that ability grouping alone is not sufficient for promoting achievement. If students at one grade level are grouped together and are ready for higher grade-level work and are not permitted to engage curricula at that level, then they do not readily achieve at that higher level unless the school provides for them to do so.

Concluding that grouping is an automatic plus for gifted learners is not warranted. Reviews of this question (Getzels & Dillon, 1973; Martinson, 1972; Rogers & Span, 1993) have added the caveat that grouping is a valuable tool when it is accompanied by quality curricula, instruction, and trained teachers. Even with this kind of knowledge, the caveat really illustrates how the research on this question has been confounded by numerous factors, such as comparison groups, ceilings on tests, uncontrolled instructional practices, and the presence of enrichment and acceleration, among others. From this research, it is impossible to sift out a single, preferred way to group students in a school. The type and number of settings depend upon the purposes of the program, the student body, and the resources of the school. Among all the possible settings for grouping children, the general trend is to group the gifted within a regular class

TABLE 7.2

Variables and Program Options Involved in Program Planning

Program Option	Acceleration	Grouping	Enrichment	Place
Out-of-school	Possible	Yes	Yes	Extraclass
Special school/ learning resource center	Possible	Yes	Possible	Intraclass
Early admission	Yes	–	–	Extraclass
Grade skipping	Yes	–	–	Extraclass
Grade telescoping	Yes	Yes	Possible	Intraclass
Subject-specific acceleration	Yes	Yes	Possible	Intraclass
Accelerated enrichment class	Yes	Yes	Yes	Intraclass, Extraclass
Special course enrichment	Rare	Yes	Yes	Extraclass
Independent study	Yes	–	Yes	Intraclass, Extraclass
Mainstreaming	No	Yes	Yes	Intraclass
Cluster grouping	Yes	Yes	Yes	Intraclass
Mentoring	Yes	Yes	Yes	Intraclass, Extraclass

most of the time—whether in a pull-out program, which appears to be the least beneficial arrangement (Martinson), or in cluster grouping, which appears to have benefits for the gifted (Rogers, 2002). Cooperative grouping is another teaching strategy and will be discussed in Chapters 9 and 10.

The grouping question involves not only how to group students, but also their actual physical placement. Are children to be served in the regular classroom, in another classroom, or somewhere outside the school? When programming occurs in a regular class, it is called "intraclass placement." When primarily others outside the regular classroom do programming, it is called "extraclass placement."

If we examine the range of possible program options (see Table 7.2) and evaluate the possibility of acceleration, enrichment, or grouping, these placements can be compared. When the evidence is taken as a whole, a pure case for any variable is impossible to find. Once children enter a program, multiple combinations are possible, and eclecticism usually prevails. The final program plan may highlight one variable, such as enrichment, and even take the term *enrichment* in its title, but almost inevitably the shape of another variable can be recognized.

Common Premises in Program Planning

In order to plan a program, regardless of the variable used, there are several premises on which proponents of all viewpoints agree. These premises form the bases for sound programming:

1. The child's strengths are to be encouraged and developed.

2. The learning environment should provide opportunities for expanding knowledge and building more effective cognitive, affective, and creative capabilities.

3. Arrangements must be made to accommodate individual differences, such as interests, abilities, learning rates, and learning styles.

4. Contact with other gifted children promotes social/emotional development.

5. A program should be responsive to the community it serves and involve families of children.

6. The curriculum should promote these premises.

7. Evaluation is an indispensable part of effective programming.

It is the disagreement over the best means of fulfilling these premises, given local resources and attitudes, that occupies educators. Schools accepting these premises are likely to start programs that evolve toward the best alternative.

SOME TYPICAL PROGRAM OPTIONS

The following program options illustrate the use of the three variables relevant to program planning (see Table 7.2). In discussing such program options, educators of the gifted have created their own jargon that can inhibit communication when used indiscriminately. Some of the programming terms used with the gifted have been placed in a glossary (see Figure 7.1).

Advanced Placement Program (APP)	Sponsored by the College Entrance Examination Board for 25 years; a wide variety of courses come under this umbrella; AP provides course description and test formats (Hanson, 1981).
Block scheduling	Two courses, such as language arts and social studies, meet during successive hours.
Cluster	A group of gifted children, usually within a regular class.
College-Level Examination Program (CLEP)	Sponsored by the College Entrance Examination Board; students can gain credit for college courses.
Individualized classroom	A variety of arrangements occur within the class; small-group and individual instruction are usually in regular class; curriculum is ungraded.
Integrated classcs	Combine gifted and nongifted in a subject area.
Pull-out program	Students leave regular classroom for another setting.
Seminars	Small discussion groups organized around special topics; seminar is sometimes used to describe special course enrichment.
Semiseparation	Similar to pull-out programs; gifted meet at one location at specific time or times.
Special interest group	Groups come together on the basis of common interest; gifted and nongifted; may be extracurricular.

Figure 7.1. Glossary of programming terms

Note. From *Schooling the Gifted* (p. 290), by L. J. Coleman, 1985, Menlo Park, CA: Addison-Wesley. Copyright ©1985 by L. J. Coleman. Reprinted with permission.

Out-of-School

"Out-of-school" is a generic phrase referring to educational opportunities that take place beyond the boundaries (time and space) of the school. Such opportunities are practiced in countries around the world (Goldstein & Wagner 1993). In some instances, the same option may be available outside of school or within a school's program. For example, academic competitions, like

279

Odyssey of the Mind, may be part of out-of-school clubs or may be connected to in-school programs.

How people become involved in out-of-school options varies. Some are opportunities that families spontaneously provide for their children. Often, children become committed to sports or music or games, like swimming, piano, or chess, because parents engage in these kinds of activities themselves. Therefore, the family seeks more advanced opportunities for their children (Sosniak, 1997). Others become involved in out-of-school activities because their parents, guardians, or caretakers believe they should be engaged in constructive activities after school and during the summer. Resources, usually in the form of money or scholarship, are needed in order to send children to special-ability programs that provide enriched or accelerated learning experiences. Summer camps, Saturday seminars, and some mentoring programs are examples of options that provide opportunities in the arts, languages, sciences, and humanities. Other students become involved in out-of-school opportunities by invitation. The talent search programs and many athletic summer camps offer opportunities for advanced learning and practice.

Special Schools

Special schools are places that admit only the gifted. They may be private or public, and admission procedures are very selective. Some schools are concerned primarily with the development of certain gifts, such as art, music, or science, rather than all abilities. Special schools are generally limited to large population centers due to the problems of finding sufficient numbers of students, inexpensive transportation, and suitably trained staff. Some exceptions are state-supported residential high schools (Kolloff, 2003). Special schools eliminate or successfully handle difficulties with which other schools must struggle, such as scheduling classes, purchasing specialized equipment, arranging flexible groups, conducting specialized courses, and finding qualified teachers.

A variation on the special school concept is the magnet school. This option is practiced at the elementary and secondary levels. Students drawn from a single school or from an entire school district report to the magnet school for instruction. Special enriched courses, accelerated special classes, seminars, and independent study might be offered.

The concept of special schools is frequently criticized for encouraging elitism and segregation on the basis of ability. While little evidence exists on which to base these criticisms, the problem of underrepresentation of minority groups is a notable identification issue. However, some special high schools for the gifted in New York City have made provisions for underachieving and minority youths (Morgan, Tennant, & Gold, 1980).

Special schools have been able to demonstrate that their graduates achieve at a high level and are admitted into highly competitive postsecondary programs. The data on residential public high schools are impressive, as well (Kolloff, 2003).

Early Admission

The principle behind early admission, also called "early entrance," to all levels of schooling is that some gifted students are ready for instruction in specific areas before their age peers and therefore should be permitted to step around the typical age barriers.

Early entrance to elementary school is one example. Although research supports this practice, it has not been widely implemented. Obstacles to early entrance come from attitudes of schools and parents, as well as schools' regulations and state laws. Identification of children who could profit from early entrance is hampered by the schools' preference for ignoring gifted children. Searching for gifted children requires personnel and a workable identification system (Robinson et al., 1979). The evidence on early entrance for selected children indicates increased achievement and slight improvement in self-esteem (Rogers, 2002).

Early admission to college is a second form of early entrance. A variety of terms have been used in conjunction with this practice, such as "advanced standing," "early graduation," and "the Advanced Placement program." Research on these practices is generally very favorable (Fox, 1979; Morgan et al., 1980), and evidence is accumulating to support this practice in subject areas. In her summary of the research, Rogers (2002) noted that "the academic effect was moderately powerful and positive," and students showed roughly a third of an additional year's gain with no substantial problems in socialization (p. 194). Kurtz (1979), a strong advocate, has argued that "students with IQs of 120, 130, 140, or 150 should have no trouble graduating from high school at ages 15, 14, 13, or 12, respectively" (p. 226).

Grade Skipping

Grade skipping, which is sometimes called "double promotion," is a time-honored practice that has been applied to the gifted for many years. The option is based on the same principle as early admission: Because gifted students are frequently several years ahead of their grade-level peers on achievement measures and, not uncommonly, up to 4 years beyond grade level (Martinson, 1972; Terman & Oden, 1947), completely skipping a grade might be highly appropriate. Objections to grade skipping persist in the face of evidence supporting its efficacy, and they follow the general criticisms of acceleration (Southern & Jones, 1991). However, "The bad reputation of grade skipping is almost wholly underserved" (Rogers, 2002, p. 167), especially since it is a cost-effective option that involves no new teachers, nor new curricula.

In general, it is best to skip grades during elementary school—the earlier, the better. Other appropriate times for grade skipping are probably at "natural transition points" between elementary and junior high, or junior and senior high. However, in a given school system, the consideration of teachers and curricular demands may make other times more appropriate.

The number of year one can skip is dependent on the child and the situation. Evidence on radical acceleration (i.e., skipping two or more grades) is positive, but data are skimpy because of the relatively few cases that have been systematically studied. However, evidence is accumulating that shows that this option is typically successful when done in a supportive environment, and many of the fears of social maladjustment are unwarranted (Rogers, 2002).

Grade Telescoping

Telescoping has elements of grade and subject compression, as in the previous two options. It exists in recognition of the fear that important content might be missed and is usually done for groups, not individuals. In essence, the content is covered in a shorter period of time. This practice is used mainly at the secondary level, but has been used in the elementary school.

Two different organizational schemes are used: one that presumes giftedness in all areas and one that does not. In the first approach, a class is formed and the group learns 3 years of work in 2 years in all subject areas. Enrichment and independent study may be part of the program. The second approach makes use of a well-organized counseling program. High school graduation requirements are met by earning credit through examination, deleting electives, and attending talent-search-type courses in varying combinations. The evidence on telescoping indicates that it benefits children academically and minimizes social misalignment (Rogers, 2002).

Subject-Specific Acceleration

Subject-specific acceleration permits a child to move through the content in a subject at a rate commensurate with his or her demonstrated achievements. Assessment is an important part of the process. Subject areas with a strong developmental sequence work better for subject-specific acceleration than subjects with a more loosely defined sequence. This practice varies in different school systems, but in general, the natural sciences and languages are more accommodating than are the humanities and social sciences.

A variety of instructional practices may be employed in subject-specific acceleration, such as computer-assisted instruction, tutors, itinerant teachers, correspondence courses, and special courses. Students sometimes enroll in talent-search-type courses (Lupkowski-Shoplik et al., 2003) or weekend or summer courses (Olszewski-Kubilius, 2003). The major obstacle is the familiar question, "If he or she does that this year, what will he or she do next year?" A second obstacle is the school not wanting to give credit for such courses, even with adequate documentation that the student has met rigorous standards (Olszewski-Kubilius, 1997).

Accelerated Enrichment Classes

Accelerated enrichment classes provide an option that has general appeal when one finds enough students of high ability in a school system. This practice can be applied to one subject area or a range of subjects. It combines provisions for a faster pace of learning, as in subject-specific acceleration, and for "relevant academic enrichment" (Stanley, 1976) for groups of children. Various programs use this model, the most researched being the Study of Mathematically Precocious Youth. A distinction between this approach and special schools is that accelerated enrichment classes involve less administrative reorganization. This option is frequently combined with instructional practices mentioned in subject-specific acceleration.

Special Course Enrichment

Special course enrichment is an option in which the intent is to broaden a child's perspective on the world and on him- or herself by introducing new, innovative courses that are indirectly linked to courses in the regular curriculum. Other terms that refer to this kind of program option are "pull-out programs" and "enrichment seminars." Special course enrichment may or may not be linked to curriculum compacting, an instructional strategy in which new activities replace content that children have already mastered.

The topics in special course enrichment may be relatively specialized, such as fossils, haiku poetry, or chess, or more broadly conceived, such as archaeology or Japanese literature. The former might entail activities and instructions lasting a few days or weeks; the latter may require a semester of study. As societal concerns change, a course that starts as a special option may become incorporated into the regular course of study. Examples are environmental studies, psychology, and career education. When the special course becomes a regular course, the procedure for letting students select courses on the basis of their own interest is lost. Because these special courses are outside the regular curriculum, they are extraclass activities.

Some teachers are resistant to letting their students leave class for enrichment classes or providing for gifted students in their classes, even when the children can do the regular work. It is unfortunately common for teachers to ask gifted students to make up missed work. As an alternative to missing class, special course enrichment can also be found in special summer programs or in extracurricular activities.

Finding staff members with suitable interests and expertise for specialized courses may be a problem, especially if a child gets committed to a subject. It is difficult to document the benefits because of confusion over the goals of specialized enrichment. Special course enrichment appears to be most effective when combined with curriculum compacting (Rogers, 2002).

Individualized Approaches:
Independent Study, Tutoring, and Mentoring

Attending to the needs of gifted children on a one-to-one basis can be the best approach. In this section, we examine three individualized approaches as administrative options. In Chapter 9, we discuss them as teaching or instructional strategies. The distinction between administrative options and teaching concerns is to clarify what is involved in implementing a program and in teaching a class.

Independent Study

Independent study is a program option that stands apart from, as well as in conjunction with, other options. When it is used within another option, independent study is not an administrative strategy, but rather a teaching strategy for helping students learn something in a more effective and personalized manner. Independent study as a program option involves building an organizational structure that permits the student access to material and personnel resources in pursuit of the answer to some question of interest. A number of different formats can meet this description of independent study; however, in most instances, a guidance role is needed. The role may be filled by teachers, tutors, or mentors who serve as facilitators to assist the student in formulating a workable goal and navigating toward it (Gold, 1980). In order to fulfill these roles, arrangements have to be made so that the student can meet with these guides for feedback. The responsibilities of both teacher and student must be clearly stated for this option to succeed. Accountability should be required for all participants in a course of independent study.

Access to resources is a critical part of an independent study program. The use of laboratories and libraries may necessitate careful scheduling in a busy school or close contact with relevant community facilities. Independent study is appropriate for all levels of schooling, although students must have developed independent study skills in order for the program to work. Leaving gifted students to pursue their interests is not sufficient enough structure to warrant the label of independent study. This practice would better be called "free time." Independent study should start from the known and proceed toward the unknown (Treffinger, 1975). Practices such as correspondence courses and programmed texts also do not deserve the label of independent study.

Tutoring and Mentoring

Tutors and mentors have somewhat different roles than teachers. Both are usually in one-to-one situations with the student. While the tutor usually has a predetermined course of study to implement, the mentor is usually an expert who exchanges ideas and experiences with a student in a less structured way. Some research has looked at student peers as tutors, either in a like-ability or high-low dyad. Like-ability tutoring produces higher achievement than the student might attain alone, but in high-low dyads the high-ability student does not gain in achievement (Rogers, 2002).

Because mentoring as a program option is practiced more widely than tutoring, we shall examine it more closely (Cox et al., 1985). In a later section in this chapter, we discuss mentors as people, while in this section we describe administrative considerations.

Mentorship programs are premised on the recognition that some children have skills and interests that are so advanced or divergent from the typical school resources that they need to be placed in situations where those resources are available.

> The matching of a promising novice with an established expert provides the novice with appropriate challenge and continued encouragement in the development of his or her talent. It can be a productive and meaningful experience for both mentor and mentee. (Clasen & Clasen, 1997, p. 218)

Mentoring seems to have particular promise for assisting minority students in reaching their potential. Most mentoring programs occur at the secondary level, but there are some elementary-level programs. Mentorship programs are attractive to schools because they seem to cost less. However, like everything in life, there is no free lunch. Unless sufficient resources and support are devoted to the program, success is unlikely.

Setting up a mentorship program is not simple, and it requires coordination among different elements. Clearly, there should be an obvious need. Recruiting appropriate mentors and pairing them with the right student requires care. Mentors can be professionals, college students, and other community members who are knowledgeable and eager to share their expertise with children (Hébert & Neumeister, 2000). Mentorships work better when the parties have a clear notion of where the relationship is going and what the outcomes are likely to be. Several sources are helpful for creating such programs (Clasen & Clasen, 2003; Siegle, 2005). In her review of the topic, Rogers (2002) reported that academic effects in specific studies "were very large—approximately a one-half year gain" (p. 146).

Mainstreaming and Inclusion

Mainstreaming is a program option whereby all programming takes place within the regular classroom. Instruction of gifted children is delivered by the regular classroom teacher and, occasionally, by itinerant resource teachers or team teachers. Learning centers are developed, and the teacher frequently implements independent studies. It is rare that mainstreaming could be called acceleration because teachers have insufficient knowledge about the myriad subjects that interest children. In late elementary school, this is a real problem because teachers are primarily generalists. Cross-grade grouping and within-class cluster grouping have been used with some success to try to provide more advanced content to students who are ready for it (Kulik & Kulik, 1997; Rogers, 2002; Slavin, 1987).

Mainstreaming causes instructional problems for teachers. Sometimes, teachers are able to superimpose an enrichment-oriented curriculum model on the regular program, such as Taylor's Multiple Talent Model, in order to help gifted children (Renzulli & Reis, 1997). The Schoolwide Enrichment Model combines mainstreaming and inclusion notions in conjunction with enrichment. Mainstreaming is an administrative problem in the sense that the use of flexible scheduling and the use of extra classroom personnel require coordination with other teachers and with other schools. An insufficient support system for regular teachers invariably leads to a collapse of this option, although it may be the least expensive.

EVALUATING PROGRAMS

Despite the generally held acceptance by educators of the importance of evaluation, it is a frequently neglected element of program planning (Callahan, 1993). Talking about evaluation is easier than implementing it.

Evaluation is more than administering tests. The purpose is to find out what is working, what needs to be improved in a program, and whether new changes work in the way they were intended. The Association for the Gifted (TAG) has long recognized that evaluation is the only means we have of consistently raising the standards of quality in programs for the gifted (House, 1970). Criticism leveled at gifted education comes from the field's inability to provide consistent evidence on the efficacy of program practices and the field's difficulty in maintaining that serious and meaningful study, rather than fun and games, is occurring in programs (Pendarvis & Howley, 1996). Of course, some people's attitudes toward gifted education are remarkably resistant to good evidence that is contrary to their opinions. No matter what evidence is presented, it will not be sufficient. The unwillingness of most schools to implement acceleration as a programming option, despite the overwhelming evidence, is the best example of this irrational and persistent resistance.

Evaluating educational programs is an arduous undertaking, and programs for the gifted add complexity to evaluation due to their design and the nature of giftedness. Our discussion will focus on evaluating special programs. Readers who wish more background are advised to consult the extensive general literature on the subject of evaluation.

Program evaluation should be a part of the design of any program. Thought should be given to it early in a project or the school year so that provisions for gathering useful information can be made. Decisions about the utility of information and program effectiveness are always heavily tied to the objectives and rationale of a program. Without a relatively clear set of statements delineating program intentions, it is difficult to conduct a meaningful evaluation.

Evaluation may be conducted to determine where changes need to be made in the program as it is being implemented (formative evaluation) and to determine what the final outcomes are (summative evaluation). Evaluation can also be carried out for reasons that do not give specific feedback about the program, but rather serve other functions like reminding people that they are accountable to others outside the program or that others in the program can evaluate them (Borland, 1997). To obtain a combination of these kinds of information, specific questions may be formulated that reflect these major concerns.

Once the kind of evaluation has been specified and questions have been raised, it is necessary to gather data. The data may be of three types: presage, process, and product. Presage data consist of information about the features of a program that are presumed to be ideal and are used to make inferences about programs. Process data are measures of teacher-pupil materials, interactions, activities, or a combination of the three that are believed to be signs of the process; however, there is no universal agreement about what signs are important for study. Product data constitute information on changes occurring in the consumers of the program. The most popular type of product data are norm-referenced or criterion-referenced scores on tests. The former compares students to other students or test norms, the latter to scores in reference to the accomplishment of a task or set of tasks. Pupil products and frequency of extracurricular activities are other types of product data. *The TAG Evaluation Sampler* (House, 1970), *A Guidebook for Evaluating Programs for the Gifted and Talented* (Renzulli & Smith, 1979), and *Designing and Utilizing Evaluation for Gifted Program Improvement* (VanTassel-Baska & Feng, 2004) have examples of techniques for gathering these different types of data.

Program evaluation may seem to some readers as a process that resembles that of conducting experimental research in which the effect of a treatment under special conditions (the program) on a group of students is studied. However, the evaluation process is considerably different (Borg, Gall, & Gall, 1996). The precision considered to be ideal in experimental research is still sought in program evaluation, but the task of program evaluation is much broader than that. It is important to use the frameworks of the stakeholders— those with an interest in a successful program—as one formulates questions and gathers data. It is as if a series of studies on identification, instruction, and curriculum design are being conducted simultaneously. The imperfections found in smaller scale studies are present, maybe even magnified, in evaluation research. Thus, the expertise of the evaluator is crucial for digesting and interpreting such imperfect data. Enthusiastic claims of program effectiveness need to be scrutinized in light of these significant limitations in research on program effectiveness.

The fundamental evaluation problem is the lack of agreement about what constitutes a proper program. Recognizing this continual dilemma, there are several other problems that hinder evaluation. It is always difficult to find a similar group with whom program participants can be compared. Another problem is measurement of program objectives stressing the mastery of abstract intellectual processes, the increase of aesthetic sensitivity, and the generation of novel thoughts and actions. While standardized tests that claim to measure some of these objectives are available, there is minimal agreement among educators for the gifted, first about their validity, and second about the tests' relationship to program objectives. Finding an instrument that measures program objectives is an even bigger problem for programs that reconstruct the curriculum. Advocates of enrichment programs are caught in this dilemma. As one departs from standard curricula, it becomes more difficult to find generally accepted forms of measurement. The difficulty in conducting good evaluation research is further complicated by problems of ceiling, reliability, and regression effect, as discussed earlier in the chapter on identification. In recent years, attempts at broadening and enriching evaluation have combined the features we have described with new information using a post-positivistic or qualitative research perspective. Borland, Schnur and Wright (2000) have provided the field with a model for doing this kind of evaluation.

In conclusion, one can see that evaluating programs for the gifted is an inexact enterprise. More work needs to be devoted to perfecting evaluation practices in order to improve the quality of programs for gifted students. For those wishing to mount a program evaluation, several publications are useful (Borland, 2003; Callahan, 1993; VanTassel-Baska & Feng, 2004).

SELECTING PERSONNEL: TEACHERS AND MENTORS

Among the seven features of gifted programs mentioned by experts, two of the seven have to do with staffing (Renzulli, 1968). The highest ranked feature is the teacher.

Attributes of a Teacher

Since the selection of high-quality teachers is crucial for effective programming, it is disturbing that few unambiguous descriptions of excellent teaching exist. Numerous lists of characteristics and competencies have been proposed, but the literature reveals a small number of meaningful, empirically demonstrated connections between teacher characteristics and learning among gifted children (Shore et al., 1991). Major reviews on this topic can be found in the literature (Feldhusen, 1997; Gold, 1965; Hansen & Feldhusen, 1994; Maker, 1975; Shore et al).

Several writers (Lindsey, 1980; Nelson & Prindle, 1992) have synthesized the literature and compiled a list of characteristics, predispositions, and behaviors relative to quality teaching. Lindsey organized her list of characteristics into progressively narrower and more specific examples. The narrowest and uppermost layer contains knowledge, skills, and attitudes that are significant for developing specific types of giftedness. This organization emphasizes that specialized teaching skills and knowledge are needed as learners move toward the outer edge of a domain (Bloom, 1985; Gold, 1979b). One implication is that teachers at the elementary level might be different from those at the secondary level.

An important source of information on teachers is direct observation of them in classrooms with gifted students. Unfortunately, the few studies available that use this procedure (Coleman, 1992; Hertzog, 1997; Story, 1985) are not closely linked to student learning.

The school district wishing to hire prospective teachers will find compilations of characteristics to be minimally helpful. It would appear that qualities attributed to good teachers in general would be applicable to the selection of teachers for the gifted. Actually, teacher selection can become a more focused process when the program has delineated its goals, objectives, and administrative organization. Personnel who have experience or skills consistent with the program's goals should be hired.

In keeping with the definition of giftedness proposed earlier, the notion that the scope of teacher expertise in a program should parallel the increasingly specialized competencies of the students may mean in many cases that the school and the teacher must be willing to put the child in contact with others outside the school. The need for expertise in an area is important so that the teacher can empathize with the difficulties experienced by students in mastering a subject and be familiar with the tacit knowledge implicit in an area (Subotnik & Coleman, 1996). Teacher preparation programs usually require teachers of the gifted to be specialists in some area. An important issue in this regard is determining what defines a subject area. Are reading, counseling, math, and biology subjects?

Bishop (1968) asked each member of a gifted high school sample to indicate the "best and most successful teacher for him—the one who made the greatest difference in his educational career" (p. 318). In a later publication, a panel of gifted children indicated what they thought were the characteristics of good teachers (AAGC, 1978). Some selected comments are paraphrased to provide some sense of what students value:

- They understand subject matter and are sensitive to emotional needs.

- They make students feel significant by taking time to talk.

- They provide access to additional work.

- They show a sense of humor.

- They set standards.

- They provide constructive criticism.

- They see students for who they are.

These comments could serve as criteria for selecting a teacher of the gifted (Baldwin, 1993).

It might appear at this point that teachers of the gifted must be gifted themselves, a conclusion that may be partially correct. One of the few studies on the subject indicated that successful teachers in an honors program possessed many characteristics associated with our portrait of giftedness: higher-than-average verbal intelligence, intellectual interests, sensitivity, organization, and imagination. The successful teachers also wanted to work with gifted students (Bishop, 1968). The idea of shared characteristics between gifted students and gifted teachers has also been reported by Brandwein (1955). While these teachers sound as though they may be gifted, it is likely that their students possess these characteristics to a greater degree than the teachers do. Thus, successful teachers of the gifted share attributes with their gifted students, but need not be gifted, or as gifted, themselves.

Because this discussion is based on limited research, one must be cautious about generalizations. The question of whether or not the teacher needs to be gifted is an important consideration in terms of administrative arrangements and school personnel practices. Given our earlier discussion about the adult adjustment of gifted children and their range of occupational choices in our society, one wonders how education can hope to have enough gifted people as teachers when other social institutions offer significantly higher monetary and status rewards. The possibility that teachers of the gifted at the elementary and secondary levels need not be gifted is encouraging in this regard. On the other hand, if gifted people are needed as teachers and they cannot be attracted, then administrative practices calling for flexibility in grouping, graduation, and so forth become increasingly important options for meeting the needs of gifted students.

Challenges Confronting Teachers of the Gifted

In setting up programs and selecting teachers, it is important to consider the problems with which teachers must deal. Teachers of the gifted have several problems related to their unique position in a school system. In new programs, the teacher of the gifted frequently stands alone as the voice of authority on the subject of giftedness (Peine, 1998; Rogers, 2002). In older programs, some of these pressures are considerably reduced due to additional personnel.

The teacher of the gifted serves as a liaison between the school and the home. This means the teacher may be the recipient of undeserved hostility from parents who have had difficulties with the school system, or he or she may be the recipient of questions about proper child-rearing practices (the chapter on families describes some of these issues in detail). A good teacher must be able to meet these challenges. The teacher must deal with aspects of the gifted role and personal association with that role. In an earlier chapter, it was proposed that the expectations of others, teachers, administrators, and the public about giftedness must be combated. Teachers need to exercise care in correcting misconceptions about the competencies of gifted children. As we know, gifted children are not good in everything, may get low grades, may have behavior problems, and may have gaps in certain skill areas. These facts must be communicated to others.

At the same time, the teacher of the gifted may have to deal with the idea of guilt by association. Aspects of giftedness pervade the teacher's life. Others may inquire whether the teacher is gifted, may think the teacher is strange to work with such children, or may even expect the teacher to be unusually competent in many areas. Sometimes, teachers get caught in a web where hostility toward the gifted is directed at them. Occasionally, teachers find themselves working hard to show they are gifted in order to justify themselves to others. This course of action is a hazardous one.

A third problem is explaining the program to others who see its nontraditional instructional activities as being "fun and games." In this respect, Renzulli (1977, 1999) has discussed the need for defensible programs. Teachers of the gifted must have a sound rationale for their instructional decisions; a series of activities strung together never represents good programming. Goals and objectives should be clear, and the teacher needs to avoid jargon in discussing programs and must be sensitive to the regular teachers' need to feel significant.

A final problem with which teachers of the gifted must contend is dealing with feelings of incompetence or failure if they don't know something about a child's particular interests. Teachers who try to compete with their students are setting the stage for bigger problems. Rather, learning how to say, "I don't know," and simultaneously showing a desire to learn about a topic are important teacher attributes that are particularly valued by gifted students. Being a continual learner is inescapable when teaching gifted students. "The teacher who can allow the gifted student's intellect to fly higher than the teacher's can ever hope to soar and to take joy in that effort has earned a special badge of maturity" (Gallagher, 1975, p. 314).

Attributes of Mentors

The idea of mentors as teachers has received wide currency, as seen by the spread of mentorship programs described earlier in this chapter (Clasen & Clasen, 2003; Gold, 1979b). Mentoring is premised on the idea that the development of competency in a field is heavily influenced by experiences with experts in the field who take a special interest in the young person. The Talent/Multiple Ability Educational Model clearly states the importance of contact between individuals of like interests, abilities, and aspirations for extended periods of time. The biographical data on famous people also point to the importance of mentors in the development of giftedness.

In essence, mentoring describes a reciprocal role relationship between a master and a novice. Each accepts the other as a worthy and capable person.

There is no fixed agenda in this relationship. Rather, there is a sharing of ideas and experience in which the novice is initiated and sustained in the pursuit of a special area of interest. The relationship ends when the mentor, the student, or both believe the student is ready to be a colleague or an independent performer in the field. It is sometimes difficult to end the relationship because of the reluctance of both parties to redefine it. The idea of mentoring may be used with different terms, such as *intern*, *sponsor*, *protégé*, and *apprenticeship*.

The importance of the mentor role has been described very well by Pepinsky (1960), where the term *sponsor* is used, but the meaning is similar to mentor:

> The sponsor is a person or agency who is not a member of the peer group, but possesses prestige or authority in the same social system. He has several significant functions: (1) regardless of his own views the sponsor encourages the other to express and to test his ideas, to think things through for himself; (2) he protects the individual from the counter reactions of his peers long enough to permit him to try out his own notions; (3) he at least keeps the structure of the situation open enough so that independence can occur. (p. 84)

Pepinsky's description raises the intriguing question of whether independence is possible in hierarchically organized institutions without the assistance of a mentor. Perhaps we should teach children to search for such people.

Under the auspices of the school, the mentor relationship is more formal than the general description above. The school seeks out individuals in the community who are willing to share their expertise in something. "An arrangement is made between the school and this individual to work on a one-to-one basis with some gifted and talented student interested in the same field" (Gold, 1979b, p. 275). This relationship can be an important aspect of independent study.

The matching of mentor to student is important because the mentor is essentially the program.

> Not everyone who is an expert can be a mentor: expertise and skill in a field are necessary but not sufficient. The mentor must be willing— even eager—to share expertise with a novice whose energy and questions may be taxing and with whom patience and understanding likely will be required. (Clasen & Clasen, 1997, p. 219)

Thus, it is crucial that a school devote time to screening and picking appropriate mentors. Clasen and Clasen (2003) provide advice on this endeavor. Particular attention is needed in programs directed at meeting the needs of disadvantaged and minority youth and young women, as mentors have the potential to help these groups overcome obstacles to high development

(Olszewski-Kubilius & Scott, 1992). Mentors can meet student needs in a highly personal way. It is the power of the relationship that seems so important. Hébert & Neumeister (2000) described a program with university students as mentors to children in an elementary program that illustrates the importance of this relationship.

EXAMPLES OF SUCCESSFUL PROGRAMS

In order to sample the various flavors of gifted education, a number of programs have been selected. Accessibility to descriptions in the literature was one criterion for selecting these programs. Another criterion was our personal experience. The programs are examples of a series of decisions about programming. The key features noted earlier in the discussion are the organizational format of this section.

The Roeper School

The Roeper School is a K–12 private school located outside Detroit, Michigan, with an enrollment of approximately 650 students. The school exists in two locations, with grades K–5 in Bloomfield Hills and 6–12 in Pontiac, three miles away. Annamarie and George Roeper created it in 1945 after they left Germany to escape the Nazis. The school is the third school begun by the Roeper family, with one in Germany and another in Switzerland.

Teaching Method
There is no preferred teaching method, per se. However, teachers' respect for the individual is a central expectation.

Curriculum
The curriculum includes mainly small, rigorous courses at the secondary level. Grades K–5 are established as levels, rather than highly distinct grades. Emphasis is placed on the child's development, rather than only on which grade the child's age determines. The curriculum emphasizes working for the common good of society. Consequently, students learn more about how to be responsible citizens than is common in other schools.

Student Selection
All children must show evidence of intellectual giftedness via traditional assessment procedures that combine outside testing data with internal interviews and observations.

Philosophy
The school's philosophy attempts to develop the self of the gifted child, paying particular attention to developing world perspectives aimed at reduc-

293

ing the likelihood of future genocide. A philosophy emphasizing the whole child is considered throughout the school's practices. Great attention is paid to engendering the Roepers' values in the areas of compassion, self-knowledge, responsibility, and civil duty. The school emphasizes social responsibility by empowering students through opportunities to develop within a school philosophy that shares power among all groups (e.g., administrators, teachers, and students).

Staff Orientation

The teachers and administrators work to create an environment where everyone knows each other and where developing talent is done with respect to those who preceded you and the knowledge of the importance of civic responsibility. Classes are kept small, with every teacher at the secondary level maintaining a homeroom. The Roeper School has a long history of providing numerous scholarships to students of limited means. In recent years, these monies have come both from tuition pools and funds raised outside the school's normal budget.

The Schoolwide Enrichment Model (SEM)

The Schoolwide Enrichment Model (SEM; Renzulli & Reis, 1985, 1997, 2003) is a comprehensive system for incorporating enrichment into schools and promoting creative productivity, the roots of which can be traced to Ward (1961). The SEM integrates Renzulli's work on definition, identification, assessment, and curriculum and implicitly moves to reforming education. The SEM recommends the use of measuring devices, management procedures, and an array of services developed by the creators.

The starting point of the Schoolwide Enrichment Model is the selection of a talent pool consisting of approximately 10–15% of the school population. The creation of the talent pool is to expand the notion of gifted behavior beyond traditional criteria and to recognize that membership in the pool is not constant. At any one time, a smaller percentage of students (about 5% of the school population) may enter of exit the program. A curriculum that originates in the regular classroom moves toward research projects on original student-selected topics conducted in a resource room. Upon completion of a project, the student may move out of the program in order to make room for another student. The program uses primarily the options of special course enrichment, independent study, and mainstreaming.

The Teacher

Two kinds of teachers are involved in the SEM. The regular teacher is seen as playing a pivotal role in identifying children for the program and in modifying the curriculum for accelerated learning so that time is available for enrichment activities. The resource teacher instructs a smaller number of students and facilitates their research. At other times, the resource teacher provides for talent-pool students who have not revolved into the resource-room enrichment activities that stimulate interests and develop skills. The resource teacher is an expert in gifted education and is fluent in assessing student interests and learning styles, as well as in providing three types of enrichment activities. The skills needed to manage a variety of independent study projects are also required. Good communication between the resource teacher and the regular teachers is a requisite for effective programming.

Curriculum

Developing the curriculum for the SEM entails modifying existing curricula, providing enrichment clusters, and adding new experiences. Curriculum compacting is the procedure for reorganizing the regular curriculum so that fast learners can buy time for engaging in enrichment activities. New experiences are organized according to the Enrichment Triad Model, which is described in the next chapter. Enrichment clusters bring groups of children together on the basis of similar interests so that the child can become a specialist. Independent study projects are the endpoint of the process.

Student Selection

There are two levels of identification in the Schoolwide Enrichment Model. The first level uses traditional screening procedures to form a talent pool. These procedures involve intelligence or achievement data, among others. In the SEM, these data are called "status information." The second level of identification uses "action information," which focuses on evidence that the child has become excited by some topic and shows that he or she has ability and commitment to that area. Data are supplied by teachers, parents, and sometimes the students themselves.

Philosophy

The philosophical underpinnings of the SEM are based on the notion that education for the talented should involve differentiation of learning experiences. The opportunity to participate in a talent program should be available throughout a student's school life. The term *gifted* is deemphasized. Children who have the capability to move faster through the regular curriculum and function at higher levels of thinking should have special provisions to accommodate these qualitative differences. The pursuit of particular projects or problems promotes the interaction of traits, such as high ability, creativity, and task commitment, which are at the heart of outstanding accomplishments. The goal is to enhance creative productivity.

Staff Orientation

A coordinated effort is made among all school personnel to identify and program for talented children. Flexibility is necessary for the system to work. Efforts are made to involve the school and the community. Staff is trained in the overall philosophy and in the use of the various instruments and forms that are part of the process.

Evaluation

The SEM recognizes the importance of evaluation. Sources of data are student products from the individual projects and questionnaires from talent-pool students, parents, teachers, and principals. Renzulli and Reis (2003) have presented data that support the model.

The Indiana Academy for Science, Mathematics, and the Humanities

The Indiana Academy for Science, Mathematics, and the Humanities is one of a dozen residential high schools in the United States supported by public funds. The North Carolina Governor's School was the first summer residential program for gifted secondary school children and has served as the prototype for other programs (Ward, 1979). The program uses accelerated enrichment options and is organized to develop students' aptitudes and interests.

The Indiana Academy is located on the campus of Ball State University and is administered by the university. The students and faculty have full access to the university's resources (e.g., library and mainframe computers). The Academy serves approximately 300 students on campus, drawing rising 11th graders from throughout the state of Indiana and an average of more than 5,000 students in Indiana and across the United States via distance learning activities (i.e., televised high school courses and electronic field trips).

The Teacher

The teachers are required to hold a master's degree, with most being in content areas. A waiver from the Indiana Department of Education allows the Academy to hire its faculty without regard for licensure issues. An average of 40–50% of the faculty hold doctoral degrees. The Academy's outreach office trains teachers in summer and monthly workshops, a faculty Fellows program, and other distance learning techniques.

Curriculum

The curriculum emphasizes coursework in science, mathematics, and humanities. The school prides itself on having this tri-emphasis. In addition to those areas, students are also required to take foreign languages, a research seminar, and colloquia emphasizing integration of knowledge. Because the school only offers an honors diploma for 11th and 12th graders, the curriculum must be highly flexible to accommodate the complex levels of skills and talents the students bring.

Student Selection

The selection process reflects the philosophy of the school by including traditional academic indicators, such as standardized test scores (both ability and achievement); grades and grade-point averages; teacher, counselor, and parent recommendations; and essays written by the applicants. The Academy attempts to recruit children of ability, with less of an emphasis on prior achievement, in an effort to transcend prior educational opportunities as a primary criterion for being admitted. Consequently, the Academy manifests a diverse culture with wide ranges in prior achievement.

Staff Orientation

The staff orientation reflects the complexity of the curricula and the organization of the school. Academic Life and Residential Life staffs work together to offer a comprehensive program. The Academic Life staff, mainly composed of teachers, focuses on providing enriched and accelerated learning experiences. The Residential Life staff, mainly composed of counselors, works to offer students opportunities in which to develop. One group of faculty stresses rigorous accelerated courses, and another stresses broadening the depth of understanding and appreciation of content. Acceleration is carried forward in the framework of Advanced Placement in science and math courses, and enrichment is emphasized in humanities and language courses. In actuality, most courses combine acceleration and enrichment as the teachers work to meet the needs of their students.

Evaluation

The Academy seeks feedback about the program in both academic and residential life. Data are gathered on graduation rate, colleges attended, and experiences at the school. Faculty actively pursue their own professional development to ensure that their classes are up to date. However, to date, little schoolwide curricular review has occurred. Individual units are engaged in self-study-yielding strategic plans. The state requires the school to participate in a performance-based assessment that reviews all aspects of the school every 5 years. This process produces some insight that provides future direction.

Talent Searches: The Center for Talented Youth

"Talent search" is a term applied to a series of programs around the United States that are based on a model postulated by Julian Stanley that has had a profound effect on programming for gifted children (Stanley, Keating, & Fox, 1974). The model, which began at the middle and secondary levels of schooling, has been expanded into the elementary level (Assouline & Lupkowski-Shoplik, 1997; Lupkowski-Shoplik et al., 2003).

The foundational principles of talent searches are the discovery of advanced ability, the description of highly able people, the development of their abilities, and the dissemination of what has been learned. At present, regional talent searches are being conducted at Johns Hopkins University, Iowa State University, Duke University, Northwestern University, Denver University, and in more localized areas, such as the Illinois Talent Search of

297

the Illinois State Board of Education. In this section, we shall describe the foundational program, the Center for Talented Youth (CTY) at Johns Hopkins University.

The Teacher

Because a variety of options are possible in the CTY program, many different teaching situations are available. In general, the teacher is a highly knowledgeable person who may also be a college professor or a graduate student. The teacher is expected to teach children what they do not know as determined by careful assessment. The general program counsels students to make wise choices about developing their abilities.

Curriculum

The curriculum for the CTY program is a series of advanced courses in mathematical, scientific, and verbal areas. Essentially, the idea is to give students the opportunity to take accelerative options in these three curricular areas. CTY advocates using curricula that are typically given only to older students with younger students of demonstrated high ability. Much of the coursework is offered in the summer at the talent search centers, and it provides revenue for continuing the programs. The special feature of the program is that the curriculum is organized so that students can learn at a rate commensurate with their abilities. In this sense, the CTY program is more of an instructional strategy than an organized curriculum. Instructional materials play an important role in the process. There is a very close tie among assessment, teaching, and evaluation.

Student Selection

The identification provision in the CTY program is central to the program's success. Ability to perform at a high level in a domain is more important than age consideration. In-grade achievement tests with national norms, routinely given to students in schools, are used to screen pupils by selecting those who score in the top 5%. This group is invited to take the Scholastic Aptitude Test, now the Scholastic Assessment Test, at 12 years of age. This practice is called *out-of-level testing*. Children scoring at the mean or better for freshmen entering college are accepted into the program.

Philosophy

The CTY program has a distinct philosophical perspective. Math is regarded as the foundation for much of modern technology and science. The program assumes that children's aptitudes are differentially distributed. Identification of talent based on average high ability, such as IQ, overlooks children who may have unusually high potentials in specific aptitudes. Standardized tests can identify these children. Unless these children are stimulated, their abilities will be lost, both to themselves and to society. The best way to aid these unusually talented children is to encourage them to grow at rates commensurate with their eagerness for such growth. Present curricula and programming cannot accommodate these children.

Staff Orientation

The personnel are committed to assisting children in mastering subject matter information at an accelerated rate. The program should be adjusted to changes in the student as needed. Special guidance considerations are matched to individual students.

Evaluation

The CTY program has an extensive evaluation capability. Attention to building a database for programmatic decision making has resulted in a large number of books and articles (Benbow & Lubinski, 1997; Stanley & Benbow, 1982). The broad documentation of the program is a standard other programs should emulate. Talent searches, unlike many other programs, have demonstrated the success of their approach over two decades.

Centerville City Schools

Centerville is a medium-sized city in Ohio with a history of receiving the highest rating from the state Department of Education. Centerville has policies for identifying gifted children and a differentiated service plan. Following the state guidelines, 2,000 children have been identified. In Ohio, identification is mandatory, but serving those children is not. As a result, Centerville—like many school districts—provides direct services to a smaller number of children from elementary to secondary level. Children who are not served directly do receive some services from teachers who do not have expertise in gifted education.

Centerville City Schools has been providing programs for gifted children since the 1970s. Since the mid-1990s, Centerville has been moving from a pull-out model of service delivery to a differentiation model where most service takes place in the general education classroom. The central administration of the school is committed to making the differentiation model work. The school district believes that, under the old system, gifted education was mistakenly viewed as a one-size-fits-all program instead of a continuum of services. As a consequence, many general education teachers doubted they had the skills to teach these students or felt little if any obligation to work with these students in their classes. When differentiation was initiated in 1996, five people were assigned to gifted education; 9 years later, 10 teachers plus a full-time coordinator are assigned to support differentiation in the classroom.

Philosophy

Centerville's philosophy is typical for U.S. public schools; yet, at the same time, it embraces differentiation as the core of educational programming. The program is premised on the notion that gifted children will spend most of their educational time with all kinds of children and that all deserve high-quality instruction. Gifted children also have the right to spend time in school with children like themselves. Cluster grouping is one way to ensure this. Centerville assumes that children have unreleased potential, and their common unmet needs are the focal point of the program. Commitment to differentiated curricula and instruction is embedded throughout the school system.

Teacher Selection and Staff Orientation

Because the teacher is believed to be crucial to the program's success, screening, selection, and staff development is a deliberate process. Centerville seeks teachers who have a commitment to differentiation. Staff development is continuous and ongoing. Teachers are scheduled to attend team meetings and biannual staff-development institutes, and they are encouraged to attend professional conferences.

New teachers and veteran teachers participate in a professional development program where they are trained to meet the needs of all students. A conscious attempt is made to create a feeling of cohesiveness and cooperation among the teachers through the training program. Learning how to listen to students is an important part of the training because Centerville believes that knowledge of students is where differentiation begins.

Centerville City has two kinds of teachers. The gifted intervention specialists (GIS) are teachers with training and state certification in gifted education. The general education teachers have training in differentiation. The school district has 10 GIS so that one is assigned to the six elementary schools, while the middle schools and high school each have one GIS. Intervention specialists often coach general education teachers, help them develop differentiated units, and deliver direct instruction to gifted children when needed.

The willingness of the general education teacher to differentiate teaching is a key variable in implementation. Cluster grouping is one way the district brings identified children and willing teachers together. Organized professional development is focused on this group. School counselors are also involved in meeting the social and emotional needs of the gifted.

Curriculum

Centerville City Schools use the standard curriculum, but the intent is to challenge students by using differentiation. Broad themes and essential questions, as well as modification of content, process, and product, are parts of the curriculum. Thematic instruction anchors learning for all. Subsequent activities are linked to the theme, but themes are school-specific. For example, across the elementary schools at the fourth-grade level, various themes include connections, systems of change, cooperation, and interdependence. The teachers often initiate alterations in content. Students are encouraged to make choices that are challenging. Instruction is tied to student interest, and there are many variations in process and product in collaboration with teachers. The curriculum is differentiated across all levels of schooling. Independent study and projects are used extensively. More differentiation occurs in the elementary and middle schools than at the secondary level. Services or programs that are linked to student interest are offered throughout the school district. At the high school, honors and Advanced Placement courses are offered, as well as postsecondary options or dual enrollment.

Student Selection

The Centerville program identifies children according to the state of Ohio guidelines. Standardized and observational data are used, and the state provides an approved list of tests. Children may be identified as superior cognitive, academic, language arts, mathematics, social studies, creative, or visual and performing arts. Children are selected using a combination of standardized measures and performance data. The commitment to differentiation means that students may be identified as their needs become apparent. Children who are most in need of service are identified in multiple areas. These students appear on the state census of gifted children being served. Other children who are gifted, but do not have a written plan are not counted as receiving service by the state. The services available for these students occur in the general classroom, in accelerated math classes, and so forth. These advanced classes are not only for those formally identified as gifted.

Evaluation

Program evaluation is done as part of the regular school policy. Standardized tests, achievement and proficiency, are common indicators. Teachers create rubrics to assess the students' products and performances. Centerville City Schools has had the highest ratings on the state report card.

The International Baccalaureate of North America (IBNA)

The International Baccalaureate of North America (IBNA) is part of a larger organization called the International Baccalaureate Office, which is headquartered in Geneva, Switzerland. The beginning of the IB Office dates back to the 1960s, when a concern was voiced about the special schooling problems of mobile students, those who accompany their parents to different job sites around the world. The problems had to do with examinations for "university-bound pupils" and educational quality across countries. More specifically, children were asked to take separate examinations in different countries that segregated learning along nationalistic lines, required students to accommodate themselves to variations in requirements within national school systems, and presented students with variations in quality of schooling from country to country. With grants from foundations such as the Ford Foundation, a group of international educators met to consider the establishment of an international examination. In 1965, the IB Office was established. By 1970, 20 schools were using it around the world.

The program is financed by application and annual membership fees, foundation grants, and government grants. In essence, "the IB program offers standards of achievement in subjects traditionally studied in the last two years of high school leading to a diploma that is recognized by universities throughout the world" (International Baccalaureate of North America, 1981, p. 1). In the United States, the IB diploma is recognized for admission and for advanced placement in more than 425 colleges and universities. Each university establishes its own policy since there is no national system of education. Examples of U.S. institutions recognizing IB diplomas are Stanford, the University of California, Yale, the University of Georgia, Harvard, and the University of Utah. IBNA holds introductory workshops and provides some materials. Teachers are expected to follow their own preference for instructional activities within the framework of the curriculum.

Curriculum

The IB curriculum offers three programs geared to different levels of schooling: the Diploma Program, which spans the last 2 years of high school; the Middle Years Program for students age 11–16; and the Primary Years Program for students age 3–12.

Coursework in the Diploma Program is to be taken in six areas: a first language, a second language, the study of humankind, experimental sciences, mathematics, and an elective. All subjects have syllabi on two levels. The student must take three subjects at the higher level and three at the subsidiary level. The higher level syllabus requires 2 years of preparatory coursework. The subsidiary level syllabus requires 1 year of coursework. Those who want an IB diploma must also take an interdisciplinary course called the Theory of Knowledge, prepare an independent research paper in a subject area, and be involved in a creative, aesthetic, or social-service activity. The Theory of Knowledge, an intriguing part of the curriculum, is a 2-year course that covers nine topics. Three of the topics are concerned with scientific knowledge and scientific proof. The second three topics examine the concepts of social science. The last three topics have a more philosophical orientation: Two explore the nature of values and one explores the question of truth.

The Middle Years Program requires students to study eight subjects: foreign language, literature taught in the student's native language, science, social studies, math, physical education, arts, and technology. The Primary Years Program is organized around these questions: Who are we? Where are we in place and time? How do we express ourselves? How does the world work? How we organize ourselves? and How do we share the planet?

Philosophy

The IB program is designed to provide a liberal education. In North America, it is offered mainly in public schools, such as comprehensive high schools and magnet schools, both urban and suburban. The program assumes that the mind may be developed to its fullest extent. The developed mind is one that can communicate, analyze, reflect, create, enjoy, and be socially responsible. The IB program assumes that high achievement in the curricular areas is an example of a well-developed mind.

Evaluation

Written examinations are a standard part of the IB program. They are given on a fixed schedule in May. The examinations come from the IB Office in Geneva. An examination may include multiple-choice and essay questions. The criteria for evaluation are published so that teachers are aware of the standards. A final grade, which includes the exam score and estimate of school performance, is given in each subject. Teachers are asked to designate a predicted score for a student and report conditions working against student success (e.g., an illness). Exams are sent to assistant examiners for grading, and these grades are reviewed by a chief examiner. Students who do not meet requirements may be given a certificate instead of a diploma. Participatory schools are monitored by the IB Office.

CONCLUSION

Most of the relatively few gifted program arrangements have precedents dating from the turn of the century, and they flow from the particular problems gifted children present to education and from three contrasting, sometimes conflicting, philosophical models: the Whole Child Model, the Talent/Multiple Ability Model, and the Basic Skills Model. Because neither the nature of giftedness nor the structure of schools is likely to change, the unsettled nature of programming will continue.

The programs that exist can be seen as attempts to manipulate three variables: acceleration, enrichment, and special group settings. A number of different viewpoints exist on the appropriateness of each variable for the gifted. Within the community of educators of the gifted, there is contention about when and for whom these variables should be used. In the larger educational community, opposition to the use of these variables is based more on opinion than on fact, especially in the case of acceleration. The resistance of general education to acceleration is not warranted, given the preponderance of evidence in its favor.

Educators of the gifted do agree on the general outline of quality programs. Many program options, ranging from the use of special schools, to independent study, to programming within the regular classroom, may yield positive results. The selection of the correct option or options for a school district depends on the nature of the student body, the nature of the regular program, and the goals of the gifted program. All programs should make provision for evaluating their effectiveness. Evaluation is a complex task, given the nature of giftedness and the curriculum. Program quality is strongly influenced by the selection of teachers, but research offers little meaningful assistance to school districts that want to hire good ones. Experience with gifted children, knowledge of their development, and competency in a field of study seem to be useful qualities to look for in a teacher. The use of mentors holds promise for educating the gifted, as well.

FOR **DISCUSSION**

1. How could we attract more talented people into the teaching profession?

2. Defend or refute: Teachers of the gifted have to be gifted themselves.

3. Taking the descriptions of the school programs in this chapter, select two and develop an advertising campaign to attract students to that program.

4. The Talent/Multiple Abilities Model and the Whole Child Model have been contrasted in the text. What are the strengths and weaknesses of each model in your view as it applies to your schooling experience? Does it have to be that way in the future?

5. Although the evidence for implementing acceleration is plentiful and convincing, opposition persists. Explain how an idea can be resisted even when the evidence supports the procedure.

6. Consider the statement: It is possible to have acceleration without enrichment, but impossible to have enrichment without acceleration. Discuss your answer.

7. What would be the implications for schooling if acceleration became a national practice?

chapter eight

CURRICULUM THEORY AND PRACTICE

KEY CONCEPTS

- Curriculum is not the same as teaching. Curriculum is the bridge between administrative arrangements and the delivery of instruction. Some curricular elements are implicit and hidden.

- The goals of programs for the gifted differ from those of general education primarily in emphasis.

- A differentiated curriculum modifies the content, processes, and products in a learning sequence.

- The models for developing curricula for the gifted are linked to the notion of a differentiated curriculum, to an image of the gifted, and to an image of an educational model.

- Curricular models are broadly categorized as direct (developed specifically for the gifted) or indirect (adapted to the gifted). The models are primarily descriptive, not prescriptive.

- Curricular models are helpful for organizing ideas about levels of learning and experience, program and materials evaluation, and staff development.

- Curricular models create a specialized jargon that tends to confuse the process of developing curricula and circumvent some basic issues.

- Relatively few validated curricula are available from which teachers can teach.

- Without a challenging curriculum, there is no defensible gifted program.

The curriculum is a major aspect of education for the gifted. It guides decision making by providing a framework for instruction. The curriculum is the glue in an educational program; it holds program organization and instruction together and, by extension, guides the interaction between teachers and students.

In this chapter, for purposes of analysis and clarity, a sharp boundary is drawn between instruction and curriculum, sharper than is possible when examining real programs. We contend that ignoring the difference between instruction and curriculum brings forth much of the confusion surrounding gifted education. Much of what passes for curricula is in reality instructional in nature. The two chapters that follow this one will illustrate this point.

When we use the term *curriculum*, we mean the planned outcomes of a program encompassing a coherent organization of knowledge and skills. The chapter does not discuss the *hidden curriculum*, which consists of teacher values and program practices that undermine the curriculum by working against it. For example, the curricular goal might be to develop creativity in students, and the hidden curriculum is the rule that students must turn in all work within narrow time limits. Another goal might be to honor the contributions of ethnic and racial groups to the development of society, and the hidden curriculum is that these contributions are mentioned solely on holidays. Many messages about social values described in Chapter 4, which implicitly devalue giftedness and talent, highlight the pervasiveness of the hidden curriculum. Special programs should guard against practices that work in opposition to curricular plans.

THE PURPOSE OF SCHOOLING

This chapter operates on the assumption that mutual support between general and special education is appropriate in a democratic society. Schools (public and private, regular and special) have generally followed the policy of preparing youths for participation in society. As the conditions within society have changed, the schools have had to adapt to the new circumstances. In the 21st century, students live in a rapidly changing, interdependent world that will require them to possess an in-depth knowledge of the world and its peoples; a knowledge of multiple realities; an awareness of alternative solutions to world problems where compromise and persuasion replace force; and a sensitivity to the consequences of one's choices.

Curricula for the gifted must mirror those changes. If not, the school is unlikely to maintain support for education of the gifted unless its purposes are seen to correspond to those of general education. The relationship between general and gifted education is sometimes strained, but an examination of the stated goals of general and special programs reveals that they are similar and compatible. Because the goals and premises of the curriculum for the gifted are consonant with those of general education, does it have to be isomorphic to that of regular education? At the level of goals, minuscule differences are apparent. At the level of the objectives and of classroom practices, there might be great differences between general and special education. These differences have been discussed extensively and are as hotly debated today as in the past (Coleman, 1996).

Educators for the gifted use the term *differentiated curriculum* to describe the attributes that should distinguish between curricula for the gifted and nongifted. More than 40 years ago, Fliegler (1961) wrote, "The quintessence for educating the gifted is curriculum differentiation—a differentiation based upon the needs of the child" (p. 380). The premise underlying differentiation is certainly as current today as it was then (VanTassel-Baska, 1998). While widespread agreement exists regarding the desirability of differentiation, less unanimity and less clarity are found regarding the rationale and meaning of differentiation (George et al., 1979; Howley et al., 1995; Kaplan, 1979; Maker, 1982). Many of the issues discussed in Chapter 7 on programming recur in discussions about differentiation.

WHAT IS A DIFFERENTIATED CURRICULUM?

The principles of differentiation highlight aspects of the curriculum that correspond to the educational needs of gifted children. Fliegler's (1961) notion that a child's needs form the foundation for curriculum development remains the rationale for differentiation. From the literature on differentiation, one might infer the argument that the needs of the gifted are somehow different from those of other children and therefore mandate special educational provisions. Is that so? What is the nature of those differences? Are the differences real? Are the differences qualitative or quantitative? The answers to these questions are examined in this section.

Real Differences?

This question is answered depending upon where the person enters the situation. No one disputes that, in any group of children, one will find varying degrees of skill, knowledge, and proficiency. Thus, it is the meaning of that observation that is the key issue. Are the differences rooted in psychological or physiological evidence, or are the differences simply attributions given to some characteristics that are valued over others? Both questions are legitimate, and the answers are probably partially correct. Being able to separate measurement from values is impossible, so that kind of argument can only take one so far.

Most people in the field of gifted education interpret those differences to reflect educationally meaningful information (Gallagher, 1996). Others believe the differences between gifted and nongifted children have no educational significance and are social value judgments (constructions) used to discriminate among children due to educationally irrelevant markers associated with class, race, and gender (Margolin, 1996; Sapon-Shevin, 1996). In other words, the characteristics of well-to-do kids are given more value, and having more of those valued characteristics leads to one being considered gifted. The often-reported fact that fewer numbers of poor and disadvantaged children are identified for gifted programs than would be predicted on the basis of probability theory seems to support that claim.

Quantitative or Qualitative Differences?

Here, the question of educational significance is turned in another direction. Are the observed differences a consequence of quantitative or qualitative differences with nongifted children? For some, the distinction is used as part of the argument for gifted education and the rationale for differentiated curriculum. Consider these quotes, which nicely capture both sides of the debate: "I know of no evidence that gifted children are in any meaningful way different than other children" (Robinson, 1977, p. 7); "*Gifted children* are 'differently abled' just as other special needs children are 'differently abled'" (Morelock, 1996, p. 11, emphasis in original).

If the gifted grow and learn in a manner that is similar in kind to other children, why have a differentiated curriculum? Must one establish a qualitative difference to argue for a differentiated curriculum?

It may not be necessary to settle the question of qualitative versus quantitative difference. Ward (1961), who was one of the early advocates for a differentiated curriculum, did not support his contention of a need for a differentiated curriculum by postulating that gifted learners are qualitatively different. Instead, he noted that the gifted possess educationally significant characteristics, such as intelligence level and learning rate, that depart so extremely from those of typical learners that differences in the gifted are tantamount, in a practical sense, to differences in kind, rather than in degree. Robinson (1996), using a slightly different premise, also pointed out that the practical meaning of the difference for the child makes the differences educationally significant. On the other hand, Morelock (1996) made the case that the inner psychological life of children who are gifted means a qualitative difference that has educational significance.

Ward (1961) continued by arguing that the social roles the gifted will likely fill as adults mean that they can benefit from and therefore need a differentiated curriculum. Thus, his rationale for differentiation rests on needs that are educationally significant and, in turn, socially relevant. The addition of the idea of future role or position in society is a new dimension that brings us back toward the issue of whether the differences are real.

Following Ward's (1961) argument, it is not necessary to resolve the question of whether or not the gifted are qualitatively different from other children to argue effectively for a differentiated curriculum. Of course, given acceptance of the rationale for a differentiated curriculum, one would still need to become more specific in order to distinguish between a differentiated and a nondifferentiated curriculum. Should the subject matter and activities look different? Are the activities used in special programs inappropriate for the nongifted? Could the nongifted learn the material?

The way in which differentiated curricula are practiced in some programs creates the impression that they are neither different nor educationally relevant. This critique is based on the contention that enrichment activities that are the staple of most programs would be suitable for all children and that those same activities are not challenging enough for advanced learners. Howley et al. (1995) have made the case that, at the heart of the problem, lays the basic anti-intellectual bias of the general education *and* gifted education communities.

Perhaps the ideal of differentiation cannot be specified in a manner that is more specific than a general discussion. Whatever the reasons are for the difficulty in explaining differentiation, one fact continues to be as evident today as when Gallagher (1979) pointed it out more than 20 years ago: There is little in the way of validated differentiated curricula for a program to use. Furthermore, many of the ideas used to describe differentiated curricula are really instructional differences, as will be demonstrated in Chapter 9.

The quest for an unambiguously differentiated curriculum may not be realizable. Although there is not universal agreement on a reliable way to distinguish differentiated from nondifferentiated curricula, a curriculum council formed by the National/State Leadership Training Institute on the Gifted and Talented (Kaplan, 1979) proposed three basic elements for determining the presence of differentiated curricula: content, process, and product. Kaplan (1980), in a later writing, added *affect* as an element. Maker (1982) has pro-

CURRICULUM THEORY AND PRACTICE

311

posed an alternative list that retains the first three elements, but replaces *affect* with *learning environments*. Tomlinson (1996) has mentioned the three repeated elements in her writings. However, in more recent work, she has presented these elements: student readiness, interest, and learning profile (Tomlinson et al., 2003).

Content refers to the knowledge to be learned in a field. It is related to the key concepts that provide for entry into the depth of a field and is associated with broad issues and themes that integrate disciplines. *Process* refers to the development of patterns of thinking and creating, both in general and in regard to particular disciplines that enable the learner to make sense of the content and to be self-directive in further learning. Skills relevant to conducting research and independent study are considered to be processes in some formulations of the term. *Product* refers to the outcomes of learning in which the learning represents what has been mastered or creates new forms of expression for a field. The products are seen as natural outcomes of the mastery of content and the processes for dealing with it. There is some assumption that the product is both personally relevant and field-relevant.

These elements provide a foothold for someone trying to create or modify existing curricula in the slippery world of curriculum development. These elements have been expanded into the principles of a differentiated curriculum for the gifted and talented:

1. Present content related to broad-based issues, themes, or problems.

2. Integrate multiple disciplines into the area of study.

3. Present comprehensive, related, and mutually reinforcing experiences within an area of study.

4. Allow for the in-depth learning of a self-selected topic within the area of study.

5. Develop independent or self-directed study skills.

6. Develop productive, complex, abstract, or higher level thinking skills.

7. Focus on open-ended tasks.

8. Develop research skills and methods.

9. Integrate basic skills and higher level thinking skills into the curriculum.

10. Encourage the development of products that challenge existing ideas and produce "new" ideas.

11. Encourage the development of products that use new techniques, materials, and forms.

12. Encourage the development of self-understanding (i.e., recognizing and using one's abilities, becoming self-directed, and appreciating likenesses and differences between oneself and others).

13. Evaluate student outcomes by using appropriate and specific criteria through self-appraisal, criterion-referenced, or standardized instruments (Kaplan, 1979, p. 5).

Differentiation does not mean more of the old curriculum, as in more assignments or more problems to complete, nor does it mean that everyone gets the same learning experiences. Rather, differentiation refers to curricula that are relevant and challenging to the gifted. Passow (1988) made the point well when he posed three questions: Would all students want to be involved in such learning experiences? Could all students participate in such learning experiences? and Should all students be expected to succeed in such learning experiences? If the answer to each question is "yes," then the curriculum is not differentiated.

MODELS USED FOR CURRICULUM BUILDING

The idea of differentiation is the background for the development of curricula for the gifted, which has been facilitated and shaped by the adoption of theoretical models from psychology, education, and sociology. The selection of models for building curricula seems to be a process of aligning three images in the minds of the curriculum builders: an image of what constitutes giftedness, an image of a differentiated curriculum, and an image of an educational model, as noted in the last chapter. Some have found models that fit their images of giftedness and possible potentials; others have not.

Curriculum models for the gifted divide into two groups: indirect and direct. The former are models based on the work of scholars outside gifted education that are applied to the gifted. The latter are models that have been developed specifically for gifted children. The appearance of more direct models is a sign of the field maturing.

The models used in curriculum development for the gifted are descriptive models (Snow, 1973). The prime characteristic of descriptive models is the classifying of phenomena into categories, such as educational objectives (Bloom, 1956), talents (Taylor, 1985), cognitive-intellectual abilities (Gardner, 1983; Guilford, 1967; Sternberg, 1985), enrichment (Renzulli, 1977; Renzulli & Reis, 1997), subject matter (VanTassel-Baska, 1986, 1997), and parallels (Tomlinson, Kaplan, Renzulli, Purcell, Leppien, & Burns, 2002). Descriptive models identify elements in a situation. They do not validate the best way to

313

achieve the goal of maximizing development in a specific time or place. Only research on curriculum can do that. Descriptive models fulfill an important function that should not be regarded lightly; however, their limitations should be recognized (Bruner, 1966). The tendency among educators of the gifted to treat descriptive models as if they were both prescriptive and descriptive causes confusion.

Direct Models

Because direct models were developed for the gifted, they have advantages over indirect models in that the creators had the three basic images in mind. Direct models have implications for the nongifted, but they were not created for that group. Examples of direct models are those of Renzulli (1977), Maker (1982), Morgan et al. (1980), Tannenbaum (1983), VanTassel-Baska (1997), Ward (1961) and Tomlinson et al. (2002). Three models are described because of their influence on the field, and a fourth model is introduced because of its presumed future influence.

Ward's Enrichment Model

In 1961, Ward published *Educating the Gifted: An Axiomatic Approach*, in which he outlined an educational theory derived from data on the gifted upon which programs and curricula could be made. Ward's image of the gifted is essentially drawn from Terman. The gifted possess a broad array of strengths, and among these, general intellectual superiority is the most significant for curriculum construction. General intellectual ability is related to high functioning in other, more specific abilities. Ward recognized some other specific aptitudes, but judged them not amenable to identification or to cultivation and, therefore, not a sound basis for curriculum construction.

Ward's image of the curriculum was found in general education, which was grounded in social reality and future social roles. The gifted person's potentials were to be developed using a broad approach. General intellectual development would foster special abilities in the natural context of development. Children "driven intrinsically" in an area of aptitude were to be supported. The modern world was seen as an ever-changing setting that required thoughtful, socially responsible, creative people. Given these considerations, Ward's curriculum emphasized intellectual activity. Experiences were to be designed to build continually more powerful modes of thought. Thus, children who are gifted should learn methods of inquiry, learn the nature of languages, and learn to apply the scientific method to life problems. Content should also include information on the foundation of civilization, the history of knowledge, literary classics, language, and principles governing personal behavior and social adjustment. Throughout, Ward tried to integrate psychological and epistemological principles into a sound educational theory.

The operationalization of many of these notions can be found in the North Carolina Governor's School (Ward, 1979) and other public residential high schools (Kolloff, 1991). The model is significant because it is a thoughtful attempt to furnish gifted education with a needed theoretical base for building curriculum and school programs. Many of Ward's ideas have been accepted, elaborated upon, and modified by others. The next model was developed by one of his students.

Renzulli's Enrichment Triad Model

The Enrichment Triad Model is a direct model of curriculum for the gifted designed to defend gifted programs from criticism (Renzulli, 1977). The image of giftedness implicit in this model has been advocated by Renzulli in the Revolving Door Identification Model (Renzulli, Reis, & Smith, 1981) and the Schoolwide Enrichment Model. Here, giftedness is essentially characterized by three attributes: high general intellectual ability, creative ability, and task commitment. Giftedness is not seen as an all-or-nothing state, but rather as one that emerges and subsides as specific interests are pursued and satisfied. The image of realized potential is a person meeting life's challenges in an independent, productive, and original manner. The school becomes the training ground for gifted behavior by providing opportunities for enriched learning experiences.

The Enrichment Triad Model classifies school experiences into three categories of related activities structured for specific purposes. Type I is general exploratory activities. The purpose is to awaken a student's personal interest in an area of study by exposing him or her to the variety of ideas and attitudes that would fuel further exploration in the world. Renzulli recommended that resource centers be set up in classrooms and in schools to provide for the varieties of information on a subject. Care should be taken so that the collection of information includes stories of others' experiences in finding information, the techniques they used, and their excitement in the search.

Type II is group training activities. The purpose here is to move from exploration to the acquisition of skills that will help the student handle content more effectively. Students are to be trained in thinking and feeling processes. Many techniques that fall under broad categories are available, such as decision-making skills, inquiry training, brainstorming, and values clarification. The techniques are designed to help students develop abilities in analyzing, creating, evaluating, imagining, and communicating. Renzulli recommended that content in typical courses, such as history and language arts, be modified to encourage the use of these processes. Both the first and second types of activities are appropriate for nongifted children, who can also profit from them. The gifted, however, are believed to thrive in this kind of experience and move naturally to the third type.

Type III consists of individual projects. Small group or individual investigations are the focus of this category. The purpose is to help gifted learners become independent investigators, a role they will have as adults. The processes and skills they need in order to study a topic independently have already begun to develop in the second type of enrichment. Students are expected to communicate their results to others. Renzulli sees the teacher as a facilitator of learning who assists students in managing their projects.

The three categories of enrichment complement and supplement each other. A student does not move in lock-step fashion from one type to the next; instead, there is movement among steps. Obviously, independent study becomes a more feasible alternative for students as they develop skills and knowledge within a content area. The Enrichment Triad Model provides a means for ordering instructional activities. It is consistent with the indirect models (to be described later) in that it is concerned with helping gifted children attain levels of performance not open to other students. In a later revision of the model provision, enrichment clusters were included to help manage children in groups (Reis, Gentry, & Maxfield, 1998).

VanTassel-Baska's Integrated Curriculum Model (ICM)

In a series of articles, books, and project reports, VanTassel-Baska (1986, 1993, 1997) has emerged as an important voice in curriculum development. The Integrated Curriculum Model (ICM) combines and extends many of the ideas advanced by authors who have models in this chapter and in the next chapter on instruction.

VanTassel-Baska was critical of the state of curriculum development because a comprehensive framework had not been developed that recognized the importance of fields of study or disciplines and was sufficiently differentiated to meet the needs of gifted students. She proposed the ICM as a synthesis of "the three best approaches to curriculum development and implementation documented in the literature" (VanTassel-Baska, 1994a, p. 128; see also Benbow & Stanley, 1983; Maker, 1982; Ward, 1961). The model has three dimensions: Advanced Content, Process-Product, and Issues/Themes. Subject matter is the foundation for learning advanced content, for engaging students in learning that leads to products consistent with the standards of the subject matter, and for studying issues that are central to that subject matter.

Using these ideas, VanTassel-Baska has conducted two national curriculum projects in science and language arts (1994b). Each of the projects used the three dimensions to organize the curriculum. Exemplary curricular units have been developed for primary, intermediate, and middle schools in each project, and reports on these projects have appeared in the literature (VanTassel-Baska, Johnson, Hughes, & Boyce, 1996), which shows the ICM's promise. Unlike the other models, the ICM has validated curricula schools could adopt.

The Parallel Curriculum

A new arrival among the direct curriculum models is the Parallel Curriculum Model (Tomlinson et al., 2002), which is a product of a committee of the National Association for Gifted Children (NAGC) with the "goal of developing a model to guide *curriculum design for the journey toward expert-*

ise" (p. xi, emphasis added). It is to serve as "a catalyst" and not to "replace existing models of curriculum development" (p. xi).

> It is our intent that the Parallel Curriculum Model represents a synthesizing of views and approaches to creating curriculum that leads toward expertise rather than reflecting any single view or approach. To that end, while we do not cite specific contributors from the field of gifted education, we acknowledge with a profound sense of heritage the work of all those who have pioneered our understanding of what it means to teach for expertise, those who have developed that understanding over the years, and those who continue to develop that understanding. (p. xi)

The Parallel Curriculum's image of giftedness is the development of expertise. Because expertise is domain-specific, the curriculum moves toward narrowing knowledge and skills and accelerating learning with fewer and fewer people being at the highest levels. The image of differentiation is also evident in the language of enrichment with the use of terms like *process, product, affect, broad themes*, and *challenge*. The image of schooling reveals a commitment to educating all children with attention to the gifted and talented.

The Parallel Curriculum gets its name from the fact that authors propose four types of curricula that exist side by side and can be used separately or jointly to develop expertise. The parallels are: the Core or Basic Curriculum (the foundation of knowledge in a discipline), the Curriculum of Connections (the interdisciplinary and cross cultural links to the discipline), the Curriculum of Practice (application of ideas and skills in the discipline), and the Curriculum of Identity (coming to understand oneself within the context of the discipline). Within each parallel, teachers are to challenge and guide students by providing for "ascending intellectual demand" (p. 13). Among the four parallels, the Curriculum of Practice seems most innovative. Readers are repeatedly invited to create curricula that follow these principles. The book is clearly intended to convince others that this is the way to do curriculum. Essentially, the Parallel Curriculum seems to be organized to be used in workshops for the future development of curriculum.

The Parallel Curriculum differs from many other curriculum models in that it introduces and emphasizes expertise, a clear departure from more conventional notions. It also differs from other models because it is the product of an organization, not an individual. While the Parallel Curriculum Model has interesting, loosely connected ideas, we were never sure what "parallel" meant in this context and why the term was chosen as the guiding concept. Because, as the writers acknowledge, few citations are made to the field of gifted education, we are led to infer it is connected to the authors' notion of curriculum. The philosophical presence of the University of Connecticut and the influence of the leadership of NAGC are evident. Earlier writings of Renzulli, Tomlinson, and Kaplan are strongly visible. One example is *The*

Multiple Menu Model: A Practical Guide for Developing Differentiated Curriculum (Renzulli, Leppien, & Hayes, 2000). At the same time, the text is full of significant ideas and connections to scholars outside the field of gifted education, some of whom are discussed under indirect curriculum models.

Is this a curriculum for the gifted? It is and it is not. The Parallel Curriculum asserts that provisions need to be made for students' varying rates of learning and interest, therefore separating learners on any other basis is unwarranted. Furthermore, the introduction of expertise as the defining element recasts giftedness as it applies to growth in a domain, which is not a mainstream concept in the schools. The term *gifted* is repeatedly used in the text, but the authors assert, *"There is no such thing as 'the' gifted learner"* (p. 19). This fuzziness between learners who are gifted and those who are not persists throughout the text.

While NAGC has launched an extensive campaign to conduct workshops and market materials connected to the Parallel Curriculum, it remains to be seen whether this model will produce appropriate curricula for the gifted. Like most of the models, we must wait for the evidence in terms of student learning and productivity.

Indirect Models

Indirect models were designed for purposes other than the education of gifted children. They organize categories of human behavior relevant to all people in a manner that suggests to advocates of gifted education the presence of less-conventional or higher levels of functioning. Because the gifted are assumed to grow toward those levels, and high-level functioning is unlikely to occur without opportunity, these models have been incorporated into gifted education. Several models are explored here, and similarities and differences are evident among them.

Why indirect models have received wide acceptance by educators of the gifted is not apparent from the literature. We speculate that the three images are operating. Gifted education is part of general education, and it is in that context that these models have received much attention. General education models are appropriate for the gifted, too, because they speak of the possibility of development to the highest levels of thinking and feeling. The aura of unfulfilled potential is noticeable. The gifted, as described without exception by writers in the field, are destined to move in this direction. The image of giftedness fits the image of potential implicit in the models. For those feeling defensive about gifted education, one could claim that what is good for all children is even better for gifted children. Indirect models provide a means for describing a differentiated curriculum that justifies the time and effort needed to help gifted children attain the levels of functioning of which they are capable.

Given the importance of intelligence testing to the emergence of the field of gifted education, it seems natural that theories of intelligence should be the basis for curriculum development. Two theories have dominated the literature:

Guilford's (1967) Structure of Intellect Model in the 1960s and 1970s and Gardner's (1983) theory of multiple intelligences in the late 1980s and 1990s. A third theorist, Robert Sternberg (1985), has also been influential in the discussion of intelligence, but less so in terms of the creation of new curricula. Calvin Taylor's (1973, 1985) multiple-talents model has also influenced the field. All of these models and theories propose the existence of multiple intelligences in the population and in single individuals. In this section, we will focus on Guilford, Taylor, and Gardner.

Guilford's Structure of Intellect Model (SI)

In 1959, the Structure of Intellect (SI) was described as an expression of Guilford's dissatisfaction with conventional notions of intelligence and IQ tests, dissatisfactions that also inspired Gardner and Sternberg. Guilford was bothered by a number of facts: People with the same IQ scores could have widely different patterns of scores; a 10-year spread in mental age from base to ceiling on the Stanford-Binet was not unusual; correlations between verbal and performance tests, as well as correlations among verbal tests themselves, were sometimes zero; creative ability was not measured on intelligence tests; and the growth of various mental abilities was not known (Guilford, 1967, 1968). In essence, Guilford took all he knew about intelligence, intelligence theory, factor analysis (a statistical technique), and morphological analysis (an analytic technique mentioned in the chapter on creativity) and created the Structure of Intellect Model.

Guilford reasoned that items on tests and tasks in life can be distinguished by looking at the kind of information people have to use (content), the way they process the information (operations), and how they organize information while processing it (products). He constructed a cubed matrix with three faces representing his categories of intellect. Each face was further subdivided into components so that there are four contents, five operations, and six products. The larger cube is composed of smaller cubes corresponding to the intersection of a content, an operation, and a product to yield a single, independent type of intelligence. Of the resulting 120 types of intelligence, close to 100 have been reported.

The SI model fits the image of the gifted as possessors of multiple abilities that need a nourishing environment for development. Furthermore, the SI model provides an explanation for the existence of multiple strengths, a place for creative behavior, and a means for looking at content in a manner that disregards subject matter. Given the mood of educational reform in the 1960s and the beginnings of the human potential movement, there was a receptive climate for the SI model. Meeker (1969, 1981) was at the forefront of applying the complete SI model to educational practice, including assessment, instruction, and curriculum. Evidence favoring the SI model's utility in general education is sketchy, however. Its use with gifted children has been fragmentary, yet influential; for example, Karnes and Bertschi (1978) described an interesting program applying SI to gifted preschoolers. However, there has been a general lack of application of the complete model to gifted education, possibly because of its highly technical nature and multiple variations of the three major dimensions.

While, the general model, using all the dimensions, has received limited attention, the operations dimension has been the focus of many efforts in gifted education. Teachers have been encouraged to organize lessons and units around the operations dimension (Sisk, 1976). Among the five operations, three operations that have generally been ignored by schools (divergent production, convergent production, and evaluation) became the centerpiece of efforts to develop and revitalize curriculum (Gowan et al., 1979). Divergent production came to be used as a synonym for creativity, and much effort went into teaching for creativity (see Chapter 6), while the other factors in the SI model received little attention.

The emphasis on operations over other components suggests that curriculum builders were committed to a perspective that emphasizes process skills or thinking ability skills. Guilford's pioneering research was conducted on adults, not children, but his model has been influential in shaping the thinking of educators of the gifted. The influence of his terminology is evident. At this point, his model demonstrates that our ability to identify SI factors (kinds of intelligence) far outstrips our ability to demonstrate effective educational strategies for developing those abilities.

Taylor's Talents Model

Calvin Taylor is an important researcher on creativity in adults who also has been concerned with identifying and developing creativity in children (Taylor, 1973, 1985). He proposed a multiple-talent model and ways to nurture talents. Taylor realized that creative performance and outstanding work in a field could not be linked to one separate talent, nor could talents be linked only to school success. In fact, when he considered American schools, one talent—academic talent—was most encouraged, while others, such as planning talent and predicting talent, were overlooked. Given Taylor's presumption that people possess many talents in differing amounts, it followed that children with high academic talent felt successful in school and, conversely, those with less academic talent, but more of another talent, felt less successful in school. If the school was to prepare children for a variety of societal roles requiring many talents, then this was an unsatisfactory way to organize it. The talents that Taylor thought were related to creative problem solving were academic, creative, planning, communicating, forecasting, decision making, and human relations. In the interrelationships among the talents, academic talent serves as an information supplier to the processing that occurs in the other talent areas.

Taylor's notions on multitalent teaching have been integrated into different programs that emphasize different talents. The Talents Unlimited Project in Mobile, Alabama, is one such program (Schlichter, 1981, 1991). The modified list of talents includes:

- *productive thinking*: to generate many, varied, and unusual ideas or solutions and to add detail to the ideas to improve on them and make them more interesting;

- *decision making*: to outline, weigh, make final judgments, and defend a decision on the many alternatives to a problem;

- *planning*: to design a means for implementing an idea by describing elements to be done, identifying the resources needed, outlining a sequence of steps to take, pinpointing possible problems, and showing improvement in the plan;

- *forecasting*: to make a variety of predictions about the possible causes or effects of various phenomena;

- *communication*: to use and interpret both verbal and nonverbal forms of communication to express ideas, feelings, and needs to others; and

- *academic*: to develop a base of knowledge and/or skills about a topic or issue through acquisition of information and concepts (Schlichter, 1991, p. 319).

Taylor's multiple talent approach is quite attractive to some educators of the gifted (Kaplan, 1974) because it assumes that varying numbers of talents may exist in one person. The talents are trainable, and developed talents will enhance potential for success in many areas of life. Again, how one can see an image of the gifted as people with multiple strengths merges with an image of furthering development. The Taylor model provides a rationale for using alternate identification and curricula by people who believe gifted programs base their identification schemes on a restricted range of abilities. For problem solving within the context of the regular curriculum, this model is useful.

While the Taylor's model has been discussed by educators of the gifted, especially as it relates to the development of creativity, research on its effectiveness with the gifted is limited (Schlichter, 1981). Several writers (Maker, 1979; Sisk, 1982) have recommended Taylor's model for use with the gifted because the talents can be nurtured in any subject. For example, Sisk provided examples of how the model may be used for furthering the moral development of gifted children. Taylor's notions received renewed interest in the 1990s (Schlichter, 1991), partially because of the encouraging results of research with nongifted children and the ability of Taylor's approach to fit into other models, such as the Enrichment Triad Model. The simple fact that Taylor's model uses familiar terms such as *communication* and *planning*, rather than psychology-oriented terms such as *cognition*, may also account for its broad appeal. Friedman and Lee (1996) reported that the model was effective in increasing the complexity of cognitive interactions in the classroom.

Gardner's Theory of Multiple Intelligences

Unlike Guilford's ideas, which became isolated to the gifted education community, Gardner's (1983) attractiveness to the larger educational community is obvious in the number of journal articles and books that reference his work. For that reason, we describe it only briefly here.

Gardner (1983) created his theory from a different perspective than Guilford's. Gardner, too, was dissatisfied with ingrained views of intelligence. After examining literature on cognitive development, anthropology, and neuroscience, Gardner determined that the notion of general intelligence was not useful and that people had multiple intelligences, hence his theory is of "multiple intelligences." He specified seven kinds of intelligence, now eight, each with a different locus and some with unconventional meanings: linguistic (verbal and nonverbal), logico-mathematical, spatial, musical, intrapersonal (self-knowledge), interpersonal (knowledge of others), bodily-kinesthetic (movement and dance), and naturalistic. These intelligences are seen as relatively autonomous, potentially present in all people, acquired through learning opportunities, and extending from limited development to extraordinary levels of development.

Gardner's ideas have been used to develop curricula for gifted children in a variety of school contexts, ranging from single classrooms to whole schools. Each intelligence can be regarded as a goal of schooling, as a thematic way of organizing the curriculum, or both. By using these eight kinds of intelligence as a guide, teachers or curriculum developers can choose, create, and orchestrate the kinds of opportunities students encounter. Maker, Nielson, and Rogers (1994) described a way to use the theory of multiple intelligences in an innovative program for gifted children from diverse communities. At present, limited research is available on the use of this theory with gifted children.

The Discipline-Specific Curriculum Model

The title of this section is conceived solely for this analysis. No actual model has this name. It is meant to represent an integration of several perspectives. The model assumes that, when children develop, they progress through stages, each of which is characterized by qualitative changes. The transition from stage to stage is marked by a child wavering back and forth. Once a stage is realized, it is difficult for the child to reconceptualize how he or she functioned at the lower stage (Kohlberg, 1969; Piaget, 1954).

The model also assumes that information can be organized into structures called *disciplines* or *subject matter areas*. These disciplines are more specific than the taxonomic notion of domains, such as the familiar Taxonomy of Educational Objectives (Bloom, 1956). While disciplines are interrelated, each has its own properties, including modes of inquiry and thinking (Bruner, 1968; Phenix, 1986; VanTassel-Baska, 1994a). Each discipline's structure builds toward greater abstractions, finer discriminations, and more powerfully generalized principles that are accessible to fewer and fewer people. The structure of a discipline evolves to more comprehensive descriptions of phenomena. This evolution is never completed, although a discipline may be incorporated into a new discipline or even abandoned (e.g., phrenology gives way to neuropsychiatry). The evolution of a discipline is a consequence of individuals creating new knowledge through development into a new stage, which is, at some point, integrated into the discipline (Feldman, 1980, 1994).

A model that elaborates and refines many of these ideas has been constructed by Feldman (1980), which was discussed in some depth in Chapter 5. In brief, Feldman proposed that learning in domains or disciplines can be considered a developmental phenomenon. Knowledge proceeds on a continuum from a point at which all people have access to it, to another point at which only one person or relatively few people comprehend it. The rate of development within a structure is largely dependent upon opportunity to learn the subject and the subject's structure.

The model seems to fit an image of the gifted as those who develop faster and achieve higher levels than others. The Discipline-Specific Model implies that education is crucial to high performance; original performance is related to subject-related factors; development can be charted within subject areas; relatively long-term involvement is needed for mastering an area; and it is reasonable that a limited number of people in a culture achieve at the most advanced levels.

The idea of a structure of knowledge within a discipline was one aspect of the curriculum reform movement of the 1960s, although the gifted were not the major group for whom curricula were developed. Curricula were developed in mathematics, biology, chemistry, physics, economics, and social studies by committees formed of educators, subject specialists, and psychologists. These group projects created an array of instructional materials to go with the curricula (Travers, 1973). The reform efforts started in the elementary schools and spread to the secondary level. Research on the effectiveness of these new structure-of-discipline-oriented curricula tended to demonstrate that the more able students received the most benefit from them. The fact that these curricula emphasized scientific models and methods while extending ideas toward more comprehensive abstractions seemed to result in a better approximation between learners' needs and curricula, at least for the gifted.

Examples of research using a stage/structure orientation that have implications for curriculum construction are available (Floyd, 1979). Other research on social relationships (Furth, 1980) and moral development (Rest, 1979) seem to be useful. The development of curricula using a stage/structure orientation has been described in social studies (Derricott & Blyth, 1979), science (Harlen, 1979), physics (Shayer, 1979), and math (Brown, 1979), which demonstrates that such an orientation has utility for curriculum development. It is also apparent that there is considerable variation among children at different stages. The nature of interactions between a subject area and cognitive development is still rather imprecise. Without greater precision and additional evidence on the benefits of curricula organized on a stage/structure basis, adoption of this perspective will probably remain limited.

In general, the Discipline-Specific Model has been in a kind of limbo. The value of disciplinary content is generally accepted, but implementation is fragmentary (Shore et al., 1991). Amidst all the turmoil about school reform in the past decade, little energy seems left for this topic. The appearance of Feldman's research, the evidence on acceleration, the sense of uneasiness about other models, the emergence of constructivism as a force in education, and renewed attention to discipline-specific curricula suggest that this curriculum model is entering a period of resurgence. VanTassel-Baska (1994b) is one voice pushing us in that direction. If a resurgence takes place, it is likely to have an impact on secondary, rather than elementary curricula because teachers have more chances to specialize in disciplines and students have already developed the necessary prerequisite skills.

Comparing the Models

Two categories of descriptive models have been examined in reference to curriculum development. The smaller category, the direct model, is constructed from ideas specifically intended for the gifted. The other category, indirect models, contains ideas developed for purposes other than the education of the gifted, but still applies to the gifted. Both types are congruent with the principles of differentiated curricula, and most have been in the literature for more than a decade.

Benefits

The models, as a whole, are useful for building better curricula and better programs. They have value because one can discriminate among the many varieties of experience, which is a first step toward effecting changes in curriculum policy for the gifted. The models can provide frameworks for constructing curricular units and for evaluating what one is doing in a program. A teacher may note, using one of the models, that certain experiences are being overemphasized. For example, when using Gardner's theory, one may recognize that linguistic intelligence is getting more attention than interpersonal intelligence.

Published materials may also be evaluated with a model. Teachers are usually bombarded by publishers selling materials that claim to teach all sorts of content and skills. A model organizes one's thoughts and gives perspective to the evaluation. For example, one might determine that Renzulli's Type I activities or Taylor's planning talent are not included in a set of materials.

The models also have utility for staff and personnel development. A school could choose to adopt one of the models as a way of thinking about curriculum. The models can be used to teach staff that multiple abilities and talents are recognizable. They illustrate that some experiences may be more likely to teach for certain outcomes than other experiences. A teacher can select from existing materials or create new experiences to nurture different abilities or talents when armed with this knowledge.

These models also point to the upper limits of performance or, in other terms, to the less-ordinary ways of thinking and feeling. It is these upper limits that fascinate educators of the gifted (Coleman, 1997). Using these models as a frame of reference tends to upgrade and freshen the educational experiences of gifted children because it provides a rationale for reconceptualizing the basics of education. These models do not denigrate the traditional basics of reading, writing, and arithmetic, but rather, place them in proper perspective. These models state that there are basic processes involved in how people experience the world. Since these processes generalize and extend into many areas of life, as do the traditional basics, they, too, are basics. By sharpening these processes, individual potential can be enhanced. The gifted have greater potentials in these basics and can profit from opportunities to develop their abilities.

Shortcomings

While these models have received much endorsement, there are problems with which they fail to deal effectively. In some ways, these problems are the reverse side of the benefits.

The ability to discriminate among models and categories is difficult for both sophisticated and unsophisticated readers. This difficulty in curriculum construction becomes a problem of deciding what the student will be doing or what the student is doing in unambiguous terms. What do concepts like "analytic intelligence," "concrete stage," or "forecasting" look like in the real world? The meaning of these concepts is shaped by the level of subject matter. Drawing parallels between analyzing the characteristics of a poem and analyzing the attributes of a concept, such as fruit, is an oversimplification. Furthermore, it is confusing to describe writing a paragraph on a topic as an activity that teaches only linguistic intelligence or planning talent.

The comprehension of descriptive models is confounded when people try to establish simplistic parallels between models, such as Gardner and Guilford or Taylor and Renzulli. One unintentional result is that the meaning of the individual model is obscured and important distinctions are lost. This situation creates a problem for researchers, teacher trainers, and teachers. An unfortunate side effect can occur when terminology associated with certain models is used in a loose, interchangeable manner. Confusion, rather than order, is created by promoting the belief that phenomena are understood when they are not and by encouraging the growth of jargon that cannot be understood with any precision either inside or outside the field. Jargon may undermine gifted programs by weakening support from general educators.

The problem of assigning objectives or activities to the proper category obviously complicates the task of evaluating a curriculum. Correctly categorizing a behavior does not mean a student actually used the process in the attain-

325

ment of a curricular objective. Designing a curriculum on the basis of some model does not guarantee that students will learn those processes. The gifted child has a choice in using one of several processes to complete many instructional tasks. For example, a student, Steve, is asked to state whether the play *Death of a Salesman* is like a Greek tragedy and to defend the answer. Steve happens to have read an article on the subject and his classmates have not. All the students' responses may seem indicative of evaluative thinking; yet, in reality, Steve simply recalled the answer.

The contention by educators of the gifted that development of higher processes is accomplished by designing curricula using these models is insufficient to turn aside critics who ask for demonstration that the goal is being reached. Demonstrating that students are better thinkers without introducing evidence of advanced content into the discussion is improbable. In other words, a fine discrimination is being made between the intent of curriculum and real performance. The use of sophisticated models provides a rationale for goals and curriculum planning, but models do not provide proof that the goals will be attained.

Unanswered Questions

Some significant issues about curriculum are poorly addressed by the curriculum models we have cited. These models tend to circumvent three questions about content—the process/development question, the content/transfer question, and the content/development question—that are basic to curriculum building. First, we will explain the questions and then follow with a discussion of how the models deal with them.

The process/development question addresses changes in the processes of thinking, feeling, and solving problems. Do these processes operate in the same way throughout the period that a child is in school? Is it possible that acquisition of some of these processes affects others? Do some processes have greater developmental significance than others? Discussion of intelligence and talent in the curriculum literature on giftedness tends to skirt the issue of changes in development. Since no one would argue that cognitive and affective processes remain constant across the dozen years of schooling, it is puzzling that a discussion of the precise adjustments recognizing these changes is difficult to find.

The content/transfer question asks whether or not some school experiences are more likely to extend to situations outside the school setting. In general, it appears that curriculum builders for the gifted assume the transfer will naturally occur as a consequence of special programs. There seems to be some implicit belief that activities that teach intellectual skills or talent are most likely to transfer outside the program. The models speak to the transfer question in a general way, yet offer little supporting evidence in response to it. Type III enrichment activities are presumed to have this quality because the ability to carry out independent investigations is a part of work in various fields. The Discipline-Specific Model also seems to speak to this point.

The content/development question examines the essential relationship between subject matter and developmental processes. Is some content better for fostering advanced development than other content? How important is the selection of content to curriculum construction for the gifted? Is there an invariant, universal developmental sequence common to all content areas, or is there a separate sequence for each content area?

A general consensus exists about the need for appropriate content, but the basis for selection of content is unclear. Statements calling for the selection of content that elicits higher levels of thinking are really too broad for application to sound decision making. Educators of the gifted are caught in a strange situation. On the one hand, there is the belief that all content has equal potential for developing basic processes. On the other hand, there is the contention that, primarily through appropriate content, processes significant to later mastery of more complex content are developed. Some sort of resolution to this situation is needed if gifted education is to rise above the perennially irrelevant process-content, or knowledge as content, debate (see Parker & Rubin, 1966). Attempts to place one over the other lead to a dead end. Only in a fantasy such as *The Wizard of Oz* could someone receive a degree in "thinkology." Gifted people in the historical record are all remembered because of significant work in an area of human endeavor. In sum, it is impossible to separate thought and feeling from the content of those thoughts and feelings. Sometimes, the controversy over acceleration and enrichment gets confused with the content debate.

None of the models has the ability to answer the above questions in an unambiguous manner. The direct models furnish more answers than the indirect models; however, they could do a better job. The Ward Enrichment, Enrichment Triad, Integrated Curriculum, and Parallel Curriculum models make proposals about selection of content and transferability. The Ward Enrichment Model seems to deal with content better than the Enrichment Triad Model, while the converse is true regarding transferability. The issue of development, as posed here, is better addressed by Ward. The Integrated Curriculum Model, by combining both perspectives, offers something about both. The Parallel Curriculum Model is more like the ICM, yet it straddles the issue.

The development issue is largely unrecognized in the indirect models. The Discipline-Specific Model proposes a sequence, yet it is tied to content considerations. The Taylor Talents Model has been organized into a sequence of sorts that claims to be independent of content. The issue of school experiences transferring to the outside is alluded to in all the indirect models, but the Taylor Talents Model and the Discipline-Specific Model deal with it most effectively. The Discipline-Specific Model seems to do a better job overall of integrating these questions into a meaningful whole for developing curricula.

One might infer from the presentation that curricula for the gifted are stalled by an overemphasis on broad skills or processes and a lack of emphasis on content. A reproachment is needed. Unless one talks about the interaction between subject matter and processes, there is little to be said about differentiated curricula (Gallagher, 1979; VanTassel-Baska, 1994a). Avoiding the construction of a curriculum that encourages the learning of advanced content and process leads to a curriculum that is appropriate for all children. The curriculum that looks as though it fits the gifted and not the nongifted only appears at the advanced levels in a given area. Renzulli (1977) recognized this problem and proposed in his Enrichment Triad Model that independent investigation of real-life problems is the province of the gifted. This approach is provocative, but is it a curriculum? It would seem to be more of an instructional strategy than a curriculum. Generating products that are more complex than typical is not a convincing example of a differentiated curriculum. Efforts must be made to specify the characteristics of an independent study worthy of a gifted child. Such efforts would require reference to the interaction of content and process and a return to the issue of what a differentiated curriculum is.

Stanley (1980) recognized, as did Renzulli, that differentiated curricula appear only at the advanced content level, but his response was decidedly different. Stanley maintained that an appropriately differentiated curriculum is already available, at least in mathematics, because advanced levels of knowledge already exist in subject areas. Moving through the discipline at a rate appropriate to individual learning ability is all that is needed. Using a somewhat different set of reasons, Howley et al. (1995) also argued that an accelerative approach is the only one that simultaneously values intellect and advantages children of varying racial, ethnic, and economic circumstances. This approach is certainly provocative, but is it a curriculum? It, too, would seem to be an instructional strategy. The curriculum is not altered; instead, the program is tailored to fit the child.

It would seem to follow from our critique that a differentiated curriculum, at least in some subject areas, is a myth. Perhaps, as Stanley has noted, curricula will never be adequate for the top learners. In any case, neither Renzulli's nor Stanley's proposals seem to satisfy the criteria for differentiated content. VanTassel-Baska (1997) recognized this problem by proposing a model that provides for what Renzulli and Stanley want within the context of specially designed units. The Parallel Curriculum Model uses a multifaceted approach to move in a similar direction. The field of gifted education needs many more examples of differentiated curricula supported by research showing their success.

AN IDEALIZED CURRICULUM?

Our discussion throughout this chapter has pointed toward the need for a comprehensive curriculum that builds toward desired goals in a program. Our presentation has implied the apparent weakness of present models for constructing curricula in a program extending over many years of schooling. The discussion in the chapter on programs suggested that a curriculum would not be readily transportable from one location to another due to local resources and values. Do these factors mean that efforts toward an idealized curriculum for the gifted are hopeless or foolish? Insisting that an idealized curriculum must fit each individual is an irrelevant point because curricula have never been designed for individuals.

The concept of an idealized curriculum is neither hopeless nor foolhardy. While unattainable, such a concept is useful. It postulates that it is possible to construct a sequence of content and skills that is more likely to optimize the development of children than a less-purposeful collection of activities. The ultimate differentiated curriculum is an idealized curriculum, and it is the task of good education to keep reorganizing and replacing school experiences in order to optimize learning as knowledge and society changes. While an idealized curriculum is a worthwhile concept, it may also be an impractical one in terms of reality. The variation among children, schools, and teachers may make it unattainable. Perhaps the only place an idealized curriculum can exist is in an ideal program. If this is the case, then what? Children, program developers, and teachers cannot wait for the idealized curriculum.

The placement of gifted children for most of their school time in a regular class has implications for curriculum development. Maybe simply conveying the idea that some experiences are better than others for children is all we can hope for. We think instruction is going to be where the difference occurs. Good teachers construct good experience. The inability of gifted education to find or approximate an idealized curriculum casts serious doubt on the enterprise of separate curriculum development for the gifted. Further, it raises several questions about the need for special programs if we cannot provide more appropriate curricula for the gifted.

CONCLUSION

Curricular practices for the gifted should be consistent with the general premises of American schooling: to have students understand reality, recognize alternatives, be sensitive to the effect of their choices, make wise choices, and implement their choices. The principles of differentiated curricula for the gifted are in harmony with general school policy and restate these premises in terms of the capabilities of gifted children.

Curriculum development for the gifted fits together three images: giftedness, human potential, and educational model. Descriptive models used for curriculum building are divided into two categories: direct and indirect. Because direct models (e.g., Ward's Enrichment Model, the Enrichment Triad Model, the Integrated Curriculum Model, and the Parallel Curriculum Model) were developed solely for the gifted, they deal with school-related issues more clearly than the indirect models (e.g., the Structure of Intellect Model, Taylor's Talents Model, and the theory of multiple intelligences). Their common features are that they were borrowed by educators for the gifted and point toward the highest levels of human development. The models present difficulties because they are too technical, are neither parallel nor synonymous, are misinterpreted, and were developed for purposes other than building curricula for the gifted.

Both categories of models are useful for training staff, evaluating materials and programs, and reconceptualizing the meaning of the basics of education. The models, both direct and indirect, have varying problems in addressing three basic questions: development of higher level processes, transfer of learning, and content. Educators of the gifted have not been able to make up their collective mind about the relationship between content and process in curriculum development, the result of which is relatively limited development and validation of curricula for the gifted. Many of the ideas touted as curricula are really better described as instruction in that they mainly address the issue of how to teach the gifted. There is an unquestionable need for more curricula to be developed for the gifted. The notion of an idealized curriculum that maximizes the learning of gifted children is a goal toward which curriculum developers should strive. At the heart of curriculum is building a structure where personalized learning takes place. Coordination between program arrangements, curriculum, and instruction is needed for quality education.

FOR **DISCUSSION**

1.   Discuss the pros and cons of differentiated curricula.

2.   Consider all the proponents of direct curriculum models and imagine them having a discussion about curricula for the gifted. Construct a script containing a dialogue among the proponents. In your script, insert points where each proponent questions the others and they respond.

3.   Specify the kind of subject matter (content) that would work best in each indirect curriculum model. What are the implications for schools?

4.   Should curricula for the gifted be different than curricula for other learners? If so, in what ways? If not, why not?

5.   In your view, why are there lots of published curricular materials, but so few that are validated? What are the implications of this situation for curriculum development?

6.   Consider the statement: I teach kids not content. Accept or rewrite the statement and justify your position.

chapter nine

TEACHING THEORY

KEY CONCEPTS

- Teaching theory makes prescriptive statements about promoting learning. Our goal is to develop such a theory for teaching children who are gifted.

- A rudimentary teaching theory for the gifted is based on 12 principles that are classified into three sets of prescriptions: content-related, diagnosis-related, and learning-related.

- Some broad approaches to teaching the gifted are defined as teaching systems because they incorporate and unify many of the principles about content, diagnosis, and learning. They illustrate embryonic forms of a teaching theory.

- General teaching methods are composed of an indeterminate number of smaller skills that are learned by teachers as a consequence of study, practice, and reflection.

- Nine general teaching methods, or repeated general patterns of classroom practice, teach knowledge objectives in a comparable fashion. These methods have varying degrees of effectiveness when teaching for other objectives, such as attitudes and creativity, with instructional groups of varying sizes.

- Given the stated objectives of programs for the gifted, some methods, such as the discussion method, independent study, simulation, and tutoring, are more likely to be used than others.

The enhancement of learning and development is the reason for special programming for gifted and talented children. Regular programs are not organized to advance gifted children's learning and development optimally; therefore, special programs are necessary. In this chapter, we do not argue the need for special programs, nor do we argue whether effective teaching can take place outside of special programs. Rather, attention is directed toward describing teaching strategies that promote learning, which means much more than clearing obstacles from a child's developmental path. The phrase "promote learning" means the active creation of situations or opportunities that increase the child's development to a level of competence beyond what would have been achieved in the absence of such assistance. Teaching practices that degrade learning should be abandoned. The evidence on child prodigies documents the crucial importance of proper teaching (Coleman, 1997; Feldman, 1980). Without excellent teaching, people do not attain the highest levels of talent.

Teaching strategies are procedures educators use to improve development and learning. A conscious decision has been made throughout this text to relegate as much general teaching information as possible to this chapter. Some of the content in the guidance, the curriculum, and the administrative chapters was structured to highlight instruction. That information is relevant here and is worthy of further study and review before reading this chapter. Organizing information about teaching procedures that actively enhance learning and development is a sensible proposition for educators of the gifted because the data on talent development are consistent with the data on teaching strategies. It is virtually impossible to find instances of giftedness if opportunity for learning and development is missing. Bloom and Sosniak's research (Bloom, 1982; Bloom & Sosniak, 1981; Sosniak, 1997), as well as the research on expertise (Ericsson, 1996; Schneider, 2000), can be interpreted as teaching strategies extending over many years. Educators of the gifted must be able to specify a set of documented workable procedures if they are to continue as an effective educational force.

Organizing information about teaching that promotes learning is also an outgrowth of our desire to move toward a theory of teaching for the gifted. An axiomatic theory that imposes a straight-jacket on teachers is not our goal; rather, we strive for the creation of a theoretical scaffold to link good practices. The idea that educational information may be separated into instructional information originates from Bruner (1966), but our conception is not identical. A theory of teaching is prescriptive and differs significantly from the descriptive models presented in the curriculum and guidance chapters. A descriptive model tells one the way things are or could be; a prescriptive model tells one what to do under certain conditions to reach a desired goal. A valid teaching model for the gifted should specify rules for teachers to use to promote the learning of knowledge and skills. The rules should be highly general in that they apply to more than one gifted child or lesson in a curricular area. The rules should assist teachers in making sound instructional choices among many alternatives. The validity of a teaching theory for classroom practice is demonstrated by an increase in the prescriptive power of teacher decisions and increases in student learning and development. Realization of such a model is not close at hand; much research is still needed. Nonetheless, the concept of teaching is a sound basis on which to organize the chapter because teaching underscores the teacher's primary goal: student learning.

Before the teacher enters the classroom situation, many decisions have already been made, and it is the teacher's job to promote learning in the face of these constraints. The goals of a program are usually set. The curriculum has frequently been determined. The students have been selected and assigned to the classroom. The administrative structure, including program options and the yearly school calendar, has been prescribed (Peine, 1998).

Yet, many decisions are still left to be made. On what information should these decisions be based? What alternatives are open to the teacher? In this chapter and the next, the decisions a teacher can make while planning, implementing, and evaluating teaching are discussed. We presume that effective teachers make decisions about when to use any of the many methods. *Intelligent choices require an understanding of the particular attributes of a given situation and teaching method.* We believe that a teacher armed with this knowledge will make better teaching choices and students will learn more.

Accordingly, this chapter presents a set of 12 teaching principles that form the basis for a new conception—systems of teaching—that explains the power and popularity of four broad approaches to teaching the gifted. The majority of this chapter is concerned with general methods that are effective with both gifted and nongifted students in terms of their merits for furthering certain curricular objectives. Chapter 10 contains more detailed examples of methods and procedures consistent with the principles proposed in this chapter.

PRINCIPLES OF TEACHING

The following 12 principles provide a template for effective teaching, and they apply to all teaching/learning situations, including self-teaching. Knowledge of them is useful for teachers when making judgments about the appropriateness of specific teaching acts. Proper application of the principles should increase the probability that students will learn. The teaching principles are classified as content-related, diagnostic-related, and learning-related.

Content-Related Principles

1. A clear statement of purpose for the learner and the teacher facilitates all other actions. The objectives are selected from the curriculum and tailored for students, both individually and in groups. Students may be involved.

2. Students are presented with challenging content in interactive situations where materials, group size, and learner preferences are considered.

3. Thoughtful, planned instruction increases learning, whether the content is presented in a thematic center or a lesson using direct teaching.

4. Content that is meaningful to students is learned more readily as the student integrates new and prior learning. Committed, involved learners can overcome major shortcomings in a teaching situation that would defeat less-committed peers.

5. Not all content is equal in an area of study. Some principles, themes, or concepts have more utility for helping students master more complex content. Teachers need to make decisions about what is important.

Diagnostic-Related Principles

6. Assessment must take into account the objectives and the content in order to start teaching near a learner's instructional level. Identification data for admission to programs are usually inadequate to this task. More specific information related to the curriculum is needed.

7. Assessment is crucial to permitting students to proceed at a rate that provides challenge. Evidence of mastery should lead to feedback for both the teacher and student, as well as the formulation of new objectives. Introduction of new content should attend to the intermediate point where the mix between new information and already acquired information occurs. Inadequate assessment wastes the time of advanced students.

Learning-Related Principles

8. Feedback is essential, and it should be minimal and specific to the task. Constructive criticism is appropriate. General, unfocused feedback is of little use. Learners profit most from errors that occur in the latter stages of learning, when they have a structure upon which to judge the error. Incidental learning situations should be planned.

9. Practice and review of newly acquired skills must be provided. Spaced reviews and practice are necessary aspects for building retention. Recognition for successful learning is important and may come from the teacher, the task, or the peer group.

10. New learning requires more immediate teacher attention, especially in remedial-type situations. Gaps in skills require close monitoring and careful sequencing.

11. Methods are better used with some objectives than with others. The match between objective and method is important. It is wise to view goals as relatively autonomous statements and look closely at objectives.

12. Different levels of mastery within a content domain require different kinds of teaching and learning. Early in the domain, methods should engender fun; middle way in a domain requires more focused learning of content and skills; and in the advanced stages of a domain, freedom to grow beyond limits is needed.

These 12 principles are statements that set the basis for decisions in a classroom. Putting all the principles into operation is a complex task, as the teacher must make many situation-relevant decisions. Teachers rarely use one principle at a time, and they make more than one decision in an active teaching period. More information about specific decisions is presented in Chapter 10.

In the next two major sections, we describe teaching systems and teaching strategies.

TEACHING SYSTEMS

"Teaching systems" is a much broader concept than "teaching methods," which is the common descriptor in the literature. Teaching systems incorporate and unify many of the principles about content, diagnosis, and teaching just presented. The principles of teaching were implicit in the three educational models for the gifted presented in Chapter 7.

We surmise that the following four systems of teaching are popular with teachers of the gifted because they incorporate the 12 principles. Thus, teachers intuitively recognize that the systems provide a coherent place to go to start teaching children. The broadest categorical names of the principles—content, diagnosis, and learning—are more evident in the models than are the 12 specific statements of teaching principles in our list. As far as we know, the developers of the systems were not using the principles as a frame of reference, yet indirectly they acknowledge them because teaching principles may be readily found.

The Diagnostic Teaching–Prescriptive Instruction System (DT-PI)

The Study of Mathematically Precocious Youth was a project begun by Julian Stanley (1979) and his associates to identify children with high mathematical reasoning ability, study them, and develop procedures for aiding their development. The DT-PI system is primarily a teaching system that has been expanded into a special program that is used in the talent searches with potential for application in other settings. Many of its key features were discussed in Chapter 7.

The DT-PI is a teaching system because it uses major principles of teaching. The content is derived from standard math curricula, but it is tailored to the individual by the diagnostic testing process. This idea is an unusually powerful instructional principle (Robinson, 1977) because the optimum teaching strategy is matching student characteristics to content as expressed in curricular goals. In essence, the DT-PI uses diagnostic testing followed by appropriate instruction. The basic principle is to "determine what the knowledgeable student does not know about a given subject and then help him or her to just learn that without having to take an entire course or wade through a textbook containing material already known" (Stanley & Benbow, 1982, p. 5).

In more specific terms, the DT-PI system uses both in-grade and out-of-level standardized tests to ascertain whether a child is good at mathematical reasoning; thus, the children to whom this instructional procedure is applied belong to a very select group, typically at least two grade levels above their chronological peers (Assouline & Lupkowski-Shoplik, 2003). The procedure was initially used with seventh graders, and now it has been extended to younger children (Assouline & Lupkowski-Shoplik, 1997; Lupkowski-Shoplik, Benbow, Assouline, & Brody, 2003).

The treatment, which a child receives after diagnostic testing, is an opportunity to select from a wide selection of special educationally accelerative opportunities. These opportunities are generally program adjustments, which include fast-paced coursework, grade skipping, double promotion, advanced placement, and opportunity to work beyond usual age considerations. The teaching strategies that predominate are the tutoring method and independent study method. The teachers are called "mentors" and may be graduate students, classroom teachers, or other gifted students. Careful attention is paid to teaching of unknown concepts and principles that were demonstrated during the testing. Students are expected to be responsible and eager to learn.

Sometimes, these children have to learn how to study. Progress is monitored carefully, and proficiency is demonstrated on course exams and standardized tests. The child is reinforced by the thrill of becoming more competent, by contact with others of like ability, and engaging with further opportunities for advanced study.

The Schoolwide Enrichment Model (SEM) System

The Schoolwide Enrichment Model is an integration and reinterpretation of a number of ideas proposed by Renzulli and his colleagues (Renzulli & Reis, 1997, 2003; Renzulli, Reis, & Smith, 1981). The SEM, like the DT-PI, is a teaching system that has been expanded into a program (Chapter 7 described its organization and philosophy). In this section, we will focus on the teaching procedures that a teacher might follow to implement instruction for a single child or group. Communication between regular educators and advocates for the gifted is a priority of this system.

The SEM has major components that can be seen as being content-related, diagnostic-related, and teaching-related principles of instruction. Once students enter into the Talent Pool, the SEM gathers information on student strengths in terms of abilities, interests, and learning styles. These data are compiled in a Total Talent Portfolio that is used for making decisions about modifying curricular content. The curriculum is adjusted so that learners are challenged, more in-depth opportunities are provided, and enrichment in different forms is introduced. The Curriculum Compactor (described in detail in Chapter 10) is used to adjust the regular curriculum in order to reduce boredom for the child by guaranteeing all concerned parties that the child can do the regular coursework and thereby buy time for enrichment. The three types of enrichment (see Chapter 8) form the basis for the creation of SEM enrichment clusters, in which nongraded groups of children who share a common interest and, sometimes, ability come together with a knowledgeable adult. The main rationale for participation in one or more clusters is that the students and teachers want to be there. The clusters emphasize the development of higher order thinking skills and their application in authentic situations.

Each step in the system involves the use of a special instrument, or form, which may be purchased from the developers. The first step is to assess student strengths in abilities, interests, and styles (Renzulli & Smith, 1979). The information on abilities is obtained from (a) the Scales for Rating Behavioral Characteristics of Superior Students and (b) standardized data. Interest assessment is accomplished with the Interest-A-Lyzer (Renzulli & Smith, 1977a). It has been used in grades 3–10 to determine students' patterns of interests in various activities, including fine arts and crafts, management, history, business, athletics, and outdoor-related activities. The third part of assessment uses the Learning Style Inventory (Renzulli & Smith, 1978a), in which students indicate preferences for teaching strategies, such as projects, drill and recitation, peer teaching, discussion, teaching games, independent study, programmed instruction, lecture, and simulation. Lastly, the Schoolwide Enrichment Model specifies a continuum of services or placement for total talent development. The continuum describes a range of services beyond what enrichment can offer to provide for students' needs. Some of these services include career counseling, mentorships, Advanced Placement courses, and special programs such as Future Problem Solving.

Problem-Based Learning System (PBL)

An emergent teaching system in gifted education is the Problem-Based Learning System, which has been practiced for some time in medical schools (Gallagher, 1997, 2001). The ideas behind PBL and the way in which it is implemented would significantly change what happens in schools.

> Problem-based learning is an approach that incorporates many of the principles of differentiated curriculum that have been the cornerstone of our field with some of the newer constructivist notions of learning and curriculum development. Students are placed in authentic problem situations in which there [is] insufficient information to comprehend and solve the problem. Students work with the help of facilitators to develop strategies for solving the problem. (Coleman & Gallagher, 1997, p. 329)

Content is an important part of the PBL system; it is neither a creative problem-solving strategy nor a means for teaching inquiry (Boyce, VanTassel-Baska, Burruss, Sher, & Johnson, 1997). The curricular content is embedded in the action of using and creating knowledge within the context of a discipline or field of study. The ill-structured problem is more than giving students a problem to solve. Rather, it is a significant real-world problem that is constructed to "cover a predefined set of knowledge, preferably integrated from many disciplines" (Gallagher, 1997, p. 338) and has intrinsic importance. As students confront different problems, they learn that knowledge is dynamic and is reformed in relation to the demands of a problem. Thus, the selection of the problem and fashioning it into an appropriate unit of instruction is important. At present, there is relatively little preconstructed curricular materials available for teachers to use. Boyce et al. described efforts that have resulted in published curricular units by the College of William and Mary in collaboration with Kendall/Hunt Publishing Company.

The student in the PBL system is assumed to be motivated or at least responsible for working on the problem. Each student brings his or her own knowledge, skills, and motivation to a problem situation, although the student's background will likely be insufficient for dealing with the problem. Thus, teaching is a crucial part of the PBL approach. In this system, instruction is as important as a well-conceived, ill-structured problem. Without good teaching, which is referred to as "tutoring" or "coaching," the PBL system cannot work as it is intended. The classroom group is turned into a collaborative team in the process.

> The job of the tutor is to maximize all of the opportunities presented by the problem. First and foremost, the tutor allows the student increasingly to take on a set of responsibilities ranging from setting the learning agenda, to facilitating the group process, to setting timelines and deadlines. (Gallagher, 1997, p. 333)

Throughout the process, the tutor, by using metacognitive questions, helps students examine their own thinking and problem solving. Examples of such questions are: "So, what kinds of questions should we be asking at this point? How do you know that? How could you find out?" (Hmelo & Ferrari, 1997, p. 413).

Self-Directed Learning (SDL) System

"Self-directed learning is concerned with creating an environment in which the learner manages and directs his or her own efforts toward the attainment of specific goals" (Treffinger, 1975, p. 48). While this description makes SDL sound as if it might be thought of as a program option, it is better characterized as a teaching system because it incorporates many principles and because it is unlikely that American schools will relinquish the control implied in the SDL system. SDL holds the promise of personalized learning. The SDL system applied to the gifted does not equate learner capabilities with the actual acquisition of skills. The system recognizes that, for gifted children to become self-directed learners, provisions must be made to teach the necessary skills (Treffinger, 1978).

The SDL system clearly demonstrates a teaching sequence that may be put into operation in many settings. The SDL model is organized around four basic teaching principles that correspond to the principles of instruction stated earlier in the chapter: specifying objectives, diagnostic testing, implementing teaching methods, and performance assessment, which is used for recycling the teaching sequence (see Figure 9.1). Each component of the basic system of instruction has been further subdivided into four steps on a continuum extending from teacher-directed to self-directed (Treffinger, 1975). These steps state a definite progression of moves toward self-direction, with teacher control being gradually replaced by learner control. It is clear that the roles of teachers and students change, but the teaching sequence stays the same, which is an important point. Teaching follows principles that are relatively independent of those associated with administrative and curricular areas.

Treffinger (1975) suggested class discussion as a basis for selecting objectives or selecting subject areas, which the teacher organizes. Implementing instruction means that decisions must be made about the teaching method,

341

Goals and Objectives

Teacher-directed:	Teacher prescribes for class or for pupils.
Self-directed, 1st step:	Teacher provides choices or options for pupils.
Self-directed, 2nd step:	Teacher involves pupil in creating options.
Self-directed, 3rd step:	Learner controls choices, teacher provides resources.

Assess Entering Behavior

Teacher-directed:	Teacher tests and makes specific prescription.
Self-directed, 1st step:	Teacher diagnoses, provides several options.
Self-directed, 2nd step:	Teacher and learner use diagnostic conference, tests employed individually, if needed.
Self-directed, 3rd step:	Learner controls diagnosis, consults teacher for assistance when unclear about needs.

Instructional Procedures

Teacher-directed:	Teacher presents content, provides exercises and activities, arranges and supervises practice.
Self-directed, 1st step:	Teacher provides options for learners to employ independently at learner's own pace.
Self-directed, 2nd step:	Teacher provides resources and options; student contracts involve learner in scope, sequence, and pace decisions.
Self-directed, 3rd step:	Learner defines projects, activities, and so forth.

Assess Performances

Teacher-directed:	Teacher implements evaluation and gives grades.
Self-directed, 1st step:	Teacher relates evaluation to objectives, gives student opportunity to react or respond.
Self-directed, 2nd step:	Peer partners used in providing feedback; teacher-student conferences for evaluation.
Self-directed, 3rd step:	Student self-evaluation.

Figure 9.1. A model of self-directed learning

Note. From "Teaching for Self-Directed Learning: A Priority for the Gifted and Talented," by D. J. Treffinger, 1975, *Gifted Child Quarterly, 19*, p. 52. Copyright © 1975 by the National Association for Gifted Children. Reprinted with permission.

the materials, and the provisions for review. Contracts are recommended as a basis for moving to self-directed learning. The assessment of performance is a significant part of the system. The SDL states that the students should learn to evaluate their own work. Treffinger suggested that teachers let students get involved in this process by discussing criteria for assessment and by participating in evaluation conferences. In sum, the SDL system advocates a partnership between teacher and student; the goal is for the learner to assume increasing control over the process.

Summary of Teaching Systems

Teaching systems are not directly concerned with the curriculum. The standard curriculum is accepted, with PBL making the biggest departure. For example, the DT-PI system deletes aspects of the curriculum or shortens the time a student spends on it, yet the curriculum is standard. The SEM repeatedly tries to prove the student has mastered the curriculum in order to justify steps for substituting various forms of enrichment implying a curricular change. The SDL moves in the direction of student choice; it is not clear whether or not the curriculum changes. The actual selection of content is loose. PBL requires the creation of units using ill-structured problems that are characteristic of a discipline or field of inquiry or profession.

The DT-PI system speaks directly to the curriculum and content-specific advanced ability as key variables. In the other teaching systems, some level of high ability is assumed, but the level need not meet as stringent a criterion as DT-PI. SEM and SDL regard student interest as a key variable in addition to above-average general ability, while DT-PI assumes it will be present.

All of the teaching systems make statements about modifying and selecting objectives to fit the gifted child. Assessment and diagnostic testing are generally recommended to individualize courses of study. The relationship between assessment and specification of student objectives is important. The DT-PI, SEM, and SDL make more or less explicit commentaries on assessment. The concern for appropriate diagnosis, unfortunately, is not always matched by a clear statement of how to achieve that goal nor what characterizes a good diagnosis. If teaching requires a judgment of where a student is in terms of intended outcomes, then good diagnosis will provide useful data for making decisions about how to help him or her reach the end point. The most useful educational data require some coordination between the assessment instrument and the content. The greater the coordination, the more useful the diagnostic data tend to be.

The DT-PI makes the clearest statement about assessment; however, even in that system, the diagnostic data still require considerable refinement. The DT-PI system regards the set of data on the advanced developmental rate of children to be the most significant piece of diagnostic information. These data are followed closely by determination of whether a child is "eager" to be in the instructional situation. Interviews are a good source of such data (Assouline &

Lupkowski-Shoplik, 2003). The PBL system says the least about assessment for beginning instruction because of the nature of ill-structured problems. The SEM recommends instruments for assessment that organize information into a potentially useful framework. Data on interests and preferred learning conditions are considered to be significant. The relationship between diagnosis and justification of content mastery is clearer than the place of these data in providing instruction in an area. The SDL system makes a strong statement about the place of assessment, but it, too, suffers from a need to put the diagnostic process into operation so that proper decisions can be made. On the other hand, the SDL approach does suggest a teaching sequence for moving toward self-diagnosis. In this sense, the content of the system is clear.

Teaching systems make statements about how to deal with variables such as speed or pacing of instruction. The systems attend to speed of learning in several ways. The SDL assumes self-pacing is the most appropriate instructional decision. The DT-PI system favors a fast-paced approach determined by careful monitoring and appropriate changes in instruction. PBL uses the tutor and the collaborative group to set the pace. The SEM falls somewhere between self-pacing and teacher pacing, although the former seems to be preferred.

Well-developed instructional systems make statements about feedback and evaluation, provisions for review, and specific teaching methods, but these systems contain few prescriptive statements. While feedback and evaluation are clearly recognized as aspects of effective teaching, when and how to provide them is not well defined. Provision for review is also a neglected aspect of teaching as defined by these systems. Among the systems, PBL promotes the use of tutoring and metacognitive coaching for this purpose.

The teaching systems have more to say about general teaching methods, which are discussed in the next section of this chapter, than about feedback and review. These statements are rarely direct in the sense that the teacher is told to use one method over another in different situations and with different objectives. In general, traditional methods, like lecture and recitation methods, are frowned upon; indirect, inquiry methods such as discussion, discovery, and independent study are the preferred approaches. However, when one should use a particular method is barely hinted at. One might infer that using nontraditional methods means the same as using special methods for the gifted. This lack of specificity about method is a serious shortcoming of these instructional systems.

These four teaching systems—the Diagnostic Teaching–Prescribed Instruction System (DT-PI), the Schoolwide Enrichment Model System (SEM), the Problem-Based Learning System (PBL), and the Self-Directed Learning System (SDL)— were selected for review because they incorporate many of the principles of teaching. These models are the result of careful thought by their developers. We intuit from the authors' work that implementation of these systems would greatly change the schools as we know them.

Each system has significant features for instruction. As a whole, they represent the beginnings of the formation of comprehensive teaching systems focused on gifted children. Yet, knowledge of them does not provide the teacher with an understanding of the general methods available for teaching gifted and talented children. We now turn to that issue.

MOVING INTO THE CLASSROOM: GENERAL TEACHING METHODS

Teaching students is a complex undertaking. Expert teachers have a vast repertoire of strategies to use in the ever-changing variations of classroom life. By looking at teachers in classrooms, some recurrent general patterns of teaching can be discerned over a variety of curricular areas.

General teaching methods are composed of an indeterminate number of smaller skills that are learned by teachers as a consequence of study, practice, and reflection. There are nine general methods, but no one method is best for teaching in all situations. While the "different teaching methods yield similar results when achievement of knowledge is used as the criterion . . . this conclusion in no way means that different teaching methods are equivalent in other ways" (Berliner & Gage, 1976, p. 17). Thus, all methods promote learning information, but some general methods are better for achieving particular objectives, such as motivation and creativity.

Decisions about the most appropriate general method in any instructional situation requires one to consider what one wants students to learn in that situation, given the particular constraints of it. Not only does this apply to general education classrooms, but also to special classes for gifted children. Variables that are frequently considered in selecting a method are student traits, instructional objectives, cost, time, and setting; however, one's objectives are the most important consideration. Given that programs for the gifted stress higher order thinking, teachers of the gifted are more likely to use some methods than others. Sometimes, teachers use methods that work against their expressed objectives. In this section, we describe general methods in order to give teachers a way to reflect on what they are doing. Each method has its advantages and disadvantages, and the careful teacher uses the method that will help students reach the objectives for that lesson or program.

Nine general teaching methods are presented. The number and names of these methods are partially derived from sources (Coleman, 1985a; Gage, 1976) and extended by us. The merits and liabilities of each general method are noted so that teachers of children who are gifted can fashion a strong rationale for determining how they might use them in their classes. Readers should also note that some of the general methods have come to be the predominant mode of all instruction in some schools.

The Recitation Method

The recitation method is so widespread across subject and grade levels that it could be called "the classroom teaching method" (Gage, 1978). In essence, the teacher asks questions and comments on student responses. Occasionally, the teacher provides summaries, and this method is frequently coupled with written materials.

The recitation method is sometimes confused with the discussion method, which is quite different. The recitation method involves verbal exchanges in the form of questions and answers about a subject by a teacher and students in which the teacher dominates the communication, little interaction occurs among students, and the teacher wants specific answers. The purpose of the recitation method is teacher-to-student interaction designed to have pupils recall information (Gall & Gall, 1976). In some ways, the method is like a quiz show where the contestants answer questions for prizes.

The point about recall is valid, but seems unnecessarily restrictive. In other words, teachers can ask more challenging questions in the recitation method, yet rarely do. However, even in those instances, the teacher's tendency is to move back to recall or knowledge-type questions.

A general assumption in this procedure is that teachers ask questions students can answer. This predisposition may influence the kinds of questions that are asked. Teachers in a variety of subject areas, including math and the social sciences, with varying age groups, elementary school to college, tend to ask similar types of questions with regularity. Approximately three quarters of all questions are recall-type questions. The remainder requires more advanced levels of thinking in accordance with Bloom (Nuthall & Snook, 1973). Similar patterns have been found in classes for the gifted (Gallagher, Aschner, & Jenne, 1967). Clearly, students respond in accord with the teacher's level of questioning (e.g., Tredway, 1995; Will, 1987). While Bloom's Taxonomy or another model can be used to generate questions, the appropriate proportion and sequence of such questions for increasing student learning is unresearched. The desire of students to learn something in a meaningful way may be more important than the level of teacher questions.

The Lecture Method

The lecture is a time-honored teaching method that is widely used with older students, especially of college age (McLeish, 1976). The lecture as an alternative for teaching various objectives should be distinguished from the lecture system in many institutions of higher education. Good lecturers are made, not born. Lecturing is a special skill that is suitable for some purposes and not others. Lecturing seems best suited for helping students pass knowledge-based tests. In this way, it is not superior to reading an appropriate textbook.

The lecture method has several advantages. A good lecturer can inspire students, fire their imaginations, integrate complex past information, introduce new information and ideas not readily available in other media, and describe future directions for research. The cost effectiveness, based on the student-to-teacher ratio, is high, and an audience of any size can be accommodated in a lecture format. However, it also has several disadvantages that make it inappropriate as the sole teaching method in a class. Teachers have great difficulty sustaining a high quality of lecturing. In most instances, it results in passive learning because there is little opportunity for students to express themselves. Lecturing tends to develop unfavorable attitudes toward subject matter because it typically fails to motivate the learner, who usually has to supplement lectures with readings.

The lecture method can be improved and used effectively in collaboration with additional techniques, including projects, workshops, tutorials, and discussion groups. Overall, the lecture has limited utility for objectives that are not knowledge-based. Its usefulness with children, especially young children, is more circumscribed because of their developmental level. Support for lecturing as a primary teaching method in elementary and secondary schools is limited, but there is a considerable literature based on its use for college-age students. However, short, well-organized, specifically oriented lectures have a place in instruction with gifted children. It can save time and enable students to move quickly to more engaging forms of learning.

The Discussion Method

The discussion method also has a long history of use. It has been used in all age and grade settings.

> The discussion method occurs when (1) a group of persons, usually in the roles of moderator/leader and participant, (2) assembles at a designated time and place, (3) to communicate interactively, (4) using speaking, nonverbal, and listening processes, (5) in order to achieve instructional objectives. (Gall & Gall, 1976, pp. 168–169)

Following this definition, group members influence each other. Who talks to whom is neither carefully prescribed, nor is the sequence of instruction or outcome. The participants are active. The direction is guided by the leader, but not controlled, and the group constructs the final outcome. An active or "true" discussion invites a variety of viewpoints. A teacher's dominance is severely minimized, and group norms permit divergence of views and freedom either to share or not to share one's viewpoint, which helps students to feel safe. This looseness means that discussions often require debriefing so the meanings that emerge are made clear to all the participants. The complexity of the discussion makes this a method preferred by gifted students (Shore et al., 1991). (Chapter 10 provides an example of the discussion method in action.)

The critical variable in the discussion method is group size (Gall & Gall, 1976). Small groups ranging in size from 2 to 20 work best, with 5 to 9 being the optimal size, although larger groups have been successful (Priles, 1993). A small, odd number of people maximizes interaction and reduces the chance for isolation. Eye contact among group members is important. Because classes are usually too large to use this method, classes need reorganization. One way is to use the discussion method with another method, such as independent study, so that a smaller group can be formed (Hawkes, Baird, & Williams, 1994). Another way is to split the class into groups with students as moderators.

Different types of discussion groups meet different instructional objectives (Gall & Gall, 1976). If mastery of subject matter is an objective, then a content-oriented discussion group is most useful. In this type of discussion group, discussion follows prior acquaintanceship with the subject matter. Topics such as vocabulary, concepts, themes, reference to other learning, and evaluation of authors may be learned (Aulls, 1998). Teacher-led discussions using higher order questions from Bloom's Taxonomy are appropriate for teaching content. The discussion method degenerates into the recitation method when one correct answer is the desired outcome. Lastly, when discussion skills are defined as the subject matter as in some programs, then the discussion method can teach those skills (Smith & Smith, 1994).

Issue-oriented discussion groups form a second type and are connected to objectives intended to increase awareness of one's own and others' viewpoints. Sometimes, attitude change is the goal. This discussion method moves a group through a succession of actions that point out the presence of attitudes in various guises and the contradictions within and among people of good faith. Analysis and evaluation of viewpoints are possible. Examples of these kinds of discussions are values-clarification-type exercises and political issues.

The third type of discussion is the problem-solving group, in which the group shares the problem and the objective is to solve it. This method assumes that the group is committed to solving the problem. Many of the teaching ideas described in the chapters on creativity (e.g., brainstorming) are variants of this category of the discussion method (Parnes, Noller, & Bondi, 1977), as are procedures described in the Problem-Based Learning System earlier in this chapter (Hmelo & Ferrari, 1997). Often, moral dilemmas or social problems are the basis of a discussion.

The discussion method has a number of advantages. It is adaptable to a variety of subject matter areas and to a variety of instructional objectives. Discussion skills themselves are worthwhile objectives, which is underscored by the fact that more and more work in the professions, academia, and business is done in collaborative groups. The discussion method can teach knowledge of subject matter and modify attitudes; it may possibly advance thinking and problem-solving skills, although the transfer of these skills to real-life situations needs additional study. The discussion method clearly can expose students to new ideas, is useful for generating independent study ideas, and can provide teachers with some indication of student learning. Teachers who wish to change attitudes and improve problem solving and collaboration should use the discussion method. It is good to use with gifted children, as they rate it highly as a preferred teaching method (Stewart, 1981).

This method's disadvantages are primarily related to the inability of the school and teacher to modify the setting. The discussion method fits small groups; use with larger groups may lead to negative attitudes toward discussion. Endless discussion leading nowhere and dominated by a few students is pointless. Teachers must change to make the method work, but some teachers have trouble relinquishing dominance in classroom discussions. Much of what is called "discussion" is really passive discussion or the recitation method in disguise. Despite the apparent utility and power of the discussion method, it cannot make an inherently dull curriculum or program meaningful and interesting. The very looseness of the method makes it difficult to direct clear feedback to individual students and monitor learning. Gifted students can sometimes manipulate group discussions to avoid learning.

The Tutoring/Coaching Method

Tutoring/academic coaching is a method with a long history. It has been used as the basis for a complete educational system, much like lecturing has. Here, tutoring is a general method for individualizing instruction with varying effects. Ellison (1976), in a comprehensive review of the method, defined tutoring as "one-to-one instruction." Although tutoring was used extensively in the past for high achievers, recently it has been used primarily for remediation. It is a method that has been underappreciated by teachers for advanced learners in schools. Tutoring is sometimes used interchangeably with the term *mentoring*, as in the DT-PI model. When someone is placed with a highly knowledgeable and experienced tutor, mentoring may be taking place.

The tutoring method is similar to teaching in general, except it is directed to one student and typically focuses on parts of a larger curricular sequence. The tutoring sequence requires setting objectives, assessment, and teaching. People or computers can tutor; the teaching activity is largely improvised in the former and carefully and tightly prestructured in the latter. In computerized tutoring, the programmer is really the teacher. Research on tutoring indicates that individual attention cannot guarantee a successful instructional episode.

> There is widespread belief among educators and laymen that individualized instruction, especially in one-to-one teaching situations, is almost infallibly effective. On occasion it may be conceded that tutoring can fail in achieving certain cognitive learning goals, but in that case tutoring is likely to be justified in terms of its "obviously" favorable effects on affective variables such as attitudes, behavior problems, or the self-concept. Much of this belief is unjustified. (Ellison, 1976, p. 133)

Careful attention to instruction, rather than simply placing two people in the same location with the same book, is what makes tutoring work. Academic coaching is a useful method when combined with assessment and the discussion or lecture methods. Searches of the literature produced scant mention of

349

this technique with gifted children, and when it was mentioned, it was in reference to gifted children tutoring others.

The tutoring/coaching method has decided advantages. It can be responsive to a wide array of individual differences. Correctly implemented, it has clear benefits for rapid learners, as well as underachievers and those missing a skill in an instructional sequence. Clear, direct feedback and appropriate pacing are important variables in this regard. Tutoring may have therapeutic benefits, and it can have affective benefits in increasing motivation and modifying values attached to a subject.

Adopting the tutoring/coaching method requires careful planning. A teacher in a typical school who uses tutoring exclusively would only have 10 minutes per day to spend with each student. When others are used as tutors—peers, aides, and parents—maintaining quality from tutor to tutor is difficult. Thus, some training is clearly needed. The general teaching problem of determining an appropriate instructional sequence is not diminished by the tutoring method. What constitutes evidence of mastery and how a tutor should react to different responses is still not resolved.

The effectiveness of the tutoring/coaching technique with gifted learners is hard to judge. The tutoring method is a good alternative when the content and skills to be learned are clearly conceived and stated. The DT-PI system uses this method well and combines it with appropriate homework (Assouline & Lupkowski-Shoplik, 2003). Tutoring is the best choice for gifted students who show deficits in specific areas when diagnostically tested. Tutoring might also be useful for establishing positive attitudes toward a subject in students who find the usual scope and sequence to be too slow or rigid and are ready to go forward.

The Simulation and Gaming Method

The simulation and gaming method has steadily grown in popularity as a teaching method since the 1970s, a consequence of the changing role of the school, the changing notion of learning (Seidner, 1976), and the increasing sophistication of computer software (Barr, 1990).

Simulations and games have both common and differing features. In both there is a set of rules for reaching specified objectives, and competition is not a required element. Simulations differ from games in that simulations abstract physical and social reality, usually in a limited way, in order to formulate rules and objectives. The simulation simplifies reality so that the players interact according to rules that reflect reality. In other words, the rules of the game apply to reality, but are not reality. Similar to reality, the success of winning in a simulation is less clear than in a game. Teachers have used games for many years, thus they are familiar. Simulations, however, are less common. The increase in the number of computer-driven simulations and games is changing the frequency with which this method is being used.

The simulation and gaming method can involve a variety of learning and expressive modes, and it is useful for teaching objectives in the areas of communication, subject matter, affect, and creativity. The evidence for the latter two is less complete than the other areas. Simulation and gaming come in many formats in many subject areas, including English, history, chemistry, physics, biology, and language arts (Seidner, 1976). The complexity of simulation is increased by the accessibility of information to the participants. Person-computer simulation greatly increases the amount of information and the number of rules. Person-person simulations, in which people assume different roles, are limited by the participants' abilities to take roles. The major difference between role-playing and simulation is that the rules and objectives are clearer with simulations.

The introduction of simulation and gaming changes the teacher's role because the game sets the sequence and the content. The simulation does the teaching, with the teacher acting as a facilitator. Selecting the game, keeping interaction moving, and preparing for the game and postgame discussion are tasks for the teacher. Careful selection of simulations and games to meet the objectives of the class is critical. There is no easy way to do this. The teacher may also author his or her own simulations and games, which can be an exciting task. Sometimes, teachers enlist students in this enterprise to create and redesign games for specific purposes.

The decision to use simulation and gaming can enliven a classroom. It is good for getting students to talk to each other, and students clearly like this method. Some data suggest that underachievers may profit from it. Simulation and gaming are primarily for small groups. The method can sensitize students to an area (such as race relations), teach content, and serve as a culminating activity in a unit. Teachers have used the method to evaluate students; however, like the discussion method, it is difficult to keep track of individual learners. Games, as distinguished from simulations, are best for reviewing content and practicing already-acquired skills. Simulation and gaming are relatively poor vehicles for teaching concepts and skills with which learners have little familiarity. Simulations can teach higher order thinking skills and attitudes, but the relationship of skills to content is problematic. Gifted students have capabilities that respond well to effectively constructed simulations that are properly facilitated by the teacher (Cardwell, 1995; May, 1997; see Sisk, 2004, for a list of well-designed simulations).

The Discovery Method

The increasing popularity of constructivist philosophical ideas of teaching (Zahorik, 1995) keeps the discovery method important. Unlike the other methods in this section, the discovery method has been offered as a model of learning and of teaching. Comments in this section will be directed toward the discovery method as one type of instructional strategy available to teachers and away from the polemics surrounding it as a general model of teaching and learning.

The discovery method, sometimes called "inquiry-based learning" (Willis, 1995), has certain characteristics that are repeatedly mentioned by its advocates. Unfortunately, the particulars of the process are variable across viewpoints, so it is difficult to isolate the method's pure aspects. Some of this difficulty is because the discovery approach welds method and objectives into an inseparable whole (Nuthall & Snook, 1973).

The discovery method is frequently linked to the higher levels of a subject area. The teacher arranges the situation such that the students inductively learn or discover a principle about a subject area. Students find themselves in a situation in which their prior learning is inadequate for finding an appropriate solution or explanation. Teachers avoid indicating the generalization or rule to be learned. At this point in the discovery method, different steps are possible for guiding students. Teachers may demonstrate examples and nonexamples of the generalization. Gagné (1976) pointed out that "minimal cues characterize the method" (p. 33). Teachers may or may not encourage verbalization between students. There is some disagreement about whether or not verbalization of the discovered rule is the same as understanding the rule.

Clearly, teachers must carefully select materials or examples of situations that illustrate a principle. The teacher should have a clear notion of the generalization and its place in the curriculum. Although the teacher's influence may not be obvious, the teacher's behavior is purposeful and directed toward the lesson's objective.

The discovery method has been instituted in a variety of subject areas, including science, social studies, and math (Gallagher, 1975). It appears that "the best discovery learning occurs in situations where there is more than one right answer" (Nuthall & Snook, 1973, p. 61). Proponents of this method view discovery as useful for learning the major principles that characterize a field of study. However, the discovery method is difficult to implement because it requires time, special materials, and usually small groups of children. It makes evaluation and feedback difficult because of multiple outcomes and the difficulty of monitoring students.

Discovery is a popular term in gifted education circles and often refers to students discovering something for themselves in an open-ended situation. This popularity may be due to the fact that the discovery method emphasizes self-directed learning and higher cognitive processes, such as creative problem solving. However, in many of those instances, independent study is the method being used (Kay, 1994), not the discovery method, because the nature of the principle of a discipline or content domain is not embedded in the instructional situation.

The Observational Method

Naming the observational method as a general method may surprise some readers because it is rarely referred to in this manner. The observational method is troublesome to define because it is described in a variety of ways in the psychological and educational literature: modeling, imitation, identifying, observational learning, and apprenticeship. Behaviorist psychologists use some of these terms, while cognitive psychologists use others. The observational method has elements of the discovery method and is implied in the recitation and simulation and gaming methods.

The observational method is best defined by describing a teaching situation. The teacher has an idea of how he or she wants students to act, such as getting along with others or writing readable compositions. The teacher acts as a model or demonstrates the appropriate attitudes or behaviors, which the students observe. The teacher has several choices. He or she can be direct or indirect, call attention to his or her own behavior, note when others are acting appropriately, or say nothing at all. In essence, the method is "Do what I do and do what I say." Thus, teachers should constantly reflect on what they do because their actions may be observed by students and therefore influence their behavior in the class. This method has potential for teaching attitudes, values, and problem-solving procedures (Gagné, 1976; Kahn & Weiss, 1973), as well as observable content. It can be applied in one-to-one, small-group, and large-group situations.

The Independent Study Method

Independent study is considered a method in this presentation because it employs a recurrent series of actions across a variety of subject areas, and it, too, cannot guarantee any higher achievement in an area than any other general method (Rogge, 1970). The independent study method, like several of the other methods, has been conceptualized as a complete educational program. It is considered to be only one among many methods in this discussion. On our continuum of techniques, independent study fits between tutoring and the discovery method.

"Independent study is the most frequently recommended instructional strategy for gifted students" (Johnsen & Goree, 2004, p. 379). It is recommended in each of the four teaching systems described earlier in this chapter and is the centerpiece of the SDL model (one variant is described in more detail in Chapter 10). The independent study method occurs when a learner pursues a topic of personal interest within an area of study by setting the objectives of the inquiry, specifying the procedures, organizing and reporting the results, and evaluating the experience under appropriate, minimal supervision. Teacher and student have joint responsibility for the experience (Doherty & Evans, 1981). The amount of supervision depends upon the student's familiarity with the topic and prior experience in independent study. The notion of minimal, appropriate supervision makes this method dissimilar to the other methods. Independent study is neither homework nor study hall, but an integral part of a school program and a useful technique for promoting growth (Kay, 1994).

Evidence of when and where to use independent study is hard to decipher because of the many variations in the methodology. The independent study method has been used with both individuals and small groups across levels of schooling, content, and student characteristics. The method is useful, but not easily accomplished. Academic aptitude, general intelligence, or both do not guarantee a successful outcome. Motivational factors, such as interests and orientation to the task, are more important. To ensure success when using the independent study method, an effort should be made to determine whether or not students have the prerequisite skills necessary to pursue their topics. These prerequisites include vocabulary, appropriate research skills, and evaluation skills. Teachers can assist students by helping to design an independent study format (Doherty & Evans, 1981; Hawkes et al., 1994; Johnsen & Goree, 2004).

The independent study method has the advantage of allowing for wide individual differences. When first used, it tends to be cumbersome until students and teachers learn the procedures. The teacher's role becomes one of facilitator and mentor. Evaluation and feedback are difficult unless clear objectives are agreed upon by teacher and students at the beginning of the process. The selection of appropriate materials can be a problem in environments with limited resources, such as small rural schools. The independent study method is useful for modifying students' perceptions of a content area from negative to positive and students' perceptions of themselves and their teachers. The method is also appropriate for teaching problem-solving strategies (Glasser, 1971) and can lead to creative outcomes (Burns, 1990). Students and teachers need a physical location where quiet study, reflection, and conferences are possible.

The Materials-Driven Method

The name "materials-driven method" meets Gage's notion of a general method because of its effect on achievement. While it is not typically thought of as a method, we see it in all the classrooms we enter. In fact, after the recitation method, the materials-driven method is what we most often observe. In essence, the curricular materials, either teacher-made or commercially prepared, are what children encounter in a lesson, and these same materials form the content and set much of the instruction. The selection of the text or other materials fixes much of what children learn. Teachers spend long hours trying to find or create the right materials for a lesson or activity. Courses in teacher preparation programs often devote considerable time to making or adapting materials.

The textbook industry, a huge, multimillion-dollar business, thrives on recognition of this fact. An attendee at any of the national or regional conferences held by professional associations of teachers and supervisors will find an array of attractive curricular materials being promoted by engaging salespeople. Publishers create materials that meet teachers' ideas of what will be attractive and engaging to students. These materials tend to be self-contained segments of instruction or organized sets of activities formed around a theme, unit, or topic. When not specified as textbooks for particular subjects or courses of study, most of these materials are called "enrichment materials."

One common denominator of gifted programs is going beyond the standard curriculum. That intent points teachers toward activities that would not typically happen in a general classroom. Since we claim enrichment as one of our tenets of programming, it is not surprising that teachers would be attracted to the materials that try to teach something that departs from the standard curriculum. Many of the special goals of gifted programs, such as teaching problem solving, critical thinking, creativity, or research skills, can be sold as packaged curricular materials designed to meet those goals, although few publishers can supply actual evidence of effectiveness. However, some of the materials are part of a larger system with some kind of validity, such as Future Problem Solving.

The crux of this method is a teacher's decision to present an activity and his or her search for materials that fit that activity. When teachers who are heavily burdened encounter attractive pieces of curricular materials, they claim them. Although good teachers adapt their purchases to fit their classes, the influence of the materials themselves is powerful because the organization and content is already set. Thus, the selection of the materials is the prime step in the materials-driven method.

The materials-driven method is often used in conjunction with other methods. One advantage of this method is that it provides a central, tangible stimulus upon which students can focus their attention, and it leads to a product the teacher and learner can see. Experienced teachers amass a collection of materials to use in their classes, resulting in learning centers and learning packages.

Two disadvantages are evident with this method. The first is that the materials tend to stay as they were originally created. They do not readily undergo the transformations that are needed as the characteristics of classes change. The second disadvantage is that the objectives conceived by the publisher are not always the same as the teacher's.

Summary of General Teaching Methods

All nine of the general teaching methods reviewed in this section are valuable methods for teaching subject matter and have similar effectiveness when teaching basic content. The differential effect of each method on some instructional outcomes and not others is important to remember. Instructional outcomes, usually favored in gifted education and reflected in the principles of differentiated curricula, are higher level thinking skills, research skills, independent learning skills, and creative problem solving. Some methods have more promise in furthering instructional outcomes other than knowledge acquisition. It is advisable, therefore, to select those methods that promote objectives other than knowledge acquisition when planning for these instructional outcomes because the general methods are similarly successful in furthering knowledge-oriented outcomes. A table summarizing these findings and showing the relationship of methods to possible outcomes as a basis for designing an instructional plan appears later in Table 10.1 in Chapter 10, where recommendations for teaching are made.

The effect of these methods on certain outcomes has been determined from general research on learners, which does not directly answer the issue of which methods work best with the gifted. But, in the absence of data showing that gifted children learn differently than other children and similarly limited data showing that there are methods that only work with gifted students, the best decisions teachers can make are to use the information on general methods to inform their practice in the classroom. Sensitive teachers will pick up on variations among students that are relevant to instruction in their classes, but the subtleties are beyond what we can generalize in a textbook.

CONCLUSION

This chapter was organized with the goal of improving learning for gifted children in schools. Our major premise is that building a theory of instruction for gifted children will lead to enhanced learning. Contained within an instructional theory are decisions for coordinating the variables in the classroom teaching environment, such as objectives and goals, learner characteristics, materials, possible teaching methods, class size, and curricula. The decisions in an instructional theory are normative and are probability statements about the course of action most likely to improve student learning. In any given situation, some choices are better than others. The teacher, in effect, makes a series of decisions in order to establish an instructional environment most conducive to learning (Coleman, 1991).

A set of teaching principles were proposed that are applicable to most teaching situations. These principles, which increase the probability of learning, are the foundation for decisions. The 12 principles fall into three categories: content, diagnosis, and teaching. The literature on teaching the gifted makes repeated references to these categories.

Although it is frequently difficult to determine which principles are being advocated in an article on teaching the gifted, a few writers have provided the field with teaching systems for the gifted—integrated views of instructional practices that emphasize more than one instructional principle. These four systems—the Diagnostic Teaching–Prescriptive Instructional System, the Schoolwide Enrichment Model System, the Problem-Based Learning System, and the Self-Directed Learning System—emphasize teaching that follows the standard curriculum with some exceptions. They make statements about modifying and selecting objectives, and they specify a relationship between diagnosis and objectives. The systems differ in the clarity of their prescriptive statements. As a group, with one significant exception, the systems frown upon the implementation of traditional teaching methods; instead, they advocate alternative methods. Those mentioned most often are versions of the discovery method, discussion, and independent study. While these systems are significant advances in the thinking about instruction for the gifted, they represent the mere beginnings of a comprehensive instructional theory for the gifted.

There are nine general teaching methods that have been used in classrooms, each of which has different objectives and are appropriately used in different situations. Not every method is appropriate for meeting all objectives. The objectives in the curriculum described in Chapter 8 lead to the inference that some methods should be used more often than other methods with gifted students. On the other hand, no method is inappropriate for instructing the gifted. Thus, teachers need to consider which method is the best for their instructional situation. The next chapter extends this discussion on teaching methods.

FOR **DISCUSSION**

1. Pick two of the teaching systems and state which of the pair is your favorite. Defend your choice on the basis of evidence in the text.

2. Consider the nine general teaching methods. Think of three classes you are taking or have recently taken. Which methods were used in each of those classes? If you could teach those classes, which methods would you use and why? Use the data in the text, as well as your experience as a student.

3. Children have varying characteristics. Take the nine teaching methods and make a list with two columns: characteristics and methods. Match up each of the characteristics to a method. Be prepared to explain your choices.

4. Assessment is a key component of teaching. Preassessment is less frequently used than postteaching assessment. Explain why preassessment is so important for gifted children. Supply evidence for your position.

5. Defend or refute the statement: I teach kids how to think, not what to think.

chapter ten

TEACHING METHODS AND BEST PRACTICES

KEY CONCEPTS

- Best practices cannot be executed the same way in every classroom.

- Teaching nonmodal gifted children requires information about diverse cultures, sensitivity, and caring, which means paying attention to what is said and done in the classroom by students and you. What is known about teaching gifted children in general is basically the same as teaching diverse learners.

- Teaching decisions should be derived from what we know about curriculum and instruction. Two categories of decisions are evident: planning and action decisions. Teaching decisions do not have guaranteed outcomes, but better decisions increase the probability of students learning.

- Five useful techniques (long-term academic planning with parents, differentiation, compacting, a cache of strategies, and conducting an active discussion) form the beginning of a basic "tool kit" for teachers.

- Special methods for often-stated goals (creative problem solving, attitudes and values about self and social responsibility, and research and study skills) of gifted education are too narrow to be defined as teaching systems, yet they extend and combine general methods for use in a variety of classes.

- Combining interesting, challenging, high-level subject matter with the special method is the best combination for teaching because it grounds the skills to be learned within meaningful learning in context.

- Evaluating unproven published materials and creating original materials is necessary to meet the objectives of different classes.

The purpose of this chapter is to bring together material that is directly applicable to teaching gifted and talented children. Chapter 9 presented general principles for teaching gifted children. We contend that, armed with that information, teachers can make more informed decisions to promote student learning. In this chapter, we shift the topic from general teaching principles and methods that teachers need to understand in order to be reflective and flexible as teachers to specific strategic decisions that we regard as best practices in the field. Two kinds of decisions—planning and action decisions—are implicit in the principles. The task of educators of the gifted is to find out when to use a particular principle. Some of these practices have an established research base; others have an emerging base. In general, best practices are determined through anecdotes, workshop presentations, and empirical research.

In the classroom, the teacher must coordinate an array of variables, including objectives and goals, learner characteristics, materials, teaching methods, class size, and the curriculum. In any specific situation, some choices are better than others; rarely is there one best decision. The teacher must make, in effect, a series of decisions in order to establish an environment most conducive to learning (Coleman, 1991). Inasmuch as the situation is dynamic, decisions do not have a guaranteed outcome; yet, some decisions do increase the probability of success in student learning.

TEACHING NONMODAL GIFTED CHILDREN

Earlier in this book, we used the term "nonmodal gifted" to refer to children who are gifted and exhibit characteristics that decrease their chances of being identified. Nonmodal gifted children were divided into two broad, not mutually exclusive categories: gifted disabled and culturally different gifted. Within each category, additional subdivisions are possible. Many of the issues in this section speak to both groups.

The largest proportion of nonmodal gifted students is culturally different, defined by Sato (1974) as those who belong to a "culture other than the dominant culture in society" (p. 573). Our definition is more narrowly defined to include only children who come from backgrounds that diverge from the Caucasian, middle-class norm. These students are frequently members of minority groups defined by race or language differences. However, a person may be a member of a minority group and not be considered culturally different according to our definition. Two terms that appear often in conversations about nonmodal children are *diversity* and *multiculturalism*. The former is often a synonym for nonmodal children; the latter refers to a philosophy of education (Banks, 1994).

Throughout the text, issues in gifted education pertinent to nonmodal children could have been interspersed, yet were not (the exceptions are in the chapters on identification and guidance). Having a separate section like this could be interpreted as relegating both nonmodal giftedness and multiculturalism to an add-on concerns, which is not our intent. Rather, this stand-alone section is intended to highlight our views and concentrate important ideas so readers can interpret what we say about teaching. Our emphasis in this chapter is on teaching because, at the classroom level, education becomes personal. The teacher is the channel for the meaning of the terms for the individual child. Also, we created a separate section because stating more than the broadest generalizations on these complex issues is difficult, and we did not want to cheapen their significance by repeating the same sentiments in the other chapters. In our experience, repeatedly admonishing people to be more attuned to others grows old and dampens the desire to confront these issues.

We appreciate the scholarly efforts that have produced works pertaining to giftedness and nonmodal children (e.g., Ford, 1996; Kitano, 1998, 1999) and have learned from them. However, we believe (although others might not concur) that writers on this topic have the same difficulty talking about curricula and instruction that we do in moving from general, transcendent statements to the specific, concrete statements that make sense to teachers in classrooms. Understanding multiculturalism and diversity is a complex undertaking; yet, understanding is much less complex than turning principles into practice. The institutions need to change, but that happens slowly; meanwhile, schooling continues.

In this section, we attempt to assist the teacher in thinking about and acting with children who are nonmodal. Anyone looking for "the answer" will not find it here. In the next pages, we make statements of the obvious and the not-so-obvious to show our position. We describe questions teachers have addressed to us in classes and workshops, and we conclude with some ideas of how to proceed in a classroom.

Statements About the Obvious

We interpret the issues surrounding nonmodal children on the basis of our formal and informal experiences. We are first-generation college graduates who have two versions of what it is like for White boys from quite modest means to reach positions where someone will publish our writings. A brief synopsis of our backgrounds: One is from the South, and one is from the urban north; one is Protestant, the other a mixture of Judaism and Catholicism; one is a teacher, the other a psychologist; one is a social radical, the other an intellectual wanderer; and so forth. These factors influence our viewpoints.

We have no doubt that we live in a society that is in a quandary about diversity. Official documents mask it and politicians decry it, but racism, classism, and sexism are unfortunately alive and virulent and are tied to inequities in income, employment, housing, and opportunity. Various perceptions compete to explain what is going on in our society, and there are often large gaps between them. In recent memory, the obvious examples of significant differences in perception are the O.J. Simpson trial, Bill Clinton's impeachment hearings, and the reasons justifying war in Iraq. We conclude that a variety of valid viewpoints exist about the world, and there are few—if any—single interpretations that hold for everything and everyone.

We concur with the idea that generalizations about minority or ethnic groups are usually inaccurate because such groups are monolithic in their makeup (Baca, 1980; Banks, 1994; Kitano, 1997b). Regional, cultural, linguistic, and other types of differences split those groups, and furthermore, generalizations about one diverse group certainly cannot be applied to another.

We have difficulty in understanding the experiences of minorities, something we believe we share with most White people. Many White people have some understanding, but those understandings are not the same as those of the minority populations. Most people, majority and minority, use overgeneralizations and stereotyping to explain the other to them. Such thinking can be dangerous to the acceptance and fostering of differences. We believe differences should be honored, not devalued, if people are to flourish. For these reasons, we support the idea of multicultural education (Banks & Banks, 1993).

We acknowledge that conflicts exist between the values of majority and minority cultures (not to mention subcultures; Kitano, 1997a). Sometimes, these values complement each other, sometimes they are in conflict, and sometimes they are irreconcilable. This means that what seems positive to one group may have a perverse effect on others. A stark example, and one that teachers find frustrating, is the notion that a minority student being successful academically is a sign of "being White" and giving up on his or her identity (Hébert, 1998). In those instances, the consequences of such differences need to be discussed, but rarely are.

Statements About the Not-So-Obvious

Some points need to be made that may not be obvious to all. First, we forget that diversity and multiculturalism have long been concerns to people in the field of gifted education (Gallagher, 1979; Tannenbaum, 1979). The majority of children who are potentially gifted are in underserved groups.

Second, the principles of good teaching are not forfeited when the students are members of minority groups. The meaning of some of the variables may change, but the basic ideas of teaching and learning are still valid. A full range of methods and other services should be available. Special programs that offer a one-set-program-for-all to all nonmodal students are just as inappropriate as they are for majority gifted students.

Third, the consensus among experts is that there are no special methods that are uniquely appropriate to gifted and talented students (Coleman, 2003; Shore & Delcourt, 1996; Tomlinson, 1996). General methods need to be fashioned to a particular learner or learners at a point in time. Some methods work better in achieving some programmatic goals than others. Evidence for using particular methods with diverse groups is no stronger than the evidence for majority learners (see Kitano, 1999).

What Does This Mean for Teachers?

As a lone teacher in a classroom with children of mixed abilities and backgrounds, what can be done? Opinion on this question overwhelms the evidence when one consults the literature. In other words, more is said about a view than there is unequivocal evidence to support that view. While most agree something is wrong, all do not agree on the solutions.

The answer to the question "What can one teacher do?" lies in understanding the basic instructional situation. Typically, a teacher and a group of students come together to learn some piece of the curriculum. The teacher needs to know the subject matter in that curriculum and know the learners in the class. This basic information enables the building of a learning bridge from where the learners are to where they are going. That is the essence of teaching.

What Does This Mean for Curricula for Nonmodal Learners?

Assuming the teacher is aware of students' characteristics, are some curricular experiences more appropriate for classes with diverse students than others? Although this is a state-level, a school-district-level, a program-level, and a classroom-level issue, here we discuss it as at the classroom level. The issue was sidestepped in the chapter on curricula because we did not want this volatile issue to muddy the discussion on appropriate curricula for gifted learners. A second reason to sidestep the issue is our belief, as stated earlier in this section, that a multicultural curriculum is appropriate for both majority and nonmodal students. However, we bring the issue up in this chapter to show that, at the classroom level, the broad issue of a multicultural curriculum is mixed with conflicting choices that mirror debates in the field, such as general enrichment/acceleration, quantitative/qualitative psychological difference, and content/process. These issues have been voiced in some form in courses we have taught.

A common worry expressed by teachers is captured by this dilemma: Is time spent on enrichment activities more valuable, as valuable, or less valuable for culturally different and poor children than time spent on learning the standard curriculum? Several scholars who are concerned about nonmodal gifted youth have differing views (Howley et al., 1995; Kitano, 1999). However, their perspectives echo some teachers' concerns about whether enrichment might not have the beneficial effect that the teachers intend. Put another way, lack of time is something teachers typically mention. Considering the limited time teachers have with nonmodal gifted students, is the students' time being used to their best advantage? Certain knowledge, skills, and experiences are prerequisites for doing well on the official forms and tests that are used for entrance to advanced training, scholarships, and education. Would it be better if teachers taught the content expected and how to take standardized tests? How can teachers justify doing what they are doing (Delpit, 1988; Tomlinson, Callahan, & Lelli, 1997)?

Some teachers reinterpret the question of enrichment and curriculum content in a different way. Aware that the standard curriculum does not tap the strengths of their nonmodal children, they look for an alternative way of understanding the differences and provide situations that develop those differences. The concept of multiple intelligences seems to attract teachers for this reason. While reasonable, adopting an approach that teaches to strengths does not really respond to the question of how best to use students' time and the long-term implications of pursuing such an agenda. Some would argue that this, too, disadvantages nonmodal children.

So, amidst these contradictions, should a teacher choose curricula by adopting a particular point of view? That is up to the individual teacher, but part of the answer is in the next section.

What Does This Mean for Teaching Diverse Learners?

Assuming the teacher is familiar with the subject and the curriculum, to what learner characteristics should the teacher attend? Among the many possibilities, we start with student interests, information and skills relevant to the particular subject of the lesson, competence to work alone or in groups, and learning rate.

Obtaining knowledge about these four possibilities requires assessment skills, which are taught in preparation programs, and sensitivity and caring, which are not readily taught in preparation programs. In our view, sensitivity and caring means learning about students in a specific class by paying attention to what they say and do. (Some of the information available on characteristics of students from ethnic and religious groups can help you to be more sensitive; but, typically, such information is not directly relevant to any one lesson.) When teachers are unsure about what they are seeing and hearing, they should give diverse students the benefit of the doubt. Never assume understanding; keep listening and watching. Keeping a journal of observations can help teachers reflect on what is happening and what is working. Sometimes, the same words and actions have dissimilar meanings between teachers and nonmodal students. (Ideas that can be adapted using this information are available later in this chapter and can help teachers make lessons more relevant and challenging.) Teachers need to be ready to learn about atypical school subjects, such as automobiles, hip-hop music, fishing, and horror films, as ways to excite children to learn. Expecting nonmodal gifted children to become mainstream gifted children is not sensible. At the same time, it also seems sensible to inform nonmodal students about the long-term effects of decisions in terms of social mobility and the majority culture's notion of success.

When all this has been said, one plain fact remains: We do not have a generally satisfactory means of handling the situation. The danger of present practices is that they may perpetuate the system of limited opportunities for nonmodal youths. The danger of applying a new approach uniformly is that it limits some children. Through their own creativity, teachers must develop means to reach their students. The field could benefit from studies of those successful teachers so we can learn from them. For broader effects, teachers should probably consider political action to obtain more resources for programs for nonmodal children. Public resources for schools is always a political issue.

KINDS OF TEACHING DECISIONS

Teachers must make planning and action decisions. These types of decisions differ largely in the time available for making them. The teacher making planning decisions has unlimited time for considering the variables because they occur in an empty classroom with no students present. Provision for the personalization, rarely individualization, of instruction is possible because arrangements can be made to attend to student differences. Alternate strategies can be formulated in case the lesson does not proceed as intended.

Between the planning and action decisions, the former are the most important because they prepare the teacher for future spontaneous, quick decisions while in a calm environment. Action decisions are made in the classroom within very narrow time frames and in the midst of a group of students. The teacher has no time for reflection; he or she must act immediately and move on with the lesson. Most action decisions are adjustments made by the teacher while evaluating children's interactions with each other, the material, or him-

or herself. Action decisions smooth instruction and correct for changes in the plan. They are important, too, but probably less so than planning decisions because of their variability and spontaneity.

The relation between planning and action can be seen in the NASA space flight program. Like teachers in classrooms, astronauts spend years planning and anticipating situations in a calm environment so they will be prepared for the unexpected action in space. Time for reflection and improvement for the next class occurs back in the empty classroom. Starting from a plan, reflection, too, can be more focused.

New teachers need to spend more time on planning decisions than more experienced teachers because new teachers do not have a reservoir, or "grey backdrop" (Coleman, 1991), of tacit knowledge to draw upon. For both new and experienced teachers, good action decisions are improved by careful planning and thoughtful reflection on past, similar teaching situations. Spontaneity is a valuable quality of teaching. Lack of spontaneity can mean a dead classroom, but overreliance on spontaneity most often leads to ineffective instruction and only a veneer of learning. When students are learning less than they would by themselves, then teachers have the responsibility and obligation to change how they are teaching.

The Basis of Teaching Decisions

Teaching decisions for gifted children grow directly from the 12 principles of instruction that were grouped as content-related, diagnostic-related, and teaching-related and enumerated in Chapter 9. The principles imply a rough sequence of decision making, as well as specific decisions in terms of each principle. In concrete terms, teaching decisions are conditional statements: If this is the case, then it is better to do that. At our present state of knowledge about teaching the gifted, these decisions are really educated statements of probability (i.e., thoughtful guesses). This presentation is intended to aid teachers in formulating decisions for teaching their gifted children. Because we are proposing recommendations for decisions in a teaching situation, this section follows the general sequence of content, diagnosis, and teaching. When teaching systems, such as those reviewed earlier (DT-PI, SEM, PBL, and SDL), are adopted, then some decisions are already made. In this section, a generalized, selective, resourceful approach using the information reviewed in earlier chapters is presented.

Background of Our Interpretation of Learning and Development

The basis of teaching decisions is buried in a set of often unvoiced beliefs held by teachers about children, learning, development, and schooling (McDiarmid, 1990), much like the different sets of beliefs that were implicit in the three competing educational models presented in the administrative chapter. Our responsibility as authors is to make explicit the beliefs that predispose us as teachers to make certain decisions and that influence our interpretation of the research on teaching gifted and talented children.

Learning occurs as a result of interaction between the child and his or her environment, with the developing student taking an increasingly active role. Higher levels of learning and development, the province of gifted education, happen under those conditions (Coleman, 1997). Individual learning is not solely a consequence of one person's actions, abilities, and attitudes, but rather is the result of the interplay of individual and context. Neither the content nor how it is learned is independent of cultural conditions.

All content is a product of human invention. In fact, each area of knowledge, also called a domain, has its own way of organizing, evaluating, and seeking information. Some domains are foundational and some are performance domains (Cross & Coleman, 2005). As students advance to the highest levels of a domain, they enter areas where fewer people understand the content, and at the outermost limits they actually create new knowledge for that domain (Feldman, 1980). Advanced development of gifted children in various domains or content areas is not an individual act independent of the subject matter and the sociocultural context (i.e., classroom, school, family, community, and society). In short, the way knowledge is represented in context sets the boundaries and potential for learning.

The language and technology of culture, which are also domains, influence higher levels of development because competence in these two areas gives children the means to be active in influencing their own development. Development moves "not in a circle, but in a spiral, passing through the same point at each new revolution [learning] while advancing to the higher level" (Vygotsky, 1978, p. 56). This progression is elaborated through a series of transformations from simple to more complex stages, with people (teachers, peers, family) and culture leading the way. In this way, learning precedes development. Therefore, one cannot readily talk about one without reference to the other.

Children learn best when the culture encourages, nudges, and challenges them to go beyond what they can readily do. This shadowy teaching borderland between potential development and learning is "the zone of proximal development" (Vygotsky, 1978, p. 86). We as teachers are the guides in this borderland. Thus, every new learning initiates the emergence of further development of higher psychological functions on the way to mastery of content and a domain.

Children learn at varying rates, which has some connection to their level of intelligence. Even in a homogeneous groups, such as children who are gifted in fourth grade, development is not uniform. Teachers are well aware that, after starting a lesson, students begin to accomplish the learning objectives differently. Some learn quickly; others take much longer. Some learn the material completely; some learn portions. In short, the students begin to stretch out across the curriculum. For the most advanced students, the range of achievement increases more rapidly than among their nongifted peers. In a practical sense, it means that, as children go through school, the range of achievement continues to broaden so widely that variation in achievement in a third-grade mixed-ability class is likely to stretch from beginning readers to those reading on a middle school level (see Gagné, 2005, for a detailed illustration of variation in a national sample).

Much of this speed of learning happens at the early stages, and it is this early learning that fosters later development. Successful teaching, which we defined earlier as promoting learning so that a child learns more than he or she could alone, results in an ever-widening range of achievement in a class. Not only does the average for the group increase, but the range of achievement does, too. There is no escaping this fact. The decisions that teachers make as they plan and conduct themselves during lessons influence what children learn, how fast they learn, and how they develop.

Planning Decisions

Decisions around planning for instruction are crucial for consistent, high-quality teaching. These empty classroom decisions are made when a teacher has time to think and consider, instead of making decisions on the fly while interacting with students.

Planning Decisions: Content-Related

Selecting objectives. Selecting objectives for students to master presumes that the goals of the program and the structure of the curriculum have already been decided. A clear statement of outcomes is the most important teaching decision. The objectives establish the selection of content and become the standard for other decisions, such as choice of methods to reach the objectives, selection of materials, and criteria for evaluation. The content, or the specific skills and knowledge, in a curricular sequence may be learned for the first time, or the content may be an expansion and refinement of previous learning. The selection of high-level curricular materials is an empirically based best practice that is a crucial part of teaching (Shore & Delcourt, 1996; Shore et al., 1991). The dumbing down of curricular materials, which has been going on for many years (Kirst, 1982), has placed advanced, higher level learning in jeopardy for all children, which is especially true for gifted children.

Selecting materials. The careful selection of materials cannot be overstated. Indiscriminate choices may result in children learning knowledge and skills that are inconsistent with the program's purpose and the curricular goals. The selection of materials is also important for surmounting limitations in a teacher's knowledge base (Gallagher, 1975). Most teachers, especially elementary teachers, are generalists. When an increase in the specificity and complexity of a topic is accompanied by a decrease in the teacher's expertise, the selection of materials becomes critical. Instructional materials in such situations must become primary sources of information, and the teacher must act as a facilitator of the materials. The scarcity of instructional materials tied to curricula for the gifted and the needs for such materials becomes most apparent in this situation.

Materials should be interesting to students, and their selection should be shaped by knowledge of a class' interests. When student-centered methods are employed, this is particularly important. Students will not take responsibility for their own learning, or at least stick with a task, unless the content is worthy of their commitment. Teaching can easily flounder on the reef of student disinterest. In the independent study and discovery approaches, materials are important not only for motivational reasons, but also because the materials exert some control over the instructional sequence. Pacing of instruction, feedback, and review, as well as exposure to knowledge and skills, are governed to a large degree by the structure of the materials.

Material should be challenging to students, meaning that they require the students to reach beyond their comfort zone. The challenge can be the introduction of new ideas, an extension of what they know, a conflict between ideas or values with no ready answer, a presentation of a real-world problem to solve, an application of learning in a new context, or a demonstration of what has been learned in different formats.

The first procedure for a teacher to follow is to search for already existent materials at the child's level. In order to determine where to begin, teachers can derive a quick estimate of a child's achievement level to use for later refinement by calculating the "Rule of Five" (Dunn, 1963), in which you take a child's mental age, subtract 5, and the result will be a rough estimate of the grade at which the child is likely to be achieving. The mental age is obtained by taking an IQ score and multiplying it by the chronological age and dividing that answer by 100. Subtracting 5 from that number yields the grade estimate. This number is useful primarily for quickly deciding which materials to begin with to examine what might be appropriate for a student.

Once the materials are chosen, compare the content against the objectives. Then, compare the format against what is known about the class interest and maturity level in that content area. The greater the similarity between the materials and the objectives, the more suitable they are. Do not trust publisher claims. Be cautious. It is rare to find perfect agreement, so compromises are necessary. One need not use all of a published set of materials; they can be adapted or modified. New materials sometimes have to be created to meet instructional objectives. More on evaluating, preparing, and adapting instructional materials is presented in a latter section of this chapter on the topic of instructional materials in general.

Planning Decisions: Diagnosis of Content Knowledge

Testing for what students already know about the content is the next instructional procedure in the empty classroom. Diagnostic testing is conducted in reference to the objectives and the associated curricular materials. The intent is to determine the content the student has learned in general, the specific content that has been learned in terms of the lesson objectives, and the appropriateness of the materials for the students. These questions are not equivalent. Most information gathered from measures that are relevant to placement and identification is irrelevant or too general for answering teaching questions.

Content in general. Understanding a child's mastery of the content in general provides a quick look at the child as a successful learner. Educators of gifted children have recognized for many years that the children are often 2–4 years beyond their chronological age in school subjects and know 40–60% of the content before they enter their chronological age-appropriate class (Terman & Oden, 1947; U.S. Department of Education, 1993). This general statement reveals nothing about what children know in specific subject areas to be taught in a teacher's class. Achievement data from general standardized tests can supply information about how a child is doing in comparison to his or her peers and get some indication of what he or she knows. The range of achievement is likely to be quite broad in any class. Gagné (2005) used a national sample from the Iowa Test of Basic Skills to demonstrate that "for any grade above second grade, the within-grade student population differs more in terms of academic achievement than the 8-year difference observed between average first and ninth graders" (pp. 148–149).

Content specifically tied to objectives. General achievement tests are linked to curricular objectives, but usually do not provide specific enough reference to unit or lesson objectives to be useful for instructional assessment. Data from more narrowly focused achievement tests that are tied to subject and grade levels provide more specific information about what content students know because the test asks more questions about the content in that range (Assouline & Lupkowski-Shoplik, 2003). Yet, even here more specificity is needed.

Documentation of the discrepancy between actual achievement level and instructional objectives is a necessary step in making good instructional decisions. Teachers of the gifted can play an important role by finding and documenting these discrepancies. Diagnostic testing shows a child has mastered many skills and missed some others. Recognition of this situation can reduce two common instructional errors. In one, a child spends time endlessly repeating and reviewing content while waiting to be taught several missed skills. In another, a child is kept working on prerequisite skills when mastery of more advanced skills has been demonstrated, such as when a child can read at the fourth-grade level, but is required to practice syllabication. In both examples, the excitement of learning is devalued. These examples raise serious questions about schools' rigid adherence to the "hypothesized" and unproven skill sequences of much of the regular curriculum, which is the practice of most schools and a hallmark of the Whole Child and Basic Skills Educational models described in Chapter 7.

Determining appropriateness of the curricular materials. The most useable diagnostic data are those that are linked to the actual content or skills to be learned. The significance of this relationship is evident in the following statement:

> Few empirical principles of human behavior are as logically compelling and empirically verifiable as the dicta (1) that learning is facilitated by an appropriate match between the material to be learned and the learner's relevant cognitive organization; and (2) that there exist substantial differences in performance on any learning task among individuals of the same chronological age. (Robinson et al., 1979, p. 192)

Diagnostic testing moves us to the point where the match can be made. That point is the instructional level, a term borrowed from reading instruction. Curriculum-based assessment (CBA) is the generic name for testing a child against the content or curricular materials to be learned. CBA takes time away from teaching, but it pays off in the long term. When teachers use instructional materials that do not have accompanying tests (which happens often), even more time is needed to create the assessment. One response a teacher can make in this situation is to test the comprehensibility of written materials for the class by using the cloze procedure (Coleman, 1977). Another response is to design a brief test, or devise a rubric, asking questions that highlight the outcomes of the unit of instruction based on the objectives. There are many Web sites with general rubrics that can be adapted to a class. Having students complete self-evaluation checklists tied to the content objectives is a third possibility. A fourth approach is to try the materials on a few typical students in order to find out where problems might exist.

Working toward a match between the learner and a particular set of materials—that is, finding when to begin instruction—is accomplished by determining what is known or unknown in an instructional sequence within a broader curricular area. The instructional level is the point at which challenge is present, frustration is controlled, and learning is possible. An old rule of thumb from reading research is that, at the appropriate instructional level, the proportion is 90% known information to 10% unknown information. Because data on this point in terms of gifted learners is unavailable, this seems to be a conservative criterion for beginning instruction with the gifted. An important mediating variable is student interest and commitment. Because there is no way to accurately account for motivation until instruction begins, a 50:50 ratio might be reasonable in some content areas. In any case, making provisions for a highly personalized program is a desirable teaching decision (Shore & Delcourt, 1996).

Other diagnostic data has been recommended in the literature, for example, learning styles, cultural and social differences, and interests or learning profile (Renzulli, 1977; Shore & Delcourt, 1996; Tomlinson et al., 2003). The utility of these data depends on other programmatic decisions, such as program orientation. For example, an enrichment-oriented program may find these data more relevant in choosing materials than an acceleration-oriented program. We have found these additional data most useful when reflecting on the strengths and weaknesses of a completed lesson or when making action decisions.

Once the diagnostic testing is complete, the teacher has a good idea of what a child knows and does not know. It is at this point that diagnostic testing turns toward teaching, which is discussed in a later section. However, teachers frequently ignore diagnostic teaching and just plunge the students into the materials. This is sometimes justifiable, given the hustle and bustle of modern classrooms. However, this practice usually opens the door to later problems of confusion, misbehavior, and inattention requiring action decisions to correct for a problem that need not have happened.

Planning Decisions: Content-Related Evaluation and Feedback

Making a provision for evaluation and feedback is a key instructional principle. Providing feedback to students and to the teacher about what was learned is important for improvement in any subject area. People need information about the correctness or suitability of a response or a product in order to improve performance. The sources of feedback are the materials, peers, audience members, experts, teachers, or the students themselves.

Given the importance of feedback, teachers' constructive criticism of incorrect answers, which is one aspect of evaluation, occupies a very small amount of instructional time in classes using a lecture-discussion method (Bellack, 1966) and in classes using an individualized instructional method (Neujahr, 1976) at the elementary level. Teacher feedback about an incorrect answer occupies only about 2% of total classroom interaction time; thus, the materials, the students' own standards, and peers provide the majority of feedback for students. If evaluation is so covert, it is difficult for everyone to see its effect, and, furthermore, it is difficult for the teacher to know how to plan for feedback.

A clear standard for judgment makes evaluation and feedback to improve learning and performance more probable. When learning the fundamentals of an area, this is especially important. In other words, early stages of instruction require immediate attention before poor habits and strategies are developed. This does not mean the teacher has to intervene or say something immediately, but he or she does need to be aware of when students are not self-correcting. Once the fundamentals are mastered, the timing of feedback is not as crucial. Because evaluation can be based on a range of student products or behaviors, it is important that criteria for acceptable work be openly discussed. Moving beyond frequency counts (e.g., number of problems correct, pages read, etc.) as a criterion for judgment is especially valuable for the growth of students' personal standards for self-direction.

Planning evaluation and feedback requires deciding what kinds of behavior, products, or demonstrations would be suitable for the unit of instruction. The possibilities are immense. Renzulli, Leppien, and Hayes (2000) have constructed a list of possible concrete and abstract products. Judging the value of the products is another matter.

An axiom of evaluation is that complex products are difficult to judge. As a student becomes more deeply involved in a field of study, the evaluation of learning demands ever more subtle discriminations among variables. For example, a beginning pianist may be judged on technique and fidelity to a score, while an accomplished pianist is judged on interpretation criteria requiring knowledge of the history of the composition and past renditions by others. In a school situation, a project on the U.S. Constitution may be judged in terms of the variety of topics covered and sources used. From a fourth grader, one might expect a summary of the roles of Alexander Hamilton, Thomas Jefferson, and James Madison and some reference to the philosophy of the new country. From a high school senior, greater sophistication, such as the use of primary sources, a rendition of arguments presented in the *Federalist Papers*, and an interpretation of the Constitution from the perspective of the European ruling class, is warranted.

Providing feedback and evaluation is the responsibility of both the teacher and the student. In fact, if our intention is to help children become self-directed learners, then they have to learn to judge their own work. The SDL teaching system suggests a model that is useful for developing students' ability to provide their own feedback. Teachers can adapt this model to their own circumstances and help students develop rubrics for evaluating their own work. Shack (1994) has offered helpful suggestions.

Evaluation can be overdone, as well as underdone. Constructive criticism seems to have a positive effect on achievement for students who have a positive academic orientation (Gage, 1978). Typically, evaluation is not done in a meaningful way. When creativity is the goal in gifted education, reference is frequently made to the overuse of evaluation, and therefore evaluation is often suspended. It is important to note that suspending evaluation is not the same thing as abandoning evaluation altogether. Suspension of evaluation is recommended primarily when one is attempting to generate a variety of ideas, trying out unusual ideas, or playing around with ideas, as in brainstorming. Often forgotten is that suspension occupies small amounts of time and should be followed by evaluation. Too little evaluation can have the perverse effect of lowering the value of an activity for gifted children or a program (Coleman & Cross, 1993). Some programs suffer from this problem because students have no standard for judging their own development.

The problem of providing meaningful evaluation and feedback at the appropriate time is exacerbated by several factors. One is that the standard of quality is so poorly defined that it is useless. A second factor is that teachers are afraid that inappropriate feedback will "kill the spark of genius," which is an understandable, yet misguided concern. Teachers of the gifted are not that powerful, nor are gifted children that weak. The positive effect of teachers on gifted children is based on long-term involvement and commitment to them (Bloom, 1985; Sosniak, 2003). Assuming that one or several infrequent mistakes will have a life-hampering effect is unreasonable. The key is providing clear, specific feedback and avoiding general statements such as "I like the way you did that." A third factor is the overreliance on frequency counts, including number of pages read, problems completed, reports written, and so on. While frequency counts are necessary, this method usually sidesteps the issue of quality. If the lesson calls for increased proficiency and demonstration of advanced thinking, then frequency counts alone are not powerful enough.

The problem of deciding what constitutes increased proficiency and advanced thinking is best handled in a straightforward manner. Three steps that follow a procedure roughly termed "concept analysis" are recommended (Coleman, 1981): (1) try to imagine examples of high-quality work in an area by students and list their attributes; (2) tell the students about the attributes and, where possible, provide examples, then have students add or amend their own examples; and (3) try the attributes out. All evaluations should conclude with a student conference that includes specific suggestions for improvement. An excellent way for conveying this process to students is to have them evaluate the teacher's work.

Evaluation and feedback are crucial parts of effective instruction. They are not to be feared; rather, they should be used to improve teaching and learning. Preplanning of evaluation decisions can aid the entire instructional process.

Planning Decisions: Teaching-Related

The key to selecting general methods is matching the method to the demands of the situation. Objectives are always the first consideration in a lesson, and a general method should be chosen that is likely to promote the objective. Table 10.1 summarizes the methods and their strengths from Chapter 9 that teachers can use for making better teaching decisions. Remember, general methods are roughly equivalent to each other in their effectiveness in teaching low-order knowledge (i.e., recall comprehension of information). Therefore, the selection of methods for a lesson or unit should be based on objectives related to higher order thinking, learning values, developing motivation, and sensitivity to others. A unit of instruction typically has several objectives that require the combining of methods and materials into some desirable sequence, such as recitation, followed by readings, which, in turn, are followed by discussion. If the objectives call for the development of higher level thinking processes or the development of values and sensitivity to others, then discussion and discovery methods should be implemented. Or, a third example, if you know from diagnostic testing that some children have mastered most of the objectives, but have some gaps, then tutoring and independent study would be useful methods.

Other variables in the situation should be considered in the selection of a method: time available for instruction, class size, student preference, teacher style, and level of student learning. The size of the class dominates a teacher's choice of methods, and teachers should never apologize for decisions based on this reality. Classes may be divided into various kinds of groupings. Table 10.1 reports the suitability of methods in relation to group size. A teacher might

TABLE 10.1

The Use of General Methods in Terms of Associated Objectives, Variants of the Methods, and Group Size in Gifted Education

Methods (Group Size)	Associated Objectives*	Variants of Methods
Lecture (all)	Information, lower order cognitive skills	Mini-lectures
Discussion (4–20)	higher order thinking skills, listening and speaking skills	Synectics, creative problem solving, problem-based learning, Future Problem Solving
Tutoring (1–3)	Knowledge, possible higher order thinking skills, higher level attitudes toward subject	Programmed materials, mentor, contracts
Simulation and gaming (1–20)	Application of information, high interest	Games, role-playing
Discovery (all)	higher order thinking skills, cognitive integrated with affect	Inquiry, learning centers
Recitation (< 40)	Low-order cognitive skills, possible higher order thinking skills with proper questioning	Quiz bowls, academic competitions
Observational (all)	Attitudes, affect (rarely used alone)	Mentors, apprenticeship
Independent Study (1)	Personally relevant learning, higher order thinking skills, affective objectives	Learning centers, instructional packages, contracts
Materials-Driven (all)	Unknown, unless check against your objectives	Books, videos, computer programs, few validated materials

Note. * All methods teach knowledge; ** HOTS = higher order thinking skills

375

select a lecture for some situations, simulation and gaming for another. Tutoring may be used with children who are particularly advanced or with students who need assistance with some missing skills.

Time available for instruction is another consideration. The beginning facts or concepts in a subject may be taught with a time-efficient method such as recitation, and the development of higher level thinking may be taught with a more time-intensive technique such as the discovery method. Initial learning usually requires more direct teacher attention.

Learner preference for a given method is another variable to consider. For example, Stewart (1981) reported that gifted students prefer independent study and discussion methods. However, the variability of learning preferences within a group of gifted children makes this consideration secondary to class size in choosing a method. Certainly, knowing students' preferences for instructional methods is valuable for grouping students, anticipating action decisions, and long-term classroom planning.

As usual, the interaction among the objectives in an area, the structure of that area, and the child's level of knowledge are important intervening variables in choosing any method. Highly structured areas of knowledge and skills, such as math, may make certain options less useful. For example, the independent study method may be less appropriate than the tutoring method in such domains.

A teacher's style is also an important consideration. For example, some teachers prefer the recitation method over the discovery method. Teachers should use methods about which they are enthusiastic not only because such enthusiasm can enhance their teaching, but also because gifted children prefer teachers with this characteristic (Coleman & Cross, 1992). However, if teacher preference is based on comfort and ease of preparation, then the choice of that specific method should be reconsidered. It is clear that one method is not appropriate for all objectives.

Planning-Related Decisions: Methods and Activities

Selecting methods is often done in conjunction with choosing an activity upon which the lesson is built. Picking an activity still requires one to consider the methods. Having an engaging activity keeps children active and occupied, but this does not necessarily lead to the lesson/unit's objectives. Using the materials-driven method and/or an associated activity without considering the objectives for the unit often results in a disconnect between the activity and the objectives. Some critics of gifted education accuse us of having children do fun and games instead of real academic learning.

Some activities are preferable because they fit a particular content area, while others are preferable because they appeal to the teacher. A cache of activities, presented later in this chapter, contains transferable ideas for building lessons in many content areas. But again, selection of any activity should be based on the idea of the objectives of the lesson. For example, a teacher might use the discussion method in the form of a Synectics-type activity to increase children's awareness of their own thinking styles and to improve creative problem-solving skills, and then follow that up with a mini-lecture on the topic, followed by a visualization skills activity.

Planning Decisions: Review and Practice

Quality teaching provides for review and practice. Gifted children need practice, too, as people typically forget 70% or more of what they initially learned after a 2-week interval. Decisions about practice should be planned. Once a child has mastered an objective, a decision is necessary about when to practice the skill. The needs of the gifted child in this regard are inseparable from those of the nongifted based on what is known at this time. There is some hint that the gifted need less practice of routine facts because of their speed of learning. Spaced practices are preferable to one mass practice; therefore, short reviews separated by varying intervals are superior to one long review. This is certainly true for remembering facts, concepts, and definitions.

The maintenance of learned skills generally follows the same pattern. Examples of skills are dividing by two-digit numbers, analyzing, planning, using the Internet to search for a source, solving quadratic equations, writing a summary, and brainstorming. The practice of skills, too, should be spaced.

Wherever possible, a good decision is to change the content area in which the knowledge or skill is applied. The content should be as real as possible and not contrived. For example, the problem of building a better mousetrap is a valid instructional procedure for teaching the skill of brainstorming. Once that initial learning is accomplished, practice in brainstorming should be used to generate hypotheses in a science experiment or to list possible outcomes of a history lesson. Later in this chapter, we provide an example of such a lesson. These examples have the mutual benefit of providing practice of a valuable skill and increasing the probability that students will generalize the skill to other settings. Helping students transfer learning to new situations is a valuable instructional decision.

Planning Decision: Forming Groups

As long as there are more students than teachers in a classroom, teachers are likely to organize children into groups. Given the range of achievement in a single class (Gagné, 2005), provisions have to be made to accommodate it, and grouping is often part of the solution. A group can be the whole class, smaller groups of varying sizes, or dyads. In this section, we are assuming that the curriculum or program of study has been settled, and the teacher is deciding what to do to accomplish the objectives of a unit. The basic questions are when to use groups and on what basis should a group be formed.

The first considerations are the purpose for the lesson, the objectives, and the methods. Grouping is relevant to some methods and not others. The discussion method works best with small groups. Obviously, in most classes, multiple groups will have to be formed. However, the groups do not have to be static, and group membership should change depending on the topic, as well as the subject area.

377

Every class also has a range of achievement, ability, and experience. The teacher's job is to decide whether these variations are important to the formation of the group. Many times, the achievement level is the basis for group formation. Cluster grouping is a viable option in which children of like achievement work together on a lesson, an approach that helps promote learning for group members (Rogers, 2002). Groups may also be formed on the basis of interest in a topic or as some aspect of a project.

A third basis for group formation is grouping children with differing perspectives or strengths to enhance learning, for example, placing a child who is analytical with a child who has more organizational skills or placing an artistically oriented child with a scientifically oriented child. Groups formed on these bases might be better at meeting objectives having to do with sense of self and social sensitivity to others than at directed academic objectives. Cooperative learning is a term that might be applied to this way of forming groups.

Cooperative learning is a teaching procedure that has wide general use at grade levels throughout school (Nelson, Gallagher, & Coleman, 1993). The value and appropriateness of cooperative learning for high-ability children is mixed and controversial (Robinson, 2003). Forming a group with children doing the same exercise or working on the same topic does not make it a cooperative learning group. To have this designation, the group must be working on a task that has a common goal and requires cooperation to reach that goal. The goal for a task might be cooperative (children are evaluated together), individual (children are judged individually), or competitive (children are rewarded for winning). The three types of goal structure have differential effects on high-ability learners in mixed-ability classes. The individual goal structure promotes learning and more positive attitudes than the others in mixed classes. While "mixed-ability cooperative learning is appropriate only in certain situations" (Rogers, 2002, p. 260), its effects are likely to be more positive in same-ability classes where all the students are gifted (Robinson).

Teachers cannot assume a group will work simply because it was formed. Students may not have the necessary skills to be able to function together. The teacher's job is to teach students how to be a group and work together without teacher supervision. Sometimes, it may be necessary to reorganize the groups in order to make them work. Groups that constantly require the teacher's attention should be reworked so that the teacher has time to spend with other groups when needed.

Planning Decision: Final Plan

The final plan for instruction coordinates the information from previous decisions. All decisions are strictly pragmatic, determining what will work best in a teacher's specific situation. The decisions for gifted children are based on clinical or teaching experience.

1. Tell students what is expected of them and what the content will be.

2. Decide how to introduce new concepts, including how new concepts relate to previously learned concepts.

3. Formulate questions to ask students when using the recitation or discussion methods; otherwise, the questions are embedded in the materials.

4. Set the sequence of activities. The materials and methods are to occur in a series.

5. Determine the procedures for making a transition from one method to another. Have a schedule or directions available on the board or in a folder so that children can proceed on their own.

6. Rethink how much you can realistically handle at one time. In a class of 30, managing more than three or four groups is arduous. The more groups and individual situations, the more preplanning and structuring are necessary. Be sensible, as you can always expand the number of groups the next year.

7. Begin instruction based on diagnostic testing. Consider whether students have prerequisite skills or must be taught them. This saves time later.

8. Be ready for students who finish early or do not finish in the planned time.

9. Set aside time to review and check what the students have done. Practice is often necessary at the early stages of learning and to learn basic facts.

10. When trying something new or innovative with a class, be ready for confusion and maybe chaos. Stick with it for several weeks before you give it up. Rarely do innovations go smoothly. Both the teacher and the students need to learn new procedures.

The final plan requires orchestrating the earlier decisions into a workable format in a classroom. Teachers should be mindful of how much they can manage at any one time. It is usually better to do something well; however, with additional planning, teachers can usually handle more than they think they can.

A Digression: Meaningless Learning and Teaching Recipes

Before proceeding with our discussion on action decisions and teaching, it is necessary to interject a note of caution. The trend in gifted education is to advocate instructional procedures that are aimed toward building higher order thinking and independent, imaginative people (Gallagher & Gallagher, 1994; Maker, 1982; Rogers, 2002). Teachers who aim to help students reach these goals should use general methods, such as discovery, independent study, observational learning, and simulation. All methods are useful with the gifted, and going overboard and using exclusively active, self-directed methods (Runco & Nemiro, 1994) is unjustified. This cautionary tale has to do with a common practice that works against the goals of gifted education.

More than 30 years ago, Ausubel and Robinson (1969) raised questions about assumptions regarding the learning processes that are conventionally held by many teachers that deserve our attention as teachers of the gifted. They postulated that learning could be thought of as being on two dimensions. The first deals with the means by which the knowledge is made available to the conscious mind of learner, either by passively receiving it or by active discovery (the reception learning/discovery learning dimension). The second distinction deals with alternate ways in which the learner may incorporate such knowledge into his or her existing structure of ideas, either meaningfully or by rote (the meaningful learning/rote learning dimension).

Ausubel and Robinson (1969) claimed the two dimensions were relatively independent, thus lessons can be taught to promote learning that exemplifies all four combinations of the meaningful/rote and reception/discovery. Thus, passive receptive learning can be meaningful, that is, meaningful reception learning. This occurs when the teacher presents the generalization in its final form and the learner relates it to his or her existing ideas in some sensible fashion. On the other hand, passive receptive learning can be rote, that is, rote reception learning. This happens if the teacher presents a generalization and the student merely memorizes it. As passive reception learning can be meaningful or rote, so can discovery learning be meaningful or rote. Meaningful discovery learning occurs if the student formulates the generalization and subsequently relates it in a sensible way to his or her existing ideas. Rote discovery learning occurs if the learner, having arrived at the generalization (typically by trial and error), subsequently commits it to memory without relating it to other relevant ideas in his or her cognitive structure.

We as teachers have an important role in helping children make learning meaningful. Rote discovery learning is an undesirable outcome that teachers of the gifted can unintentionally foster in their classrooms. When teachers give students recipes, formulaic steps, or rubrics when approaching new situations, they may be contributing to the learning of rote ways of solving problems, which is contrary to the purpose of programs for the gifted. For example, repeatedly reminding students of the five steps to effective problem solving may teach children to mouth the steps, but they are not likely to acquire the flexible understanding that is necessary for solving real problems. Teachers should be wary of children who approach problems in this manner and assist them in overcoming this habit.

Action Decisions

Action decisions are made during the act of teaching. They are specific responses to particular circumstances, and for that reason, our discussion of action decisions is rather limited in scope when compared to planning decisions. Planning decisions help in making action decisions because the teacher has the experience of reasoning out earlier decisions for use in quick recall, reexamination, and possible reaffirmation of reasons for specific decisions.

While conducting lessons in the busy, student-filled classroom, there are some behaviors and attitudes the teacher of gifted children can use to guide action decisions (Shore et al., 1991):

1. An indirect style of soliciting remarks, enlarging on student ideas, praising student efforts, and being accepting of varying viewpoints is positively related to achievement. This style is more effective at the secondary level than at the elementary level (Gage, 1978).

2. Gifted children do not accept undue praise when they know the task was easy.

3. The way the teacher acts is a powerful message. The observational method is a valuable tool with gifted children, who tend to be more sensitive than other students to social cues (Whitmore, 1980).

4. Fighting the tendency to ask mainly low-order cognitive questions and, consequently, asking more higher order questions may raise the level of student thinking (Gallagher et al., 1967).

5. Drill and practice should be minimized.

6. In the long term, the longer students spend learning some area, the more they learn. Thus, efforts to help students stick to a task are worthwhile (Berliner & Gage, 1976; Sosniak, 2003).

7. Teachers who move frequently about the classroom noting what students are doing and demonstrating an awareness of student behavior and academic needs get better results.

8. If teachers are attentive to nonverbal signs of frustration or boredom, they can modify the pace of instruction. The materials and methods influence pacing.

9. Students need an opportunity to be active while learning. Young students need to touch and feel what they are learning. Both young and older students need concrete, visual evidence of their success.

381

10. Teachers should be ready to deal with what they do not know about a subject and be willing to show students how they learn. Beginning teachers probably learn more than their students do.

11. Reflect systematically after class about what worked and what could have worked better. Keeping a written record will help you find patterns that can be altered. Solutions to random events are unlikely.

Teachers can prepare themselves for action decisions by reflecting on how their class went in comparison to their plan and keeping a journal, as already noted. Other ways to prepare for action decisions are visiting the classes of others who are successful, keeping a diary of what works in certain circumstances, and forming a support group. There are no shortcuts to building a repertoire of action decisions, or what one teacher called the "grey backdrop" to classroom teaching (Coleman, 1991).

The next part of this chapter presents some examples of strategies implying planning and action decisions as carried out by teachers. These are intended to deepen your understanding of the meaning of planning and action decisions.

USEFUL TECHNIQUES FOR TEACHERS

In this section, we distill from conferences and journal articles those ideas that have had utility in classrooms across the nation. These techniques compose the beginnings of a basic toolkit for teachers. To keep up to date, teachers have to consult the journals and attend conferences and in-service events. They also need to engage in long-term academic planning with the parents of gifted children. Until recently, when faced with questions such as "What is the academic future for my students?" and "What does this all mean?," teachers have had to fall back on vague generalities that point toward future college entrance. With the growth of the national talent searches, data has emerged demonstrating more specific educational paths for students based on their performance on out-of-level tests. Table 10.2 organizes the scores on the SAT or ACT into three ranges. Options for each range are presented for acceleration, in-school enrichment, and access to advanced or college-level work. The table shows that, as scores increase, the kinds of options change. Teachers should collaborate with parents to ensure that as many options as possible are available for all children.

In the following sections, we present five strategy options: program options, differentiation, compacting, a cache of techniques, and conducting an active discussion. We present these strategies with some trepidation because rushing to use them without bearing in mind the ideas in Chapters 7, 8, and 9 can lead to underestimating seriously the complexity of teaching gifted and talented children.

TABLE 10.2

At-A-Glance Program Options
for Talent Search Students

	"A" Range Scores • 230–470 on SAT-V • 200–510 on SAT-M or • 0–21 on ACT-Eng or ACT-Read • 0–17 on ACT-Math	"B" Range Scores • 480–580 on SAT-V • 520–600 on SAT-M or • 22–27 on ACT-Eng or ACT-Read • 18–23 on ACT-Math	"C" Range Scores • 580+ on SAT-V • 600+ on SAT-M or • 28+ on ACT-Eng or ACT-Read • 24+ on ACT-Math
Options for acceleration	Homogeneous grouping for acceleration at one year above grade level in area of strength	Homogeneous grouping for accelerated, fast-paced, or telescoped classes at least one year above grade level	Special gifted school placement
		Grade placement in area of strength 1 to 2 years above grade level and early access to higher levels of schooling (e.g., attending high school for math instruction)	Grade placement in area of strength 3 to 4 years above grade level
	Differentiation of assign-ments, homework, and projects in area of strength	In-class clustering for acceleration in area of strength	Individualized program of study in area of strength, including independent studies, mentorships, etc.
Options for in-school enrich-ment	Resource room or pull-out program for enrich-ment or project work, at least 5 hours per week	Resource room or pull-out program for inde-pendent study or project work, at least 5 hours per week	
	In-class clustering for enrichment in area of strength		
Option for access to advanced or college-level work	Access to AP in grades 11 and 12	Access to AP in grade 10	Access to AP in grade 9
	International Baccalaureate program	International Baccalaureate program	Early entrance into college
		Dual enrollment (for college courses) in grade 11 and 12	Dual enrollment (for college courses) begin-ning in grade 9 or 10
Options for extracurriculars	Extracurricular activities (contests, internships, study abroad, summer pro-grams, etc.) in area of strength		

Note. From At-A-Glance Program Options for Talent Search Students by Center for Talent Development, Northwestern University, 2004, Evanston, IL: Author. Copyright ©2004 by Center for Talent Development.

Differentiation in the Classroom

Special education for the gifted is rooted in the idea that gifted and talented learners present demands on the school for which the institution is ill prepared. Gifted children exhibit four attributes that cause teaching problems more than other children: wide range of ability, advanced knowledge in areas, rapid learning rate, and intense involvement in some topics. Differentiation is a process of accepting and dealing with these issues.

Differentiation, as discussed in Chapter 8, describes the appropriate educational changes that are needed for gifted students. Here we are more specific about how differentiation might be implemented while taking into account the information from Chapters 7, 8, and 9. In essence, the one-method-fits-all school has to be transformed into a place where multiple methods, multiple outcomes, and diversity are valued. Differentiation tries to do that. It is appropriate in programs that favor acceleration, as well as those that favor enrichment, although most discussion seems to emphasize the latter.

The range of individual differences in a class is broad, whether in a general education or a special education class. A goal of excellent teachers is to increase the class' average achievement and to expand the range of differences within the class more than would happen by chance. Expert teachers recognize that they can only deal with a limited number of differences among students at any one time. Like most goals of teaching, striving for the goal of meeting every child's need is an ideal, not an end state, for building a career.

Differentiation is not at the end of a single path; many factors intercede. So, if there is no one way, how do you know when it is being implemented, and how can you defend that differentiation is being done appropriately? A simple, yet powerful starting point is the definition itself (Tomlinson, 1995). A set of criteria is needed so teachers can judge whether differentiation has been realized in their class. Recognizing this imperative, we present two scholars' notions of the criteria for judging the success of differentiation.

In summarizing the research on differentiation, Tomlinson et al. (2003) asserted that effective differentiation meets the following standards:

1. It is proactive, rather than reactive.

2. It employs flexible use of small teaching-learning groups in the classroom.

3. It varies the materials used by individuals and small groups of students in the classroom.

4. It uses variable pacing as a means of addressing learner need.

5. It is knowledge-centered.

6. It is learner-centered.

Montgomery (personal communication, 1999), with a colleague and a group of teachers, generated four standards that also capture what differentiation should do and says it even more succinctly:

- No learner should have to spend time learning something he or she already knows.

- No learner should have to spend time learning something he or she is not ready to learn.

- All learners should be responsible for demonstrating competence in a general curriculum in well-articulated scope and sequence.

- The curricula for the gifted are encased between the needs of the gifted learner and the planned differentiation (faster, broader, deeper) from the general curriculum.

Starting to differentiate in one's class is not an easy task. Using the dimensions of content, process, and product, Table 10.3 presents possibilities for a classroom. Good ideas are also available from other sources. Tomlinson (1995, 1996) provided explanations for carrying out differentiation in schools and at the classroom level. Winebrenner (1992) offered many other ideas for differentiation. Hughes (1999), a general education teacher, reported her practices and how she got feedback about her effectiveness from her students and parents through action research. Noble (2004) has devised a flexible planning tool that combines the theory of multiple intelligences with the Revised Bloom Taxonomy (Anderson & Krathwohl, 2001).

Curriculum Compacting

Curriculum compacting, a time-tested procedure, is a method that combines diagnostic assessment and curriculum planning so that students spend more time doing new work than languishing in the standard curriculum. Curriculum compacting is a three-step procedure in its simplest form. Renzulli and Smith (1978b) have summarized the procedure and placed it in a form known as the Compactor, which has three sections corresponding to the three steps (see Table 10.4).

The top section uses assessment data to justify the curricular area to be compacted. The curriculum is considered from one of two perspectives: a time period or a topic. In the time period approach, the curriculum is examined over a set time frame, such as the marking period or school year. In the topic approach, a curricular sequence or unit is the time frame for compacting.

The middle section of the Compactor is concerned with describing procedures for compacting the regular curricular material. Fluent use of diagnostic testing and familiarity with the standard curriculum are necessary for these

TABLE 10.3

Differentiation by Dimension

Content	Process	Product
Differentiation through:	*Differentiation through:*	*Differentiation through:*
• multiple texts and supplementary print resources • varied computer programs • varied audio-visuals • varied support mechanisms • varied time allotments • interest centers • contracts • compacting • triarchic-based orientation	• tiered assignments • learning centers • triarchic model assignments • multiple-intelligence assignments • graphic organizers • simulation • learning logs • concept attainment • concept development • synectics	• tiered product assignments • independent study • community-based products • negotiated criteria • graduated rubrics • triarchic-based orientations • multiple intelligence-based orientations

Note. From "Good Teaching for One and All: Does Gifted Education Have an Instructional Identity?," by C. Tomlinson, 1996, *Journal for the Education of the Gifted, 20,* p. 162. Copyright ©1996 by The Association for the Gifted. Adapted with permission.

procedures. Again, the section justifies the need for compacting in a more specific way by delineating the material to be left out in the time frame or some curricular area by specifying what is to be taught and by stating how evaluation that guarantees proficiency is to be carried out.

The last, or bottom, section is used to specify the acceleration or enrichment in the curricular areas that the previous sections have justified. In short, "a decision must be made regarding whether the time that has been bought will be devoted to acceleration or enrichment in this particular area" (Renzulli & Smith, 1979, p. 21). Compacting information can also be used to form groups or enrichment clusters (Reis et al., 1998).

Compacting is a procedure that is easier to illustrate than it is to carry out. It requires sensitive attention to the needs of children and to teachers who are not specialists in gifted education. Implementing compacting requires a support network of colleagues who are committed to trying it and willing to share

TABLE 10.4

The Compactor Used With Two Students

Brenda (third grade)	Bill (sixth grade)

Curricular Areas to Be Considered for Compacting

Unit 2, Level 14—Hand Stands	Chapter 3—Elementary School Math Book (Addison-Wesley)
Objectives—see p. 64 in Teacher's Edition (attached). All items on Pretest (attached) correct with exception of questions dealing with grapheme-phoneme correspondence.	Objectives—see p. T39a in Teacher's Edition. Student has straight-A average in math during the past 5 years. He has scored in the 99th percentile on achievement tests for the past 3 years.

Procedures for Compacting

Do p. 23 in Workbook and Skill Reinforcement Master No. 6. Check proficiency by using Activity No. 3 p. 76 in Teacher's Edition and Criterion Reference Test items dealing with decoding (Workbook pp. 133, 1–4).	pp. 78–79—Administered chapter review to student. Answer all items correctly.

Acceleration and/or Enrichment Activities

Guide independent reading; ask librarian to meet with Brenda for 7 hours per week; help her to obtain mystery stories from the high school and the city library; help her draw up a summer reading plan.	Meet with people from computer center at Manchester Community College. Develop logic problems guidebook for hand calculators and microcomputers.
Work with gifted program resource teacher on creative writing of mystery stories.	Teach course (using Guidebook) during spring minicourse week.
Work with art teacher and other students to produce puppet dramatizations of her mystery stories.	Develop display boards (with aid of other students) and enter work in regional science and math fair.

Note. From "Curriculum Compacting: An Essential Strategy," by J. S. Renzulli, L. H. Smith, and S. Reis, 1982, *Elementary School Journal, 82,* p. 188. Copyright © 1982 by The Journal Press.

TABLE 10.5

Teaching Strategies

Strategy	Description
Paradoxes	common notion not necessarily true in fact; self-contradictory statements or observations
Attributes	inherent properties, conventional symbols of identities, ascribing qualities
Analogies	situations of likeness, similarities between things, comparing one thing to another
Discrepancies	gaps of limitations in knowledge, missing links in information, what is not known
Provocative Questions	inquiry to bring forth meaning, incite knowledge exploration, summon to discovering new knowledge
Examples of Change	demonstrate the dynamics of change, provide opportunities for making alterations, modifications, or substitutions
Examples of Habit	effects of habit-bound thinking, building sensitivity against rigidity in ideas and well-tried ways
Organized Random Search	using a familiar structure to go at random to build another structure. An example from which new research approaches occur at random
Skills of Search	search for ways something has been done before (historical search); search for current status of something (descriptive research); set up an experimental situation and search for what happened (experimental research)

Tolerance for Ambiguity	provide situations that puzzle, intrigue, or challenge thinking; pose open-ended situations that do not force closure
Intuitive Expression	feeling about things through all the senses, skills of expressing emotion, be sensitive to inward hunches or nudges
Adjustment to Development	learn from mistakes and failures; develop, rather than adjust, to something; develop many options or possibilities
Study People and Processes	analyze traits of eminently creative people and study processes that lead to problem solving, invention, incubation, and insight
Evaluate	decide upon possibilities by the consequences and situations implications; and check to verify ideas and guesses against the facts
Visualization Skill	express ideas in visual forms, illustrating thoughts and feelings, describing experiences through illustrations

Note. From *Classroom Ideas for Encouraging Thinking and Feeling* (p. 202), by F. E. Williams, 1970, Buffalo, NY: D.O.K. Copyright ©1970 by F. Williams & L. Schaffer. Reprinted with permission.

the successes and failures. Starting with a small group, rather than the whole class, is a manageable way to learn the procedures. Compacting cannot work unless the teacher has or is prepared to create a list of activities to replace the eliminated material.

A Cache of Techniques

Teachers are frequently at a loss as to where to turn in order to generate new lessons. Among the many possibilities for lessons, some techniques have multiple applications across the curriculum. Williams' (1970, 1979) Model for Implementing Cognitive-Affective Behavior in the Classroom has this feature. Although not strictly developed for the gifted, this model is widely cited in the literature. One part of the model is illustrated in Table 10.5, which presents 15 strategies along with their descriptions. Williams incorporated ideas from indirect curricular models (see Chapter 8) and some of the information on instructional systems (see Chapter 9) into a usable, meaningful framework for teachers.

The value and usefulness of Williams' ideas have been demonstrated in many classrooms over several decades, and they continue to be teacher-friendly (Friedman & Lee, 1996). Some of his strategies are applicable within general teaching methods, such as discussion, tutoring, and discovery. Some excellent suggestions for the content and materials in lessons are also implied in the list of strategies. The model has considerable flexibility, and it can be reorganized within various curricular arrangements. The methods have utility in enrichment-oriented and acceleration-oriented classrooms. Many ideas similar to Williams' can be found in other more recent sources of techniques (e.g., Rogers, 2000). The basic way to use his idea is to take a unit or a course of study and adapt the strategies to that content. A second way to use the 15 strategies is as a starting point for generating ideas of your own.

Conducting Active Discussions

The use of the discussion method is evident in almost every program for the gifted. Many of the techniques directed at developing higher order thinking and creativity are connected to this method. Some research indicates that the gifted may learn more with this technique than other children (Michell & Lambourne, 1979). Chapter 9 has already explained the discussion method and some of its variants, and in this section, an example of the method is presented.

While much has been written on the importance of the discussion method, only one study (Coleman, 1992) has shown how a skilled discussion leader actually conducts classes with gifted children. We use the story of Alex to illustrate how a teacher might conduct a discussion. Alex's voice exemplifies one successful active discussion. His description is not meant to be the only way a teacher can conduct a discussion; rather, it is a template against which a teacher of the gifted might reflect on his or her own practice.

Behavior Prior to Conducting a Discussion (Planning Decisions)

Alex is teaching a mixed-gender group of 11 gifted children, ages 12–18, in a summer program. The topic is the meaning of time. Before the discussion begins, Alex has a good idea of where it should go, his role in it, and the discussion's specific parts. Alex reviews the questions he intends to ask, silently asks himself those questions, and answers them as if he were having a dialog. Then, Alex reviews his expectations for a good discussion. He wants to create a warm environment where students actively share ideas and feelings about the topic. During the discussion, he expects ideas to flow and move at a pace that seems right for that moment. He knows he can influence, but he cannot control the class and have an active discussion. In the course of the class, he works to help students move from the safe world of abstractions toward "making it concrete" so that what they are saying can be seen or applied in their world.

Moving Through the Discussion (Action Decisions)

Alex uses the term *moves* to refer to his actions and thoughts during a discussion. The moves are smaller teaching techniques, actually action decisions, within the larger discussion method.

- *Seizing the opportunity*: Wait for children to make comments and use them to bring up an important point.

- *Moving on*: Estimate when enough has been said and proceed to another part of the discussion. The most direct way is to ask, "Can we move on?"

- *Saying nothing*: Be silent. Do not follow each student comment with your own. Ignore a dominating student or student comments that seem irrelevant when they have been followed by a relevant comment. Let the students control the discussion.

- *The quick go-around*: Move quickly around the group to get a fast survey of information or opinions to use later.

- *Pushing kids:* Probe for deeper comments. Making an idea concrete is one suggestion. Sometimes be kind, other times, demanding. Talk to the students as needed after class about the low quality of their participation.

- *It is not working*: When students are not involved, keep trying by building on a student's comments and asking provocative questions.

- *Telling outrageous stories*: Provide examples that are absurd, improbable, or funny to keep the discussion flowing.

- *Restatement* (the most common behavior): Summarize what was said, have a student who has not been participating do it, suggest alternative wording, or recall a previous comment by a student and name the student.

These eight behaviors are integrated throughout the course of a discussion. To illustrate the point, we use the following excerpt from part of a taped discussion (Coleman, 1992, pp. 12–13), although not all of the moves are evident. Note how the discussion builds in a kind of spiral pattern with twists and turns as the meaning of the topic is explored and expanded.

A student has been describing her sense of time during dreaming.

Alex: (*pushing kids*) Just recalling other dreams, days, whatever, when you are more aware of the dream. Does the time of the dream seem to be as the time like now?

391

ML: Like what you are picturing in the dream?

Alex: Yeah, the time in the dream, when you are in the dream.

ML: It seems like it takes the entire time you are asleep.

Alex: (*moving on*) Okay, somebody else, I'm sorry.

ML: Aren't dreams supposed to be really short or something?

Alex: (*seizing the opportunity; reemphasizing the point*) That's what people say, but they are not to the person who is dreaming.

ML: [*laughs*] Huh.

AH: I don't see how, now that you mention it, I was really thinking about . . . how long you dream. I don't think there is any way you can know . . . because you're still asleep. I don't see how you can think, "Well, I'm now starting my dream. Well, let's see how long."

Alex: Some people do. Some people are totally aware of what goes on in their dreams, have total recall; some people don't.

AH: I can remember a lot of stuff, but I can't remember how long it is.

Alex: I'm not asking you how long it was when you wake up. I'm really trying to ask you how long was it while you were doing it. How do you experience time (*pushing kids*)? Is time the same in that dream state as it is right now? Is it different?

AH: [*pause*] I don't see how you would have any way of knowing it.

Alex: (*restatement*) Okay, for you there is no difference or no way of knowing. (*moving on*) How about someone else?

ML: Okay, I kind of understand. Like, while you are dreaming, the stuff you are seeing seems to be like everybody's going real, real fast, or it did to me.

Alex: Okay. (*saying nothing*)

ML: It's like over a period of a couple of days that I dreamed about, like the days went real fast [*snaps fingers*], the whole thing.

Alex: (*restatement; quick group summary*) All right, that is something like I'm asking you to pick up on. All right, so . . . there are other kinds of time,

392

bathroom time, that kind of stuff. You know the time you have to go to the bathroom and you can't get in [*laughter*]? Here it doesn't necessarily happen with multiple toilets and stuff. (*telling outrageous stories*) [*Two quick stories follow: one based on his father using the toilet in a one-bathroom house and a story of returning from a long trip and wanting to get into the bathroom and can't.*] So you are hopping all around [*laughter*]. Those kind of things, those are all experiences of time. Uh, all right, so there's all that stuff. Now (*moving on*), we have different kinds of time people were talking about, different experiences of time.

Obviously, conducting an active discussion is an acquired, complex set of behaviors. Skill in the discussion method can be developed by planning carefully, trying it out, recording yourself or having someone observe you, analyzing what you hear, and keeping a discussion journal. Discussion is a skill that has applicability across the curriculum. Notice, in Alex's discussion, the many opportunities for higher levels of thinking.

SPECIALIZED METHODS TIED TO SPECIAL GOALS

We now turn from generalized methods that are commonly used in classes for the gifted to more specialized methods that appear in the literature. Presentations at conferences for and by teachers of the gifted tend to focus on special methods that foster learning for three goals: (a) creative problem solving, (b) attitudes and values about self and social responsibility, and (c) research and study skills. These special methods are too narrow to be thought of as teaching systems; yet, they combine general methods and are relevant to a variety of content areas. Because these special methods are so widespread, teachers need to reflect on how they compare to our discussion of general methods and their own teaching preferences. Within each special category, there are numerous methods from which to choose. We have selected people with pioneering ideas or cogent synthesis to present in each goal area.

Creativity and Problem Solving

Creative thinking and problem solving are frequently stated goals of gifted programs. Many techniques can be subsumed under this rubric. A significant portion of Chapter 6 was devoted to teaching for creativity; that discussion is not replicated here and should be reviewed. Three important concepts, not previously described, by de Bono (1970, 1971), Polya (1945/1973), and Papert (1980) are summarized because they offer perspectives with significant teaching implications. Evidence on the effectiveness of these approaches (whether in the form advocated by these writers or other versions of inquiry and problem solving) with gifted children is limited (Plucker & Beghetto, 2003; Shore et al., 1991; Treffinger et al., 1993).

393

Lateral thinking. de Bono (1970, 1971) approaches creative problem solving in a deliberate, practical way. He believed that the human mind is "a self-organizing information system" that inevitably creates patterns of information that have strengths and liabilities. In his view, there are two types of thinking: vertical and lateral. Vertical thinking is logical, consistent, in search of the best result. It is a closed system that rejects wrong information. Lateral thinking is open-ended, illogical, unfocused, and explorative in its search for possibilities. Lateral and vertical thinking are complementary because of their opposing strengths and weaknesses.

de Bono believed thinking patterns can be restructured; therefore, lateral thinking can be improved by adopting a positive attitude toward change, avoiding vertical thinking, and learning new techniques. The idea of postponing judgment is evident. Recognizing current ideas is crucial so a person can grasp what is dominating his or her thinking. de Bono makes no attempt to change ideas, only to be cognizant of them so that he can avoid them and escape the dominance of current thinking. Examples of techniques are: (a) ask why; (b) enter the problem at a point other than the beginning; (c) set a quota of ideas; (d) drop a concept and use another one; and (e) divide a concept into parts. Changing ideas from within by altering ideas in an unreasonable manner, such as reversing ideas and exaggerating an idea or part of a solution to an extreme point, is recommended. Many of de Bono's ideas are similar to those who advocate brainstorming.

In our experience, many teachers have difficulty connecting creative problem-solving techniques, like brainstorming, with subject matter. A good example of the integration of subject and creative problem solving is a two-lesson procedure for creating science units in which the teacher and student roles are modified (Knutsen, 1979). In lesson one, the children learn the brainstorming procedure. In lesson two, the teacher sets "the formula" for a unit. In Table 10.6, the formula is presented by outlining the jobs needed to complete the unit and the people responsible.

The unit follows a general problem-solving sequence paralleling the scientific method in which brainstorming is an embedded procedure for defining the problem, forming hypotheses, and designing experiments. The teacher acts as a facilitator and has the significant job of starting the process, providing basic concepts and data, and conducting the evaluation (the zinger). The latter term is also used in promoting independent study (Strother, 1997). Note how Knutsen's methodology incorporates creativity, problem solving, and research skills, while also using aspects of general methods, such as lecture, recitation, discussion, and observation, as he follows the formula.

Building problem solving. Polya (1945/1973) pointed out that learning problem-solving skills comes from experience in solving problems and in watching others solve problems. In his classic text, *How to Solve It*, Polya advocated the study of heuristics, the study of mental operations used in solving problems applicable to many subject matters. Polya contended that there are

TABLE 10.6

A Prototypical Approach Incorporating General and Special Methods in a Subject Area

Lesson One: Brainstorming—explain steps; let students do it so they learn

Lesson Two: Present "The Formula" for creating a unit with roles

Job	Person(s) Responsible
Presenting the problem	Teacher
Defining/delimiting the problem	Students
Basic tool (foundation)	Teacher
Collecting data	Students
Forming hypotheses	Students
Designing experiments	Students
Controlling variables	Students
Running control groups	Students
Specific job assignments	Students
Presenting results	Students
Drawing conclusion	Students
The Zinger	Teacher

Note. From "Teaching 50 Gifted Science Units in 2 Easy Steps," by L. Knutsen, 1979, *Science and Children, 50,* 51–53. Copyright ©1979 by the National Science and Teachers Association Publications, 1840 Wilson Blvd., Arlington, VA 22201-3000. Reprinted with permission.

four parts to solving a problem, each of which can be aided by the judicious application of questions to help that part of the process along:

1. Understand the problem.
   - What is the unknown?
   - What are the data?
   - What are the conditions?

2. Devise a plan.
   - Do you know a related problem?
   - Look at the unknown. Think of a familiar problem with similar unknowns.
   - Look at a related problem that was solved before. Could you use it?

3. Carry out the plan.
   • Check each step.

4. Look back.
   • Check the result. Can you do it differently?

Powerful and neglected aspects of Polya's methodology are the systematic procedures and, most importantly, Step 4. He urged problem solvers to spend time reviewing the manner in which the problem was solved, not only to improve upon the solution, but also to reflect about how one solves a problem. By engaging in metacognition, in which you comprehend your own thought processes and relate what you have done in other instances of problem solving, you increase the probability that problem solving will transfer to other subject areas. In today's parlance, reflecting on one's thinking is being advocated. The revisions of Bloom's Taxonomy pay particular attention to metacognitive processes in learning (Anderson & Krathwohl, 2001).

Somewhat related to Polya's ideas is the work of Papert (1980), who believed that children need to be aware of their thinking. Computers are an excellent medium for creating "microworlds" in which children can discover strategies for solving problems. Papert contended that schools typically teach a child that answers to problem situations are right or wrong. Thus, children learn to avoid errors and devalue situations filled with error. These kinds of learning are contrary to problem solving. Children need to learn that errors are always expected; in fact, rarely can one be correct the first time. Through the study of their errors, children learn whether or not something is correctable. Papert believed that children should acquire the attitude that many situations are fixable, mistakes are natural, and there are ways to go about improving a situation. Learning to program a computer using LOGO, a computer language, helps children learn this attitude and discover procedures for solving problems that are encountered in a microworld.

Teaching children to become better thinkers and problem solvers requires that they think about how they approach problems and about the adequacy or inadequacy of their systems for solving real phenomena. Children need to be involved in what they are learning and supported for doing these activities if they are to become better learners. The writings of de Bono, Polya, and Papert, in combination with the literature on creativity, provide a group of techniques for teaching creative problem solving. According to Sternberg (2003b), using techniques like those proposed requires that teacher "decide for creativity" (p. 119) by incorporating these 21 ideas into their classes:

• Redefine the problem.

• Question and analyze assumptions.

• Do not assume that creative ideas sell themselves. Sell them.

- Encourage idea generation.

- Recognize that knowledge is a double-edged sword and act accordingly.

- Encourage children to identify and surmount obstacles.

- Encourage sensible risk taking.

- Encourage tolerance of ambiguity.

- Help children build self-efficacy.

- Help children find what they love to do.

- Teach children the importance of delaying gratification.

- Model creativity.

- Cross-fertilize ideas.

- Allow time for creative thinking.

- Instruct and assess for creativity.

- Reward creativity.

- Allow mistakes.

- Teach children to take responsibility for both successes and failures.

- Encourage creative collaboration.

- Teach children to imagine things from others' points of view.

- Maximize person-environment fit (pp. 119–131).

Deciding for creativity can be done in all content areas. A review of articles on instruction for the gifted invariably makes reference to these characteristics. For a compilation of materials related to these terms, consult books and articles (Callahan, 1978; Feldhusen & Treffinger, 1980; Karnes & Collins, 1980; Treffinger et al., 1993) or catalogs put out by various publishers.

Attitudes and Values

A second often-stated goal of gifted programs is "the development of self-understanding, that is, recognizing and using one's abilities, becoming self-directed, appreciating likenesses and differences between one's self and others" (Kaplan, 1979, p. 5). Educators of the gifted accept the principle that the learning of attitudes and values by gifted children follows the same course of development that it follows for the nongifted, except the gifted proceed at an accelerated rate in various domains. Techniques used for the gifted are virtually identical to those used with nongifted children. Thus, many of the conflicting claims about the effectiveness of various techniques with the nongifted can be found in the literature on the gifted. If a teacher is looking for special methods appropriate primarily for the gifted and less appropriate for the nongifted in developing attitudes and values, those methods are unavailable. What teachers must do is select procedures that fit their program's philosophy. The discussion method is commonly employed. The observational method, where teachers model the attitudes and values, is appropriate and frequently overlooked. Significant changes in attitudes or modifications rarely occur as a result of random, discontinuous lessons. The classroom has to demonstrate consistently that the desired attitudes are valued.

Many of the procedures referred to in the literature on developing attitudes in gifted children are modeled after Drews' (1964, 1972) pioneering work. She advocated enabling children to explore their capabilities and values and come in contact with role models, either vicariously through print or film or directly through personal contact. Another technique for increasing self-understanding is boundary-breaking questions (Sisk, 1982). The idea is to give children an opportunity to think about themselves and others in an intuitive manner in a small-group discussion. Students sit in a circle, a question is stated, and everyone takes turns answering it. Students may decline to respond, or pass. The following are examples of boundary-breaking questions: "If you had one hour of free time, how would you spend that time?" (p. 4); "If you could change one thing about yourself, what would that be?" (p. 5). The technique is also useful for beginning lessons and units.

While these techniques are appealing and involving to children and teachers, their indiscriminate use has been interpreted as fun and games and inappropriately reserved for the gifted alone. Renzulli (1977) has argued that many of these techniques are necessary prerequisites to developing independent learners, but teaching should move on toward that goal. Teachers of the gifted need to be aware that regular educators, especially in middle school and later, take a dim view of activities that appear irrelevant to the regular curriculum and reserved for the gifted students only (Sapon-Shevin, 1996). Teachers of the gifted are advised to fashion exercises so that they deal more directly with content-related values and attitudes, thus, lending credence and power to Renzulli's argument.

Research Skills and Independent Study Skills

A third often-stated goal of gifted education is mastery of research skills and independent study skills. Obviously, these two are interrelated. Research skills may be viewed as being generic skills or as being skills tied to particular kinds of research, such as historical research, descriptive research, and experimental research. Interestingly, generic research skills may also be viewed as prerequisites to the teacher's use of general methods, such as discovery and independent study.

Generic research skills are information-gathering and information-presenting skills. Examples of the former are note taking, outlining, interviewing, conducting experiments, and library usage. Information-presenting skills are report writing, audiovisual presentations, and debating. A search of ERIC will yield many references and publisher's catalogs. Teachers must realize that gifted children need assistance in developing these skills. It is unrealistic to expect otherwise. Students and teachers are likely to develop distaste for independent projects unless sufficient preparation has been undertaken (Burns, 1990; Doherty & Evans, 1981; Hawkes et al., 1994; Rogge, 1970). However, not all of these skills need to be mastered before students can pursue topics on their own.

The conduct of independent study is advocated in the Schoolwide Enrichment Model and the Self-Directed Learning System, both of which were discussed in Chapter 8. Teachers often report difficulty implementing independent study in association with the curriculum. One approach uses three successive phases—teacher-led, independent study, and summary—to teach independent study skills in conjunction with predetermined units of instruction (Doherty & Evans, 1981). Students select from three possible units, such as optics, the future, and etymology, which are to be studied for 10–15 weeks. During the teacher-led phase, children are introduced to the topic through exploratory training exercises based on a cache of techniques (see this chapter) and Taylor's ideas (see Chapter 8). Learning centers and simulations are methods used to teach for content and affective objectives.

In the second phase—independent study—the student chooses an issue-oriented problem in the area of an interest for study. Doherty and Evans (1981) outlined a nine-step procedure to guide children through the process.

1. The student selects a topic that is issue-oriented.

2. The student establishes a schedule.

3. The student develops five or more questions (first objective) to direct the research.

4. The student secures references and seeks sources or raw data.

5. The student researches the topic, collects raw data, and takes notes.

6. The student develops five final objectives using Bloom's Taxonomy.

7. The student has a conference with the teacher, who evaluates the depth of knowledge and the idea production.

8. The student makes a product showing some of his or her new ideas.

9. The student's product is displayed, evaluated with a friend, and examined by an expert. (p. 109)

Most of these steps are self-explanatory, but some need further explanation. Step 2 gets the child organized so that later progress can be assessed. Step 3 defines the parameters of the study. Steps 4 and 5 require some pretraining of students, alluded to earlier. Step 6 asks the student to use the newly acquired knowledge in an original way, using Bloom's Taxonomy as a model (the revised taxonomy would work, as well), and these objectives are used for the evaluation phase. The process ends in the third or summary phase when the student communicates what was learned. This is an important aspect of the process and an inherent part of real-world creative work. Doherty and Evans' (1981) process corresponds significantly with other ideas about independent, self-initiated learning (see Reis & Renzulli, 1992, for a description of how a library media specialist can promote the independent study process, and Dove & Zitkovich, 2003, for an integration of independent study, technology, and group investigations).

Summary

In this section, we organized special methods into three categories that correspond to major outcomes or curricular goals in gifted programs: creative thinking and problem solving, attitudes and values, and research and independent study skills. Pioneering techniques were selected to represent special methods relevant to the attainment of objectives in those areas. Additional methods are available within each area, and more can be found in ERIC and on the Internet.

Several conclusions are warranted. The overwhelming majority of teaching methods reported in the literature on gifted education are variations on creativity and problem-solving themes. Their major characteristics involve suspension of judgment, practice in generating responses, and opportunities for children to consider how they think (metacognition). Special methods for teaching values and attitudes to the gifted are nonexistent. In other words, methods used in general education are appropriate for the gifted. Variations of the discussion method are the most common teaching procedures. The observational method could be used more extensively. Research skills are important prerequisites for children if teachers are going to move toward a personalized approach to learners.

In short, different outcomes call for different instructional procedures. *Recommended Practices in Gifted Education* (Rogers, 2002) is a good source for evidence on what works. Finally, we must make a point that can be overlooked in a presentation on special methods: The use of high-level content and special methods is the best combination for teaching because it grounds the skills in a context associated with meaningful content.

INSTRUCTIONAL MATERIALS AND MEDIA

A major element in a teaching situation is the manner in which information is brought into the lesson. The learner interacts with a book, a program, a videocassette, a computer, a film, or a learning center. The materials are a stable system of information because the message in the material is consistent in each presentation (Rothkopf, 1976).

When a teacher selects materials, a critical teaching decision is made. In a sense, the focus for a lesson subtly switches from the teacher to the material. Much of the credit for success or discredit for failure can be tied to this decision. If the learner cannot comprehend what is presented, and the content is inappropriate for an instructional objective, then the teacher's selection of material is at fault. The materials clearly act as the mediator between the learner and the objectives. Therefore, the teacher should be careful in selecting and preparing materials.

Because there are multiple ways in which the content of a lesson may be structured, the teacher should be familiar with materials and select the appropriate medium for attaining a particular set of objectives. Written materials continue to be the most common mode of communication. Classrooms are typically filled with textbooks, workbooks, and other written materials because the materials are recognized as effective and efficient transmitters of complex bodies of information. Books are useful vehicles for providing detailed information that is not available from the teacher alone, bringing learners into contact with the thoughts of experts in a variety of fields or providing vicarious experiences that are unlikely to be encountered in the student's immediate environment.

Even with all these possibilities, books have only the potential to engage the learner in higher levels of thought. Unless the reader has some commitment to integrating the information into some personally meaningful context, higher level thinking will not occur.

> The most carefully written and edited text will not produce the desired instructional results unless the student acts in a suitable way. The student has complete veto power over the success of written instruction. The student also has the opportunity to extend its scope substantially. (Rothkopf, 1976, p. 94)

Actually, this statement is true for all media. The teacher plays a pivotal role in enhancing the instructional value of any instructional materials. On the other hand, a highly motivated learner can overcome the obstacle of poor materials.

401

The addition of video (television, DVDs, videotapes, and the Internet) into the classroom has been a boon to educators and students. Unfortunately, it can also be a liability when it is used indiscriminately to compensate for bored teachers and unimaginative curricula and teaching. Digital technology can present uncommon or complex experiences that are inaccessible to schools in real time, dynamic information that is invisible to the naked eye, and animated information, and it can repeat those images endlessly. On the other hand, video is not yet able to respond easily to students in real time, foster the practice of new learning and provide meaningful feedback, and respond to individual differences. This situation is changing with the emergence of faster computers.

Computers, in conjunction with video or by themselves, are able to manipulate multiple variables associated with sound principles of instruction. The computer can present content in various formats, monitor student responses, rearrange the instructional sequence on the basis of those data, and provide for practice. With the constant expansion of the Internet, search engines, databases, and digital libraries make access to information easy, inexpensive, and voluminous (Dove & Zitkovich, 2003). Thus, teaching methods that were powerful modes for promoting learning before computers, such as independent study, tutoring, simulation, and discovery, become even more powerful when used with the computer.

In essence, computers have the capability of interacting with learners. Theoretically, there is no limit to what is programmable. Yet, practically speaking, computers are no better than the quality of their designers and programmers. The majority of educational applications are efforts to individualize instruction so that students may learn in a manner that is consistent with their educational histories, rates of learning, and particular abilities (Bunderson & Faust, 1976; Shore et al., 1991). Notice, in this description, that the standard curriculum is maintained within a new technology.

A different perspective on the use of computers was developed by Papert, as discussed earlier. In his view, computers should be used to restructure education in a meaningful way so that learning takes place in terms of a child's personal knowledge of the world. The computer can be programmed to create a microworld, which is governed by programmable rules that approximate the structure of a discipline, such as geometry. The child interacts and plays with the computer, much like the child does in the real, noncomputerized world, by searching, experimenting, and trying to understand problems encountered in this environment. Successes are based upon the child developing better, more efficient procedures for solving problems. While Papert's microworlds have been used with children of varying ages, abilities, and handicaps, relatively little has been done to realize fully his vision (Subhi, 1999).

Evaluating and Preparing Instructional Materials

Commercially sold materials have one common feature: preparation by someone who is unfamiliar with the learners with whom they are to be used.

The abundance of materials is overwhelming. Teachers are bombarded with claims from publishers, both through the mail and at professional meetings. Teachers should realize two obvious facts: First, the publisher is selling materials to make money; and, second, rarely have materials been field tested with gifted students (an important exception is the curricular materials developed by the Center for Gifted Education at the College of William and Mary).

The teacher faced with no verifiable information on the quality of commercial materials must make estimates about their potential (Karnes & Collins, 1980). Criteria for screening materials combine questions relevant to the principles of instruction, the reality of classroom teaching, and the principles of a differentiated curriculum. When judging the quality of materials, one should ask the following questions:

1. Do the objectives stated by the publisher suit your programs, goals, and objectives? Look beyond the claims.

2. Is the material to be used singly, in small groups, or in large groups?

3. Is the material consistent with the range of developmental levels and backgrounds?

4. Is the material highly structured and sequenced?

5. Is there provision or suggestion for diagnostic testing, assessment, and evaluation?

6. Is the material adaptable to changing needs and consistent with your teaching style?

7. Are there suggestions for teaching that are consistent with your knowledge of general methods?

8. Is teacher preparation time reduced enough to justify purchase? Are they renewable materials, are the graphics highly motivating, and is there a list of resources?

9. Can you obtain the material on a trial basis?

10. Is the material truly different from what you have, or can you use the ideas in the material without purchasing it?

While these questions are guides to selecting materials for the gifted, they parallel those asked by general educators.

After examining materials, a teacher may find that they are inappropriate or too costly. In this situation, the teacher must create new materials, adapt other materials, or restructure existent materials into a new instructional package.

Adapting Materials

The adaptation of commercial materials is widespread, which is not surprising given that it is unlikely that a set of materials is completely appropriate for any class and few materials have been validated for gifted students. The process of adapting materials involves making them consistent with a program's curricular goals. "One of the primary needs in materials adaptation for the gifted is restructuring the content so as to incorporate concepts, thinking skills, cognitive processes, and other dimensions of learning that are appropriate for gifted students" (Karnes & Collins, 1980, p. 28). Materials should also be modified to conform to sound instructional principles. A teacher can adapt commercial instructional materials in the following ways:

1. Eliminate activities and content not related to the class goals.

2. Design a series of pretests and posttests to determine entry, exit, and acceleration points (diagnostic testing).

3. Change the recommended teaching methods, including lecture, discussion, and so forth, to meet student preferences (selecting the method).

4. Alter the recommended teaching sequence in accord with three questions: Do the skills and knowledge treated as more complex in the materials deserve that label? Is there a way to provide for large "try-out" jumps to higher levels to see if lower level material is already known? Is unnecessary repetition eliminated?

5. Differentiate between teacher-led and student-led activities.

6. Add resources, such as readings, films, and people, to broaden content.

7. Select materials that are typically geared for older learners and modify them for younger students. Special attention should be given to the location of prerequisite learning, which may be missing in younger students.

8. Include activities that lead to the development of skills for self-directed learning, higher order thinking, and creativity.

9. Make provision for sufficient practice.

10. Make provisions, other than tests, for evidence of student learning that include a full range of expressive behaviors, such as written reports, slides, newspaper articles, poems, pictures, essays, plays, and tutoring others.

These practices for adapting materials are appropriate for large and small units of instruction.

Creating Materials

The creation of instructional materials from nothing but the teacher's mind is an arduous task. The amount of time a teacher has available for the task is an important variable. Before beginning, the teacher should be sure that other materials are not available. This information can be found in journals and texts, publisher's catalogs, and on the Internet.

Designing a General Unit

Developing a unit is really devising a pattern through which learners may move toward some specified objective. The reason for the unit is furthering learning, not restricting it. The curricular pattern is never perfect for any learner and should not be reified. Teachers must be ready to let the child move beyond any point in the pattern. The more appropriate the curriculum is for a topic and a group of students, the more learning will take place and the less adjustment will be needed.

The erecting of a curricular pattern follows two rules. The primary rule is to teach from known to unknown from the students' perspective. A subsidiary, or clarifying, rule is to proceed from the concrete (actual experience) to the abstract. The progression from known to unknown is especially important if one is to avoid repetition and promote the transfer of content and skills acquired in one unit to another unit. Teachers need to be particularly alert to children applying apparently unrelated learning, as far as the teacher can see, to a new setting. Problems with repetition can be related to the phenomenon of a student being able to relate something learned in one place to another, as well as the surprising ability of some children to skip or jump over sections of a curricular pattern.

Many teachers hunt for available resources and work backward by selecting parts to use and devising a suitable rationale for a unit. This reverse sequence is a good survival mechanism; but, if it becomes the typical mode of unit construction, it works against comprehensive programming. The procedure we recommend is a rational, deductive sequence:

1. *Select a topic.* The topic may be administratively designated, teacher-selected, or student-selected. The purpose may be to teach a content area or teach an authentic activity related to adult roles.

405

2. *Write a rationale.* Reasons for selecting a unit should be made evident. The reasons should tie into students' short-term needs and long-range curricular goals. A strong rationale is the first line of defense for curricular innovation. It is wise to write a rationale because most teachers and administrators have not clearly thought out their reasons for school practices.

3. *Generate content objectives.* Using a brainstorming approach, list all that a child should learn from the unit. Some items may be unrealistic. Remember, objectives are attainable; goals are not.

4. *Rank the objectives.* The objectives should be organized into a useable format. Rank the objectives on a continuum from "all must learn," to "some should learn," to "few could learn" (Coleman, 1985a).

5. *Establish the priorities.* Within each level, it should be possible to select the key objectives necessary for performing at that level. From the remaining objectives, place them in a concrete-to-abstract sequence and fit some objectives near others of similar complexity. The latter group of objectives is suitable for providing enrichment.

6. *Specify the processes.* List the skills that are important to learning the content and other similar content. The skills may be those already mastered in other units or those needing further development. Some of the skills needing development may be related to content, while others may be related to a general model (assuming one has been adopted). Select skills to develop that logically fit content objectives. Avoid teaching skills in isolation. This can be done in specialized units.

7. *Decide on assessment and evaluation.* How will the students' knowledge and skills be tested? Is it assumed that all students need identical experiences, at least in the beginning of the unit? Is the evaluation going to be through tests, work sample-like tasks, or teacher judgment? The idea is to select points for judging student progress. Look for key points where content and skills converge, which are appropriate spots to ask successful students if they wish to accelerate in the unit.

8. *Conduct a resource search.* Look for resources, including people, films, books, and published curricula, that fit the unit. Some of this information may influence you to reorganize your plans. Available guides may be used as much as you wish. In the absence of empirical evidence or curricula on the topic, teachers should trust their judgment. Armed with a completed outline of the curriculum, the teacher is ready to make instructional decisions. Whenever possible, it is wise to have

several teachers work on a unit. In any case, the time devoted to a curricular unit is never wasted because it can be improved the next time.

Creating a Problem-Based Unit

This kind of unit fits within the Problem-Based Learning System described in Chapter 8. We include it here because the principles for forming units of this type are quite different from those just described. In this approach, the typical assumptions about classroom interactions and the relationship between students and the teacher are changed.

Stepien and Pyke (1997) described how to design a PBL unit. The centerpiece is an ill-structured problem "that (a) contains significant content, (b) fits curriculum outcomes for a specific course or program, (c) is appropriate for the targeted audience, and (d) can be managed effectively by students in the time available" (Stepien & Pyke, p. 399). Once the problem is set, the teacher has to build a "problem map" in order to plot out the "flow of activity." Students must then wrestle with this problem in order to comprehend the issues implicit in the problem, search out relevant knowledge, and construct possible solutions. Designing a PBL unit is a complex procedure, and we urge readers to consult Stepien and Pyke's work for more specific information.

Summary

Teachers are faced with the task of selecting from published materials, making new materials, or adapting existing materials. Few materials have been field-tested for the gifted; therefore, it is necessary to evaluate materials. When a teacher cannot find suitable materials for a class or cannot afford new materials, old materials must be adapted, new materials must be assembled, or new units must be constructed.

CONCLUSION

The chapter began with an exposition on teaching and decision making, with special attention paid to teaching diverse learners. There are two types of decisions: planning and action. These decisions take the form of conditional statements: If this is happening or desired in a lesson, then do this. Planning decisions occur in the empty classroom and are more important than action decisions because they build the structure for instruction. Action decisions are spontaneous readjustments to student needs during instruction. Planning decisions aid in decision making by following a general sequence of content, diagnosis, evaluation, and feedback; choosing among various methods; review and practice; forming groups and a final plan; and teaching. The decisions are best characterized as eclecticism with a purpose. It is important for teachers of the gifted to be wary of teaching their students to be mechanical, rote problem solvers instead of spontaneous, meaningful problem solvers.

The general methods (lecture, discussion, tutoring, simulation and gaming, discovery, recitation, observation, independent study, and materials-driven) are frequently recast into the form of specialized methods for the gifted. Just as there is limited evidence to support the effectiveness of any one general method over others for teaching the gifted, there is also limited evidence that special methods advocated for the gifted are effective. Recognizing these findings and the special goals of gifted programs, the techniques that are useful in most teaching situations are differentiation, curriculum compacting, a cache of techniques, and conducting discussions. There are also special methods designed to teach for the often-stated goals of creativity and problem solving, attitudes about self and social responsibility, and research and study skills.

A major element in teaching is how information is brought into a lesson. Instructional materials usually perform this function. If, in some instances, appropriate materials cannot be found, decisions must be made about creating and adapting materials, as well as designing units of instruction in a typical fashion or using a problem-based learning format.

FOR **DISCUSSION**

1. Discuss the difference between planning and action decisions and their relative merit in teaching the gifted.

2. Differentiation can occur through modifying content, process, product, or affect in a teaching situation. In a social studies lesson on tariffs and trade or migration from farms to cities, which would you be most likely to modify? Explain your choices.

3. Some teachers adapt existing materials and others create their own. On what basis would you decide to adapt or create? Defend your decision.

4. Defend or refute: Teaching gifted children is easier than teaching other children because they learn more readily.

5. If you had the power to institute only two changes for gifted children in the schools, what would they be? Defend your answer.

REFERENCES

Abraham, W. (1977). Parents talk. In National/State Leadership Training Institute on the Gifted and the Talented, *Gifts, talents, and the very young* (pp. 27–42). Ventura, CA: Office of the Superintendent of Public Schools.

Achter, J., Lubinski, D., & Benbow, C. (1996). Multipotentiality among the intellectually gifted: "It was never there and already it's vanishing." *Journal of Counseling Psychology, 43,* 65–76.

Adams, C. (1996). Gifted girls and science: Revisiting the issues. *Journal of Secondary Gifted Education, 7,* 447–458.

Albert, R. S. (1980). Exceptional gifted boys and their parents. *Gifted Child Quarterly, 24,* 174–179.

Albert, R., & Runco, M. (1986). The achievement of eminence: A model based on a longitudinal study of exceptionally gifted boys and their families. In R. Sternberg & J. Davidson (Eds.), *Conceptions of giftedness* (pp. 332–357). New York: Cambridge University Press.

Alvino, J., McDonnel, R., & Richert, S. (1981). National survey of identification practices in gifted and talented education. *Exceptional Children, 48,* 124–132.

Amabile, T. M. (1983). *The social psychology of creativity.* New York: Springer-Verlag.

American Association for Gifted Children (AAGC). (1978). *On being gifted.* New York: Walker.

Anastasi, A. (1976). *Psychological testing* (4th ed.). London: Collier-MacMillan.

Anastasi, A., & Schaefer, C. E. (1969). Biographical correlates of artistic and literary creativity. *Journal of Applied Psychology, 53,* 267–283.

Anastasi, A., & Urbina, S. (1997). *Psychological testing* (7th ed.). Upper Saddle River, NJ: Prentice Hall.

Anderson, L., & Krathwohl, D. (2001). *A taxonomy for learning, teaching, and assessing: A revision of Bloom's taxonomy of educational objectives.* New York: Longman.

Arieti, S. (1981, March). *Simple but undervalued: Attitudes and conditions fostering creativity.* Paper presented at the National/State Training Institute on the Gifted and Talented Second National Conference on Creativity, Memphis, TN.

Arnold, K. (1993a). The Illinois valedictorian project: Early adult careers of academically talented female high school students. In R. F. Subotnik & K. D. Arnold (Eds.), *Beyond Terman: Longitudinal studies in contemporary gifted education.* Norwood, NJ: Ablex.

Arnold, K. (1993b). The lives of female high school valedictorians in the 1980s. In K. D. Hulbert & D. T. Schuster (Eds.), *Women's lives through time: Educated American women of the 20th century.* San Francisco: Jossey-Bass.

Assouline, S., & Lupkowski-Shoplik, A. (1997). Talent searches: A model for the discovery and development of academic talent. In N. Colangelo & G. A. Davis (Eds.), *Handbook of gifted education* (2nd ed., pp. 170–179). Boston: Allyn and Bacon.

Assouline, S., & Lupkowski-Shoplik, A. (2003). *Developing mathematical talent: A guide for challenging and educating gifted students.* Waco, TX: Prufrock Press.

Aulls, M. (1998). Contributions of classroom discourse to what content students learn during curriculum enactment. *Journal of Educational Psychology, 90,* 56–69.

Austin, A. B., & Draper, D. C. (1981). Peer relationship of the academically gifted: A review. *Gifted Child Quarterly, 25,* 129–133.

Ausubel, D. P., & Robinson, F. G. (1969). *School learning: An introduction to educational psychology.* New York: Holt, Rinehart, & Winston.

Baca, L. (1980). Issues in the education of culturally diverse exceptional children. *Exceptional Children, 46,* 583.

Bachtold, L. M. (1976). Personality characteristics of women of distinction. *Psychology of Women Quarterly, 1,* 70–78.

Bachtold, L. M. (1978). Reflections of gifted learners. *Gifted Child Quarterly, 22,* 116–124.

Bachtold, L. (1980). Speculation on a theory of creativity: A physiological basis. *Perceptual and Motor Skills, 50,* 699–702.

Bachtold, L. M., & Werner, E. E. (1970). Personality profiles of gifted women: Psychologists. *American Psychologist, 25,* 234–243.

Bachtold, L. M., & Werner, E. E. (1972). Personality characteristics of women scientists. *Psychological Reports, 32,* 391–396.

Bachtold, L. M., & Werner, E. E. (1973). Characteristics of creative women. *Perceptual and Motor Skills, 33,* 391–396.

Baer, J. (1994). Performance assessments of creativity: Do they have long-term stability? *Roeper Review, 17,* 7–11.

Baird, L. J. (1972). The Torrance Tests of Creative Thinking. In O. K. Buros (Ed.), *The seventh mental measurement yearbook* (pp. 836–838). Highland Park, NJ: Gryphon Press.

Baker, J., Bridger, R., & Evans, K. (1998). Models of underachievement among gifted preadolescents: The role of personal, family, and school factors. *Gifted Child Quarterly, 42,* 5–15.

Baldwin, A. Y. (1977). Tests can underpredict: A case study. *Phi Delta Kappan, 58,* 620–621.

Baldwin, A. (1993). Teachers of the gifted. In K. A. Heller, F. J. Mönks, & A. H. Passow (Eds.), *International handbook of research and development of giftedness and talented* (pp. 621–629). New York: Paradigm.

Ball, O., & Torrance, E. P. (1980). Effectiveness of new materials developed for training and streamlined scoring of the Torrance Test of Creative Thinking, Figural A and B forms. *Journal of Creative Behavior, 4,* 199–202.

Bandura, A. (1986). *Social foundation of thought and action: A social cognitive theory.* Englewood Cliffs, NJ: Prentice Hall.

Banks, J. A. (1994). Multicultural education: Historical development, dimensions, and practices. In L. D. Darling-Hammond (Ed.), *Review of research in education* (pp. 3–49). Washington, DC: American Educational Research Association.

Banks, J. A., & Banks, C. A. (Eds.). (1993). *Multicultural education: Issues and perspectives* (2nd ed.). Boston: Allyn and Bacon.

Barbe, W. B. (1963). *One in a thousand.* Columbus, OH: Department of Public Instruction.

Barr, D. (1990). A solution in search of a problem: The role of technology in educational reform. *Journal for the Education of the Gifted, 14,* 79–95.

Barren, F. (1968). The measurement of creativity. In D. K. Whitla (Ed.), *Handbook of measurement and assessment in behavioral sciences* (pp. 338–366). Reading, MA: Addison-Wesley.

Baum, S. M., & Olenchak, F. R. (2002). The alphabet children: GT, ADHD, and more. *Exceptionality, 10*(2), 77–91.

Baum, S., Emerick, L. J., Herman, G. N., & Dixon, J. (1989). Identification programs and enrichment strategies for gifted learning disabled youth. *Roeper Review, 12*, 48–53.

Bayley, N. (1970). Development of mental abilities. In P. H. Mussen (Ed.), *Manual of child psychology* (3rd ed., pp. 163–209). New York: Wiley.

Bellack, A. A. (1966). *The language of the classroom.* New York: Teachers College Press.

Benbow, C. P., & Lubinski, D. (1994). Individual differences among the gifted: How can we best meet their educational needs? In N. Colangelo, S. G. Assouline, & D. L. Ambrosen (Eds.), *Talent development II: Proceedings from the 1993 Henry B. and Jocelyn Wallace National Research Symposium on Talent Development* (pp. 83–100). Dayton: Ohio Psychology Press.

Benbow, C. P., & Lubinski, D. (1997). Intellectually talented children: How can we best meet their needs? In N. Colangelo & G. A. Davis (Eds.), *Handbook of gifted education* (2nd ed., pp. 155–169). Boston: Allyn and Bacon.

Benbow, C. P., & Stanley, J. C. (1980). Intellectually talented students: Family profiles. *Gifted Child Quarterly, 24*, 119–122.

Benbow, C., & Stanley, J. (1983). *Academic precocity: Aspects of its development.* Baltimore, MD: Johns Hopkins University Press.

Bennett, G. K., Seashore, H. G., & Wesman, A. G. (1990). *The differential aptitudes test* (5th ed.). San Antonio, TX: Psychological Corporation.

Berliner, D. C., & Gage, N. L. (1976). The psychology of teaching methods. In N. L. Gage (Ed.), *The psychology of teaching methods* (pp. 1–20). Chicago: University of Chicago Press.

Bernal, E. M. (2002). Three ways to achieve a more equitable representation of culturally and linguistically different students in GT programs. *Roeper Review, 24*, 82–88.

Bernal, E. M., Jr. (1979). The education of the culturally different gifted. In A. H. Passow (Ed.), *The gifted and the talented: Their education and development* (Vol. 78, pp. 395–400). Chicago: University of Chicago Press.

Bernal, E. M., Jr., & Reyna, J. (1975). Analysis and identification of giftedness in Mexican-American children: A pilot study. In B. O. Boston (Ed.), *A resource manual of information on educating the gifted and talented* (pp. 53–60). Reston, VA: Council for Exceptional Children.

Bessemer, S. P., & Treffinger, D. J. (1981). Analysis of creative products: Review and syntheses. *Journal of Creative Behavior, 15*, 158–178.

Betts, G. (1988). The autonomous learner model. In J. S. Renzulli & S. M. Reis (Eds.), *Systems and models for developing programs for the gifted and talented* (pp. 134–156). Mansfield Center, CT: Creative Learning Press.

Binet, A., & Simon, T. (1905). Methodes nouvelles pour le diagnostique du niveau intellectuel des anormaux. *L'annee Psychologique, 11*, 245–336.

Bishop, W. E. (1968). Successful teachers of the gifted. *Exceptional Children, 34*, 317–325.

Blake, K. (1981). *Educating exceptional pupils.* Reading, MA: Addison-Wesley.

Blaubergs, M. S. (1978). Overcoming the sexist barriers to gifted women's achievement. In National/State Leadership Training Institute of the Gifted and the Talented, *Advantage: Disadvantaged gifted* (pp. 7–39). Ventura, CA: Office of the Superintendent of Public Schools.

Bloom, B. S. (Ed.). (1956). *Taxonomy of education objectives: The classification of educational goals. Handbook I: Cognitive domain*. New York: Longmans Green.

Bloom, B. S. (1982). The role of gifts and markers in the development of talent. *Exceptional Children, 48,* 510–522.

Bloom, B. S. (Ed.). (1985). *Developing talent in young people*. New York: Ballantine.

Bloom, B. S., & Sosniak, L. A. (1981). Talent development vs. schooling. *Educational Leadership, 39*(2), 86–94.

Bondi, A. M., & Koubik, N. A. (1980). Ask . . . and you shall conceive. *Journal of Creative Behavior, 14,* 235–241.

Boodoo, G., Bradley, C., Frontera, R., Pitts, J., & Wright, L. (1989). A survey of procedures used for identifying gifted learning disabled children. *Gifted Child Quarterly, 33,* 110–114.

Borg, W. R. (1964). *The evaluation of ability grouping* (Cooperative Research Project No. 577). Logan: Utah State University.

Borg, W., Gall, M., & Gall, J. (1996). *Educational research: An introduction* (6th ed.). White Plains, NY: Longman.

Borland, J. (1978). Teacher identification of the gifted: A new look. *Journal for the Education of the Gifted, 2,* 22–32.

Borland, J. H. (1989). *Planning and implementing programs for the gifted.* New York: Teachers College Press.

Borland, J. (1996). Gifted education and the threat of irrelevance. *Journal for the Education of the Gifted, 19,* 129–147.

Borland, J. (1997). Evaluating gifted programs. In N. Colangelo & G. A. Davis (Eds.), *Handbook of gifted education* (2nd ed., pp. 253–268). Boston: Allyn and Bacon.

Borland, J. (2003). Evaluating gifted programs: A broader perspective. In N. Colangelo & G. A. Davis (Eds.), *Handbook of gifted education* (3rd ed., pp. 293–310). Boston: Pearson Education.

Borland, J., Schnur, R., & Wright, L. (2000). Economically disadvantaged children in a school for the academically gifted: A postpositivistic inquiry into individual and family adjustment. *Gifted Child Quarterly, 44,* 13–32.

Borland, J., & Wright, L. (1994). Identifying young, potentially gifted, economically disadvantaged students. *Gifted Child Quarterly, 38,* 164–171.

Bostick, L. (1980). Parent advocacy. In National/State Leadership Training Institute on the Gifted and the Talented, *Educating the preschool/primary gifted and talented* (pp. 183–194). Ventura, CA: Office of the Superintendent of Public Schools.

Boyce, L., VanTassel-Baska, J., Burruss, J., Sher, B., & Johnson, D. (1997). A problem-based curriculum: Parallel learning opportunities for students and teachers. *Journal for the Education of the Gifted, 20,* 363–379.

Brandwein, P. (1955). *The gifted student as future scientist*. New York: Harcourt-Brace.

Brody, L. E., & Mills, C. J. (1997). Gifted children with learning disabilities: A review of the issues. *Journal of Learning Disabilities, 30,* 282–286.

Bronfenbrenner, U. (1979). *The ecology of human development.* Cambridge, MA: Harvard University Press.

Bronfenbrenner, U. (1986). Ecology of the family as a context for human development: Research perspectives. *Developmental Psychology, 22,* 723–742.

Bronfenbrenner, U. (1994). Ecological models of human development. In T. Husen & T. N. Postlethwaite (Eds.), *International encyclopedia of education* (2nd ed., Vol. 3, pp. 1643–1647). Oxford: Pergamon Press/Elsevier Science.

Bronowski, J. (1973). *The ascent of man*. Boston: Little, Brown.

Brown, L. (1993). *The new shorter Oxford English dictionary* (Vol. 1). Oxford, England: Oxford University Press and Clarendon Press.

Brown, L., Sherbenou, R. J., & Johnsen, S. K. (1997). *Test of nonverval intelligence–3rd ed. (TONI-3)*. Austin, TX: PRO-ED.

Brown, M. (1979). Cognitive development and the learning of mathematics. In A. Floyd (Ed.), *Cognitive development in the school years* (pp. 351–373). New York: Wiley.

Bruch, C. B. (1971). Modification of procedures for identification of the disadvantaged gifted. *Gifted Child Quarterly, 15,* 267–272.

Brunelle, E. (Ed.). (1979). Apollo and Dionysius. *Journal of Creative Behavior, 5*(1), 37–43.

Bruner, J. S. (1966). *Toward a theory of instruction*. Cambridge, MA: Belknap.

Bruner, J. S. (1968). *On knowing*. New York: Atheneum.

Bull, K. S., & Davis, G. A. (1980). Evaluating creative potential using the statement of past creative activities. *Journal of Creative Behavior, 14,* 249–257.

Bullough, V., Bullough, B., & Mauro, M. (1981). History and creativity: Research problems and some possible solutions. *Journal of Creative Behavior, 15,* 102–116.

Bunderson, C. V., & Faust, G. W. (1976). Programmed and computer-assisted instruction. In N. L. Gage (Ed.), *The psychology of teaching methods* (pp. 44–90). Chicago: University of Chicago Press.

Burks, B. S., Jensen, D. W., & Terman, L. (1930). *The promise of youth: Follow–up studies of a thousand gifted children: Genetic studies of genius, Vol. 3*. Stanford, CA: Stanford University Press.

Burns, D. (1990). The effects of group training activities on students' initiation of creative investigations. *Gifted Child Quarterly, 34,* 31–36.

Busse, T. V., & Mansfield, R. S. (1980). Theories of the creative process. *Journal of Creative Behavior, 14,* 91–103.

Callahan, C. M. (1978). *Developing creativity in the gifted and talented*. Reston, VA: Council for Exceptional Children.

Callahan, C. (1993). Evaluation programs and procedures for gifted education: International problems and solutions. In K. A. Heller, F. J. Mönks, & A. H. Passow (Eds.), *International handbook of research and development of giftedness and talented* (pp. 605–618). New York: Paradigm.

Callahan, C. (1996). A critical self-study of gifted education: Healthy practice, necessary evil, or sedition? *Journal for the Education of the Gifted, 19,* 148–163.

Callahan, C. M., Cunningham, C. M., & Plucker, J. A. (1994). Foundations for the future: The socio-emotional development of gifted, adolescent women. *Roeper Review, 17,* 99–105.

Callahan, C. M., Tomlinson, C. A., & Pizatt, P. M. (Eds.). (1996). *Contexts for promise: Noteworthy practices and innovations in the identification of gifted students*. Charlottesville: National Research Center on the Gifted and Talented, University of Virginia.

Cardwell, P. (1995). Role-playing games and the gifted student. *Gifted Educational International, 11,* 39–46.

413

Casserly, P. L. (1979). Helping able young women take math and science seriously in school. In N. Colangelo & R. T. Zaffrann (Eds.), *New voices in counseling the gifted* (pp. 346–369). Dubuque, IA: Kendall/Hunt.

Cassidy, J. (1981). Parental involvement in gifted programs. *Journal for the Education of the Gifted, 4,* 284–287.

Castille, L. (1998). The effect of analogy instruction on young children's metaphor comprehension. *Roeper Review, 21,* 27–31.

Cattell, R. B. (1950). *Handbook for the individual of group Culture Fair Intelligence Test. Scale I.* Champaign, IL: I.P.A.T.

Center for Talent Development, Northwestern University. (2004). *Recommended planning and resource guide, Midwest Talent Search.* Evanston, IL: Author.

Chambers, J. A., Barren, F., & Sprecher, J. W. (1980). Identifying gifted Mexican-American students. *Gifted Child Quarterly, 24,* 123–128.

Chan, D. W. (2004). Social coping and psychological distress among Chinese gifted students in Hong Kong. *Gifted Child Quarterly, 48,* 30–41.

Ciha, T. E., Harris, R., Hoffman, C., & Potter, M. (1974). Parents as identifiers of giftedness: Ignored but accurate. *Talents and Gifts, 18,* 191–195.

Clark, B. (1988). *Growing up gifted: Developing the potential of children at home and at school* (3rd ed.). Columbus, OH: Merrill.

Clark, B. (1992). *Growing up gifted: Developing the potential of children at home and at school* (4th ed.). Columbus, OH: Merrill.

Clark, B. (1997). *Growing up gifted: Developing the potential of children at home and at school* (5th ed.). Columbus, OH: Merrill.

Clark, G., & Zimmerman, E. (1987). Tending the special spark: Accelerated and enriched curricula for highly talented art students. *Roeper Review, 10,* 10–17.

Clark, G., & Zimmerman, E. (2001). Identifying artistically talented students in four rural communities in the United States. *Gifted Child Quarterly, 45,* 104–114.

Clasen, D., & Clasen, R. (1997). Mentoring: A time-honored option for education of the gifted and talented. In N. Colangelo & G. A. Davis (Eds.), *Handbook of gifted education* (2nd ed., pp. 218–229). Boston: Allyn and Bacon.

Clasen, D. R., & Clasen, R. E. (2003). Mentoring the gifted and talented. In N. Colangelo & G. A. Davis (Eds.), *Handbook of gifted education* (3rd ed., pp. 254–267). Boston: Pearson Education.

Cohn, S. J. (1979). Acceleration and enrichment: Drawing the base lines for further study. In W. C. George, S. J. Cohn, & J. C. Stanley (Eds.), *Educating the gifted: Acceleration and enrichment* (pp. 3–12). Baltimore, MD: Johns Hopkins University Press.

Cohen, L. M., & Frydenberg, E. (1996). *Coping for capable kids: Strategies for parents, teachers, and students.* Waco, TX: Prufrock Press.

Colangelo, N. (1991). Counseling gifted students. In N. Colangelo & G. A. Davis (Eds.), *Handbook of gifted education* (pp. 273–284). Boston: Allyn and Bacon.

Colangelo, N. (1997). Counseling gifted students: Issues and practices. In N. Colangelo & G. A. Davis (Eds.), *Handbook of gifted education* (2nd ed., pp. 353–365). Boston: Allyn and Bacon.

Colangelo, N. (2000). Counseling gifted students. In K. A. Heller, F. J. Mönks, R. J. Sternberg, & R. F. Subotnik (Eds.), *International handbook of giftedness and talent* (2nd ed., pp. 595–607). Amsterdam: Elsevier.

Colangelo, N. (2003). Counseling gifted students. In N. Colangelo & G. A. Davis (Eds.), *Handbook of gifted education* (3rd ed., pp. 373–387). Boston: Allyn and Bacon.

Colangelo, N., Assouline, S., & Gross, M. (2004). *A nation deceived: How schools hold back America's brightest students.* Iowa City, IA: The Connie Belin and Jacqueline Blank International Center for Gifted Education and Talent Development.

Coleman, J. M. (1981, December). *Self-concept and the gifted classroom: The role of social comparisons.* Paper presented at the Council for Exceptional Children/The Association for the Gifted National Conference on the Gifted and Talented Child, Orlando, FL.

Coleman, L. J. (1975). *Interpersonal evaluation of the gifted associated with the sociometric structure of special classes.* Unpublished doctoral dissertation, Kent State University, Kent, OH.

Coleman, L. J. (1976, February). *A systematic procedure for school districts to use for identifying gifted/talented children from varying cultural settings.* Paper presented at the Regional Conference on Culturally Different Gifted, Nashville, TN.

Coleman, L. J. (1977). An evaluation of seven techniques for evaluating the comprehensibility of instructional materials and recommendations for their use. *Education and Training of the Mentally Retarded, 12,* 339–344.

Coleman, L. J. (1981). Reducing reading levels: Simplify the verb. *Teaching Exceptional Children, 13,* 62–65.

Coleman, L. J. (1983, May/June). An unsolved mystery: Interpreting grade scores or how come my seven year old scored at the sixth grade level and she can't do fourth grade work. *G/C/T, 28,* 24–27.

Coleman, L. (1985a). *Schooling the gifted.* Menlo Park, CA: Addison-Wesley.

Coleman, L. J. (1985b, April). *Using a decision-making protocol to improve instructional prescriptions for the gifted.* Paper presented at the annual meeting of the Council for Exceptional Children, Anaheim, CA.

Coleman, L. J. (1991). The invisible world of professional practical knowledge of a teacher of the gifted. *Journal for the Education of the Gifted, 14,* 151–165.

Coleman, L. J. (1992). The cognitive map of a master teacher of the gifted conducting discussions with gifted children. *Exceptionality, 3,* 1–16.

Coleman, L. (1994). Portfolio assessment: A key to identifying hidden talents and empowering teachers of young children. *Gifted Child Quarterly, 38,* 65–69.

Coleman, L. (1995). The power of specialized educational environments in the development of giftedness: The need for research on social context. *Gifted Child Quarterly, 38,* 171–176.

Coleman, L. J. (Ed.). (1996). Critical appraisals of gifted education [Special issue]. *Journal for the Education of the Gifted, 19*(2).

Coleman, L. J. (1997). Studying ordinary events in a field devoted to the extraordinary. *Peabody Journal of Education, 72,* 117–132.

Coleman, L. J. (2003.) Gifted child pedagogy: Meaningful chimera? *Roeper Review, 25,* 163–165.

Coleman, L., & Cross, T. L. (1988). Is being gifted a social handicap? *Journal for the Education of the Gifted, 11,* 41–56.

Coleman, L. J., & Cross, T. L. (1992). Gifted high school students' advice to science teachers. *Gifted Child Today, 15*(5), 25–26.

Coleman, L. J., & Cross, T. L. (1993). Relationships between programming practices and outcomes in a summer residential school for gifted adolescents. *Journal for the Education of the Gifted, 16,* 420–441.

Coleman, L. J., & Cross, T. L. (2000). Social-emotional development and the personal experience of giftedness. In K. A. Heller, F. J. Mönks, R. J. Sternberg, & R. F.

415

Subotnik (Eds.), *International handbook of giftedness and talent* (2nd ed., pp. 203–212). Amsterdam: Elsevier.

Coleman, L. J., & Cross, T. L. (2001). *Being gifted in school: An introduction to development, guidance, and teaching.* Waco, TX: Prufrock Press.

Coleman, L., & Gallagher, S. (1997). Notes from the editor's desk. *Journal for the Education of the Gifted, 20,* 329–331.

Coleman, L. J., & Sanders, M. D. (1993). Social needs, social choices, and masking one's giftedness. *Journal of Secondary Gifted Education, 5,* 22–25.

Coleman, L., Sanders, M., & Cross, T. L. (1997). Perennial debates and tacit assumptions in the education of gifted children. *Gifted Child Quarterly, 41,* 1–11.

Cooke, G. (1976). Peer nominations: A useful tool for identifying gifted and talented students. *Talents and Gifts, 19*(1), 3.

Cooke, G., & Baldwin, A. Y. (1979). Unique needs of a special population. In A. H. Passow (Ed.), *The gifted and the talented: Their education and development* (Vol. 78, pp. 388–394). Chicago: University of Chicago Press.

Cornell, D. (1984). *Families of gifted children.* Ann Arbor, MI: UMI Research Press.

Cornell, D., Callahan, C., Bassin, L., & Ramsay, S. (1991). Affective development in accelerated students. In W. T. Southern & E. D. Jones (Eds.), *The academic acceleration of gifted children* (pp. 74–101). New York: Teachers College Press.

Cornish, R. L. (1968). Parents', pupils', and teacher perception of a gifted child's ability. *Gifted Child Quarterly, 12,* 14–17.

Cox, C. M. (1926). *The early mental traits of three hundred geniuses: Genetic studies of genius, Vol. II.* Stanford, CA: Stanford University Press.

Cox, J., Daniel, N., & Boston, B. (1985). *Educating able learners: Programs and promising practices.* Austin: University of Texas Press.

Crockenberg, S. B. (1972). Creativity tests: A boon or boondoggle for education? *Review of Educational Research, 42*(1), 27–45.

Cross, T. (1997a). *Report of the evaluation of the 1996 Governor's Institutes of Vermont.* Unpublished manuscript.

Cross, T. (1997b). Psychological and social aspects of educating gifted students. *Peabody Journal of Education, 72,* 180–200.

Cross, T. L. (2004). *On the social and emotional lives of gifted children: Issues and factors in their psychological development* (2nd ed.). Waco, TX: Prufrock Press.

Cross, T., Coleman, L., & Stewart, R. (1993). The social cognition of gifted adolescents: An exploration of the stigma of giftedness paradigm. *Roeper Review, 16,* 37–40.

Cross, T., Coleman, L., & Stewart, R. (1995). Psychological diversity of gifted adolescents: An exploration of the stigma of giftedness paradigm. *Roeper Review, 16,* 37–40.

Cross, T., Coleman, L., & Terharr-Yonkers, M. (1991). The social cognition of gifted adolescents in schools: Managing the stigma of giftedness. *Journal for the Education of the Gifted, 15,* 44–55.

Cross, T., & Coleman, L. (2005). School-based conception of giftedness. In R. Sternberg & J. Davidson (Eds.), *Conceptions of giftedness* (2nd. ed, pp. 52–63). New York: Cambridge University Press.

Csikszentmihalyi, M. (1996). *Creativity: Flow and psychology of discovery and invention.* New York: HarperCollins.

Csikszentmihalyi, M., & Getzels, J. (1971). Discovery-oriented behavior and the originality of creative products: A study of artists. *Journal of Personality and Social Psychology, 19,* 47–52.

Csikszentmihalyi, M., Rathunde, K., & Whalen, S. (1993). *Talented teenagers: The roots of success and failure*. New York: Cambridge University Press.

CTB/McGraw-Hill. (2003). *California achievement test, sixth edition (CAT/6)*. Monterey, CA: Author.

Dai, D. Y, & Schader, R. (2001). Parents' reasons and motivation for supporting their child's music training. *Roeper Review, 24*, 23–31.

Dai, D. Y, & Schader, R. (2002). Decisions regarding music training: Parental beliefs and values. *Gifted Child Quarterly, 46*, 135–144.

Damiani, V. (1996). The individual family support plan: A tool to assist special populations of gifted learners. *Roeper Review, 18*, 293–297.

Daurio, S. P. (1979). Educational enrichment vs. acceleration: A review of the literature. In W. C. George, S. J. Cohn, & J. C. Stanley (Eds.), *Educating the gifted: Acceleration and enrichment* (pp. 13–63). Baltimore, MD: Johns Hopkins University Press.

Davis, G. A., & Rimm, S. (1979). Identification and counseling of the creatively gifted. In N. Colangelo & R. T. Zaffrann (Eds.), *New voices in counseling the gifted* (pp. 225–336). Dubuque, IA: Kendall/Hunt.

Davis, G., & Rimm, S. (1989). *Education of the gifted and talented*. Englewood Cliffs, NJ: Prentice Hall.

Day Hulbert, K., & Tickton Schuster, D. (1993). *Women's lives through time: Educated American women of the twentieth century*. San Francisco: Jossey-Bass.

de Bono, E. (1970). *Lateral thinking: Creativity step by step*. New York: Harper & Row.

de Bono, E. (1971). *Lateral thinking for measurement*. New York: American Management Association.

DeHaan, R. F., & Wilson, R. C. (1958). Identification of the gifted. In DeHaan et al. (Eds.), *Education for the gifted* (Vol. 57; pp. 166–192). Chicago: University of Chicago Press.

Delcourt, M. (1994). Characteristics of high-level creative productivity: A longitudinal study of students identified by Renzulli's three-ring conception of giftedness. In R. F. Subotnik & K. D. Arnold (Eds.), *Beyond Terman: Contemporary longitudinal studies of giftedness and talent* (pp. 401–426). Norwood, NJ: Ablex.

Delisle, J. (1987). Preventing discipline problems with gifted students. *Teaching Exceptional Children, 19*, 32–38.

Delisle, J. (1992). *Guiding the social and emotional development of youth*. New York: Longman.

Delph, J. L. (1980). How to live successfully with the gifted child. In National/State Leadership Training Institute on the Gifted and the Talented, *Educating the preschool/primary gifted and talented* (pp. 167–182). Ventura, CA: Office of the Superintendent of Public Schools.

Delpit, L. (1988). The silenced dialogue: Power and pedagogy in educating other people's children. *Harvard Educational Review, 58*, 280–298.

Dembinski, R. J., & Mauser, A. J. (1978). Parents of the gifted: Perceptions of psychologists and teachers. *Journal for the Education of the Gifted, 1*, 5–14.

Dettman, D. F., & Colangelo, N. (1980). A functional model for counseling parents of gifted students. *Gifted Child Quarterly, 24*, 158–161.

Derricott, R., & Blyth, A. (1979). Cognitive development: The social dimension. In A. Floyd (Ed.), *Cognitive development in the school years* (pp. 284–316). New York: Wiley.

d'Heurle, A., Mellinger, J., & Hapgood, E. (1959). Personality, intellectual, and achievement patterns in gifted children. *Psychological Monographs, 73*(483), 1–28.

417

Doherty, E., & Evans, L. (1981). Independent study process: They can think, can't they? *Journal for the Education of the Gifted, 4,* 106–111.

Dove, M., & Zitkovich, J. (2003). Technology-driven group investigations for gifted elementary student. *Information Technology in Childhood Education Annual,* 223–241.

Drew, P., & Drew, E. (1979). Behavioral contracting for gifted and talented students. In N. Colangelo & R. T. Zaffrann (Eds.), *New voices in counseling the gifted* (pp. 483–489). Dubuque, IA: Kendall/Hunt.

Drews, E. M. (1963). The four faces of able adolescents. *Saturday Review, 46*(7), 68–71.

Drews, E. M. (1964). The creative intellectual style in gifted adolescents. In *Being and becoming: A cosmic approach to counseling and curriculum* (Third report of Title VII, Project No. 647–I, National Defense Act of 1958. Grant No. 7–32–0410–140.) Washington, DC: Department of Health, Education, and Welfare.

Drews, E. M. (1972). *Learning together: How to foster creativity, self-fulfillment, and social awareness in today's students and teachers.* Englewood Cliffs, NJ: Prentice Hall.

Dunn, L. (1963). *Exceptional children in the schools.* New York: Holt, Rinehart, & Winston.

Dunn, L. M., & Dunn, L. M. (1997). *Peabody picture vocabulary test–third edition (PPVT-III).* Circle Pines, MN: AGS.

Eberle, R. (1996). *Scamper: Games for imagination development.* Waco, TX: Prufrock Press.

Ellison, D. G. (1976). Tutoring. In N. L. Gage (Ed.), *The psychology of teaching methods* (pp. 130–165). Chicago: University of Chicago Press.

Ericsson, K. A. (1996). (Ed.) *The road to excellence: The acquisition of expert performance in the arts, sciences, sports, and games.* Mahwah, NJ: Erlbaum.

Ericsson, K. A., & Charness, N. (1994). Expert performance: Its structure and acquisition. *American Psychologist, 49,* 725–747.

Ericsson, K. A., Krampe, R. T., & Tesch-Römer, C. (1993). The role of deliberate practice in the acquisition of expert performance. *Psychological Review, 100,* 363–406.

Evans, R. J., Bickel, R., & Pendarvis, E. D. (2000). Musical talent: Innate or acquired? Perceptions of students, parents, and teachers. *Gifted Child Quarterly, 44,* 80–90.

Feldhusen, J. (1993). Talent development as an alternative to gifted education. *Journal of Secondary Gifted Education, 5,* 5–9.

Feldhusen, J. (1994). Educating teachers for work with talented youth. In N. Colangelo & G. A. Davis (Eds.), *Handbook of gifted education* (pp. 547–552). Boston: Allyn and Bacon.

Feldhusen, J. (1997). Educating teachers for work with talented youth. In N. Colangelo & G. A. Davis (Eds.), *Handbook of gifted education* (2nd ed., pp. 547–552). Boston: Allyn and Bacon.

Feldhusen, J. F., Bahlke, S. J., & Treffinger, D. J. (1969). Teaching creative thinking. *Elementary School Journal, 70,* 48–53.

Feldhusen, J. F., Buska, L. K., & Womble, S. (1981). Using standard scores to synthesize data in identifying the gifted. *Journal for the Education of the Gifted, 4,* 177–186.

Feldhusen, J., & Clinkenbeard, P. (1986). Creativity instructional materials: A review of research. *Journal of Creative Behavior, 20,* 153–182.

Feldhusen, J. F., & Treffinger, D. J. (1979). The role of instructional material in teaching creative thinking. In J. C. Gowan, J. Khatena, & E. P. Torrance (Eds.), *Educating the ablest* (pp. 102–110). Itasca, IL: Peacock.

Feldhusen, J. F., & Treffinger, D. J. (1980). *Creative thinking and problem solving in gifted education*. Dubuque, IA: Kendall/Hunt.

Feldman, D. H. (1980). *Beyond universals in cognitive development*. Norwood, NJ: Ablex.

Feldman, D. H. (1994). *Beyond universals in cognitive development* (2nd ed.). Norwood, NJ: Ablex.

Feldman, D. H. (1997, August). *Developmental theory and the expression of talent*. Paper presented at the 12th World Conference of the World Council for Gifted and Talented Children, Seattle, WA.

Feldman, D. (2000). Was Mozart at risk? A developmentalist looks at extreme talent. In R. Friedman & B. Shore (Eds.), *Talents unfolding: Cognitive and developmental frameworks* (pp. 251–264). Washington, DC: American Psychological Association.

Feldman, D. H., & Fowler, R. C. (1997). The nature(s) of developmental change: Piaget, Vygotsy, and the transition process. *New Ideas in Psychology, 15*, 195–210.

Festinger, L. A. (1954). Theory of social comparison processes. *Human Relations, 7*, 117–140.

Fetterman, P. M. (1988). *Excellence and equality*. Albany: State University of New York Press.

Feuerstein, R. (1980). *Instrumental enrichment*. Baltimore, MD: University Park Press.

Fisher, E. (1981). Modeling behavior. In B. S. Miller & M. Price (Eds.), *The gifted child, the family, and the community* (pp. 67–72). New York: Walker.

Fishkin, A., & Johnson, A. (1998). Who is creative? Identifying children's creative abilities. *Roeper Review, 21*, 40–46.

Fliegler, L. A. (1961). *Curriculum planning for the gifted*. Englewood Cliffs, NJ: Prentice Hall.

Fliegler, L. A., & Bish, C. E. (1959). The gifted and talented. *Review of Educational Research, 29*, 408–450.

Fleming, E. S., & Hollinger, C. L. (1994). Project CHOICE: A longitudinal study of the career development of talent. In R. F. Subotnik & K. D. Arnold (Eds.), *Beyond Terman: Contemporary longitudinal studies of giftedness and talent* (pp. 316–348). Norwood, NJ: Ablex.

Floyd, A. (Ed.). (1979). *Cognitive development in the school years*. New York: Wiley.

Ford, D. Y. (1996). *Reversing underachievement among gifted Black students: Promising practices and programs*. New York: Teachers College Press.

Ford, D. Y., & Harris, J. J., III. (1999). *Multicultural gifted education*. New York: Teachers College Press.

Ford, D. Y., Harris, J. J., III , Tyson, C. A., & Trotman, M. F. (2002). Beyond deficit thinking: Providing access for gifted African American students. *Roeper Review, 24*, 52–58.

Fox, L. H. (1979). Programs for the gifted and talented: An overview. In A. H. Passow (Ed.), *The gifted and the talented: Their education and development* (Vol. 78, pp. 104–126). Chicago: University of Chicago Press.

Fox, L. H., Brody, L., & Tobin, D. (Eds.). (1974). *Women and the mathematical mystique*. Baltimore, MD: Johns Hopkins University Press.

Fox, L. E., Brody, L., & Tobin, D. (Eds.). (1983). *Learning disabled/gifted children: Identification and programming*. Baltimore, MD: University Park Press.

Frank, A. J., & McBee, M. T. (2003). The use of *Harry Potter and the Sorcerer's Stone* to discuss identity development with gifted adolescents. *Journal of Secondary Gifted Education, 15*, 33–39.

Frasier, M. M. (1974). Decision-making skills for life planning (DLP). *Talents and Gifts, 17*, 25–26.

Frasier, M. M. (1981). Minority gifted children. In B. S. Miller & M. Price (Eds.), *The gifted child, the family, and the community* (pp. 54–59). New York: Walker.

Frasier, M. M. (1997). Gifted minority students: Reframing approaches to their identification and education. In N. Colangelo & G. A. Davis (Eds.), *Handbook of gifted education* (2nd. ed., pp. 498–515). Boston: Allyn and Bacon.

Frasier, M. M., & McCannon, C. (1981). Using bibliotherapy with gifted children. *Gifted Child Quarterly, 25*, 81–85.

Freehill, M. (1961). *Gifted children*. New York: MacMillan.

Freeman, J. (1979). *Gifted children*. Baltimore, MD: University Park Press.

Friedman, P., Jenkins-Friedman, R., & Van Dyke, M. (1984). Identifying the leadership gifted: Self, peer, or teacher nominations? *Roeper Review, 7*, 91–94.

Friedman, R., & Lee, S. (1996). Differentiating instruction for high-achieving/gifted children in regular classrooms: A field test of three gifted-education models. *Journal for the Education of the Gifted, 19*, 405–436.

Frierson, E. (1968). The gifted child with learning disabilities. *Exceptional Children, 34*, 387–388.

Fuchs-Beauchamp, K., Karnes, M., & Johnson, L. (1993). Creativity and intelligence in preschoolers. *Gifted Child Quarterly, 35*, 113–117.

Furth, H. G. (1980). *The world of grown-ups: Children's conceptions of society*. New York: Elsevier North Holland.

Gage, N. L. (Ed.). (1976). *The psychology of teaching methods*. Chicago: University of Chicago Press.

Gage, N. L. (1978). *The scientific basis of the art of teaching*. New York: Teachers College Press.

Gagné, F. (1985). Giftedness and talent: Reexamining a reexamination of the definition. *Gifted Child Quarterly, 29*, 103–112.

Gagné, F. (1993). How well do peers agree among themselves when nominating the gifted and talented? *Gifted Child Quarterly, 37*, 39–45.

Gagné, F. (1995). From giftedness to talent: A developmental model and its impact on the language of the field. *Roeper Review, 18*, 103–111.

Gagné, F. (1998). A proposal for subcategories within gifted and talented populations. *Gifted Child Quarterly, 42*, 87–95.

Gagné, F. (1999) My convictions about the nature of abilities, gifts, and talents. *Journal for the Education of the Gifted, 22*, 109–136.

Gagné, F. (2003). Transforming gifts into talents: The DMGT as a developmental theory. In N. Colangelo & G. A. Davis (Eds.), *Handbook of gifted education* (3rd ed., pp. 60–74). Boston: Allyn and Bacon.

Gagné, F. (2005). From noncompetence to exceptional talent: Exploring the range of academic achievement within and between grade levels. *Gifted Child Quarterly, 49*, 139–153.

Gagné, R. M. (1976). The learning basis of teaching methods. In N. L. Gage (Ed.), *The psychology of teaching methods* (pp. 21–43). Chicago: University of Chicago Press.

Galbraith, J. (1985). The eight great gripes of gifted kids: Responding to special needs. *Roeper Review, 8*, 15–18.

Gall, M. D., & Gall, J. P. (1976). The discussion method. In N. L. Gage (Ed.), *The psychology of teaching methods* (pp. 166–216). Chicago: University of Chicago Press.

Gallagher, J. J. (1975). *Teaching the gifted child* (2nd ed.). Boston: Allyn and Bacon.

Gallagher, J. J. (1979). Issues in education of the gifted. In A. H. Passow (Ed.), *The gifted and the talented: Their education and development* (Vol. 78, pp. 28–44). Chicago: University of Chicago Press.

Gallagher, J. (1996). A critique of critiques. *Journal for the Education of the Gifted, 19*, 234–249.

Gallagher, J. J., Aschner, M. J., & Jenne, W. (1967). *Productive thinking of gifted children in classroom interaction.* Washington, DC: Council for Exceptional Children.

Gallagher, J. J., & Gallagher, S. A. (1994). *Teaching the gifted* (4th ed.). Boston: Allyn and Bacon.

Gallagher, S. (1997). Problem-based learning: Where did it come from, what does it do, and where is it going? *Journal for the Education of the Gifted, 20*, 332–362.

Gallagher, S. (2001). Adapting problem-based learning for gifted students. In F. A. Karnes & S. M. Bean (Eds.), *Methods and materials for teaching the gifted* (pp. 369–397). Waco, TX: Prufrock Press.

Gallagher, J. (2003). Issues and challenges in the education of gifted students. In N. Colangelo & G. A. Davis (Eds.), *Handbook of gifted education* (3rd ed., pp. 11–23). Boston: Pearson Education.

Gardner, J. (1961). *Excellence . . . Can we be equal and excellent too?* New York: Harper & Row.

Gardner, H. (1983). *Frames of mind: The theory of multiple intelligences.* New York: BasicBooks.

Gardner, H. (1993). *Frames of mind: The theory of multiple intelligences* (10th Anniversary Edition). New York: BasicBooks.

Gardner, H. (1997). *Extraordinary minds.* New York: BasicBooks.

Gardner, H. (2000). The "Giftedness Matrix" from a multiple intelligence perspective. In R. Friedman & B. Shore (Eds.), *Talents unfolding: Cognitive and developmental frameworks* (pp. 77–88). Washington, DC: American Psychological Association.

Gear, G. (1976). Accuracy of teacher judgment in identifying intellectually gifted children. *Gifted Child Quarterly, 20*, 478–490.

Gear, G. (1978). Effects of training on teachers' accuracy in identifying gifted children. *Gifted Child Quarterly, 22*, 90–97.

Gelbrich, J. A. (1997). Identifying the gifted infant. In J. F. Smutny (Ed.), *The young gifted child: Potential and promise: An anthology* (pp. 16–30). Cresskill, NJ: Hampton Press.

George, W. C. (1979). On A. K. Kurtz's acceleration vs. enrichment—the tenth rule of three-cubed. In W. C. George, S. J. Cohn, & J. C. Stanley (Eds.), *Educating the gifted: Acceleration and enrichment* (pp. 225–236). Baltimore, MD: Johns Hopkins University Press.

George, W. C., Cohn, S. J., & Stanley, J. C. (Eds.). (1979). *Educating the gifted: Acceleration and enrichment.* Baltimore, MD: Johns Hopkins University Press.

Gerencser, S. (1979). The Calasanctius experience. In A. H. Passow (Ed.), *The gifted and the talented: Their education and development* (Vol. 78, pp. 127–137). Chicago: University of Chicago Press.

Getzels, J. W. (1979). From art student to fine artist: Potential, problem finding, and performance. In A. H. Passow (Ed.), *The gifted and the talented: Their education and development* (Vol. 78, pp. 372–387). Chicago: University of Chicago Press.

Getzels, J. W., & Dillon, J. T. (1973). The nature of giftedness and the education of the gifted. In R. M. W. Travers (Ed.), *Second handbook of research on teaching* (pp. 689–731). Chicago: Rand McNally.

Getzels, J. W., & Jackson, F. (1962). *Creativity and intelligence.* New York: Wiley.

Ghiselin, B. (Ed.). (1952). *The creative process.* Berkeley: University of California Press.

Gilliam, J. E., Carpenter, B. O., & Christensen, J. R. (1996). *Gifted and talented evaluation scales (GATES).* Austin, TX: PRO-ED.

Gilligan, C. (1982). *In a different voice: Psychological theory and women's development.* Cambridge, MA: Harvard University Press.

Gilman, B. (2004). *Closing statement: Promising new or still valuable tests or portions of tests.* Retrieved June 1, 2004 from http://www.neiu.edu/~ourgift/Archives/Kearney_Gilman/Gilman_Closing_Statement.htm

Glasser, J. F. (1971). *The elementary school learning center for independent study.* West Nyack, NY: Parker.

Glasser, W. (1969). *Schools without failure.* New York: Harper & Row.

Goertzel, V., & Goertzel, M. (1962). *Cradles of eminence.* Boston: Little, Brown.

Goertzel, M., Goertzel, V., & Goertzel, T. (1978). *300 eminent personalities.* San Francisco: Jossey-Bass.

Goertzel, V., Goertzel, M., Goertzel, T. G., & Hansen, A. M. W. (2004). *Cradles of eminence: Childhoods of more than 700 famous men and women* (2nd ed.). Scotsdale, AZ: Great Potential Press.

Goffman, E. (1963). *Stigma.* Englewood Cliffs, NJ: Prentice Hall.

Gold, M. J. (1965). *Education of the intellectually gifted.* Columbus, OH: Merrill.

Gold, M. J. (1979a). Acceleration: Simplistic gimmickry. In W. C. George, S. J. Cohn, & J. C. Stanley (Eds.), *Educating the gifted: Acceleration and enrichment* (pp. 188–189). Baltimore, MD: Johns Hopkins University Press.

Gold, M. J. (1979b). Teachers and mentors. In A. H. Passow (Ed.), *The gifted and the talented: Their education and development* (Vol. 78, pp. 272–288). Chicago: University of Chicago Press.

Gold, M. J. (1980). Secondary level programs for the gifted and the talented. In H. J. Morgan, C. G. Tennant, & M. J. Gold (Eds.), *Elementary and secondary level programs for the gifted and talented* (pp. 32–65). New York: Teachers College Press.

Goldstein, D., & Wagner, H. (1993). After school program, competition school, olympics, and summer programs. In K. A. Heller, F. J. Mönks, & A. H. Passow (Eds.), *International handbook of research and development of giftedness and talented* (pp. 593–604). New York: Paradigm.

Golomb, C. (2004). Individual differences and cultural diversity in the art forms of children talented in the visual arts. In D. Boothe & J. C. Stanley (Eds.), *In the eyes of the beholder: Critical issues for diversity in gifted education* (pp. 33–47). Waco, TX: Prufrock Press.

Goodenough, F. L., & Harris, D. B. (1963). *Goodenough-Harris drawing test.* San Antonio, TX: PsychCorp.

Gordon, E. E. (1995). Musical aptitude profile (Rev. ed.). Chicago: GIA.

Gordon, W. J. J. (1961). *Synectics.* New York: Harper & Row.

Gordon, W. J. J. (1971). *The metaphorical way of learning and knowing.* Cambridge, MA: Porpoise Books.

Gottfried, A. E., & Gottfried, A. W. (2004). Toward the development of a conceptualization of gifted motivation. *Gifted Child Quarterly, 48*, 121–132.

Gowan, J. C. (1955). The underachieving gifted child: A problem for everyone. *Exceptional Children, 21,* 247–250.

Gowan, J. C. (1972). *Development of the creative individual.* San Diego, CA: R. K. Knapp.

Gowan, J. C. (1977). An editorial on a differentiated guidance for the gifted: A developmental view. *Gifted Child Quarterly, 21,* 282–291.

Gowan, J. C. (Ed.). (1979). Creativity [Special issue]. *Gifted Child Quarterly, 23*(4).

Gowan, J. C., & Bruch, C. G. (1971). *The academically talented student and guidance.* Boston: Houghton-Mifflin.

Gowan, J. C., & Demos, D. G. (1964). *The education and guidance of the ablest.* Springfield, IL: Thomas.

Gowan, J. C., Khatena, J., & Torrance, E. P. (Eds.). (1979). *Educating the ablest* (2nd ed.). Itasca, IL: Peacock.

Grant, T. E., & Renzulli, J. (1981). *Relative aspects of potential (RAP) inventory.* Marlborough, CT: RAP Researchers.

Greenstadt, W. M. (1981). Parents of gifted children. In B. S. Miller & M. Price (Eds.), *The gifted child, the family, and the community* (pp. 77–82). New York: Walker.

Gridley, B. E., Norman, K. A., Rizza, M. G., & Decker, S. L. (2003). Assessment of gifted children with the Woodcock-Johnson III. In F. A. Schrank & D. P. Flanagan (Eds.), *WJ-III, clinical applications* (pp. 385–317). San Diego: Academic Press.

Gross, M. (1993). *Exceptionally gifted children.* London: Routledge.

Gross, M. U. M. (1998). The "me" behind the mask: Intellectually gifted students and the search for identity. *Roeper Review, 20,* 167–174.

Gross, M. U. M. (1999). Small poppies: Highly gifted children in the early years. *Roeper Review, 21,* 207– 214.

Gross, M. U. M. (2004). *Exceptionally gifted children* (2nd ed.). London: Routledge Falmer.

Gross, M., & van Vliet, H. (2003). *Radical acceleration of highly gifted children: An annotated bibliography of international research on high gifted young people who graduate from high school three or more years early.* Sydney, Australia: Gifted Education Research, Resource, and Information Centre, University of New South Wales, Sydney, Australia.

Guilford, J. P. (1950). Creativity. *American Psychologist, 5,* 444–454.

Guilford, J. P. (1959). Three faces of intellect. *American Psychologist, 14,* 469–479.

Guilford, J. P. (1967). *The nature of human intelligence.* New York: McGraw-Hill.

Guilford, J. P. (1968). *Intelligence, creativity, and their educational implications.* San Diego, CA: Knapp.

Guilford, J. P. (1975). Varieties of creative giftedness, their measurement, and development. *Gifted Child Quarterly, 19,* 107–121.

Guilford, J. P. (1979). Some incubated thoughts on incubation. *Journal of Creative Behavior, 13,* 1–8.

Guilford, J. P., & Christensen, P. R. (1973). The one-way relation between creative potential and IQ. *Journal of Creative Behavior, 7,* 247–252.

Gust, K., Waldron, D., & Cross, T. (1997). Characteristics of gifted children referred to a school psychology clinic. *Research Briefs, 11,* 45–60.

Hagen, E. (1980). *Identification of the gifted.* New York: Teachers College Press.

Hall, E. G., & Skinner, N. (1980). *Somewhere to turn: Strategies for parents of the gifted and talented.* New York: Teachers College Press.

423

Hammill, D. D. (1987). Assessing students in schools. In D. D. Hammill (Ed.), *Assessing the abilities and instructional needs of students* (pp. 5–37). Austin, TX: PRO-ED.

Hansen, J., & Feldhusen, J. (1994). Comparison of trained and untrained teachers of gifted students. *Gifted Child Quarterly, 38,* 115–123.

Hanson, H. P. (1981). Twenty-five years of encouraging able students. *Education Digest, 46*(7), 48–51.

Harcourt-Brace Educational Measurement. (1996). *Stanford achievement test–9th edition (SAT).* San Antonio, TX: Author.

Harcourt-Brace Educational Measurement. (2001). *Metropolitan achievement tests, eighth edition (MAT/8).* San Antonio, TX: Author.

Harlen, W. (1979). Matching the learning environment to children's development: The progress in learning science project. In A. H. Floyd (Ed.), *Cognitive development in the school years* (pp. 317–339). New York: Wiley.

Hauck, B. B., & Freehill, M. F. (1972). *The gifted case studies.* Dubuque, IA: Brown.

Havighurst, R. J., Hersey, J., Meister, M., Cornog, W. H., & Terman, L. M. (1958). The importance of education for the gifted. In N. B. Henry (Ed.), *Education for the gifted.* (Vol. 47, pp. 3–20). Chicago: University of Chicago Press.

Hawkes, M., Baird, H. J., & Williams, D. D. (1994). What we learned as developers of self-paced, self-instructional program for gifted high school students. *Journal of Instructional Psychology, 21,* 25–30.

Hébert, T. P. (1998). Gifted Black males in an urban high school: Factors that influence achievement. *Journal for the Education of the Gifted, 21,* 385–414.

Hébert, T. P. (2002). Gifted Black males in a predominantly White university. Portraits of high achievement. *Journal for the Education of the Gifted, 26,* 25–64.

Hébert, T. P., & Beardsley, T. M. (2001). Jermaine: A critical case study of a gifted Black child living in rural poverty. *Gifted Child Quarterly, 45,* 85–103.

Hébert, T., & Neumeister, K. (2000). University mentors in an elementary classroom: Supporting the intellectual, motivational, and emotional needs of high-ability learners. *Journal for the Education of the Gifted, 24,* 122–148.

Hébert, T. P., & Speirs Neumeister, K. L. (2001). Guided viewing of film: A strategy for counseling gifted teenagers. *Journal of Secondary Gifted Education, 14,* 224–235.

Herrnstein, R., & Murray, C. (1994). *The bell curve: Intelligence and class structure in American life.* New York: The Free Press.

Hertzog, N. (1997). Open-ended activities and their role in maintaining challenge. *Journal for the Education of the Gifted, 21,* 54–81.

Hildreth, G. H. (1966). *Introduction to the gifted.* New York: McGraw-Hill.

Hitchfield, E. M. (1973). *In search of promise.* London: Longman.

Hmelo, C., & Ferrari, M. (1997). The problem-based learning tutorial: Cultivating higher order thinking skills. *Journal for the Education of the Gifted, 20,* 401–422.

Hollinger, C. L. (1991). Facilitating the career development of gifted young women. *Roeper Review, 13,* 135–139.

Hollingworth, L. S. (1942). *Children above 180 IQ, Stanford-Binet: Origin and development.* Yonkers, NY: World Book.

Hong, E., & Milgram, R. (1991). Original thinking in preschool children: A validation of ideational fluency measures. *Creativity Research Journal, 4,* 253–260.

Hong, E., Milgram, R., & Gorsky, H. (1995). Original thinking as a predictor of creative performance in young children. *Roeper Review, 18,* 147–148.

Hoover, H. D., Dunbar, S. B., & Frisbie, D. A. (2001). *Iowa tests of basic skills (ITBS)*. Itasca, IL: Riverside.

Horner, M. (1972). The motive to avoid success and changing aspirations in college women. In J. Bardwick (Ed.), *Readings in the psychology of women* (pp. 62–67). New York: Harper & Row.

House, E. R. (Ed.). (1970). *TAG evaluation sampler*. Reston, VA: Council for Exceptional Children.

House, P. A. (1979). Through the eyes of their teachers: Stereotypes of gifted pupils. *Journal for the Education of the Gifted, 2*, 220–224.

Howieson, N. (1981). A longitudinal study of creativity—1965–1975. *Journal of Creative Behavior, 15*, 117–134.

Howley, A., Howley, C., & Pendarvis, E. (1986). *Teaching gifted children: Principles and strategies*. Boston: Little, Brown.

Howley, C., Howley, A., & Pendarvis, E. (1995). *Out of our minds: Anti-intellectualism and talent development for American schooling*. New York: Teachers College Press.

Hoyt, K. B., & Hebeler, J. R. (Eds.). (1974). *Career education for gifted and talented students*. Salt Lake City, UT: Olympus.

Hughes, L. (1999). Action research: How can I meet the needs of the high-ability students within my regular education classroom? *Journal for the Education of the Gifted, 22*, 282–297.

Hughes, L. C., & Killian, J. B. (1977). A practical approach to screening for intellectually gifted kindergarten children. *Talents and Gifts, 19*(3), 21–22.

Hunsaker, S. & Callahan, C. (1995). Creativity and giftedness: Published instrument uses and abuses. *Gifted Child Quarterly, 39*, 110–114.

Institute for Behavioral Research in Creativity. (1974). *Identification of academic, creative, and leadership talent from biographical data: Final report*. Raleigh, NC: Department of Public Instruction.

International Baccalaureate of North America. (1981). *Restoring a challenge to secondary education: The International Baccalaureate Program*. New York: Author.

Jackson, P., & Messick, S. (1965). The person, the product, and the response: Conceptual problems in the assessment of creativity. *Journal of Personality, 33*, 309–329.

Jacobs, J. (1971). Effectiveness of teacher and parent identification as a function of school level. *Psychology in the Schools, 8*, 140–142.

Jarosewich, T., & Stocking, V. B. (2003). Talent search: Student and parent perceptions of out-of-level testing. *Journal of Secondary Gifted Education, 14*, 137–150.

Jensen, A. (2004). The mental chronometry of giftedness. In D. Booth & J. C. Stanley (Eds.), *In the eyes of the beholder: Critical issues for diversity in gifted education* (pp. 157–166). Waco, TX: Prufrock Press.

Johnsen, S. K. (2003). Issues in the assessment of talent development. In J. H. Borland (Ed.), *Rethinking gifted education* (pp. 201–214). New York: Teachers College Press.

Johnsen, S., & Corn, A. (1987). *Screening assessment for gifted elementary students (SAGES)*. Austin, TX: PRO-ED.

Johnsen, S., & Corn, A. (1992). *Screening assessment for gifted elementary students—Primary (SAGES-P)*. Austin, TX: PRO-ED.

Johnsen, S., & Corn, A. (2002). *Screening assessment for gifted elementary students—2nd ed. (SAGES-2)*. Austin, TX: PRO-ED.

Johnsen, S. K., & Goree, K. K. (2004). Teaching gifted student through independent study. In F. A. Karnes & S. M. Bean (Eds.), *Methods and materials for teaching the gifted* (2nd ed., pp. 379–408). Waco, TX; Prufrock Press.

Kahn, S. B., & Weiss, J. (1973). The teaching of affective responses. In R. M. W. Travers (Ed.), *Second handbook of research on teaching* (pp. 759–804). Chicago: Rand McNally.

Kamphaus, R. W. (2001). *Clinical assessment of child and adolescent intelligence* (2nd ed.). Boston: Allyn and Bacon.

Kanevsky, L. (2000). Dynamic assessment of gifted students. In K. A. Heller, F. J. Mönks, R. J. Sternberg, & R. F. Subotnik (Eds.), *International handbook of giftedness and talent* (2nd ed., pp. 283–295). Amsterdam: Elsevier.

Kanigher, H. (1977). *Everyday enrichment.* Ventura, CA: Office of the Superintendent of Public Schools.

Kaplan, S. N. (1974). *Providing programs for the gifted and talented: A handbook.* Ventura, CA: Office of the Superintendent of Public Schools.

Kaplan, S. N. (Ed.). (1979). *Inservice training manual: Activities for developing curriculum for the gifted/talented.* Ventura, CA: Office of the Superintendent of Public Schools.

Kaplan, S. N. (1980). Curricular and programmatic concerns. In S. N. Kaplan (Ed.), *Educating the preschool/primary gifted and talented* (pp. 61–101). Ventura, CA: Office of the Superintendent of Public Schools.

Karnes, F. A., & Collins, E. C. (1980). *Handbook of instructional resources and references for teaching the gifted.* Boston: Allyn and Bacon.

Karnes, F. A., & McGinnis, C. (1995). Self-actualization and locus of control of gifted children in fourth through eighth grades. *Psychological Reports, 76,* 1039–1042.

Karnes, M. B., & Bertschi, J. B. (1978). Identifying and educating gifted/talented nonhandicapped and handicapped preschoolers. *Teaching Exceptional Children, 10,* 114–119.

Kaufmann, F. A. (1976). *Your gifted child and you.* Reston, CA: Council for Exceptional Children.

Kaufmann, F. A. (1981). The 1964–1968 presidential scholars: A follow-up study. *Exceptional Children, 48,* 164–169.

Kay, S. (1994). From theory to practice: Promoting problem-finding behavior in children. *Roeper Review, 16,* 195–197.

Kay, S. (1998). Curriculum and the creative process: Contributions in memory of A. Harry Passow. *Roeper Review, 21,* 5–13.

Kay, S., & Subotnik, R. (1994). Talent beyond words: Unveiling spatial, expressive, kinesthetic, and musical talent in young children. *Gifted Child Quarterly, 38,* 70–74.

Keating, D. P. (1975). Testing those top percentiles. *Exceptional Children, 41,* 435–436.

Keating, D. P. (1980). Four faces of creativity: The continued plight of the intellectually underserved. *Gifted Child Quarterly, 24,* 57–61.

Kelly, A. (1978). *Girls and science.* Stockholm, Sweden: Amquest & Wiksell International.

Kerr, B. A. (2000). Guiding gifted girls and young women. In K. A. Heller, F. J. Mönks, R. J. Sternberg, & R. F. Subotnik (Eds.), *International handbook of giftedness and talent* (2nd ed., pp. 649–657). Amsterdam: Elsevier.

Kerr, B. A., & Cohn, S. J. (2001). *Smart boys: Talent, manhood, and the search for meaning.* Scottsdale, AZ: Gifted Psychology Press.

Kerr, B. A., & Nicpon, M. F. (2003). Gender and giftedness. In N. Colangelo & G. A. Davis (Eds.), *Handbook of gifted education* (3rd ed., pp. 493–505). Boston: Allyn and Bacon.

Khatena, J. (1972). Developmental patterns in production by children aged 9 to 19 of original images as measured by "Sounds and Images." *Psychological Reports, 30,* 649–650.

Khatena, J. (1982). *Educational psychology of the gifted.* New York: Wiley.

Khatena, J., & Fisher, S. (1974). A four-year study of children's responses to ono-matopoeic stimuli. *Perceptual and Motor Skills, 39,* 1062.

Khatena, J., & Torrance, E. P. (1976). *Manual for the Khatena-Torrance Creative Perception Inventory.* Chicago: Stoelting.

Kimball, M. M. (1989). A new perspective on women's math achievement. *Psychological Bulletin, 105,* 198–214.

Kindlon, D., & Thompson, M. (1999). *Raising Cain: Protecting the emotional lives of boys.* New York: Ballantine.

Kingore, B. (1997). Seeking advanced potentials: Developmentally appropriate procedures for identification. In J. F. Smutny (Ed.), *The young gifted child: Potential and promise: An anthology* (pp. 31–51). Cresskill, NJ: Hampton Press.

Kirschenbaum, R. (1998). The creativity classification system: An assessment theory. *Roeper Review, 21,* 20–26.

Kirst, M. (1982). How to improve schools without spending more money. *Phi Delta Kappan, 64,* 6–8.

Kitano, M. (1991). A multicultural perspective on serving the culturally diverse gifted. *Journal for the Education of the Gifted, 15,* 4–19.

Kitano, M. (1997a). Gifted Asian American women. *Journal for the Education of the Gifted, 21,* 3–37.

Kitano, M. (1997b). Gifted Latina women. *Journal for the Education of the Gifted, 21,* 131–159.

Kitano, M. (1998). Gifted African American Women. *Journal for the Education of the Gifted, 21,* 254–287.

Kitano, M. (1999). Bringing clarity to "This thing called giftedness": A response to Dr. Renzulli. *Journal for the Education of the Gifted, 23,* 87–101.

Kitano, M. K., & DiJiosia, M. (2002). Are Asian and Pacific Americans overrepresented in programs for the gifted? *Roeper Review, 24,* 76–80.

Knutsen, L. (1979). Teaching fifty gifted science units in two easy steps. *Science and Children, 16,* 51–53.

Kogan, N., & Pankove, E. (1974). Long-term predictive validity of divergent-thinking lists: Some negative evidence. *Journal of Educational Psychology, 66,* 802–810.

Kohlberg, L. (1969). Stage and sequence: The cognitive-developmental approach to socialization. In D. Goslin (Ed.), *Handbook of socialization theory and research* (pp. 347–480). New York: Rand McNally.

Kolloff, P. (1991). Special residential high schools. In N. Colangelo & G. A. Davis (Eds.), *Handbook of gifted education* (pp. 198–206). Boston: Allyn and Bacon.

Kolloff, P. (2003). State-supported residential high schools. In N. Colangelo & G. A. Davis (Eds.). *Handbook of gifted education* (3rd. ed., pp. 238–246) Boston: Pearson Education.

Kranz, B. (1975). From Lewis Terman and Matina Horner: What happens to gifted girls. *Talents and Gifts, 37*(3), 31–36.

427

Krippner, S., Dreistadt, T., & Hubbard, C. C. (1979). The creative person and non-ordinal reality. In J. C. Gowan, J. Khatena, & E. P. Torrance (Eds.), *Educating the ablest* (pp. 445–470). Itasca, IL: Peacock.

Kulieke, M., & Olszewski-Kubilius, P. (1989). The influence of family value and climate on the development of talent. In J. L. VanTassel-Baska & P. Olszewski-Kubilius (Eds.), *Patterns of influence on gifted learners: The home, the self, and the school* (pp. 40–59). New York: Teachers College Press.

Kulik, J. (1992). *An analysis of the research on ability grouping: Historical and contemporary perspectives* (Research-Based Decision Making Series No. 9204). Storrs: The National Research Center on the Gifted and Talented, University of Connecticut.

Kulik, J. A., & Kulik, C. C. (1984). Synthesis of research of effects of accelerated instruction. *Educational Leadership, 42*, 84–89.

Kulik, C., & Kulik, J. (1991). Ability grouping and gifted students. In N. Colangelo & G. A. Davis (Eds.), *Handbook of gifted education* (pp. 178–196). Boston: Allyn and Bacon.

Kulik, C., & Kulik, J. (1997). Ability grouping. In N. Colangelo & G. A. Davis (Eds.), *Handbook of gifted education* (2nd ed., pp. 230–242). Boston: Allyn and Bacon.

Kurtz, A. K. (1979). Acceleration vs. enrichment—the tenth rule of three-cubed. In W. C. George, S. J. Cohn, & J. C. Stanley (Eds.), *Educating the gifted: Acceleration and enrichment* (pp. 225–226). Baltimore, MD: Johns Hopkins University Press.

Lajoie, S., & Shore, B. M. (1981). Three myths? The overrepresentation of the gifted among dropouts, delinquents, and suicides. *Gifted Child Quarterly, 25*, 138–143.

LaRose, B. (1978). A quota system for gifted minority children: A viable solution. *Gifted Child Quarterly, 22*, 394–403.

Lehman, H. C. (1953). *Age and achievement.* Princeton, NJ: Princeton University Press.

Lehman, P. R. (1968). *Tests and measurements in music.* Englewood Cliffs, NJ: Prentice Hall.

Lindsey, M. (1980). *Training teachers of the gifted and talented.* New York: Teachers College Press.

Lohman, D. F., & Hagen, E. P. (2001). *Cognitive abilities test (CogAT).* Itasca, IL: Riverside.

Lorge, I., & Thorndike, R. M. (1954). *Lorge-Thorndike intelligence tests.* Boston: Houghton-Mifflin.

Lucito, L. (1963). Gifted children. In L. M. Dunn (Ed.), *Exceptional children in the schools* (pp. 179–238). New York: Holt, Rhinehart, & Winston.

Ludwig, A. (1995). *The price of greatness: Resolving the creativity and madness controversy.* New York: The Guilford Press

Lupkowski-Shoplik, A., & Assouline, S. (1994). Evidence of extreme mathematical precocity: Case studies of talented youths. *Roeper Review, 16*, 144–51.

Lupkowski-Shoplik, A., Benbow, C., Assouline, S., & Brody, L. (2003). Talent searches: Meeting the needs of academically talented youth. In N. Colangelo & G. A. Davis (Eds.), *Handbook of gifted education* (3rd ed, pp. 204–218). Boston: Pearson Education.

Maccoby, E. E., & Jacklin, C. N. (1974). *The psychology of sex differences.* Stanford, CA: Stanford University Press.

MacKinnon, D. W. (1964). The creativity of architects. In C. W. Taylor (Ed.), *Widening horizons in creativity* (pp. 359–378). New York: Wiley.

Maker, J. C. (1975). *Training teachers for the gifted and talented: A comparison of models.* Reston, VA: Council for Exceptional Children.

Maker, J. C. (1977). *Providing programs for the gifted handicapped.* Reston, VA: Council for Exceptional Children.

Maker, J. C. (1979). Developing multiple talents in exceptional children. *Teaching Exceptional Children, 11,* 120–124.

Maker, J. C. (1981). The gifted hearing-impaired student. *American Annals of the Deaf, 126,* 631–645.

Maker, J. C. (1982). *Curriculum development for the gifted.* Rockville, MD: Aspen Systems.

Maker, J. (1992). Intelligence and creativity in multiple intelligences: Identification and development. *Educating Able Learners, 17*(4), 12–19.

Maker, J. C., Morris, E., & James, J. (1981). The Eugene Field Project: A program for potentially gifted young children. In National/State Leadership Training Institute on the Gifted and Talented (Ed.), *Balancing the scale for the disadvantaged child* (pp. 117–175). Ventura, CA: Office of the Superintendent of Public Schools.

Maker, J., Nielson, A., & Rogers, J. (1994). Giftedness, diversity, and problem solving. *Teaching Exceptional Children, 27*(1), 4–19.

Maker, J., Rogers, J., Nielson, A., & Bauerle, P. (1996). Multiple intelligences, problem solving, and diversity in the general classroom. *Journal for the Education of the Gifted, 19,* 437–460.

Malone, C., & Noonan, W. J. (1975). Behavioral identification of gifted children. *Gifted Child Quarterly, 19,* 301–306.

Manor-Bullock, R. (1995). Is giftedness socially stigmatizing? The impact of high achievement on social interactions. *Journal for the Education of the Gifted, 18,* 319–338.

Margolin, L. (1996). A pedagogy of privilege. *Journal for the Education of the Gifted, 19,* 164–180.

Marion, R. L. (1980). Parenting the gifted: Working with parents of the disadvantaged or culturally different child. *Roeper Review, 2,* 32–34.

Marland, S. P., Jr. (1972). *Education of the gifted and talented: Report to the Congress of the Unites States by the U.S. Commissioner of Education and background papers submitted to the U.S. Office of Education,* 2 vols. Washington, DC: U.S. Government Printing Office. (Government Documents Y4.L 11/2:G36)

Martinson, R. (1961). *Educational programs for gifted pupils.* Sacramento: California State Department of Education.

Martinson, R. (1972). Research on the gifted and talented: Its implications for education. In S. P. Marland, Jr., *Education of the gifted and talented: Report to the Congress of the Unites States by the U.S. Commissioner of Education and background papers submitted to the U.S. Office of Education,* 2 vols (pp. 79–118). Washington, DC: U.S. Government Printing Office. (Government Documents Y4.L 11/2:G36)

Martinson, R. (1975). *The identification of the gifted and talented.* Reston, VA: Council for Exceptional Children.

Martinson, R., & Seagoe, M. V. (1967). *The abilities of young children.* Washington, DC: Council for Exceptional Children.

Maslow, A. (1968). *Toward a psychology of being* (2nd ed.). New York: Van Nostrand Reinhold.

429

Mathews, F. N. (1981). Influencing parents' attitudes toward gifted education. *Exceptional Children, 48*, 140–144.

May, D. G. (1997). Simulations: Active learning for gifted students. *Gifted Child Today, 20*(2), 28–30, 32, 34–35.

McClelland, D. C. (1958). *Talent and society*. Princeton, NJ: Van Nostrand Reinhold.

McCoach, D. B., & Siegle, D. (2003). Factors that differentiate underachieving gifted students from high-achieving gifted students. *Gifted Child Quarterly, 47*, 144–154.

McDiarmid, G. (1990). Challenge prospective teachers' beliefs during field experience: A quixotic undertaking? *Journal of Teacher Education, 41*(3), 12–20.

McLeish, J. (1976). The lecture method. In N. L. Gage (Ed.), *The psychology of teaching methods* (pp. 252–301). Chicago: University of Chicago Press.

Mednick, S. A., & Mednick, M. T. (1967). *Remote associates test*. Boston: Houghton-Mifflin.

Meeker, M. (1969). *The structure of intellect: Its interpretation and uses*. Columbus, OH: Merrill.

Meeker, M. (Ed.). (1981). *A book of collected readings on application of the Guilford S-I to educational practice*. El Segundo, CA: Structure of Intellect Institute.

Mercer, J. K. (1973). *Labeling the mentally retarded*. Berkeley: University of California Press.

Mercer, J. K., & Lewis, J. F. (1978). Using the System of Multicultural Pluralistic Assessment (SOMPA) to identify the gifted minority child. In A. Y. Baldwin, (Ed.), *Educational planning for the gifted: Overcoming cultural, geographic, and socioeconomic barriers* (pp. 59–66). Reston, VA: Foundation for Exceptional Children.

Michell, L., & Lambourne, R. (1979). An association between high intellectual ability and an imaginative analytic approach to the discussion of open questions. *British Journal of Educational Psychology, 49*, 60–72.

Milgram, R., & Hong, E. (1993). Creative thinking and creative performance in adolescence as predictors of creative attainments in adults: A follow up after 18 years. *Roeper Review, 15*, 135–140.

Milgram, R., & Milgram, N. (1976). Group versus individual administration in the measurement of creative thinking in gifted and nongifted children. *Child Development, 47*, 563–565.

Moon, S. M., & Hall, A. S. (1998). Family therapy with intellectually and creatively gifted children. *Journal of Marital and Family Therapy, 24*(1), 59–80.

Miller, B. S., & Price, M. (Eds.). (1981). *The gifted child, the family, and the community*. New York: Walker.

Moon, S. M., & Thomas, V. (2003). Family therapy with gifted and talented adolescents. *Journal of Secondary Gifted Education, 14*, 107–113.

Moon, S., Jurich, J., & Feldhusen, J. (1998). Families of gifted children. In R. Friedman & K. Rodgers (Eds.), *Talent in context: Historical and social perspectives on giftedness* (pp. 81–99). Washington, DC: American Psychological Association.

Morelock, M. J. (1996). On the nature of giftedness and talent: Imposing order on chaos. *Roeper Review, 19*, 4–12.

Morelock, M. (1997). Imagination, logic, and the exceptionally gifted. *Roeper Review, 19*, A1–A4.

Moreno, J. T. (1952). Psychodramatic production technique. *Group Psychotherapy, 4*, 243–273.

Morgan, H. J., Tennant, C. G., & Gold, M. J. (1980). *Elementary- and secondary-level programs for the gifted and talented.* New York: Teachers College Press.

Morris, J. E. (2002). African American students and gifted education: The politics of race and culture. *Roeper Review, 24,* 59–62.

Mumford, M. (1998). Creative thought: Structure, components, and educational implications. *Roeper Review, 21,* 14–19.

Naglieri, J. A. (2003). *Naglieri nonverbal ability test.* San Antonio, TX: The Psychological Corporation.

Naglieri, J. A., & Ford, D. Y. (2003). Addressing the underrepresentation of gifted minority children using the Naglieri Nonverval Ability Test (NNAT). *Gifted Child Quarterly, 47,* 155–160.

Nathan, C. N. (1979). Parental involvement. In A. H. Passow (Ed.), *The gifted and the talented: Their education and development* (Vol. 78, pp. 255–271). Chicago: University of Chicago Press.

Neihart, M. (1999). The impact of giftedness on psychological well-being: What does the empirical literature say? *Roeper Review, 22,* 10–17.

Nelson, K., & Prindle, N. (1992). Gifted teacher competencies: Ratings by rural principals and teachers compared. *Journal for the Education of the Gifted, 15,* 357–369.

Nelson, S., Gallagher, J., & Coleman, M. (1993). Cooperative learning from two different perspectives. *Roeper Review, 16,* 117–121.

Neujahr, J. L. (1976). *The individualized instruction game.* New York: Teachers College Press.

Newland, T. E. (1976). *The gifted in socio-educational perspective.* Englewood Cliffs, NJ: Prentice Hall.

Newland, T. E. (1980). Psychological assessment of exceptional children and youth. In W. M. Cruickshank (Ed.), *Psychology of exceptional children and youth* (4th ed., pp. 74–135). Englewood Cliffs, NJ: Prentice Hall.

Nicholls, J. G. (1972). Creativity in the person who will never produce anything original and useful: The concept of creativity as a normally distributed trait. *American Psychologist, 27,* 717–727.

Nichols, R. C., & Davis, J. A. (1964). Characteristics of students of higher-academic aptitude. *Personnel and Guidance Journal, 42,* 794–800.

Noble, T. (2004). Integrating the revised Bloom's taxonomy with multiple intelligences: A planning tool for curriculum differentiation. *Teachers College Record, 106*(1), 193–211.

Nuthall, G., & Snook, I. (1973). Contemporary models of teaching. In R. M. W. Travers (Ed.), *Second handbook of research on teaching* (pp. 47–76). Chicago: Rand McNally.

Oakes, J., & Lipton, M. (1992). Detracking schools: Early lessons from the field. *Phi Delta Kappan, 73,* 448–454.

Oden, M. H. (1968). The fulfillment of promise: 40-year follow-up of the Terman gifted group. *Generic Psychology Monographs, 77,* 3–93.

Olszewski, P., Kulieke, M., & Buescher, T. (1987). The influence of the family environment on the development of talent: A literature review. *Journal for the Education of the Gifted, 11,* 6–28.

Olszewski-Kubilius, P. (1997). Special summer and Saturday programs for gifted students. In N. Colangelo & G. A. Davis (Eds.), *Handbook of gifted education* (2nd ed., pp. 180–188). Boston: Allyn and Bacon.

Olszewski-Kubilius, P. (2003). Do we change gifted children to fit gifted programs, or do we change gifted programs to fit gifted children? *Journal for the Education of the Gifted, 26,* 304–313.

Olszewski-Kubilius, P., & Scott, J. (1992). An investigation of the college and career counseling needs of economically disadvantaged, minority gifted students. *Roeper Review, 14,* 141–148.

Olton, R. A. (1979). Experimental studies of incubation: Searching for the elusive. *Journal of Creative Behavior, 13,* 9–22.

Ortman, H. L. (1966). How psychodrama fosters creativity. *Group Psychotherapy, 19,* 210–212.

Osborn, A. F. (1953). *Applied imagination.* New York: Scribner's.

O'Shea, M. V. (Ed.). (1924). *The child: His nature and his needs.* New York: Children's Foundation.

Otis, A. S., & Lennon, R. T. (2003). *Otis-Lennon school ability test, 8th ed. (OLSAT-8).* San Antonio, TX: Harcourt Assessment.

Owens, L. (1979). Programs for the gifted and talented in Anchorage, Alaska. In W. C. George, S. J. Cohn, & J. C. Stanley (Eds.), *Educating the gifted: Acceleration and enrichment* (pp. 205–207). Baltimore, MD: Johns Hopkins University Press.

Papert, S. (1980). *Mindstorms: Children, computers, and powerful ideas.* New York: BasicBooks.

Parker, J., & Rubin, L. (1966). *Process as content.* Chicago: Rand McNally.

Parker, M., & Colangelo, N. (1979). An assessment of values of gifted students and their parents. In N. Colangelo & R. T. Zaffrann (Eds.), *New voices in counseling the gifted* (pp. 408–414). Dubuque, IA: Kendall/Hunt.

Parnes, S. J. (1967). *Creative behavior guidebook.* New York: Scribner's.

Parnes, S. J., Noller, R., & Bondi, A. (1977). *Guide to creative action.* New York: Scribner's.

Passow, A. H. (Ed.). (1979). *The gifted and the talented: Their education and development* (Vol. 78). Chicago: University of Chicago Press.

Passow, A. H. (1988). The educating and schooling of the community artisans in science. In P. Brandwein & A. H. Passow (Eds.), *Gifted young in science: Potential through performance* (pp. 27–38). Washington, DC: National Teachers Association.

Paulus, P., & Nijastad, B. (Eds.). (2003). *Group creativity: Innovation through collaboration.* New York: Oxford University Press.

Paulus, P., & Paulus, L. (1997). Implications of research on group brainstorming for gifted education. *Roeper Review, 19,* 225–229.

Pegnato, C. W., & Birch, J. W. (1959). Locating gifted children in junior high schools: A comparison of methods. *Exceptional Children, 25,* 300–304.

Peine, M. (1998). Practical matters. *Journal for the Education of the Gifted, 22,* 37–55.

Pendarvis, E., & Howley, A. (1996). Playing fair: The possibilities of gifted education. *Journal for the Education of the Gifted, 19,* 215–233.

Pepinsky, P. N. (1960). Study of productive nonconformity. *Gifted Child Quarterly, 4,* 81–85.

Perrone, P. (1991). Career development. In N. Colangelo & G. A. Davis (Eds.), *Handbook of gifted education* (pp. 321–327). Boston: Allyn and Bacon.

Peters, W. A. M., Grager-Loidl, H., & Supplee, P. (2000). Underachievement in gifted children and adolescents: Theory and practice. In K. A. Heller, F. J. Mönks, R. J. Sternberg, & R. F. Subotnik (Eds.), *International handbook of giftedness and talent* (2nd ed., pp. 609–620). Amsterdam: Elsevier.

REFERENCES

Phenix, P. (1986). *Realms of meaning: A philosophy of the curriculum for general education.* Ventura, CA: National/State Leadership Training Institute on the Gifted and Talented.

Piaget, J. (1954). *The construction of reality in the child.* New York: BasicBooks.

Piirto, J. (1999). *Talented children and adults: Their development and education* (2nd ed.). Columbus, OH: Merrill.

Piirto, J. (2004). *Understanding creativity.* Scottsdale, AZ: Great Potential Press.

Plomin, R. (1997). Genetics and intelligence. In N. Colangelo & G. A. Davis (Eds.), *Handbook of gifted education* (2nd ed., pp. 67–74). Boston: Allyn and Bacon.

Plowman, P. D. (1981). Training extraordinary leaders. *Roeper Review, 3,* 13–17.

Plucker, J., & Runco, M. (1998). The death of creativity measurement has been greatly exaggerated: Current issues, recent advances, and future directions in creativity assessment. *Roeper Review, 21,* 36–39

Plucker, J. A., & Beghetto, R. A. (2003). Why not be creative when we enhance creativity? In J. Borland (Ed.), *Rethinking gifted education* (pp. 215–226). New York: Teachers College Press

Pollard, G., & Howze, J. (1981). School-wide talented and gifted program for the deaf. *American Annals of the Deaf, 26,* 600–606.

Pollack, W. (1998). *Real boys: Rescuing our sons from the myths of boyhood.* New York: Holt.

Polya, G. (1973). *How to solve it.* Princeton, NJ: Princeton University Press. (Original work published 1945)

Porath, M. (1996). A narrative performance in verbally gifted children. *Journal for the Education of the Gifted, 19,* 276–292.

Potok, C. (1972). *My name is Asher Lev.* Greenwich, CT: Fawcett Crest.

Pratt, S. I., & Moreland, K. L. (1998). Individuals with other characteristics. In J. Sandoval, C. L. Frisby, K. F. Geisinger, J. D. Scheuneman, & J. R. Grenier (Eds.), *Test interpretation and diversity* (pp. 349–371). Washington, DC: American Psychological Association.

Pressey, S. L. (1949). *Educational acceleration, appraisal, and basic problems.* Columbus: Bureau of Educational Research, Ohio State University.

Preuss, L. J., & Dubow, E. F. (2004). A comparison between intellectually gifted and typical children in their coping responses to a school and a peer stressor. *Roeper Review, 26,* 105–111.

Priles, M. (1993). The fishbowl discussion: A strategy for large honors classes. *English Journal, 82,* 49–50.

Pyryt, M. (1998). Effectiveness of training children in divergent thinking: A meta-analytic review. In A. Fishkin, B. Cramond, & P. Olszewski-Kubilius (Eds.), *Investigating creativity in youth: Research and methods* (pp. 351–366). Cresskill, NJ: Hampton Press.

Raffaele Mendez, L. M. (2000). Gender roles and achievement-related choices: A comparison of early adolescent girls in gifted and general education programs. *Journal for the Education of the Gifted, 24,* 149–169.

Raph, J. B., Goldberg, M. L., & Passow, A. H. (1966). *Bright underachievers: Studies of scholastic underachievement among intellectually superior high school students.* New York: Teachers College Press.

Raven, J. C., Raven, M., & Styles, I. (1998). *Raven's progressive matrices.* Oxford, England: Oxford Psychologists Press.

433

Reis, S. M. (1998). *Work left undone: Choices & compromises of talented females.* Mansfield Center, CT: Creative Learning Press.

Reis, S. M. (2003). Gifted girls, twenty-five years later: Hopes realized and new challenges found. *Roeper Review, 25*, 154–157.

Reis, S. M., & McCoach, D. B. (2000). The underachievement of gifted students: What do we know and where do we go? *Gifted Child Quarterly, 44*, 152–170.

Reis, S. M., Gentry, M., & Maxfield, L. R. (1998). The application of enrichment clusters to teachers' classroom practices. *Journal for the Education of the Gifted, 21*, 310–334.

Reis, S., & Renzulli, J. (1991). The assessment of creative products in programs for gifted and talented students. *Gifted Child Quarterly, 35*, 128–134.

Reis, S. M., & Renzulli, J. S. (1992). The library media specialists' role in teaching independent study to high ability students. *School Library Media Quarterly, 21*, 27–35.

Renzulli, J. S. (1968). Identifying key features in programs for the gifted. *Exceptional Children, 35*, 217–221.

Renzulli, J. S. (1977). *The enrichment triad model: A guide for developing defensible programs for the gifted and talented.* Wethersfield, CT: Creative Learning Press.

Renzulli, J. S. (1979). Some concerns about educational acceleration for intellectually talented youth, or are treadmills really different if we run them at a faster rate? In W. C. George, S. J. Cohn, & J. C. Stanley (Eds.), *Educating the gifted: Acceleration and enrichment* (pp. 190–191). Baltimore, MD: Johns Hopkins University Press.

Renzulli, J. S. (1986). The three-ring conception of giftedness: A developmental model for creative productivity. In R. J. Sternberg & J. E. Davidson (Eds.), *Conceptions of giftedness* (pp. 53–92). Cambridge, England: Cambridge University Press.

Renzulli, J. S. (1992). A general theory for the development of creative productivity through pursuit of ideal acts of learning. *Gifted Child Quarterly, 36*, 170–182.

Renzulli, J. S. (1999). What is this thing called giftedness, and how do we develop it? A twenty-five year perspective. *Journal for the Education of the Gifted, 23*, 3–54.

Renzulli, J. S., Hartman, R. H., & Callahan, C. M. (1971). Teacher identification of superior students. *Exceptional Children, 38*, 211–214, 243–248.

Renzulli, J. S., Leppien. J., & Hayes, T. (2000). *The multiple menu model: A practical guide for developing differentiated curriculum.* Mansfield, CT: Creative Learning Press.

Renzulli, J. S. & Reis, S. M. (1985). *The schoolwide enrichment model: A comprehensive plan for educational excellence.* Mansfield, CT: Creative Learning Press.

Renzulli, J. S., & Reis, S. M. (1997). *The schoolwide enrichment model: A how-to guide for educational excellence* (2nd ed.). Mansfield, CT: Creative Learning Press.

Renzulli, J. S., & Reis, S. M. (2003). The Schoolwide Enrichment Model: Developing creative and productive giftedness. In N. Colangelo & G. A. Davis (Eds.), *Handbook of gifted education* (3rd. ed., pp. 184–203). Boston: Pearson Education.

Renzulli, J. S., Reis, S. M., & Smith, L. H. (1981). The revolving door model: A new way of identifying the gifted. *Phi Delta Kappan, 62*, 648–649.

Renzulli, J. S., & Smith, L. H. (1977a). *The interest-a-lyzer.* Mansfield Center, CT: Creative Learning Press.

Renzulli, J. S., & Smith, L. H. (1977b). Two approaches to identification of gifted students. *Exceptional Children, 43*, 512–518.

Renzulli, J. S., & Smith, L. H. (1978a). *The learning styles inventory.* Mansfield Center, CT: Creative Learning Press.

Renzulli, J. S., & Smith, L. H. (1978b). *The compactor*. Mansfield Center, CT: Creative Learning Press.

Renzulli, J. S., & Smith, L. H. (1979). A practical model for designing individualized education programs (IEPs) for gifted and talented students. In S. M. Butterfield, S. Kaplan, M. Meeker, J. S. Renzulli, L. Smith, and D. Treffinger (Eds.), *Developing IEPs for the gifted/talented* (pp. 11–24). Ventura, CA: Office of the Superintendent of Public Schools.

Renzulli, J. S., Smith, L. H., & Reis, S. (1982). Curriculum compacting: An essential strategy for working with gifted students. *Elementary School Journal, 82*, 185–194.

Renzulli, J. S., Smith, L., White, A., Callahan, C., Hartman, R., & Westberg, K. (2002). *Scales for Rating the Behaviorial Characteristics of Superior Students: Technical and administration manual* (Rev. ed.). Mansfield Center, CT: Creative Learning Press.

Rest, J. R. (1979). *Development in judging moral issues*. Minneapolis: University of Minnesota Press.

Reyna, J., & Bernal, E. M., Jr. (1974). Alternate identification strategies for Mexican-American youngsters at the primary level. *Talents and Gifts, 17*(1), 5–16.

Rice, J. S. (1970). *The gifted: Developing total talent*. Springfield, IL: Thomas.

Richert, E. S. (1991). Rampant problems and promising practices in identification. In N. Colangelo & G. A. Davis (Eds.), *Handbook of gifted education* (pp. 81–96). Boston: Allyn and Bacon.

Rieger, M. P. (1983). Life patterns and coping strategies in high and low creative women. *Journal for the Education of the Gifted, 6*, 98–110.

Rimm, S. B. (1990). *How to parent so children will learn*. Watertown, WI: Apple Valley Press.

Rimm, S. B. (1994). *Keys to parenting the gifted child*. New York: Barron's Educational Series.

Rimm, S. B. (1997). Underachievement syndrome: A national epidemic. In N. Colangelo & G. A. Davis (Eds.), *Handbook of gifted education* (2nd ed, pp. 416–434). Needham Heights, MA: Allyn and Bacon.

Rimm, S., & Davis, G. A. (1976). GIFT: An instrument for the identification of creativity. *Journal of Creative Behavior, 10*, 178–182.

Rimm, S., & Davis, G. A. (1980). Five years of international research with GIFT: An instrument for the identification of creativity. *Journal of Creative Behavior, 14*, 35–46.

Roach, A. A., Wyman, L. T., Brookes, H., Chavez, C., Heath, S. B., & Valdes, G. (1999). Leadership giftedness: Models revisited. *Gifted Child Quarterly, 43*, 13–24.

Robinson, A. (2003). Cooperative learning and high ability students. In N. Colangelo & G. A. Davis (Eds.), *Handbook of gifted education* (3rd ed., pp. 282–292). Boston: Pearson Education.

Robinson, H. B. (1977). Current myths concerning gifted children. In National/State Leadership Training Institute on the Gifted and Talented, *Gifts, talents, and the very young* (pp. 1–11). Ventura, CA: Office of the Superintendent of Public Schools.

Robinson, H. B., Roedell, W. C., & Jackson, N. E. (1979). Early identification and intervention. In A. H. Passow (Ed.), *The gifted and the talented: Their education and development* (Vol. 78, pp. 138–154). Chicago: University of Chicago Press.

Robinson, N. (1996). Counseling agendas for gifted young people. *Journal for the Education of the Gifted, 20*, 128–137.

Robinson, N., & Noble, K. (1991). Social-emotional development and adjustment of gifted children. In M. Wang, M. Reynolds, & H. Walberg (Eds.), *Handbook of special education: Research and practice. Vol. 4: Emerging programs: Advances in education* (pp. 57–76). Oxford, England: Pergamon Press.

Roe, A. (1953). *The making of a scientist.* New York: Dodd, Mead.

Roedell, W. C., Jackson, N. E., & Robinson, H. B. (1980). *Gifted young children.* New York: Teachers College Press.

Rodenstein, J., Pfleger, L. R., & Colangelo, N. (1979). Career development of gifted women. In J. C. Gowan, J. Khatena, & E. P. Torrance (Eds.), *Educating the ablest* (2nd ed., pp. 383–390). Itasca, IL: Peacock.

Rogers, K. (1991). *The relationship of grouping practices to the education of the gifted and talented.* Storrs: National Research Center on the Gifted and Talented, University of Connecticut.

Rogers, K. B. (1999). The lifelong productivity of the female researchers in Terman's genetic studies of genius longitudinal study. *Gifted Child Quarterly, 43,* 150–169.

Rogers, K. B. (2002). *Re-forming gifted education: How parents and teachers can match the program to the child.* Scottsdale, AZ: Great Potential Press.

Rogers, K. B., & Span, P. (1993). Ability grouping with gifted and talented students: Research and guidelines. In K. A. Heller, F. J. Mönks, & A. H. Passow (Eds.), *International handbook of research and development of giftedness and talent* (pp. 585–592). New York: Paradigm.

Rogge, W. (1970). Independent study, talent development, and responsibility. *Gifted Children Newsletter, 12,* 1–4.

Roid, G. H. (2003). *Stanford-Binet intelligence scales, fifth edition.* Itasca, IL: Riverside.

Root, W. T., Jr. (1931). A socio-psychological study of fifty-three supernormal children. *Psychological Monographs, 23,* 1–133.

Ross, A. O. (1979). The gifted child in the family. In N. Colangelo & R. T. Zaffrann (Eds.), *New voices in counseling the gifted* (pp. 402–407). Dubuque, IA: Kendall/Hunt.

Rothkopf, E. A. (1976). Writing to teach reading to learn: A perspective on the psychology of written instruction. In N. L. Gage (Ed.), *The psychology of teaching methods* (pp. 91–129). Chicago: University of Chicago Press.

Rowley, S. J., & Moore, J. A. (2002). Racial identity in context for the gifted African American. *Roeper Review, 24,* 63–67.

Rubenzer, R. L., & Twaite, J. A. (1979). Attitudes of 1,200 educators toward the education of the gifted and talented: Implications for teacher preparation. *Journal for the Education of the Gifted, 2,* 202–213.

Ruf, D. L. (2003). *Use of the SB5 in the assessment of high abilities* (Stanford-Binet Intelligence Scales, Fifth Edition Assessment Service Bulletin No. 3). Itasca, IL: Riverside.

Runco, M. (1987). The generality of creative performance in gifted and nongifted children. *Gifted Child Quarterly, 31,* 121–125.

Runco, M. (1993). Divergent thinking, creativity, and giftedness. *Gifted Child Quarterly, 37,* 16–22

Runco, M., & Mraz, W. (1992). Scoring divergent thinking tests using ideational output and a creativity index. *Educational and Psychological Measurement, 52,* 213–221.

Runco, M., & Nemiro, J. (1994). Problem finding, creativity, and giftedness. *Roeper Review, 16,* 235–241.

Runnells, M., & Martin, M. (1993). Identifying Hispanic gifted children using the Screening Assessment for Gifted Elementary Students. *Psychological Reports, 70,* 939–942.

Ryser, G. R., & Johnsen, S. K. (1998). *Test of mathematical abilities for gifted students (TOMAGS).* Austin, TX: PRO-ED.

Ryser, G. R., & McConnell, K. (2003). *Scales for identifying gifted students (SIGS).* Waco, TX: Prufrock Press.

Safter, N. T., & Bruch, C. (1981). Use of the DGG Model for differential guidance for the gifted. *Gifted Child Quarterly 25,* 167–174.

Salvia, J., & Ysseldyke, J. E. (1995). *Assessment in special and remedial education* (6th ed.). Boston: Houghton-Mifflin.

Samuda, R. J. (1975). *Psychological testing of American minorities: Issues and consequences.* New York: Dodd, Mead.

Sandborn, M. P. (1979a). Career development of gifted and talented students. In N. Colangelo & R. T. Zaffrann (Eds.), *New voices in counseling the gifted* (pp. 284–300). Dubuque, IA: Kendall/ Hunt.

Sandborn, M. P. (1979b). Working with parents. In N. Colangelo & R. T. Zaffrann (Eds.), *New voices in counseling the gifted* (pp. 396–401). Dubuque, IA: Kendall/Hunt.

Sapon-Shevin, M. (1994). *Playing favorites: Gifted education and the disruption of community.* Albany: State University of New York Press.

Sapon-Shevin, M. (1996). Beyond gifted education: Building a shared agenda. *Journal for the Education of the Gifted, 19,* 194–214.

Sarouphim, K. (2001). DISCOVER: Concurrent validity, gender differences, and identification of minority students. *Gifted Child Quarterly, 45,* 130–138.

Sarouphim, K. (2002). DISCOVER in high school: Identifying gifted Hispanic and Native American students. *Journal of Secondary Gifted Education, 14,* 30–38.

Sarouphim, K. (2004). DISCOVER in middle school: Identifying gifted minority students. *Journal of Secondary Gifted Education, 15,* 61–69.

Sattler, J. M. (1988). *Assessment of children: Cognitive applications* (3rd ed.). San Diego, CA: Author.

Sato, I. S. (1974). The culturally different gifted child—the dawning of his day. *Exceptional Children, 40,* 572–576.

Sawyer, R. K., John-Steiner, V., Moran, S., Sternberg, R. J., Feldman. D. H., Nakamura, J., & Csikszentmihalyi, M. (2003). *Creativity and development.* New York: Oxford Univerwsity Press.

Schaefer, C. E., & Anastasi, A. (1968). A biographical inventory for identifying creativity in adolescent boys. *Journal of Applied Psychology, 521,* 42–48.

Schiever, S., & Maker, J. (1997). Enrichment and acceleration. In N. Colangelo & G. A. Davis (Eds.), *Handbook of gifted education* (2nd ed., pp. 99–110). Boston: Allyn and Bacon.

Schiever, S. W., & Maker, C. J. (2003). New directions in enrichment and acceleration. In N. Colangelo & G. A. Davis (Eds.), *Handbook of gifted education* (3rd. ed., pp. 163–173). Boston: Pearson Education.

Schlichter, C. L. (1981). The multiple talent approach in mainstream and gifted programs. *Exceptional Children, 48,* 144–150.

Schlichter, C. (1991). Talent unlimited model in programs for gifted students. In N. Colangelo & G. A. Davis (Eds.), *Handbook of gifted education* (pp. 318–327). Boston: Allyn and Bacon.

437

Schneider, W. (2000). Giftedness, expertise, and (exceptional) performance: A developmental perspective. In K. A. Heller, F. J. Mönks, R. J. Sternberg, & R. F. Subotnik (Eds.), *International handbook of giftedness and talent* (2nd ed., pp. 165–178). Amsterdam: Elsevier.

Schorr, D. N., Jackson, N. E., & Robinson, H. B. (1980). Achievement test performance of intellectually advanced preschool children. *Exceptional Children, 46,* 646–648.

Science Research Associates. (1992). SRA achievement series. Monterey, CA: CTB/McGraw-Hill.

Sears, P. S. (1979). The Terman Genetic Studies of Genius, 1922–1972. In A. H. Passow (Ed.), *The gifted and the talented: Their education and development* (Vol. 78, pp. 75–96). Chicago: University of Chicago Press.

Sears, R. R. (1977). Sources of life satisfactions of the Terman gifted men. *American Psychologist, 32,* 119–128.

Seidner, C. J. (1976). Teaching with simulations and games. In N. L. Gage (Ed.), *The psychology of teaching methods* (pp. 217–251). Chicago: University of Chicago Press.

Sellin, D. F., & Birch, J. W. (1980). *Educating gifted and talented learners.* Rockville, MD: Aspen Systems.

Shack, G. (1993). Effects of a creative problem-solving curriculum on students of varying ability levels. *Gifted Child Quarterly, 37,* 32–38.

Shack, G. (1994). Authentic assessment procedures for secondary students' original research. *Journal of Secondary Gifted Education, 6,* 38–43.

Shavelson, R. J. (1976). Teachers' decision making. In N. L. Gage (Ed.), *The psychology of teaching methods* (pp. 372–414). Chicago: University of Chicago Press.

Shayer, M. (1979). Conceptual demands in the Nuffeld O-level physics course. In A. Floyd (Ed.), *Cognitive development in the school years* (pp. 340–350). New York: Wiley.

Shore, B. M., Cornell, G., Robinson, A., & Ward, V. (1991). *Recommended practices in gifted education: A critical analysis.* New York: Teachers College Press.

Shore, B., & Delcourt, M. (1996). Effective curricular and program practices in gifted education and the interface with general education. *Journal for the Education of the Gifted, 20,* 138–154.

Shore, B., Kanevsky, L., & Rejskind, F. (1991). Learning and the needs of gifted students. In R. Short, L. Stewin, & S. McCann (Eds.), *Educational psychology: Canadian perspectives* (pp. 372–400). Toronto: Hans Huber.

Siegle, D. (2005). *Developing mentorship programs for gifted and talented students.* Waco, TX: Prufrock Press.

Silverman, L. (1980). Secondary programs for gifted students. *Journal for the Education of the Gifted, 4,* 30–42.

Silverman, L. K. (1993). The gifted individual. In L. K. Silverman (Ed.), *Counseling the gifted and talented* (pp. 3–28). Denver: Love.

Silverman, L. K. (1997a). *Paradigms and perspectives: Essays in psychology.* Lanham, MD: University Press of America.

Silverman, L. K. (1997b). The construct of asynchrony. *Peabody Journal of Education 72*(2 & 3), 36–58.

Silverman, L. K. (1998). Through the lines of giftedness. *Roeper Review, 20,* 204–210.

Silverman, L. K. (2003). Gifted children with learning disabilities. In N. Colangelo, & G. A. Davis (Eds.), *Handbook of gifted education* (3rd ed., pp. 533–543). Boston: Allyn and Bacon.

Simonton, D. K. (1979). The eminent genius in history: The critical area of creative development. In J. C. Gowan, J. Khatena, & E. P. Torrance (Eds.), *Educating the ablest* (2nd ed., pp. 79–87). Itasca, IL: Peacock.

Simonton, D. (1997). When giftedness becomes genius: How does talent achieve eminence. In N. Colangelo & G. A. Davis, *Handbook of gifted education* (2nd ed., pp. 335–349). Boston: Allyn and Bacon.

Simonton, D. K. (1999). *Origins of genius: Darwinian perspectives on creativity*. Oxford, England: Oxford University Press.

Simpson, J. (1979). Developmental process theory as applied to mature women. In J. C. Gowan, J. Khatena, & E. P. Torrance (Eds.), *Educating the ablest* (2nd ed., pp. 371–383). Itasca, IL: Peacock.

Sisk, D. A. (1976). *Teaching gifted children*. Tampa: University of South Florida.

Sisk, D. A. (1982). Caring and sharing: Moral development of gifted students. *Elementary School Journal, 82*, 221–229.

Sisk, D. A. (1997). The importance of early identification of gifted children and appropriate educational intervention. In J. F. Smutny (Ed.), *The young gifted child: Potential and promise: An anthology* (pp. 73–90). Cresskill, NJ: Hampton Press.

Sisk, D. A. (2004). Teaching the gifted through simulation. In F. A. Karnes & S. M. Bean (Eds.), *Methods and material for teaching the gifted* (2nd ed., pp. 543–574). Waco, TX: Prufrock Press.

Slavin, R. (1987). Ability grouping and student achievement in elementary schools: A best-evidence synthesis. *Review of Educational Research, 57*, 293–350.

Slocumb, P. D., & Payne, R. K. (2000). *Removing the mask: Giftedness in poverty*. Highlands, TX: aha! Process.

Slosson, R. L., Nicholson, C. L., & Hibpsham, T. H. (1991). *Slosson intelligence test for children and adults*. East Aurora, NY: Slosson Educational Publications.

Smidchens, U., & Sellin, D. F. (1976). Attitudes toward mentally gifted learners. *Gifted Child Quarterly, 20*, 109–113.

Smith, L., & Smith, D. L. (1994). The discussion process: A simulation. *Journal of Reading, 37*, 582–5.

Smutny, J. F. (Ed.). (1997). *The young gifted child: Potential and promise: An anthology*. Cresskill, NJ: Hampton Press.

Snow, R. E. (1973). Theory construction for research on teaching. In R. M. W. Travers (Ed.), *Second handbook of research on teaching* (pp. 77–112). Chicago: Rand McNally.

Solow, R. (1995). Parents' reasoning about the social and emotional development of their intellectually gifted children. *Roeper Review, 19*, 142–146.

Sosniak, L. (1997). The tortoise, the hare, and the development of talent. In N. Colangelo & G. A. Davis, *Handbook of gifted education* (2nd ed., pp. 207–217). Boston: Allyn and Bacon.

Sosniak, L. (2003.) Developing talent: Time, task, and context. In N. Colangelo & G. A. Davis (Eds.), *Handbook of gifted education* (3rd ed., pp. 247–253). Boston: Pearson Education.

Southern, W. T., & Jones, E. D. (1991). Academic acceleration: Background and issues. In W. T. Southern & E. D. Jones (Eds.), *The academic acceleration of gifted children* (pp. 1–29). New York: Teachers College Press.

Spangler, R. S., & Sabatino, D. A. (1995). Temporal stability of gifted children's intelligence. *Roeper Review, 17*, 20–23.

Stanley, J. C. (1973). Accelerating the educational progress of intellectually gifted youth. *Educational Psychologist, 10,* 133–146.

Stanley, J. C. (1976). Identifying and nurturing the intellectually gifted. *Phi Delta Kappan, 58,* 234–237.

Stanley, J. C. (1979). The study and facilitation of talents for mathematics. In A. H. Passow (Ed.), *The gifted and the talented: Their education and development* (Vol. 78, pp. 169–185). Chicago: University of Chicago Press.

Stanley, J. C. (1980). On educating the gifted. *Educational Researcher, 9*(3), 8–13.

Stanley, J. C., & Benbow, C. P. (1982). Educating mathematically precocious youths: Twelve policy recommendations. *Educational Researcher, 11*(5), 4–9.

Stanley, J. C., & Benbow, C. P. (1986). Youths who reason exceptionally well mathematically. In R. J. Sternberg & J. E. Davidson (Eds.), *Conceptions of giftedness* (pp. 361–387). New York: Cambridge University Press.

Stanley, J., Keating, D., & Fox, L. (1974). *Mathematical talent: Discovery, description, and development.* Baltimore, MD: Johns Hopkins University Press.

Stark, E. W., & Stanley, J. C. (1978). Bright youth dispel persisting myths. *Gifted Child Quarterly, 22,* 220–234.

Starko, A. (1986). *It's about time: Inservice strategies for curriculum compacting.* Mansfield Center, CT: Creative Learning Press.

Starko, E. (1988). Effects of the Revolving Door Model Identification Model on creative productivity and self efficacy. *Gifted Child Quarterly, 32,* 291–297.

Stein, M. I. (1974). *Stimulating creativity: Individual procedures* (Vol. 1). New York: Academic Press.

Stein, M. I. (1975). *Stimulating creativity: Group procedures* (Vol. 2). New York: Academic Press.

Stepien, W., & Pike, S. (1997). Designing problem-based learning units. *Journal for the Education of the Gifted, 20,* 380–400.

Sternberg, R. J. (1985). *Beyond IQ.* Cambridge, England: Cambridge University Press.

Sternberg, R. J. (Ed.). (1999). *Handbook of creativity.* Cambridge, England: Cambridge University Press.

Sternberg, R. J. (2003a). Giftedness according to the theory of successful intelligence. In N. Colangelo & G. A. Davis (Eds.), *Handbook of gifted education* (3rd ed., pp. 88–99). Boston: Allyn and Bacon.

Sternberg, R. J. (2003b). *Wisdom, intelligence, and creativity synthesized.* Cambridge, England: Cambridge University Press.

Sternberg, R. J., Kaufman, J. C., & Pretz, J. E. (2002). *The creativity conundrum: A propulsion model of kinds of creative contributions.* New York: Psychology Press.

Sternberg, R., & Lubart, T. (1993). Creative giftedness: A multivariate investment approach. *Gifted Child Quarterly, 37,* 7–15.

Sternberg, R., & Lubart, T. (1995). *Defying the crowd: Cultivating creativity in a culture of conformity.* New York: The Free Press.

Sternberg, R. J., & O'Hara. L. A. (1999). Creativity and intelligence. In R. J. Sternberg (Ed.), *Handbook of creativity* (pp. 251–272). Cambridge, England: Cambridge University Press.

Sternberg, R. J., & Zhang, L. (1995). What do we mean by giftedness? A pentagonal implicit theory. *Gifted Child Quarterly, 29,* 88–94.

Stewart, E. (1981). Learning style among gifted/talented students: Instructional technique preferences. *Exceptional Children, 48,* 134–138.

Stogdill, R. M. (1974). *Handbook of leadership.* New York: The Free Press.

Stone, G. L. (1980). *A behavioral-cognitive approach to counseling psychology*. New York: Praeger.

Story, C. (1985). Facilitators of learning: A micro of hemisphere study of the teachers of the gifted. *Gifted Child Quarterly, 29*, 155–159.

Strang, R. (1960). *Helping your gifted child*. New York: Dutton.

Strother, P. (1997). A jump start zinger. *Gifted Child Today, 20*(3), 34–37.

Subhi, T. (1999). The impact of LOGO on gifted children's achievement and creativity. *Journal of Computer Assisted Learning, 15*(2), 98–109.

Subotnik, R. F., & Arnold, K. D. (1993). Longitudinal studies of giftedness: Investigating the fulfillment of promise. In K. A. Heller, F. J. Mönks, & A. H. Passow (Eds.), *International handbook of research and development of giftedness and talent* (pp. 149–160). New York: Pergamon.

Subotnik, R. F., & Coleman, L. J. (1996). Establishing the foundations for a talent development school: Applying principles to creating an ideal. *Journal for the Education of the Gifted, 20*, 175–189.

Subotnik, R. F., Stone, K. M., & Steiner, C. (2001). Lost generation of elite talent in science. *Journal of Secondary Gifted Education, 13*, 33–43.

Swiatek, M. A. (2002). Social coping among gifted elementary school students. *Journal for the Education of the Gifted, 26*, 65–86.

Swiatek, M., & Benbow, C. (1991). Ten-year longitudinal follow-up of ability-matched accelerated and unaccelerated gifted students. *Journal of Educational Psychology, 83*, 528–38.

Tannenbaum, A. J. (1958). History of interest in the gifted. In N. B. Barry (Ed.), *Education of the gifted* (Vol. 57, pp. 21–38). Chicago: University of Chicago Press.

Tannenbaum, A. J. (1962). *Adolescent attitudes towards academic brilliance*. New York: Teachers College Press.

Tannenbaum, A. J. (1979). Pre-Sputnik to post-Watergate concern about the gifted. In A. H. Passow (Ed.), *The gifted and the talented: Their education and development* (Vol. 78, pp. 5–27). Chicago: University of Chicago Press.

Tannenbaum, A. (1983). *Gifted children: Psychological and educational perspectives*. New York: Macmillan.

Tannenbaum, A. (1993). History of giftedness and "gifted education" in world perspective. In K. A. Heller, F. J. Mönks, & A. H. Passow (Eds.), *International handbook of research and development of giftedness and talented* (pp. 3–28). New York: Paradigm.

Tannenbaum, A. (1997). The meaning and making of giftedness. In N. Colangelo & G. A. Davis (Eds.), *Handbook of gifted education* (2nd ed., pp. 155–169). Boston: Allyn and Bacon.

Tannenbaum, A. (1998). Programs for the gifted: To be or not to be. *Journal for the Education of the Gifted, 22*, 3–36.

Tannenbaum, A. J. (2003). Nature and nurture of giftedness. In N. Colangelo & G. A. Davis (Eds.), *Handbook of gifted education* (3rd ed., pp. 45–59). Boston: Allyn and Bacon.

Tannenbaum, A. J., & Neuman, E. (1980). *Reaching out: Advocacy for the gifted and talented*. New York: Teachers College Press.

Taylor, C. W. (1973). Developing effectively functioning people—the accountable goal of multiple talent teaching. *Education, 94*, 99–110.

Taylor, C. (1985). Cultivating multiple creative talents in students. *Journal for the Education of the Gifted, 8*, 187–198.

441

Taylor, C. W., & Ellison, R. L. (1967). Biographical predictors of scientific perform-ance. *Science, 155,* 1075–1080.

Terman, L. M. (1925). *Mental and physical traits of a thousand gifted children: Genetic studies of genius, Vol. I.* Stanford, CA: Stanford University Press.

Terman, L. M., & Oden, M. H. (1947). *The gifted child grows up: Twenty-five years' fol-low-up of a superior group: Genetic studies of genius, Vol. IV:.* Stanford, CA: Stanford University Press.

Terman, L. M., & Oden, M. H. (1959). *The gifted group at mid-life: Thirty-five years' follow-up of a superior group: Genetic studies of genius, Vol. V.* Stanford, CA: Stanford University Press.

Tews, T. C. (1981). A high school for the creative arts. In National/State Leadership Training Institute on the Gifted and the Talented, *Secondary programs for the gifted and talented* (pp. 59–67). Ventura, CA: Office of the Superintendent of Public Schools.

The Association for the Gifted (TAG). (2001, April). *Diversity and developing gifts and talents: A national action plan.* Reston, VA: Council for Exceptional Children.

Thorndike, R. L., Hagen, E., & Sattler, J. (1986). *Stanford-Binet intelligence scale, fourth edition (SBIV).* Itasca, IL: Riverside.

Tidwell, R. (1980). A psycho-educational profile of 1,593 gifted high school students. *Gifted Child Quarterly, 24,* 63–68.

Toffler, A. (1970). *Future shock.* New York: Random House.

Tomchin, E., Callahan, C., Sowa, C., & May, K. (1996). Coping and self concept. *Journal of Secondary Gifted Education, 8,* 16–27.

Tomlinson, C. (1995). Deciding to differentiate instruction in middle school: One school's journey. *Gifted Child Quarterly, 39,* 77–87.

Tomlinson, C. (1996). Good teaching for one and all: Does gifted education have an instructional identity? *Journal for the Education of the Gifted, 20,* 155–174.

Tomlinson, C., Callahan, C., & Lelli, K. (1997). Challenging expectations: Case stud-ies of high-potential, culturally diverse young children. *Gifted Child Quarterly, 41,* 5–18.

Tomlinson, C. A., Brighton. C., Hertberg, H., Callahan, C., Moon, T. R., Brimijoin, K., Conover, L. A., & Reynolds, T. (2003) Differentiating instruction in response to student readiness, interest, and learning profile in academically diverse class-rooms: A review of literature. *Journal for the Education of the Gifted, 27,* 119–145.

Tomlinson, C. A., Kaplan, S. N., Renzulli, J. S., Purcell, J. H., Leppien, J. H., & Burns, D. E. (2002). *The parallel curriculum model: A design to develop high potential and challenge high ability learners.* Thousand Oakes, CA: Corwin Press.

Tomlinson-Keasey, C., & Little, T. D. (1990). Predicting educational attainment, occupational achievement, intellectual skill, and personal adjustment among gifted men and women. *Journal of Educational Psychology, 82,* 442–455.

Torrance, E. P. (1962a). *Guiding creative talent.* Englewood Cliffs, NJ: Prentice Hall.

Torrance, E. P. (1962b). Non-test ways of identifying the creatively gifted. *Gifted Child Quarterly, 6*(3), 71–75.

Torrance, E. P. (1965). *Rewarding creative behavior.* Englewood Cliffs, NJ: Prentice Hall.

Torrance, E. P. (1968). A longitudinal examination of the fourth grade slump in cre-ativity. *Gifted Child Quarterly, 12,* 195–199.

Torrance, E. P. (1969). Creative positives of disadvantaged children and youth. *Gifted Child Quarterly, 13,* 71–81.

Torrance, E. P. (1972). Career patterns and peak creative achievements of creative high school students twelve years later. *Gifted Child Quarterly, 16*, 75–88.

Torrance, E. P. (1974). *Torrance tests of creative thinking.* Bensenville, IL: Scholastic Testing Service.

Torrance, E. P. (1977). *Discovery and nurturance of giftedness in the culturally different.* Reston, VA: Council for Exceptional Children.

Torrance, E. P. (1979a). An instructional model for enhancing innovation. *Journal of Creative Behavior, 13*, 23–35.

Torrance, E. P. (1979b). Unique needs of the creative child and adult. In A. H. Passow (Ed.), *The gifted and the talented: Their education and development* (Vol. 78, pp. 352–371). Chicago: University of Chicago Press.

Torrance, E. P. (1980). Psychology of gifted children and youth. In W. Cruicksank (Ed.), *Psychology of exceptional children and youth* (pp. 469–496). Englewood Cliffs, NJ: Prentice Hall.

Torrance, E. P. (1981, October). *Growing up creatively gifted: A twenty-two year longitudinal study.* Paper presented at the National/State Training Institute on the Gifted and Talented Second National Conference on Creativity and the Gifted/Talented, Memphis, TN.

Torrance, E. P., & Hall, L. K. (1980). Assessing the further reaches of creative potential. *Journal of Creative Behavior, 14*, 1–19.

Torrance, E. P., Khatena, J., & Cunnington, B. F. (1973). *Thinking creatively with sounds and words.* Lexington, MA: Personnel Press.

Torrance, E. P., & Myers, R. E. (1970). *Creative learning and teaching.* New York: Dodd, Mead.

Torrance, E. P., Reynolds, C. R., Riegel, T., & Ball, O. (1977). Your style of learning and thinking, forms A & B. *Gifted Child Quarterly, 21*, 563–573.

Torrance, E. P., & Wu, T. (1981). A comparative longitudinal study of adult creative achievements of elementary school children identified as highly intelligent and highly creative. *Creative Child and Adult Quarterly, 6*, 71–76.

Travers, R. M. W. (Ed.). (1973). *Second handbook of research on teaching.* Chicago: Rand McNally.

Tredway, L. (1995). Socratic seminars. *Educational Leadership, 53*, 26–29.

Treffinger, D. J. (1975). Teaching for self-directed learning: A priority for the gifted and talented. *Gifted Child Quarterly, 19*, 46–59.

Treffinger, D. J. (1978). Guidelines for encouraging independence and self-direction among gifted students. *Journal of Creative Behavior, 12*, 14–20.

Treffinger, D. J. (1980). The progress and peril of identifying creative talent among gifted and talented students. *Journal of Creative Behavior, 14*, 20–34.

Treffinger, D. (1986). *Blending gifted education with the total school program.* Buffalo, NY: D.O.K.

Treffinger, D. J., & Poggio, P. (1972). Needed research on the measurement of creativity. *Journal of Creative Behavior, 6*, 253–267.

Treffinger, D., Sortore, D., & Cross, J. (1993). Programs and strategies for nurturing creativity. In K. A. Heller, F. J. Mönks, & A. H. Passow (Eds.), *International handbook of research and development of giftedness and talented* (pp. 555–567). Oxford: Pergamon.

U.S. Department of Education, Office of Educational Research and Improvement. (1993). *National excellence: A case for developing America's talent.* Washington, DC: U.S. Government Printing Office.

443

Vail, P. (1979). *The world of the gifted child.* New York: Walker.

VanTassel-Baska, J. (1986). Effective curriculum and instructional models for the gifted. *Gifted Child Quarterly, 30,* 164–169.

VanTassel-Baska, J. (1993). Theory and research on curriculum development for the gifted. In K. A. Heller, F. J. Mönks, & A. H. Passow (Eds.), *International handbook of research and development of giftedness and talented* (pp. 365–386). New York: Paradigm.

VanTassel-Baska, J. (1994a). What matters in curriculum for gifted learners: Reflections on theory, research, and practice. In N. Colangelo (Ed.), *Handbook of gifted education* (pp. 126–135.) Boston: Allyn and Bacon.

VanTassel-Baska, J. (1994b). The national curriculum development projects for high ability learners: Key issues and findings. In N. Colangelo, S. Assouline, & D. Ambroson (Eds.), *Talent development II: Proceedings from the 1993 Henry B. and Jocelyn Wallace National Research Symposium on Talent Development* (pp. 19–38). Dayton: Ohio Psychology Press.

VanTassel-Baska, J. (1997). What matters in curriculum for gifted learners: Reflections on theory, research, and practice. In N. Colangelo & G. A. Davis (Eds.), *Handbook of gifted education* (2nd ed., pp. 113–125). Boston: Allyn and Bacon.

VanTassel-Baska, J. (1998). Appropriate curriculum for the talented learner. In J. VanTassel-Baska (Ed.), *Excellence in educating gifted and talented learners* (3rd ed., pp. 339–361). Denver: Love.

VanTassel-Baska, J., & Baska, L. (1993). The roles of educational personnel in counseling gifted students. In L. Silverman (Ed.), *Counseling the gifted and talented* (pp. 181–200). Denver: Love.

VanTassel-Baska, J., & Feng, A. X. (Eds.). (2004). *Designing and utilizing evaluation for gifted program improvement.* Waco, TX: Prufrock Press.

VanTassel-Baska, J., Johnson, D., & Avery, L. D. (2002). Using performance tasks in the identification of economically disadvantaged and minority gifted learners: Findings from Project STAR. *Gifted Child Quarterly, 46,* 110–123.

VanTassel-Baska, J., Johnson, D., Hughes, C., & Boyce, L. (1996). A study of language arts curriculum effectiveness with gifted learners. *Journal for the Education of the Gifted, 19,* 461–480.

VanTassel-Baska, J., Patton, J. M., & Prillaman, D. (1991). *Gifted youth at risk: A report of a national study.* Reston, VA: Council for Exceptional Children.

Von Karolyi, C., Ramos-Ford, V., & Gardner, H. (2003). Multiple intelligences: A perspective on giftedness. In N. Colangelo & G. A. Davis (Eds.), *Handbook of gifted education* (3rd ed., pp. 100–112). Boston: Allyn and Bacon.

Vygotsky, L. (1978). *Mind in society: The development of higher psychological processes* (Trans. M. Cole, V. John-Steiner, S. Scribner, E. Souberman). Cambridge, MA: Harvard University Press.

Walberg, H. J., Rasher, S. P., & Parkerson, J. (1979). Childhood eminence. *Journal of Creative Behavior, 13,* 225–231.

Walberg, H. J., Williams, D. B., & Zeiser, S. (2003). Talent, accomplishment, and eminence. In N. Colangelo & G. A. Davis (Eds.), *Handbook of gifted education* (3rd ed., pp. 350–357). Boston: Allyn and Bacon.

Walker, S. Y. (1991). *The survival guide for parents of gifted teens.* Minneapolis, MN: Free Spirit.

Wallach, M. A. (1972). The Torrance Tests of Creative Thinking. In O. K. Buros (Ed.), *The seventh mental measurement yearbook* (pp. 448–449). Highland Park, NJ: Gryphon Press.

Wallach, M. A., & Kogan, N. (1965). *Modes of thinking in young children*. New York: Holt, Rhinehart, & Winston.

Wallach, M. A., & Wing, C. (1969). *The talented student: A validation of the creativity-intelligence distinction*. New York: Holt, Rhinehart, & Winston.

Wallas, G. (1926). *The art of thought*. New York: Harcourt, Brace.

Ward, V. S. (1961). *Educating the gifted: An axiomatic approach*. Columbus, OH: Merrill.

Ward, V. S. (1979). The Governor's School of North Carolina. In A. H. Passow (Ed.), *The gifted and the talented: Their education and development* (Vol. 78, pp. 209–217). Chicago: University of Chicago Press.

Warren, J. R., & Heist, P. A. (1960). Personality attributes of gifted college students. *Science, 132*, 330–337.

Webb, J., Meckstroth, E., & Tolan, S. S. (1982). *Guiding the gifted child: A practical source for parents and teachers*. Columbus: Ohio Psychology Press.

Wechsler, D. (1991). *Wechsler intelligence scale for children–third edition (WISC-III)*. Austin, TX: Harcourt Assessment.

Wechsler, D. (2001). *Wechsler individual achievement test–second edition (WIAT-II)*. San Antonio, TX: Harcourt Assessment.

Wechsler, D. (2003). *Wechsler intelligence scale for children–fourth edition (WISC-IV)*. San Antonio, TX: Harcourt Assessment.

Whitmore, J. R. (1979). Discipline and the gifted child. *Roeper Review, 2*(2), 42–46.

Whitmore, J. R. (1980). *Giftedness, conflict, and underachievement*. Boston: Allyn and Bacon.

Whitmore, J. R. (1981). Gifted children with handicapping conditions: A new frontier. *Exceptional Children, 48*, 106–114.

Will, H. C. (1987). Asking good follow-up questions. *Gifted Child Today, 10*(1), 32–34.

Williams, F. E. (1970). *Classroom ideas for encouraging thinking and feeling*. Buffalo, NY: D.O.K.

Williams, F. E. (1971). How do you feel about yourself? In F. E. Williams (Ed.), *A total creativity program for elementary school teachers*. Englewood Cliffs, NJ: Educational Technology Publications.

Williams, F. E. (1979). Williams' strategies orchestrating Renzulli's triad. *Gifted, Creative, and Talented, 9*, 2–10.

Williams, R. L., & Long, J. D. (1991). *Manage your life* (4th ed.). Boston: Houghton-Mifflin.

Willis, S. (1995, Summer). Reinventing science education: Reformers promote hands-on, inquiry-based learning. *Curriculum Update*. Alexandria, VA: Association for Supervision and Curriculum Development. (ERIC Reproduction Service No. ED387324)

Winebrenner, S. (1992). *Teaching gifted children in the regular classroom: Strategies and techniques every teacher can use to meet the academic needs of the gifted and talented*. Minneapolis, MN: Free Spirit.

Winner, E., & Martino, G. (1993). Giftedness in the visual arts and music. In K. A. Heller, F. J. Mönks, & A. H. Passow (Eds.), *International handbook of research and development of giftedness and talent* (pp. 253–281). Oxford: Pergamon Press.

Witty, P. A. (1940). A genetic study of fifty gifted children. In G. M. Whipple (Ed.), *Intelligence: Its nature and nurture* (Vol. 39, pp. 401–409). Chicago: University of Chicago Press.

Wolleat, P. L. (1979). Guiding the career development of gifted females. In N. Colangelo & R. T. Zaffrann (Eds.), *New voices in counseling the gifted* (pp. 331–344). Dubuque, IA: Kendall/Hunt.

Wolf, J., & Gygi, J. (1981). Learning disabled and gifted: Success or failure? *Journal for Education of the Gifted, 4*, 199–206.

Wolf, M. H. (1981). Talent search and development in the visual and performing arts. In National/State Leadership Training Institute on the Gifted and the Talented, *Balancing the scale for the disadvantaged gifted* (pp. 103–116). Ventura, CA: Office of the Superintendent of Public Schools.

Woodcock, R. W., McGrew, K. S., & Mather, N. (2001). *The Woodcock-Johnson III (WJ III)*. Itasca, IL: Riverside.

Yamamoto, K. (1965). Effects of restriction of range and test unreliability on correlation between measures of intelligence and creative thinking. *British Journal of Educational Psychology, 35*, 300–305.

Yewchuk, C. R. (1995). The "mad genius" controversy: Implications for gifted education. *Journal for the Education of the Gifted, 19*, 3–29.

Yewchuk , Y., & Lupart, J. (2002). Inclusive education for gifted students with disabilities. In K. A. Heller, F. J. Mönks, R. J. Sternberg, & R. F. Subotnik (Eds.), *International handbook of giftedness and talent* (2nd ed., pp. 659–670). Amsterdam: Elsevier.

Yoshida, R. K. (1978). Parental involvement in the special education pupil planning process: The school's perspective. *Exceptional Children, 44*, 531–534.

Zaffrann, R. T., & Colangelo, N. (1979). Counseling with gifted and talented students. In J. C. Gowan, J. Khatena, & E. P. Torrance (Eds.), *Educating the ablest* (pp. 167–181). Itasca, IL: Peacock.

Zahorik, J. A. (1995). *Constructivist teaching*. Bloomington, IN: Phi Delta Kappa.

Ziv, A. (1977). *Counseling the intellectually gifted child*. Toronto: University of Toronto.

Zuckerman, H. (1977). *Scientific elite*. New York: The Free Press.

INDEX